D0021497

Biographical Dictionary of Modern American Educators

FREDERIK OHLES,
SHIRLEY M. OHLES,
and
JOHN G. RAMSAY

GREENWOOD PRESS
WESTPORT, CONNECTICUT • LONDON

Library of Congress Cataloging-in-Publication Data

Ohles, Frederik, 1953–
Biographical dictionary of modern American educators / Frederik Ohles, Shirley M. Ohles, and John G. Ramsay.
p. cm.
Includes bibliographical references and index.
ISBN 0–313–29133–0 (alk. paper)
1. Educators—United States—Biography—Dictionaries. I. Ohles, Shirley M. II. Ramsay, John G. III. Title.
LA2311.055 1997
370'.92'2—dc21
[B] 97–6413

British Library Cataloguing in Publication Data is available.

Library of Congress Catalog Card Number: 97–6413
ISBN: 0–313–29133–0

First published in 1997

Greenwood Press, 88 Post Road West, Westport, CT 06881
An imprint of Greenwood Publishing Group, Inc.

Printed in the United States of America

The paper used in this book complies with the Permanent Paper Standard issued by the National Information Standards Organization (Z39.48–1984).

10 9 8 7 6 5 4 3 2 1

**In memory of
John F. Ohles
1920–1988**

CONTENTS

PREFACE

The *Biographical Dictionary of Modern American Educators* continues the *Biographical Dictionary of American Educators*, which John F. Ohles edited and Greenwood Press published in 1978. The subject of the *Dictionary* is persons who marked education in the United States. By marking education, we mean that their work changed it in more than the common ways that the teaching, scholarship, service, and opinions of innumerable excellent members of the profession enrich the educational community.

By design, we have chosen to sketch a diverse group of educators. They represent all fifty states, they worked in many different areas within education broadly conceived, and they had a wide variety of backgrounds. We have not limited our sketches to eminent or famous persons. Some of the educators sketched here did not have distinguished reputations or achieve prominence in their lifetimes, nor have they always figured conspicuously in historical accounts since, but each of them made a distinctive contribution to a facet of education in this country.

The results may sometimes seem surprising. The originator of driver education, Amos Neyhart, is included, although his name is hardly familiar. Several well-remembered popular pundits, culture mavens, and citizens of the airwaves from his generation are excluded, although they were more famous. Neyhart contributed a notable change in the curriculum of secondary schools that drew unfavorable comment from Jacques Barzun, also sketched here. Neyhart's better-known contemporaries shaped public opinion but did not necessarily mark education. Yet we have included some critics, such as Barzun, by the same standard, because they changed opinions about education, and more important, they affected educational practice.

There was a time when college presidents and school superintendents were educators by definition, but since the middle decades of the twentieth century they have often been either managers or public personalities instead. Rising high in an educational bureaucracy or becoming well known in the nation or in a state has not in itself persuaded us to include someone in the *Dictionary*. Nor have we thought we should acknowledge fame in another field coupled with a tangential connection to education. We have not been tempted to imitate the national hamburger restaurant chain that put "great American teachers" on its paper place mats a decade ago. For this honor the kings of the burger realm chose persons who had taught very briefly before becoming famous for entirely different reasons. To mention two striking cases, Lyndon B. Johnson taught school for one year before he was U.S. senator and president, and Vince Lombardi was also a teacher for a short time before his famous career as a football coach.

Great institutional leaders find their place in the *Biographical Dictionary of Modern American Educators* when the greatness of their leadership transcended their own institutions and when their accomplishments were significantly in education, not just in politics, public service, the scholarship of one discipline, entertainment, sports, or finance—all areas that can make people famous without making them educators. If the impact of college and university presidents, union officials, politicians, public administrators, or scholars on educational topics was notable for their state, their region, or the nation; or if their work fashioned a subject of fundamental significance for educational issues, such as urban studies or reading; or if they were notable in a subject within education, such as the development of community colleges or educational television—then we have included them. Otherwise, as with everyone's favorite elementary school teacher, we have left their remembrance to other occasions.

In some instances, we have included representative leaders in a field, selecting them from a larger number of persons who were active in the same area and might have been sketched in the *Dictionary*. It is arguable that every great child psychologist had an impact on education, but we have included only some of the most notable ones. Also in the case of recently developed fields, such as African-American studies and women's studies, we have made sure to represent these fields, but we have tended to be cautious, leaving for inclusion in a future edition some persons just recently retired or deceased whose contribution can be measured better later.

At the same time, it has been our conscious aim to represent the breadth and variety of American society as seen in its educational ideas, practices, and institutions. One means of accomplishing that goal is to make special efforts to include members of groups that have a history of being underrepresented in the published record of American education, particularly women and racial minorities. Sometimes the claim of representation has taken precedence in our selections; other times the question of what mark the person made has seemed to us to matter more.

Our work is intentionally historical. The 410 biographical sketches in this volume bring the chronological range of the *Biographical Dictionary of American Educators* further into the twentieth century, though, by design, not up to the present. We have included only persons who were born before January 1, 1935, or are now deceased, in order to consider the whole of a career. Most of our sketches are about persons who were active professionally in the early and middle decades of the twentieth century. A smaller number of them date from the nineteenth century. In some cases we have been able to include persons who surely would have been in the original *Dictionary* twenty years ago, if only the source collections, particularly on women and racial minorities, had been as well developed then as they are today.

Our biographies are brief. Each one includes basic information from the personal history, a statement on the significance of the biographee in education, a capsule history of his or her education and career, titles of notable publications, significant honors received, and a list of references. In many cases we have been able to point out professional relationships among the educators in this volume (by using "q.v.") and in the *Biographical Dictionary of American Educators* (BDAE). We have divided the references into two parts, first, standard works, which we present alphabetically in abbreviated form, then other works presented in full, again alphabetically. A guide to the abbreviations follows this preface.

While we have written the sketches ourselves, our work has been possible only because of the assistance that many persons and organizations lent to the project. As we began, we wrote to the college of education in the largest public university, the historical society, the education association, and the principal government agency for education in each state and territory of the United States, asking for suggestions on educators we might include. We also wrote to some of the persons who had contributed sketches to the *Biographical Dictionary of American Educators* two decades ago and to a group of members in the International Society for Educational Biography.

The suggestions we received, along with names we gathered ourselves, made a pool of nearly 1,500 candidates. We researched approximately 850 of them in order to make our selections for the *Biographical Dictionary of Modern American Educators*. Although we have not been able to incorporate all of the interesting and accomplished educators recommended to us, we are extremely grateful that so many people made thoughtful recommendations, which helped us to see the possibilities and frame our choices.

We owe special thanks to the late William W. Brickman for his suggestions to John F. Ohles and to Kim Sebaly for his suggestions to us; each brought into the *Dictionary* several educators whose distinctive contributions we would have missed otherwise. The sketch of Willard Walcott Beatty owes its origin to a letter that Frederick J. Stefon wrote to John F. Ohles after the *Biographical Dictionary of American Educators* appeared. The following entries are based on sketches written for the earlier work but ultimately not included in it: Thomas Higdon Gentle by Donald C. Jones; Guy Loraine Bond by John P. Madison; Charles Harris Congdon, Haim Ginott, Rowland Haynes, Cyrus Taggart Mills, and Jesse Brundage Sears by John F. Ohles.

We are grateful for advice and assistance from Dale G. Andersen, Phyllis André, Deborah Appleman, Anton Armstrong, Roland Baumann, Maurice R. Berube, Judith A. Billings, Barney Bloom, Richard W. Bodman, Robert K. Bruce, Charles F. Bryan, Jr., Frederick S. Buchanan, Robert F. Bullough, Jr., Emma Cecilia Busam, Peggy Catzen, Margaret Cowperthwaite, Patti Cox, Ivan J. K. Dahl, William D. Dawson, Filomena DiCarlo, Susan Franzosa, Timothy Fuller, Loretta Zwolak Greene, Mary Harris, James E. Hartmann, Elizabeth H.

Helms, Robert M. Hendrickson, Larry Hickman, Ann J. Hinson, Julie Holzer, John O. Holzhueter, Joan Hori, M. Vivian Ivantic, Stan Ivie, Michael E. James, Franklin Ross Jones, Roger H. Jones, Stanley N. Katz, Michael Kelly, Karen M. Kennelly, Ginny Kiefer, Colleen Kirby, Eileen Libby, Barbara A. Love, Margharita Machione, Nancy McCoy, Robert McGinty, Judith Metz, Nancie Mitchell, Jerry R. Mohrig, John Molyneux, Marjorie Murfin, Beverly Nagel, James O'Hanlon, Janet A. Ohles, Judy Ohles Kooistra, Barbara Peltzman, Hugh Petrie, Rodney J. Reed, David Riesman, Earl M. Rogers, Peter A. Rubba, Rita S. Saslaw, Helen Scott, Vernon Lee Sheeley, Michael Sherman, Robert R. Sherman, Brian Shovers, Lytton Smith, Samuel F. Stack, Jr., Lynn Arthur Steen, Carol Steinberg, Frank A. Stone, Lee Sylvester, Jill M. Tarule, Maureen Taylor, Lowell Thompson, Lucy Townsend, Lorett Treese, Martha T. Wallace, Douglas M. Warren, W. Michael Westbrook, Vickie C. Woodcock, and Solveig Zempel.

Assistance to us also came from the reference staff of the Kent State University Library, reference and interlibrary loan staffs of the Rølvaag Memorial Library at St. Olaf College, South Dakota State Archives, office of the provost of the University of Wisconsin at Madison, Stanford University Alumni Association, Wainwright-Bernhardt Funeral Home in Vineland, New Jersey, and University of Illinois Archives.

We have had indispensable aid from student research assistants, including Carrie H. Zwiebel at Carleton College and Trista J. Anderson, Janet A. Dopf, and Jonathan R. Kibler at St. Olaf College. We acknowledge gratefully the kind help of our coworkers in clerical roles, particularly Lois H. Messal at Carleton College, Jennifer S. Peterson and Jane Weis at St. Olaf College, and Lee Fredericks at Illinois College. It is quite possible that we have neglected to mention someone else whose help we ought to acknowledge, and for that we apologize.

Frederik Ohles
Illinois College
Jacksonville, Illinois

Shirley M. Ohles
Kent, Ohio

John G. Ramsay
Carleton College
Northfield, Minnesota

ABBREVIATIONS

AAW	Dorothy C. Salem, ed., *African-American Women* (Garland, 1993).
AR	Alden Whitman, ed., *American Reformers* (Wilson, 1985).
ASL	William McGuire and Leslie Wheeler, *American Social Leaders* (ABC-CLIO, 1993).
AWM	Judith A. Leavitt, *American Women Managers and Administrators* (Greenwood, 1985).
AWS	Martha J. Bailey, *American Women in Science: A Biographical Dictionary* (ABC-CLIO, 1994).
BBD	Nicholas Slonimsky, reviser, *Baker's Biographical Dictionary of Musicians*, 7th ed. (Schirmer, 1984).
BCAW	Mabel W. Cameron, comp., *Biographical Cyclopedia of American Women* (Gale, 1974).
BDAE	John F. Ohles, ed., *Biographical Dictionary of American Educators* (Greenwood, 1978).
BDAL	Gary M. Fink, ed., *Biographical Dictionary of American Labor* (Greenwood, 1974).
BDIA	*Biographical Dictionary of Indians of the Americas* (American Indian, 1983).
BDP	Leonard Zusne, *Biographical Dictionary of Psychology* (Greenwood, 1984).
BDSW	Walter I. Tratter, ed., *Biographical Dictionary of Social Welfare in America* (Greenwood, 1986).
BWA	Darlene Clark Hine, ed., *Black Women in America: An Historical Encyclopedia*, 2 vols. (Carlson, 1993).
CA	*Contemporary Authors* (Gale, 1962–96). (1–144 are volumes from the original series; 1R indicates original series revised; NR–1 indicates new revised series; P–1 indicates permanent series.)
CB	*Current Biography* (H. H. Wilson, 1940–96).
CHE	*Chronicle of Higher Education.*
DAB	Allen Johnson et al., eds., *Dictionary of American Biography* (Scribner's, 1937–94).

DALB	Bohdan S. Wynar, ed., *Dictionary of American Library Biography* (Libraries Unlimited, 1978).
DANB	Rayford W. Logan and Michael R. Winston, eds., *Dictionary of American Negro Biography* (Norton, 1982).
DARB	Henry Warner Bowden, *Dictionary of American Religious Biography*, 2nd ed. (Greenwood, 1993).
EAB	John A. Garraty, ed., *Encyclopedia of American Biography* (Harper and Row, 1974).
EBA	W. Augustus Low and Virgil A. Clift, eds., *Encyclopedia of Black America* (McGraw-Hill, 1981).
ECE	Wilma Bardwell and Rose F. Spicola, *Early Childhood Education: Personalities* (1974).
ECP	Robert I. Watson, ed., *Eminent Contributors to Psychology*, vol. 1: *A Biography of Primary References* (Springer, 1974).
ESW	John B. Turner, ed., *Encyclopedia of Social Work*, 16th and 17th eds. (National Association of Social Workers, 1971 and 1977).
FWC	*Foremost Women in Communications* (Bowker, 1970).
HAWH	Angela Marie Howard Zophy, ed., *Handbook of American Women's History* (Garland, 1990).
IESS	David L. Sills, ed., *International Encyclopedia of the Social Sciences* (Macmillan, 1968).
LE	J. M. Cattell et al., eds., *Leaders in Education* (Science Press, 1932–74).
LW	Robert McHenry, ed., *Liberty's Women* (Merriam-Webster, 1980).
NAW	Edward T. James, ed., *Notable American Women*, 3 vols. (Harvard University Press, 1971).
NAW (Mod)	Barbara Sicherman and Carol Hurd Green, eds., *Notable American Women: The Modern Period* (Harvard University Press, 1980).
NBAW	Jessie Carney Smith, ed., *Notable Black American Women* (Gale, 1992).
NCAB	*National Cyclopedia of American Biography* (White, 1891–1984). (Entries provide volume number or letter, followed by page number.)
NGD	H. Wiley Hitchcock and Stanley Sadie, eds., *The New Grove Dictionary of American Music* (Grove's Dictionaries of Music, 1986).
NNAA	Duane Champagne, ed., *Native North American Almanac* (Gale, 1994).
NYT	*New York Times.*
PC	John F. Ohles and Shirley M. Ohles, *Private Colleges and Universities* (Greenwood, 1983).

PR	Carl Murchison, ed., *Psychological Register*, vol. 3 (Clark University Press, 1932).
q.v.	See another biographical entry in this *Dictionary*.
RPE	Derek L. Burleson, ed., *Reflections: Personal Essays by 33 Distinguished Educators* (Phi Delta Kappa, 1981).
UNESCO	United Nations Educational, Scientific and Cultural Organization.
WAB	Charles Van Doren, ed., *Webster's American Biographies* (Merriam, 1974).
WD	*Writer's Directory* (St. James Press, 1974–96).
WEUS	Maxine Schwartz Seller, ed., *Women Educators in the United States, 1820–1993, A Bio-Bibliographical Sourcebook* (Greenwood, 1994).
WP	*Washington Post.*
WR	Marion Tinling, *Women Remembered: A Guide to Landmarks of Women's History in the United States* (Greenwood, 1986).
WS	Mary Jo Deegan, ed., *Woman in Sociology: A Bio-Bibliographical Sourcebook* (Greenwood, 1991).
WW	*Who's Who in America* (Marquis, 1899–1996).
WWAW	*Who's Who of American Women* (Marquis, 1958–96).
WWBA	*Who's Who Among Black Americans* (Gale Research, 1976–94/1995).
WWE	Mark Blaug, ed., *Who's Who in Economics* (MIT Press, 1986).
WWW	*Who Was Who in America* (Marquis, 1899–1993).

A

ACKERMAN, Carl William. b. January 16, 1890, Richmond, Indiana, to John F. and Mary Alice (Eggemeyer) Ackerman. Married May 24, 1914, to Mabel Vander Hoof. Children: one. d. October 9, 1970, New York City.

Carl W. Ackerman was dean of the school of journalism at Columbia University for a quarter century. He transformed it from an undergraduate to a graduate institution and emphasized practical training in its curriculum.

Ackerman attended Indiana University and Earlham College, where he received B.A. (1911) and M.A. (1917) degrees. He was in the first graduating class of twelve students from the Columbia University School of Journalism, earning the B.Litt. degree in 1913.

He wrote for United Press International and the *New York Tribune* before becoming a war correspondent for the *Saturday Evening Post* (1917–18) and the *New York Times* (1918–19), reporting from Mexico, Western Europe, and Siberia. He directed the foreign news service of the *Philadelphia Ledger* for two years, then opened a public relations business, Carl W. Ackerman, Inc., which he operated from 1921 to 1930. In 1930 he became assistant to the president of General Motors Corporation. The next year he was named dean at Columbia.

Ackerman led the development of a one-year master's curriculum in journalism, eliminating the longer baccalaureate course of study. He was an adviser on journalism education in China and South America, administered the Pulitzer Prize competition, and was a vigorous advocate of press freedom in the United States and abroad. He retired in 1956.

As a journalist Ackerman wrote books on current events in Germany, Mexico, and Russia; later he was the author of biographies of Charles Dawes and George Eastman. He was a cofounder of the American Press Institute.

REFERENCES: CA (73–76, 29–32R); CB (1945, 1970); NYT, October 10, 1970, p. 28; WWW (5); Donald Paneth, *The Encyclopedia of American Journalism* (Facts on File, 1983).

ADLER, Mortimer Jerome. b. December 28, 1902, New York City, to Ignatz and Clarissa (Manheim) Adler. Married May 2, 1927, to Helen Leavenworth Boynton; 1963 to Caroline Sage Pring. Children: two.

With the publication of *The Paideia Proposal: An Educational Manifesto*

(1982), Mortimer Adler achieved a rare feat for a philosopher of education—a wide and serious readership on the reform of American public education. Two elaborating texts followed quickly: *Paideia Problems and Possibilities* (1983) and *The Paideia Program: An Educational Syllabus* (1984). The last book contained essays by other members of Adler's Paideia Group, which included Jacques Barzun (q.v.), Leon Botstein, Ernest Boyer (q.v.), Adele Simmons, and Theodore Sizer (q.v.).

Adler's educational career began inauspiciously when he dropped out of high school after a dispute with the principal. Because he was unwilling to take Columbia University's swimming test, he also received no bachelor's degree. He graduated from Columbia with the Ph.D. degree in psychology in 1928. He was granted the B.A. degree belatedly from Columbia College in 1983.

Adler taught at Columbia (1923–30) and was assistant director of the People's Institute (1927–29) before joining the faculty of the University of Chicago (1930–52) at the instigation of Robert Maynard Hutchins (BDAE), his longtime friend and scholarly collaborator. In 1937 Adler also began an association with Saint John's College (Maryland), where he was a visiting lecturer. He directed the Institute for Philosophic Research in Chicago from 1952. He was president of San Francisco Productions (1954–94) and chair of the board of editors of the *Encyclopedia Britannica* from 1974. At the age of eighty-five he became a university professor at the University of North Carolina at Chapel Hill (1988–91).

In 1946 Adler initiated the Great Books Program, a continuing liberal education program for adults that focused on classical texts of Western civilization. He was editor with Hutchins of *Great Books of the Western World* (1954), which *Encyclopedia Britannica* and the University of Chicago sponsored. In fifty-four volumes they presented works of seventy-four authors from Homer to Sigmund Freud. Adler also wrote a best-seller, *How to Read a Book: The Art of Getting a Liberal Education* (1940).

Over a period of almost seventy years, Adler was author or coauthor of more than forty books. They included *Dialectic* (1927), *The Revolution in Education* (with Milton Mayer, 1958), *Reforming Education* (1977), *A Guidebook to Learning* (1986), and *Reforming American Education: The Opening of the American Mind* (1989). He also wrote *Philosopher at Large: An Intellectual Autobiography* (1977) and *A Second Look in the Rear-view Mirror: Further Reflections of a Philosopher at Large* (1992).

REFERENCES: CA (NR–33); CB (1952); WAB; WD (1994–96); WW (1996); Joselito Bernardo Jara, ''The Educational Philosophy of Mortimer J. Adler'' (Ph.D. diss., University of Illinois at Urbana-Champaign, 1976); *Time* 125 (May 6, 1985): 68.

AIKIN, Wilford Morton. b. September 22, 1882, New Concord, Ohio, to James Henderson and Mary Jane (Dew) Aikin. Married February 21, 1907, to Lena Graham; April 27, 1940, to Marjorie Jackson. Children: three. d. February 16, 1965, Palo Alto, California.

Wilford Aikin chaired the Commission on the Relation of School and College of the Progressive Education Association, which conducted the ''Eight-Year Study'' (1932–40). The study reexamined the purpose and effectiveness of high school education. Twenty-eight high schools participated in the study, among them some of the best, public and private, in America. The study suggested that many varieties of high school study would lead to success in college. It urged abandonment of existing admissions requirements that prescribed the content of high school curricula and called for schooling to emphasize communication skills, quantitative reasoning, and good citizenship.

Aikin graduated from Muskingum College with the B.S. degree in 1907. He was a high school teacher in Bowling Green, Ohio (1907–8), and Jackson, Michigan (1908–10), then taught in Ann Arbor, Michigan (1910–13), while completing requirements at the University of Michigan for the M.A. degree, which he received in 1913. He studied at Columbia University during 1917–18 but took no further degrees.

He was principal of the Ann Arbor High School from 1913 to 1916, served on the faculty at Ohio State University (1916–18), then returned to school administration as director of the Scarborough (New York) School (1918–22). While serving as director of the John Burroughs School in Clayton, Missouri (1922–35), Aikin took responsibility for the Eight-Year Study. In 1935 Aikin returned to Ohio State University as professor of education and research associate in the Bureau of Educational Research. In 1942 he became chief of civilian training in the U.S. Department of War. For a time after 1946 he represented the U.S. Office of Education at Sixth Army headquarters in San Francisco.

In addition to *The Story of the Eight-Year Study* (1942), Aikin wrote *English Literature* (1914) and *American Literature* (with Thomas Rankin, 1916).

REFERENCES: LE (1948); WWW (4); Raymond Blaine Fosdick, *Adventure in Giving: The Story of the General Education Board* (Harper and Row, 1962).

ALBERS, Josef. b. March 19, 1888, Bottrop, Westphalia, Germany, to Lorenz and Magdalena (Schumacher) Albers. Married May 25, 1925, to Anni Fleischmann. Children: no. d. March 25, 1976, New Haven, Connecticut.

Josef Albers was best known as an influential teacher of design and color, first at the Bauhaus, then at Black Mountain College in North Carolina, and finally at Yale University. He presented his artistic and pedagogical ideas in the book *Interaction in Color* (1963). In teaching color, Albers emphasized that theory should follow practice, and he exhorted his students to see on their own, rather than according to rules.

Albers began his education at a teachers' academy in Büren, Westphalia, where he studied from 1905 to 1908. He was a student at the Royal Art School of Berlin (1913–15), Art Academy of Munich (1919–20), and the Bauhaus in Dresden (1920–23), where at the age of thirty-two he was the oldest student in its inaugural class. At the Bauhaus Albers began to merge the art he had been studying with the crafts of his family heritage.

Albers was an art teacher in public schools in several German towns, 1908–13 and 1916–19. In 1923 he began teaching at the Bauhaus, becoming a ''master'' teacher in 1925. The national socialists closed the Bauhaus in 1933.

With his wife, also an artist and teacher, he joined the faculty of newly founded Black Mountain College, where he stayed sixteen years (1933–49). Black Mountain was established with the intention that art be central in the curriculum. Albers continued to teach drawing and design there, while beginning the work in color that would be his most notable achievement. He served also on the governing Board of Fellows.

Albers directed the Department of Design at Yale University from its establishment in 1950 until his retirement in 1958. He was a visiting professor and lecturer in Cuba, Chile, and Peru and at many universities in the United States. His prominence as an artist came only after his retirement, in the period of op art and pop art. The Federal Republic of Germany inducted him into its Order of Merit in 1957, and he was a Ford Foundation fellow in 1959.

His art was the subject of more than 100 one-man shows. In addition to *Interaction of Color*, Albers was author of *Poems and Drawings* (1958) and several articles, including ''Art as Experience,'' *Progressive Education* 12 (October 1935): 391–93.

REFERENCES: CA (NR-3, 65–68); CB (1962, 1976); NYT, March 26, 1976, p. 38; WWW (7); Emile de Antonio and Mitch Tuchman, *Painters Painting* (Abbeville Press, 1984); Werner Spies, ed., *Albers* (Henry N. Abrams, 1975); Jane Turner, ed. *The Dictionary of Art* (Grove's Dictionaries, 1996); Nicholas Fox Weber et al., *Josef Albers: A Retrospective* (Solomon R. Guggenheim Foundation, 1988).

ALEXANDER, (Richard) Thomas. b. May 3, 1887, Smicksburg, Pennsylvania, to William John and Mary Elizabeth (Wilhelm) Alexander. Married October 5, 1916, to Grace Elizabeth Andrews. Children: two. d. October 16, 1971, Waynesville, North Carolina.

Thomas Alexander founded and led the experimental New College of Teachers College, Columbia University, during the 1930s. It emphasized new methods in teacher training, including seminars and independent projects. Students spent a summer on a farm, often one the school operated in Canton, North Carolina. They also spent time in industry and in social work and a summer abroad. Alexander wanted to integrate their training with these other experiences. A master's degree was earned after a teaching internship. Peter Sammartino (BDAE), founder and president of Fairleigh Dickinson University, used New College ideas. New College closed in 1939 due to lack of funds.

Alexander received B.Ped. and M.Ped. degrees from the State Normal School (later, Truman State University) in Kirksville, Missouri, and was a principal in Kirksville schools (1905–6). He taught at Heathcote Preparatory School in New York City (1910–12). He taught science at Robert College, Constantinople, Turkey (1907–9), studied at the University of Jena, Germany (1909), and was an exchange teacher in Prussia (1913–14). From 1914 to 1923 Alexander served as professor of elementary education at George Peabody College for Teachers (later, part of Vanderbilt University). He became professor of education at Teachers College in 1924 and retired in 1951. Alexander was a visiting professor and directed foreign study at Adelphi College (later, University, 1952–71).

After World War II he was chief of the education branch (1945–47) and educational adviser (1948–49) of the American Military Government for Germany. He received the Grand Merit Cross from the Federal Republic of Germany.

Alexander wrote *Prussian Elementary Schools* (1918), *Training of Elementary Teachers in Germany* (1929), and *New Education in the German Republic* (with Beryl Parker, 1929). He coauthored *The Teacher of the Social Studies* (with William C. Bagley, BDAE, 1937), *Teaching as a Profession* (with Agnes Snyder, 1932), *Extracurricular Activities in the Elementary Schools* (with others, 1937), and *Supervision and Teaching of Reading* (with others, 1927).

REFERENCES: NYT, October 20, 1971, p. 50; WWW (5).

ALEXANDER, William Marvin. b. February 19, 1912, McKenzie, Tennessee, to E. Marvin and Lillis (McElroy) Alexander. Married June 6, 1935, to Nell McLeod. Children: two. d. August 27, 1996, Gainesville, Florida.

The "father of the American middle school," William M. Alexander led the movement to change junior high schools into middle schools. The University of Florida established the first program in middle school teacher education under Alexander's leadership.

After receiving the B.A. degree from Bethel College in McKenzie, Tennessee, in 1934, Alexander taught in McKenzie public schools for two years. He earned the M.A. degree from George Peabody College for Teachers (later, part of Vanderbilt University) in 1936. While assistant director of curriculum in Cincinnati, Ohio (1939–41), he received the Ph.D. degree from Columbia University (1940). Alexander was associate professor of education (1941–43) at the University of Tennessee; assistant superintendent of schools in Battle Creek, Michigan (1946–49); and superintendent of the Winnetka, Illinois, schools (1949–50). During World War II he was on active duty with the U.S. Naval Reserve (1943–46).

Alexander served as professor of education at the University of Miami (1950–58) and professor of education and chairman of the department at George Peabody College for Teachers (1958–63) before becoming professor of education at the University of Florida (1963–77). At Florida he was chair of the Division of Curriculum and Instruction (1963–66), director of the Institute for Curriculum Improvement (1966–69), and chair of the Department of Instructional Leadership (1975–77).

A prolific writer, Alexander's books included *Secondary Education: Basic Principles and Practices* (with J. Galen Saylor, BDAE, 1950), *Curriculum Planning for Better Teaching and Learning* (with Saylor, 1954), *Are You a Good Teacher?* (1959), *Independent Study in Secondary Schools* (with others, 1967), and *The Emergent Middle School* (with others, 1968). He edited *The High*

School of the Future: Memorial to Kimball Wiles (BDAE) (1969) and ''Rinehart Education Pamphlets'' (1957–62). His books were translated into several languages.

Alexander was a Fulbright scholar at the University of Teheran (1974–75). He was on the Board of Directors of the Joint Council on Economic Education (1951–64) and president of the Association for Supervision and Curriculum Development (1959–60). He received the John H. Lounsbury Award from the National Middle School Association (1981) and an award from the American Educational Research Association (1983).

REFERENCES: CA (33–36R); NYT, August 29, 1996, p. D19; RPE; WW (1980–81); C. Kenneth McEwin, ''William M. Alexander, Father of the American Middle School,'' *Middle School Journal* 23 (May 1992): 32–38.

AMES, Louise Bates. b. October 29, 1908, Portland, Maine, to Samuel Lewis and Annie Earle (Leach) Bates. Married May 22, 1930, to Smith Whittier Ames. Children: one. d. October 31, 1996, Cincinnati, Ohio.

Louise Bates Ames joined the Yale Clinic of Child Development, directed by Arnold Gesell (BDAE), in 1933 as a graduate student; she served at the clinic and its successor, the Gesell Institute, for more than sixty years. Ames was author and coauthor of several dozen books on children's behavior and school readiness, most of them in collaboration with Gesell and Frances L. Ilg (q.v.).

She earned the A.B. degree at the University of Maine in 1930 and the M.A. there in 1933. Yale University awarded her the Ph.D. in 1936.

Ames was an instructor in the Yale Medical School (1940–44) and an assistant professor as well as curator of the Yale Films of Child Development, a project of Gesell's clinic (1944–50). After Gesell's retirement, Yale closed the clinic, but Ilg and Ames obtained other quarters and continued operations, initially without pay during 1950–52, then with income from a syndicated newspaper column (''Parents Ask''), a television program (*Child Behavior*), and grants. Ames was director of research (1950–65), associate director of the institute (1965–70), codirector (1971–77), acting director (1978), and associate director (from 1978).

Her books included *The First Five Years of Life* (with Arnold Gesell and others, 1940), *The Child from Five to Ten* (with Gesell and others, 1946), *Youth: The Years from Ten to Sixteen* (with Gesell and Frances L. Ilg, 1956), *The Guidance Nursery School* (with Evelyn Goodenough Pitcher, 1964), *School Readiness* (with Frances L. Ilg, 1965), *Is Your Child in the Wrong Grade?* (1967), *Stop School Failure* (1972), and *Don't Push Your Preschooler* (with Joan A. Chase, her daughter, 1974).

Ames was president of the Society for Projective Techniques (1969–70). Yale University awarded her the title of assistant professor emeritus in 1993, when she was eighty-five years old.

REFERENCES: CA (NR–39); CB (1956, 1997); FWC; WW (1996); Louise Bates Ames, *Arnold Gesell—Themes of His Work* (Human Sciences Press, 1989), Chapter 26; Gwendolyn Stevens and Sheldon Gardner, *Women of Psychology*, vol. 2 (Schenkman, 1982), pp. 83–86.

ANDERSON, Charles Arnold. b. January 13, 1907, Platte, South Dakota, to Edward Thomas and Edith (Orvis) Anderson. Married July 18, 1942, to Mary Jean Bowman. Children: one. d. June 20, 1990, Chicago.

C. Arnold Anderson was a founder and leader of comparative education. He served as first director of the University of Chicago's Comparative Education Center (1958–72). In nearly 200 articles, he made important contributions to cross-national research methodology, the study of education and social mobility, and education in less-developed nations. He edited the *American Journal of Sociology* between 1967 and 1973.

After public schooling in the Dakotas and Minnesota, Anderson took the B.A. (1927), M.A. (1928), and Ph.D. (1932) degrees at the University of Minnesota, where Pitirim Sorokin was his mentor. Anderson went with Sorokin to Harvard University, teaching there from 1930 to 1935, when he moved to Iowa State University (1936–43). After wartime service in government (1943–45), Anderson taught at the University of Kentucky (1945–58), with leaves to teach at the University of California, Berkeley, and the Universities of Lund and Uppsala in Sweden. At Uppsala he was a Fulbright professor. In 1958 he became director of Chicago's Comparative Education Center, which Robert Havighurst (BDAE) and Francis Chase had established. At Iowa State and Chicago, Anderson was a close colleague of Theodore Schultz (q.v.), an expert in the economics of education.

Anderson was coauthor and editor of several books, including *Where Colleges Are and Who Attends* (with others, 1973) and *Social Selection in Education and Economic Development* (1983), but he was known better for his many scholarly articles. He was president of the Comparative and International Education Society (1962–63) and an honorary fellow of the society (1986). He received an honorary doctorate from the University of Stockholm and was elected to the Swedish Royal Academy.

REFERENCES: WWW (10); Erwin H. Epstein, "On the Wings of a Gadfly: C. Arnold Anderson," *CIES Newsletter* 95 (September 1990): 3–4; Erwin H. Epstein, "Editorial," and Philip Foster, "C. Arnold Anderson: A Personal Memoir," *Comparative Education Review* 35 (May 1991): 211–14 and 215–21.

ANDERSON, John Edward. b. June 13, 1893, Laramie, Wyoming, to John August and Julia (Wilhelmson) Anderson. Married December 3, 1918, to Dorothea Lynde. Children: five. d. May 10, 1966, Chattanooga, Tennessee.

John E. Anderson was founding director of the Institute of Child Welfare (later, Institute of Child Development) at the University of Minnesota from 1925 to 1954. He pioneered research in developmental psychology and was a founder of the Society for Research in Child Development. With Florence L. Goodenough (q.v.) he developed the Minnesota Occupational Scale. His book *Child*

Care and Training (with M. O. Faegre) appeared in eight editions between 1928 and 1958. His research encompassed parent education, early childhood education, and gerontology.

Raised in Wyoming, Anderson received the A.B. degree from the University of Wyoming in 1914. At Harvard University he earned A.M. (1915) and Ph.D. (1917) degrees. During 1917–19 he served in the U.S. Army as chief psychological examiner at Camps Devens (Massachusetts) and Greenleaf (Georgia) and instructor in the School of Military Psychology.

Anderson taught at Yale University from 1919 to 1925, when he went to the University of Minnesota. In 1954 he relinquished direction of the Institute of Child Development, but he remained as a graduate teacher and researcher until retirement in 1961. Established in his honor were the John E. Anderson Lecture Series in 1961 and the John E. Anderson Research Fund in 1963.

Anderson was president of the Society for Research in Child Development (1942–44), having chaired the editorial board of its *Monographs* (1934–38). He was president of the American Psychological Association (1942–43) and editor of the *Psychological Bulletin.* Anderson was a member of the White House Conference on Children in 1930 and chaired its Committee on the Infant and Pre-school Child, which led to studies on the status and welfare of children.

Anderson wrote more than 150 articles in professional journals. Among his books were *Happy Childhood: The Development and Guidance of Children and Youth* (1933), *The Psychology of Development and Personal Adjustment* (1949), and *Psychological Aspects of Aging* (1956). With Florence L. Goodenough he wrote *Your Child Year by Year* (1930) and *Experimental Child Study* (1931).

REFERENCES: NCAB (52: 59); WWW (4); Robert H. Beck, "Educational Leadership, 1906–1956," *Phi Delta Kappan* 37 (January 1956): 159; *Minneapolis Morning Tribune*, May 11, 1966, p. 1; Mildred C. Templin, "John E. Anderson: 1893–1966," *Child Development* 39 (September 1968): 657–70.

ANDERSON, Robert Henry. b. July 28, 1918, Milwaukee, Wisconsin, to Robert Dean and Eleanor (Weil) Anderson. Married July 19, 1941, to Mary Jane Hopkins; January 24, 1979, to Karolyn J. Snyder. Children: four.

Robert Anderson was an exponent of open education, an idea expressed through means such as team teaching across grade levels, flexible space plans in school buildings, extension of learning into the community, and providing children with choice in what they learn and how they learn it.

Anderson graduated with the B.A. degree (1939) from the University of Wisconsin, where he also earned the M.A. (1942). He received the Ph.D. degree at the University of Chicago in 1949.

He was a school teacher in Oconomowoc, Wisconsin (1940–43), and served in the U.S. Navy (1943–46). While pursuing graduate study, he was a school principal in River Forest, Illinois (1947–49). He was superintendent of schools in Park Forest, Illinois, from 1949 until his appointment to the faculty of the Graduate School of Education at Harvard University (1954–73). At Harvard he directed elementary school internships and led a team teaching project in the Lexington, Massachusetts, public schools. Anderson served as dean of education at Texas Tech University (1973–83) and was a professor of education at the University of South Florida (from 1984). He was founder and president of a consulting firm, Pedamorphosis.

Anderson wrote *The Nongraded Elementary School* (with John Goodlad, q.v., 1959), *Teaching in a World of Change* (1966), *Opting for Openness* (1973), and, with Karolyn J. Snyder, *Managing Productive Schools* (1986) and *Coaching Teaching* (1988). He served on the U.S. Department of State's Overseas Schools Advisory Committee and the Board of Directors of the Association for Supervision and Curriculum of the National Education Association. He was a consulting editor of *Colloquy*.

REFERENCES: CA (NR-27); ECE; LE (1974); WW (1996); John H. Johansen et al., *American Education* (W. C. Brown, 1982), pp. 292–93.

ANDRUS, Ethel Percy. b. September 21, 1884, San Francisco, California, to George Wallace and Lucretia Frances (Duke) Andrus. Married: no. d. July 13, 1967, Long Beach, California.

Ethel Percy Andrus was instrumental in changing the status of retired teachers as founder of the National Retired Teachers Association (NRTA) in 1947. She served as its president until her death in 1967.

Andrus attended schools in Chicago. She received the Ph.B. degree from the University of Chicago in 1903 and the B.S. degree from the Lewis Institute (later, Illinois Institute of Technology) in 1918. She received M.A. (1928) and Ph.D. (1930) degrees from the University of Southern California.

After teaching at the Lewis Institute, beginning in 1903, she moved to California in 1910 and taught in Los Angeles high schools. In 1916 she became the first woman principal in California. She served as principal of Abraham Lincoln High School to her retirement in 1944. Active in the community, Andrus established the Opportunity School for Adults at Lincoln. She taught summer school at several universities in Los Angeles.

Andrus helped secure low-cost health insurance for NRTA members and established branches in all states. She edited the *NRTA Journal*, founded in 1950.

In 1958 she founded the American Association of Retired Persons (AARP). She later founded and edited *Modern Maturity*, a monthly journal. Andrus also established the Retirement Research and Welfare Association in 1961 and the Institute for Lifetime Learning in 1963. She served on the national advisory committee for the White House Conference on Aging in 1961. The Ethel Percy Andrus Gerontology Center at the University of Southern California was named in her honor.

REFERENCES: DAB (supp. 8); NAW (Mod); NYT, July 15, 1967, p. 25; WWAW (1961); WR; Dorothy Crippen et al., comps., *The Wisdom of Ethel Percy Andrus* (National Retired Teachers Association, 1968); Marion Smith, ''The Oldsters Come of Age,'' *Minnesota Journal of Education* 48 (March 1968): 22.

ANRIG, Gregory Richard. b. November 18, 1931, Englewood, New Jersey. Married June 29, 1957, to Charlotte Schlott. Children: three. d. November 14, 1993, Princeton, New Jersey.

Though he served with distinction as education commissioner of Massachusetts and worked in the U.S. Office of Education, Gregory Anrig was remembered best for his leadership of the Educational Testing Service (ETS) during the turbulent 1980s. Anrig became president of ETS in 1981, the year after publication of Allan Nairn's highly critical book *The Reign of ETS: The Corporation That Makes Up Minds*. David Owen's book *None of the Above: Behind the Myth of Scholastic Aptitude* (1985) extended Nairn's critique and included personal information about Anrig. In 1988 the motion picture *Stand and Deliver* portrayed Latino students of a charismatic teacher investigated by ETS officials who suspected cheating. Through this adversity, Anrig remained a forceful defender of ETS, its methods, standards, and products.

Anrig graduated from Western Michigan University (1953) and earned M.A.T. (1956) and Ed.D. (1963) degrees from the Harvard Graduate School of Education. He served with the U.S. Army in Korea (1953–55). He was a high school teacher and principal (1956–64) in White Plains, New York, and superintendent of the Mount Greylock Regional School District of Williamstown, Massachusetts (1964–67). He served in the U.S. Office of Education as director of the equal opportunities division (1967–69) and executive assistant to the commissioner of education (1969–70). From 1970 to 1973 Anrig directed the Institute of Learning and Teaching at the University of Massachusetts, Boston. As commissioner in Massachusetts (1973–81) he devoted much of his attention to school desegregation in Boston and sixteen other cities.

In 1989 Anrig received the Harvard Graduate School of Education's Alumni Council Award, and in 1993 a medal for distinguished service from Teachers College, Columbia University. One month before his death, the College Entrance Examination Board awarded him its Medal for Distinguished Service.

REFERENCES: NYT, November 16, 1993, p. B14; WW (1994); George R. Kaplan, "Shining Lights in High Places: Education's Top Four Leaders and Their Heirs," *Phi Delta Kappan* 67 (September 1985): 7+.

ARTICHOKER, John Hobart. b. January 17, 1930, Pine Ridge, South Dakota, to John and Emily (Lessert) Artichoker. Married to June Boettiger.

Soon after establishment in 1949 of an Office of Indian Education within the South Dakota Department of Public Instruction, John Artichoker became its first long-term director (1951–62). Artichoker earned B.A. and M.A. degrees at the University of South Dakota. His revised master's thesis was published as *The Sioux Indian Goes to College* (with Neil M. Palmer, 1959). It presented the results of a study of seventy-two Native American college students, half of them bilingual, the other half speakers only of English. Artichoker found that Indian youth who were less assimilated into the majority culture faced greater challenges in college, due to poor academic preparation, insufficient resources, and difficulty in social adjustment.

Artichoker went from state service to a second career in the U.S. Bureau of Indian Affairs, where he was a tribal relations officer in Montana (1962–63) and a reservation superintendent in Montana and Arizona (1963–82). In retirement he worked in the development of Native American economic enterprises.

REFERENCES: BDIA; NNAA; T. Emogene Paulson and Lloyd R. Moses, *Who's Who among the Sioux* (Institute of Indian Studies, University of South Dakota, 1988).

AUSTIN, Mary Carrington. b. January 10, 1915, Sherrill, New York, to Curtis and Anna A. (Lynch) Carrington. Married July 30, 1939, to George H. Austin. Children: no.

Mary Austin served as director of the Harvard-Carnegie Reading Study, a survey of reading curricula and policies in teacher preparation programs at seventy-four colleges and universities. As principal author of *The Torchlighters: Tomorrow's Teachers of Reading* (1961), she recommended higher admission requirements for teacher preparation programs and urged greater emphasis on reading instruction for all teachers.

With a three-year diploma earned in 1935 at the Oswego College of Education (later, State University of New York College at Oswego), Mary Austin became a high school teacher in Phoenix, New York (1935–44). She resumed her formal education at Syracuse University, where she received B.S. (1944), M.S. (1945), and Ed.D. (1949) degrees. She was a member of the faculty in education at Western Reserve (later, Case Western Reserve) University from 1948 to 1955. In 1955 Austin went to the Graduate School of Education at Harvard University, where she was a lecturer until 1963. Austin taught again at Western Reserve University (1963–69) and the University of Hawaii (1969–81). During the last part of her career, her scholarship shifted to the positive effects of multicultural literature on children's learning.

She was coauthor of the "Sheldon Reading Series" (1957), *The First R: The Harvard Report on Reading in Elementary Schools* (with Coleman Morrison, 1963), and *The Torchlighters Revisited* (with Morrison, 1977), *Reading Evaluation* (1961), *Literature for Children about Asians and Asian-Americans* (1987), and *Promoting World Understanding through Literature* (1983); and coeditor of *The Sound of Poetry* (1963). She served as president of the International Reading Association (1960–61) and the National Conference on Research in English.

REFERENCES: CA (5–8R); WWAW (1976).

AUSUBEL, David Paul. b. October 25, 1918, Brooklyn, New York, to Herman and Lillian (Leff) Ausubel. Married November 21, 1943, to Pearl Liebowitz. Children: two.

What works in classrooms was the focus David Ausubel preferred for educational psychology. Ausubel's research built on the premise that new learning takes place most effectively when it fits into schemes that already exist in students' minds. His advocacy of reception learning and expository teaching brought the expression "advance organizers" into the common vocabulary and practice of classroom teachers.

Ausubel studied at the University of Pennsylvania (A.B., 1939). He earned the M.D. degree at Middlesex University in 1943 and M.A. (1940) and Ph.D. (1950) degrees in developmental psychology at Columbia University.

Ausubel was an assistant surgeon and psychiatric resident with the U.S. Public Health Service and worked in Germany in the medical treatment of displaced persons immediately after World War II.

He taught at the University of Illinois from 1950 to 1966. He was professor of psychology, education, and medical education at the University of Toronto (1966–68) before going to the City University of New York, where he headed the doctoral program in educational psychology until his retirement in 1975. From 1981 he was a psychiatrist at Rockland Children's Psychiatric Center.

Ausubel's many books included *Ego Development and the Personality Disorders* (1952), *Theory and Problems of Adolescent Development* (1954), *Theory and Problems of Child Development* (1958), *Maori Youth: A Psychoethnological Study of Cultural Deprivation* (1961), *The Psychology of Meaningful Verbal Learning* (1963), *School Learning: An Introduction to Educational Psychology* (with Floyd G. Robinson, 1969), and *The Fern and the Tiki: An American View of New Zealand National Character, Social Attitudes, and Race Relations* (1977). He was a Fulbright scholar in New Zealand during 1957–58.

REFERENCES: *Directory of the American Psychological Association* (American Psychological Association, 1993); *Who's Who in World Jewry* (Pitman, 1972).

B

BAIRD, Albert Craig. b. October 20, 1883, Vevay, Indiana, to William J. and Sarah (Hedden) Baird. Married June 26, 1923, to Marion Peirce. Children: one. d. March 18, 1979, Iowa City, Iowa.

A. Craig Baird was a leader in the field of speech education. His book, *Public Discussion and Debate* (1928), was a pioneer text in the field.

After graduation from high school in Vevay, Indiana, Baird spent one year working in a steel mill in Youngstown, Ohio. He graduated with the A.B. degree in 1907 from Wabash College, then attended McCormick Theological Seminary in Chicago for one year. At Union Theological Seminary in New York City, he received the B.D. degree in 1910. Columbia University awarded him the A.M. degree in 1912.

Baird taught at Ohio Wesleyan University (1910–11), Dartmouth College (1911–13), and Bates College (1913–25). In addition to teaching argumentation and composition, he headed debate programs. Baird organized the State of Maine Debate League in 1914 and the international debating program in 1921.

In 1925 Baird went to the University of Iowa. He directed the Iowa High School Forensic League until 1948. He became interested in public address and initiated yearly publication of *Representative American Speeches* by H. W. Wilson Company. He was its editor from 1938 to 1960. Baird was president of the Speech Association of America in 1939. Among his books were *Public Discussion and Debate* (1928), *Discussion: Principles and Types* (1943), *Argumentation, Discussion, and Debate* (1950), *American Public Addresses, 1740–1952* (1956), and *Rhetoric: A Philosophic Inquiry* (1965).

REFERENCES: CA (P–1); WWW (7); Owen Peterson, "A. Craig Baird (1883–1979)," *The Southern Speech Communication Journal* 47 (Winter 1982): 130–34; Loren Reid, ed., *American Public Address: Studies in Honor of Albert Craig Baird* (University of Missouri Press, 1961); *Wilson Library Bulletin* 34 (January 1960): 381.

BAKER, Frank Elmer. b. September 10, 1877, Clymer, New York, to Horace and Amelia Wilhelmina (Simmelinke) Baker. Married June 14, 1911, to Florence Howard Fowler; November 1, 1926, to Ruth Mary Geiser. Children: two. d. April 19, 1961, Mountain Home, North Carolina.

Frank Baker was an innovative leader in teacher training, bringing to the subject extensive experience as a schoolteacher and principal. He graduated with a diploma from Clarion State Normal School (later, Clarion University of Pennsylvania) in 1895 and earned the A.B. degree at Allegheny College in 1905 and the A.M. at Harvard University in 1909.

With his normal school training, he served as teacher and principal in several rural schools in northwestern Pennsylvania and southwestern New York, moving every year or two (1895–1903). After graduation from Allegheny College, he was high school principal in Greensburg, Pennsylvania (1905–8). He chaired the science department at Brooklyn Polytechnic Institute Preparatory School during 1909–11.

In 1911 he took the first of three successive assignments directing normal schools. He was principal of Edinboro State Normal School (1911–20, later, Edinboro University of Pennsylvania), East Stroudsburg State Normal School (1920–23, later, East Stroudsburg University of Pennsylvania), and Milwaukee State Teachers College (1923–46, later, University of Wisconsin–Milwaukee), where after two years the position was retitled president.

Baker was a proponent of the "integrated course" approach to preparation for elementary school teaching, which alternated field experiences in schools with academic study. This method attracted national attention and led to studies in the 1930s and 1940s by the American Council on Education and the Harvard Graduate School of Education.

Baker contributed to yearbooks of the John Dewey Society as well as to teacher education journals. He was president of the American Association of Teachers Colleges (1933–34) and the American Association of Teacher Education Institutions in Metropolitan Areas (1941) and was on the executive board of the Progressive Education Association.

REFERENCES: NCAB (45: 28); WWW (5).

BALLARD, Louis Wayne. b. July 8, 1931, Devil's Promenade, Oklahoma, to Charles Guthrie and Leona Mae (Quapaw) Ballard. Married to Ruth Dové; December 6, 1965, to Ruth Sands. Children: three.

As a composer and music educator, Louis Ballard sought to preserve Native American musical traditions and bring them into the consciousness of mainstream American culture. Ballard gained his early education at an Indian boarding school, a reservation school, and a Baptist mission school in Oklahoma. He studied at Northeast Oklahoma Agricultural and Mechanical College and the University of Tulsa, where he graduated with the B.A. degree in 1954. He earned the master of music degree there in 1962.

He was a teacher of music in public schools in Oklahoma (1954–58), taught music privately (1959–62), then was music director (1962–65) and performing arts director (1965–69) at the Institute of American Indian Arts in Santa Fe, New Mexico. For a decade (1969–79) in the U.S. Bureau of Indian Affairs, Ballard was responsible for music education in Native American schools. In all of these roles Ballard emphasized the distinctiveness and value of the Native American musical tradition. As a composer his orchestrations used western and

Native American instruments to present Native American themes. From 1979 he worked independently as a composer in Santa Fe.

Ballard wrote ballets and many other musical forms. He was author of *My Music Reaches to the Sky* (1973) and *Music of North American Indians* (1975). He was a four-time recipient of awards from the National Endowment for the Arts. He received a National Indian Achievement Award in 1972 and the Catlin Peace Pipe Award of the National Indian Lore Association in 1976, among many other honors.

REFERENCES: BBD; NGD; WW (1996); Jane B. Katz, ed., *This Song Remembers: Self-Portraits of Native Americans in the Arts* (Houghton Mifflin, 1980), pp. 132–38; Barry T. Klein, ed., *Reference Encyclopedia of the American Indian* (Todd, 1986); Sharon Malinowski, ed., *Notable Native Americans* (Gale Research, 1995).

BANDURA, Albert. b. December 4, 1925, Mundare, Alberta, Canada, to Joseph and Jessie (Berazanski) Bandura. Married to Virginia B. Varnes. Children: two.

Albert Bandura's emphasis on imitative behavior in his social learning theory strongly influenced educators' assumptions about aggressive behavior and heightened their concerns about television violence. Later in his career, he developed an empowerment model for at-risk children based on the premise that successful interpersonal competencies could be achieved through effective modeling.

After schooling in northern rural Alberta, Canada, Bandura studied at the University of British Columbia, earning the B.A. degree in 1949. At the University of Iowa he was awarded M.A. (1951) and Ph.D. (1952) degrees in psychology. He was a postdoctoral intern at the Wichita (Kansas) Guidance Center during 1952–53.

An important influence on Bandura when he joined the Psychology Department at Stanford University in 1953 was Robert Sears (q.v.), then department chair. Bandura remained at Stanford all of his career, becoming David Starr Jordan Professor of Social Science in 1974.

With R. H. Walters, Bandura wrote *Adolescent Aggression* (1959) and *Social Learning and Personality Development* (1963). He was also author of *Principles of Behavior Modification* (1969), *Aggression: A Social Learning Analysis* (1973), and *Social Foundations of Thought and Action* (1986). His book *Social Learning Theory* (1971) was translated into four languages.

Bandura was president of the American Psychological Association (1974) and the Western Psychological Association. He was a fellow of the Center for Advanced Study in the Behavioral Sciences (1969–70) and a Guggenheim fellow (1972). He received the James McKeen Cattell Award in 1977 and became a fellow of the American Academy of Arts and Sciences in 1980, among other honors.

REFERENCES: CA (13–16R); ECE; WD (1994–96); WW (1996); *American Psychologist* 36 (January 1981): 27–34; Richard I. Evans, *Albert Bandura: The Man and His Ideas—A Dialogue* (Praeger, 1989); Joan E. Grusec, "Social Learning Theory and

Developmental Psychology: The Legacies of Robert Sears [q.v.] and Albert Bandura,'' *Developmental Psychology* 28 (September 1992): 776–86; Vernon J. Nordby and Calvin S. Hall, *A Guide to Psychologists and Their Concepts* (W. H. Freeman, 1974).

BARKER, Mary Cornelia. b. January 20, 1879, Atlanta, Georgia, to Thomas Nathaniel and Dora Elizabeth (Lovejoy) Barker. Married: no. d. September 15, 1963, Atlanta, Georgia.

Mary Barker was a schoolteacher and principal who provided leadership in the earliest years of teachers' unions in the city of Atlanta and nationally.

She graduated with a diploma from Agnes Scott College in 1900. For the next four years she taught in rural schools and at the Orphans Home of Decatur, Georgia. In 1904 she became a teacher in the Atlanta public schools and in 1922 a principal, the role she filled until her retirement in 1944.

Barker was a prominent member of the Atlanta Public School Teachers' Association from its founding in 1905. She led its affiliation with the American Federation of Teachers (AFT, 1919) and Atlanta Federation of Trades (1920), placing it firmly in the labor movement. She was president of the Atlanta teachers' organization (1923–25) and of the AFT (1925–31). As president of the national union, she led the expansion of its membership and the establishment of a set of common goals focused on improvement of teaching conditions.

She was an organizer of the Southern Summer School for Women Workers in Industry and chair of its central committee (1927–44).

REFERENCES: BDAL; NAW (Mod); Solon De Leon, ed., *American Labor Who's Who* (Hanford Press, 1925); Joseph Whitworth Newman, ''A History of the Atlanta Public School Teachers' Association, Local 897 the American Federation of Teachers 1919–1956'' (Ph.D. diss., Georgia State University, 1978).

BARNETT, Marguerite Ross. b. May 21, 1942, Charlottesville, Virginia, to Dewey Ross and Mary (Douglass) Barnett. Married December 18, 1962, to Stephen A. Barnett; June 30, 1980, to Walter Eugene King. Children: one. d. February 26, 1992, Wailuku, Hawaii.

Marguerite Ross Barnett was the first African-American woman to head a major university. Barnett was an advocate for urban universities' having a strong role in urban society. She became president of the University of Houston in 1990 but died of cancer less than two years later.

Barnett had gone to Houston from the chancellorship of the University of Missouri–St. Louis, which she headed from 1986 to 1990. At both institutions she established programs that aided disadvantaged students in their transition to college. Her program received the Anderson Medal of the American Council on Education in 1991 as an outstanding public school initiative. At St. Louis the program was called Partnerships for Progress, and at Houston, the Texas Center for University–School Partnerships.

Barnett was raised in Buffalo, New York, where she graduated from Bennett High School. She received the A.B. degree from Antioch College (1964) and

M.A. (1966) and Ph.D. (1972) degrees from the University of Chicago. She taught political science at the University of Chicago (1969–70), Princeton University (1970–76), and Howard University (1976–80), where she also headed the Department of Political Science (1977–80). From 1980 to 1983 at Columbia University Barnett directed the Institute for Urban and Minority Education.

In 1983 Barnett became vice chancellor for academic affairs at the City University of New York (CUNY), where she established a transition program for disadvantaged high school students. Barnett served as a consultant to many organizations dealing with racial, public policy, and urban problems. In 1981 her book *The Politics of Cultural Nationalism in South India* (1976) received a prize from the American Political Science Association. She coedited *Public Policy for the Black Community: Strategies and Perspectives* (with James A. Refner, 1976), *Comparing Race, Sex, and National Origin Desegregation* (1985), and *Educational Policy in an Era of Conservative Reform* (1986). She received many public service awards.

REFERENCES: BWA; CHE, June 25, 1986, p. A3, and March 6, 1991, p. A3; NBAW; NYT, February 27, 1992, p. B7; WWBA (1985); WWW (10).

BARON, Salo Wittmayer. b. May 26, 1895, Tarnow, Austrian Galicia (later, Poland), to Elias and Minna (Wittmayer) Baron. Married June 12, 1934, to Jeannette G. Meisel. Children: two. d. November 25, 1989, New York City.

More than anyone else, Salo W. Baron gave shape to the interdisciplinary field of Jewish studies in the United States. At Columbia University, he was the first American professor of Jewish studies. He was author of *A Social and Religious History of the Jews* in eighteen volumes, from their origins to the twelfth century.

As a child, Baron was tutored at home and trained with his father to be a commodities broker. When he was eighteen, his family moved to Vienna, capital of the Austro-Hungarian Empire. There his studies brought him ordination as a rabbi (1920) and doctorates from the University of Vienna in philosophy (1917), political science (1922), and law (1923). He lectured on history at the Jüdisches Pädagogium in Vienna from 1919 to 1925, when he emigrated to the United States.

Baron taught at the Jewish Institute of Religion in New York City from 1926 to 1930, serving concurrently as acting librarian and director of the Department of Advanced Studies. In 1930 he was appointed to the Miller Chair of Jewish History, Literature, and Institutions at Columbia University, where he continued to teach until he retired in 1963. He held concurrent appointment on the faculty of the Jewish Theological Seminary (1954–72).

In addition to writing eighteen of the thirty-two volumes he had planned of his major work (second edition, 1952–83), Baron was author of *Modern Nationalism and Religion* (1947), *The Russian Jew under Tsars and Soviets* (1964), and *Economic History of the Jews* (with Arcadius Kahan, 1975), among many other works. His command of twenty languages aided his scholarship.

He was a fellow of the American Academy of Arts and Sciences, president of the American Academy for Jewish Research during four terms totaling nineteen years between 1940 and 1979, founder and president of the Conference of Jewish Social Studies (1941–55, 1959–68), and president of the American Jewish Historical Society (1953–55). He served as president of the Academic Council of Hebrew University in Jerusalem (1940–50) and sat on the Boards of Governors of the Universities of Haifa and Tel Aviv.

REFERENCES: CA (69–72, 130); IESS (18); NYT, May 6, 1975, p. 31, February 27, 1985, p. III 20, and November 26, 1989, p. 44; WWW (10); Abraham J. Karp, ''Professor Salo Wittmayer Baron: A Tribute,'' and Salo W. Baron, ''Reply,'' *American Jewish History* 71 (June 1982): 493–500; Robert J. Liberles, *Salo Wittmayer Baron: Architect of Jewish History* (New York University Press, 1995).

BARZUN, Jacques Martin. b. November 30, 1907, Créteil, France, to Henri Martin and Anna-Rose (Martin) Barzun. Married August 1936 to Mariana Lowell; June 1980 to Marguerite Davenport. Children: three.

Jacques Barzun immigrated to the United States from France at eleven years of age. He enrolled in Columbia University when he was fifteen, earning B.A. (1927), M.A. (1928), and Ph.D. (1932) degrees there. The university would remain his professional home over a long career as professor and administrator.

Barzun was renowned for the range of his learning and the sharpness of his opinions on culture and education. He championed liberal arts against specialization in universities and colleges and modeled the difference through his own scholarship, which ranged across history, art, music, literature, philosophy, and contemporary affairs. In *The House of Intellect* (1959), he objected to the democratic tendency of public schooling in the United States, where, in his view, driver education had replaced Latin. He was dean of graduate faculties at Columbia University from 1955 to 1958 and provost from 1958 to 1967. Upon his retirement from Columbia as University Professor in 1975, he became a literary adviser to Scribner's publishing house.

Among Barzun's many books were *The French Race* (1932), *Darwin, Marx, Wagner* (1941), *Romanticism and the Modern Ego* (1943), *The Teacher in America* (1945), *Berlioz and the Romantic Century* (1950), *Music in American Life* (1956), *The Modern Researcher* (1957), *Science, the Glorious Entertainment* (1964), *The American University* (1968), *Clio and the Doctors* (1974), *A Stroll with William James* (1983), *The Culture We Deserve* (1989), and *Begin Here: On Teaching and Learning* (1990).

Barzun was a member of the editorial board of *The American Scholar* (1946–76) and a frequent contributor to it. He served twice as president of the American Academy and Institute of Arts and Letters (1972–75, 1977–78). He was a Chevalier of the French Legion of Honor and received the George Polk Memorial Award for his achievement as editor of *Modern American Usage*.

REFERENCES: CA (NR-22); CB (1964); NYT July 11, 1975, p. C38; WD (1994–96); WW (1996); John Thomas Holton, ''The Educational Thought of Jacques Barzun: Its

Historical Foundation and Significance for Teacher Education'' (Ph.D. diss., Ohio State University, 1980).

BASCOM, Florence. b. July 14, 1862, Williamstown, Massachusetts, to John (BDAE) and Emma (Curtiss) Bascom. Married: no. d. June 18, 1945, Northampton, Massachusetts.

Florence Bascom was a noted geologist who spent most of her career at Bryn Mawr College, where she introduced geology as a major and taught the leading women geologists of her era. Under her leadership the Bryn Mawr graduate program in geology gained a national reputation.

Bascom attended high school in Madison, Wisconsin, and received bachelor's degrees from the University of Wisconsin, where her father, John Bascom, was president. After graduation she taught for one year without pay at Hampton Institute (later, University). She earned a master's degree in geology at Wisconsin in 1887, then taught high school Greek and physical geography for one year. At Rockford (Illinois) Seminary (later, College) Bascom taught geology and chemistry for two years. In 1893 she was the first woman to earn the Ph.D. degree from Johns Hopkins University and the first woman in America to receive a doctorate in geology. From 1893 to 1895 she was an assistant in geology to Edward Orton (BDAE) at Ohio State University. In 1895 she went to Bryn Mawr College, where she remained until her retirement in 1928. She had been asked to introduce geology in the Departments of Biology and Chemistry. A separate Geology Department was formed after three years.

In addition to teaching, Bascom was with the U.S. Geological Survey from 1896 to 1936, the first woman member of the survey. She participated in mapping some of the Mid-Atlantic Piedmont region. Her work published in Geological Survey Folios included *Volcanic Rocks of South Mountain, Pennsylvania* (1896), *Geological and Mineral Resources of the Quakertown–Doylestown District, Pennsylvania and New Jersey* (1931), and *Fairfield–Gettysburg Folio, Pennsylvania* (with George W. Stose, 1929). She was the first woman elected a fellow of the Geological Society of America in 1894. From 1896 to 1905 she was an associate editor of *American Geologist.*

REFERENCES: AWS; BCAW; DAB (supp. 3); LW; NAW; NYT June 20, 1945, p. 23; WWAW (1914); WWW (2); Lois Barber Arnold, *Four Lives in Science: Women's Education in the Nineteenth Century* (Schocken Books, 1984); *The Biographical Cyclopaedia of American Women*, vol. 2 (Franklin W. Lee, 1925; Gale Research, 1974); G. Kass-Simon and Patricia Farnes, eds., *Women of Science: Righting the Record* (Indiana University Press, 1990).

BEATTY, Willard Walcott. b. September 17, 1891, Berkeley, California, to William Adam and Mabel (Walcott) Beatty. Married December 13, 1913, to Elise Hersey Biedenbach. Children: two. d. September 29, 1961, Washington, D.C.

Willard Beatty was a prominent innovator in the progressive education movement. He was one of the developers of the "Winnetka technique" of individually paced learning and the originator of the "Bronxville experiment," which emphasized socialization of schoolchildren for responsible citizenship, racial tolerance, and sexual awareness.

Beatty earned B.S. (1913) and A.M. (1921) degrees at the University of California, Berkeley. He pursued graduate study during the 1920s at the University of Chicago and Teachers College of Columbia University but did not complete further degrees. He taught drawing in the Oakland, California, public schools (1913–14) and was managing editor of *California Outlook* (1914–15), a weekly magazine, before joining the faculty of San Francisco State Normal School (later, University). There he headed the departments of arithmetic (1915–17) and history and civics (1917–20), directed teacher training (also 1917–20), and was an associate of Frederic Burk (BDAE) and Carleton Washburne (BDAE). Beatty taught next at the Presidio Open Air School of San Francisco (1920–22).

In 1922 he became junior high school principal and assistant superintendent of schools in Winnetka, Illinois. With Washburne, who was superintendent, he developed the "Winnetka technique." In 1926 Beatty went to Bronxville, New York, site of the "Bronxville experiment," to be superintendent of schools. During his ten years at Bronxville, he became a leader of the Progressive Education Association, serving as its president (1933–37) and treasurer (1941–44).

Beatty was director of education in the U.S. Bureau of Indian Affairs from 1936 to 1952. In the initial years of his term he replaced boarding with day schools and promoted a bilingual curriculum for Native American children. In later years, he was unable to sustain these reforms. He served as deputy director of UNESCO in Paris, France (1951–53); as an educational consultant to Perkins and Will, an architectural firm (1953–58); and as executive vice president of the Save the Children Federation (1958–61).

Beatty was editor of *Indian Education* (1936–51) and author of *Education for Action* (1944) and *Education for Cultural Change* (1953).

REFERENCES: DAB (supp. 7); NYT, September 30, 1961, p. 25; WWW (4); letter from Frederick J. Stefon to John F. Ohles, October 12, 1981.

BECKER, Gary Stanley. b. December 2, 1930, Pottsville, Pennsylvania, to Louis William and Anna (Siskind) Becker. Married September 19, 1954, to Doria Slote; October 31, 1979, to Guity Nashat. Children: four.

After attending public schools in New York City, Gary S. Becker studied at Princeton University, where he earned the A.B. degree with highest honors in 1951. He was awarded A.M. (1953) and Ph.D. (1955) degrees at the University of Chicago. Becker taught at the University of Chicago from 1954 to 1957 and again from 1969. In the interim he was on the faculty of Columbia University.

Becker's scholarship focused on the boundaries between economics and other social sciences, including education. His book *Human Capital: A Theoretical and Empirical Analysis, with Special Reference to Education* (1964) examined rates of investment in education and rates of return in the form of future earnings. His observation that persons with the lowest levels of education were wasted in the American economy led him to support educational vouchers and expanded vocational training programs. Becker was also author of *Economics of Discrimination* (1957), *Economic Theory* (1971), *The Allocation of Time and Goods over the Life Cycle* (1975), and *A Treatise on the Family* (1981), among other works. In 1992 he received the Nobel Prize in economics. He was a founder of the National Academy of Education and recipient of the John Bates Clark Medal of the American Economic Association (1967).

REFERENCES: CA (NR-11); CB (1993); LE (1974); WD (1994–96); WW (1996); WWE; J. R. Shackleton, "Gary S. Becker: The Economist as Empire-Builder," in J. R. Shackleton and Gareth Locksley, eds., *Twelve Contemporary Economists* (John Wiley and Sons, 1981).

BEGLE, Edward Griffith. b. November 27, 1914, in Saginaw, Michigan, to Ned G. and Cornelia (Campbell) Begle. Married August 14, 1937, to Elise Aiken Pierce. Children: seven. d. March 2, 1978, Palo Alto, California.

When the launch of the Sputnik satellite by the Soviet Union in 1957 raised concerns about the adequacy of science and mathematics education in American schools, Edward G. Begle became a leader in the development of "new math." Begle emphasized the importance of mathematical principles over the traditional focus on memorization and computational skills. Under his leadership the School Mathematics Study Group (SMSG) reconceptualized the learning of mathematics at all grade levels and developed teaching materials to fit the new concept.

Begle graduated with B.A. (1936) and M.A. (1937) degrees from the University of Michigan. He studied topology at Princeton University, where he earned the Ph.D. degree in mathematics in 1940. After holding a National Research Council Fellowship (1941–42), Begle joined the faculty of Yale University, where he was assistant and associate professor from 1942 to 1961. At Stanford University (1961–79) he was professor of mathematics and education. He directed SMSG from 1958 to 1972. He also led in the development of the National Longitudinal Study of Mathematical Abilities.

Begle wrote *Introductory Calculus, with Analytic Geometry* (1954) and *Critical Variables in Mathematics Education: Findings from a Survey of the Empirical Literature* (1979). He served the American Mathematical Society as secretary during 1951–56. In 1969 the Mathematical Association of America presented him its Distinguished Service Award.

REFERENCES: LE (1974); NYT, March 3, 1978, p. B2; WWW (7); *American Mathematical Monthly* 85 (October 1978): 629–31; William Wooten, *SMSG: The Making of a Curriculum* (Yale University Press, 1965).

BELKIN, Samuel. b. December 12, 1911, Swislicz, Poland, to Solomon and Mina (Sattir) Belkin. Married November 19, 1935, to Selma Ehrlich; January 3, 1963, to Abby Polesie. Children: two. d. April 18, 1976, New York City.

In the thirty-two years that Samuel Belkin served as president of Yeshiva

University, he led its development into a major university remaining true to its Orthodox Jewish commitments.

Belkin was seventeen years old when he earned ordination in 1929 as a rabbi at Radun Theological Seminary in his native Poland. The same year he emigrated to the United States. He studied at Harvard and Brown universities, receiving the Ph.D. degree in Greek literature at Brown in 1935.

On arrival in this country, Belkin taught Talmud for one year at New Haven Rabbinical Seminary in Cleveland, Ohio. In 1935 he began an affiliation at Yeshiva College that would continue until his death. Beginning as instructor of Greek and Talmud, he soon became dean and professor of Hellenistic literature (1940–43), then president (1943–75). In 1943 Yeshiva became a university. In 1955 it began offering medical training through Albert Einstein College of Medicine. Through the entire period of Belkin's administrative leadership, from 1940 to 1976, he was also dean of the university's theological seminary.

Belkin was author of *The Alexandrian Halakhah in Apologetic Literature* (1936), *Philo and Oral Law* (1940), *Essays in Traditional Jewish Thought* (1956), and *In His Image* (1961). He was a member of the National Advisory Commission on the Bicentennial of the American Revolution.

REFERENCES: CA (NR-6, 65–68); CB (1952, 1976); LE (1974); NCAB (G: 373); WWW (7); *Jewish Education* 44 (Spring/Summer 1976): 17; *Newsweek* 39 (June 23, 1952): 86.

BELL, Derrick Albert, Jr. b. November 6, 1930, Pittsburgh, Pennsylvania, to Derrick Albert and Ada Elisabeth (Childress) Bell. Married June 26, 1960, to Jewell Allison Hairston; July 1992 to Janet Dewart. Children: three.

Derrick Bell's commitment to creating educational opportunities for African Americans led him to positions that were often controversial. In 1971 he was the first African American tenured at Harvard Law School. There he developed a perspective on legal studies known as "critical race theory." True to his principle of teaching future lawyers to take risks for their beliefs and values, Bell took unpaid leave from Harvard in 1990, protesting the absence of a tenured woman of color. Two years later Harvard revoked Bell's tenure.

Bell earned the A.B. degree at Duquesne University in 1952 and after military service gained the LL.B. at the University of Pittsburgh in 1957. Even though he ranked third in his class and had served on the law review, because of his race he received no employment offers from major law firms. He became an attorney in the civil rights division of the U.S. Department of Justice (1957–59) but left after refusing an order to resign his membership in the National Association for the Advancement of Colored People (NAACP).

Bell was briefly executive director of the Pittsburgh NAACP, then first assistant counsel of the NAACP Legal Defense and Educational Fund in New York (1960–66), where he worked with Thurgood Marshall and James Nabrit (q.v.) to gain admission to the University of Mississippi for James Meredith. Bell returned to Washington as deputy director of the Office of Civil Rights in the

Department of Health, Education, and Welfare (1966–68). Frustrated by the slow pace of the bureaucracy, he resigned and became executive director of the Western Center on Law and Poverty at the University of Southern California. One year later he moved to Harvard Law School.

Between two periods of teaching at Harvard (1969–79, 1985–91), Bell was visiting professor at Stanford University and dean of the University of Oregon Law School (1981–85). He was visiting professor at New York University Law School from 1991. He received fellowships from the Ford Foundation (1972, 1975) and National Endowment for the Humanities (1980–81). In 1985 he received the Society of American Law Schools Teacher of the Year Award.

He was author of the widely used text *Race, Racism and American Law* (1973); *We Are Not Saved: The Elusive Quest for Racial Justice* (1987); *Faces at the Bottom of the Well: The Permanence of Racism* (1992), and a memoir titled *Confronting Authority: Reflections of an Ardent Protester* (1994). He edited *Shades of Brown: New Perspectives on School Desegregation* (1980).

REFERENCES: CA (104); CB (1993); EBA; NYT, May 21, 1990, p. A18, November 21, 1990, p. B11, and October 28, 1992, p. C1; WW (1996); WWBA (1994/95).

BELL, Terrel Howard. b. November 11, 1921, Lava Hot Springs, Idaho, to Willard Dewain and Alta (Martin) Bell. Married August 1, 1957, to Betty Ruth Fitzgerald. Children: four. d. June 22, 1996, Salt Lake City, Utah.

Recruited by President Ronald Reagan to dismantle the U.S. Department of Education, Terrel H. Bell served as secretary of the department from 1981 to 1985. Bell appointed the commission that produced the report *A Nation at Risk* (1983), which argued that national economic viability was threatened by an inadequate public school system. For refocusing public and political attention on the plight of public schools, Bell earned credit from educational conservatives for launching the ''excellence movement'' of the 1980s.

His undergraduate education at Southern Idaho College of Education (B.A., 1946) was interrupted by duty in the U.S. Marine Corps during World War II. He received the M.S. degree in educational administration from the University of Idaho (1954), undertook further study at Stanford University as a Ford Foundation fellow (1954–55), and earned the Ed.D. from the University of Utah (1961).

Bell was a science teacher and coach in Eden, Idaho, and superintendent in Rockland Valley, Idaho; Afton, Wyoming; and Ogden, Utah, before becoming chairman and professor of educational administration at Utah State University in 1962. From 1963 to 1970 he served as state superintendent of public instruction and executive director of the Board for Vocational Education in Utah.

He arrived in Washington, D.C., in 1981 quite familiar with the city and its federal government bureaucracies. In 1970 he had accepted appointment as associate commissioner for regional office coordination in the U.S. Office of Education, only to become acting commissioner two months later upon President Richard Nixon's firing of James Allen (BDAE). In 1971 Bell returned to Utah as superintendent of schools in Granite. Bell went once again to Washington in 1974 as commissioner of education, a post he held until 1976. He was Utah commissioner of higher education from 1976 to 1981. After his service as secretary of the U.S. Department of Education he became professor of education at the University of Utah in 1985.

Bell wrote *Effective Teaching: How to Recognize and Reward Competence* (1960), *A Philosophy of Education for the Space Age* (1962), *Your Child's Intellect—A Parent's Guide to Home-Based Preschool Education* (1972), and *How to Shape Up Our Nation's Schools* (1991). His most widely read work was *The Thirteenth Man* (1988), his inside account of his years as secretary of education. He received Distinguished Service Awards from the National Council of Chief State School Officers (1971) and Association of State Boards of Education (1973).

REFERENCES: CA (144); CB (1976, 1996); CHE, January 16, 1985, p. 26; LE (1974); NCAB (N63: 31); NYT, January 8, 1981, p. 10, and June 24, 1996, p. B8; WP, August 19, 1991, p. A19; WW (1996).

BENSON, Charles Scott. b. May 20, 1922, Atlanta, Georgia, to Marion Trotti and Sallie May (Bagley) Benson. Married June 8, 1946, to Dorothy Ruth Merrick. Children: three. d. July 2, 1994, Carlsbad, California.

Charles Benson was an authority on educational finance and the relationship between government and education. In the latter part of his career he became increasingly involved in discussions about the role of vocational education as a vehicle for improving the quality of learning available to most youth.

Benson was awarded the A.B. degree at Princeton University (1943) and, after service in the U.S. Navy (1943–46), M.A. (1948) and Ph.D. (1955) degrees at Columbia University. With a grant from the Ford Foundation, he studied educational finance in England and Wales during 1962–63.

He taught economics at Bowdoin College (1950–55) and education at Harvard University (1955–64) before joining the faculty of the University of California at Berkeley in 1964. From 1968 he was professor of the economics of education. He was a visiting professor at Stanford University during 1980–81. At Berkeley he also served as associate dean (1986–89). He directed the National Center for Research in Vocational Education from 1988 until his death.

Benson was a consultant to local, state, and national governments, including Pakistan, Nigeria, and Egypt. He was a member of the Presidential Advisory Panel on Financing Elementary and Secondary Education (1979–81) and served as president of the American Educational Finance Association (1977–78). He was most notable for his voluminous writings. He was author of *Teachers' Salaries* (1959); *The Economics of Public Education* (1961), which was the standard work on the subject; *The Cheerful Prospect: A Statement on the Future of American Education* (1965); *Cost and Financing of Elementary and Secondary Education* (1972); *Implementing the Learning Society* (with Harold Hodgkinson, 1974); and *From Mass to Universal Education: The Experience of the State of California and Its Relevance to European Education in the Year 2000* (with Guy Benveniste, 1976). In addition, he was author, coauthor, or contributor to many reports and policy documents prepared for government agencies.

REFERENCES: CA (NR-8, 146); LE (1974); NYT, July 8, 1994, p. A19; WW (1992–93); *Journal of Vocational Education Research* 18 (1993): 97–99.

BEREDAY, George Zygmunt Fijalowski. b. July 15, 1920, Warsaw, Poland, to Zygmunt B. and Halina (Piwko-Barylska) Bereday. Married December 21, 1954, to Mary Hale Gillam. Children: three. d. October 22, 1983, New York City.

The United States was George Bereday's third home, after Poland, where he was born, and England, where he began his studies. After service in the Polish cavalry (1938–40), he was a paratroop officer in British service (1940–45), rising to battlefield battalion commander. He earned the degrees of B.Sc. (1944) at the University of London, B.A. (1950) and M.A. (1953) at the University of Oxford, Ph.D. at Harvard University (1953), and J.D. (1976) at Columbia University.

Bereday was an assistant professor of history at Boston College (1954–55) before joining the faculty of Columbia University, where he became professor of comparative education in Teachers College in 1959. In addition he was professor of juvenile law and sociology of education from 1978. He was an exchange professor in Moscow in 1961 and Tokyo in 1962.

Bereday was legendary for his energetic approach to scholarship. While his interests ranged widely, he was best known for writings in comparative education. In his book *Comparative Method in Education* (1964), he proposed a systematic approach to comparative education as a new interdisciplinary social science focused on schools. Bereday was founding editor of the *Comparative Education Review* from 1957 to 1967 and in the same period was joint editor of the *World Year Book of Education.* When these publications first appeared, the study of comparative education was new; Bereday was likely its first full-time practitioner in the United States. He was also author of *Modernization and Diversity in Soviet Education* (with others, 1971) and *Universities for All* (1973), sponsored by the United Nations Organization for Educational and Cultural Development (OECD). He edited *The Politics of Soviet Education* (with Jaan Pennar, 1960), *The Changing Soviet School* (with William W. Brickman, BDAE, and Gerald H. Read, BDAE, 1960), and *Essays on World Education: The Crisis of Supply and Demand* (1969).

Bereday distinguished himself in combining concerns about education, family, and law. His scholarship was aided by his mastery of eight languages, including Russian and Japanese.

REFERENCES: CA (NR-4, 111); LE (1974); NYT, May 8, 1966, and October 26, 1983, p. D27; WWW (8); *Comparative Education Review* 28 (February 1984): 1–9; *Slavic Review* 43 (Spring 1984): 182; *Western European Education* 15 (Fall 1983): 94–95.

BERRY, George Packer. b. December 29, 1898, Troy, New York, to George Titus and Carrie Electa (Packer) Berry. Married July 10, 1924, to Elizabeth L'Estrange Duncan. Children: two. d. October 5, 1986, Princeton, New Jersey.

George Berry was a national leader in developing methods to maintain excellence in medical education during a period of rapid scientific change.

After graduation from Princeton University with the A.B. degree (1921) and Johns Hopkins University with the M.D. degree (1925), Berry was a medical resident and instructor for four years at Johns Hopkins. From 1929 to 1932 he was an assistant and associate at the Rockefeller Institute for Medical Research (later, University). At the University of Rochester, he was a professor of bacteriology and administrator (1932–49) before accepting appointment as dean of the Harvard Medical School, where he remained until his retirement (1949–65). He was also president of the Harvard Medical Center (1956–65), an association of the medical school and seven teaching hospitals, which he organized.

While dean at Harvard, Berry was a consultant to the U.S. Department of Health, Education, and Welfare and Massachusetts Department of Public Health. In retirement, he was a special consultant to the president of Princeton University. He was a director of the Josiah Macy Foundation, trustee of the American University in Beirut, vice president of the Sex Information and Education Council of the United States, and member of the medical advisory committee of the Boston Museum of Science and science advisory committee of the Howard Hughes Medical Institute, among many services in the profession and the nation. He served for twelve years in the U.S. Naval Reserve.

Berry was president of the American Association of Immunologists (1939–40) and American Association of Medical Colleges (1951–52).

REFERENCES: NYT, October 9, 1986, p. D26; WWW (9); *Time* 86 (July 9, 1965): 55.

BESTOR, Arthur Eugene, Jr. b. September 20, 1908, Chautauqua, New York, to Arthur Eugene (BDAE) and Jeanette Louise (Lemon) Bestor. Married 1931 to Dorothea Nolte; March 5, 1939, to Anne Carr; November 23, 1949, to Dorothy Alden Koch. Children: three. d. December 13, 1994, Seattle.

Beginning in 1952 with a speech entitled ''Aimlessness in Education,'' Arthur Bestor was one of progressive education's most formidable critics. He aimed his critique at professors of education who placed greater value on teaching methodologies than intellectual disciplines. He argued that such approaches were both anti-intellectual and antidemocratic.

Bestor made his case in *Educational Wastelands: The Retreat from Learning in Our Public Schools* (1953), followed by corrective suggestions in *The Restoration of Learning: A Program for Redeeming the Unfulfilled Promise of American Education* (1955). During the 1950s he also wrote many articles on education and schooling, published in periodicals as various as *Teachers College Record* and *Good Housekeeping*.

After completing the high school program at the Lincoln School conducted by Teachers College of Columbia University, Bestor enrolled at Yale University, which granted him Ph.B. (1930) and Ph.D. (1938) degrees. While pursuing graduate study in history he was editor in chief of the *Chautauquan Daily* (1931–33) at the Chautauqua Institution, where his father was president.

He taught at Teachers College (1936–42) and Stanford University (1942–46), before moving to the University of Illinois (1947–62). He was Harmsworth Professor of American History at Oxford University during 1956–57. He finished his career at the University of Washington (1962–76).

Bestor's early scholarship was in American intellectual history and resulted in the book *Backwoods Utopias* (1950), which won the Beveridge Award of the American Historical Association. Later, his attention focused on American constitutional history and the separation of powers. He edited and contributed to many publications.

He was president of the Council for Basic Education (1956–57) and served on its Board of Directors until 1977. He was a fellow of the Newberry Library in 1946 and the Guggenheim Foundation in 1953–54 and 1961–62.

REFERENCES: CA (NR-6); CB (1958, 1995); NYT, December 17, 1994, p. 24; WD (1994–96); WW (1976–77); Clarence J. Karier and Foster McMurray, "Retrospectives," *Educational Wastelands* (2d ed., 1985), pp. 233–87; Oliver M. Keels, "The Bestor Resolution and the Changing Image of the High School History Teacher," *International Journal of Social Education* 8 (Spring 1993): 31–41; Delbert H. Long, "Arthur Bestor on Education of Teachers," *Educational Forum* 48 (Summer 1984): 423–48.

BIGELOW, Karl Worth. b. May 10, 1898, Bangor, Maine, to Bert Elmer and Florence (Worth) Bigelow. Married September 15, 1921, to Margaret Johnson. Children: four. d. April 2, 1980, New York City.

Trained as an economist, Karl Bigelow became a national figure in discussions of teacher education during the 1940s. In the decades of the 1950s and 1960s, he extended his work in education internationally, with a focus on Africa.

Bigelow received the B.A. degree from Clark College (later, University) in 1920. His studies had been interrupted by service in the U.S. Navy during 1917–19. He earned the Ph.D. degree in economics at Harvard University in 1929.

While teaching economics at the University of Buffalo (1930–37, later, State University of New York at Buffalo), Bigelow served concurrently as headmaster of the Park School (1933–35). One year later he moved to Teachers College of Columbia University as a visiting professor. He received a permanent appointment there in 1937. He retired in 1963.

Under auspices of the Progressive Education Association, Bigelow chaired a study of social studies in secondary schools (1936–40) that led to publication of *The Social Studies in General Education* (1940). He was on leave from Teachers College for six and one-half years while directing the Commission on Teacher Education (1938–44) of the American Council on Education. Its final report was *The Improvement of Teacher Education* (1946).

Bigelow represented the National Conference of Christians and Jews at UNESCO during 1949–52. In the same period he began conducting studies and organizing conferences on education in Africa. He was founder and executive director of the Afro-Anglo-American Program for Teacher Education in Africa (1960–69), with support from the Carnegie Corporation.

He was coauthor of *Teachers in Our Times* (1944) and *Education and Foreign Aid* (1965).

REFERENCES: CA (97–100); CB (1949, 1980); LE (1974); NYT, April 3, 1980, p. D17; WWW (7); Andrew Taylor, ed., *Insights into African Education: The Karl W. Bigelow Memorial Lectures* (Teachers College Press, 1984).

BISHOP, Nathan. b. August 12, 1808, Vernon, New York, to Elnathan and Statira (Sperry) Bishop. Married 1858 to Caroline (Caldwell) Bleecker. Children: one. d. August 7, 1880, Saratoga Springs, New York.

During Nathan Bishop's superintendency of Providence, Rhode Island, schools, they gained recognition throughout the nation. He was named to the new post of superintendent in 1839 and oversaw construction of thirteen schools in the next two years. In 1851 Bishop became superintendent of Boston schools, remaining there until 1857.

The eldest son in a farming family, Bishop had come late to formal schooling. He attended Hamilton (New York) Academy. In 1837 he graduated from Brown University, having taken one year out to teach school. He served at Brown as a tutor during 1838–39, became a trustee of the university in 1842, and served on the Board of Fellows (1854–61).

After leaving Boston for New York City in 1857 he lived from his investments and engaged in philanthropic endeavors. He was chairman of the U.S. Christian Commission during the Civil War, a trustee of the American Bible Society beginning in 1865, and a member of the Board of New York State Commissioners for Public Charities from 1867 and was active in the American Baptist Home Mission Society. Bishop was one of the original trustees of Vassar College. In 1869 President Ulysses Grant appointed Bishop to the board of the U.S. Indian Commissioners to look into conditions in the Indian Territory. There he contracted malaria, which led to his death a decade later.

REFERENCES: DAB; DARB; WWW (H); NYT, August 8, 1880, p. 5; *The Biographical Cyclopedia of Representative Men of Rhode Island* (National Biographical Publishing Co., 1881); Norman Fox, *A Layman's Ministry: Notes on the Life of Nathan Bishop, LL.D.* (1883).

BLACKMER, Alan Rogers. b. December 26, 1902, Oak Park, Illinois, to Ernest Alfred and Emma Agnes (Morton) Blackmer. Married to Josephine Bedford. Children: four. d. November 1, 1975, New London, New Hampshire.

Alan Rogers Blackmer played a leading role in discussions during the early 1950s that led to establishment of the Advanced Placement Program.

Blackmer attended schools of Oak Park, Illinois, and Williams College, where he received the B.A. degree in 1924. He earned the M.A. degree at the University of Chicago in 1925 and studied in Paris, France, at the Sorbonne (1927–

28). He began his long career at Phillips (Andover, Massachusetts) Academy in 1925. At Andover, he was head of the English Department (1941–44), director of studies (1952–56), dean of the faculty (1953–68), and acting headmaster (1961–66).

Development of the Advanced Placement Program came rapidly during 1950–54, though from an improbable beginning. A curriculum study at Phillips Andover, which Blackmer chaired, led to discussions with alumni on the awkward transition for the ablest students from school to college. With support from the Ford Fund for the Advancement of Education, Blackmer led a study by school and college representatives. Their report, *General Education in School and College* (1953), argued that first-year college courses too often wasted students' time and failed to motivate them. At their urging, the College Entrance Examination Board (CEEB) developed a new examination series, Advanced Placement, that was immediately popular.

Blackmer was a member of the committee on examinations of CEEB and a consultant to the National Association of Independent Schools and the Upward Bound program. At the behest of Calvin Gross (q.v.), he introduced a curriculum for gifted children in Pittsburgh public schools.

REFERENCES: NCAB (59: 105); NYT, November 2, 1975, p. 67; Frederick S. Allis, Jr., *Youth From Every Quarter: A Bicentennial History of Phillips Academy, Andover* (Phillips Academy; distributed by University Press of New England, 1979); College Entrance Examination Board, *Annual Report* (1954–56).

BLOOM, Allan David. b. September 14, 1930, Indianapolis, to Allan and Malvina Dorothea (Glasner) Bloom. Married: no. d. October 7, 1992, Chicago.

With publication of the best-selling book *The Closing of the American Mind* (1987), Allan Bloom emerged from relative obscurity as a professor of political philosophy to a high public profile as a critic of prevailing values and practices in American higher education.

Bloom was educated in Indianapolis public schools until the age of sixteen, when his family moved to Chicago, and he enrolled in the University of Chicago. There he earned the A.B. degree in 1949, the A.M. in 1953, and the Ph.D., from the Committee on Social Thought, in 1955. He also studied at the Universities of Paris (1953–55) and Heidelberg (1957).

He taught at Chicago (1955–60), Yale (1960–63), and Cornell (1963–70) Universities, and the University of Toronto (1970–79) before returning to Chicago as a professor in the Committee on Social Thought, the position he held until his death. He was author of *Shakespeare's Politics* (with Harry V. Jaffa, 1964), *Giants and Dwarfs* (1990), and *Love and Friendship* (1993), as well as translator and editor of works by Plato and Jean-Jacques Rousseau.

Bloom believed *The Closing of the American Mind* vindicated classical liberal concepts about society and education, particularly the enduring value of "Great Books" and the need for elite education. Both supporters and detractors interpreted it, however, as a highly political attack on dominant tendencies in American universities and society at large. It became a touchstone in the debate on ''political correctness'' in academe.

He was honored with fellowships from the Rockefeller (1957–58) and Guggenheim (1975–76) Foundations and the Jean-Jacques Rousseau Prize of the city of Geneva (1987).

REFERENCES: CA (131, 139); CB (1988, 1992); NYT, October 8, 1992, p. B29; WD (1994–96); WWW (10); James Atlas, ''Chicago's Grumpy Guru,'' NYT *Magazine*, January 3, 1988, p. 13.

BLOOM, Benjamin Samuel. b. February 21, 1913, Lansford, Pennsylvania. Married: yes. Children: two.

Benjamin S. Bloom's scholarship and teaching made ''higher-order thinking skills'' part of the vocabulary of reform in American education. His ''taxonomy of educational objectives'' became a standard tool for planning and evaluating instruction across the curriculum.

Bloom believed schools put too much emphasis on rote learning and competition. He wanted schools to teach problem solving and cultivate ''mastery learning,'' in which students were helped in learning each step before going on to more advanced tasks. He hoped in this way to equalize educational attainment. Bloom received B.A. and M.S. degrees from Pennsylvania State University (1935). He was a researcher for the Pennsylvania Youth Commission (1935–36) and American Youth Commission (1936–38) and research assistant for the Cooperative Study in General Education (1939–40). In 1942 Bloom earned the Ph.D. degree from the University of Chicago. The next year he began a long career at the university. He was a research assistant for the board of examinations and college–university examiner (1943–59), rose from instructor to distinguished professor (1943–70), and in 1970 was named Charles H. Swift Distinguished Service Professor. He was a fellow at the Center for Advanced Study in the Behavioral Sciences (1959–60) and Jacks Distinguished Visiting Professor of Education at Stanford University (1969–70). From 1983 to 1989 Bloom was professor of education at Northwestern University.

Bloom headed the Development of Talent Research Project, which resulted in *Developing Talent in Young People* (1985), which he edited. A prolific writer, among his books were *Problem-Solving Processes of College Students* (with Lois J. Broder, 1950), *The Use of Academic Predicting Scales for Counseling and Selecting College Entrants* (with Frank R. Peters, 1961), *Stability and Change in Human Characteristics* (1964), *Compensatory Education for Cultural Deprivation* (with Allison Davis and Robert Hess, q.v., 1965), *Human Characteristics and School Learning* (1976), and *All Our Children Learning* (1981). He edited *Research Problems of Education and Cultural Deprivation* (1965), *Taxonomy of Educational Objectives: The Classification of Educational Goals Handbook I: Cognitive Domain* (with others, 1956), and *Handbook II: The Affective Domain* (with D. R. Krathwohl and B. B. Masia, 1965).

Bloom was educational adviser to the governments of India (1957–59) and Israel (1963 and 1968). He was a founding member of the International Association for the Evaluation of Educational Achievement (IEA, 1959) and the International Curriculum Association (1972). He was president of the American Educational Research Association (1965–66) and in 1970 received an award for distinguished contributions to education from that association and Phi Delta Kappa. Bloom was honored by the John Dewey Society (1968) and received the Edward L. Thorndike (BDAE) Award (1972) from the American Psychological Association, of which he was a fellow.

REFERENCES: WW (1996); Ronald S. Brandt, ''On Talent Development: A Conversation with Benjamin Bloom,'' *Educational Leadership* 43 (September 1985): 33–35; Paul Chance, ''Master of Mastery,'' *Psychology Today* 21 (April 1987): 43–46; *Educational Leadership* 37 (November 1979): 157–61; *NASSP Bulletin* 70 (November 1986): 53–69.

BOATWRIGHT, Frederic William. b. January 28, 1868, White Sulphur Springs, West Virginia, to Reuben Baker and Maria Elizabeth (Woodruff) Boatwright. Married December 23, 1890, to Ellen Moore Thomas. Children: two. d. October 31, 1951, Richmond, Virginia.

Frederic W. Boatwright spent his career at the University of Richmond. Having enrolled at the age of fifteen in Richmond College, he graduated with the M.A. degree in 1888. He became a professor of modern languages in 1890 and president in 1894. At the time he was the youngest college president in the nation. During the previous twenty-five years the college had been governed by a faculty chairman. His appointment was controversial and prompted three professors to resign.

Boatwright led the institution through a period of growth and directed expansion of the curriculum. Women were admitted in 1898. The college was moved to a new suburban campus in 1914 and in 1920 was renamed the University of Richmond. Boatwright served as president until 1946. During his fifty-two-year tenure the college grew from 183 students and a faculty of 9 to more than 4,000 students and a faculty of 100.

Boatwright's early education had been provided by his father. He attended private and public schools in Marion, Virginia, then worked at a printing office in Marion before he enrolled at Richmond College. While a student he was an assistant in Greek and director of the gymnasium. His graduate study was done at the University of Halle and the Sorbonne in 1889–90 and at the University of Leipzig in 1892.

He wrote *Syllabi of French and German Literatures* (1894) and *Education in Richmond* (1937).

REFERENCES: NCAB (46: 254); WWW (3); NYT, November 1, 1951, p. 29; Reuben E. Alley, *Frederic W. Boatwright* (University of Richmond, 1973); Woodford B. Hackley, *Faces on the Wall* (Virginia Baptist Historical Society, 1972).

BOK, Derek Curtis. b. March 22, 1930, Bryn Mawr, Pennsylvania, to Curtis and Margaret Adams (Plummer) Bok. Married May 7, 1955, to Sissela Ann Myrdal. Children: three.

Derek Bok was an advocate of liberal education who held that ethics was a central element of effective education. His presidency of Harvard University (1971–91) brought a renewed focus on education of undergraduates, founding of the Kennedy School of Government, and establishment of the Harvard Management Corporation, which invested the university's assets. His annual reports as president addressed major issues in American higher education.

Bok attended Harvard School, a secondary school in North Hollywood, California. He received the A.B. degree from Stanford University (1951), the J.D. from Harvard University (1954), and the A.M. from George Washington University (1958). He was a Fulbright scholar at the University of Paris (1954–55) and served in the U.S. Army (1956–58). At the Harvard University Law School (1958–71) Bok taught antitrust and labor law. With Archibald Cox he edited *Cases and Materials On Labor Law* (1962), a widely used casebook. He served as dean of the Harvard Law School from 1968 to 1971, when he became president of the university. As dean he added classes on criminal and environmental law, established joint degree programs with other schools in the university, recruited female and black students, and addressed student protests. In 1991 Bok became 300th Anniversary University Professor of Harvard University.

Bok was author of *The First Three Years of the Schuman Plan* (1955), *Labor in the American Community* (1970), *Beyond the Ivory Tower* (1982), *Higher Learning* (1986), *Universities and the Future of America* (1990), and *The Cost of Talent* (1993). He was chair of the American Council on Education (1981–82), a member of the Commission on Federal Paperwork, and a fellow of the Center for Advanced Study in the Behavioral Sciences (1991–92).

REFERENCES: CA (106); CB (1971); CHE, March 18, 1982, p. 1+ and November 14, 1990, p. 15+; LE (1974); WD (1994–96); WW (1996); Bernard Murchland, *Voices in American Education* (Prakken, 1990); *Newsweek* 77 (January 18, 1971): 70–72; *Time* 128 (September 8, 1986): 63.

BOND, Guy Loraine. b. May 3, 1904, Cooperville, Washington, to Elias and Florence (Westover) Bond. Married August 19, 1936, to Fredericka Hoffa. Children: two.

Guy L. Bond was noted internationally for his contributions in the area of reading education, a field that his research shaped substantially. Bond received the B.S. degree (1932) from the University of Alabama and M.A. (1933) and Ph.D. (1935) degrees from Columbia University. He was professor of education and director of research at the New York State Teachers College at Fredonia (1936–37, later, State University of New York College at Fredonia) and served on the faculty of education at the University of Minnesota from 1937 until his retirement.

His major publications included *Methods of Determining Reading Readiness* (with Arthur I. Gates, BDAE, and David H. Russell, 1938), *Developmental Reading in the High School* (with Eva Bond, 1941), *Teaching the Child to Read* (with Eva Bond Wagner, 1943), *Living Literature Series* (fourteen volumes with W. W. Theisen, 1945), *Adapting Instruction to Individual Differences in Reading* (with Bertha Handlan, 1948), *Developmental Reading Series* (1949), *Child Growth in Reading* (with Eva Bond Wagner, 1955), *Diagnosis and Treatment of Learning Difficulties* (with Leo J. Brueckner, BDAE, 1955), *Reading Difficulties* (with Miles A. Tinker, 1957), and *Developmental Reading Series* (with others, four volumes, 1958). In 1948, he was a major contributor to the *Forty-Seventh Yearbook* of the National Society for the Study of Education.

REFERENCES: WW (1960–61); Robert H. Beck, *Beyond Pedagogy: A History of the University of Minnesota College of Education* (North Central, 1980).

BOOKER, Matilda Moseley. b. 1887, Halifax County, Virginia. Married 1916 to Samuel G. Booker. d. 1957.

Little is known about the early or late years of Matilda Moseley Booker's life. As a young woman she attended the Thyne Institute in Mecklenburg County, Virginia. There she received a third-class teaching certificate in 1909. She was a "Jeanes teacher" and principal in rural Henrico County schools for the next four years. Her mentor was Virginia E. Randolph (q.v.).

From 1913 until 1920 she was supervisor of two dozen schools for African-American children in Cumberland County. With financial support from the Anna T. Jeanes Foundation and Julius Rosenwald Fund, she was able to extend the school term from as little as two months to seven months annually, improve qualifications and salaries of teachers, and construct and repair school buildings. She went to Mecklenburg County in 1920 as supervisor of four dozen schools and remained there until 1935. Booker arranged summer study for teachers. In a county where there had been no high schools for African Americans, she opened two.

REFERENCES: NBAW; Mary Jenness, *Twelve Negro Americans* (Friendship Press, reprinted by Chadwick-Healey, 1936), pp. 24–33.

BORCHARDT, Selma Munter. b. December 1, 1895, Washington, D.C., to Newman and Sara (Munter) Borchardt. Married: no. d. January 30, 1968, Washington, D.C.

Selma Borchardt combined a career as a high school English teacher with service as an officer and legislative liaison of the American Federation of Teachers (AFT).

She earned A.B. (1919) and B.S. (1922) degrees at Syracuse University, the LL.B. from Washington College of Law (1933, later, part of American University), and the A.M. in sociology from Catholic University (1937). She was a playground instructor before becoming director of teacher training (1919–20) and supervisor of rural schools (1920–21) in Montgomery County, Maryland.

In 1922 Borchardt began teaching in the public schools of the District of

Columbia, where she continued to work until her retirement in 1960. She was on leave during 1941–45, when she served on the Wartime Commission of the U.S. Office of Education. For two years (1941–43) she directed its High School Victory Corps.

Borchardt was an early participant in the Teachers Union of the District of Columbia and served as its executive secretary. She was a vice president of the AFT beginning in 1924. In 1929 she became chair of the Education Committee of the American Federation of Labor (AFL), a position she held until 1955. She was a director of the World Federation of Education Associations (1927–46) and its vice president for the Americas (1937–46). She was also a director of the Institute on World Studies (1946–48) and a U.S. commissioner to UNESCO (1946–51). For many years she was an adviser on education to the Women's Joint Congressional Committee and the American Association of University Women.

Studies that Borchardt wrote for the AFT and World Federation of Education Organizations included *Who Selects Our Textbooks* (1926), *The Relation of School Attendance Laws and Child Labor Laws* (1930), *Labor's Program for the Prevention of Juvenile and Youth Delinquency* (1943), *The Teaching of International Cooperation in the Secondary Schools of the United States* (1945), *The Structure and Work of the International Teacher Organizations* (1945), *Getting and Keeping Children in School* (1954), *A Citizen's Responsibility for the Education of Children and Youth* (1954), *Program for Accelerated Training of Earlier School Drop Out* (1960), and *Balancing the Rights of the Individual and the Rights of Society* (1960).

REFERENCES: BDAL; NAW (Mod); NYT, February 1, 1968, p. 34; WWW (5).

BOWEN, Howard Rothmann. b. October 27, 1908, Spokane, Washington, to Henry Grant and Josephine Katherine (Menig) Bowen. Married August 24, 1935, to Lois B. Schilling. Children: two. d. December 22, 1989, Claremont, California.

Howard Bowen made his greatest mark on American education through a series of studies over nearly twenty years on the costs and finances of higher education in the United States. Even before the series began, however, he was well known as an academic economist and administrator.

Because his mother sent him to first grade at the age of four, Bowen graduated from high school at the age of sixteen. He earned the B.A. degree at the State College of Washington (later, Washington State University) in 1929, worked for three years as a jewelry salesman, then returned and took the M.A. in 1933. He received the Ph.D. at the University of Iowa in 1935 and pursued postdoctoral studies at the University of Cambridge and London School of Economics during 1937–38 on a fellowship from the Social Science Research Council.

Bowen taught at the University of Iowa (1935–42), was an economist for the U.S. Department of Commerce (1942–44) and Congress (1944–45), and was vice president and chief economist of Irving Trust Company (1945–47) before his appointment as dean of commerce and business administration at the University of Illinois (1947–50). Changes he sought there soon led to his dismissal. He remained at Illinois for one and a half years conducting a study of graduate programs in economics, then was professor of economics at Williams College (1952–55) before holding presidencies at Grinnell College (1955–64) and the University of Iowa (1964–69). At Claremont University Center he was president (1969–70) and chancellor (1970–74). During the early 1950s he was also an economic consultant to the Central Intelligence Agency.

With support from the Carnegie Foundation for the Advancement of Teaching, Bowen was author of four studies: *The Finance of Higher Education* (1969), *Efficiency in Liberal Education* (with Gordon Douglass, 1971), *Investment in Learning* (1977), and *The Costs of Higher Education* (1980). Among his other books were *Toward Social Economy* (1948), *Social Responsibilities of the Businessman* (1953), *Christian Values and Economic Life* (1954), *The State of the Nation and the Agenda for Higher Education* (1982), and *American Professors: A National Resource Imperiled* (with Jack Schuster, 1986). For the last two books Bowen received the Ness Prize of the Association of American Colleges (later, and Universities). He also wrote a memoir, *Academic Recollections* (1988).

He was a consultant to the National Council of Churches (1949–53) and a member of the Committee for Economic Development (1955–59), the Federal Advisory Commission on Intergovernmental Relations (1961–64), and the National Commission on Non-Traditional Study (1970–72), among numerous public services. He was president of the American Association for Higher Education and Western Economic Association.

REFERENCES: CA (NR-8, 130); LE (1974); WWE; WWW (10); *Economic Inquiry* 28 (July 1990): iii; Clark Kerr (BDAE), ''Howard R. Bowen (1908–1989): Fiat Lux et Justitio Omnibus,'' *Change* 22 (March/April 1990): 78–79.

BOWEN, William Gordon. b. October 6, 1933, Cincinnati, Ohio, to Albert A. and Bernice (Pomert) Bowen. Married August 25, 1956, to Mary Ellen Maxwell. Children: Two.

William G. Bowen first predicted inexorable increases in the costs of higher education and the arts and their deleterious effects, then worked to counteract them as a university and foundation executive.

Bowen earned the B.A. degree at Denison University in 1955 and the Ph.D. at Princeton University three years later. He remained at Princeton as a member of the faculty, becoming a professor at the age of thirty-one, provost at thirty-four, and president at thirty-eight. He also served as director of graduate studies in the Woodrow Wilson School for Public and International Affairs (1964–66). At Princeton as provost and president, Bowen strengthened institutional resources, finances, and academic quality, while he weakened the grip of tradition. He promoted the admission of women as undergraduates and the establishment of on-campus residential colleges to counteract the social sway of off-campus eating clubs.

After fifteen years as Princeton's president (1972–87), Bowen became president of the Andrew W. Mellon Foundation (from 1987). He continued the foundation's emphasis on support of education, while urging universities and colleges to operate more efficiently.

He was author of *The Wage-Price Issue: A Theoretical Analysis* (1960), *Wage Behavior in the Postwar Period: An Empirical Analysis* (1960), *Economic Aspects of Education: Three Essays* (1964), *Performing Arts: The Economic Dilemma* (with W. J. Baumol, 1966), *The Economics of Labor Force Participation* (with T. A. Finegan, 1969), *Prospects for Faculty in the Arts and Sciences: A Study of the Factors Affecting Demand and Supply, 1987 to 2012* (with Julie Ann Sosa, 1987), and *In Pursuit of the Ph.D.* (with Neil L. Rudenstine, 1992).

REFERENCES: CB (1973); LE (1974); NYT, January 25, 1987, p. 26, and May 10, 1987, p. C6; WD (1994–96); WW (1996).

BOWMAN, John Gabbert. b. May 18, 1877, Davenport, Iowa, to John R. and Mary Ann (Gabbert) Bowman. Married June 29, 1908, to Florence Berry. Children: two. d. December 2, 1962, Bedford, Pennsylvania.

John G. Bowman was a builder of institutions and programs, including the American College of Surgeons, the University of Iowa and its medical school, the University of Pittsburgh and its forty-two-story academic skyscraper, the "Cathedral of Learning," but, most notably for American education, the "Carnegie classification" of universities and colleges.

Bowman taught for one year in a one-room rural Iowa school before enrolling in 1896 at the University of Iowa, where he was awarded the A.B. degree in 1899. He was a newspaperman in Iowa and Illinois for the next several years, then returned to the University of Iowa and obtained the A.M. degree in 1904. After one year of graduate study and teaching in the field of English at Columbia University, he went to the newly founded Carnegie Foundation for the Advancement of Teaching with responsibility for establishing a system of classification among institutions of higher education. His scheme distinguished institutions according to admission standards and instructional programs. In 1907 he was named secretary of the foundation.

Bowman returned to the University of Iowa as president (1911–14). He was founding director of the American College of Surgeons (1915–21) and then long-term chancellor of the University of Pittsburgh (1921–45). In each case he enacted ambitious plans, even in relatively short tenures. At Pittsburgh he relieved serious overcrowding of facilities and built strong ties with businesses, while relationships with liberal faculty and students were strained.

Bowman served as consultant about hospitals to the U.S. Department of the Treasury (1921–23) and was a trustee of the Henry C. Frick Educational Commission. He wrote a book of verse for children, *Happy All Day Through* (1917), and a memoir of his early years, *The World That Was* (1926).

REFERENCES: NCAB (F: 100); NYT, December 3, 1962, p. 31; WWW (4); Raymond F. Howes, "Sweetness and Light in Pittsburgh," *Outlook and Independent* 153 (December 4, 1926): 522–26+.

BOYCE, Frank Gordon. b. April 8, 1917, Binghamton, New York, to Clarence and Ethel (Wilcox) Boyce. Married September 5, 1941, to Joan A. Sweet. Children: three. d. December 9, 1987, Brattleboro, Vermont.

Frank Boyce led the Experiment in International Living (later, World Learning) in its development as a premier provider of international education opportunities for youth of the United States and other countries.

He graduated from Colgate University with A.B. (1939) and A.M. (1948) degrees. Following college, he was a reporter with the *Binghamton Sun* newspaper (1939–41) and served in the U.S. Navy (1941–45). He returned to Colgate as assistant to the president in 1946, remaining until 1950. From 1950 to 1974 he was president of the Experiment in International Living.

Initially, the organization limited its programs to summer opportunities for 1,000 students in a handful of countries. By the time Boyce left, its range of offerings had expanded to include academic year programs, and it served 5,000 participants yearly. Under Boyce's leadership, the School for International Training was established in 1964 as an affiliate of the Experiment in International Living. It awarded its first degrees in 1970.

Boyce was later executive director of the Vermont Federation of Independent Colleges (1976–83), director of international programs at Nathaniel Hawthorne College (1976–79), and counselor on international programs to Nasson College in Maine and Green Mountain College in Vermont (1983–87).

In 1961 Boyce served briefly as first director of the division of private and international organizations in the U.S. Peace Corps. He was a member of the U.S. commission to UNESCO (1965–70). He received the Order of Merit of the Federal Republic of Germany, the Legion de O'Higgins of Chile, and the Order of Sacred Treasure of Japan.

REFERENCES: NYT, December 13, 1987, p. 60; WP, December 16, 1987, p. C6; WWW (9); William Peters, *Passport to Friendship: The Story of the Experiment in International Living* (Lippincott, 1957).

BOYER, Ernest LeRoy. b. September 13, 1928, Dayton, Ohio, to Clarence and Ethel (French) Boyer. Married August 26, 1950, to Kathryn Garis Tyson. Children: four. d. December 8, 1995, Princeton, New Jersey.

Ernest Boyer was a highly skilled administrator and policymaker as chancellor of the State University of New York and U.S. commissioner of education, but he made his most significant contributions to American education as long-term president of the Carnegie Foundation for the Advancement of Teaching. At Carnegie he wrote many books, including three that were particularly influential, *High School: A Report on Secondary Education in America* (1983), *College: The Undergraduate Experience in America* (1987), and *The Basic School*

(1995). The Carnegie Foundation sponsored a network of thirteen schools dedicated to implementing the educational ideals of *The Basic School.* The book and the network exemplified Boyer's exceptional ability to articulate an educational vision and marshal resources for it. ''To help shape the debate is at least half the battle,'' Boyer believed. ''Defining the right issues to discuss is the first step to achieving responsible change.'' He was one of the most quoted and consulted experts on American schools by virtue of his honest criticism and relentless advocacy for improvement.

Boyer graduated from Greenville (Illinois) College in 1950 and after further study at Ohio State University earned a master's degree in speech pathology (1955) and a doctorate in audiology (1957) at the University of Southern California. After serving as a postdoctoral fellow in medical audiology at the University of Iowa and teaching speech pathology and forensics at Upland College (California) and Loyola University of Los Angeles, he became academic dean at Upland in 1956. His reputation as a consensus builder and problem solver grew through his work with the Western College Association, where he dealt with the rancorous issue of the professional preparation of teachers. As the director of the Center for Coordinated Education at the University of California at Santa Barbara (1962–65), Boyer oversaw school improvement projects. He was founding executive dean (1965–70) and chancellor (1970–77) of the State University of New York system. Under his leadership, the university established Empire State College and other units serving nontraditional students.

In 1977, President Jimmy Carter appointed Boyer to be U.S. commissioner of education. He was the last chief national education official to serve before the Office of Education was made a cabinet-level department. As president of the Carnegie Foundation from 1979 until his death in 1995, Boyer extended its mission from higher education to include schooling.

Boyer was also author of *Campus Life* (1990) and *Ready to Learn* (1991). The National Humanities Center conferred upon him its Charles Frankel Prize in the Humanities (1994). He was a Fulbright fellow in India (1985) and Chile (1989). Among other honors, in 1990 the newsmagazine *U.S. News and World Report* named him ''Educator of the Year.''

REFERENCES: CA (110); CB (1988, 1996); CHE, January 16, 1985, p. 26, and January 5, 1996, p. 18; LE (1974); NYT, July 31, 1970, p. 32, March 16, 1977, p. B5, November 13, 1977, p. XII 10, June 26, 1979, p. C1, and December 9, 1995, p. 52; RPE; WW (1996); *Change* 14 (January/February 1982): 18–21; *Education Week* 67 (May 24, 1994): 24–29; *Educational Record* 61 (Winter 1980): 4–9; George R. Kaplan, ''Shining Lights in High Places: Education's Top Four Leaders and Their Heirs,'' *Phi Delta Kappan* 67 (September 1985): 7+.

BRADEMAS, (Stephen) John. b. March 2, 1927, Mishawaka, Indiana, to Stephen John and Beatrice Cenci (Goble) Brademas. Married July 9, 1977, to Mary Ellen Briggs. Children: no.

John Brademas bridged the realms of politics and education, serving first as a U.S. congressman who devoted much of his attention to legislation on behalf of education, then as a university president.

Brademas studied at the University of Mississippi, Harvard University (B.A., 1949), and Oxford University, where he was a Rhodes scholar (D. Phil., 1954). His field of scholarship was recent European history.

Upon his return to the United States, Brademas was three times a candidate for the U.S. House of Representatives from Indiana, losing in 1954 and 1956, then winning in 1958. In the several years before his election, he worked as a legislative assistant in Washington, D.C., and executive assistant to Adlai Stevenson in the presidential election campaign of 1956. He also taught political science at St. Mary's (Indiana) College (1957–58).

In twenty-two years as a congressman, Brademas was a leader in the development of legislation in support of education, including laws that assisted states in establishing technical and community colleges; created loan programs for colleges and their students; launched the Head Start program for disadvantaged preschool children; and established the National Institute of Education, a research agency within the federal government. In 1976 he became majority whip of the House of Representatives. He lost in the election of 1980.

A year later Brademas became president of New York University (1981–92). There he was noted for improving financial resources, emphasizing the liberal arts, and raising the residential profile of the university.

Brademas was the author of *Washington, D.C. to Washington Square* (1986) and coauthor of *The Politics of Education: Conflict and Consensus on Capitol Hill* (1987). Among numerous honors, he was decorated by the governments of France and Greece. He was a director and adviser to corporations and public service organizations and chaired the board of the Federal Reserve Bank of New York.

REFERENCES: CB (1977); CHE, September 30, 1987, pp. A18–21; NYT, July 11, 1990, p. B6; RPE; WW (1996); Brock Brower, ''Big Man on Campus: NYU Feels the Whip,'' *New York* 17 (December 3, 1984): 102+; J. Anthony Lukas, ''The Moving Force at N.Y.U.,'' NYT *Magazine*, June 2, 1985, p. 44+.

BRANCH, Mary Elizabeth. b. 1881, Farmville, Virginia, to Clement Tazewell and Harriet Lacey Branch. Married: no. d. July 6, 1944, Camden, New Jersey.

Mary Elizabeth Branch received her earliest education at home, where her father, a shoemaker and former slave, led the family in reading. At a school for white girls where her mother worked she was allowed to attend as an auditor. She enrolled at Virginia Normal and Industrial Institute (later, Virginia State University), where she completed high school and normal school studies, graduating in 1897. She later earned Ph.B. (1922) and M.A. (1925) degrees at the University of Chicago.

Upon completion of her normal studies, Branch taught elementary school in Blackstone, Virginia, for three years. In 1900 she returned to Virginia Normal, where she taught English until 1920. After studies at the University of Chicago, she went to St. Louis, where from 1925 to 1930 she was dean of women at Vashon High School, the nation's largest school for African-American girls at the time.

In 1930 Branch accepted a request from the American Missionary Association to be president of Tillotson (later, Huston-Tillotson) College in Austin, Texas. The college was near collapse, with an inadequate library and a dilapidated campus. Branch ended the high school program, oversaw the rebuilding of facilities, improved the library collection to meet accrediting association standards, and instituted a work-study program on campus that involved almost all students. Enrollment grew from fewer than 150 women in 1930 to 500 women and men at the time of Branch's death fourteen years later.

REFERENCES: AAW; NBAW; Mary Jenness, *Twelve Negro Americans* (Friendship Press, reprinted by Chadwick-Healey, 1936), pp. 85–100; Frank Lincoln Mather, ed., *Who's Who of the Colored Race* (1915, reprinted by Gale Research, 1976); Milton A. Maxwell, "Mary E. Branch," *Advance* (September 1944), reprinted in Elizabeth L. Ihle, ed., *Black Women in Higher Education: An Anthology of Essays, Studies and Documents* (Garland, 1992), pp. 177–78.

BRAZELTON, Thomas Berry, II. b. May 10, 1918, Waco, Texas, to Thomas Berry and Pauline (Battle) Brazelton. Married December 3, 1949, to Christina Lowell. Children: four.

T. Berry Brazelton extended the work in "parent education" initiated by Benjamin Spock (q.v.) in directions that altered basic assumptions in medical education and early childhood education. He pressed for redirection of training in pediatric medicine, away from pathology, toward study of the "well baby." His Neonatal Behavioral Assessment Scale (1973) emphasized that most infants are normal. Through books, essays, television programs, and lectures that reached large audiences, he worked to educate parents on infant behavior and communication.

After schooling in Waco, Texas, and at Episcopal High School in Alexandria, Virginia, Brazelton enrolled at Princeton University, where he graduated with the A.B. degree in 1940. He earned the M.D. degree at Columbia University in 1943. He served one year of medical internship and one year in the U.S. Naval Reserve, followed by residencies in Boston during 1945–50 in general medicine, pediatrics, and child psychology. He opened a private practice in pediatrics in Cambridge, Massachusetts, in 1950. The next year he joined the faculty of the Harvard Medical School, remaining a member until his retirement in 1988.

In 1972 Brazelton was cofounder of the Child Development Unit, a component of Children's Hospital Medical Center in Boston. He was an active proponent of national family leave legislation.

Among his many books were *Infants and Mothers: Individual Differences in Development* (1969), *Toddlers and Parents* (1974), *Doctor and Child* (1976), *Working and Caring* (1981), and *What Every Baby Knows* (1987). He was also featured in a daily television program titled, *What Every Baby Knows* (from 1984) and wrote a column in *Family Circle* magazine.

Brazelton was head of the child development section of the American Academy of Pediatrics (1970), president of the Society for Research in Child Development (1987–89) and National Center for Clinical Infant Programs (1988–91), and a member of the National Commission on Children (1989). He received many honors, among them the Cine Gold Eagle of the Educational Development Center in 1973 for *Gabriel*, the American Film Festival's first prize in 1978 for *Newborn*, and *Parents Magazine*'s Medal for Outstanding Service to Children (1977).

REFERENCES: CA (97–100); CB (1993); ECE; WW (1996); *Newsweek* 113 (February 13, 1989): 72; *Scholastic Pre-K Today* 7 (August/September 1992): 81–84; Sybil Steinberg, ''PW Interviews: T. Berry Brazelton,'' *Publishers Weekly* 232 (November 13, 1987): 57–58.

BREWSTER, Kingman, Jr. b. June 17, 1919, Longmeadow, Massachusetts, to Kingman and Florence Foster (Besse) Brewster. Married November 30, 1942, to Mary Louise Phillips. Children: five. d. November 8, 1988, Oxford, England.

Kingman Brewster, Jr., was known for his strong advocacy of the liberal arts. As a university president, he navigated the disruptions of the 1960s with adeptness and an enduring commitment to liberal values, even in the face of sharp criticism.

Brewster was chairman of the *Yale Daily News* in his senior year at Yale University, where he received the A.B. degree in 1941. After work in the U.S. Office of Inter-American Affairs (1941–42) and service as a naval aviator (1942–45), he entered Harvard Law School, where he was an editor of the *Harvard Law Review* and earned the LL.B. degree in 1948.

He was assistant general counsel in the office of the U.S. special representative in Europe (1948–49) for the Marshall Plan and research associate in economics at the Massachusetts Institute of Technology (1949–50). He returned to Harvard Law School as a member of the faculty in 1950 and remained there for a decade. In 1960 he went to Yale University as professor of law and provost-designate, becoming provost the following year. In 1963, after the death of A. Whitney Griswold, Brewster was named Yale's president.

In the fourteen years (1963–77) of his presidency, Brewster oversaw a dramatic change in the composition of the Yale University student body, with fewer sons of alumni, fewer private school graduates, more African Americans, and, beginning in 1969, the admission of women. He was an outspoken critic of the war in Vietnam and a supporter of the civil rights movement, stances that drew unfavorable attention from some alumni and the federal government. He was the model for President King in the ''Doonesbury'' comics.

Brewster left Yale to serve as ambassador to Great Britain (1977–81). He was a partner in New York and London of the law firm of Winthrop, Stimson, Putnam, and Roberts (1981–86). In 1986 he was elected master of University College, Oxford University, where he remained until his death.

He was author of *Anti-Trust and American Business Abroad* (1959) and coauthor with Milton Katz of *Law of International Transactions and Relations* (1960). He was a trustee of the Carnegie Endowment for International Peace and a member of the national advisory commission on selective service in 1966–67, among many public service roles.

REFERENCES: CB (1979, 1989); EAB; LE (1974); NYT, November 9, 1988, p. A1; WWW (9).

BRONK, Detlev Wulf. b. August 13, 1897, New York City, to Mitchell and Marie (Wulf) Bronk. Married September 10, 1921, to Helen Alexander Ramsey. Children: three. d. November 17, 1975, New York City.

Detlev Bronk conducted research in biophysics that shaped the discipline, pressed for increased flexibility between undergraduate and graduate education as president of Johns Hopkins University, and developed the Rockefeller Institute for Medical Research (later, University) from a research organization into a graduate university. He was a model of the academic scientist in national service.

Bronk graduated with the A.B. degree from Swarthmore College (1920) after service as a naval aviator during World War I. He earned M.S. (1922) and Ph.D. degrees (1926) at the University of Michigan, where he also taught.

He taught for three years (1926–29) at Swarthmore College, being promoted in rank each year, and served as dean of men during the last two years. He was professor of biophysics and director of research in medical physics at the University of Pennsylvania (1929–49).

In 1949 he succeeded Isaiah Bowman (BDAE) as president of Johns Hopkins University. Bronk instituted the ''Hopkins Plan,'' which allowed students to determine their own rate of progress through undergraduate and graduate studies. He was the first president of the Rockefeller Institute (later, University) from 1953 until his retirement in 1968.

Bronk chaired the National Research Council (1946–50), was president of the National Academy of Sciences (1950–62), and chaired the National Science Foundation board (1956–64), among many public service roles. He received the Presidential Medal of Freedom in 1964.

REFERENCES: CB (1949, 1976); DAB (supp. 9); NYT November 18, 1975, p. 40; WWW (7); Frank Brink, Jr., ''Detlev Wulf Bronk,'' *National Academy of Sciences Biographical Memoirs*, vol. 50 (National Academy of Sciences, 1979), pp. 2–87; *Science* 19 (December 5, 1975): 941; Charles Van Doren, ed., *Webster's American Biographies* (G. and C. Merriam, 1979).

BROWN, Sterling Allen. b. May 1, 1901, Washington, D.C., to Sterling Nelson and Adelaide (Allen) Brown. Married September 1927 to Daisy Turnbull. Children: one. d. January 13, 1989, Takoma Park, Maryland.

As a teacher, poet, and literary critic, Sterling Brown played a central part in establishing African-American literature as a subject of scholarly study. Brown's father served as a Congregational minister and taught religion at Howard University, where the son would spend most of his career. His mother imbued in her son a love of poetry that would figure prominently in his life's work.

Brown received the B.A. degree from Williams College in 1922. One year later he earned the M.A. degree at Harvard University. He taught at Virginia Seminary and College (1923–26), Lincoln University in Missouri (1926–28), and Fisk University (1928–29) before joining the faculty at Howard University, where he remained until his retirement in 1969.

His first book of poems, *Southern Road*, appeared in 1932. Unable to find a publisher for a second volume of verse, Brown refocused his creative efforts on literary studies. The first result, *An Outline for the Study of the Poetry of American Negroes*, was published in 1931. His seminal essay, "Negro Character as Seen by White Authors," appeared in the *Journal of Negro Education* in 1933. Two books followed it in 1937: *Negro Poetry and Drama* and *The Negro in American Fiction.* Brown was coeditor of *The Negro Caravan* (1941), a noted anthology of African-American literature.

As much as through his writings, Brown helped to form the study of his people and their creative work through the students he taught, including the writers Toni Morrison and Amiri Baraka and the psychologist Kenneth B. Clark (q.v.). After an intensely productive period of scholarship in the 1930s, Brown and his work were neglected outside Howard University. For three decades he devoted himself principally to teaching. In the late 1960s both the man and his writing achieved renewed recognition and popularity. Awards of honorary degrees from major universities and colleges followed during the 1970s, and his books, including the poetry, found publishers again.

Brown was national editor for Negro affairs in the Federal Writers' Project of the New Deal (1936–39) and in the same period contributed to the Carnegie Corporation study of race relations in the United States, led by Gunnar Myrdal, which resulted in the book *What the Negro Wants* (1948). He was a Guggenheim fellow during 1937–38.

Brown was also author of *The Last Ride of Wild Bill, and Eleven Narrative Poems* (1975) and *Collected Poems* (1980), coauthor of *The Negro Newcomers in Detroit* and *The Negro in Washington* (both 1970), and contributor to many other books and periodicals.

REFERENCES: CA (NR-26, 127); CB (1982, 1989); NYT, January 17, 1989, p. 11; WP, January 16, 1989, pp. B6 and D1, January 17, 1989, p. D3, and January 19, 1989, p. A26; *Contemporary Poets* (St. Martin's Press, 1980); Saunders Redding (q.v.), *To Make a Poet Black* (University of North Carolina Press, 1939).

BROWNELL, Samuel Miller. b. April 3, 1900, Peru, Nebraska, to Herbert (BDAE) and May (Miller) Brownell. Married June 23, 1927, to Esther Delzell. Children: four. d. October 12, 1990, New Haven, Connecticut.

Samuel Miller Brownell was a career educational administrator who served as U.S. commissioner of education from 1953 to 1956. He reorganized the Office of Education, which was under the Department of Health, Education, and Welfare. He initiated studies to deal with dropout rates and illiteracy, made plans to assist school districts in efforts to integrate schools, and established the Committee on Education beyond the High School.

Brownell's father was president of Peru (Nebraska) State Teachers College (later, State College). The son served in the U.S. Army in 1918 and graduated from the University of Nebraska with the A.B. degree in 1921. He was a science teacher and principal in the demonstration school of Peru State Teachers College. At Yale University he earned the A.M. degree in 1923 and the Ph.D. in 1926.

After one year teaching at Albany (New York) State College (later, State University of New York at Albany), he served as superintendent of schools in Grosse Pointe, Michigan (1927–38). It was regarded as an outstanding system, and after he left a school was named for him. Brownell became professor of educational administration at Yale University in 1938, conducting surveys in many school systems. In 1947 Brownell became concurrently president of New Haven State Teachers College (later, Southern Connecticut State University), where he oversaw the development of a new campus. When President Dwight Eisenhower appointed him U.S. commissioner of education in 1953, he resigned from the presidency of the teachers college and took a leave of absence from Yale.

Leaving government service in 1956, Brownell became superintendent of schools in Detroit, where he remained until 1966. As first superintendent from outside the system, he opened administrative posts to outside competition, increased opportunities for African-American teachers, emphasized the role of schools as community and cultural centers, and worked to maintain racial integration in the schools.

Brownell was an early advocate of the use of radio and television in classrooms. He was chairman of the Midwest Council on Airborne Television Instruction. From 1966 until his 1972 retirement, Brownell was again at Yale as professor of urban educational administration. He wrote many journal articles and two books.

REFERENCES: CB (1954, 1991); CHE, January 16, 1985, p. 26; LE (1974); RPE; WWW (10); NYT, October 14, 1990, p. 34; *Higher Education* 10 (November 1953): 33–34, and 13 (September 1956): 1–2; Edgar Logan, "Samuel Brownell: Champion of Children," *Clearing House* 41 (April 1967): 491–93; Marjorie E. Porter, "Samuel M. Brownell: Uncompromising Purist," *Saturday Review* 44 (August 19, 1961): 44+.

BRUNER, Herbert Bascom. b. December 18, 1892, Montserrat, Missouri, to Calhoun and Elizabeth (Richardson) Bruner. Married June 6, 1918, to Lucile Munday. Children: two. d. August 2, 1974, Boca Raton, Florida.

Herbert Bruner earned the A.B. degree at Central College (Missouri) in 1913, the M.A. at the University of Missouri in 1915, and the Ph.D. at Teachers College of Columbia University in 1925. He taught high school in Mexico,

Missouri (1913–14), and served as superintendent of schools in Lathrop, Missouri (1916–18), and Okmulgee, Oklahoma (1918–24).

In Okmulgee, Bruner conducted a five-year curricular experiment on which he wrote his dissertation, published in 1925 as *The Junior High School at Work.* To counter high levels of school dropout in the seventh and eighth grades, Bruner developed classes that invited pupils to explore their interests, to broaden their acquaintance with subjects and vocations, and thus to give them a basis for determining what they should study in senior high school. At the same time the new classes were designed to help schoolteachers and administrators know better their pupils' aptitudes and abilities. The project began a lifelong interest by Bruner on effective means for schools to develop responsible and productive citizens.

At Teachers College, where he remained after graduate study, Bruner was an associate in curriculum research (1924–29), professor of education (1929–43), director of the curriculum laboratory (1929–40), and chair of the Department of Exceptional Children (1940–43). In 1941 he was principal author of *What Our Schools Are Teaching*, which presented the results of a content analysis of 85,000 curricula for science, social science, and industrial arts in grades four through twelve. He and his coauthors lamented the gap between school curricula and challenges of modern life.

He served as superintendent of schools in Oklahoma City (1943–48) and in Minneapolis (1948–50) before returning to New York, where he was professor of education at New York University (1950–63) and at St. John's University (1963–68). During 1953–54 he directed an educational organization for dependents of U.S. Army personnel.

Bruner was coauthor of *Children's Interests in Poetry* (1927), *Social Studies: Intermediate Grades* (1936), *Conserving Our Natural Resources* (1938), *Language Arts for Modern Youth* (1939), and *Adventuring in Science* (1940).

REFERENCES: NYT, August 4, 1974, p. 45; WWW (6).

BRUNER, Jerome Seymour. b. October 1, 1915, New York City, to Herman and Rose (Glucksmann) Bruner. Married November 10, 1940, to Katherine Frost; January 16, 1960, to Blanche Marshall McLane. Children: two.

Under the sponsorship of the National Academy of Sciences, Jerome Bruner chaired the Woods Hole Conference on science education in September 1959. He established himself as one of the nation's leading learning theorists when he published his account of "the major themes, the principal conjectures, and the most striking tentative conclusions" of the conference under the title *The Process of Education* (1962). Arguing from his experience and research in cognitive psychology, Bruner insisted that children learn through intuition and discovery. He urged teachers to encourage students' respect for their own curiosity and their ability to make "interesting informed guesses."

Bruner was blind until two years of age. After his father's death, when he was twelve years old, the family moved frequently, and he attended six high schools in four years, the last year at a preparatory school in New York state. He received the A.B. degree from Duke University (1937) and began graduate work there. In 1938 he went to Harvard University, working with Edwin G. Boring (BDAE) and receiving M.A. (1939) and Ph.D. (1941) degrees. During World War II he worked for the Foreign Broadcast Monitoring Service, Office of Public Opinion Research at Princeton University, and Anglo-American Psychological Warfare Division of the Supreme Headquarters Allied Expeditionary Force Europe.

After the war Bruner returned to Harvard to the Psychology Department. He spent the 1951–52 sabbatical year at the Princeton, New Jersey, Institute for Advanced Study and had a Guggenheim Fellowship to Cambridge University (1955–56). In 1960 Bruner and George A. Miller founded the Center for Cognitive Studies at Harvard, which Bruner directed until 1972. Bruner's experimental social studies course for fifth graders, Man: A Course of Study, received favorable reviews and prizes but later was attacked by the John Birch Society and ''creationists.''

In 1972 Bruner was Watts Professor of Psychology and fellow of Wolfson College at Oxford University. He spent the year 1979 at the Netherlands Institute for Advanced Study in the Humanities and Social Sciences. From 1981 to 1988 he was George Herbert Mead Professor at the New School for Social Research. Beginning in 1984 Bruner was research professor of psychology and senior research fellow in law at New York University.

A prolific author, his books included *Mandate from the People* (1944), *A Study of Thinking* (with others, 1956), *Idealism in Education* (1966), *Toward a Theory of Instruction* (1966), *Studies in Cognitive Growth* (with others, 1966), *The Relevance of Education* (1971), *Child's Talk* (1983), *Actual Minds, Possible Worlds* (1986), *Acts of Meaning* (1990), and *The Culture of Education* (1996). He edited *The Developing Child* (with others, 1977). *The Process of Education* was translated into nineteen languages.

Bruner was president of the American Psychological Association (1964–65) and Society for the Psychological Study of Social Issues. He received the G. Stanley Hall Medal, Merrill-Palmer Institute Citation, and Distinguished Scientific Award of the American Psychological Association. He wrote *In Search of Mind: Essays in Autobiography* (1983); *The Social Foundations of Language and Thought: Essays in Honor of Jerome S. Bruner* (1980) was edited by Jeremy M. Anglin and others.

REFERENCES: CA (NR-1); CB (1984); LE (1974); WD (1994–96); WW (1978–79); Elizabeth Devine et al., eds., *Thinkers of the Twentieth Century* (Gale Research, 1983); Elizabeth Hall, ''Schooling Children in a Nasty Climate,'' *Psychology Today* 16 (January 1982): 57–63; *Human Development* 33 (November-December 1990): 325–55; Maya Pines, ''Jerome Bruner Maintains—Infants Are Smarter Than Anybody Thinks,'' NYT *Magazine*, November 19, 1970; *Time* 78 (October 13, 1961): 78+, and 95 (January 19, 1970): 50.

BUCHANAN, Scott Milross. b. March 17, 1895, Sprague, Washington, to William Duncan and Lillian Elizabeth (Bagg) Buchanan. Married February 5, 1921, to Miriam Damon Thomas. Children: one. d. March 25, 1968, Santa Barbara, California.

While an undergraduate at Amherst College, Scott Buchanan took note of the relentless, interrogative style of college president Alexander Meiklejohn (BDAE). As dean of St. John's College in Annapolis, Maryland (1936–47), Buchanan became one of the nation's leading theoreticians and practitioners of liberal education through Great Books and intellectual discipline through Socratic questioning.

Buchanan was raised in Jeffersonville, Vermont. After his graduation from Amherst College with the B.A. degree (1916), he remained there as instructor in Greek (1917–18) and served briefly in the U.S. Navy (1918) before taking up a Rhodes Scholarship at the University of Oxford in England (1919–21). He taught high school in Amherst. He received the Ph.D. degree in philosophy from Harvard University in 1925.

Buchanan taught (1924–25) at the College of the City of New York (later, City University of New York) and was assistant director of the People's Institute (1925–29), a New York organization that promoted adult education. He also taught at the University of Virginia (1929–36).

In 1936 Buchanan began a collaboration with Stringfellow Barr (BDAE) when both were called to the University of Chicago by its president, Robert Maynard Hutchins (BDAE), to aid him with educational innovations there. One year later Barr became the president, and Buchanan the dean, of St. John's College. There Buchanan put in place the Great Books curriculum for which the college became well known.

He directed Liberal Arts, Inc., a private consulting organization (1947–49), was a consultant to the Foundation for World Government (1948–58), and chaired the Department of Religion and Philosophy at Fisk University (1956–57) before working again with Hutchins as a consultant to the Fund for the Republic, beginning in 1957. Buchanan's writings included *Possibility* (1927), *Poetry and Mathematics* (1929), *The Doctrine of Signatures: A Defense of Theory in Medicine* (1938), and *Essay in Politics* (1953). He edited *The Portable Plato* (1948).

REFERENCES: CB (1962, 1968); DAB (supp. 8); NYT, March 29, 1968, p. 41; WWW (5); Harris Wofford, Jr., ed., *Embers of the World: Conversations with Scott Buchanan* (Center for the Study of Democratic Institutions, 1970).

BUNTING, Mary Alice Ingraham. b. July 10, 1910, Brooklyn, New York, to Henry A. and Mary T. (Shotwell) Ingraham. Married June 22, 1937, to Henry Bunting; 1979 to Clement A. Smith. Children: four.

Mary Ingraham Bunting was both a model and an advocate for educated women to combine professional opportunities with family responsibilities. She was an accomplished scientist in the field of microbial genetics who later entered academic administration. At Rutgers University, where she was dean of Douglass College, and at Radcliffe College, where she was president, she established programs that allowed women beyond traditional college age to return to academic endeavors.

After schooling at the Packer Collegiate Institute in Brooklyn, New York, Mary Ingraham attended Vassar College, where she majored in physics and earned the B.A. degree in 1931. She studied agricultural bacteriology and chemistry at the University of Wisconsin, receiving the M.A. degree in 1932 and the Ph.D. in 1934. She was a research assistant at Wisconsin for two years, taught biology at Bennington College (1936–37) and Goucher College (1937–38), and was a research assistant at Yale University (1938–40) before the birth of her first child brought a hiatus to her scientific work.

During 1946–47, while her husband conducted research in Cambridge, Massachusetts, Mary Ingraham Bunting lectured in botany at Wellesley College. She was again a research assistant at Yale University (1948–52) and a lecturer there (1953–55), while active in the community of Bethany, Connecticut, where she and her family lived. She served on the planning committee for a regional high school (1950–53) and on the school board (1952–55), among other civic roles. The death of her husband, a professor of medicine, in 1954, triggered her return to full-time academic employment, but now in administration of women's institutions.

After four years as dean of Douglass College, Rutgers University (1955–59), she served twelve years as president of Radcliffe College (1960–72). In 1960 she founded the Radcliffe Institute for Independent Study, which provided support for women's research and creativity. She took leave from her post during 1964–65 to serve on the Atomic Energy Commission. Upon retirement from Radcliffe, she became assistant to the president for special projects at Princeton University (1972–75).

Bunting was the author of scientific papers. She chaired the American Council on Education's Commission on the Education of Women (1958–59) and served on the President's Commission on the Status of Women, among many other public and professional service roles. She received the Eminent Achievement Award of the American Women's Association (1961) and the Gold Medal of the National Institute of Social Scientists (1962).

REFERENCES: AWS; CB (1967); LE (1974); NCAB (J: 374); WW (1976–77); William P. Rayner, *Wise Women* (St. Martin's Press, 1983), pp. 59–66; *Time* 78 (November 3, 1961): 68–73 (cover story).

BUROS, Oscar Krisen. b. June 14, 1905, Lake Nebagamon, Wisconsin, to Herman Roy and Tona (Ferguson) Buros. Married December 21, 1925, to Luella Gubrud. Children: no. d. March 19, 1978, New Brunswick, New Jersey.

Oscar Buros was editor and publisher of *Mental Measurements Yearbook*. It described and evaluated educational and psychological tests and cataloged research on them. The first edition included more than 200 reviews of more than 1,000 testing instruments by 133 contributors. There were eight editions between 1938 and 1978.

Buros studied at Superior (Wisconsin) State Normal School (later, University of Wisconsin–Superior) and the University of Minnesota, from which he received the B.S. degree in 1925. He was awarded the M.A. degree by Teachers College of Columbia University in 1928.

He was a high school teacher in Wisconsin (1926–27) and a principal in New Jersey (1930–32) before joining the faculty of Rutgers University (1932–65). At Rutgers he directed the Institute of Mental Measurements (1946–78). He was also president of Gryphon Press, which published *Mental Measurements.*

Buros directed testing for specialized training and reviewed military testing while on active duty in the U.S. Army during World War II. He taught in Uganda (1956–57) on a Fulbright Award and in Kenya (1965–66), where he also was a Ford Foundation adviser on testing. In 1973 he was honored by the Educational Testing Service with its distinguished service award.

REFERENCES: BDP; CA (77–80); NCAB (60: 281); NYT, March 21, 1978, p. 28; Barbara S. Plake et al., "The Buros Institute of Mental Measurements: Commitment to the Tradition of Excellence," *Journal of Counseling and Development* 69 (May/June 1991): 449–55; Harold Ordway Rugg, *Foundations for American Education* (World Book, 1947), pp. 751, 771.

BURRITT, Elihu. b. December 8, 1810, New Britain, Connecticut, to Elihu and Elizabeth (Hinsdale) Burritt. Married: no. d. March 6, 1879, New Britain, Connecticut.

"The learned blacksmith," Elihu Burritt was an early and striking example of "self-culture" or adult education. Largely on his own he acquired some knowledge of thirty languages, including not only French, German, Spanish, Italian, Greek, and Latin but also Bohemian, Danish, Syriac, Sanskrit, Hindustani, Arabic, and Turkish. Although his formal education was quite limited, he gained entree to major public lecture halls and brought broad public attention to the possibility of language learning.

As a youth, Burritt attended district schools during the winter in Connecticut. Upon his father's death he was apprenticed to a blacksmith; intermittently, he practiced that trade from 1828 to 1839. In the same period he studied briefly in a school conducted by a brother, studied on his own in New Haven, and declined an offer of admission to Harvard College. He found work as a peddler and grocer.

Burritt was a guest of the American Antiquarian Society in 1838 and delivered sixty-four public lectures during 1841–42, including at the Lowell (Massachusetts) Lyceum. In Worcester, Massachusetts, he was publisher of *The Literary Gemini* (1839–40) and *Christian Citizen* (1844–45) and, after a period of several years' residence in England, editor of the *Peace Advocate* (1849–51).

He was a founder of the Universal Brotherhood in London in 1846 and an organizer of the 1848 Brussels Peace Congress. During 1863–70 he served as U.S. consul in Birmingham, England. Among his published works were *Sparks from the Anvil* (1848), *Olive Leaves* (1853), *Handbook of the Nations* (1856), and *Thoughts and Notes at Home and Abroad* (1868).

REFERENCES: AR; WWW (H); James Grant Wilson and John Fiske, eds., *Appleton's Cyclopedia of American Biography* (D. Appleton, 1888); Charles Northend, ed., *Elihu Burritt: A Memorial Volume* (D. Appleton, 1879); Peter Tolis, *Elihu Burritt: Crusader for Brotherhood* (Archon Books, 1968); Ronald G. Walters, *American Reformers 1815–1860* (Hill and Wang, 1978).

BURROUGHS, Nannie Helen. b. May 2, 1879, Orange Springs, Virginia, to John and Jennie (Poindexter) Burroughs. Married: no. d. May 20, 1961, Washington, D.C.

''We specialize in the wholly impossible,'' was the motto Nannie Burroughs gave to the National Training School (later, Trade and Professional School) for Women and Girls, which she founded in Washington, D.C. When Burroughs was four years old, she moved with her sister and mother, a former slave, to Washington. There she attended the Colored (also known as M Street, later, Dunbar) High School, from which she graduated in 1896. She studied for one year at Strayer Business College in Washington.

Disappointed at being shut out of employment in District of Columbia schools and federal civil service because of her color, Burroughs worked briefly in Philadelphia on the staff of the *Christian Banner*, a Baptist newspaper, and in Washington in clerical and custodial jobs before moving to Louisville, Kentucky, in 1900. There she was a secretary and bookkeeper at the Foreign Mission Board of the National Baptist Convention.

In Louisville, Burroughs organized the Woman's Industrial Club and through it offered evening classes to women in secretarial and household skills. She was a founder of the National Baptist Woman's Convention in 1900, serving as its corresponding secretary (1900–1948) and president (1949–61). From the beginning of the new century she campaigned in the Baptist conventions for establishment of a women's training school. When the National Training School opened in Washington in 1909, initially with support from the Woman's Convention, Burroughs became director, a post she held the rest of her life. Calling it the ''School of the 3 B's (Bible, bath, and broom),'' she offered African-American women and girls classes in household arts, clerical skills, and trades such as printing and barbering. From 1956 on there was only a summer school. In 1964 the institution was renamed in her memory and made an elementary school.

In the 1920s with Mary McLeod Bethune (BDAE), Burroughs founded the National Association of Wage Earners, a short-lived association. She later was also founder of Cooperative Industries, Inc., in Washington and chaired a presidential committee studying the housing of African Americans.

Burroughs was a frequent contributor to periodicals; editor of the *Worker*, the newspaper of her school; and author of *The Slabtown District Convention*, a popular one-act play, as well as ''Nannie Burroughs Says,'' a column syndicated in African-American newspapers. She served on the executive committee of Baptist World Alliance (1950–55).

REFERENCES: AAW; AWM; BWA; DANB; DARB; NAW; NBAW; NYT, May 22, 1961, p. 31; WEUS; WR; Evelyn Brooks Barnett, ''Nannie Burroughs and the Education of Black Women,'' in Sharon Harley and Rosalyn Terborg Penn, eds., *The Afro-American Woman: Struggles and Images* (National University, 1978), pp. 97–108; Opal V. Easter, *Nannie Helen Burroughs* (Garland, 1995).

BUTLER, Selena Sloan. b. January 4, 1872?, Thomasville, Georgia, to William Sloan and Winnie Williams. Married May 3, 1893, to Henry Rutherford Butler. Children: one. d. October 7, 1964, Los Angeles.

Selena Butler led in the establishment of parent–teacher organizations for African Americans, when existing bodies were not open to them. She enrolled in the high school program of Spelman Seminary (later, College) in 1882, graduated in 1888, and later studied public speaking at the Emerson School (later, College) in Boston (1894). From about the age of sixteen (her birthdate is uncertain) she taught English, first in Atlanta public schools, (1888–91), then at the State Normal School (later, Florida Agricultural and Mechanical University, 1891–93).

From the time of her marriage, Butler was a night school teacher, private tutor, and editor of a monthly newspaper for African-American women, *Woman's Advocate*. When her son, Henry, Jr., and other children in their neighborhood were ready for kindergarten, Butler started one at home. She organized a parent–teacher association at her son's elementary school in 1911. She was founding president of the Georgia Colored Parent–Teacher Association (from 1920) and the National Congress of Colored Parents and Teachers (from 1926). Through Butler's efforts, the new organization and its white counterpart cooperated until their merger in 1970. Butler served in many other civic organizations, including the National Association of Colored Women, Georgia Commission on Interracial Cooperation, and Georgia Federation of Colored Women's Clubs, of which she was also the first president.

After her husband's death in 1931, she lived with her son and his family in England, Arizona, and California, except for a brief period in Atlanta. She is remembered as one of three national founders of parent–teacher associations.

REFERENCES: BWA; NAW (Mod); NBAW; WR.

C

CAIN, Leo Francis. b. July 30, 1909, Chico, California, to Edmund Joseph and Myrtle (Perdue) Cain. Married August 17, 1940, to Margaret Brennan. Children: three.

At San Francisco State College (later, University) as first director of special education, Leo Cain established a model program to train teachers of the mentally retarded. He was codeveloper of the Cain Levine Social Competency Scale (1963) and conducted research that demonstrated the importance of parent-teacher cooperation in the development of mentally retarded children.

Cain graduated with the A.B. degree from Chico State College (later, California State University at Chico) in 1931. He earned M.A. (1935) and Ph.D. (1939) degrees at Stanford University.

He was a public school teacher in California even before he completed his college studies. After serving also as a principal, he was research associate for the American Council on Education in 1939 before joining the faculty at the University of Maryland, where he taught during 1940–43. He served concurrently as director of education in the U.S. Department of Justice. Cain was professor of education at the University of Oklahoma (1946–47) before becoming director of special education at San Francisco State College. He remained there as dean of educational services and summer session (1951–57) and vice president (1957–62). In 1962 he became president of California State University at Dominguez Hills, staying until 1976.

After his retirement as a college president, Cain was associate director of the accrediting commission of the Western Association of Schools and Colleges (1976–78) and director of the Institute for Research on Exceptionality at San Francisco State University (1976–84).

Among many public service roles, Cain was a consultant on education and youth in the Federal Republic of Germany (1953), Liberia (1961), and Saudi Arabia (1975–81). He chaired the mental health council of the Western Interstate Commission for Higher Education (1969–72). By appointment of Lyndon Johnson he was a member of the President's Commission on Mental Retardation (1967–73).

Cain wrote *Effects of Community and Institutional School Programs on Trainable Mentally Retarded Children* (1963) and *Mental Retardation in School and Society* (with Donald L. MacMillan, 1977).

REFERENCES: LE (1974); WW (1996); *Mental Retardation* 15 (August 1977): n.p.

CALDWELL, Bettye McDonald. b. December 24, 1924, Smithville, Texas, to Thomas Milton and Juanita (Mayes) McDonald. Married June 8, 1947, to Fred T. Caldwell, Jr. Children: two.

Bettye M. Caldwell was principal of the Kramer School in Little Rock, Arkansas, which had an innovative program in integrating infancy, preschool, and elementary grades. It engaged in research and curriculum development. The program was recognized nationally. It operated in conjunction with the University of Arkansas at Little Rock, where Caldwell became professor of education in 1974 and Donaghey Distinguished Professor in 1978. From 1969 to 1974 she was at the University of Arkansas at Fayetteville as professor of education and director of the Center for Early Development and Education.

Caldwell received the A.B. degree from Baylor University in 1945 and the M.A. from the University of Iowa in 1947. She was a student and an assistant in medical psychology in the Department of Pediatrics and Psychiatry at Washington University School of Medicine (1947–53) and received the Ph.D. degree in psychology from Washington University in 1951. After two years (1953–55) as assistant professor of psychology at Northwestern University Caldwell returned to Washington University as director of the child evaluation clinic (1956–58).

In Syracuse, New York, Caldwell was at the State University of New York Upstate Medical Center as a research associate in the Department of Pediatrics (1959–65). From 1965 to 1969 she was professor of child development in the College of Home Economics at Syracuse University. With Julius Richmond she worked on projects on early mother–infant interaction. A day care center for infants was organized in 1964. She developed readiness scales with which to evaluate Head Start programs.

Caldwell was editor of *Child Development* from 1968 to 1972. She published more than 100 articles and was coeditor of *Review of Child Development Research*, vol. 3 (1973). With Robert H. Bradley she wrote *Assessing the Home Environment* (1982) and *Child Development and Education* (1982). Caldwell produced motion pictures in the field of child development. She was a member of the juvenile research committee of the National Institute of Mental Health (1970–73), was on the governing board of the Society for Research in Child Development (1977–81), and was president of the National Association for the Education of Young Children (1982–84). In 1976 she was *Ladies' Home Journal* Woman of the Year in humanitarian and community service.

REFERENCES: CA (104); ECE; FWC; LE (1974); WW (1993–94).

CAMPBELL, Olive Dame. b. March 11, 1882, Medford, Massachusetts, to Lorin Low and Isabel (Arnold) Dame. Married March 21, 1907, to John C. Campbell. Children: no. d. June 14, 1954, Nantucket, Massachusetts.

The John C. Campbell Folk School, which Olive Dame Campbell founded in Brasstown, North Carolina, was fashioned on Danish folk schools. Its purpose was to enrich the lives of the people in the Southern Highland region. Classes began in 1927. The school had no admission requirements, offered no credits, and required no examinations.

Campbell graduated in 1903 from Tufts College (later, University) and taught school before her marriage. She traveled with her husband throughout Appalachia under a grant he had from the Russell Sage Foundation to study the needs of the region. When he died in 1919, she completed the book he had begun, *The Southern Highlander and His Homeland* published under his name in 1921. John Campbell had also founded the Conference of Southern Mountain Workers. Olive Campbell was executive secretary of the organization from his death until 1928. She also had an interest in mountain ballads and collaborated with Cecil Sharp in the editing of *English Folk Songs of the Southern Appalachians* (1917).

As she became interested in the Danish folk school movement, Philander P. Claxton (BDAE) encouraged her to visit Scandinavia. She won a fellowship from the American–Scandinavian Foundation and traveled with Marguerite Butler to study folk schools and cooperatives in Scandinavia during 1922. Campbell put forth her plans for a folk high school at a 1924 meeting of the Conference of Southern Mountain Workers. A site at Brasstown, North Carolina, was chosen with 30 acres donated and another 60 purchased acres. Eventually, the site was 200 acres. By 1929 a community building was erected for boarding students.

In addition to offering courses the school helped to organize a credit union and the Mountain Valley Creamery. In the early years the school provided a public health nurse, a small lending library, and a hot lunch program at a public school. It offered recreational programs and operated a demonstration farm. Campbell initiated a meeting at Penland in 1928, hosted by Lucy Morgan (q.v.), at which the Southern Highlands Handicraft Guild was formed.

Campbell retired in 1946. She was the author of journal articles and *The Danish Folk School* (1928).

REFERENCES: WR; William S. Powell, ed., *Dictionary of North Carolina Biography*, vol. 1 (University of North Carolina Press, 1979); Pat McNelley, ed., *The First 40 Years: John C. Campbell Folk School* (N.p., 1966); David E. Whisnant, "The Cultural Work of Olive Dame Campbell, 1908–1948," in *All That Is Native and Fine* (University of North Carolina Press, 1983), pp. 103–79.

CAMPBELL, Roald Fay. b. December 4, 1905, Ogden, Utah, to Ulysses Fay and Pearl (Wilson) Campbell. Married May 29, 1931, to Della Jones; December 29, 1980, to Margaret Adamson. Children: four. d. September 17, 1988, Pocatello, Idaho.

As dean of the University of Chicago Graduate School of Education, Roald Campbell organized the National Conference on the Educational Dimension of the Model Cities Program, drawing over ninety of the nation's experts on city schools. Campbell was known for raising timely issues, bringing diverse scholars and policymakers together, and serving as mentor to hundreds of school administrators and professors of educational administration. When he died, the former

U.S. secretary of education, Terrel Bell (q.v.), wrote, "The giant of educational administration is gone."

Campbell earned an associate's degree at the Idaho Technical Institute (later, State University) in 1925. After one year as a rural teacher and principal in Idaho, two and a half years as a Mormon missionary (including one year as elementary school principal in a Mormon community in east Texas), and a short period farming, he enrolled in 1929 at Brigham Young University, where he received the A.B. degree in 1930.

He studied summers for the M.A. degree, which Brigham Young awarded him in 1933, while he served for three years as superintendent of schools in Moore, Idaho, overseeing seven teachers and 150 pupils. In 1933 he moved to the larger community of Preston, Idaho, where he was superintendent until 1942, the year he completed the Ed.D. degree at Stanford University.

At the University of Utah (1942–51) Campbell headed the Department of Elementary Education, directed the laboratory school, and began teaching educational administration. He was a professor at Ohio State University (1952–57, 1970–74). At the University of Chicago he directed the Midwest Administration Center (1957–64) and was dean of the Graduate School of Education (1964–70). He was Distinguished Adjunct Professor at the University of Utah from 1970 until his death.

Campbell coauthored or coedited many books, among them *Dynamics of School Community Relations* (1955), *Introduction to Educational Administration* (1958), *Organization and Control of American Schools* (1965), *Educational Administration as a Social Process* (1968), and *A Study of Professors of Educational Administration* (1973). He also wrote *The Making of a Professor: A Memoir* (1981).

He was founding editor of *Educational Administration Quarterly* (1964–67), a charter member of the National Academy of Education (1965), and president of the American Educational Research Association (1969–70).

REFERENCES: LE (1974); WW (1972–73); *Educational Administration Quarterly* 25 (May 1969): 124–25; *Educational Evaluation and Policy Analysis* 11 (Spring 1989): 2; *Kappa Delta Pi Record* 6 (April 1970): 131–32.

CARHART, Raymond Theodore. b. March 28, 1912, Mexico City, Mexico, to Raymond Albert and Edith (Noble) Carhart. Married August 2, 1935, to Mary Ellen Westfall; March 31, 1973, to Jeanette (Davis) Grunig. Children: three. d. October 2, 1975, Evanston, Illinois.

At Northwestern University Raymond Carhart initiated courses in audiology, a term he created. He was the first professor of audiology in the nation and did extensive research in the field.

Carhart's early education was in Mexico, where his father was a missionary. He received the A.B. degree in speech and psychology (1932) from Dakota Wesleyan University and M.A. (1934) and Ph.D. (1936) degrees from Northwestern University. He continued at Northwestern as instructor in speech reed-ucation, becoming professor of audiology in 1947. From 1942 to 1947 he was director of education for the deaf and hard of hearing. During World War II in the U.S. Army Medical Corps, he was director of the Acoustical Clinic at a Butler, Pennsylvania, hospital.

At Northwestern Carhart established the Diagnostic Hearing Clinic in 1947, with George E. Shambaugh, Jr., and directed it until 1953. He also headed the Division of Audiology in the School of Speech. In the Medical School, from 1948, Carhart taught otolaryngology. He developed a diagnostic procedure for otosclerosis called Carhart's Notch. In 1950 Carhart spoke in Stockholm, Sweden, at the First International Congress of Audiology.

Carhart was a member of the national advisory council of the National Institute of Neurological Disease and Stroke and received its research career award in 1963. In 1960 he was granted an award of merit from the American Academy of Ophthalmology and Otolaryngology. He was a fellow of the American Laryngological, Rhinological, and Otological Society and American Speech and Hearing Association (president, 1957), from which he received an Honors Award in 1960. He was a director of the American Board of Examiners in Speech Pathology and Audiology (1960–62). Carhart served as a consultant on audiology to the Veterans Administration and on aural problems to the surgeon general of the army (1946–52).

REFERENCES: NCAB (62: 143); WWW (7); *Journal of Speech and Hearing Disorders* 22 (March 1957): 131.

CARLSON, William Samuel. b. November 18, 1905, Ironwood, Michigan, to Samuel and Mary (Lamsted) Carlson. Married December 17, 1932, to Maryjane Rowe; Claire Callan. Children: one. d. May 8, 1994, Belleair Bluffs, Florida.

William S. Carlson served as president of four state universities. At the University of Delaware, where he was president from 1946 to 1950, degrees were awarded to African-Americans for the first time, doctoral programs were begun, and a new biological science department was established. Carlson spent two years as president of the University of Vermont (1950–52), then became second president of the State University of New York system (1952–58), succeeding Alvin C. Eurich (BDAE). He guided the University of Toledo from a small municipal college to a state university during his years as its president (1958–72).

Carlson trained as a geologist. His degrees, earned at the University of Michigan, were B.A. (1930), M.S. (1932), and Ph.D. (1937). He went on University of Michigan expeditions to Greenland in 1928–29 and 1930–31, when he was expedition leader. During 1931–32 he attended the University of Copenhagen, Denmark, as a fellow of the American-Scandinavian Foundation.

In Michigan Carlson taught at Ironwood High School (1933–34) and was principal of Wakefield (1934–36) and East Lansing (1936–37) high schools. In 1937 he went to the University of Minnesota as assistant professor and director of the training school. He became director of admissions and records in 1941.

During World War II he was with the U.S. Army Air Force as consultant on arctic problems, for which he received the Legion of Merit in 1946. He returned to Minnesota, becoming dean in 1946 just before going to the University of Delaware as president.

Carlson wrote *Greenland Lies North* (1940), *Student Teachers Handbook* (with C. W. Boardman, 1940), *Report of the Northern Division of the Fourth University of Michigan Greenland Expedition* (1941), *Lifelines through the Arctic* (1962), and *The Municipal University* (1962). He edited *Manual for the Supervising Teacher* (1940).

REFERENCES: CA (1–4R, 145); CB (1952, 1994); LE (1974); NCAB (I: 132); NYT, May 11, 1994, p. D25; WW (1980–81); *Time* 59 (January 14, 1952): 67.

CARROLL, John Bissell. b. June 5, 1916, Hartford, Connecticut, to William J. and Helen M. (Bissell) Carroll. Married September 6, 1941, to Mary Elizabeth Searle. Children: one.

John B. Carroll was known for his scholarship on psychological and pedagogical issues in language learning and psychometrics. His work ranged widely between theory and praxis, including seminal articles on broad concepts related to the ability to learn. He also wrote the Modern Language Aptitude Test.

Carroll earned the B.A. degree at Wesleyan University in 1937 and the Ph.D. at the University of Minnesota in 1941. He taught at Mount Holyoke College (1940–42) and Indiana University (1942–43). After naval service during World War II he was a research psychologist for the Department of Defense (1946–49). He was a member of the faculty of Harvard University from 1949 to 1967. After seven years as a research psychologist at the Educational Testing Service Carroll went to the University of North Carolina at Chapel Hill, where from 1974 until his retirement in 1983 he was Kenan Professor of Psychology and director of the Thurstone Psychometric Laboratory.

Carroll wrote *The Study of Language: A Survey of Linguistics and Related Disciplines in America* (1953), *Modern Language Aptitude Test* (1958), *Language and Thought* (1964), *The Teaching of French as a Foreign Language* (1975), and *Human Cognitive Abilities: A Survey of Factor-Analytic Studies* (1993). He edited *Language, Thought, and Reality* (1956), *Language Comprehension and the Acquisition of Knowledge* (with Roy O. Freedle, 1972), and *Toward a Literate Society* (with Jeanne S. Chall, q.v., 1975). His essays included "A Model of School Learning" (*Teachers College Record*, 1963), which stimulated much subsequent research on adaptive education, and "Words, Meanings, and Concepts" (*Harvard Educational Review*, 1968).

Carroll was president of the Psychometric Society (1960–61) and the Educational Psychology Division of the American Psychological Association 1967–68) and a founding member and vice president of the National Academy of Education. He received the Edward L. Thorndike (BDAE) Award in educational psychology (1970); the Diamond Jubilee Medal of the Institute of Linguistics,

London, England (1971); and a distinguished service award from the Educational Testing Service (1980).

REFERENCES: CA (NR-3); LE (1974); WW (1996); Lorin W. Anderson, ed., *Perspectives on School Learning: Selected Writings of John B. Carroll* (L. Erlbaum Associates, 1985).

CASEY, Ralph Droz. b. May 8, 1890, Aspen, Colorado, to James and Linda (Droz) Casey. Married May 26, 1921, to Lois Elda Osborne. Children: no. d. July 16, 1977, Seattle.

Ralph Casey was an early leader in both the education of journalists and the development of scholarship on public opinion and propaganda. He was the first American to obtain a doctorate in journalism as a social science. He emphasized the importance of grounding journalism as an academic subject in research.

Casey earned the A.B. degree at the University of Washington in 1913. He went to work as a reporter for the *Seattle Post-Intelligencer*, rising to assistant city editor before leaving in 1916. He taught in schools of journalism at the University of Montana (1916–19) and the University of Washington (1919–20) before returning to newspaper work for two further years, first at the *New York Herald*, then at the *Post-Intelligencer* again. He was concurrently associate editor of the *Pacific Review*.

He taught journalism at the University of Oregon (1922–30), with a two-year hiatus while completing the Ph.D. degree at the University of Wisconsin (1929). Casey made his major contributions to journalism education at the University of Minnesota as professor of journalism (1930–58) and director of the School of Journalism, which was established in 1941. During World War II he was a consultant to the U.S. Office of War Information and Bureau of the Budget (1942–43).

Casey was twice president of the American Association of Schools and Departments of Journalism (1931, 1957). He was a member of the Committee on Pressure Groups and Propaganda of the Social Science Research Council (1930–34) and the Peabody Radio Awards Committee (1942–47). He held a Guggenheim Fellowship during 1937–38. Sigma Delta Chi and Kappa Tau Alpha honored him in 1946 for his contributions to journalism research.

He wrote *Principles of Publicity* (with Glenn Quiet, 1926) and edited *Journalism Quarterly* (1935–45), as well as several other books on topics in journalism.

REFERENCES: NYT, July 17, 1977, p. 42; WWW (8); Gary L. Whitby and Lynn K. Whitby, "Ralph Casey and Propaganda Analysis," in William David Sloan, ed., *Makers of the Media Mind: Journalism Educators and Their Ideas* (L. Erlbaum Associates, 1990), pp. 134–41.

CAVAZOS, Lauro Fred. b. January 4, 1927, King Ranch, Texas, to Lauro Fred and Tomasa (Quintanilla) Cavazos. Married December 28, 1954, to Peggy Ann Murdock. Children: ten.

In 1988 Lauro Cavazos was the first Hispanic American to serve in a presidential cabinet when appointed secretary of education by Ronald Reagan. He was reapppointed by President George Bush and served until 1990.

Cavazos was born on the King Ranch in Texas, where his father was a foreman. When he was in third grade, the family moved to Kingsville, where he and his siblings were the first Mexican Americans to attend public schools. After service in the U.S. Army (1945–46) Cavazos first attended Texas A & I University and then Texas Technical College (later, University), where he received B.A. (1949) and M.A. (1951) degrees. He was a research assistant at Iowa State University, where he earned the Ph.D. degree in physiology in 1954.

While on the faculty of the Medical College of Virginia (1954–64) Cavazos served on the editorial board of the *Medical College of Virginia Quarterly*. At Tufts University Medical School (1964–80) he was professor of anatomy, department chair (1964–72), and dean (1975–80). He also was on the scientific staff of New England Medical Center Hospital (1974–80). As president of Texas Tech University and Health Science Center (1980–88) he cut administrative costs and increased enrollment of Hispanics.

Cavazos published articles in professional journals and was on the editorial boards of *Anatomical Record* (1970–73), *Tufts Health Science Review* (1972–80), and *Journal of Medical Education* (1980–85). He served on the Texas Governor's Task Force on Higher Education (1980–82). In 1984 President Reagan presented him an Outstanding Leadership Award in Education. He was in the Hispanic Hall of Fame (1987) and received a Medal of Merit of the Pan-American Union (1988).

REFERENCES: CB (1989); CHE, November 30, 1988, p. A23+, December 14, 1988, p. A17+, and December 19, 1990, p. A1+; NYT, August 11, 1988, p. 20, and October 20, 1988, p. B8; WW (1996); Nicolas Kanellos, ed., *The Hispanic-American Almanac* (Gale Research, 1993), pp. 277, 722–23; Matt S. Meier, *Mexican-American Biographies* (Greenwood Press, 1988); *Newsmakers* (1989); *Time* 133 (May 29, 1989): 76, and 136 (December 24, 1990): 64; Amy L. Unterburger, ed., *Who's Who Among Hispanic Americans* (Gale Research, 1994–95).

CHALL, Jeanne Sternlicht. b. January 1, 1921, Shendisov, Poland, to Hyman and Eva (Kreinik) Sternlicht. Married June 8, 1946, to Leo P. Chall. Children: no.

As a theorist and researcher on reading, Jeanne S. Chall had widespread influence. She made significant contributions to the understanding of readability, fourth-grade slump, and literacy challenges of low-income children. Chall promoted direct reading instruction because it built phonemic awareness. In her book *Stages of Reading Development* (1983), she introduced a scheme for describing and explaining the path mature readers travel from decoding to constructive and reconstructive reading.

Chall received the B.B.A. degree from City College (later, of the City University of New York) in 1941. She was an assistant in the Institute of Psychological Research at Teachers College of Columbia University (1943–45). As a research assistant (1945–57) and instructor (1947–49) at the Bureau of Educational Research of Ohio State University she worked with Edgar Dale (BDAE); they devised the Dale-Chall Readability Formula. Chall received M.A. (1947) and Ph.D. (1952) degrees from Ohio State. She was on the faculty of the City College of New York from 1950 to 1965, when she went to the Harvard Graduate School of Education to direct the Harvard Reading Laboratory, retiring in 1991.

Chall served on editorial boards for *Reading Research Quarterly* (1965–69), *Education Review*, and *Education Digest*. Among her writings were *Roswell-Chall Diagnostic Reading Test of Word Analysis Skills* (with Florence G. Roswell, 1956), *Readability: An Appraisal of Research and Application* (1958), *Learning to Read: The Great Debate* (1967), *An Analysis of Textbooks in Relation to Declining S.A.T. Scores* (with Sue S. Conard and Susan H. Harris, 1977), *Chall-Popp Reading Books* (with Helen M. Popp, 1986), *The Reading Crisis: Why Poor Children Fall Behind* (with Vicki A. Jacobs and Luke E. Baldwin, 1990), *Do Textbooks Challenge Students?: A Case for Easy or Hard Textbooks* (with Sue S. Conard, 1991), *Creating Successful Readers* (with Florence G. Roswell, 1994), and *Readability Revisited* (1995). She edited *Toward a Literate Society: Report of the Committee on Reading of the National Academy of Education* (with John B. Carroll, q.v., 1975) and *Education and the Brain* (with Allan Mirsky, 1978).

Chall was president of the National Conference on Research in English (1965). She was on the Boards of Directors of the National Society for the Study of Education (1972–78) and the International Reading Association (1961–65), from which she received a Certificate of Merit in 1979. She received the National Reading Conference Annual Publication Award for contributions to reading education (1975), the Edward L. Thorndike (BDAE) Award from the American Psychological Association (1982), and the American Educational Research Association Award (1982, 1986). She was elected to the Reading Hall of Fame (1979).

REFERENCES: CA (NR-10); LE (1974); RPE; WW (1996); WWAW (1981–82); Charlotte Cox, "Learning to Read, Reading to Learn: An Interview with J. S. Chall," *Curriculum Review* 22 (December 1983): 11–15; *Phi Delta Kappan* 70 (November 1988): 226–40, and (March 1989): 521–38; *Reading Teacher* 43 (February 1990): 370–80.

CHEEK, James Edward. b. December 4, 1932, Roanoke Rapids, North Carolina, to King Virgil and Lee Ella (Williams) Cheek. Married June 14, 1953, to Celestine Juanita Williams. Children: two.

Over a long career as their president, James Cheek brought improvement to two historically black universities. Not shy about controversy, he held views considered radical early in his life. In later years his associations with Republican politicians brought student protests against his leadership and led to his early retirement.

Cheek earned the B.A. degree at Shaw University in 1955, the B.D. at Colgate Rochester Divinity School in 1958, and the Ph.D. at Drew University in 1962. He taught theology at Union Junior College (1959–60) and Virginia Union University (1960–63) before returning to his alma mater as president. In the five years that Cheek led Shaw University he arrested a financial crisis and introduced black studies into the curriculum.

In 1969 Cheek left Shaw to be president of Howard University, the sole congressionally chartered, historically black university in the country, widely regarded as the premier institution among such universities. During his twenty years as president, Howard grew through expansion of research and graduate programs and establishment of a school of theology. Cheek's invitation to Lee Atwater, chairman of the Republican National Committee, to join the university's board led to student protests that forced Cheek to retire in 1989.

He was a member of the President's Commission on Campus Unrest (1970). He received Rockefeller and Lilly Fellowships and the Medal of Freedom in 1983 from President Ronald Reagan.

REFERENCES: EBA; LE (1974); WW (1996); *Contemporary Newsmakers* (1987); *Time* 92 (December 27, 1968): 48.

CHILDS, John Lawrence. b. January 11, 1889, Eau Claire, Wisconsin, to John Nelson and Helen Janette (Smith) Childs. Married July 22, 1915, to Grace Mary Fowler. Children: no. d. January 31, 1985, Rockford, Illinois.

John Childs graduated from the University of Wisconsin with the A.B. degree in 1911. In his senior year he was editor in chief of the *Cardinal*, the student newspaper. He later earned the M.A. (1924) and Ph.D. (1931) degrees at Columbia University.

Childs was graduate secretary of the Young Men's Christian Association (YMCA) in Madison, Wisconsin (1911–12), before joining the national staff of the YMCA's Intercollegiate Department (1912–16) as a field-worker in the Midwest. In 1916 he went to Beijing, China, where he was YMCA foreign secretary (1916–22). When John (BDAE) and Alice Dewey were guests in his home during July 1919, an affiliation began that changed the direction of Childs' career from the YMCA to educational philosophy. He studied at Union Theological Seminary and Teachers College of Columbia University (1922–24), then returned to Beijing, where he was on the staff of the YMCA once more, now in an industrial program (1924–27).

Childs taught at Teachers College from 1928 until his retirement in 1954. The moral concerns that guided his YMCA work continued to be important for him, now applied to education. He became a major interpreter of pragmatism and progressivism in education. He was also active in progressive politics through the American Federation of Teachers, American Labor Party, and Liberal Party. In retirement he held visiting appointments at the Universities of Michigan and Illinois and at Southern Illinois University.

Childs was coauthor with John Dewey and others of *The Educational Frontier*

(1933). He wrote *Education and the Philosophy of Experimentalism* (1931), *Education and Morals* (1950), and *American Pragmatism and Education* (1956). He was honored by the League for Industrial Democracy and the John Dewey Society and received the Kilpatrick Award.

REFERENCES: WWW (8); Jean Ahlberg, ''John Childs and the Reflective Thinking of Experimentalism'' (Ph.D. diss., Southern Illinois University at Carbondale, 1987); Lawrence J. Dennis, *From Prayer to Pragmatism: A Biography of John L. Childs* (Southern Illinois University Press, 1992); Lawrence Leo Loveall, ''The Implication of John L. Childs' Concept of Moral Education for Philosophy of Education'' (Ph.D. diss., Southern Illinois University at Carbondale, 1985); William Van Til (BDAE), ''John L. Childs: An Appreciation,'' *Contemporary Education* 58 (Fall 1986): 21.

CLAPP, Elsie Ripley. b. 1882. Married: no. d. 1965.

Elsie Ripley Clapp was an innovator in developing schools as community centers, particularly in very poor, rural settings. Information is sparse about the early and later years of Clapp's life.

Barnard College awarded her the B.A. degree in 1908 with a major in English. The next year she earned the M.A. in philosophy from Columbia University. Though she took no further degree, Clapp completed coursework for the Ph.D. in both English and philosophy. Between 1911 and 1927 she worked often as a graduate assistant with John Dewey (BDAE). She was head of Rosemary Junior School, a progressive primary school affiliated with Rosemary Hall, in Greenwich, Connecticut, from 1924 to 1929.

In 1929 Clapp went to Jefferson County, Kentucky, where she headed the Roger Clark Ballard Memorial School. She reviewed the needs of the community in establishing its curriculum. Pupils studied aspects of life in Kentucky and dramatized their research. The school offered clinics for mothers and babies and sponsored a cooperative market. Boys learned home repairs, while girls sewed clothing. There were 4-H projects and a school garden. Clapp saw the school as a place for community recreation and entertainment as well as education.

Invited to confer about the kind of school needed for a new homestead community in West Virginia, Clapp became head of the Arthurdale School and director of community activities (1934–36). Though a public school of Preston County, during its first two years the Arthurdale School received private funds for its experiment in community education. With a curriculum similar to that of the Ballard School, the Arthurdale School focused on community problems, including health. Among its activities were a school and community newspaper, clubs, and square dances. Members of the Arthurdale School's National Advisory Committee included Eleanor Roosevelt, John Dewey, W. Carson Ryan (BDAE), and Lucy Sprague Mitchell (q.v.). At the end of two years Clapp transferred the school to county and state authorities.

Clapp was the first woman vice president of the Progressive Education Association and headed its Committee on Community School Relations. She became editor of *Progressive Education* in October 1937 but served only until May 1939. While she edited the journal, its attention shifted from prosperous, suburban school settings to impoverished, rural communities. Clapp was the author of *Arthurdale, a School* (1935), *Community Schools in Action* (1939), and *The Use of Resources in Education* (1952), the latter two with prefaces by John Dewey.

REFERENCES: Elsie Ripley Clapp, ''Plays in a Kentucky County School,'' *Progressive Education* 8 (January 1931): 34–39, and ''A Rural Community School in Kentucky,'' *Progressive Education* 10 (March 1933): 123–28; Charlene Haddock Seigfried, *Pragmatism and Feminism* (University of Chicago Press, 1996), pp. 47–52; Steward Wagner, ''School Buildings: Arthurdale, West Virginia,'' *Progressive Education* 15 (April 1938): 304–16; Clapp's books.

CLAPP, Hannah Kezia. b. 1824, near Albany, New York, to Orrin and Hannah (Bangs) Clapp. Married: no. d. October 8, 1908, Palo Alto, California.

Hannah Clapp was a pioneer in women's and girls' education in the West. How she received her own education is unknown. She was a teacher during 1849–54 at Union Seminary, a private school in Ypsilanti, Michigan; principal of the Female Seminary in Lansing, Michigan; and a founding member of the faculty at Michigan Female College. She taught for one year (1859–60) in Vacaville, California, having gone there by wagon train with her brother and his family.

In 1860 Clapp moved to Carson City, Nevada, where there was no public school. She organized Sierra Seminary, a private coeducational school. Incorporated in 1861, it was known as ''Miss Clapp's School.'' A new building was erected in 1865, and with the help of the assistant principal, Eliza C. Babcock, Clapp made it into an important school in Nevada. Clapp invested in early business ventures in Nevada, particularly mining, and saw her fortunes rise and fall with the frontier economy. During the 1880s, under financial duress, she served as a clerk in the Nevada Assembly to supplement her income and keep her school open.

In 1887 Clapp was named preceptress and professor of history and English at the University of Nevada in Reno; she and the president were the entire founding faculty. From 1891 she no longer taught but was university preceptress and librarian. She retired in 1901 at the age of seventy-seven and moved to California.

REFERENCES: WR; Kathryn Dunn Totton, ''Hannah Keziah Clapp: The Life and Career of a Pioneer Nevada Educator, 1824–1908,'' *Nevada Historical Society Quarterly* 20 (Fall 1977): 167–83.

CLARK, Felton Grandison. b. October 13, 1903, Baton Rouge, Louisiana, to Joseph Samuel and Octavia Eleanor (Head) Clark. Married August 22, 1958, to Allene J. Knighten. Children: no. d. July 5, 1970, New Orleans.

As its longtime president, Felton Clark built Southern University from the foundation laid by his father. The son was a leader among historically black universities and colleges in a period that saw both rapid expansion of opportunities for their students and racial desegregation that challenged the premises on which these institutions had been built.

Joseph Clark had refounded Southern University and Agricultural and Mechanical College at Scotts Bluff, Louisiana, in 1914, after the closing of its predecessor institution in New Orleans. From its founding in the Reconstruction era, it had been a land grant institution for African Americans. Felton Clark succeeded his father as president in 1938.

After two years of diploma-level study at Southern, Felton Clark attended Beloit College and earned the A.B. degree (1924). One year later he completed studies for the M.A. at Teachers College of Columbia University; he received the Ph.D. in educational administration there in 1933.

Clark taught psychology and education at Wiley College (1925–27), Southern University (1927–30), and Howard University (1931–33), while completing graduate study. He returned to Southern in 1933 as dean and director of instruction, posts he held until 1937. From 1936 to 1938 he directed the National Survey of Vocational Education and Guidance of Negroes in the U.S. Office of Education.

He was president of Southern University for thirty-one years (1938–69). To its existing campus at Scotts Bluff, he added two more, in New Orleans and Shreveport. The university grew to include professional schools of law, engineering, and business, as well as a graduate school. Clark's cooperation with the governor of Louisiana in disciplining students who were active in the civil rights movement brought him unwelcome attention and led to a temporary closing of the university in 1962.

Clark was president of the Land Grant Colleges Presidents' Conference (1940–41), the Association of Colleges and Secondary Schools for Negroes (1944–45), and the Interracial Conference of Louisiana Colleges and Universities (1968). He served on the Board of Foreign Scholarships overseeing the Fulbright Program (1956–63), the executive committee of the American Association of Land Grant Colleges and Universities (1960–62), and the World Alliance Commission on Race Relations in Geneva, Switzerland, among many public service roles.

He was the author of *The Control of State-Supported Teacher-Training Programs for Negroes* (1934), which foresaw a greater role for African Americans in the governance of their own institutions of higher education. He served also on the editorial board of the *Journal of Negro Education* (1942–52).

References: DAB (supp. 8); EAB; NCAB (57: 37); NYT, July 6, 1970, p. 31; WWW (5); Iris J. Perkins, "Felton Grandison Clark: Louisiana Educator" (Ed.D. diss., Louisiana State Agricultural and Mechanical College, 1976).

CLARK, Kenneth Bancroft. b. July 24, 1914, Panama Canal Zone, to Arthur Bancroft and Miriam (Hanson) Clark. Married April 14, 1938, to Mamie Phipps. Children: two.

Kenneth B. Clark modeled applications of social science research to societal problems, particularly to improving education of African Americans. He was a vigorous opponent of racial segregation and of racial separatism, a stance that brought him into conflict with whites and blacks.

Clark immigrated to the United States from the Panama Canal Zone at the age of four. After attending racially integrated public schools in New York City, he earned A.B. (1935) and M.S. (1936) degrees at Howard University. He taught at Howard for one year, then undertook graduate study in experimental psychology at Columbia University, where he received the Ph.D. degree in 1940.

Clark taught briefly at Hampton Institute (later, University, 1940–41) but resigned because its president wanted him to encourage accommodation to segregated society. He was a research analyst in the Office of War Information during 1941–42, examining wartime morale among African Americans. In 1942 he began a long association with City College of New York, where in 1960 he was the first African American promoted to professor and in 1970 was named a Distinguished University Professor. He retired from City College in 1975.

He was concurrently research director of the Northside Center for Child Development in Harlem, New York (1946–66), providing therapy, testing, research, and advocacy of educational opportunity for poor children; acting chairman of Harlem Youth Opportunities Unlimited (1962–64); president of Metropolitan Applied Research Center (1967–75); chairman and president of Clark, Phipps, Clark and Harris (1975–86), a consulting firm on affirmative action and race relations; and president of Kenneth B. Clark and Associates (from 1986).

With his wife, who also held a doctorate in psychology, Clark conducted research from the 1930s that documented the low self-esteem of black children enrolled in segregated schools. The findings convinced him that improvement in education was essential for the civil rights of African Americans. He was a consultant to the National Association for the Advancement of Colored People (NAACP) from 1951 and a principal author of "The Effects of Segregation and the Consequences of Desegregation: A Social Science Statement," submitted to the U.S. Supreme Court as evidence in the landmark case *Brown v. Board of Education of Topeka, Kansas* (1954).

Among other works, Clark was author of *Prejudice and Your Child* (1955), *Dark Ghetto* (1965), *A Possible Reality* (1972), and *The Pathos of Power* (1974); coauthor of *A Relevant War against Poverty* (with Jeannette Hopkins, 1968); and coeditor of *The Negro American* (with Talcott Parsons, 1966).

He was president of the Society for the Psychological Study of Social Issues (1959–60), American Association for the Advancement of Science (1970–71), and American Psychological Association (1970–71). He was a member of the Regents of the State of New York (1966–86) and the Woodrow Wilson International Center for Scholars (1980–87). He received the Spingarn Medal of the NAACP (1961), the Kurt Lewin Memorial Award of the Society for the Psychological Study of Social Issues (1966), and the Medal for Distinguished Service to Education of the College Entrance Examination Board (1980), among other honors.

REFERENCES: ASL; CA (33–36R); CB (1964); CHE, May 21, 1986, p. 3; EBA; LE (1974); WD (1994–96); WW (1996); *American Psychologist* 34 (January 1979): 65–68; Nat Hentoff, "The Integrationist," *New Yorker* 58 (August 23, 1982): 37–40+; Gerald Markowitz and David Rosner, *Children, Race, and Power: Kenneth and Mamie Clark's Northside Center* (University Press of Virginia, 1996); Charles V. Willie, *Five Black Scholars* (University Press of America, 1986), pp. 41–57.

CLARK, Septima Poinsette. b. May 3, 1898, Charleston, South Carolina, to Peter Porcher and Victoria Warren (Anderson) Poinsette. Married May 1920 to Nerie David Clark. Children: two. d. December 15, 1987, Johns Island, South Carolina.

After several decades as a schoolteacher in South Carolina, Septima Clark undertook a second career, training teachers of reading for adult African Americans throughout the South, in order to help them overcome restrictive voter registration laws.

Clark earned the Licentiate of Instruction at Avery Normal Institute in Charleston, South Carolina, in 1916, qualifying her as a schoolteacher. Teachers at the institute urged her to study at Fisk University, but her family could not afford the cost. Not until 1942 did she earn the B.A. degree at Benedict College. The M.A. degree followed in 1946, from Hampton Institute (later, University).

She taught on Johns Island (1916–19), at Avery Normal Institute (1919–20), and in McClellansville (1920–21), all in South Carolina. During the early 1920s she married, bore two children, one of them surviving infancy, and was widowed. She taught again on Johns Island (1926–29) before moving to Columbia, South Carolina, where she was a teacher for eighteen years. She returned to her native city of Charleston, teaching there (1947–56) until her dismissal for being a member of the National Association for the Advancement of Colored People (NAACP).

In the summer of 1954 Clark attended the Highlander Folk School in eastern Tennessee, an interracial institution directed by Myles Horton (q.v.). Two years later, Horton invited her to join its resident staff. As director of workshops (1956) and director of education (1957–61), she trained teachers for the hundreds of "citizenship schools" that would help to end exclusion of African Americans from politics in the South. Clark remained until public officials closed the school in 1961. From 1962 until her retirement in 1970, Clark continued her work in literacy and citizenship education as a representative of the United Church of Christ, assigned to the Southern Christian Leadership Conference's Dorchester Cooperative Community Center in McIntosh, Georgia.

In retirement, Clark served on the Charleston (South Carolina) County School Board (1976–83). In 1981 she was awarded back pay of the salary she would have earned during 1956–64, had she not been dismissed. She was honored with a Living Legacy Award by President Jimmy Carter in 1979 and the Order of the Palmetto by the state of South Carolina in 1982. Her autobiography, *Echo in My Soul*, appeared in 1962.

REFERENCES: AAW; BWA; CA (5–8R, 124); NBAW; NYT, December 17, 1987, p. 130; WEUS; Cynthia Stokes Brown, ed., *Ready from Within: Septima Clark and the Civil Rights Movement—A First Person Narrative* (Africa World Press, 1990).

COBB, Henry Van Zandt. b. February 22, 1909, East Orange, New Jersey, to Sanford Ellsworth and Margaret Brown (Macleish) Cobb. Married August 3, 1932, to Florence Ruth Crozier. Children: five.

Henry Cobb came to the study of mental retardation indirectly, after scholarly training and teaching experience in philosophy and psychology. In South Dakota as a parent of a retarded child, he took leadership in the development of state, national, and international organizations on behalf of mentally retarded persons. By the 1970s he was author of a major retrospective study of studies on mental retardation. He was also principal author of *Century of Decision* (1976), the ten-year report of the President's Commission on Mental Retardation.

Cobb was awarded the A.B. degree at Pomona College (1930), where he studied English literature, and the Ph.D. degree in philosophy at Yale University (1936). He taught philosophy at Carleton College (1936–44) and was in the U.S. Naval Reserve (1944–45). He then began a long term as chair at the University of South Dakota of what was first the combined Department of Philosophy and Psychology (1946–58) and, later, Psychology alone (1958–67). He was also dean of the College of Arts and Sciences (1967–69) and academic vice president (1969–74).

After retiring from South Dakota, Cobb was visiting scholar (1974–76) and clinical professor (1977–81) at the University of North Carolina at Chapel Hill. During 1964–65 he was visiting professor at Teachers College, Columbia University.

Cobb's many contributions to his profession and his community included founding president of the South Dakota Association for Retarded Children (1955–57), president of the National Association for Retarded Citizens (1964–65) and the International League of Societies for the Mentally Handicapped (1966–70), member of the President's Commission on Mental Retardation (1973–79), and consultant to the Peace Corps in Kenya (1977–78).

He broadcast a weekly radio program *Our Children*, with his wife during 1952–53. He wrote *Man's Way: A First Book in Philosophy* (1942), *Forecast of Fulfillment* (1972), and *Mental Retardation, Past and Present* (1977).

REFERENCES: LE (1974); WW (1996); *Mental Retardation* 15 (August 1977): n.p.

COBB, Jewell Plummer. b. January 17, 1924, Chicago, to Frank V. and Carriebel (Cole) Plummer. Married 1954 to Roy Paul Cobb. Children: one.

Jewell Cobb applied her talents as a scientist and college administrator to bringing African-American students the opportunities for careers in science and medicine that her family had had. The daughter of a physician in Chicago, she graduated from Talladega College with the A.B. degree in 1944. She earned M.S. (1947) and Ph.D. (1950) degrees at New York University.

Cobb's scholarship was in cell physiology, with a research interest in melanin and melanomas. She was a postdoctoral fellow at the National Cancer Institute (1950–52) and a researcher at the Harlem Hospital Cancer Research Foundation (1955). She taught at the University of Illinois College of Medicine (1952–54), Hunter College of the City University of New York (1956–60), and Sarah Lawrence College (1960–69). She was dean of Connecticut College (1969–76) and Douglass College, Rutgers University (1976–81), before being appointed president of California State University, Fullerton, in 1981. Upon retiring in 1990, she was named a trustee professor of the California State University System.

Cobb began a program at Connecticut College that encouraged minority students to pursue careers in medicine and dentistry. It became a model for programs at many other colleges. As trustee professor in California she returned to this work in a collaboration with six colleges.

She was well known for her article ''Filters for Women in Science,'' which appeared in 1979 in the *Annals of the New York Academy of Sciences*. In it she argued that the sciences filtered out women more than men. She was the author of many research articles, as well as articles on women and minorities in the sciences. She was a member of the National Science Board (1974–80).

REFERENCES: AAW; BWA; LE (1974); NBAW; WW (1996); WWBA (1994/95).

COLEMAN, James Samuel. b. May 12, 1926, Bedford, Indiana, to James Fox and Maurine (Lappin) Coleman. Married February 5, 1949, to Lucille Richey; 1973 to Zdzislawa Walaszek. Children: four. d. March 25, 1995, Chicago.

The Coleman Report was the name commonly given to a study commissioned by the U.S. Office of Education in 1965 and published the following year as *Equality of Educational Opportunity*. Written principally by James Coleman, it identified educational opportunity and social circumstance as key factors in determining the quality of education available in American schools. It underlined the importance of schools in improving opportunities for African-American youth and suggested that the quality of school facilities alone made little difference to educational outcomes. The report was often cited as a basis for busing to desegregate schools, a remedy that Coleman later disavowed. It was the first of several controversial books he wrote on American education.

James Coleman served in the U.S. Navy (1944–46) before earning the B.S. degree with a major in chemical engineering at Purdue University in 1949. Following two years of employment by Eastman-Kodak Company, in 1951 he took up graduate study of sociology at Columbia University, where he was awarded the Ph.D. (1955). After one year as a fellow of the Center for Advanced Study in the Behavioral Sciences at Palo Alto, California, and three years teaching at the University of Chicago, Coleman joined the faculty at Johns Hopkins University in social relations (1959–73). He later returned to the University of Chicago as professor of sociology (1973–95).

Coleman directed a federally funded study of high schools and youth culture that resulted in *The Adolescent Society* (1961) and *Adolescents and the Schools* (1965). Among his many other books were *Union Democracy* (with others, 1956), *Community Conflict* (1957), *Youth* (1973), *High School Achievement* (1982), *Public and Private High Schools* (1987), and *Equality and Achievement in Education* (1990).

Coleman received a Guggenheim Foundation Fellowship in 1966–67, a fellowship of the Wissenschaftscolleg Berlin in 1981–82, and a Fulbright Senior Scholar Award to the European Universities Institute in 1993. Columbia University bestowed upon him the Nicholas Murray Butler (BDAE) Award.

REFERENCES: CA (13–16R); CB (1970, 1995); CHE, November 6, 1978, p. 5; NYT, March 28, 1995, p. B11; RPE; WD (1994–96); WW (1996); ''Integration, Yes; Busing, No,'' NYT *Magazine*, August 24, 1975, pp. 10–11+; *Education Week* 14 (April 5, 1995): 15; *High School Journal* 63 (November 1979): 48–53; Harold G. Shane (q.v.), ''An Interview with James S. Coleman on the Problems of Youth,'' *Today's Education* 64 (March 1975): 74+.

COLES, Robert (Martin). b. October 12, 1929, Boston, to Philip Winston and Sandra (Young) Coles. Married July 4, 1960, to Jane Hallowell. Children: three.

Robert Coles used his training as a child psychiatrist, his passion for literature, and his involvement with movements for social justice to elicit the hopes, fears, and ideals of children and youth. His talent for turning familial stories and crayon drawings into national moral narratives earned him the Pulitzer Prize in 1973 for the second and third volumes of his five-volume work, *Children of Crisis* (1967–78). As a sociologist of children, children's book author, and teacher of literature to students in professional schools, Coles was a guide through the inner workings of conscience and character in young people.

He graduated from Boston Latin School in 1946 and received the A.B. degree in 1950 from Harvard College, where his major was English. He wrote his senior thesis on the poem ''Paterson,'' by William Carlos Williams, who encouraged Coles to study medicine. Coles earned the M.D. degree from the Columbia University College of Physicians and Surgeons in 1954. He interned at the University of Chicago the following year. During 1955–58 he was a resident in psychiatry at Massachusetts General Hospital in Boston, McLean Hospital in Belmont, and Judge Baker Guidance Center of Children's Hospital in Roxbury, all in Massachusetts, as well as a teaching fellow at Harvard Medical School.

While a captain in the U.S. Air Force, Coles was chief of the neuropsychiatric unit at Keesler Air Force Base at Biloxi, Mississippi (1958–60). In that period in New Orleans he first met Ruby Bridges, a solitary student in an integrated school that whites were boycotting. This experience led to Coles' study on children of crisis. Coles returned to the South during 1961–63, working with the Southern Regional Council as a research psychiatrist.

He was a psychiatric fellow at the Judge Baker Guidance Center (1960–61) and member of the psychiatric staff at Massachusetts General Hospital. At Harvard Medical School he was a teaching assistant to Erik Erikson (q.v.), research psychiatrist from 1963, and professor of psychiatry and medical humanities from 1978. Coles eventually taught in various professional schools at Harvard, using literature as his vehicle, on topics such as Charles Dickens and the law in the Law School and moral inquiry in the Business School.

Among his many other activities, Coles testified before the U.S. Congress on conditions in the South and traveled with presidential candidate Robert Kennedy during 1967–68. The many awards he received included the Family Life Book Award of the Child Study Association of America, Four Freedoms Award of B'nai B'rith, Ralph Waldo Emerson Prize of Phi Beta Kappa, McAlpin Medal of the National Association for Mental Health, Holzheimer Award for research from the American Psychiatric Association, and MacArthur Foundation Award. He was a fellow of the American Academy of Arts and Sciences and served on many national boards and committees.

Among Coles' many books were *Still Hungry in America* (1969), *Erik H. Erikson: The Growth of His Work* (1970), *The Geography of Faith* (with Daniel Berrigan, 1971), *Irony in the Mind's Life* (1974), *Women of Crisis* (with Jane Hallowell Coles, 1978–80), *The Moral Life of Children* (1986), *The Political Life of Children* (1986), *The Spiritual Life of Children* (1990), *Their Eyes Meeting the World: Drawings and Paintings of Children* (1992), and *The Story of Ruby Bridges* (1995). He contributed columns to *The New Republic*, *New Oxford Review*, and *American Poetry Review* and was on editorial boards of *American Scholar*, *Contemporary Psychoanalysis*, and *Child Psychiatry and Human Development*.

REFERENCES: CA (NR-32); CB (1969); CHE, April 9, 1986, pp. 6–8; NYT, September 1, 1995, p. B1; WD (1994–96); WW (1996); Milton Esterow, ''How to Look at a Mountain,'' *Art News* 92 (March 1993): 92–99; Bernard Murchland, *Voices in American Education* (Prakken, 1990); Bruce A. Ronda, *Intellect and Spirit: The Life and Work of Robert Coles* (Continuum, 1989); *U.S. News and World Report* 109 (December 3, 1990): 66–69; Philip Yancey, ''The Crayon Man,'' *Christianity Today* 31 (February 6, 1987): 14–20.

COMER, James Pierpont. b. September 25, 1934, East Chicago, Indiana, to Hugh and Maggie (Nichols) Comer. Married June 20, 1959, to Shirley Ann Arnold. Children: two.

While director of the Yale Child Study Center, James Comer developed his ''school intervention model'' based on study in the New Haven, Connecticut, public school system. His training as a child psychiatrist and vivid recollections of upbringing by his mother led him to focus on the quality of the personal relationships between teachers and students and the strength of school collaboration with parents. The ''Comer model'' set forth trust-building principles and activities aimed at bringing families and professionals into harmonious teams. In 1990, the Rockefeller Foundation granted $15 million to introduce the ''Comer model'' in schools throughout the United States.

Comer received the B.A. degree from Indiana University (1956), M.D. from

Howard University (1960), and M.P.H. from the University of Michigan (1964) and engaged in postdoctoral study at Yale University (1964–67). He was a fellow in child psychiatry at the District of Columbia's Children's Hospital (1967–68). In 1968 Comer went to Yale University as assistant professor at the Child Study Center. He also directed pupil services of the Baldwin-King School Program in New Haven (1968–73). He was associate dean of the Medical School from 1969 and Maurice Falk Professor of Psychiatry beginning in 1976.

Comer's books included *Beyond Black and White* (1972), *School Power: Implications of an Intervention Project* (1980), and *Maggie's American Dream: The Life and Times of a Black Family* (1988), about his own growing up in an urban setting. With Alvin F. Poussaint (q.v.) he wrote *Black Child Care* (1975), which won the Child Study Association/Wel-Met Family Life Book Award, and *Raising Black Children* (1992). He was a columnist for *Parents Magazine* and served on editorial boards of the *American Journal of Orthopsychiatry* (1976–77), *Youth and Adolescence* (1971–87), and *Journal of Negro Education* (1978–83).

Comer was cofounder of the Black Psychiatrists of America. His many honors and awards included the Harold W. McGraw, Jr., Prize in education (1990), three awards from the American Psychiatric Association (1990), Vera S. Paster Award from the American Orthopsychiatric Association (1990), Charles A. Dana Prize in Education (1991), and James Bryant Conant (BDAE) Award from the Education Commission of the States (1991).

REFERENCES: CA (NR-43): CB (1991); CHE, April 11, 1990, p. A3; RPE; WW (1996); WWBA (1994/95); *Black Enterprise* 15 (September 1984): 38–39; *Educational Leadership* 43 (February 1986): 13–17, and 48 (September 1990): 40–42; *Newsweek* 114 (October 2, 1989): 50, and 121 (January 25, 1993): 55.

COMMONS, John Rogers. b. October 13, 1862, Hollansburg, Ohio, to John and Clarissa (Rogers) Commons. Married December 25, 1890, to Ella Brown Downey. Children: five. d. May 11, 1945, Raleigh, North Carolina.

The writings of John R. Commons and his students, including Selig Perlman (q.v.), became known as the "Wisconsin school" of labor history. Commons was a leader in institutional economics and made the study of labor an academic subject.

Commons graduated from Winchester, Ohio, High School in 1882 and from Oberlin College with the B.A. degree in 1888. For two years he studied at Johns Hopkins University under Richard Ely (BDAE) but left without completing the Ph.D. degree. He taught at Wesleyan University (1890–91), Oberlin College (1891–92), Indiana University (1892–95), and Syracuse University (1895–99). His early publications included *The Distribution of Wealth* (1893), *Social Reform and the Church* (1894), and *Proportional Representation* (1896). Because of a reputation for radicalism Commons became a controversial public figure. He left teaching for other employment, including research for the Democratic National Campaign Committee (1899–1900), and worked for the U.S. Industrial

Commission (1902–4). In 1904 Commons returned to academe when Ely invited him to join the Department of Political Economy at the University of Wisconsin. Commons was a professor of economics at Wisconsin from 1904 to 1933.

Commons and his students completed *A Documentary History of American Industrial Society* (eleven volumes, 1910–11), which Ely had begun. *A History of Labour in the United States* (with others) was published in 1918 and 1935, two volumes each year. Commons served on the editorial staff of *Survey Magazine*. In 1917 he was president of the American Economic Association. A prolific writer, his other books included *Races and Immigrants in America* (1915), *Industrial Goodwill* (1919), *Legal Foundations of Capitalism* (1924), *Institutional Economics* (1934), and the autobiography *Myself* (1934).

Commons drafted civil service and public utility laws and a workers' compensation act for Wisconsin. He served on the Wisconsin Industrial Commission (1911–13), which he had helped to create, and on the U.S. Commission on Industrial Relations (1913–15), National Bureau of Economic Research (associate director, 1920–28), National Monetary Association (president, 1922–23), National Consumers' League (president, 1923–35), and Wisconsin Minimum Wage Board. He was among the first four persons selected for the Labor Hall of Fame.

REFERENCES: AR; ASL; BDAL; BDSW; DAB (supp. 3); IESS; NCAB (13: 511); WWE; WWW (2); Philip Arestis and Malcolm Sawyer, eds., *A Biographical Dictionary of Dissenting Economists* (Edward Elgar, 1992); Jack Barbash, "John R. Commons: Pioneer of Labor Economics," *Monthly Labor Review* 112 (May 1989): 44–49; *Dictionary of Wisconsin Biography* (State Historical Society of Wisconsin, 1960); Howard D. Marshall, *The Great Economists* (Pitman, 1967); Selig Perlman, "John Rogers Commons, 1862–1945," *American Economic Review* 45 (September 1945): 782–86.

CONGDON, Charles Harris. b. December 18, 1856, Nelson, Pennsylvania, to Benjamin D. and Sarah (Campbell) Congdon. Married April 29, 1887, to Anna R. McWilliams. Children: two. d. March 23, 1928, Marshall's Creek, Pennsylvania.

Although little is known about the career of Charles Congdon, he was an early, innovative, and effective advocate for music instruction in public schools.

Congdon graduated from the State Normal School in Mansfield, Pennsylvania (later, Mansfield University of Pennsylvania), in 1876, then taught in rural schools for two years. He introduced music instruction in the Brainerd, Minnesota, public schools (1884–85) and was director of music for the St. Paul public schools (1885–98). From St. Paul he moved to Chicago, where he collaborated with Robert Foresman and Eleanor Smith in using songs rather than scales as the basis for elementary instruction in music.

He was the author of the *Congdon Music Readers* (1908–23) and, with Charles B. Gilbert, the *Congdon Pamphlet Readers* (1910). He also developed teaching aides such as charts for instruction in music and reading.

REFERENCES: NYT, March 25, 1928, p. 31; WWW (1).

CONWAY, Jill Kathryn Ker. b. October 9, 1934, Hillston, New South Wales, Australia, to William Innes and Evelyn Mary (Adames) Ker. Married December 22, 1962, to John Conway. Children: no.

As a historian of women in America and as first woman president of Smith College, Jill Ker Conway raised the status of women as students, scholars, and subjects of scholarship.

After receiving her earliest education at home on a remote sheep station in Australia, she completed high school in Sydney and studied at the University of Sydney, where she received the B.A. degree in 1958. She went to Harvard University as a Fulbright scholar in 1960, receiving the Ph.D. degree in history there in 1969.

Her first teaching was as a lecturer at the University of Sydney (1958–60). At the University of Toronto she served on the faculty (1964–75) and was vice president of internal affairs (1973–75). For ten years (1975–85) she was president of Smith College. At Smith, Conway reaffirmed its importance as an institution for the education of women, and she established a model program for older women to study in college. Subsequently, she was a visiting scholar at the Massachusetts Institute of Technology (from 1985).

She was author of *The Female Experience in Eighteenth- and Nineteenth-Century America: A Guide to the History of American Women* (1982), *The First Generation of American Women Graduates* (1987), and two autobiographical works, *The Road from Coorain* (1989) and *True North* (1994). She coedited *Learning about Women* (1989) and edited *Written by Herself: Autobiographies of American Women* (1992). Conway chaired the American Antiquarian Society.

REFERENCES: AWM; CA (130); CB (1991); WD (1994–96); WW (1996).

COOKE, Flora Juliette. b. December 25, 1864, Bainbridge, Ohio, to Sumner and Rosetta (Ellis) Hannum. Adopted in 1881 by Charles and Luella (Miller) Cooke. Married: no. d. February 21, 1953, Chicago.

Flora J. Cooke was a leader in progressive education who served for thirty-three years as the founding director of the Francis W. Parker School in Chicago. Under her leadership, the school was well known for its experiments in teaching.

Cooke attended Youngstown, Ohio, schools. She taught in rural schools and at the Hellman Street School in Youngstown (1885–89), where she was also principal (1887–89). From 1889 to 1899 Cooke was on the faculty of the Cook County (Illinois) Normal School (later, Chicago State University). In 1899 she was a student at the Chicago Institute, directed by Francis W. Parker (BDAE), and the next year she joined its faculty. Becoming director in 1901, Cooke continued to 1934 and was a trustee until 1948. The institute was renamed the Francis W. Parker School. It enrolled children from varied backgrounds. Cooke developed programs and supported the rights of individual students. She participated in the Eight-Year Study of the Progressive Education Association.

Cooke wrote *Nature Myths and Stories for Little Children* (1895) and *Reading in the Primary Grades* and was editor of the *Francis W. Parker Studies in*

Education (1912–34). She was a founder of the North Shore Country Day School in Winnetka, Illinois.

REFERENCES: AWM; NAW (Mod); NYT, February 22, 1953, p. 63; WWW (3); *Chicago Tribune*, February 22, 1953.

COOLEY, Anna Maria. b. September 16, 1874, New York City, to Charles Wallace and Emma (Davin) Cooley. Married: no. d. May 6, 1955, Pawling, New York.

Anna M. Cooley was an influential professor of home economics early in the twentieth century and the author of popular textbooks on the subject for high schools and colleges. Her writings exemplified the shifting character of the case made for the study of home economics.

Cooley earned diplomas at the New York Normal College (1893), Jenny Hunter Kindergarten Training School (1894), and Barnard College (1896). She received the B.S. degree and a baccalaureate diploma in teaching household arts at Teachers College of Columbia University in 1903.

In the last years of the nineteenth century Cooley was a high school teacher in Michigan. In Muskegon, Michigan, she was principal of household arts and sciences in 1903. She served on the faculty of Teachers College from 1904, achieved the rank of professor in 1923, and retired in 1941.

In *Domestic Arts in Woman's Education* (1911), Cooley argued for the importance of home economics in elementary, secondary, and college curricula and wrote that it merited a greater place than the liberal arts in women's colleges, being ''so vital an expression of [woman's] nature.'' By 1922, however, when *Teaching Home Economics* appeared with Cooley as lead author, the effects of the world war on women's work and the passage of woman suffrage were reflected by a much more moderate posture. Cooley also wrote *Occupations for Little Fingers* (with Elizabeth Sage, 1905); *Household Arts*, a high school textbook in two volumes (with Helen Kinne, 1913); a three-volume textbook series for rural schools (with Kinne, 1916); and *Household Arts for Home and School*, in two volumes (with Wilhelmina H. Spohr, 1920).

REFERENCES: NYT, May 8, 1955, p. 89; WWW (5); *Journal of Home Economics* 47 (September 1955): 467.

COOLEY, Rossa Belle. b. 1873. Married: no. d. September 24, 1949, Greenport, New York.

Rossa B. Cooley succeeded Laura Towne (q.v.) as head of the Penn School on South Carolina's St. Helena Island. She changed the direction of the school to include agriculture and trades in order to educate African Americans for life on the island. Because of Cooley's efforts living conditions for the islanders improved.

Cooley was a graduate of Vassar College in 1893. She taught many subjects and several grades at Hampton Institute (later, University), before going to St. Helena Island in 1901. After traveling throughout the island to observe the residents in their homes and at work, she devised a new plan for the school, which was modeled after Hampton and involved the entire community. In 1904 a two-story, eight-room building was erected, and a school farm was added. The institution was named the Penn Normal, Industrial and Agricultural School. For a time academic training continued as before. Later, agricultural and industrial education was begun. The farm became an experimental and demonstration unit. Practical work for girls included home management, housekeeping, gardening, and sewing.

A school library was provided for Penn students, and the children owned some books. By 1916 the school had seven years of elementary grades; by 1930, eleven grades. Penn School also prepared elementary school teachers. An ungraded school on the grounds provided a place for practice teaching. In later years many of the teachers were Penn School graduates who trained at Hampton Institute. The first agricultural cooperative in South Carolina was established by Penn School, along with a credit union. Cooley wrote *Home of the Freed* (1926) and *School Acres: An Adventure in Rural Education* (1930).

REFERENCES: NYT, September 26, 1949, p. 25; Gerald Robbins, "Rossa B. Cooley and Penn School: Social Dynamo in a Negro Rural Subculture, 1901–1930," *Journal of Negro Education* 33 (Winter 1964): 43–51; T. J. Woofter, Jr., *Black Yeomanry: Life on St. Helena Island* (Holt, 1930).

COONS, Arthur Gardiner. b. June 13, 1900, Anaheim, California, to Richard LaSalle and Mary Ella (Gardiner) Coons. Married February 9, 1927, to Mary Edna Palmer. Children: one. d. July 26, 1968, Newport Beach, California.

Arthur G. Coons was a successful private college president but better known for chairing the commission that developed the Master Plan for Higher Education in California and then defending the results.

Coons graduated from Occidental College with A.B. (1920) and M.A. (1922) degrees. The University of Pennsylvania awarded him the Ph.D. in economics (1927). He was a high school and junior college teacher in Anaheim and Fullerton, California (1922–24), and taught economics at the University of California at Los Angeles (1924–25 and 1926–27).

Returning to Occidental College in 1927, Coons was executive secretary to the president (1927–31) and dean of men (1931–38) as well as a member of the faculty in economics. After five years at the Claremont Colleges (1938–43), Coons again went to Occidental College in 1943 as dean of the faculty. He was president from 1946 until his retirement in 1965. During and after World War II he served as a planner and adviser on regional, state, national, and international economic issues.

The California Master Plan study of 1959–60 followed rapid growth in state college and junior college enrollments and uncertainty about the future roles for the University of California, state colleges, and junior colleges. Clark Kerr (BDAE), president of the University of California, and Roy Simpson (BDAE), superintendent of public education, chose Coons to lead the nine-person study team. Coons was a member of the subsequent Coordinating Council for Higher Education in California from 1960 and chaired it during 1965–68.

The master plan established governing boards for the university and state colleges, provided broad access to higher education, established admissions standards, and set institutional missions. By the mid-1960s it came under frequent attack amid controversies over siting new campuses, the possibility of doctoral study at state colleges, and governance of the university. Coons defended the plan in *Crises in California Higher Education: Experience under the Master Plan and Problems of Coordination, 1959 to 1968* (1968), completed shortly before his death.

He was president of the Association of American Colleges (later, & Universities, 1956) and a member of the President's Committee on Education Beyond the High School (1956–57). He served on the Council for Financial Aid to Education (1953–67) and the College Entrance Examination Board (1961–64), among numerous public and professional services. He wrote *The Foreign Public Debt of China* (1930) and *An Economic and Industrial Survey of the Los Angeles and San Diego Areas* (with Arjay R. Miller, 1941), as well as pamphlets on economic and educational issues. He was an honorary commander of the Order of the British Empire (1967).

REFERENCES: NCAB (55: 181); NYT, July 28, 1968, p. 65; WWW (5); Irving Hendrick, *California Education: A Brief History* (Boyd and Fraser, 1980), pp. 63–65.

COOPER, Anna Julia Haywood. b. August 10, 1858 or 1859, Raleigh, North Carolina, to George Washington Haywood and Hannah Stanley. Married June 21, 1877, to George A. C. Cooper. Children: no. d. February 27, 1964, Washington, D.C.

Anna Cooper was an advocate for academic training for African Americans. She believed that academic aptitude should be the only factor in receiving an education. While not opposed to vocational education, she thought talented students should have higher education, and she wanted higher education available to African-American women.

Cooper's mother was a slave, and her father a slave master. As a child Cooper attended St. Augustine's Normal School and the Collegiate Institute in Raleigh. When eight years old, she coached older students. At about the age of eighteen she was married; she was widowed two years later. She attended Oberlin College, where she received the A.B. degree in 1884. She taught at Wilberforce (Ohio) University (1884–85) and St. Augustine's Normal School (later, College, 1885–87). In recognition of her teaching experience Oberlin awarded her the M.A. degree in 1888.

In 1887 Cooper became a teacher of Latin at the Preparatory High School for Colored Youth, also known as Washington High School, in Washington, D.C. It was named M Street High School in 1891 and Dunbar High School in 1916. In 1901 she was appointed principal of the school. She maintained college preparatory goals and stressed high academic standards. Some students received scholarships to prestigious colleges. Cooper refused to use inferior textbooks and curriculum or to stop seeking scholarships for her students, so she was not reappointed in 1906. From 1906 to 1910 she was chair of languages at Lincoln Institute (later, University) in Missouri, with her summers spent in Oberlin.

In 1910 Cooper returned to the M Street High School as a Latin teacher. Her summers were spent studying in France (1911–13) and at Columbia University (1914–17), where she began work on a doctorate. Because she could not complete residency requirements at Columbia, she later transferred to the Sorbonne in Paris. She completed her thesis in French and received the Ph.D. degree in 1925.

Cooper retired from public school teaching in 1930. Shortly after, she became second president of the Frelinghuysen Group of Schools for Employed Colored Persons (later, Frelinghuysen University) in Washington, D.C., serving until 1942. Her home was used for classes.

Cooper was guardian for seven children. In 1893 she addressed the Congress of Representative Women at the Columbian Exposition, and in 1900 she spoke at the Pan-Africa Conference in London. She wrote *A Voice from the South: By a Black Woman of the South* (1892), *The Life and Writings of the Grimke Family* (1951), and *The Third Step* (1950).

REFERENCES: AAW; AMW; BWA; NAW (Mod); NBAW; WEUS; WP, February 29, 1964; Paul Phillips Cooke, ''Anna J. Cooper: Educator and Humanitarian,'' *Negro History Bulletin* 45 (January-March 1982): 5–7; Leona C. Gabel, *From Slavery to the Sorbonne and Beyond: The Life and Writings of Anna J. Cooper* (Smith College Press, 1982); Sharon Harley, ''Anna J. Cooper: A Voice for Black Women, '' in Sharon Harley and Rosalyn Terborg-Penn, eds., *The Afro-American Woman: Struggles and Images* (National University, 1978); Bert J. Loewenberg and Ruth Bogin, eds., *Black Women in Nineteenth-Century American Life* (Pennsylvania State University Press, 1976).

COOPER, (Jere) Frank Bower. b. September 17, 1855, Mount Morris Township, Illinois, to William Thomas and Barbara Theophania (Wallace) Cooper. Married August 24, 1880, to Mattie M. Hazeltine. Children: no. d. November 23, 1930, Seattle.

Frank B. Cooper led the Seattle school system in progressive and innovative methods during twenty-one years as superintendent.

Cooper's formal education was limited to high school in Polo, Illinois, and one year at Cornell University (1878–79). In Iowa, he was superintendent of schools at Le Mars (1883–90), professor of education at the University of Iowa (1890–91), and superintendent of Des Moines schools (1891–99). For two years he was school superintendent in Salt Lake City before going to Seattle in 1901.

Cooper went to Seattle as an innovator. In a period of growth for the city he erected new school buildings and introduced progressive teaching methods. Less attention was paid to memorization, with students taught to think through problems. In 1909 the Seattle schools began a program using auxiliary teachers to aid with small group instruction. Elementary schools were seen as neighborhood centers. Classes were begun in music, art, domestic science, manual training, and physical education. Evening and summer schools opened, and part-time classes became available for working pupils.

During World War I a Seattle division of the American Protective League, which monitored patriotism, opposed Cooper's ways. The school board changed also, refused to adopt an American history textbook advocated by Cooper, and fired a teacher deemed unpatriotic. In the early 1920s the board sought to cut taxes by reducing the payroll and curriculum, emphasizing ''basic'' courses with fewer extracurricular activities. Cooper resigned in 1922.

REFERENCES: WWW (4); Bryce E. Nelson, ''Frank B. Cooper: Seattle's Progressive School Superintendent, 1901–22,'' *Pacific Northwest Quarterly* 74 (October 1983): 167–77; *Seattle Post Intelligencer*, November 24, 1930, p.1.

COOPER, William John. b. November 24, 1882, Sacramento, California, to William James and Belle Stanley (Leary) Cooper. Married August 19, 1908, to Edna Curtis. Children: three. d. September 19, 1935, Kearney, Nebraska.

From positions of influence, first in the state of California and then nationally, William Cooper advocated school reforms in order to adjust to modern conditions.

Cooper earned B.A. (1906) and M.S. (1917) degrees from the University of California, Berkeley. Most of his career was spent in California. He taught Latin and history in Stockton (1907–10), directed history in the junior and senior high schools of Berkeley (1910–15), and supervised social studies in Oakland public schools (1915–18). During 1918–19 he was briefly employed in education and training work for the U.S. Department of War.

Returning to California, Cooper was superintendent of schools in Piedmont (1918–21), Fresno (1921–26), and San Diego (1926–27). In 1927 he became superintendent of public instruction and director of evaluation for the state of California. Two years later he was appointed U.S. commissioner of education (1929–33).

Cooper held that the time had come for education in the United States to end its dependence on European traditions and that it was necessary to create a new manner of education rooted in the culture of the New World. As the nation's commissioner of education, he called for consolidation of rural school districts and for greater guidance of schools by the states. He inaugurated surveys of educational practices in high schools nationwide, of teacher education, and of school finance.

Cooper was a professor of education at George Washington University (1933–35). While returning to California, he died unexpectedly in 1935. He was the author of articles on topics in education and wrote *Economy in Education* (1933) and *Education of Negro Teachers* (with Ambrose Caliver, BDAE, 1933).

REFERENCES: CHE, January 16, 1985, p. 26; DAB; LE (1932); NCAB (28: 371); NYT, September 20, 1935, p. 21; WWW (1).

COPELAND, Melvin Thomas. b. July 17, 1884, Brewer, Maine, to Salem Dwight and Livonia (Pierce) Copeland. Married June 25, 1912, to Else Helbling. Children: two. d. March 27, 1975, Annisquam, Massachusetts.

Credited with devising the term "marketing" in 1914, Melvin T. Copeland made an important contribution to the direction of courses in marketing in U.S. universities. He also influenced the use of the case method in business schools. In 1919 Dean Wallace Donham (q.v.) of the Harvard Business School asked Copeland to write a casebook. The result was *Marketing Problems* (1920), with later editions titled *Problems in Marketing*. Copeland believed the best foundation for business was a liberal education.

Copeland received the A.B. degree from Bowdoin College in 1906 and A.M. (1907) and Ph.D. (1910) degrees from Harvard University. He taught economics at Harvard (1909–10) and at New York University (1911–12). His book *The Cotton Manufacturing Industry of the United States* (1912) received the David A. Wells Prize for 1911–12. He returned to Harvard in 1912 and remained until 1953, becoming the George F. Baker Professor of Administration. From 1916 to 1926 he was director of the Bureau of Business Research, which administered Harvard's case research program. The case method came to be used by other business schools. On his retirement in 1953 the Melvin T. Copeland Award was established in his honor.

Copeland wrote extensively in the fields of marketing and commodity prices. Among his books were *Principles of Merchandising* (1924), *Cases on Industrial Marketing* (1930), *Raw Materials and Business Conditions* (1933), *The Executive at Work* (1951), and *And Mark an Era: The Story of the Harvard Business School* (1958). He coauthored *Merchandising of Cotton Textiles* (1933), *The Board of Directors and Business Management* (1947), and *The Saga of Cape Ann* (1960) and edited *Business Statistics* (1917).

Among commissions and boards he served on were the Massachusetts Commission on the Cost of Living (1916–17), the Conservation Division of the War Industries Board (executive secretary, 1918), and Massachusetts Commission on Postwar Adjustment (chair, 1941–46).

REFERENCES: CA (P-2, 57–60); NYT, March 29, 1975, p. 26; WWW (6); Malcolm P. McNair, "Melvin T. Copeland, 1884–," *Journal of Marketing* 22 (October 1957): 181–84.

COYLE, Grace Longwell. b. March 22, 1892, North Adams, Massachusetts, to John Patterson and Mary Allerton (Cushman) Coyle. Married: no. d. March 8, 1962, Cleveland, Ohio.

Grace Coyle led the development of social group work theory and advocated its integration into the field of social work, where it was added to individual and casework methods as a third disciplinary orientation.

Coyle had an eclectic education in the social sciences and brought practical experience to her academic work. She earned the B.A. degree at Wellesley College in 1914. The following year she was awarded a certificate for studies at the New York School of Philanthropy (later, Columbia University Graduate School of Social Work). Further studies led to the M.A. degree (1928) in economics and the Ph.D. (1931) in sociology, both from Columbia University.

Coyle was a settlement house worker in the coal region of northeast Pennsylvania (1915–17), field-worker for the Young Women's Christian Association (YWCA) in Pittsburgh (1917–18), and industrial secretary of the YWCA national board in New York City (1918–26). She directed research for the YWCA as executive of its national laboratory division (1930–34).

In 1934 Coyle joined the faculty of the School of Applied Social Sciences at Western Reserve (later, Case Western Reserve) University, where she taught until her death. During World War II she worked in the War Relocation Authority. She was president of the National Conference of Social Work (1940), the American Association of Social Workers (1942–44), and the Council on Social Work Education (1958–60). She was author of *Social Process in Organized Groups* (1930), *Group Experience and Democratic Values* (1947), *Group Work and American Youth* (1948), *Social Science in the Professional Education of Social Workers* (1958), and *Social Process in the Community and the Group* (1958) and editor of *Studies in Group Behavior* (1937).

REFERENCES: DAB (supp. 7); HAWH; NAW (Mod); NYT, March 10, 1962, p. 22; *Encyclopedia of Social Work* (National Association of Social Workers, 1977); *Social Casework* 43 (July 1962): 376; *Social Service Review* 36 (June 1962): 232–33.

CREMIN, Lawrence Arthur. b. October 31, 1925, New York City, to Arthur T. and Theresa (Borowick) Cremin. Married September 19, 1956, to Charlotte Raup. Children: two. d. September 4, 1990, New York City.

Lawrence Cremin's three-volume historical synthesis *American Education* (1970–88) altered assumptions guiding research by focusing on the educative value of institutions, people, and ideas external to schools. Cremin's broad definition of education was the intergenerational and intercultural transmission of knowledge, attitudes, skills, values, and sensibilities. He set the work of schools within a larger context of families, churches, libraries, the mass media, and other agencies with their own curricula and distinctive purposes.

Cremin's parents were founders of the New York Schools of Music. He graduated from Townsend Harris High School, received the B.S.S. degree from City College of City University of New York (1946) and A.M. (1947) and Ph.D. (1949) degrees from Teachers College of Columbia University. In 1949 he joined the Teachers College faculty; he become Frederick A. P. Barnard Professor of Education in 1961. He was director of the Division of Philosophy, Social Sciences, and Education (1958–74) and Institute of Philosophy and Politics of Education (1965–74). He served as Teachers College president from 1974 to 1984.

Cremin edited the Teachers College ''Classics in Education'' series and was on the board of editors of *The American Scholar*. Among his writings were *The American Common School: An Historic Conception* (1951), *A History of Edu-*

cation in American Culture (with R. Freeman Butts, BDAE, 1953), *The Genius of American Education* (1965), *The Wonderful World of Ellwood Patterson Cubberley* (BDAE, 1965), and *Popular Education and Its Discontents* (1990). He won the Bancroft Prize in American history in 1962 for *The Transformation of the School: Progressivism in American Education, 1876–1957* (1961). For volume 2 of *American Education* Cremin received the Pulitzer Prize in history in 1981.

Cremin was a trustee of the Center for Advanced Study in the Behavioral Sciences (1984–89) and Carnegie Foundation for the Advancement of Teaching (1979–87). He chaired the U.S. Office of Education Curriculum Improvement Panel (1963–65) and Carnegie Commission on Education of Educators (1966–70). He was a founding member of the National Academy of Education (1965) and its president (1969–73), as well as president of the National Society of College Teachers of Education (1961), History of Education Society, and Spencer Foundation (from 1985).

He was a Guggenheim fellow (1957). Among many awards he received were those from the American Educational Research Association (1969) and New York University for Creative Educational Leadership (1971).

REFERENCES: CA (NR-29, 132); LE (1974); WWW (10); NYT, September 5, 1990, p. D21, and June 23, 1974, p. 11; Ellen Condliffe Lagemann and Patricia Albjerg Graham, ''Lawrence A. Cremin: A Biographical Memoir,'' *Teachers College Record* 96 (Fall 1994): 102–13; Diane Ravitch, ''Lawrence A. Cremin,'' *The American Scholar* 61 (Winter 1992): 83–89; Kevin Ryan, Katherine K. Newman, and John M. Johnson, ''An Interview with Lawrence A. Cremin,'' *Phi Delta Kappan* (October 1978): 112–16.

CRIM, Alonzo Aristotle. b. October 1, 1928, Chicago, to George and Hazel (Howard) Crim. Married June 1, 1949, to Gwendolyn Motley. Children: three.

Alonzo Crim served in the U.S. Naval Reserve (1945–46). He attended George Williams College, received the B.A. degree from Roosevelt College (later, University) in 1950, and was a social worker until 1954. Crim was with the Chicago public schools as an elementary teacher (1954–63); principal of Whittier Elementary School (1963–65), which had an all-white student body; principal of Phillips High School (1965–68); and a district superintendent (1968–69). He studied under John Goodlad (q.v.) at the University of Chicago, where he earned the M.A. degree in 1958. In 1965 at the Adult Education Center Crim developed a curriculum for literacy.

Crim received the Ed.D. degree from Harvard University (1969), where Herold Hunt (q.v.) was his adviser. He went to California, where he was superintendent of Compton Union High School District (1969–70) and Compton Unified School District (1970–73). From 1973 until his 1988 retirement Crim was superintendent of schools in Atlanta, Georgia, where Benjamin Mays (BDAE) was president of the school board. Crim emphasized improvement of academic performance, particularly in reading and mathematics. He was professor of educational administration at Georgia State University (1988–91) and professor of education at Spelman College (from 1991), where he directed the Ford Scholars Program.

Crim received the Vincent Conroy Award from the Harvard Graduate School of Education (1970), Eleanor Roosevelt Key Award from Roosevelt University (1974), and Distinguished Educators Award from Teachers College of Columbia University (1980).

REFERENCES: RPE; WW (1996); WWBA (1994/95); Alonzo A. Crim, ''Community of Believers,'' *Educating Our Citizens: The Search for Excellence* (1983), pp. 15–24.

CROGMAN, William Henry, Sr. b. May 5, 1841, Phillipsburg, St. Martin, West Indies, to William and Charlotte (Chippendale) Crogman. Married July 10, 1878, to Lavinia C. Mott. Children: eight. d. October 15, 1931, South Atlanta, Georgia.

In the debate at the close of the nineteenth century on what should receive emphasis in the education of African Americans, liberal or vocational education, William Crogman advocated an education based in the classics. While he respected the work of institutions such as Tuskegee Institute (later, University), during his presidency at Clark (later, Clark–Atlanta) University, he dropped vocational programs from the curriculum.

Orphaned at the age of twelve, Crogman worked for more than a decade as a sailor on ships of B. L. Boomer, shipowner from Middleboro, Massachusetts, who became his guardian. When Crogman was twenty-seven years old, with Boomer's encouragement he enrolled at Pierce Academy, a high school in Middleboro, where he graduated in 1868. After three years as the first African-American teacher of English at Claflin College, in Orangeburg, South Carolina, he enrolled as a student of classics at Atlanta (later, Clark–Atlanta) University. There he was awarded the A.B. degree as a member of the first graduating class in 1876. He received the A.M. degree, also from Atlanta University, in 1879.

Crogman was professor of classics from 1880 until 1921 at Clark University. He was first African-American president of the institution during 1903–10. He was secretary of its Board of Trustees from 1885 to 1922.

He was author of *Talks for the Times* (1896) and coauthor of *Progress of a Race* (with Henry F. Kletzing, 1897).

REFERENCES: DANB; EBA; NCAB (14: 367); WWW (1); Frank Lincoln Mather, ed., *Who's Who of the Colored Race* (1915; reprinted by Gale Research, 1976); William J. Simmons, *Men of Mark* (G. M. Rewell, 1887; reprinted by Arno Press, 1968).

CUBAN, Larry. b. October 31, 1934, Passaic, New Jersey, to Morris and Fanny (Janoff) Cuban. Married June 15, 1958, to Barbara Joan Smith. Children: two.

Over a long and many-sided career, Larry Cuban became one of the nation's leading authorities on how schools both change and resist innovation. Beginning in 1957, Cuban worked to remediate the invisibility of the African-American experience in schoolbooks. From materials he collected and tested in his own classroom, he developed *The Negro in America* (1964). As a teacher, school administrator, and professor of education, Cuban produced a remarkably diverse set of written observations on American education.

He earned the B.A. degree in 1955 at the University of Pittsburgh and the M.A. in 1958 at Western Reserve (later, Case Western Reserve) University. He was a public school teacher for one year in Pennsylvania and from 1956 at Glenville High School in Cleveland, Ohio. In 1963 Cuban went to Washington, D.C., to participate in the Cardozo Project in Urban Teaching, initially as a master teacher of history (to 1965), then as director (1965–67). During the next several years he alternated teaching history in the District (1967–68, 1970–71) with brief periods as director of the U.S. Commission on Civil Rights (1968) and director of staff development for District schools (1969–70).

Cuban received the Ph.D. degree from Stanford University in 1974. His doctoral thesis was published two years later as *Urban School Chiefs under Fire* (1976). In Arlington, Virginia, he was superintendent of schools (1974–81) before returning to Stanford on the faculty of the School of Education.

Among Cuban's other books were *To Make a Difference: Teaching in the Inner City* (1970), *The Promise of America* (with Philip Roden, 1971), *Youth as a Minority* (editor, 1972), *How Teachers Taught: Constancy and Change in American Classrooms, 1890–1980* (1984), *Teachers and Machines: The Classroom Use of Technology since 1920* (1986), and *Tinkering toward Utopia* (with David Tyack, q.v., 1995). During 1967–69 he served on the President's Advisory Committee on the Teacher Corps.

REFERENCES: CA (NR-12); RPE.

CULBERTSON, Jack Arthur. b. July 16, 1918, Nickelsville, Virginia, to Otto Cecil and Lola (Fuller) Culbertson. Married August 12, 1952, to Mary Virginia Pond. Children: two.

For nearly a quarter century, Jack Culbertson was executive director of the University Center for Educational Administration (UCEA) at Ohio State University. Through conferences, research programs, and publications, the center stimulated innovation in programs of graduate study for school administrators.

Even before he earned the A.B. degree at Emory and Henry College (1943), Culbertson was an elementary school teacher in rural southwestern Virginia (1937–41). He was a high school teacher in Winston-Salem, North Carolina (1943–44), then completed the M.A. degree at Duke University (1946). Returning to southwestern Virginia, Culbertson was teaching principal of a community school during 1947–49.

In 1949 he moved to California, where he was first a high school teacher in El Centro (to 1951), then superintendent of schools in Santa Barbara (1951–53). Culbertson returned to graduate school, obtaining the Ph.D. degree at the University of California, Berkeley, in 1955. From 1955 to 1959, he taught educational administration at the University of Oregon.

Culbertson directed UCEA from 1959 to 1981. Among its programs the center developed the Monroe City Simulation Materials, resources for administrative role playing. Culbertson coedited publications of the center, including *Preparing Administrators: New Perspectives* (1962), *The Professorship in Educational Administration* (1964), *Social Science Content for Preparing Educational Leaders* (1973), and *Linking Processes in Educational Improvement* (1977). He continued to teach at Ohio State University after 1981.

Culbertson was a consultant to the Ford and W. K. Kellogg foundations, vice president of the American Educational Research Association (1966–68), and an editorial board member of *Educational Administration Quarterly* (from 1965).

REFERENCES: RPE; Richard S. Podemski, ''Reflections on the Administration of Education: A Conversation with Jack A. Culbertson,'' *Phi Delta Kappan* 63 (March 1982): 473–76; *Who's Who in the Midwest* (1978–79).

D

D'AMICO, Victor Edmond. b. May 19, 1904, New York City. Married to Mabel D'Amico. d. March 30, 1987, Southampton, New York.

As director of art education at the Museum of Modern Art in New York City (1937–69), Victor D'Amico spearheaded the use of museums as settings for creative education. The programs he initiated emphasized the creative potential of children. His writings echoed these themes.

During the 1920s, D'Amico was a student at the Cooper Union, Pratt Institute, and Teachers College of Columbia University. At the Fieldston Schools, he directed the Art Department beginning in 1926, a role he continued in until 1948. In 1935 he conducted a study for the Rockefeller Foundation on art education in public schools. He taught art at Columbia University (1934–42) and New York University (1965–72). At the Museum of Modern Art D'Amico opened the Young People's Gallery in 1937, the War Veterans' Art Center in 1945, and the People's Art Center in 1949, all of them offering studio classes.

His books included *Theater Art* (1931), *The Visual Arts in General Education* (1940), *Creative Teaching in Art* (1942), *How to Make Pottery and Ceramic Sculpture: 20 Graded Projects* (1947), *Art for the Family* (1954), and *Experiments in Creative Art Teaching* (1960).

REFERENCES: NYT, April 3, 1987, p. B5; Prabha Sahasrabudhe, ''Victor D'Amico: Expressing the Creative,'' *School Arts* 93 (January 1994): 34–35.

DAVIS, Hallie Flanagan. *See* FLANAGAN, Hallie Mae Ferguson.

DAVIS, Jackson. b. September 25, 1882, Cumberland County, Virginia, to William Anderson and Sally Wyatt (Guy) Davis. Married May 9, 1911, to Corinne Mansfield. Children: two. d. April 15, 1947, Cartersville, Virginia.

Jackson Davis was noted for his interest in the education of African Americans, particularly in the South. He attended school in Richmond, Virginia, and received the B.A. degree from the College of William and Mary in 1902. In Virginia he spent one year each as a school principal in Williamsburg, assistant secretary of the Roanoke Young Men's Christian Association, and principal in Marion. In 1905 Davis became superintendent of schools in Henrico County and visited all schools in his district, both white and black. Impressed by the teaching of Virginia Randolph (q.v.), he approached James Dillard, trustee of the Jeanes Fund, to finance Randolph's visits to black schools in the county. Within three years there were more than 100 Jeanes teachers in thirteen southern states.

In 1908 Davis earned the Ph.D. degree from Columbia University. He served on the state board of examiners and as inspector for the Virginia Board of Education (1909–10). From 1910 to 1915 he was the first state agent for black rural schools. In 1915 the General Education Board appointed him general field agent. For two years he was in Richmond before moving to New York City. He became assistant director of the General Education Board in 1929, associate director for southern education in 1933, and vice president and director in 1946. The board's work centered on education in the South.

Davis was a trustee of the Phelps–Stokes Fund from 1939 and became its vice president in 1940 and president in 1946. He was a Carnegie visitor to Africa in 1935. He wrote *Africa Advancing* (1945) with Margaret Wrong and Thomas M. Campbell. Davis served on the International Education Board (1923–38), was a member of the Interracial Commission and the Advisory Committee on Education in Liberia, and was president of the Booker T. Washington Institute in Liberia.

REFERENCES: NCAB (37: 267); NYT, April 16, 1947, p. 25; WWW (2); Raymond B. Fosdick, *Adventure in Giving: The Story of the General Education Board* (Harper and Row, 1962); *Journal of Negro History* 32 (July 1947): 401–3; *School and Society* 65 (April 26, 1947): 307.

DEARBORN, Walter Fenno. b. July 19, 1878, Marblehead, Massachusetts, to Josiah Weare and Martha Mehitable (Dinsmore) Dearborn. Married September 24, 1917, to Ellen Kedean. Children: two. d. June 21, 1955, St. Petersburg, Florida.

Walter Dearborn conducted foundational research on intelligence, intelligence testing, and reading. He established a typology of readers and demonstrated that complex factors affect success at reading. On intelligence, Dearborn's research underlined the separateness of physical and mental growth.

Dearborn was schooled at Phillips Academy in Exeter, New Hampshire. He earned A.B. (1900) and A.M. (1903) degrees at Wesleyan University. At Columbia University he was awarded the Ph.D. degree in 1905 for his studies in educational psychology under James McKeen Cattell (BDAE). He studied also in Germany at the Universities of Göttingen, Heidelberg, and Munich, taking the M.D. degree at Munich in 1913.

Dearborn taught at the University of Wisconsin (1905–9) and the University of Chicago (1909–12) before going to Harvard University, where he remained until his retirement in 1947. From 1947 to 1953 he was director of the Psycho-Educational Clinic at Lesley College. He was author of *Dearborn Group Tests of Intelligence* (1920), *Predicting the Child's Development* (with J.W.M. Rothney, 1941), *Reading and Visual Fatigue* (with Leonard Carmichael, 1947), and *Psychology of Teaching Reading* (1952).

Dearborn served as a trustee of the Massachusetts State Infirmary (1913–14 and 1915–33) and the Fernald School for the Blind (1943–55). The Hungarian Society of Education made him an honorary member.

REFERENCES: BDP; ECP; NYT, June 22, 1955, p. 29; PR; WWW (3); Herbert S. Langfeld, ''Walter Fenno Dearborn: 1878–1955,'' *American Journal of Psychology* 68 (December 1955): 679–81.

DEMMERT, William G., Jr. b. March 9, 1934, Klawock, Alaska.

William G. Demmert graduated from Seattle Pacific College (later, University) and received Ed.M. and Ed. D. (1973) degrees from Harvard University, where he directed the American Indian Program at the Graduate School of Education. He was a teacher in Forks, Washington (1960–64), and Fairbanks, Alaska (1965–68) and administered public schools in Klawock, Alaska (1968–70). He attended the First Convocation of American Indian Scholars at Princeton University in 1969.

Demmert served as a consultant in the U.S. Senate for the Indian Education Act of 1972. From 1972 he was employed by the U.S. Office of Education in the area of Indian education. He was deputy commissioner of education during 1975–76. At the Bureau of Indian Affairs (1976–78), he was director of Indian education. He returned to Alaska to serve as commissioner of education from 1987 to 1990. Later, he was visiting professor of education at Stanford University.

Lauro Cavazos (q.v.) established the Indian Nations at Risk Task Force in 1990 and appointed Demmert and Terrel H. Bell (q.v.) as cochairs. The task force established goals in 1991 to improve schools serving Native Americans, including Alaskans. Among their recommendations were training more native teachers and renewing language and cultural identities. Demmert was treasurer of the National Indian Education Association. In 1977 he was named Indian Educator of the Year by the National Education Association.

REFERENCES: NNAA; *Biographical Dictionary of Indians of the Americas* (1983); Sharon Malinowski, ed., *Notable Native Americans* (Gale Research, 1995); Peter West, ''Task Force to Propose New Indian-Education Post,'' *Education Week*, September 4, 1991.

DILLER, Angela. b. August 1, 1877, Brooklyn, New York, to William A. M. and Mary Abigail (Welles) Diller. Married: no. d. May 1, 1968, Stamford, Connecticut.

In 1921 Angela Diller founded the Diller-Quaille School of Music in New York City with Elizabeth Quaille. The curriculum they developed integrated theory with practice and had a major influence on music pedagogy. Students were taught musicianship in groups and then put it into practice with individual lessons. Diller and Quaille authored the Diller–Quaille series of music books in forty volumes. Two million copies were sold by 1958. Diller was director of the school until 1941, then became director emeritus.

Diller's given name was Mary Angelina. She changed it to Angela. She began playing the piano at a very young age and even gave lessons to other children but took her first lesson at the age of twelve. At seventeen she began teaching at St. John the Baptist School for Girls in New York. She studied with Edward McDowell (1896–1903) and also at Barnard College (1896–1901). Columbia University awarded her the first Mosenthal Fellowship for composition in 1899.

Diller taught at the Music School Settlement and headed its theory department (1899–1916). There she met Elizabeth Quaille. They both taught at the Mannes School of Music, from its founding in 1916 by David Mannes (BDAE) and Clara Damrosch Mannes (BDAE) until 1921. Diller also headed its theory department. She helped Margaret Dessoff found the Dessoff Choirs in the 1920s. In 1953 she was awarded a Guggenheim Fellowship. Among her many books were *First Theory Book* (1921), *Keyboard Harmony* (1936), and *The Splendor of Music* (1957). She also collaborated on publications with Harold Bauer and Kate Stearns Page.

REFERENCES: BBD; NGD; NAW (Mod); NYT, May 2, 1968, p. 47; WR; Angela Diller, "Personal Recollections of a Music Teacher," *Music Journal* 16 (April–May 1958): 36; *New Yorker* 34 (September 20, 1958): 33–34; César Saerchinger, ed., *International Who's Who in Music* (Current Literature, 1918).

DOLL, Edgar Arnold. b. May 2, 1889, Cleveland, Ohio, to Arnold and Katherine (Rademacher) Doll. Married June 30, 1914, to Agnes Louise Martz; December 28, 1938, to S. Geraldine Longwell. Children: four. d. October 22, 1968, Bellingham, Washington.

As research director (1925–49) at the Training School in Vineland, New Jersey, E. A. Doll developed the Vineland Social Maturity Scale. It provided a basis for measuring social competence of the mentally retarded. He pioneered in assisting children with cerebral palsy and developed ways to measure their capabilities. He also developed a classification system for use in prisons. While a consulting psychologist in Bellingham, Washington, in the 1960s, he developed the Preschool Attainment Record.

Doll attended public schools in Lakewood, Ohio. He graduated from Cornell University in 1912 with the A.B. degree and taught experimental psychology at the University of Wisconsin the following year. From 1913 to 1917 Doll was research and clinical psychologist at the Vineland Training School. He received the Pd.M. degree from New York University in 1916. His *Clinical Studies in Feeble-Mindedness* was published in 1917. From 1917 to 1919 he served in the U.S. Army Sanitary Corps on the Psychological Examining Board. Doll earned the Ph.D. in psychology from Princeton University in 1920, while chief psychologist and director in the Division of Education of the New Jersey Department of Institutions and Agencies (1917–23). For two years he taught at Ohio State University before returning to Vineland Training School.

Doll's work with the mentally deficient at Vineland became well known. The Vineland Social Maturity Scale (1935) developed the concept of social quotient

(SQ) and was widely used. With Winthrop Phelps and Ruth Taylor Melcher he wrote *Mental Deficiency Due to Birth Injury* (1932), concerning cerebral palsy. *The Measurement of Social Competence* appeared in 1953.

From 1949 to 1953 Doll coordinated research at the Devereux Schools in Devon, Pennsylvania. In 1953 he went to Bellingham, Washington, as consulting psychologist.

Doll served as associate editor of several journals, including *Training School Bulletin*, *Journal of Consulting Psychology*, and *Applied Psychology Monographs*. He was a fellow of the American Association on Mental Deficiency and the American Association of Applied Psychology. In 1972 the Edgar A. Doll Developmental Center was built in Bellingham to provide programs for mentally retarded persons.

REFERENCES: BDP; NCAB (62: 162); NYT, November 2, 1968, p. 37; PR; WW (1960–61); Eugene A. Doll, "Edgar Arnold Doll, 1889–1968," *American Journal of Mental Deficiency* 73 (March 1969): 681–82; *Journal of Special Education* 4 (Spring–Summer 1970): 126; *Training School Bulletin* 65 (February 1969): 115; Commemorative Issue Honoring Edgar Arnold Doll, *Training School Bulletin* 47 (June 1950).

DONHAM, Wallace Brett. b. October 26, 1877, Rockland, Massachusetts, to George E. and Sarah A. (Studley) Donham. Married April 7, 1903, to Mabel Higgins. Children: three. d. November 29, 1954, Cambridge, Massachusetts.

Wallace B. Donham was a pioneer in education for business. As second dean of the Harvard Business School (1919–42), he advocated the case method, and established it as an integral part of a reorganized curriculum.

Donham received the A.B. degree from Harvard College in 1898 and graduated from Harvard Law School in 1901. He was employed by the Old Colony Trust Company, where he was vice president from 1906 to 1919. In 1919 A. Lawrence Lowell (BDAE), president of Harvard University, asked Donham to serve as dean of the Graduate School of Business Administration.

Donham organized courses by subject matter instead of by industry, as had been done previously. He asked Melvin Copeland (q.v.) to prepare a casebook text. By 1924 study of cases became the principal method of instruction, and most other business schools came to use case study for instruction. There was continual curricular change throughout Donham's administration. Business ethics was taught from 1928 until 1935, when it was incorporated into other courses.

Donham raised funds to build a new campus at Soldiers Field, across the Charles River from Harvard Yard. The school moved into its new quarters in 1927. Donham planned the *Harvard Business Review*, first published in 1922. When the Business Historical Society was chartered in 1924, Donham arranged for the Business School Library to be a depository for its collections.

Donham retired as dean in 1942. He was George F. Baker Professor of Business Administration until 1948. He introduced a course in human relations at Harvard College and helped to develop a program in human relations at Colgate

University (1948–49). He was a trustee, chairman of the board (1934–54), and managing director (1950–54) of the Harvard-Yenching Institute. He was author of *Business Adrift* (1931), *Business Looks at the Unforeseen* (1932), *Education for Responsible Living: The Opportunity for Liberal Arts Colleges* (1944), and *Administration and Blind Spots: The Biography of an Adventurous Idea* (1952).

REFERENCES: NYT, November 30, 1954, p. 29; WWW (3); Melvin T. Copeland, *And Mark an Era: The Story of the Harvard Business School* (Little, Brown, 1958); Serge Elisseeff, "Wallace Brett Donham (1877–1954)," *Harvard Journal of Asiatic Studies* 18 (1955): vii–ix.

DORSON, Richard Mercer. b. March 12, 1916, New York City, to Louis Jasper and Gertrude (Lester) Dorson. Married 1940 to Dorothy Diamond; August 8, 1953, to Gloria Irene Gluski. Children: four. d. September 11, 1981, Bloomington, Indiana.

Richard M. Dorson made the study of folklore a recognized academic field. He influenced fieldwork theory and technique. He was a field-worker in regional groups throughout the country.

Dorson received A.B. (1937), M.A. (1940), and Ph.D. (1943) degrees in American history from Harvard University and was an instructor there (1943–44). At Michigan State University, where he taught history from 1944 to 1956, he rose from instructor to professor. He attended summer sessions of the Folklore Institute of America at Indiana University and began to offer an occasional course in folklore.

After one year in Japan teaching American studies as a Fulbright fellow (1956–57), Dorson went to Indiana University in 1957 as professor of history and folklore. In 1963 he became director of the Folklore Institute and in 1971 Distinguished Professor of History and Folklore. He was chair of the Folklore Department. He restructured the folklore program. It became internationally known, with many conferences brought to the campus.

Dorson was a Guggenheim fellow on three occasions and was twice a fellow of the American Council of Learned Societies. He served as president of the American Folklore Society (1966–68). He was editor of the *Journal of American Folklore* (1957–62) and founder and editor of the *Journal of the Folklore Institute* (1962–81). Dorson published more than 200 articles, edited many volumes, and wrote many books, including *Jonathan Draws the Long Bow: New England Popular Tales and Legends* (1946), *Bloodstoppers and Bearwalkers: Folk Traditions of the Upper Peninsula* (1952), *Negro Folktales in Michigan* (1956), *American Folklore* (1959), *Folk Legends of Japan* (1961), *Buying the Wind: Regional Folklore in the United States* (1964), *American Folklore and the Historian* (1971), *America in Legends: Folklore from the Colonial Period to the Present* (1973), and *Folklore and Fakelore: Essays toward a Discipline of Folk Studies* (1976).

REFERENCES: CA (106, 105); WWW (8); NYT, September 23, 1981, p. D23; Jan Harold Brunvand, "Obituary: Richard M. Dorson (1916–1981)," *Journal of American*

Folklore 95 (July/September 1982): 347–53; Christopher Winters, ed., *International Dictionary of Anthropologists* (Garland, 1991).

DOUGLASS, Aubrey Augustus. b. February 26, 1887, Eureka, Kansas, to Clifford Hannibal and Ella Erwin (Mains) Douglass. Married April 20, 1918, to Mary Evelyn Fitzsimmons. Children: two. d. May 8, 1952, Sacramento, California.

Aubrey Douglass played a leading role in the establishment of the state colleges of California, which began with institutions in Sacramento, Los Angeles, and Long Beach and grew into the California State University system with many campuses. Earlier in his career, he was an acknowledged expert on secondary education.

Douglass earned the A.B. degree from Kansas State Teachers College (later, University, 1912) and A.M. (1915) and Ph.D. (1917) degrees from Clark University. He served in the U.S. Army during 1917–19.

Douglass taught in Wamego, Kansas (1910–12), and was principal of its high school (1912–14). He served on the faculties of the State College of Washington (later, Washington State University, 1919–24) and the Harvard Graduate School of Education (1924–26). He became professor of education at Pomona College in 1926. With the opening of instruction at Scripps College, second of the Claremont Colleges, the following year, Douglass taught there as well, until his first California state assignment, chief of secondary education in the Department of Education (1935–37). He directed graduate studies in the Claremont Colleges (1937–38) before returning to state service as chief of secondary education and assistant superintendent of public instruction (1938–43). He was superintendent of schools in Modesto, California (1943–47). From 1947 until his death in 1952, he was associate superintendent of public instruction with responsibility for state colleges and teacher education.

Books by Douglass included *The Junior High School* (1917), *Secondary Education* (1927), *The American School System* (1934), and *Modern Secondary Education* (1938).

REFERENCES: NCAB (41: 186); WWW (3).

DOUGLASS, Sarah Mapes. b. September 9, 1806, Philadelphia, to Robert and Grace (Bustill) Douglass. Married July 23, 1855, to William Douglass. Children: no. d. September 18, 1882, Philadelphia.

Sarah Douglass was noted for her training of black youth in Philadelphia, many of whom became schoolteachers.

Douglass was born into a free black, Quaker family. They were friends of Sarah and Angelina Grimke and Charlotte Forten Grimke (BDAE). Douglass was privately tutored until entering a school founded in 1819 by her mother and James Forten. She taught for a short time in New York City. About 1828 she opened a school in Philadelphia for black children. She helped to found the

Philadelphia Female Anti-Slavery Society and in 1838 received support from them for her school.

In 1853 she began teaching at the Institute for Colored Youth (a forerunner of Cheyney University of Pennsylvania), in charge of the girls' primary department. After 1869 she worked under the direction of Fanny Coppin (BDAE). Except for the years of her marriage (1855–61) she taught at the institute until her retirement in 1877. From 1855 to 1858 Douglass took the medical course at Ladies' Institute of the Pennsylvania Medical University, being the first African American to attend. She introduced scientific subjects such as physiology into the curriculum of the institute.

Douglass lectured on health and physiology to black groups in New York and Philadelphia. In 1859 she began the Sarah Mapes Douglass Literary Circle. She served as vice chair of the Women's Pennsylvania Branch of the American Freedmen's Aid Commission. Douglass was active in abolitionist endeavors and contributed articles to *The Liberator*.

REFERENCES: AAW; AR; BWA; DANB; NAW; NBAW; WEUS; Sylvia G. L. Dannett, *Profiles of Negro Womanhood* (Educational Heritage, 1964); Marianna W. Davis, ed., *Contributions of Black Women to America* (Kenday Press, 1982); Gerda Lerner (q.v.), *Black Women in White America* (Pantheon Books, 1972); Marie J. Lindhorst, "Sarah Mapes Douglass: The Emergence of an African American Educator/Activist in Nineteenth Century Philadelphia (Pennsylvania)" (Ph.D. diss., Pennsylvania State University, 1995).

DOYLE, Sarah Elizabeth. b. March 23, 1830, Providence, Rhode Island, to Thomas and Martha Dorrance (Jones) Doyle. Married: no. d. December 21, 1922, Providence, Rhode Island.

In an era when women had few opportunities for higher education, Sarah Doyle looked for alternatives. She was founder and president (1876–84) of the Rhode Island Woman's Club, founding secretary of the coeducational Rhode Island School of Design (1877–99), and a director of the Providence Atheneum (1899–1903). She also participated in the formation of the General Federation of Women's Clubs.

Doyle was a pupil in the first class of the Girls' Department at Providence High School (1843–46), then taught in private schools for a decade. She returned to her alma mater as a teacher (1856–78) and principal (1872–92). Elisha Andrews (BDAE), president of Brown University, invited Doyle in 1895 to lead a campaign to raise funds for a building to house the recently formed Women's College (later, Pembroke College). In 1896 the Rhode Island Society for the Collegiate Education of Women was chartered, with Doyle as president (until 1919). With the funds her group raised, Pembroke Hall was erected in 1897.

In 1884 Doyle was the first woman to preside at a session of the National Education Association; in 1894 she was the first woman to receive an honorary degree (M.A.) from Brown, although she held no earned collegiate degrees.

REFERENCES: DAB; NAW; WR; WWW (1); Polly Welts Kaufman, ed., *The Search for Equity: Women at Brown University, 1891–1991* (Brown University; distributed by University Press of New England, 1991).

DOZIER, Edward Pasqual. b. April 23, 1916, Santa Clara Pueblo, New Mexico, to Thomas Sublette Dozier and Leocadia Gutiérrez. Married to Claire Butler; Marianna Fink. Children: three. d. May 2, 1971, Tucson, Arizona.

Of Tewa, Anglo, and Spanish background, Edward P. Dozier was raised in the Tewa Santa Clara Pueblo in New Mexico. He was a respected scholar and interpreter of Pueblo Indians. He established the interdisciplinary American Indian Studies program at the University of Arizona, where he was professor of anthropology and linguistics from 1960 to his death in 1971.

Dozier attended a Bureau of Indian Affairs grammar school and graduated from St. Michael's High School in Santa Fe, New Mexico. He attended the University of New Mexico, served in the air force during World War II, then returned to the university and earned the B.A. degree in 1947. His M.A. degree (1949), also from the University of New Mexico, was in Pueblo linguistic studies. Dozier was a Whitney fellow in 1950–51 and taught at the University of Oregon in 1951–52. He was awarded the Ph.D. degree from the University of California at Los Angeles in 1952, his thesis being on the ethnography of the Hopi-Tewa.

Following a year as Wenner-Gren Foundation Research fellow, Dozier taught at Northwestern University from 1953 to 1958. He participated in the Southwest Project in Comparative Psycholinguistics. Dozier wrote the section on the Rio Grande Pueblos in Edward H. Spicer's *Perspectives in American Indian Culture Change* (1961). After a year as a research fellow at the Center for Advanced Study in the Behavioral Sciences, he went to the University of Arizona in 1960.

Dozier served on the board (1957–71) and was vice president of the Association on American Indian Affairs. He wrote *The Hopi-Tewa of Northern Arizona* (1954), *Hano, a Tewa Indian Community in Arizona* (1966), and *The Pueblo Indians of North America* (1970). His research in the northern Luzon area of the Philippines resulted in publication of *Mountain Arbiters: The Changing Life of a Philippine Hill People* (1966) and *The Kalinga of the Northern Luzon, Philippines* (1976). He testified at Congressional hearings on conditions of Native Americans.

REFERENCES: NNAA; NYT, May 4, 1971, p. 50; *Biographical Dictionary of Indians of the Americas* (American Indian, 1983); Frederick J. Dockstader, *Great North American Indians* (Van Nostrand Reinhold, 1977); Fred Eggan and Keith Basso, ''Edward P. Dozier,'' *American Anthropologist* 74 (June 1972): 740–46; Marion Eleanor Gridley, *Indians of Today* (Sponsored by Indian Council Fire, 1960); Sharon Malinowski, ed., *Notable Native Americans* (Gale Research, 1995); *Newsweek* 39 (March 24, 1952): 67–68; Marilyn Jane Norcini, ''Edward P. Dozier: A History of Native American Discourse in Anthropology'' (Ph.D. diss., University of Arizona, 1995); Christopher Winters, ed., *International Dictionary of Anthropologists* (Garland, 1991).

DRAKE, (John Gibbs) St. Clair. b. January 2, 1911, Suffolk, Virginia, to John Gibbs St. Clair and Bessie Lee (Bowles) Drake. Married June 17, 1942, to Elizabeth Dewey Johns. Children: two. d. June 5, 1990, Palo Alto, California.

When Stanford University recruited St. Clair Drake to direct its model black studies program, he brought to the task three decades of experience elsewhere as a researcher and teacher on the subject.

Drake graduated from Hampton Institute (later, University) with the B.S. degree in 1931 and from the University of Chicago with the Ph.D. in 1954. The year after he finished his baccalaureate studies, he participated in a Quaker "peace caravan." It began with a training program at Haverford College, then traveled through the United States promoting world peace.

Drake was a teacher at the Christiansburg Institute, a private school in Virginia, from 1932 to 1935, when he went to Dillard University as a research assistant and a member of the faculty in anthropology (1935–37, 1941–42). He was research supervisor under the New Deal's Works Progress Administration in Chicago (1937–40) and associate director of the Illinois State Commission on Conditions of the Urban Colored Population (1940–41). His research in Chicago led to publication of *Black Metropolis: A Study of Negro Life in a Northern City* (with Horace A. Cayton, 1945), a monumental sociological and anthropological study of African Americans in their communities in south Chicago and in their relationships with whites.

During World War II Drake served as a pharmacist's mate and statistician in the U.S. Merchant Marine. He joined the faculty of Roosevelt College (later, University) in 1946, remaining there until his appointment as professor of sociology and anthropology and director of the Afro-American studies program at Stanford in 1969. While on leave (1958–61) he headed the Department of Sociology at the University of Ghana.

Drake was author of *The Redemption of Africa and Black Religion* (1970) and *Black Folk Here and There* (1987) and at the time of his death was writing *White Folks I Have Known*. He wrote and narrated *The War against Fascism*, a film in the series *Black Heritage: A History of Afro-Americans*, produced by Columbia University and CBS television (1969).

Drake was an adviser to the government of Ghana and assisted in training Peace Corps volunteers to Africa. He received the Dubois-Johnson-Frazier Award from the American Sociological Association (1973) for scholarship and teaching.

REFERENCES: CA (65–68, 131); CB (1946, 1990); NYT, June 21, 1990, p. B7; WW (1976–77); WWBA (1990–91); *American Ethnologist* 15 (November 1988): 762–81; Christopher Winters, ed., *International Dictionary of Anthropologists* (Garland, 1991).

DREXEL, Mary Katharine. b. November 26, 1858, Philadelphia, to Francis Anthony and Hannah Jane (Langstroth) Drexel. Married: no. d. March 3, 1955, Cornwells Heights, Pennsylvania.

Mother Mary Katharine Drexel founded the Sisters of the Blessed Sacrament for Indians and Colored People. The order established many schools and Xavier University in New Orleans. She used her fortune to fund the schools, spending more than $100,000 annually.

Born Catherine Drexel in a prominent Philadelphia family, she was educated by private tutors. The family traveled extensively and gave generously to missions for Native Americans and African Americans. Drexel visited missions in the West and considered joining a contemplative order. With her sisters she inherited a large fortune. When she met Pope Leo XIII to ask him for missionary nuns to serve Native Americans and African Americans, he suggested that she become a missionary.

In 1889 Drexel entered the novitiate of the Sisters of Mercy in Pittsburgh for two years of training. She took the name Mary Katharine and made her vows in 1891. Drexel was appointed superior of a new congregation, Sisters of the Blessed Sacrament for Indians and Colored People. Twelve sisters went from Pittsburgh to Philadelphia and for a time were housed in the Drexel estate until a new place was erected for them. They opened a home for African-American children. For seventeen years Drexel served as mistress of novices.

Drexel traveled throughout the West, visiting missions and establishing schools. Many of the schools were built with her funds. She also gave to missions and schools outside her order. In Virginia she purchased 700 acres of land to build an African-American girls' high school. She opened St. Michael's School for Navajos in the Southwest and a number of schools for African Americans along the Mississippi delta of Louisiana. Later schools were built in Columbus, Chicago, St. Louis, Cincinnati, and the Harlem district of New York City. In 1915 the old Southern University property in New Orleans was bought to be used for Xavier Academy, an institution for African Americans. A junior college was added, and a liberal arts college was established in 1925.

In 1937 after several years of ill health, Drexel's term as superior ended. At her death the order had forty-nine houses and conducted sixty-three schools, Xavier University, and social service agencies. In 1988 Drexel was beatified by Pope John Paul II.

REFERENCES: AWM; DAB (supp. 5); DARB; NAW (Mod); NYT, March 4, 1955, p. 23, and November 21, 1988, p. B14; WEUS; WR; Katherine Burton, *The Golden Door: The Life of Katharine Drexel* (Kenedy, 1957); Consuela Marie Duffy, *Katharine Drexel: A Biography* (P. Reilly, 1966); Glenn D. Kittler, *Profiles in Faith* (Coward-McCann, 1962); *New Catholic Encyclopedia* (McGraw-Hill, 1967); Francis Paul Prucha, *The Churches and the Indian Schools, 1888–1912* (University of Nebraska Press, 1979).

DUBOIS, Rachel Davis. b. January 25, 1892, near Woodstown, New Jersey, to Charles Howard and Bertha Priscilla (Haines) Davis. Married June 19, 1915, to Nathan Stewart DuBois. Children: no. d. March 30, 1993, Woodstown, New Jersey.

Rachel Davis DuBois (or Davis-DuBois, as she often called herself in her books) was an advocate for intercultural education, a name she helped to give it, at a time when assimilationist assumptions dominated in American education. Beginning in the 1930s, she directed her skills in writing and organization to affirm the positive aspects of ethnic and racial difference in the United States.

DuBois earned the Ph.B. degree at Bucknell University in 1914, the M.A. at Teachers College of Columbia University in 1933, and the Ed.D. at New York University in 1941. She was a teacher and principal in Glassboro, New Jersey, schools (1914–20) and a high school social studies teacher in Woodbury, New Jersey (1924–29). Between those assignments, she lectured on behalf of the Woman's International League for Peace and Freedom (1921–23).

In 1934 she founded the Service Bureau for Education in Human Relations (later, for Intercultural Education). She directed it until 1940, when a dispute with its Board of Directors led her to found the Intercultural Education Workshop, under which she continued to write and consult with schools on "cultural democracy" and intercultural relations. Its advisory board included W.E.B. Du Bois (BDAE).

Her written works emphasized practical approaches to affirming diversity, such as "neighborhood-home festivals." They included *The Jews in American Life* and *The Germans in American Life* (both 1935, edited with Emma Schweppe), which were to have been the first of ten volumes on ethnic groups; *Americans All—Studies in Intercultural Education* (the 1942 National Education Association yearbook); *Get Together Americans: Friendly Approaches to Racial and Cultural Conflicts through the Neighborhood-Home Festival* (1943); *Build Together Americans: Adventures in Intercultural Education for the Secondary School* (1945); and *The Art of Group Conversation* (with Mew-Soong Li, 1963); as well as pamphlets. During 1938–39 she organized *Americans All—Immigrants All*, a radio series sponsored by the U.S. Office of Education and Works Progress Administration and broadcast on the Columbia Broadcasting System. With Corann Okorodudu, DuBois wrote her autobiography, *All This and Something More: Pioneering in Intercultural Education* (1984).

REFERENCES: NYT, April 1, 1993, p. D24; WWAW (1958). Her papers are in the Immigration History Center, University of Minnesota.

DUMKE, Glenn S. b. May 5, 1917, Green Bay, Wisconsin, to William Frederick and Marjorie (Schroeder) Dumke. Married February 3, 1945, to Dorothy Deane Robison. Children: no. d. June 29, 1989, Los Angeles.

Glenn S. Dumke served for twenty years as chancellor of the California State University system, a model, multicampus public institution of higher education. It was one of three vocations Dumke had, for he was also an accomplished historian of the American West and a writer of historical novels.

As a small boy Dumke moved from Wisconsin to California. He graduated from Occidental College with the A.B. degree in 1938 and earned the M.A. there the following year. The University of California, Los Angeles, awarded him the Ph.D. in 1942.

Dumke returned to Occidental College in 1940 as a member of the faculty.

In 1950 he was promoted to professor and named dean of the faculty, a position he held until 1957. That year he became president of San Francisco State College (later, University). He was vice chancellor for academic affairs of the new California State University system during 1961–62. When Buell Gallagher (q.v.) resigned after only eight months as the founding chancellor, Dumke succeeded him and was chancellor until retirement in 1982. He was subsequently president of the Institution for Contemporary Studies (1982–86) and the Foundation for the 21st Century (1986–89).

Dumke served with Arthur Coons (q.v.) on the study group that in 1959–60 developed the Master Plan for Higher Education in California. He was chairman of the Western Interstate Commission for Higher Education (1976–77).

His scholarly books included *The Boom of the Eighties in Southern California* (1944), *Mexican Gold Trail* (1945), and *History of the Pacific Area in Modern Times* (with Osgood Hardy, 1949). Under the pseudonym Glenn Pierce he wrote two novels, *The Tyrant of Bagdad* (1955) and *King's Ransom* (1986); he wrote *Cavern of Silver* (1982) as Jordan Allen. He was decorated by the governments of the United Kingdom, Sweden, and Taiwan and received several professional awards upon his retirement as chancellor.

REFERENCES: CA (NR-31, 129); LE (1974); NYT, July 1, 1989, p. 10; WWW (10); *Los Angeles Times*, July 1, 1989, sec. 2 p. 1.

E

EDWARDS, Richard. b. December 23, 1822, Cardiganshire, Wales, to Richard Hugh and Anne (Jones) Edwards. Married July 5, 1849, to Betsey Josselyn Samson. Children: ten. d. March 7, 1908, Bloomington, Illinois.

Under Richard Edwards' leadership the Illinois State Normal School gained a national reputation. He developed its Model School, which he considered especially important in training teachers. Edwards believed strongly in education as a profession and in free public education.

Edwards' earliest schooling was in Wales. When he was ten years old, he emigrated with his family to Ravenna, Ohio. He attended a district school part-time, became a carpenter's apprentice, and taught school briefly in Ohio. In 1844 he moved to Massachusetts, where he taught in Hingham and Waltham. He entered Bridgewater Normal School (later, State College) in 1845 and received a normal school diploma in 1846. He received the B.S. degree from Rensselaer Polytechnic Institute in 1847 and completed a course in civil engineering the next year.

He returned to teach at Bridgewater and was assistant principal. He made improvements in instruction, did oral teaching, and minimized memorization of textbooks. He also lectured at lyceums and institutes. In Salem, Massachusetts, he was principal of Bowditch High School. For a time he was an agent of the Massachusetts State Board, headed by Barnas Sears (BDAE).

In 1854 Edwards was named acting principal of the newly opened Salem (Massachusetts) Normal School (later, State College); he became principal in 1855. He served also as editor of *Massachusetts Teacher*. In 1858 he moved to St. Louis, Missouri, to head St. Louis Normal School (later, Harris-Stowe State College). There he used public schools for demonstration and practice.

Edwards went to Illinois State Normal School (later, University) as a mathematics teacher in the spring of 1862; he became principal later that year. At Illinois State Edwards organized teacher institutes to instruct common school teachers. For a number of years he served as editor of the *Illinois Teacher*. In 1856 Edwards helped to organize the American Normal School Association. It became part of the National Teachers Association (begun in 1857) in 1870 and later was renamed the National Education Association (NEA).

Edwards was coauthor of *The Analytical Series of Readers* (1866), *The Analytical Speller*, and *The Student's Reader* (1877). He left the normal school in

1876 and then served at a church in Princeton, Illinois, for nine years, having been ordained in 1873. In 1885 he was financial agent for Knox College. From 1887 to 1891 he was state superintendent of public instruction in Illinois and saw compulsory education laws enacted. He was defeated for reelection. After one year as president of Blackburn College, he moved to Bloomington, Illinois, where he spent his remaining years.

REFERENCES: WWW (1); Charles A. Harper, *A Century of Public Teacher Education* (American Association of Teachers Colleges, 1939); Homer Hurst, *Illinois State Normal University and the Public Normal School Movement* (George Peabody College for Teachers, 1948); Helen E. Marshall, *Grandest of Enterprises, Illinois State Normal School, 1857–1957* (Illinois State Normal University, 1956).

EGGERTSEN, Claude Andrew. b. February 25, 1909, Thistle, Utah, to Claude E. and Helen El Deva (Blackett) Eggertsen. Married June 3, 1931, to Nita Wakefield. Children: three. d. February 9, 1995, Ann Arbor, Michigan.

At the University of Michigan Claude Eggertsen established programs in international education, which included exchange programs in England and Scotland. He also developed teacher education programs in India at the Universities of Bombay and Baroda.

Eggertsen was raised in Mantai, Utah. He received B.A. (1930) and M.A. (1933) degrees from Brigham Young University. From 1930 to 1933 he was a teacher in the Carbon County (Utah) School District. After initial graduate study at Stanford University, he followed Harold Benjamin (BDAE) to the University of Minnesota, where he taught (1934–39) and received the Ph.D. degree (1939) under Edgar B. Wesley (BDAE).

He began teaching at the University of Michigan in 1939, becoming professor of education in 1953 and remaining until retirement in 1979. While in the Naval Reserve (1944–46) he organized and operated the Navy Pacific University and received a Bronze Star.

Eggertsen helped to found the History of Education Society and the Comparative and International Education Society and was president of the latter (1963–64). He was a visiting professor at universities in the United States, England, Japan, India, and Hong Kong. He served the National Society of College Teachers of Education as secretary-treasurer (1948–60). Eggertsen was editor of *Studies in the History of American Education* (1947), *Studies in the History of Higher Education in Michigan* (1950), and *Studies in the History of the School of Education, University of Michigan* (1955). He was editor of the *History of Education Journal* from 1949 to 1960.

REFERENCES: WW (1995); "Claude Eggertsen Retires," *Innovator* 11 (July 27, 1979); Kim P. Sebaly, "Claude A. Eggertsen (1909–95) and Comparative Education," *Comparative Education Review* 40 (May 1996): 107–15.

EISNER, Elliot Wayne. b. March 19, 1933, Chicago, Illinois, to Louis and Eva E. Eisner. Married January 6, 1957, to Eleanor Ann Rose. Children: two.

Elliot Eisner was an advocate of curriculum reform and believed teachers needed to be involved in curriculum planning. He insisted that conditions in schools must change before real reform could take place.

Eisner received the B.A. degree from Roosevelt College (later, University) of Chicago (1954), the M.S. degree from the Illinois Institute of Technology (1955), and M.A. (1958) and Ph.D. (1962) degrees from the University of Chicago. He taught art at Carl Schurz High School in Chicago (1956–58) and at Ohio State University (1960–61) and was assistant professor of education at the University of Chicago (1961–65).

Eisner went to Stanford University in 1965, becoming professor of art and education in 1970. He directed the Charles F. Kettering Foundation Curriculum Development Project (1967–69). Eisner was president of the National Art Education Association (1977–79) and vice president of Division B of the American Educational Research Association (AERA, 1981–83) and received the AERA's Palmer O. Johnson Memorial Award (1967). He was a Fulbright scholar in Australia (1979).

Among Eisner's books were *Educating Artistic Vision* (1972), *English Primary Schools: Some Observations and Assessments* (1974), *The Educational Imagination* (1979), *Cognition and Curriculum: A Basis for Deciding What to Teach* (1982), *The Art of Educational Evaluation: A Personal View* (1985), and *The Enlightened Eye: Qualitative Inquiry and the Enhancement of Educational Practice* (1991). He edited volumes, including *Confronting Curriculum Reform* (1971), *The Arts, Human Development, and Education* (1976), *Reading, the Arts, and the Creation of Meaning* (1978), *Learning and Teaching the Ways of Knowing* (1985), and *Evaluating and Assessing the Visual Arts in Education: International Perspectives* (with others, 1996).

REFERENCES: CA (123); LE (1974); RPE; WW (1984–85); Ron Brandt, ''On Discipline-Based Art Education: A Conversation with Elliot Eisner,'' *Educational Leadership* 45 (December 1987/January 1988): 6–9; *Who's Who in American Art* (R. R. Bowker, 1991–92).

ELIOT, Abigail Adams. b. October 9, 1892, Boston, to Christopher Rhodes and Mary (May) Eliot. Married: no. d. October 29, 1992, Concord, Massachusetts.

Abigail Adams Eliot was an early leader in nursery and childhood education and in training teachers for nursery schools. With Elizabeth W. Pearson she founded the Ruggles Street Nursery School in Boston in 1922. Eliot served as director until 1952. Providing teacher training, the school became the Ruggles Street Nursery School and Training Center and later the Nursery Training School of Boston. In 1951 it became a part of Tufts University as the Eliot-Pearson Department of Child Study.

Eliot received the A.B. degree from Radcliffe College in 1914 and was a social worker in Boston for six years. She studied nursery education under Margaret McMillan in England in 1921 at the Rachel McMillan School; her travel sponsor was the Woman's Education Association of Boston. In 1926 Eliot received a master's degree and in 1930 the Ph.D. from Harvard University. She was a member of the advisory group that organized the National Association for Nursery Education (later, National Association for the Education of Young Children) and served as secretary-treasurer in the 1930s. Eliot was a member of the National Advisory Committee for emergency nursery schools for needy children and supervisor of its New England region.

After her 1952 retirement Eliot taught at Pacific Oaks College. She returned to Massachusetts in 1954 to teach four-year-olds at the Brooks School in Concord (1954–57) and to teach at Garland Junior College (1955–58).

REFERENCES: ECE; NYT, November 2, 1992, p. D11; WWAW (1958); Samuel J. Braun and Esther P. Edwards, *History and Theory of Early Childhood Education* (C. A. Jones, 1972); *Young Children* 48 (March 1993): 52.

ELKIND, David. b. March 11, 1931, Detroit, to Peter and Betsy (Nelson) Elkind. Married December 21, 1960, to Sally Faye Malinsky. Children: three.

Through his interpretation and application of the behavioral theories of Jean Piaget, David Elkind had a substantial influence on early childhood education in the United States. His work illuminated the relationships between stages of development and pedagogical strategies in subjects as varied as mathematics, natural science, social science, and reading. His research suggested that very early education was unlikely to have a lasting effect.

At the University of California, Los Angeles (UCLA), Elkind earned both B.A. (1952) and Ph.D. (1955) degrees. He was a research assistant at the Austen Riggs Center in Stockbridge, Massachusetts (1956–57), and staff psychologist at Beth Israel Hospital in Boston (1957–59) before taking up academic appointments at Wheaton (Massachusetts) College in psychology (1959–61), the UCLA School of Medicine in medical psychology (1961–62), and the University of Denver, where he directed the Child Study Center (1962–66). Elkind was professor of psychology at the University of Rochester (1966–78) and concurrently headmaster of Mt. Hope School in Rochester (1974–77). In 1978 he went to Tufts University as professor of child study and Psychology Department chair.

Elkind was editor and cotranslator of Jean Piaget's *Six Psychological Studies* (1968) as well as the editor of *Studies in Cognitive Development: Essays in Honor of Jean Piaget* (with John H. Flavell, 1969). He wrote *Children and Adolescents: Interpretive Essays on Jean Piaget* (1970), *Exploitation in Middle Class Delinquency: Issues in Human Development* (1971), *A Sympathetic Understanding of the Child: Six to Sixteen* (1971), *Development of the Child* (1978); *The Child's Reality: Three Developmental Themes* (1978), and *The Child and Society* (1979).

He held a National Science Foundation senior postdoctoral fellowship for research in Geneva, Switzerland (1964–65), won the Nicholas Hobbs Award of the American Psychological Association, and was president of the National Association for the Education of Young Children (1986–88).

REFERENCES: CA (NR-1); ECE; WW (1996); Ellis D. Evans, *Contemporary Influences on Early Childhood Education* (Holt, Rinehart, and Winston, 1971).

ELLIS, John Tracy. b. July 30, 1905, Seneca, Illinois, to Elmer Lucian and Ida Cecelia (Murphy) Ellis. Married: no. d. October 16, 1992, Washington, D.C.

On the basis of indisputably strong scholarship, John Tracy Ellis criticized the ''ghetto mentality'' and intellectual timidity of Roman Catholicism in the United States, particularly in its institutions of higher education. He raised these concerns as a priest with clear support from the Vatican, and he coupled his criticism with genuine enthusiasm for other aspects of American Catholicism. Although not without detractors, his views were widely accepted. He was credited with prompting a movement in the 1950s and 1960s to increase intellectual rigor in Roman Catholic colleges and universities.

Ellis earned the A.B. degree at St. Viator College (1927) in Bourbonnais, Illinois, and A.M. (1928) and Ph.D. (1930) degrees at the Catholic University of America. He worked throughout his career at colleges and universities of the church. After graduate study he taught at St. Viator College (1930–32) and the College of St. Teresa (1932–34) in Winona, Minnesota.

When he was thirty years old, Ellis began studies for the priesthood, a vocation he had first considered long before. After four years at the Sulpician Seminary in the District of Columbia, he was ordained in 1938. Ellis taught church history at the Catholic University of America (1947–64), the University of San Francisco (1964–76), and again at the Catholic University of America (1977–89). From 1941 to 1962 he was executive secretary of the American Catholic Historical Association and editor of its journal.

His writings were voluminous, encompassing church history, Catholics in America, documentary collections, and essays. They included *Anti-Papal Legislation in Medieval England* (1930), *Cardinal Consalvi and Anglo-Papal Relations* (1942), *The Formative Years of the Catholic University of America* (1946), *A Select Bibliography of the History of the Catholic Church in the United States* (1947), *The Life of James Cardinal Gibbons, Archbishop of Baltimore* (1952), *American Catholics and the Intellectual Life* (1956), *American Catholicism* (1956), *Catholics in Colonial America* (1965), and *The Catholic Priest in the United States* (1971).

REFERENCES: CA (NR-46, 139); CB (1990, 1993); NYT, October 17, 1992, p. 15; WWW (10).

ENGELMANN, Siegfried. b. November 26, 1931, Chicago, to Victor E. and Rose (Onixt) Engelmann. Married June 28, 1953, to Therese Piorkowski. Children: four.

With Carl Bereiter, Siegfried Engelmann developed a controversial and highly structured approach to teaching underprivileged preschool children. Under their plan children received intense, small-group instruction in language, mathematics, and reading. They believed that disadvantaged children needed to be taught at an accelerated rate if they were to have the opportunity to succeed in school.

Engelmann received the B.A. degree from the University of Illinois (1955), was an investment counselor (1955–60), and worked in advertising (1960–64). In 1964 he returned to the University of Illinois, where he was first at the Institute for Research on Exceptional Children and then senior educational specialist (1966–70). From 1970 he was professor of special education at the University of Oregon. He cofounded the Engelmann-Becker Corporation in Oregon. The U.S. Office of Education supported Engelmann's research.

A prolific writer, his books included *Teaching Disadvantaged Children in the Preschool* (with Bereiter, 1966), *Give Your Child a Superior Mind* (with Therese Engelmann, 1966), *Your Child Can Succeed* (1975), *Preventing Failure in the Primary Grades* (1969), *Direct Instruction* (1980), *Theory of Instruction* (with Douglas Carnine, 1982), and *Generalized Compliance Training* (with Geoffrey Colvin, 1983). Engelmann also developed packaged skill development programs and in 1967 designed the Basic Concept Inventory.

REFERENCES: CA (NR-13); ECE.

ENGLE, Paul Hamilton. b. October 12, 1908, Cedar Rapids, Iowa, to Hamilton Allen and Evelyn (Reinheimer) Engle. Married July 3, 1936, to Mary Nomine Nissen; May 14, 1971, to Hualing Nieh. Children: two. d. March 22, 1991, Chicago.

Paul Engle taught creative writing at the University of Iowa for fifty years. He was director of Iowa's famous Creative Writing Program from 1937 to 1965, then was founding director of the International Writing Program from 1966 until his retirement in 1987.

Engle graduated in 1931 with the B.A. degree from Coe College, where his major was geology. He earned the M.A. in literature the following year at the University of Iowa. After graduate study at Columbia University during 1932–33, he went to Merton College of Oxford University as a Rhodes scholar. At Oxford he received A.B. (1936) and A.M. (1939) degrees.

By the time of Engle's return to the University of Iowa, he was author of three volumes of poetry: *Worn Earth* (1932), *American Song* (1934), and *Break the Heart's Anger* (1936). As director, he brought the Writers' Workshop national recognition as the foremost program of its kind in the country. Engle presented it as a Ph.D. program for the imagination. Under his leadership it came to have separate tracks in poetry, fiction, and translation.

Other books he wrote included *Corn* (1939), *New Englander* (1940), *Always the Land* (1941), *West of Midnight* (1941), *American Child* (1945), *The Word of Love* (1957), *Golden Children* (1962), and *Women in the American Revolution* (1976). With his second wife, he translated *Poems of Mao Tse-Tung* (1972). He was editor of the annual *Prize Stories: The O. Henry Award* during 1954–59, as well as *Reading Modern Poetry* (1955), *Midland: Twenty-Five Years of Fiction and Poetry from the Writing Workshops of the State University of Iowa* (with Henri Coulette, 1961), and *Midland II* (1970). He was coeditor of the quarterly journal *American Prefaces* (1935–43).

Engle received three Guggenheim Fellowships and a Ford Foundation Fellowship.

REFERENCES: CA (NR-5, 134); CB (1942, 1991); NYT, March 24, 1991, p. 38; WWW (10); Stephen Wilbers, *The Iowa Writers' Workshop* (University of Iowa Press, 1980).

ERIKSON, Erik Homburger. b. June 15, 1902, Frankfurt on the Main, Germany, to unnamed parents. Married April 1, 1930, to Joan Mowat Serson. Children: three. d. May 12, 1994, Harwich, Massachusetts.

In the United States Erik Erikson became a major reinterpreter of the work of Sigmund Freud, particularly on identity and life stages. His theories were profoundly influential on the field of child development and indirectly on educational psychology. He originated the term "identity crisis."

Born from a brief liaison of Danish parents, Erik Erikson was raised as Erik Homburger, having been given the surname of his stepfather, a Jewish pediatrician in Karlsruhe, Germany. The boy graduated in 1920 from the Humanistische Gymnasium in Karlsruhe. For the next seven years, he traveled, studied art in Karlsruhe and Munich, and earned his living as an itinerant artist. In 1927 at the invitation of a friend from his youth, he went to Vienna, where he was certified as a Montessori teacher. In 1930 he began a three-year course of analysis and study under Anna Freud at the Vienna Psychoanalytic Institute. Upon completing his psychoanalytic training in 1933, he immigrated to the United States, where he took the surname Erikson.

Erikson was an analyst in private practice in Boston and also served on the staffs of Massachusetts General Hospital and Harvard Psychological Clinic. He began Ph.D. studies but dropped them soon to accept appointment to the research staff of the Yale University Institute of Human Relations (1936–39). He also taught in the Yale School of Medicine.

He taught at the San Francisco Psychoanalytic Institute and the University of California, Berkeley from 1939 to 1950, when he left the university rather than sign a loyalty oath that he was not a communist. For the next decade Erikson was a senior member of the staff at the Austen Riggs Center, a private psychiatric clinic in Stockbridge, Massachusetts, and visiting professor at the Western Psychiatric Institute of the University of Pittsburgh School of Medicine, where he worked in cooperation with Benjamin Spock (q.v.). Erikson was professor of human development at Harvard University from 1960 until his retirement in 1970.

His renown came largely from the success of his books, which included *Childhood and Society* (1950); *Young Man Luther* (1958); *Identity: Youth and Crisis* (1968); *Gandhi's Truth* (1969), which won him the National Book Award and Pulitzer Prize in 1970; *Toys and Reasons* (1976); and *Vital Involvement in Old Age* (1986). Erikson received the Aldrich Award of the American Academy of Pediatrics in 1971, the Montessori Medal of the American Montessori Society in 1973, and the research award of the National Association for Mental Health in 1974.

REFERENCES: CA (NR-33, 145); CB (1971, 1994); NYT, June 14, 1988, pp. 15–17, and May 13, 1994, p. B9; WD (1994–96); WW (1994); *American Psychologist* 50 (September 1995): 796–97; Robert Coles (q.v.), *Erik H. Erikson: The Growth of His Work* (Little, Brown, 1980); Elizabeth Devine et al., eds., *Thinkers of the Twentieth Century* (Gale Research, 1983); David Elkind (q.v.), ''Erik Erikson's Eight Ages of Man,'' NYT *Magazine*, April 5, 1970, p. 25; Henry W. Maier, *Three Theories of Child Development: The Contributions of Erik H. Erikson, Jean Piaget, and Robert R. Sears* (q.v.) *and Their Applications* (Harper and Row, 1969).

F

FAHS, Sophia Blanche Lyon. b. August 2, 1876, Hangchow, China, to David and Mandana (Doolittle) Lyon. Married June 14, 1902, to Charles Harvey Fahs. Children: five. d. April 17, 1978, Hamilton, Ohio.

Sophia Lyon Fahs was an advocate for reform of children's religious education. She was dissatisfied with Sunday school teaching, felt more attention should be paid to children, opposed authoritarian Sunday schools, and desired longer time for instruction. She advocated centers for research and experimentation in religious concerns.

Fahs was a daughter of Presbyterian missionaries. She grew up in Wooster, Ohio, with her mother and siblings while her father was in China. She was valedictorian at Wooster High School in 1893 and graduated from the College of Wooster in 1897. She spent two years with the Student Volunteer Movement, then worked for the University of Chicago Young Women's Christian Association (YWCA) and studied at the university. Moving to New York City after her marriage, Fahs took classes at Teachers College of Columbia University. When Frank McMurry (BDAE) told her of a new experimental Sunday school sponsored by Teachers College, Fahs became a teacher at the school. She received the M.A. degree from Teachers College in 1904. From 1919 to 1921 she was director of religious education at Leonia (New Jersey) Methodist Church.

At the age of forty-seven Fahs became a student at Union Theological Seminary. She received the bachelor of divinity degree in 1926 with a thesis on developing a curriculum for religious education. The seminary conducted the Union School of Religion, a Sunday school, where Fahs became a supervisor in 1925 and, later, principal. In 1927 she became one of the first two women on the faculty of the seminary. The Union School of Religion closed in 1929, but Fahs continued at the seminary, teaching there until 1944. Her subjects were the psychology and philosophy of religious education for young children and curriculum planning and methods. From 1933 to 1942 she served on the staff of Riverside Church in New York City, first as fourth grade teacher, then as supervisor of the junior department.

Fahs began revising Beacon Course material for the Unitarian Church when appointed children's editor in 1927. She was coauthor with Verna Hills of the Martin and Judy books and served with Abigail Eliot (q.v.) on the Unitarian curriculum committee. When she retired as curriculum editor in 1951, she received the Unitarian Award for meritorious service to the denomination. Fahs remained a consultant until 1964. At the age of eighty-two Fahs was ordained at the Montgomery County (later Cedar Lane) Unitarian Church in Bethesda, Maryland.

Among her books were *Uganda's White Man of Work* (1907), *Red, Yellow and Black: Tales of Indians, Chinese and Africans* (1918), *Beginnings of Earth and Sky* (1937), *Jesus, the Carpenter's Son* (1945), *Today's Children and Yesterday's Heritage, a Philosophy of Creative Religious Development* (1951), and *Worshipping Together with Questioning Minds* (1965). She wrote extensively in journals and conducted religious education summer workshops.

REFERENCES: CA (77–80); DARB; NYT, April 19, 1978, p. B10; WWAW (1961); Edith F. Hunter, *Sophia Lyon Fahs: A Biography* (Beacon Press, 1966); Lina Mainiero, ed., *American Women Writers*, vol. 2 (Ungar, 1980); *Religious Education* 51 (September–October 1956): 323–59, 61 (July-August 1966): 257–59, 62 (July–August 1967): 306, and 84 (Fall 1989): 538–52.

FAIRBANK, John King. b. May 24, 1907, Huron, South Dakota, to Arthur Boyce and Lorena C. V. (King) Fairbank. Married June 29, 1932, to Wilma Cannon. Children: two. d. September 14, 1991, Cambridge, Massachusetts.

More than any other individual, John Fairbank shaped Chinese studies in the United States from the 1950s to the 1980s. As a professor at Harvard University, he trained several generations of scholars, while he was the leading academic exponent of a moderate and accommodating stance toward the People's Republic of China.

Fairbank studied for two years at the University of Wisconsin before enrolling in Harvard University, where he earned the A.B. degree in 1929. While at Oxford University on a Rhodes Scholarship his scholarly focus shifted from Britain to China. He spent the years 1932–36 in China, principally in Beijing, learning Chinese, lecturing at Tsing Hua University, and conducting research for a thesis that earned him the Ph.D. degree at Oxford in 1936.

Fairbank returned to Harvard that year; he was Francis Lee Higginson Professor from 1959 to 1977. He was founding director of Harvard's East Asia Research Center. During World War II he took leave from the university for government service in Washington and Beijing, initially in the Office of Strategic Services, then as special assistant to the U.S. ambassador in China, acting deputy director of Far Eastern operations in the Office of War Information, and in the first postwar years director of the U.S. Information Service in China.

His scholarship emphasized the importance of a strong documentary basis for understanding China. The first edition of his book *The United States and China* appeared in 1948. The study that had begun as his doctoral thesis, *Trade and Diplomacy on the China Coast: The Opening of the Treaty Ports*, was published in 1954. He was author, with others, of *Modern China: A Bibliographic Guide to Chinese Works, 1898–1937* (1950), *Documentary History of Chinese Communism, 1921–50* (1952), *China's Response to the West: A Documentary Sur-*

vey, 1839–1923 (1954), and *Japanese Studies of Modern China: A Bibliographic Guide to Historical and Social Science Research on the 19th and 20th Centuries* (1955). He was coauthor of a leading textbook in two volumes, *East Asia*. He was coeditor of a twelve-volume series, *The Cambridge History of China*; author of *China Perceived* (1974) and *Chinabound: A Fifty-Year Memoir* (1982); and editor of many other works. For Fairbank's sixtieth birthday in 1967 Albert Feuerwerker, Rhoads Murphey, and Mary Wright edited a festschrift, *Approaches to Modern Chinese History*.

Fairbank served as president of the Association for Asian Studies (1959) and the American Historical Association (1968). He was a fellow of the Rockefeller Foundation (1934–36) and the Guggenheim Foundation (1952–53 and 1960). He received an award for distinguished accomplishment in the humanities from the American Council of Learned Societies (1964).

REFERENCES: CA (NR-3, 135); CB (1966, 1991); IESS (18); NYT, September 16, 1991, p. B12; WD (1994–96); WWW (10); Paul A. Cohen and Merle Goldman, comps., *Fairbank Remembered* (John K. Fairbank Center for East Asian Research, Harvard University; distributed by Harvard University Press, 1992); Roderick MacFarquhar, ''John King Fairbank: A Memoir,'' *China Quarterly* 127 (September 1991): 613–15.

FANTINI, Mario D. b. c. 1927, Philadelphia, to Mariano and Carolina Fantini. Married to Temmy Fantini. Children: four. d. October 6, 1989, Woodland Hills, California.

As an advocate for alternative schools and as a university administrator, Mario Fantini brought innovative ideas to difficult problems. He engineered the decentralization of New York City's public schools in the late 1960s and called for adaptation of Thomas Peters' eight attributes of successful business enterprises to education in the 1980s. His combination of optimism and pragmatism made him an influential reformer.

Fantini received B.S. (1957) and M.A. (1958) degrees from Temple University and the Ed.D. degree (1961) from the Harvard Graduate School of Education. He was a senior research associate at Syracuse University (1962–64), directing an urban teachers education program and special projects for the Syracuse City schools. After one year as program officer with the Ford Foundation's Fund for the Advancement of Education (1964–65) directing its Elementary School Teaching Project (ESTP), he served on Mayor John Lindsay's Advisory Panel on Decentralization of New York City Schools and was a consultant to school systems in Los Angeles and Washington, D.C.

As dean of the College of Education at the State University of New York College at New Paltz (1970–76) he was project director of a grant for regional cooperation. He was dean of the School of Education at the University of Massachusetts, Amherst, from 1976 to 1987. Fantini's extensive writings included *Toward a Contact Curriculum* (with Gerald Weinstein, 1967), *The Disadvantaged: Challenge to Education* (with Gerald Weinstein, 1968), *Community Control and the Urban School* (with Marilyn Gittell and Richard Magat, 1970),

Designing Education for Tomorrow's Cities (with Milton A. Young, 1970), *Decentralization: Achieving Reform* (with Marilyn Gittell, 1973), *Public Schools of Choice* (1973), *What's Best for the Children?: Resolving the Power Struggle Between Parents and Teachers* (1974), and *Regaining Excellence in Education* (1986). He edited *Toward Humanistic Education* (with Gerald Weinstein, 1970), *Alternative Education* (1976), and *Parenting in a Multicultural Society* (with Rene Cardenas, 1980) and was on the editorial board of *Principal.*

REFERENCES: CA (77–80, 129); NYT, October 12, 1989, p. B12.

FARNSWORTH, Dana Lyda. b. April 7, 1905, Troy, West Virginia, to Henry Lyda and Isabell (Waggoner) Farnsworth. Married March 18, 1931, to Elma Morris. Children: no. d. August 2, 1986, Watertown, Massachusetts.

As a psychiatrist and director of major university health services, Dana Farnsworth provided leadership to higher education on issues concerning the emotional well-being of college students and the organization of their health care. In an era of extensive youthful experimentation with illegal drugs, he took a strong position by pointing to the long-term damage they caused.

Farnsworth earned the A.B. degree at West Virginia University (1927) and B.S. (1931) and M.D. (1933) degrees at Harvard University. At Massachusetts General Hospital, he was an intern (1933–35), and at Boston City Hospital, an assistant resident (1935) before going to Williams College as assistant director (1935–41) and, later, director of health (1945–46). During 1941–45 he served in the U.S. Marine Corps.

He was professor and medical director at Massachusetts Institute of Technology (1946–54) and acting dean of students (1950–51). At Harvard University, Farnsworth was first a lecturer in the School of Medicine (1952–54), then Oliver Professor of Hygiene and director of the university health service (1954–71). He held concurrent appointment at Massachusetts General Hospital as staff physician from 1950 to 1966.

His books included *Mental Health in College and University* (1957), *Perspectives on Living: Readings for College Health Courses* (1962), *Textbook of Psychiatry* (1963), *College Health Administration* (1964), *Psychiatry, Education and the Young Adult* (1966), *Psychiatry, the Clergy, and Pastoral Counseling: The St. John's Story* (1969), and *Counseling and the College Student* (edited with Graham B. Blaine, Jr., 1970).

Farnsworth served on editorial boards of the *American Journal of Psychiatry* (1965–73), *New England Journal of Medicine* (1970–73), and *Psychiatric Annals* (1971–86). He was vice chair of the National Commission on Marijuana and Drug Abuse (1971–73). He served as president of the American College Health Association (1953–54) and the Group for the Advancement of Psychiatry (1957–59) and was board chair of Medicine in the Public Interest (1973–86). Among many distinctions, he received the Pax Christi Award from St. John's University.

REFERENCES: CA (61–64, 119); NYT, August, 5, 1986, p. D22; WW (1970–71).

FELDMAN, Marvin Jerome. b. May 24, 1927, Rochester, New York, to Max and Blanche Feldman. Married July 29, 1954, to Dorothy Owens. Children: two. d. November 26, 1993, New York City.

Marvin Feldman was an advocate of vocational education. Under his presidency, the Fashion Institute of Technology in New York City, part of the State University of New York, expanded its curriculum and began awarding degrees.

Feldman served in the U.S. Navy (1944–46). After study at the U.S. Military Academy (1948–51) he received the A.B. degree from San Francisco State University (1953). He was a public school mathematics teacher in San Francisco (1952–57) and vice president of Cogswell College (1958–64). He was with the Ford Foundation as an officer in the Division of International Education and Research (1964–69) and with the U.S. Office of Education and Office of Economic Opportunity (1969–71). Northeastern University awarded him the Ph.D. degree in 1973.

Feldman became president of the Fashion Institute of Technology in 1971 and served until his retirement in 1992. Enrollment increased from 5,000 to 12,000 students, and the campus grew from two buildings to eight. The number of majors also increased. Bachelor's degrees were offered beginning in 1975 and master's degrees in 1979, though most students remained in a two-year program. An Advanced Apparel Manufacturing Technology Demonstration Facility was organized, and a Small Business Center opened in 1983.

Feldman was a member of the National Advisory Council on Vocational Education (1968–79) and received the council's meritorious award in 1972, 1976, and 1978. In 1993 the Fashion Institute of Technology's administration and technology center was named the Marvin Feldman Center.

REFERENCES: CHE, August 5, 1992, p. 5; NYT, November 28, 1993, p. 58; WW (1992–93); *Vocational Education Journal* 69 (February 1994): 51.

FENICHEL, Carl. b. December 30, 1905, New York City. Married to Joan Fenichel. Children: two. d. September 25, 1975, Brooklyn, New York.

Carl Fenichel was a pioneer in the treatment of emotionally disturbed children, including autistics and schizophrenics. He founded (1953) and directed the League School for Seriously Emotionally Disturbed Children in Brooklyn, New York. The school was a day facility that provided therapeutic education for mentally ill children while allowing their families to keep the children at home.

Fenichel received the B.S.S. degree from City College (later, of the City University of New York) in 1928, the M.A. from the New School for Social Research in 1951, and the Ed.D. from Yeshiva University in 1959. He also earned a certificate from the William Alanson White Institute of Psychiatry (1953). From 1948 to 1952 he was a therapist and special education teacher at Kings County Hospital and the psychiatric division of the School for Disturbed Children. Fenichel was also professor of special education at Teachers College of Columbia University and lecturer at the State University of New York Downstate Medical College. He served in the U.S. Army during World War II (1943–45).

The League School based instruction for each child on the child's level of development. In 1966 the school began a home training program, and in the 1970s it developed mininetworks of day care centers in New York City and other cities throughout the United States.

Fenichel received citations for his work from New York state and New York City. He was a consultant to the Congressional Committee on Education of the Handicapped and served on the review board of the National Institute of Mental Health.

REFERENCES: NYT, September 26, 1975, p. 76; *American Men of Science* (1960); Carl Fenichel, Harold Coopchik, and Tommanie Walker, "New Resources for Severely Disturbed Young Children and Their Parents," *Phi Delta Kappan* 55 (April 1974): 548–49; Carl Fenichel, Alfred M. Freedman, and Zelda Klapper, "A Day School for Schizophrenic Children," *American Journal of Orthopsychiatry* 30 (January 1960): 130–43.

FISHER, Welthy Blakesley Honsinger. b. September 18, 1879, Rome, New York, to Abraham Walker and Welthy Blakesley (Sanford) Honsinger. Married June 18, 1924, to Frederick Bohn Fisher. Children: no. d. December 16, 1980, Southbury, Connecticut.

Known as the "first lady of literacy," Welthy Honsinger Fisher lived many years in China and India, where she led efforts to make education available to girls and to provide literacy to rural people.

She attended Syracuse University, graduating in 1900. For the next six years she was a music teacher, first in a one-room schoolhouse, then at the high school in Englewood, New Jersey. In 1906 she committed herself to missionary work, going to Nanchang, China, where she was principal (1906–20) of the Baldwin, or Bao Lin, School for Young Ladies, which she expanded to include a high school program (later, Middle School Number Ten). During 1917–19 she was on leave from the school working with the Young Women's Christian Association in wartime France. She was editor (1920–24) of *World Neighbors*, a Methodist magazine published in New York City. She lived in India from her 1924 marriage to Frederick Fisher, Methodist bishop of Calcutta and Burma, until 1930. Returning to the United States, they lived in Ann Arbor, Michigan, until his death in 1938. Welthy Fisher was later an officer of the East-West Association, working with Pearl Buck.

In 1951 Welthy Honsinger Fisher returned to India as a government consultant on literacy. In Lucknow, India, in 1953, she founded Saksharta Niketan, or Literacy House, a place where many thousands were trained to teach reading and writing in rural India. In 1958 the school was incorporated as World Education, which Fisher served as president until 1972, when she was ninety-two years old.

From her early Asian experiences she wrote *Twin Travelogues* (1922), *Beyond the Moongate: Being a Diary of Ten Years in the Interior of the Middle Kingdom* (1924), *The Top of the World* (1926), *A String of Chinese Pearls* (1927), and *Freedom* (1930). Later books included *Frederick Bohn Fisher—World Citizen* (1944), *Handbook for Ministers' Wives* (1950), and her autobiography, *To Light a Candle* (1962).

Honors conferred on Fisher included the Ramon Magsaysay Award (1964), the first Nehru Literary Award (1968), an honorary doctor of laws degree from Delhi University, and a commemorative Indian stamp, the last two awarded in 1980, when she was 100 years old.

REFERENCES: CA (NR-2, 102); (CB 1969, 1981); FWC; NYT, September 18, 1969, p. 49, and December 17, 1980, p. A33; WWAW (1970); Colleen A. Kelly, "Welthy Honsinger Fisher: Three Dawns, 1879–1980," *Delta Kappa Gamma Bulletin* 59 (Fall 1992): 36–42+; John Spencer, *Workers for Humanity* (George C. Harrap, 1962).

FLANAGAN, Hallie Mae Ferguson. b. August 27, 1889, Redfield, South Dakota, to Frederic Miller and Louisa (Fischer) Ferguson. Married December 25, 1912, to (John) Murray Flanagan; April 27, 1934, to Philip H. Davis. Children: two. d. July 23, 1969, Old Tappan, New York.

Hallie Flanagan was a pioneer of experimental theater in the college curriculum, developing model programs of study and performance at Vassar College and Smith College. Her public achievements came amid repeated personal adversities. She was left a widow with two young sons in 1918; lost the older child, aged seven, to meningitis in 1922; was denounced in 1938 by members of the House Un-American Activities Committee for "communistic tendencies" they discerned in the Federal Theater Project that she directed; was widowed a second time in 1940; and from the mid-1940s had Parkinson's disease.

After graduation from Grinnell College with the B.A. degree in 1911, Hallie Ferguson taught English in high school for one year. She resumed teaching as the widowed Hallie Flanagan in 1918–19 at Grinnell's high school. She taught drama at Grinnell College (1919–25), with a year off (1923–24) to study at Harvard University under George Pierce Baker (BDAE) in his 47 Workshop. Radcliffe College awarded her the A.M. degree in 1924.

Flanagan was director of the Vassar (College) Experimental Theatre from 1925 until 1942. As one of the first recipients of a Guggenheim Fellowship, Flanagan spent 1926–27 in Europe and the Soviet Union studying theater, an experience she recounted in her first book, *Shifting Scenes of the Modern European Theatre* (1928). She was on leave from Vassar College during 1935–39 while directing the Federal Theatre Project, under the Works Progress Administration. With a Rockefeller Foundation grant, she wrote *Arena: The History of the Federal Theatre* (1940). In *Dynamo: The Story of a College Theatre* (1943) she recounted her work at Vassar College.

Flanagan was dean of Smith College (1942–46) and taught theater there until her retirement in 1955. She received a Creative Arts Award (1957) from Brandeis University and a citation from the National Theatre Conference (1968).

Both Vassar and Smith Colleges named their theaters for her. She was born one year earlier (1889) than the date she gave.

REFERENCES: AWM; NAW (Mod); NYT, July 24, 1969, p. 37, and August 3, 1969, p. B3; WR; Joanne Bentley, *Hallie Flanagan: A Life in the American Theatre* (Knopf, 1988); Alice M. Robinson, Vera Mowry Roberts, and Milly S. Barranger, eds., *Notable Women in the American Theatre* (Greenwood Press, 1989).

FOGHT, Harold Waldstein. b. December 7, 1869, Fredrikshald, Norway, to John E. and Laura (Arneberg) Foght. Married December 28, 1897, to Alice Mabel Robbins. D. April 25, 1954, Minneapolis, Minnesota.

Harold Foght served education on the American prairie, first as a school and college teacher, then as an educational research and policy officer of the federal government, and finally as a university president.

He received his primary schooling in Norway and his high school education in Ord, Nebraska. Before beginning his higher education, Foght was a rural school teacher from 1890 to 1893. He was a student at the University of Nebraska (1893–95), Iowa State College (later, University, A.B., 1897), Augustana College in Rock Island, Illinois (A.M., 1900), the University of Copenhagen (1900–1), and after an interruption of a dozen years, at American University (Ph.D., 1918).

Foght taught history and sociology at Elk Horn (Iowa) College (1895–97) and was headmaster (1897–99) of its high school. It was the first institution in America to be modeled on Danish folk high schools. When its Danish Lutheran immigrant sponsors merged it with Blair (later, Dana) College in 1899, Foght went along to the Nebraska college for one year as professor of history and education. He was president of Ansgar College in Hutchinson, Minnesota (1901–3), and principal of the academy (1903–6) and professor of history and education (1906–8) at Midland College, in Atchison, Kansas (later, Midland Lutheran College, Fremont, Nebraska).

Foght made his mark as an expert on rural education, which he taught from 1908 to 1912 at Missouri State Teachers College (later, Truman State University). He was on the staff of the U.S. Bureau of Education as a specialist in rural education (1912–14), specialist in rural school practice (1914–17), and chief of the rural school division (1917–19). In these roles he wrote many reports on rural schools published in the Bureau of Education's bulletin series, including "Rural Denmark and Its Schools" (1915), "The Rural Teacher and His Work" (1915), "Rural and Agricultural Education at the Panama-Pacific Exposition" (1916), and "A Survey of the Educational Institutions of the State of Washington" (1916). As the nation urbanized rapidly, Foght emphasized the need for "pioneer schools" to consolidate into district graded schools, to be subject to common standards, and to have trained teachers.

After completing his doctorate and rising to division chief in federal service, Foght returned to the prairie as president of Northern Normal and Industrial School (later, Northern State College) in Aberdeen, South Dakota (1919–27), and the Municipal University of Wichita (later, Wichita State University, 1927–33). At Wichita, Foght led the recovery of a nearly defunct institution that the city had recently taken over. In retirement he was a superintendent in the U.S. Bureau of Indian Affairs.

He was author of *Trail of the Loup* (1906), *The American Rural School* (1910), and *Unfathomed Japan* (with Alice Foght, 1928). He chaired the Commission of 100 on Rural Education of the National Education Association in 1923 and was association vice president in 1925.

REFERENCES: WWW (3); U.S. Office of Education Research Reports, 1913–19.

FORBES, Jack D. b. January 7, 1934, Long Beach, California, to George Theodore and Dorothy Hazel (Rufener) Forbes. Married December 21, 1956, to Barbara Ann Alexander; November 26, 1975, to Carolyn L. Johnson. Children: two.

Jack D. Forbes was cofounder of Degoniwida-Quetzalcoatl (D-Q) University in Davis, California, and served on its Board of Trustees. A Powhaten American Indian trained in ethnic history, he taught Native American studies and wrote many books about American Indians.

Forbes received A.B. (1955), M.A. (1956), and Ph.D. (1959) degrees from the University of Southern California. He taught at Citrus College in Azusa, California, for one year (1959–60) and taught history at California State University, Northridge (1960–64). At the University of Nevada, Reno, he was director of the Center for Western North American Studies and associate professor of history (1964–67). Forbes served at the University of California, Berkeley, as research program director in the Far West Laboratory for Educational Research and Development (1967–69).

In 1969 he went to the University of California, Davis, as professor of Native American studies and department head. Among his publications were *Apache, Navaho, and Spaniard* (1960), *The Indian in America's Past* (1964), *Warriors of the Colorado* (1965), *Nevada Indians Speak* (1967), *Afro-Americans in the Far West: A Handbook for Educators* (1968), *Native Americans of California and Nevada* (1968), and *American Words: The Influence of Native American Languages on English* (1979). He also wrote poetry and short stories. Forbes received Guggenheim and Fulbright awards. He served as first chair of the American Indian College Committee.

REFERENCES: BDIA; CA (NR-4); NNAA; WW (1996); Barry T. Klein, *Reference Encyclopedia of the American Indian* (Todd, 1995); Sharon Malinowski, ed., *Notable Native Americans* (Gale Research, 1995).

FOREMAN, Stephen. b. October 22, 1807, Rome, Georgia, to Anthony Foreman and Elizabeth Gurdaygee. Married to Sarah Watkins Riley; to Ruth Riley Candy. Children: fourteen. d. December 8, 1881, Park Hill, Indian Territory (Oklahoma).

Stephen Foreman organized the school system of the Cherokee Nation in 1841 and served as its first superintendent of public instruction.

Foreman's mother was Cherokee, and his father was of Scotch background. He attended school in Cleveland, Tennessee, and at a mission in Candy's Creek, Tennessee. After his father's death he received instruction in Georgia from Samuel Worcester, a Congregational minister. Foreman was a student at Union Theological Seminary in Virginia and graduated from Princeton Theological Seminary. In 1835 he was licensed to preach by a Tennessee presbytery.

Foreman worked with Worcester on translating several books of the Bible into Cherokee. He was associate editor of the *Cherokee Phoenix*. Because he supported Cherokee resistance to removal, he was jailed in 1838. He became a member of the Cherokee National Supreme Court in 1844 and was executive councilor of the Cherokees from 1847 to 1855. During the Civil War he was a missionary in Texas.

REFERENCES: BDIA; Frederick J. Dockstader, *Great North American Indians: Profiles in Life and Leadership* (Van Nostrand Reinhold, 1977); Arlene Hirschfelder and Paulette Molin, The *Encyclopedia of Native American Religions* (Facts on File, 1992); Carl Waldman, *Who Was Who in Native American History* (Facts on File, 1990).

FOSTER, Luther Hilton, Jr. b. March 21, 1913, Lawrenceville, Virginia, to Luther Hilton and Daisy (Poole) Foster. Married August 27, 1941, to Vera Adrienne Chandler. Children: two. d. November 27, 1994, East Point, Georgia.

Tuskegee Institute (later, University) prospered during the administration of Luther Hilton Foster, Jr., who served as president from 1953 to 1981, a time of civil rights and antiwar movements. After a two-year self-study the College of Arts and Sciences was established in 1957 with a common course of study for all students. Foster strengthened professional programs and phased out precollegiate programs.

Foster grew up on the campus of Virginia State College in Petersburg, Virginia, where his father was business manager and, later, president. The son attended an experimental school on the campus. He earned B.S. degrees from Virginia State College (later, University) in 1932 and Hampton Institute (later, University) in 1934. After receiving the M.B.A. degree from Harvard University in 1936, Foster served as budget officer at Howard University from 1936 to 1940. In 1941 he became business manager at Tuskegee, continuing in that position until being named president in 1953. He received the Ph.D. degree in educational administration from the University of Chicago in 1951.

After retirement Foster was chairman of the Academy for Educational Development. He was president of the United Negro College Fund, director of the Joint Center for Political and Economic Studies, and a member of advisory bodies for the U.S. Agency for International Development (AID), Air Force Academy, and the American Revolution Bicentennial Commission.

REFERENCES: LE (1974); NYT, December 2, 1994, p. D20; WWBA (1994/95); WW (1995); John Scanlon, "Luther Foster of Tuskegee," *Saturday Review* 47 (May 16, 1964): 76, 88.

FOSTER, Marcus Albert. b. March 31, 1923, Athens, Georgia. Married: yes. Children: one. d. November 6, 1973, Oakland, California.

In a life cut short by assassination, Marcus A. Foster strove to transform urban schools by instilling a sense of pride in their minority students, decentralizing administration, building school–community connections, and using discipline to rid schools of drugs and violence. His success in making urban schools more effective won widespread praise but also the enmity of African-American militants such as the Black Panthers.

As a child, Foster moved to Philadelphia, where he attended public schools. He graduated from Cheyney State College (later, Cheyney University of Pennsylvania), a historically black institution, and earned a doctorate at the University of Pennsylvania in 1971.

Foster was author of *Making Schools Work: Strategies for Changing Education* (1971), based principally on his experiences in the Philadelphia public schools, where he served from 1957 to 1970 as a teacher, principal, and associate superintendent for community relations. He went to Oakland, California, as superintendent of schools in 1970, serving there until his death by shooting three years later.

The Bok Foundation honored Foster in 1969 for his contributions to the Philadelphia public schools.

REFERENCES: Carson Carr, Jr., ''Marcus A. Foster, Urban Educational Manager'' (Ed.D. diss., Syracuse University, 1982); *Los Angeles Times*, November 8, 1973, p. 10; Jesse J. McCorry, *Marcus Foster and the Oakland Public Schools* (University of California Press, 1978); Harry C. Silcox, ''In Memory of Marcus A. Foster, 1923–1973,'' *Harvard Educational Review* 44 (February 1974): 1–5.

FRANKLIN, John Hope. b. January 2, 1915, Rentiesville, Oklahoma, to Buck Colbert and Mollie Lee (Parker) Franklin. Married June 11, 1940, to Aurelia E. Whittington. Children: one.

John Hope Franklin distinguished himself as a historian of the South and the African-American experience; as a leader among historians; and as a forceful advocate of racial justice and integration in education as well as in other social institutions. While on the faculty of Howard University, Franklin provided historical documentation on the deleterious effects of segregation that Thurgood Marshall used in the successful 1954 litigation of *Brown v. Board of Education of Topeka, Kansas*. Through his scholarship, his academic appointments, and his leadership in professional associations, Franklin modeled the integration of African Americans within a predominantly European–American society.

He graduated with the A.B. degree from Fisk University (1935) and at Harvard University earned A.M. (1936) and Ph.D. (1941) degrees. He returned to Fisk (1936–37) as a member of the faculty in history and taught at St. Augustine's College (1939–43), North Carolina College at Durham (1943–47, later, North Carolina Central University), and Howard University (1947–56) before chairing the Department of History at Brooklyn College (1956–64). He was professor of history and sometime department chair at the University of Chicago (1964–82) and concluded his long career in the History Department (1982–85) and Law School (1985–92) of Duke University. He also held a visiting professorship at Cambridge University (1962–63) and was a Fulbright professor in Australia (1960) and Zimbabwe (1986).

Franklin was author of *The Free Negro in North Carolina, 1790–1860* (1943), *From Slavery to Freedom: A History of African Americans* (1947), *The Militant South, 1800–1860* (1956), *Reconstruction after the Civil War* (1961), *The Emancipation Proclamation* (1963), *Illustrated History of Black Americans* (1970), *A Southern Odyssey* (1976), *Racial Equality in America* (1976), *George Washington Williams: Biography* (1985), *Race and History* (1990), and *The Color Line: Legacy for the 21st Century* (1993). He edited *A Fool's Errand* by Albion Tourgee (1961), as well as other books. He served on the editorial board of *The American Scholar* (1972–77 and from 1994).

Franklin was president of the Southern Historical Association (1970–71), Organization of American Historians (1974–75), and American Historical Association (1978–79). He was a member (1962–66) and chair (1966–69) of the Board of Foreign Scholarships. Among many honors, he received Guggenheim Fellowships (1950–51, 1973–74), a President's Fellowship of Brown University (1952–53), the Jefferson Medal of the National Endowment for the Humanities (1976), and a Senior Mellon Fellowship at the National Humanities Center (1980–82).

REFERENCES: ASL; CA (NR-26); CB (1963); CHE, January 9, 1978, p. 7, and May 30, 1984, p. 7; WD (1994–96); WW (1996); Peter Applebome, "Keeping Tabs on Jim Crow: John Hope Franklin," NYT *Magazine*, April 23, 1995, pp. 34–37; *Black Issues in Higher Education* 10 (January 13, 1994): 16+; James J. Flynn, ed., *Negroes of Achievement in Modern America* (Dodd, Mead, 1970); Edgar A. Toppin, *A Biographical History of Blacks in America since 1528* (David McKay, 1971); *U.S. News and World Report* 109 (September 17, 1990): 52–53.

FRAZIER, Maude. b. April 4, 1881, Sauk County, Wisconsin, to William Henry and Mary Emma (Presnall) Frazier. Married: no. d. June 20, 1963, Las Vegas.

Maude Frazier graduated in 1905 from Stevens Point State Teachers College (later, University of Wisconsin–Stevens Point), then taught for one year in Wisconsin schools. From 1906 to 1921, Frazier was a teacher and principal in public schools of western and southern Nevada, at Genoa, Lovelock, Seven Troughs, Beatty, Goldfield, and Sparks.

In 1921 she became deputy state superintendent of public instruction, with responsibility for 3,000 pupils and 150 teachers in four counties that spanned 40,000 square miles of southern Nevada. She was superintendent of the Las Vegas Union School District and principal of its high school from 1927 to 1946. Because of construction of the Hoover Dam at nearby Boulder, war industry, and tourism, the school district grew rapidly.

In retirement, Frazier ran unsuccessfully as a Democratic candidate from Clark County for the state legislature in 1948. She ran again in 1950 and was elected. She chaired the education committee during six legislative sessions (1951–61), guiding passage in 1955 of a school reorganization act that reduced the number of districts in the state from more than 200 to 17. At the age of eighty-one in July 1962, she was appointed to serve briefly as lieutenant governor.

REFERENCES: NAW (Mod); WR; Elbert B. Edwards, ''Maude Frazier: Nevadan'' (1970); Mary Ellen Glass, ''Nevada's Lady Lawmakers: The First Half Century,'' *Nevada Public Affairs Report* 14 (October 1975).

FRED, Edwin Broun. b. March 22, 1887, Middleburg, Virginia, to Samuel Rogers and Catherine Conway (Broun) Fred. Married June 21, 1913, to Rosa Helen Parrott. Children: two. d. January 16, 1981, Madison, Wisconsin.

''Wisconsin's greatest builder,'' E. B. Fred spent almost all of his career at the University of Wisconsin, beginning as an assistant professor and eventually serving as dean of the graduate school, dean of agriculture, and president. His administrative leadership came in a period when the university expanded rapidly.

After attending Randolph Macon Academy in Front Royal, Virginia, Fred received B.S. (1907) and M.S. (1908) degrees from Virginia Polytechnic Institute. In 1911 he was granted the D. Phil. degree in bacteriology from the University of Göttingen, Germany. He returned to Virginia Polytechnic as an assistant professor (1912–13), then went to the University of Wisconsin, where he became known as an outstanding bacteriologist. He was active in agricultural extension work with Wisconsin canners and farmers, in addition to his campus activities.

In 1934 Fred was named dean of Wisconsin's Graduate School. He chaired a National Academy of Sciences study of biological warfare in 1941 and was a consultant to the secretary of war during World War II, earning the Medal of Merit for his service. Fred became dean of the College of Agriculture at Wisconsin and director of the Agricultural Experiment Station in 1943.

In 1945 he was named president of the university, serving until 1958. During his presidency extension centers were developed throughout the state to accommodate rapid postwar enrollment increases.

Fred coauthored *Laboratory Manual of Soil Bacteriology* (1916), *Textbook of Agricultural Bacteriology* (1923), *Laboratory Manual of Microbiology* (1928), and *Root Nodule Bacteria and Leguminous Plants* (1932). He served as president of the Society of American Bacteriologists (1932) and was vice chair of the National Science Board. He was a member of the National Advisory Health Council, U.S. Advisory Commission on Educational Exchange (1949–54), and the Board of Trustees of the Carnegie Foundation for the Advancement of Teaching (1946–58). He received the Golden Diploma from the University of Göttingen.

REFERENCES: CB (1950); NCAB (F: 244); WWW (7); Ira L. Baldwin, ''Edwin Broun

Fred,'' *National Academy of Sciences Biographical Memoirs*, vol. 55 (National Academy of Sciences, 1985), pp. 247–90; Diane Johnson, *Edwin Broun Fred: Scientist, Administrator, Gentleman* (University of Wisconsin Press, 1974); Clarence A. Schoenfeld, ''A Tradition of Leadership at the University of Wisconsin: A Time of Plenty,'' *Change* 13 (May/June 1981): 34+.

FRY, Edward Bernard. b. April 4, 1925, Los Angeles, to Eugene Bert and Frances (Dreier) Fry. Married 1950 to Carol Addison; 1974 to Cathy Boyce. Children: two.

Edward Bernard Fry was noted for the Fry Readability Graph. From 1989 he was a writer of curriculum materials.

Fry served in the U.S. Merchant Marine (1943–45). He received the B.A. degree from Occidental College (1949) and M.A. (1954) and Ph.D. (1960) degrees from the University of Southern California. From 1954 to 1963 he was associate professor of education at Loyola University in Los Angeles. Fry was at Rutgers University from 1963 to 1987 as professor of education and director of the Reading Center. In 1988–89 he was a visiting professor at the University of California at Riverside.

Fry authored many articles and books, including *Teaching Machines: An Annotated Bibliography* (with Glenn L. Bryan and Joseph Rigney, 1960), *A Survey and Analysis of Current Teaching-Machines Programs and Programming* (1961), *Current Teaching-Machine Programs and Programming Techniques* (with Joseph Rigney, 1961), *Teaching Machines and Programmed Instruction* (1963), *First Grade Reading Instruction Using a Diacritical Marking System, the Initial Teaching Alphabet and a Basic Reading System* (1965), *The Emergency Reading Teachers Manual* (1969), *Typing Course for Children* (1969), *Ninety-Nine Phonics Charts* (1971), *Reading Instruction for Classroom and Clinic* (1972), *Elementary Reading Instruction* (1977), *Skimming and Scanning* (1978), *Dictionary Drills* (1980), *Graphical Comprehension* (1981), *Fry's Instant Word Puzzle and Activities* (1987), and *How to Teach Reading* (1992). He coauthored the *Jamestown Heritage Readers* and was on the Board of Directors of the National Reading Conference.

REFERENCES: CA (NR-5); LE (1974); WD (1994–96).

FRY, Emma Viola Sheridan. b. October 1, 1864, Painesville, Ohio, to George A. and Emma Christina (Huther) Sheridan. Married 1890 to Alfred Brooks Fry. Children: one. d. 1936, Westwood, New Jersey.

Trained as an actress, Emma Fry played in professional companies before turning her attention to children's and community theater. She practiced and advocated educational dramatics, which emphasized the development of expressive individuals, community contributions to theatrical events, and the primacy of getting ready for a stage show over the show itself.

She was a graduate of the New York Normal (later, Hunter) College and the American Academy of Dramatic Arts (1885). In 1903 she founded the Children's and Young People's Theatre, later called the Children's Educational Theatre, under auspices of the Educational Alliance of New York City. There she adapted popular dramas so that they could be played more readily by children and youth. She left the Children's Educational Theatre in 1908 after its Sunday performances ran afoul of restrictive ordinances on weekend entertainments; it was discontinued in 1909. With her encouragement, some of the players continued their work as the Educational Players.

Fry was dramatic director of the Educational Dramatic League of the People's Institute of New York from 1912 to 1916. She taught educational dramatics at Columbia University Extension (1916), in Cincinnati (about 1920), and at Mills College (1927) and the University of California at Berkeley (1928). She wrote of her methods and purposes in *Educational Dramatics* (1913).

REFERENCES: BCAW; Beatrice L. Tukesbury, "Emma Sheridan Fry and Educational Dramatics," *Educational Theater Journal* 16 (December 1964): 341–48; John W. Leonard, ed., *Woman's Who's Who of America* (American Commonwealth, 1914).

G

GAGE, Nathaniel Lees. b. August 1, 1917, Union City, New Jersey, to Hyman and Rose (Lees) Gage. Married June 27, 1942, to Margaret Elizabeth Burrows. Children: four.

In April 1977, N. L. Gage delivered the Julius and Rosa Sachs Memorial Lectures at Teachers College, Columbia University. Thc lectures served as the basis for Gage's *The Scientific Basis of the Art of Teaching* (1978), culminating a career committed to the value of educational research for improving teachers' classroom practices. With W. W. Charters (BDAE), Gage edited the *Handbook of Research on Teaching* (1963), a model for publications of the American Educational Research Association.

Gage studied for two years at the City College of New York and then at the University of Minnesota, where he received the A.B. degree in 1938. As an undergraduate he was a research assistant for B. F. Skinner (BDAE). Gage worked in the Aviation Psychology Program of the U.S. Army Air Force (1943–45). Before the war he had begun graduate study at Purdue University, where he earned the Ph.D. degree (1947) and taught (1947–48).

At the University of Illinois (1948–62), Gage was on the staff of the Bureau of Educational Research and professor of education (1956–62) and psychology (1961–62). At Stanford University (1962–87) he was professor of education and psychology and Margaret Jacks Professor of Education (1981–87). He codirected (1965–68) the Center for Research and Development in Teaching and chaired its executive board (1968–76).

Gage was president of the American Educational Research Association (1963–64); chair of the National Society for the Study of Education (1971), Council for Educational Development and Research (1970–71), and American Council on Education (1972–73); and a visiting scholar at the National Institute of Education (1974). He was a fellow at the Center for Advanced Study in the Behavioral Sciences (1965–66 and 1987–88) and held Guggenheim (1976–77) and U.S. Public Health Service (1965–66) Fellowships.

Among Gage's books were *Educational Measurement and Evaluation* (with H. H. Remmers, 1943), *Principles of Democracy* (with others, 1960), *Teacher Effectiveness and Teacher Education* (1972), and *Educational Psychology* (with David C. Berliner, 1975). He edited *The Psychology of Teaching Methods* (1976). He was a consulting editor for the *Journal of Abnormal and Social*

Psychology (1956–64), *American Educational Research Journal* (1964–70), *Journal of Educational Psychology* (1963–75), and *Contemporary Psychology* (1967–73).

In 1986 Gage received an outstanding writing award from the American Association of Colleges for Teacher Education and the Edward L. Thorndike (BDAE) Award.

REFERENCES: CA (69–72); LE (1974); RPE; WW (1996).

GALAMIAN, Ivan Alexander. b. January 23, 1903, Tabriz, Iran, to Alexander J. and Sarah (Khounoutz) Galamian. Married November 22, 1941, to Judith Johnson. Children: no. d. April 14, 1981, New York City.

Ivan Galamian was a noted teacher of violin. Many of his pupils became world-renowned performers. He also was interested in the education of future teachers, violinists in quartets, and concertmasters. He was founder of the Meadowmount School in Essex County, New York, a summer school for string players.

Galamian was born of Armenian parents who moved to Russia when he was one year old. Beginning at the age of fourteen, he studied violin at the Moscow Philharmonic School. He studied in France and made his Paris debut in 1924. From 1924 to 1937 he taught at the Russian Conservatory in Paris and toured Europe as a performer.

In 1937 Galamian came to the United States, where he opened a private studio in New York. He joined the faculty of the Curtis Institute in Philadelphia as a professor in 1944. At the invitation of William Schuman (q.v.) he moved to the Juilliard School in New York in 1946. In addition, he kept his private studio.

Galamian taught every summer at the Meadowmount School of Music, established in 1944 in the Adirondacks. Josef Gingold (q.v.) and Leonard Rose taught chamber music there. Galamian authored *Principles of Violin: Playing and Teaching* (1962) and *Contemporary Violin Technique* (1966).

REFERENCES: BBG; CA (108); NGD; NYT, April 15, 1981, p. B6; WWW (7); *American String Teacher* 30 (Spring 1985): 48–49; Faubion Bowers, "Music: Ivan Galamian," *Atlantic Monthly* 229 (February 1972): 100–104; Joseph Edgar Koob II, "The Violin Pedagogy of Ivan Galamian" (Ed.D. diss., University of Illinois at Urbana–Champaign, 1986); Boris Schwarz, *Great Masters of the Violin* (Simon and Schuster, 1983); *Time* 92 (December 6, 1968): 53–54.

GALLAGHER, Buell Gordon. b. February 4, 1904, Rankin, Illinois, to Elmer David and Elma Maryel (Poole) Gallagher. Married September 1, 1927, to June Lucille Sampson. Children: two. d. August 30, 1978, New York City.

As a college president, Buell G. Gallagher made an exceptional commitment to the education of African Americans. In a southern, rural, historically black college and a northern, urban, multiracial university, he focused institutional commitments and resources on building academic strength. Through his books he was a well-known commentator on issues of race, religion, and education in the United States.

As a child, Gallagher was schooled in Montana, North Dakota, and Minnesota, as his father took ministerial assignments with Congregational churches in those states. Gallagher was educated at Carleton College (B.A., 1925), Union Theological Seminary (B.D., 1929), and Columbia University (Ph.D., 1939). After brief periods studying at the University of London, teaching at Doane College, serving as secretary of the Interseminary Movement, and in a New Jersey pastorate, at the age of twenty-nine Gallagher became president (1933–43) of Talladega (Alabama) College. There he wrote *American Caste and the Negro College* (1939), in which he made the case that the purpose of higher education should be to promote an equal opportunity society, a project he called "prophetic education." At Talladega College, Gallagher worked closely with Charles S. Johnson (BDAE) and Horace Mann Bond (BDAE), distinguished African-American college educators.

Gallagher taught at the Pacific School of Religion (1944–49) and was consultant and assistant commissioner in the U.S. Office of Education (1950–52) before becoming president of the City College of New York, where he served from 1952 to 1969, with the exception of an eight-month period in 1961–62, when he was founding chancellor of the California State Colleges (later, University). He ran unsuccessfully for a seat in the U.S. House of Representatives in 1948.

Gallagher's writings included *Campus in Crisis* (1974), his summation of issues confronting higher education. He served from 1934 to 1976 on the Board of Directors of the National Association for the Advancement of Colored People (NAACP), the last five years as vice chair. He chaired the international assembly of the World University Service (1962–66) and served on the commission on religion and race of the National Council of Churches (1962–78). The government of France made him a chevalier of the Legion of Honor and the U.S. Army awarded him its Outstanding Civilian Service Medal (1961).

REFERENCES: CA (65–68); CB (1953, 1979); NCAB (J: 121); NYT, November 6, 1978, p. 56; WWW (7).

GANS, Bird Stein. b. May 29, 1868, Allegheny City, Pennsylvania, to Solomon and Pauline (Bernhard) Stein. Married April 1888 to Louis Sternberger; July 1908 to Howard S. Gans. Children: two. d. December 29, 1944, Tuckahoe, New York.

When she was a young girl, Bird Stein moved from western Pennsylvania to New York City, where she attended private schools. She studied law at New York University. As a young wife and mother, she developed a strong interest in the education and care of children.

From 1897 to 1938, she was president of the Society for the Study of Child Nature, which was later known as the Federation for Child Study and eventually as the Child Study Association of America. Sponsored initially by Felix Adler

(BDAE), the association led in the development of "parent education." Gans initiated summer play schools through the association in 1917.

She was also vice president of the League for the Improvement of Children's Comic Supplements and chaired the National Committee for Better Films.

REFERENCES: NYT, December 31, 1944, p. 26; *The Biographical Cyclopaedia of American Women* vol. 1 (Halvord, 1924; Gale Research, 1974).

GANS, Roma. b. February 22, 1894, Saint Cloud, Minnesota, to Hubert W. and Mary Anne (Ley) Gans. Married: no. d. October 4, 1996, Pittsfield, Massachusetts.

Roma Gans was an authority in the teaching of reading. She did extensive research in the field and was a great influence on many reading teachers. At Teachers College of Columbia University, where she taught from 1929 until her retirement in 1959, her course The Teaching of Reading was very popular.

Gans attended St. Cloud (Minnesota) Normal School (later, State University) for two years and received a teaching certificate there. Her career in education began as a teacher of junior high school science and high school music in Clearwater, Minnesota (1917). She taught mathematics in St. Cloud from 1918 to 1923. After one year in St. Louis, Missouri (1924–25), she became assistant superintendent of schools and director of research in Superior, Wisconsin, for two and one-half years. She was also an editor of textbooks for a Philadelphia concern. In 1926 she received a bachelor's degree from Teachers College and in 1940 the Ph.D. Gans became an assistant professor at Teachers College in 1929 and a professor in 1940. From 1940 to 1949 she was chair of the Department of Early Childhood Education.

Gans believed teachers should encourage children to explore. She disliked emphasis on speed in reading, particularly on standardized tests. She advocated that teachers should not be tied to special curricula, but use good literature in teaching reading. Gans had a questioning mind and thought teachers should stand up for their beliefs. At Teachers College she introduced and taught a course, The Work of the Teacher, which explored current critical issues. An all-night bus tour through New York City was also provided as a lesson in social studies.

Gans was active in the American Federation of Teachers and served on the Commission of Educational Reconstruction with Selma Borchardt (q.v.), John Childs (q.v.), Milton Eisenhower (BDAE), Floyd Reeves (q.v.), and others. A prolific writer, she published more than 100 articles in professional journals. She was the author of *A Study of Critical Reading Comprehension in the Intermediate Grades* (1940), *Guiding Children's Reading through Experiences* (1941), *Reading Is Fun* (1949), *Teaching Young Children* (with Celia Burns Stendler and Millie Almy, 1952), *Common Sense in Teaching Reading* (1963), and *Facts and Fiction about Phonics* (1964). The "Let's Read-and-Find-Out" series of science books was supervised and edited by Gans and Franklyn M. Branley (1963–86). Gans was inducted into the Reading Hall of Fame in 1981.

REFERENCES: CA (NR-32); ECE; Millie Almy, "Roma Gans: Teacher of Teachers," *Childhood Education* 67 (Winter 1990): 98+; Joanna Sullivan, "Roma Gans: Still Writing at 95," *Journal of Reading* 34 (December 1990/January 1991): 270–72.

GARDNER, David Pierpont. b. March 24, 1933, Berkeley, California, to Reed Snow and Margaret (Pierpont) Gardner. Married June 27, 1958, to Elizabeth Fuhriman. Children: four.

As president of the Universities of Utah and California, David P. Gardner demonstrated an exceptional ability to steer complex institutions in difficult times. The path to leadership in higher education showed itself early to Gardner. He grew up in the neighborhood of the Berkeley campus of the University of California.

After earning the B.S. degree at Brigham Young University (1955) and the M.A. in political science at Berkeley (1959), he took the Ph.D., also at Berkeley, in the field of higher education (1966). By then he was already assistant to the Santa Barbara campus chancellor.

Gardner served in the U.S. Army during 1955–57. He was an administrative assistant with the California Farm Bureau Federation (1960–62) before becoming field and scholarship director of the California Alumni Foundation at Berkeley (1962–64). After three years as assistant to the chancellor at Santa Barbara, he was successively assistant chancellor (1967–69), vice chancellor (1969–70), and system wide vice president for public service and extension programs (1971–73).

He left the University of California in 1973 to become president of the University of Utah. Ten years later he returned as president of the University of California, serving until 1993. In his decade of leadership at each institution he was known for his commitment to excellence and equal opportunity. In 1993 Gardner became president of the Hewlett Foundation.

During 1981–83 he chaired the President's Commission on Excellence in Education, which issued the report, *A Nation at Risk*. In 1987 he was a Fortieth Anniversary Distinguished Fellow of the Fulbright Scholar Program.

REFERENCES: CA (21–24R); NYT, August 6, 1983, p. 13; WW (1996); *Time* 121 (March 14, 1983): 73.

GARDNER, John William. b. October 8, 1912, Los Angeles, to William Frederick and Marie Flora (Glover) Gardner. Married August 18, 1934, to Aida Marroquin. Children: two.

John W. Gardner had several careers, in which he directed attention to the civic purposes of education and the pursuit of excellence in a free society. He collaborated often with James B. Conant (BDAE) and Francis Keppel (q.v.).

Gardner earned A.B. (1935) and A.M. (1936) degrees at Stanford University and the Ph.D. (1938) degree in psychology at the University of California at Berkeley. He taught at Connecticut College for Women (later, Connecticut College, 1938–40) and Mount Holyoke College (1940–42) before wartime service as head of the Latin American section of Foreign Broadcast Intelligence in the Federal Communications Commission (1942–43) and as an officer in the U.S. Marine Corps (1943–46).

Joining the staff of the Carnegie Corporation in 1946, he rose quickly to be vice president (1949–55) and president (1955–65). Concurrently he held the presidency of the Carnegie Foundation for the Advancement of Teaching. Gardner supported James B. Conant's study of the American high school and the new math initiative.

Gardner was an adviser to U.S. presidents, notably Lyndon Johnson, particularly on issues in education. He chaired the education section of the Commission on National Goals established by President Dwight Eisenhower in 1959 and the White House Conference on Education convened by President Johnson in 1965. Shortly after the White House Conference, Johnson nominated Gardner to be secretary of health, education, and welfare, a position he held until 1968. In the president's cabinet, Gardner withdrew federal financial aid to racially segregated school districts in southern states. His efforts toward school integration were criticized as too severe by southern conservatives and too moderate by northern liberals.

Gardner was chair of the National Urban Coalition (1968–70), founder and chair of Common Cause (1970–77), and founder and chair of the Independent Sector (from 1980). He was a special adviser to the Aspen Institute. Among many books he wrote were *Excellence: Can We Be Equal and Excellent Too?* (1961), *Self-Renewal: The Individual and the Innovative Society* (1964), and *Know or Listen to Those Who Know* (with Francesca Gardner Reese, 1975). He received the Presidential Medal of Freedom (1964).

REFERENCES: CA (NR-4); CB (1976); LE (1974); NYT, July 22, 1965, p. 16, and July 28, 1965, pp. 1+; WW (1996); Nelson Lichtenstein, ed., *Political Profiles: The Johnson Years* (Facts on File, 1976), pp. 201–3.

GATTEGNO, Caleb. b. November 11, 1911, Alexandria, Egypt, to a Spanish merchant. Married to Shakti Gattegno. Children: four. d. July 28, 1988, Paris, France.

Caleb Gattegno was ignored largely in American scholarship, although he invented geoboards, was first translator (with F. M. Hodgson) of Jean Piaget's works into English, and developed striking, original theories and techniques on how mathematics, reading, and foreign languages can be learned. Gattegno's mind ranged unusually far, taking in not just mathematics and language but psychology and epistemology as well. His prose was elusive, as was his person: the public record offers only hints of his biography. He was as much at home in Europe and the Middle East as in the United States.

Gattegno studied in France and Switzerland, earning a doctorate in mathematics at the University of Basel and another in psychology at the University of Lille. He was director of the Institute of Higher Scientific Studies in Cairo, Egypt, from 1937 to 1945, then taught at the Universities of Liverpool and

London in the period 1945–57. He also worked in Ethiopia for the United Nations Technical Assistance Board developing teaching materials and in Switzerland as an editor in the field of mathematics education. In New York City from 1966 until his death, he was founder and president of Schools for the Future and Educational Solutions, Inc., the first a research center, and the second, a publishing and consulting venture that disseminated his ideas.

In 1952 he was a founder in Britain of the Association for Teaching Aids in Mathematics (later, Association of Teachers of Mathematics); he became a frequent contributor to its journal, *Mathematics Teaching.* Gattegno advocated treating mathematics as a natural part of life and a birthright of every person. During the 1980s he developed "Visible and Tangible Mathematics" computer programs for learning elementary mathematics on Apple computers. He created instructional "Pop-Ups" that were shown with children's television programs on the National Broadcasting Corporation network.

Among his books were *Introduction à la psychologie de l'affectivité* (1952), *Numbers in Color* (with G. Cuisenaire, 1954), *Teaching Mathematics to Deaf Children* (1958), *A Teacher's Introduction to the Cuisenaire–Gattegno Methods of Teaching Arithmetic* (1960), *Teaching Foreign Languages in Schools* (1963), *L'Enseignement des mathématiques* (with Jean Piaget, Jean Nicolet, and others, 1965), *Towards a Visual Culture* (1969), *Reading with Words in Colour: A Scientific Study of the Problems of Reading* (1969), *What We Owe Children* (1970), and *An Experimental School* (1973). Translations of his works appeared in German, Italian, Spanish, and Portuguese.

REFERENCES: CA (126); LE (1974); NYT, August 4, 1988, p. D21; *Los Angeles Times*, August 13, 1988, p. 28; *Mathematics Teaching* 125 (December 1988): 9; the prefaces and appendixes of Gattegno's books.

GAVER, Mary Virginia. b. December 10, 1906, Washington, D.C., to Clayton Daniel and Ruth Lydia (Clendening) Gaver. Married: no. d. December 31, 1991, Danville, Virginia.

Mary Virginia Gaver was a leader in the development of school libraries and library education. In 1960 she participated in the development of national school library standards. She was president of the American Association of School Librarians (AASL) and the American Library Association (ALA).

Gaver grew up in Schoolfield, Virginia, a Dan Rivers company town. She graduated from Randolph-Macon Institute and in 1927 received the B.S. degree from Randolph-Macon Woman's College. At George Washington High School in Danville, she taught English for one year, then served as the school librarian. She earned B.S. (1932) and M.S. (1938) degrees in library science from Columbia University. During 1937–38 she held a Carnegie Fellowship. She was technical director of a library program in Virginia under the Works Progress Administration (1938–39). From 1939 to 1942 Gaver was high school librarian in Scarsdale, New York, where she also oversaw four elementary libraries.

In 1942 Gaver began a long career as a professor of library science. At New

Jersey State Teachers College (later, College of New Jersey), she became supervisor of the school library program. She spent a semester during 1952–53 as a library specialist in Tehran, Iran. Gaver went to Rutgers University in 1954 as associate professor at the new Graduate School of Library Science. She taught children's and young adult literature and developed the Ph.D. program. She also taught at Emory University and the University of Virginia. After her 1971 retirement Gaver was vice president and director of library consulting services of Bro-Dart Industries. She was general editor of the Bro-Dart guide, *The Elementary School Library Collection*, first through eighth editions (1965–73).

Gaver was president of the New Jersey Library Association (1954–55), AASL (1959–60), ALA (1966–67), and Women's National Book Association. While president of the ALA, she established its Committee on Library Instruction. She chaired the AASL Knapp School Libraries Project Advisory Committee for three years. She studied school libraries in Puerto Rico.

Among her many publications were *Research Paper* (with Lucyle Hook, 1944), *School Libraries of Puerto Rico* (with Gonzalo Velasquez, 1963), *Libraries for the People of New Jersey* (with Lowell A. Martin, 1964), *Services of Secondary School Media Centers* (1971), and *A Braided Cord: Memoirs of a School Librarian* (1988). She compiled *Background Readings in Building Library Collections* (two volumes, 1969) and edited *State-Wide Library Planning* (1963). She directed a study for the U.S. Office of Education, published as *Effectiveness of Centralized Library Service in Elementary Schools (Phase I)*. In 1963 Gaver received the Herbert Putnam Honor Award for contributions to librarianship, in 1973 the Constance Lindsay Skinner Award for contributions to the world of books, and in 1980 the AASL President's Award.

REFERENCES: CA (NR-34, 136); CB (1966, 1992); FWC; NYT, January 3, 1992, p. A18; WW (1980–81); *The ALA Yearbook* (American Library Association, 1977); *Library Journal* 98 (October 15, 1973): 3101; *Library Quarterly* 31 (July 1961): 270; *School Libraries* 13 (October 1963): 49; *Wilson Library Bulletin* 66 (February 1992): 14.

GENTLE, Thomas Higdon. b. August 1, 1870, Farmington, Illinois, to James B. and Maggie (McMullen) Gentle. Married October 18, 1892, to Carrier M. Kessler. Children: five. d. May 21, 1951, Monmouth, Oregon.

Thomas Gentle was considered the foremost exponent in the United States of the educational theories of Johann F. Herbart, the German educational psychologist whose emphasis on environmental factors influenced the progressive education movement in America.

Gentle was a student at Danville (Illinois) Normal College, Illinois State University, and the University of Illinois. He studied at the University of Jena, where he won acquaintance with the work of Herbart and his successors.

After teaching at Platteville (Wisconsin) State Teachers College (later, University of Wisconsin–Platteville), he moved to Oregon, where he was director of teacher training at the Normal School in Monmouth from 1911 to 1928. One year after his arrival in Oregon, normal schools in the state closed for a three-year period for lack of legislative appropriation. When they reopened, Gentle reorganized the teacher training program at Monmouth on a Herbartian basis. The extensive influence he came to have on teacher education in Oregon was muffled in 1928, when the president of Monmouth Normal School dismissed him, apparently for personal reasons. After his forced retirement, Gentle taught in the extension division of the University of Oregon (1928–31).

REFERENCES: William H. Burton (BDAE), "Last of the Jena Group," *Oregonian*, June 3, 1951, p. 31; *Capitol's Who's Who for Oregon* (1948–49); letter from Donald C. Jones to John F. Ohles, October 29, 1975; *Oregon Daily Journal*, May 22, 1951, p. 7; *Oregonian*, May 22, 1951, p. 15.

GIDDINGS, Thaddeus Philander Woodbury. b. February 19, 1869, Anoka, Minnesota, to A. W. and Mary E. (Simons) Giddings. Married: no. d. March 4, 1954, Clermont, Florida.

T. P. Giddings spent his career as a supervisor of public school music, principally with the Minneapolis schools. He was known for the innovations he brought to public school music programs, including sight reading of music for all children and in-school piano classes. He cofounded the famous National Music Camp at Interlochen, Michigan.

Giddings attended Anoka, Minnesota, public schools and graduated from high school in 1885. He studied at the University of Minnesota for one year. On being hired to teach music in Anoka, he took a one-hour lesson in public school music in Minneapolis. He taught in Anoka (1886–89) and Anoka County (1889–91). During this time he studied at the American Institute of Normal Methods at Lake Geneva, Wisconsin, and in Highland Park, Illinois. Giddings went to Moline, Illinois, for three years (1891–94) as supervisor of music. His high school students there sang the oratorio *Creation*, one of the first performances of an oratorio by a high school in the country. He supervised music in the schools of Oak Park, Illinois, from 1894 to 1910.

Giddings was supervisor of music in Minneapolis public schools from 1910 until his retirement in 1942. When visiting classes, he heard the children sing almost the entire time, spending little time telling about music but rather emphasizing participation. He taught public school music at the University of Minnesota from 1915 to 1928 and music education at MacPhail College of Music in Minneapolis from 1923 to 1942.

In 1907 Giddings was a founder, along with Philip Hayden (q.v.), of the Music Supervisors (later, Educators) National Conference (MENC) in Keokuk, Iowa. He served as chairman of its executive committee. Giddings persuaded Joseph E. Maddy (BDAE) to become a music teacher and with him founded the Interlochen, Michigan, National Music Camp in 1928. Giddings was vice president of the camp.

Among Giddings' publications were *Grade School Music Teaching* (1910); with Joseph Maddy, *Instrumental Technique for Orchestras and Bands* (1926) and *Instrumental Class Teaching* (1928); with Wilma A. Gilmer, *Giddings' Pub-*

lic School Class Method for the Piano (1916); with Elbridge W. Newton, *The Junior Song and Chorus Book* (1915); and with Will Earhart (BDAE), Ralph L. Baldwin, and Elbridge W. Newton, *Music Educators Series* (1923–31).

REFERENCES: NGD; John Berry, "The Legacy of Maddy and Giddings," *Music Educators Journal* 79 (March 1993): 36–40; "Early Events in the Professional Life of T. P. Giddings Written by Himself in 1927," *Music Educators Journal* 43 (January 1957): 52–53; Karl O. Kuersteiner, "The Functional Mister Giddings," *Music Educators Journal* 34 (September–October 1947): 28–29; Charles Maynard McDermid, "Thaddeus P. Giddings: A Biography" (Ph.D. diss., University of Michigan, 1967); César Saerchinger, ed., *International Who's Who in Music* (Current Literature, 1918); *Who Was Who among North American Authors, 1921–1939* (Gale Research, 1976).

GINGOLD, Josef. b. October 28, 1909, Brest-Litovsk, Russia, to Meyer and Anna (Leiserowitz) Gingold. Married October 14, 1934, to Gladys Anderson. Children: no. d. January 11, 1995, Bloomington, Indiana.

At the height of a successful violin performance career, Josef Gingold switched to full-time university teaching. Renowned as a violinist and violin teacher, he continued a busy studio schedule past the age of eighty.

When Gingold came to the United States from Russia at the age of eleven, he was already an accomplished violin student. He debuted at Aeolian Hall in New York City when he was sixteen years old and continued his studies under Eugène Ysaÿe in Brussels (1927–30). He was first violinist of the NBC Orchestra (1937–43), concertmaster of the Detroit Symphony Orchestra (1943–46) and the Cleveland Orchestra (1947–60), and a member of the Primrose (1939–42) and NBC String (1941–43) Quartets. While continuing his performance career, he taught at Western Reserve (later, Case Western Reserve) University (1950–60). Recruited by Ivan Galamian (q.v.), he also taught at the summer Meadowmount School of Music (1955–81).

In 1960 Gingold left the Cleveland Orchestra to be professor of music at Indiana University. His presence on its faculty contributed to its development as an outstanding school of music. He was named distinguished professor in 1965. He was often a visiting professor at other American universities and taught master classes in Paris and Tokyo. The American String Teachers Association named Gingold "Teacher of the Year" in 1968.

He edited *Orchestral Excerpts from the Symphonic Repertoire* (1953–62), a three-volume standard textbook for the violin.

REFERENCES: BBD; NGD; NYT, January 13, 1995, p. A24; WW (1986–87); *New Yorker* 66 (February 4, 1991): 34+; Boris Schwarz, *Great Masters of the Violin* (Simon and Schuster, 1983), pp. 554–55; Jeffrey Wagner, "Josef Gingold: Remembrance of a Life in Music," *Instrumentalist* 39 (January 1985): 18–24.

GINOTT, Haim G. b. August 5, 1922 in Tel Aviv, Israel. Married Alice Lasker. Children: two. d. November 4, 1973, New York City.

Haim Ginott was a very public and humorful practitioner of what later came to be called parent education. While his work was principally as a clinical psychologist and graduate professor of that subject, it was through his popular books, his newspaper columns, and his role as resident psychologist on the *Today* television program that he was widely known.

Ginott received bachelor's (1948), master's (1949), and Ed.D. (1952) degrees from Columbia University. He was a clinical psychologist in private practice, adjunct professor of psychology at New York University, and clinical professor of psychotherapy at Adelphi University.

In several books, he sought to assist teachers and parents in improving spoken communication with children. He was the author of *Group Psychotherapy with Children* (1961), *Between Parent and Child* (1965), *Between Parent and Teenager* (1969), and *Teacher and Child* (1972). The books offered practical guidance and were sprinkled with sample dialogues between adults and children.

Ginott wrote a weekly newspaper column, "Between Us," conducted workshops in child and group psychotherapy and parent guidance throughout the United States and abroad, and was a consultant to mental health centers. He was a consultant on behalf of UNESCO to the Ministry of Education of Israel and a participant in the 1970 White House Conference on Children.

REFERENCES: NYT, November 7, 1973, p. 36; *Publishers Weekly*, November 19, 1973, p. 31; Lynn Smith, "Stepfather Knows Best," *Los Angeles Times*, April 13, 1994, p. E1.

GLAZER, Nathan. b. February 25, 1923, New York City, to Louis and Tillie (Zacharevich) Glazer. Married September 26, 1943, to Ruth Slotkin; October 4, 1962, to Sulochana Raghavan. Children: three.

Nathan Glazer came to the study of education in the United States from the perspective of sociology. In books and essays that defied easy categorization according to usual political, theoretical, or disciplinary rubrics, he offered a complex analysis of the interrelationships among race and ethnicity, urban life, politics, education, and cultural values. Glazer challenged the cultural assumptions of advocates of busing to achieve racially balanced schools, affirmative action in university admissions, and multicultural education.

His education was long, unusual, and intertwined with his career. After public schooling in the Bronx, he earned the B.S.S. degree at the City College of New York in 1944 and the A.M. in linguistics the same year at the University of Pennsylvania. Columbia University awarded him the Ph.D. in 1962 upon submission of his book *The Social Basis of American Communism* (1961); he had begun doctoral studies at Columbia during the late 1940s.

Glazer served on the editorial staff of *Contemporary Jewish Record* (later, *Commentary*) during 1944–53. He was on leave from the magazine during 1948–50 while collaborating with David Riesman (BDAE) and Reuel Denney on writing *The Lonely Crowd* (1950). With Riesman he also wrote *Faces in the Crowd* (1952). Glazer was an editor at Anchor Books, Doubleday and Company during 1954–57. In the period 1956–60 he held one-year appointments teaching sociology at the University of California, Berkeley; Bennington College; and

Smith College. After a year spent in Japan studying its language and society, he joined the Housing and Home Finance Agency as an urban sociologist (1962–63).

By 1963, when he returned to the University of California, Berkeley, as professor of sociology, Glazer was also author of *American Judaism* (1957) and *Beyond the Melting Pot* (with Daniel Patrick Moynihan, 1963). He became professor of education and social structure in the Harvard Graduate School of Education in 1969. Among Glazer's later books were *Remembering the Answers: Essays on the American Student Revolt* (1970), *Affirmative Discrimination* (1975), *Ethnic Dilemmas, 1964–82* (1983), *The Limits of Social Policy* (1988), and *We Are All Multiculturalists Now* (1997). He was coeditor of *The Public Interest* magazine from 1973.

Glazer had Guggenheim Fellowships in 1954 and 1966. He was inducted into the American Academy of Arts and Sciences and the National Academy of Education.

REFERENCES: CA (5–8R); CB (1970); CHE, April 11, 1997, pp. A16, A18; LE (1974); WD (1994–96); WW (1994–95); Nathan Glazer, ''From Socialism to Sociology,'' in Bennet M. Berger, ed., *Authors of Their Own Lives: Intellectual Autobiographies by Twenty American Sociologists* (University of California Press, 1990), Chapter 8; ''An Interview with Nathan Glazer,'' *New Perspectives* 17 (Fall 1985): 27–30.

GLEASON, Eliza Valeria Atkins. b. December 15, 1909, Winston-Salem, North Carolina, to Simon Green and Oleona (Pegram) Atkins. Married November 5, 1937, to Maurice F. Gleason. Children: one.

Eliza Atkins Gleason was the first dean of the School of Library Service at Atlanta (later, Clark–Atlanta) University and one the nation's preeminent library educators. Under Gleason's guidance this new school became the center for the training of professional African-American librarians, replacing a defunct program at Hampton Institute (later, University).

Gleason was raised in Winston-Salem, where her father was president of Slater Industrial Academy (later, Winston-Salem State University). In 1930 she received the A.B. degree from Fisk University, in 1931 the B.S. degree from the library school at the University of Illinois, and in 1936 the M.A. degree in library science from the University of California at Berkeley.

Gleason was a librarian at Louisville Municipal College (1931–32), headed the reference department at Fisk University (1932–36), and was library director at Talledaga College (1936–37). When she received the Ph. D. degree from the University of Chicago in 1940, she became the first African-American doctoral recipient in library science. Her dissertation was published as *The Government and Administration of Pubic Library Service to Negroes in the South.*

Gleason was founding dean of the Atlanta University library school beginning in 1940. When she moved to Chicago in 1946, she was succeeded at Atlanta University by Virginia Lacy Jones (q.v.). Gleason was head reference librarian at Wilson Junior College in 1953 and at Chicago Teachers College (later, Chicago State University) in 1953–54. Later Gleason was associate professor of library science at Illinois Teachers College (1954–63), assistant librarian at John Crerar Library (1964–67), and professor of library science at Illinois Institute of Technology (1967–70). At the Chicago Public Library (1970–73) she was assistant chief librarian of the regional centers. She was a professor at Northern Illinois University (1974–75).

Gleason was the first African American to serve on the Council of the American Library Association (1942–46). In 1979 she served on the Board of Directors of the Chicago Public Library.

REFERENCES: BWA; NBAW; WWAW (1974–75); WW (1990–91); WWBA (1994–95); Robert Wedgeworth, ed., *ALA World Encyclopedia of Library and Information Services* (American Library Association, 1980).

GLUECK, Nelson. b. June 4, 1900, Cincinnati, Ohio, to Morris and Anna (Rubin) Glueck. Married March 26, 1931, to Helen R. Iglauer. Children: one. d. February 12, 1971, Cincinnati, Ohio.

While Nelson Glueck was best known to a wide public for his discovery of King Solomon's mines during the 1930s and his archaeological explorations in the Negev Desert during the 1950s and 1960s, he was also a leader of biblical and rabbinical education for Reformed Judaism in America. During a quarter century as president of Hebrew Union College–Jewish Institute of Religion, he developed it into an international institution on four campuses.

Glueck enrolled at Hebrew Union College in 1915 and earned the bachelor of Hebrew literature degree there in 1918. At the University of Cincinnati he took the A.B. degree in 1920. In 1923 he was ordained a rabbi at Hebrew Union College and awarded a Morgenthau Traveling Fellowship for study in Europe. He enrolled at the Universities of Berlin, Heidelberg, and Jena, receiving the D.Phil. degree at Jena in 1927. He studied archaeology at the American School of Oriental Research in Jerusalem during 1927–28.

In 1928 he joined the faculty of Hebrew Union College, teaching Hebrew, and later Bible and biblical archaeology. He was on leave during much of the 1930s and 1940s, conducting archaeological research. From 1942 until 1947, while director of the American School for Oriental Research and its field director in Baghdad, he was also an intelligence agent for the Office of Strategic Services.

In 1947 Glueck became president of Hebrew Union College. In 1950 it was united with the Jewish Institute of Religion in New York City, and a third campus opened in Los Angeles. In 1963 at Glueck's instigation the institution added a fourth campus, the Biblical and Archaeological Center in Jerusalem.

Glueck's publications included *The Other Side of the Jordan* (1940), *The River Jordan* (1946), and *Rivers of the Desert: A History of the Negev* (1959).

REFERENCES: CA (P-2); CB (1969, 1971); DAB (supp. 9); NCAB (56: 170); NYT, February 14, 1971, p. 75; WWW (5); Fritz Bamberger, "The Mind of Nelson Glueck," in James A. Sanders, ed., *Near Eastern Archaeology in the Twentieth Century: Essays in Honor of Nelson Glueck* (Doubleday, 1970), pp. xvii–xxiv; Reuben G. Bullard, ''A Biography of Nelson Glueck,'' in Gisela Walberg, *Nelson and Helen Glueck Collection of Cypriot Antiquities, Cincinnati* (Astrov, 1992), pp. 36–66; Ellen Norman Stern, *Dreamer in the Desert: A Profile of Nelson Glueck* (KTAV Publishing House, 1980).

GOLDSMITH, Grace Arabell. b. April 8, 1904, St. Paul, Minnesota, to Arthur William and Arabell Louise (Coleman) Goldsmith. Married: no. d. April 28, 1975, New Orleans.

In the 1940s Grace Goldsmith introduced nutrition into the medical school curriculum. She helped to found the Tulane School of Public Health and Tropical Medicine and was its first dean.

Goldsmith attended the University of Minnesota and received the B.S. degree from the University of Wisconsin in 1925. She served as education director of the New Orleans Young Women's Christian Association before deciding to enter the medical field. Goldsmith received the M.D. degree from Tulane University in 1932 at the top of her class. She was an intern in New Orleans and a fellow in internal medicine at the Mayo Clinic in Rochester, Minnesota (1933–36). She received the M.S. degree in medicine from the University of Minnesota (1936).

Goldsmith became an instructor at the Tulane University School of Medicine in 1936. She served as dean from 1967 to 1973 and remained at Tulane until her death in 1975. She surveyed the nutrition of Louisiana schoolchildren in 1943 and studied diets in Newfoundland in 1944 and 1948. Her early research centered on vitamin C deficiency and B-complex vitamins. Later, she studied the relationship of nutrition to disease.

Goldsmith contributed to many books and wrote *Nutritional Diagnosis* (1959). She served on the editorial boards of the *American Journal of Clinical Nutrition* (1952–53), *Journal of Nutrition* (1954–58), *Physiological Reviews* (1961–67), *Journal of Atherosclerosis Research* (1962–68), and *Archives of Internal Medicine* (1966–69). She was a member of the science advisory committee of the Nutrition Foundation (1948–64 and 1972–75), the nutrition study section of the U.S. Public Health Service (1959–63), member (1948–69) and chair (1958–69) of the Food and Nutrition Board of the National Research Council, member (1951–63) and chair (1954–56) of the Food and Nutrition Research Advisory Committee for Agricultural Research Service of the U.S. Department of Agriculture, and consultant to the Louisiana Board of Health (1962–67).

Goldsmith was president of the American Institute of Nutrition (1965), American Board of Nutrition (1966–67), and American Society for Clinical Nutrition (1972–73). In 1959 she received the Osborne-Mendel Award from the American Institute of Nutrition, in 1964 the Goldberger Award in clinical nutrition from the American Medical Association, and in 1970 the Axson-Choppin Award from the Louisiana Public Health Association and the Seale-Harris award from the Southern Medical Association.

REFERENCES: NAW (Mod); NCAB (J: 204); NYT, April 29, 1975, p. 36; WWAW (1972–73); WR; WWW (6); *Nutrition Reviews* 33 (October 1975): 314–15.

GOODENOUGH, Florence Laura. b. August 6, 1886, Honesdale, Pennsylvania, to Linus North and Alice (Day) Goodenough. Married: no. d. April 4, 1959, Lakeland, Florida.

Florence L. Goodenough was an influential teacher and an outstanding researcher in the field of developmental child psychology. She joined the Institute of Child Welfare at the University of Minnesota in 1926 and remained until her retirement in 1947. John E. Anderson (q.v.), director, and Goodenough were the first two staff members of the institute. It gained a national reputation for its research and was noted for test development. Goodenough was credited with innovations in the testing field. She developed time sampling and event sampling. She was in charge of psychological research at the institute and devised the Minnesota Preschool Scale, with Katharine M. Maurer and others, to judge the intellectual capacity of very young children.

Goodenough developed the nonverbal Draw-a-Man test, which was used extensively and published as *Measurement of Intelligence by Drawings* (1926). The test was later known as the Goodenough-Harris drawing test. Goodenough also studied the social and emotional development of children and in 1931 wrote *Anger in Young Children*. With John Anderson she wrote *Your Child Year by Year* (1930) and *Experimental Child Study* (1931).

Goodenough attended school in Rileyville, Pennsylvania. She received a bachelor of pedagogy degree from Millersville Normal School (later, Millersville University of Pennsylvania) in 1908 and taught in rural schools in Pennsylvania. At Columbia University she earned B.S. (1920) and M.A. (1921) degrees. She was director of research in the schools of Rutherford and Perth Amboy (New Jersey) from 1919 to 1921. At Stanford University Goodenough studied under Lewis Terman (BDAE) and received the Ph.D. degree in 1924. She was a contributor to Terman's *Genetic Studies of Genius* (1925).

In 1925 Goodenough went to Minnesota as chief psychologist at the Minneapolis Child Guidance Clinic. Among her books were *Minnesota Preschool Scale* (with J. C. Foster and Marvin J. Van Wagenen, 1932), *Developmental Psychology* (1934), *The Mental Growth of Children from Two to Fourteen Years* (with Katharine M. Maurer, 1942), and *Mental Testing: Its History, Principles and Applications* (1949). She served as president of the Society for Research in Child Development, the Division on Childhood and Adolescence of the American Psychological Association, and the National Council of Women Psychologists.

Goodenough's retirement came when she developed an illness that led to blindness and partial deafness. She learned Braille and wrote two of her books after she became blind. *Exceptional Children* (1956) was begun before her loss of vision and completed with the assistance of her niece, Lois M. Rynkiewicz.

REFERENCES: AWS; BDP; ECP; LE (1948); NAW (Mod); PR; Dale B. Harris, ''Florence L. Goodenough, 1886–1959,'' *Child Development* 30 (1959): 305–6; Agnes N. O'Connell and Nancy Felipe Russo, eds., *Women in Psychology: A Bio-Bibliographic Sourcebook* (Greenwood Press, 1990); Gwendolyn Stevens and Sheldon Gardner, *The Women of Psychology*, vol. 1: *Pioneers and Innovators* (Schenkman, 1982).

GOODLAD, John Inkster. b. August 19, 1920, North Vancouver, British Columbia, Canada, to William James and Mary (Inkster) Goodlad. Married August 23, 1945, to Evalene M. Pearson. Children: two.

During the 1980s and 1990s, John Goodlad became one of the nation's most influential advocates for systemic educational reform. As an advocate of open education, he criticized the dull didacticism of many American classrooms. His research led him to argue forcefully for wide-ranging school–university collaboration. As director of the Center for Educational Renewal and president of the American Association of Colleges for Teacher Education (1988–90), he urged teachers to retrain themselves in professional development schools.

Goodlad received a teaching certificate from the Vancouver Normal School in 1939. In British Columbia he taught in a one-room school, was teacher/principal at an elementary school in Surrey, and was director of education at the Provincial Industrial Training School for Boys. He earned the B.A. degree from the University of British Columbia (1945) and the Ph.D. from the University of Chicago (1949). In 1949 he went to Emory University, where he was director of the Division of Teacher Education (1950–56) and of the Agnes Scott College–Emory University teacher education program.

At the University of Chicago (1956–60), Goodlad was professor and director of the Center for Teacher Education. From 1960 to 1985 he was professor and director of the University Elementary School at the University of California at Los Angeles (UCLA), where he also served as dean of the Graduate School of Education (1967–83). He directed the Center for Educational Renewal and (to 1981) the Research and Development division of the Institute for Development of Educational Activities. He was a professor at the University of Washington from 1985 to 1991. In 1993 he was named the first Distinguished Visiting Scholar in Educational Policy at the Hoover Institution.

Among Goodlad's many writings were *The Nongraded Elementary School* (with Robert H. Anderson, q.v., 1959), judged an outstanding education book by the Enoch Pratt Library; *School Curriculum Reform in the United States* (1964); *School, Curriculum, and the Individual* (1966); *The Dynamics of Educational Change* (1975); *What Schools Are For* (1979); *A Place Called School* (1984); and *Teachers for Our Nation's Schools* (1990). His coedited volumes included *The Elementary School in the United States* (with Harold Shane, q.v., 1973), chosen an outstanding education book by Phi Lambda Theta; *The Ecology of School Renewal* (1987); *The Moral Dimensions of Teaching* (1990); and *Integrating General and Special Education* (1993). He served on the editorial boards of *Child's World* (1952–75), *International Review of Education* (1971–

79), *Journal of Aesthetic Education* (1976–78), and *New Standard Encyclopedia* (from 1953). His books were translated into Hebrew, Italian, Japanese, and Spanish.

Goodlad was a founding member of Global Perspectives in Education, Inc. (1974–86) and National Academy of Education. He was on the Board of Directors of the Council for the Study of Mankind (1965–71, chair 1969–71), National Foundation for the Improvement of Education (1970–74), and National Humanities Faculty (1972–76). He was president of the National Society of College Teachers of Education (1962–63) and American Educational Research Association (1967–68). He served on the President's Task Force on Early Education (1966–67) and on Education of the Gifted (1967–68). He was a fellow of the Ford Foundation (1952–53) and received many awards, including the Distinguished Contribution to Curriculum Award (1983) and Outstanding Book Award (1985) from the American Educational Research Association.

REFERENCES: CA (NR-43); LE (1974); CHE, March 15, 1989, p. A3, and October 17, 1990, p. A17; RPE; WD (1994–96); WW (1996); *Educational Leadership* 52 (March 1995): 82–85.

GOODYKOONTZ, Bess. b. August 21, 1894, Waukon, Iowa, to Edward Warren and Lela (Sherman) Goodykoontz. Married: no. Children: one adopted. d. July 29, 1990, South Newfane, Vermont.

During her long career in the U.S. Office of Education, Bess Goodykoontz contributed to an increased federal role in research and support of education. Her work focused initially on elementary education and later on international education. She founded the State Consultants in Elementary Education, an association of administrators in state departments of education that raised the profile of elementary school concerns. She was an early advocate of the educational uses of films.

After graduation from high school, Goodykoontz was an elementary school teacher in rural Iowa (1912–16). At the University of Iowa, she earned B.A. (1920) and M.A. (1922) degrees. She also taught (1920–21) and was principal (1921–22) of the Experimental School, which Ernest Horn (q.v.) had founded at the University of Iowa.

From Iowa, Goodykoontz went to Green Bay, Wisconsin, as supervisor of elementary education (1922–24), and to the University of Pittsburgh, where she taught elementary education (1924–29). In 1929 the U.S. commissioner of education, William John Cooper (q.v.), selected her for the new position of assistant commissioner, with responsibility for elementary education. Having agreed to a two-year term, she stayed in the Office of Education for forty-three years. From 1946 she directed the Division of Elementary Education. In 1949 she became associate commissioner with broad responsibilities for administration and research. She later served as director of comparative education (1952–56) and director of international education relations (1956–62) in the Division of International Education.

Goodykoontz participated in the U.S. Educational Mission to Germany in 1946, headed by James B. Conant (BDAE). She was president of the World Organization for Early Childhood Education (1958–60); chair of the Committee on Supply, Preparation, and Certification of Teachers of the National Education Association; chair of the board of the National Society for the Study of Education; first president of the Association for Supervision and Curriculum Development (1946–47); and president of the American Education Research Association (1939–40), National Council of Administrative Women in Education (1953–57), and Pi Lambda Theta, educational honor society for women (1933–37). She was author of many articles.

REFERENCES: LE (1948); NYT, August 4, 1990, p. 29; WWAW (1958–59); WWW (10); Paul E. Blackwood, ''Bess Goodykoontz: 1894–1990,'' *Childhood Education* 67 (Summer 1991): 265–70.

GOSLIN, Willard Edward. b. September 24, 1899, Harrisburg, Missouri, to William E. and Maggie (Long) Goslin. Married June 28, 1924, to Marion Gregory. Children: two. d. March 6, 1969, Nashville, Tennessee.

Willard Goslin, a nationally acclaimed school superintendent, became a symbol of the end of educational progressivism when he was forced to resign from the Pasadena, California, schools in November 1950. Goslin's ouster was a victory for citizens' groups that deemed his support of racial understanding, outdoor education, child guidance, and mental health as evidence of subversive, un-American values.

Goslin was raised on a Missouri farm. He began teaching in rural schools of Boone County in 1916. After receiving the B.S. degree from Northeast Missouri State Teachers College (later, Truman State University) in 1922, he was principal (1922–23) and superintendent (1923–28) in Slater, Missouri. He earned the A.M. degree at the University of Missouri (1928) and served as superintendent in Webster Groves, Missouri (1930–44). While superintendent of Minneapolis schools (1944–48), Goslin was named one of the five outstanding public school administrators in the country.

In 1948 Goslin became superintendent of Pasadena, California, schools, succeeding a superintendent who had been in the office for twenty years. Goslin's first year passed peacefully; a bond issue was passed, and construction of new schools began. However, he soon faced opposition from a new group, the Pasadena School Development Council. Its members opposed programs they deemed progressive and were joined by a group named Pro America. The School Development Council demanded loyalty oaths for teachers and sought to oust Goslin. When he lost school board support, Goslin resigned. These events attracted nationwide attention.

Goslin served as professor of education and chair of the Division of Educational Administration and Community Development at George Peabody College for Teachers (later, part of Vanderbilt University) from 1951 until his retirement in 1966. He was president of the Missouri State Teachers Association (1939) and American Association of School Administrators (1948–49). In 1952 he received an American Education Award from the National Education Association. He coordinated a teacher education project for South Korea.

REFERENCES: LE (1948); NYT, March 8, 1969, p. 27; WW (1954–55); *American School Board Journal* 122 (January 1951): 70; David Hurlburd, *This Happened in Pasadena* (Macmillan, 1952); Charles L. Lee, "A Case Study in Educational Leadership: Willard E. Goslin" (Ph.D. diss., Stanford University, 1950); Carey McWilliams, "The Enemy in Pasadena," *Christian Century* 68 (January 3, 1951): 10–15; *Nation's Schools* 47 (January 1951): 25, 76; *Time* 56 (November 27, 1950): 85–87.

GRAMBS, Jean Dresden. b. April 6, 1919, Pigeon Point, California, to Abraham and Esther (Dresden) Schwartz. Married June 18, 1945, to Harold P. Grambs. Children: three. d. September 30, 1989, Riverdale, Maryland.

Jean D. Grambs wrote widely in the fields of human development and education, particularly social studies education.

Grambs received the A.B. degree from Reed College in 1940 and the M.A. degree from Stanford University in 1941. She taught in junior and senior high schools in Oakland and San Andreas, California, from 1941 to 1943. After earning the Ed.D. degree from Stanford in 1948, she remained there as assistant professor until 1953. She was a Ford Foundation fellow during 1952–53.

Moving to Maryland, Grambs served as a supervisor of adult education in Prince George's County (1955–57). She joined the faculty of the University of Maryland in 1961 as an associate professor of secondary education, becoming professor in 1967. From 1979 until she retired in 1988 she was a member of the Department of Human Development. Grambs served as a consultant to many school systems and agencies serving youth.

Among her books were *Modern Methods in Secondary Education* (with William J. Iverson, 1952), *Education in a Transition Community* (1955), *Foundation of Teaching: An Introduction to Modern Education* (with L. Morris McClure, 1964), *Society and Education: Readings* (with James D. Raths, 1965), *Schools, Scholars, and Society* (1965), *Intergroup Education: Methods and Materials* (1968), *Women over Forty: Visions and Realities* (with Marilyn R. Block and Janice L. Davidson, 1981), and *Sex Differences and Learning: An Annotated Bibliography of Educational Research, 1979–1989* (with John C. Carr, 1991). She coedited *Counseling the Disadvantaged Youth* (1968), *Education in the World Today* (1972), and *Black Self-Concept: Implications for Education and Social Science* (1972).

Grambs was a director of the National Council for the Social Studies (NCSS, 1970–73) and at the time of her death was coordinator of NCATE Folio Reviews for NCSS.

REFERENCES: CA (NR-7, 129); FWC; LE (1974); NYT, October 3, 1989, p. B10; WWAW (1977); WW (1980–81); *Social Education* 54 (April/May 1990): 232.

GRAY, Hanna Holborn. b. October 25, 1930, Heidelberg, Germany, to Hajo and Annemarie (Bettmann) Holborn. Married June 19, 1954, to Charles Montgomery Gray. Children: no.

Hanna Gray was the first woman to lead a major American research university, first as acting president of Yale University, then as president of the University of Chicago.

As a small child, she emigrated from Germany with her mother, a scholar of classical philology, and her father, a well-known professor of history dismissed for his opposition to national socialism. At the age of fifteen she enrolled at Bryn Mawr College, where she earned the A.B. degree (1950). Harvard University awarded her the Ph.D. degree (1957). She was a Fulbright scholar at Oxford University (1950–51) and held teaching appointments in European history at Bryn Mawr (1953–54) and Harvard (1955–60), before joining the faculty of the University of Chicago (1961–72). For two years (1972–74) she was dean of arts and sciences of Northwestern University.

Gray was provost (1974–78) and acting president (1977–78) of Yale before returning to the University of Chicago, where she was president for fifteen years (1978–93). At Chicago she emphasized educational quality, increased the size of the undergraduate college, and worked against large budgetary constraints much like the ones she had faced at Yale. Upon retiring from the presidency, she returned to the faculty and taught history.

She was coeditor with Charles Gray of the *Journal of Modern History* (1965–70); a fellow of the Center for Advanced Study in the Behavioral Sciences (1966–67); a member of the National Council on the Humanities (1972–78); a recipient of the Medal of Liberty award (1986), Presidential Medal of Freedom (1991), and the Jefferson Medal of the American Philosophical Society (1993); a trustee of the Andrew W. Mellon Foundation; and a director of many corporations. She chaired the American Council on Education (1979) and the Association of American Universities (1990).

REFERENCES: AWM; CB (1979); CHE, January 22, 1979, pp. 4–5, and May 18, 1991, p. 11+; LE (1974); LW; WW (1996); WWAW (1993–94); Kathryn McDonald Nelson, ''Interview: Hanna Holborn Gray,'' *College Board Review* 108 (Summer 1978): 2–9+; *Newsmakers* (Gale Research, 1992); *Time* 110 (December 5, 1977): 96, 98.

GREEN, Richard Reginald. b. May 27, 1936, Mennifee, Arkansas, to James and Gertrude (Howelton) Green. Married February 4, 1960, to Gwendolyn Tolbert. Children: four. d. May 10, 1989, New York City.

From an impoverished childhood in a Minneapolis public housing project Richard Green rose to be the city's superintendent of schools. He went on to New York City as school chancellor. In both cities he was the first African American to fill the leadership role. After not much more than a year in New York, he died suddenly.

Green moved with his mother and sister to Minneapolis when he was one year old. As a youth he was assigned briefly to a reform school. He graduated from Vocational High School in Minneapolis and earned the B.A. degree at Augsburg College in 1959. At St. Cloud State College (later, University) he received a master's degree in special education in 1968. While working in the Minneapolis public schools, with financial assistance from local business executives, he studied at the Harvard Graduate School of Education, obtaining the Ed.D. degree in 1972.

He taught in the Minneapolis public schools beginning in 1959. In 1972 he became administrative assistant to the superintendent for desegregation and integration. He was also principal of North Community High School before becoming superintendent in 1980. As leader of the Minneapolis public schools, Green introduced benchmark testing of all students. He closed underenrolled schools and established magnet programs. He was known for his intense dedication to schoolchildren. The move to a much larger school system in New York proved challenging, but his death came too early to know how he would have fared in a highly politicized situation.

REFERENCES: NYT, January 3, 1988, p. A23, May 11, 1989, p. 1+, B4, May 13, 1989, p. 27+, and August 26, 1989, p. A27; Elizabeth Kaibel, "Twin Citians of the Decade," *Mpls. St. Paul* 18 (January 1990): 52–57.

GREENE, Maxine Meyer. b. December 23, 1917, New York City, to Max C. and Lillian (Greenfield) Meyer. Married March 19, 1938, to Joseph M. Krimsley; August 2, 1947, to Orville N. Greene. Children: two.

Maxine Greene was one of the most influential philosophers of education of her generation. She argued that literature and the arts should liberate students' and teachers' imaginations from the constraints of bureaucratic schools and a technological social order.

Greene earned the B.A. degree at Barnard College of Columbia University (1938) and M.A. (1949) and Ph.D. (1955) degrees at New York University. She taught at New York University during 1949–56. At Montclair State College (later, University) she was assistant professor of English for one year before returning to New York University (1957–62). She was a member of the faculty in education at Brooklyn College of the City University of New York (1962–65). At Teachers College of Columbia University she taught English and philosophy of education from 1965 and was William F. Russell Professor of Foundations of Education from 1975. During 1965–70 she edited *Teachers College Record.*

Greene was a consultant to many organizations, including the U.S. Office of Education (1965–67), University of Illinois (1965–67), and Lincoln Center Institute of Arts in Education (from 1976). She was president of the Philosophy of Education Society (1966–67) and Middle Atlantic States Philosophy of Education Society (1965–67), as well as chairman of the John Dewey Society from 1970. She was the first woman and first humanities scholar to be president of the American Educational Research Association (1971–72).

Her books included *The Public School and the Private Vision: A Search for America in Education and Literature* (1965), *Existential Encounters for Teachers* (1967), *The Birthmark and Other Stories* (1968), *Teacher as Stranger: Educational Philosophy for the Modern Age* (1973) *Education, Freedom, and Possibility* (1975), *Landscapes of Learning* (1978), and *The Dialectic of Freedom* (1988). She was coauthor of *The Master Teacher Concept: Five Perspectives* (1984).

REFERENCES: CA (NR-13); LE (1974); RPE; WW (1996).

GRENNAN, Jacqueline. *See* WEXLER, Jacqueline Grennan.

GROSS, Calvin Edward. b. April 8, 1919, Los Angeles, to Harry Edward and Telah May (Calvin) Gross. Married March 29, 1946, to Bernice Marjorie Hayman. Children: three. d. March 14, 1987, San Antonio, Texas.

Calvin Gross was an educational administrator, particularly noted for his innovations during his superintendency in Pittsburgh. Gross believed in reading as a basis for all education. He wanted emphasis on academics and regarded subjects such as driver education as frills. However, he also encouraged new ideas such as team teaching.

Gross grew up in Los Angeles. After receiving the A.B. degree with honors in mathematics from the University of California at Los Angeles (1940), he was a graduate assistant in mathematics at Oregon State University (1940–41). He served as a captain in the U.S. Army (1941–46). He was with the Los Angeles City Schools (1946–50) as a teacher, mathematics department chair, registrar, and vice principal. Gross received the M.S. degree from the University of Southern California (1947). After one year on a fellowship at the Harvard Graduate School of Education (1950–51) he was superintendent of schools in Weston, Massachusetts (1951–56). In 1957 Gross earned the Ed.D. degree from Harvard. He was superintendent of the Niskayuna Central School District, outside Schenectady, New York (1956–58).

Gross was superintendent of Pittsburgh schools from 1958 to 1963. He sponsored academic innovations there, including initiation of the nation's largest team teaching project. The Hill Project, financed by the Ford Foundation, offered culturally deprived students trips to museums and concerts. Gross began a Directed Studies Program for gifted students. Teachers' salaries were raised, paid through a wage tax that Gross helped steer through the legislature.

In 1963 a committee headed by Francis Keppel (q.v.) recommended to the New York City school board that they hire Gross as superintendent. He was the first superintendent chosen from outside the city. New York City schools faced many problems, including one-third of the teachers being substitutes. The teachers' union was threatening to strike, and civil rights leaders were threatening a boycott, while de facto segregation continued to increase. After two years the board requested Gross' resignation, feeling he had not been forceful enough in organizational reform.

Gross was dean of the School of Education at the University of Missouri–Kansas City (1965–72). From 1972 to 1978 he was president of the National College of Education in Evanston, Illinois. From 1978 until his death in 1987 he was superintendent of schools at Alamo Heights, San Antonio, Texas.

Gross was a member (1970–74) and chair (1972–73) of the National Council for Accreditation of Teacher Education and a member of the Advisory Committee on New Educational Media for the U.S. Department of Health, Education, and Welfare. He was a trustee of the Educational Testing Service and the Joint Council on Economic Education. He was on the editorial advisory board of *Nation's Schools* and was coauthor of *Research for Tomorrow's Schools: Discipline Inquiry for Education* (1969).

REFERENCES: LE (1974); NYT, March 16, 1987, p. D11; WW (1976–77); *Newsweek* 65 (March 15, 1965): 88–89; *Saturday Review* 45 (December 15, 1962): 47+; *Time* 82 (November 15, 1963): 86–92.

GROSS, Richard Edmund. b. May 25, 1920, Chicago, to Edmund Nicholas and Florence (Gallistel) Gross. Married May 25, 1943, to Jane Clare Hartl. Children: four.

In social studies education, Richard Gross played a leading role in the United States and internationally through his books and professional activity. He had a particular interest in the development of citizenship education.

After two years of study at the Wright Branch of Chicago City College (later, Wright College), Gross enrolled at the University of Wisconsin, where in 1942 he received the B.S. degree. He remained in Madison, Wisconsin, as a high school teacher (1943–48). Wisconsin awarded him the M.S. degree in 1946. While pursuing graduate study at Stanford University, he taught in the Menlo College School of Business Administration (1948–51). After receiving the Ed.D. degree at Stanford (1951), he served on the faculty of Florida State University (1951–55). He then returned to Stanford, where he remained for the rest of his career.

His international experiences included a Fulbright lecturing award at the University of Wales, Swansea (1961–62), a visiting professorship at the University of Frankfurt (1968–69), another at Monash University in Australia (1976), and consultation for the Chilean Ministry of Education (1973). He was president of the National Council for the Social Studies (1966–67) and editor of *California Social Science Review* (1962–68).

Gross wrote *How to Handle Controversial Issues* (1952) and coauthored *The Sociology of the School* (1957), *Educating Citizens for Democracy* (1958), *Civics in Action* (1965), *Man's World: A Physical Geography* (1966), *Quest for Liberty* (1971), *Problem-Centered Social Studies Instruction* (1971), *Teaching Social Studies Skills* (1971), *The Human Experience* (1974), *Social Studies for Our Times* (1978), and *American Citizenship: How We Govern* (1979). He edited California's *Report of the State Central Committee on Social Studies* (1959), *The Heritage of American Education* (1962), *British Secondary Education*

(1965), *Teaching the Social Studies: What, Why, and How* (with others, 1969), and *Learning to Live in Society: Toward a World View of the Social Studies* (1980).

REFERENCES: CA (NR-1); LE (1974); WD (1994–96); WW (1996).

GUINIER, Ewart G. b. May 17, 1910, Panama City, Canal Zone, to Howard Manoah and Marie Louise (Beresford) Guinier. Married July 1, 1933, to Doris I. Cumberbatch; October 16, 1945, to Eugenia Paprin. Children: four. d. February 4, 1990, Bedford, Massachusetts.

Ewart Guinier organized the Department of Afro-American Studies at Harvard University in 1969, served as its chairman from 1969 to 1976, and remained a professor until 1980.

Guinier came to the United States in 1925 and graduated from Boston English High School. He attended Harvard College for two years (1929–31). He received the B.S. degree from City College of New York in 1935 and the M.A. degree from Columbia University in 1939. In New York City, Guinier was assistant vice president of the Harlem Research Laboratory (1933–35), director of intake in the New York Welfare Department (1935–37), and examiner and director of the Service Rating Bureau (1937–42).

From 1942 to 1946 he served in the U.S. Army, where he organized guidance and educational programs. He was regional director and then international secretary-treasurer of the Congress of Industrial Organizations (CIO) Public Workers Union (1946–53). Guinier then worked in real estate and insurance. After earning a law degree from New York University in 1959, he directed the Queens (New York) Urban League (1962–68).

In 1968 Guinier went to Columbia University to direct its Urban Center. The next year he began his tenure at Harvard University. From 1969 to 1974 Guinier also served as director of Harvard's W.E.B. DuBois Institute for Afro-American Research. He was on the Board of Directors of the Center for Urban Education and received several awards, including the Carter G. Woodson (BDAE) Award.

REFERENCES: NCAB (N-63: 63); NYT, February 7, 1990, p. B7; WWW (10); *Negro History Bulletin* 33 (January 1970): 20.

H

HAGERTY, William Walsh. b. June 10, 1916, Holyoke, Minnesota, to William Walsh and Alice Amanda (Lindberg) Hagerty. Married September 30, 1939, to Mary Elizabeth McKay. Children: three. d. January 14, 1986, Savannah, Georgia.

William W. Hagerty was a leader in engineering education who served as president of Drexel Institute of Technology from 1963 until his 1984 retirement. In 1970 the institution was renamed Drexel University. The university was the first in the United States to require all freshmen to own a personal computer.

Hagerty received the B.S. degree in mechanical engineering (1939) from the University of Minnesota and M.S. (1943) and Ph.D. (1947) degrees from the University of Michigan. In Saint Paul, Minnesota, he worked for the Great Lakes Pipe Line Company (1935–39) and was a junior engineer with the U.S. Gypsum Company (1939–40).

Hagerty taught mechanical engineering at Villanova College (later, University, 1940–41) and the University of Cincinnati (1941–42). From 1942 to 1955 he was at the University of Michigan, rising to professor of engineering mechanics. He was professor of engineering and dean of the School of Engineering at the University of Delaware (1955–58) and professor of engineering mechanics, director of the Bureau of Engineering Research, and dean of the College of Engineering at the University of Texas (1958–63) before assuming the presidency at Drexel.

Hagerty coauthored *Engineering Mechanics* (with Harold J. Plass, Jr., 1962). He served on the Board of Directors of the Communications Satellite Corporation, was an adviser to the National Aeronautics and Space Administration (1964–70), member of the Commission on Presidential Scholars (1964–69), board member of the National Science Foundation (1964–70), and member of the Philadelphia Commission on Higher Education.

REFERENCES: LE (1974); NYT, January 15, 1986, p. B11; WWW (9).

HAMILTON, (Amy) Gordon. b. December 26, 1892, Tenafly, New Jersey, to George and Bertha (Torrance) Hamilton. Married: no. d. March 10, 1967, Victoria, British Columbia, Canada.

Gordon Hamilton was a leader in social work education. She became a faculty member of the New York School of Social Work in 1923 and served as its associate dean from 1951 to 1955. She remained at the school until her 1957 retirement. Hamilton helped to develop a doctoral program in social work. The school later became the Columbia University Graduate School of Social Work. Hamilton's book *Theory and Practice of Social Case Work*, published in 1940 and revised in 1951, was a major social work textbook. She was a developer of the psychosocial school of social work.

Hamilton was educated at home. After graduation from Bryn Mawr College in 1914, she was employed by the American Red Cross. In 1920 she became a caseworker and later research secretary for the New York Charity Organization Society. During her teaching career she continued to be active in social work practice as a consultant to the Social Service Department of Presbyterian Hospital (1925–36), social service director for the New York State Temporary Emergency Relief Administration (1935–36), and research counselor to the Jewish Board of Guardians (1947–50). She also worked for the Federal Emergency Relief Administration, Church World Service, and United Nations Relief and Rehabilitation Administration (1944–52).

From 1956 to 1962 Hamilton was the first editor of *Social Work*, journal of the newly organized National Association of Social Workers. Among her publications were *A Medical Social Terminology* (1927), *Social Case Recording* (1936), *Principles of Social Case Recording* (1946), and *Psychotherapy in Child Guidance* (1947).

REFERENCES: BDSW; ESW; HAWH; NAW (Mod); NYT, March 11, 1967, p. 29; Batya Shneider Shoshani, ''Gordon Hamilton: An Investigation of Core Ideas'' (D.S.W. diss., Columbia University, 1984); *Social Casework* 38 (July 1957): 375.

HANSEN, Carl Francis. b. January 18, 1906, Wolbach, Nebraska, to Peder and Barbara (Cutler) Hansen. Married June 11, 1929, to Ruth Williams. Children: three. d. August 27, 1983, Washington, D.C.

During two decades of marked change in race relations and increasing pressure on schools from court decisions on race issues, Carl Hansen was a key administrator in District of Columbia public schools. He began as associate superintendent of curriculum of white elementary schools (1947–55), then became assistant superintendent of senior high schools (1955–58), and superintendent (1958–67). An advocate of integration, Hansen supported the *Bolling v. Sharpe* Supreme Court ruling that racial segregation in the District was a denial of due process. At first he won praise for his role in helping to desegregate Washington's schools. Hansen established innovative programs, including the four-track system, which critics attacked as discriminatory toward minority groups. The decision in the case of *Hobson v. Hansen* ruled de facto segregation in Washington unconstitutional. When a federal appeals court agreed in 1967 and ordered busing, Hansen resigned.

Hansen received B.A. (1927) and M.A. (1940) degrees from the University of Nebraska. He taught at Wolbach High School beginning in 1925. While teaching at Grand Island, Nebraska, he organized the Grand Island Teachers

Association. During 1935–36 he worked for the Works Progress Administration in Nebraska as a personnel officer. Beginning in 1936 he taught at Omaha (Nebraska) Technical High School, where he developed curriculum materials. He headed the Language Arts Department from 1940 to 1945, then from 1945 to 1947 was principal. He also taught at the Municipal University of Omaha. In 1944 Hansen received the Ed.D. degree from the University of Southern California.

In 1968 he published *Danger in Washington: My Twenty Years in the Schools in the Nation's Capital*. He became a consultant to the California State Department of Education in 1969.

REFERENCES: CA (NR-2, 110); CB (1962); LE (1974); WP, August 29, 1983, p. B10; Larry Cuban (q.v.), *Urban School Chiefs under Fire* (University of Chicago Press, 1976); Victor Gold, "Defeat of an Educator," *National Review* 21 (January 14, 1969): 28; James D. Koerner, "Carl F. Hansen of Washington, D.C.," *Saturday Review* 44 (December 16, 1961): 49–51; *Time* 86 (July 9, 1965): 56.

HAUGEN, Einar Ingvald. b. April 19, 1906, Sioux City, Iowa, to John and Kristine (Gorset) Haugen. Married June 18, 1932, to Eva Lund. Children: two. d. June 20, 1994, Cambridge, Massachusetts.

Two early experiences helped to shape Einar Haugen's career. He grew up speaking English and Norwegian in the home of his immigrant parents, and when he was in his teens, the family lived for two years in Norway. He became an expert on dialect, lexicographer, scholar of immigration, and innovator in techniques for mastering spoken foreign languages. His oral method of teaching Norwegian to American soldiers under time pressure during World War II became a model for language instruction in peacetime, too.

Haugen attended Morningside College (1924–27) and earned the B.A. degree at St. Olaf College (1928). He received the M.A. (1929) and Ph.D. (1931) degrees at the University of Illinois. He taught for many years at the University of Wisconsin (1931–64), holding the titles of Thompson Professor of Scandinavian Languages and Vilas Research Professor of Scandinavian Languages and Linguistics before moving to Harvard University as Victor S. Thomas Professor of Scandinavian Languages and Lingustics (1964–75). He taught in the United States Army (1943–44) and was cultural attaché at the U.S. Embassy in Oslo, Norway (1945–46).

Haugen wrote more than two dozen books, including *Norsk i Amerika* (1939), *Reading Norwegian* (1940), *Norwegian Word Studies* (two volumes, 1941), *Voyages to Vinland* (1941), *Spoken Norwegian* (1946), *Norwegian Language in America: A Study in Bilingual Behavior* (1953), *Bilingualism in the Americas: A Guide to Research* (1957), *Norwegian-English Dictionary* (1965), *Language Conflict and Language Planning: The Case of Modern Norwegian* (1966), *Riksspråk og folkemål* (1969), *Ecology of Language* (1972), *Scandinavian Languages: Introduction to Their History* (1976), *Land of the Free* (with Eva L. Haugen, 1978), *Bjørnson's Vocabulary* (1978), *Ibsen's Drama: Author to*

Audience (1979), *Scandinavian Language Structures* (1982), *Oppdalsmålet* (1982), *Blessings of Babel* (1987), and *Ole Bull* (with Camilla Cai, his daughter, 1993). He edited and translated many other works.

He was a Guggenheim fellow (1942–43) and twice a Fulbright scholar (1951–52 in Oslo; 1976–77 in Uppsala, Sweden), among other awards and prizes. He served as a special lecturer abroad sponsored by the U.S. Department of State. Haugen was president of the Linguistic Society of America (1950), American Dialect Society (1965), Ninth International Congress of Linguists (1962), and the Permanent International Committee on Linguistics (1966–72). He served on the board of editors of the Norwegian American Historical Society. *Studies for Einar Haugen: Presented by Friends and Colleagues*, edited by Evelyn Scherabon Firchow and others, was published in 1972. Haugen was awarded the Order of St. Olaf, First Class, by Norway and the Order of the North Star by Sweden.

REFERENCES: CA (NR-25, 110); NYT, June 23, 1994, p. B8; WD (1994–96); WW (1992–93); *Language* 71, no. 3 (1995): 558–64; *Norway Times*, December 13, 1990.

HAYDEN, Philip Cady. b. November 20, 1854, Brantford, Ontario, Canada, to Joel Babcock and Fannie J. (Van Brocklin) Hayden. Married October 12, 1886, to Mary Neely Ralston. Children: two. d. June 1, 1925, Keokuk, Iowa.

Philip Cady Hayden organized the Music Supervisors' National Conference and was instrumental in beginning the publication of *School Music Monthly* (later, *School Music*).

Hayden attended New York University (1876–77) and Oberlin College (1878–81) and Conservatory (1883). He was supervisor of music in the public schools of Quincy, Illinois (1888–1900). While there he served as president of the Illinois Music Teachers' Association (1896–97).

In 1892 Hayden became supervisor of music in Keokuk, Iowa, where he remained until his death. He established the independent journal *School Music Monthly* in 1900 and was its editor and publisher. In 1907 he issued an invitation to music educators, including T. P. Giddings (q.v.), to a meeting in Keokuk that led to the founding of the Music Supervisors' (later, Educators) National Conference. Hayden served as first president.

Hayden was active in the National Education Association (NEA), particularly its Department of Music Education, of which he was president (1899) and secretary (1904–7 and 1909). He lectured to music teachers' associations and wrote children's songs.

REFERENCES: WWW (4); Chester Newhall Channon, ''The Contributions of Philip Cady Hayden to Music Education in the United States'' (Ed.D. diss., University of Michigan, 1959); *Music Supervisors' Journal* 12 (October 1925): 8; César Saerchinger, ed., *International Who's Who in Music* (Current Literature, 1918).

HAYES, Samuel Perkins, Sr. b. December 17, 1874, Baldwinsville, New York, to M. D. L. and Mary Ellen (Perkins) Hayes. Married July 23, 1903, to Agnes Hayes Stone. Children: five. d. May 7, 1958, Princeton, New Jersey.

Samuel Perkins Hayes applied his extensive understanding of the psychology of blindness to advances in education of the blind. He brought to the subject a wide variety of interests and experiences.

Hayes graduated from Amherst College with the A.B. degree in 1896. He enrolled several years later at Union Theological Seminary and Columbia University, earning both the B.D. at Union and the M.A. in sociology at Columbia in 1902. He began graduate study of psychology at Clark University (1902–3), continuing it at the Universities of Berlin (1903–4) and Paris (1904). He completed the Ph.D. at Cornell University in 1906.

Between baccalaureate and graduate studies, Hayes sold insurance. From Cornell he went to Mount Holyoke College as associate professor and director of the psychology laboratory. He retired from the college in 1940, only to take up a new appointment directing teacher training at the Perkins Institution and Massachusetts School for the Blind (1940–54). He held a concurrent appointment as lecturer in the Harvard Graduate School of Education. His second retirement came at the age of seventy-nine.

Until a fire in 1917 destroyed the psychology laboratory at Mount Holyoke College and with it Hayes' lecture and research notes from twenty years, blindness was but one of several areas in which he worked. He had focused initially on color blindness. In 1916 he began a consultation at the Pennsylvania Institute for the Instruction of the Blind, where he adapted achievement and intelligence tests for use with blind pupils. In 1919 he became a consultant to the Perkins Institution and in 1925 to the American Federation for the Blind.

Hayes was author of *Contributions to the Psychology of Blindness* (1941) and numerous pamphlets published by the state schools for the blind in Pennsylvania and Massachusetts. He contributed many articles to encyclopedias, journals, and books. He chaired the National Committee on Psychological Research for the Blind beginning in 1949.

REFERENCES: CB (1954, 1958); LE (1948); NYT, May 9, 1958, p. 23; PR; WWW (3); *American Men of Science* (1949).

HAYNES, Rowland. b. July 30, 1878, Worcester, Massachusetts, to Charles Thaddeus and Sybel (Wallace) Haynes. Married July 3, 1906, to Wilhelmena Rigby Gill. Children: three. d. October 18, 1963, Omaha, Nebraska.

Rowland Haynes was an early advocate for recreation education. He graduated from Williams College with the A.B. degree (1902) and Clark University with the A.M. degree (1905). He studied at Union Theological Seminary and Columbia University (1902–4 and 1905–7).

Haynes taught at the University of Chicago (1906–7) and University of Minnesota (1907–11). He served as field secretary of the Playground and Recreation Association of America (1911–15) and made a pioneer survey of the Milwaukee, Wisconsin, city recreation program (1912). He was secretary for recreation of the Board of Estimate and Apportionment of New York City (1916–17) and director of the New York City War Camp Community Service (1917–20).

In Cleveland, Ohio, Haynes served as director of the recreation council (1920–22) and the Cleveland Welfare Federation (1922–27). Haynes was secretary of the University of Chicago (1927–31), regional adviser to the President's Organization for Unemployment Relief (1931–39), and field representative for the Emergency Relief Division of the Reconstruction Finance Corporation (1932–33) and for the Federal Emergency Relief Administration (1933). He served as state administrator of federal relief for the state of Nebraska (1933–35).

In 1935 Haynes became president of the University of Omaha (later, University of Nebraska at Omaha), where he served until his retirement in 1948. Haynes was the author of *A Community Recreation Program* (1920) and *Public Provision for Recreation* (with Stanley P. Davies, 1920).

REFERENCES: NCAB (50: 631): WWW (4).

H'DOUBLER, Margaret Newell. b. April 26, 1889, Beloit, Kansas. Married 1934 to Wayne Claxton. Children: no. d. March 26, 1982, Springfield, Missouri.

Margaret H'Doubler founded modern dance as a subject in college programs. She broke with former techniques, which had been based on classical ballet movements to develop fundamentals of dance. H'Doubler based her techniques on a scientific understanding of dance movements, applying knowledge of anatomy, physiology, and physics to understand how the body works.

H'Doubler attended school in Warren, Illinois. She received the B.A. degree with a major in biology (1910) and the M.A. (1924) from the University of Wisconsin. While an undergraduate she participated in sports. She held an assistantship and taught physical education at Wisconsin after graduation. At Teachers College of Columbia University (1916–17) she was asked to find a new form of dance instruction. She returned to Wisconsin in 1917 and in 1919 organized a performing group, named Orchesis, which was the prototype of other dance organizations. H'Doubler developed the first course in dance at an American college. Beginning in 1927 the program in dance in the School of Education led to a degree; until 1931 Wisconsin was the only university to offer this degree. Dance majors also studied art, history, and music. Graduates of the program were in demand. Eventually, the program led to master's and doctoral programs. H'Doubler retired in 1954.

H'Doubler gave demonstrations abroad and was a guest teacher and lecturer. In 1953 she was honored by the Wisconsin Association for Health, Physical Education and Recreation. In 1963 she received the Heritage Honor of the National Association of Dance of the American Association for Health, Physical Education and Recreation (AAHPER) and in 1971 the Luther Halsey Gulick Award from AAHPER. She authored the dance section of the *Encyclopedia of the Arts*, as well as *A Manual of Dance* (1921), *Dance and Its Place in Education* (1925), *Rhythmic Form and Analysis* (1932), *Dance: A Creative Art Experience* (1940), and *Movement and Its Rhythmic Structure* (1946).

REFERENCES: Judith Anne Gray, "To Want to Dance: A Biography of Margaret H'Doubler" (Ph.D. diss., University of Arizona, 1978); *Journal of Health–Physical Ed-*

ucation–Recreation 42 (May 1971): 42; Mabel Lee (BDAE), *A History of Physical Education and Sports in the U.S.A.* (John Wiley and Sons, 1983); *Dance Magazine* 40 (April 1966): 33+, and 56 (August 1982): 87; Robert Lindsay, "Margaret H'Doubler: Initiator of Orchesis and of the College Major in Dance," *Dance Magazine* 321 (April 1957): 36–39; Mildred C. Spiesman, "Dance Education Pioneers," *Journal of Health–Physical Education–Recreation* 31 (January 1960): 25–27.

HEALY, Timothy Stafford. b. April 25, 1923, New York City, to Reginald Stafford and Margaret Dean (Vaeth) Healy. Married: no. d. December 30, 1992, Newark, New Jersey.

From positions of educational leadership, Timothy Healy was a vigorous advocate for educational opportunity for the poor and a builder of institutions. Healy was a Jesuit priest who challenged assumptions in and out of the Roman Catholic Church on the relationship between ecclesiastical authority and academic freedom.

Healy entered the Society of Jesus in 1940 and was ordained a priest in 1953. He received the B.A. degree at Woodstock College in Maryland in 1946, the M.A. at Fordham University in 1953, and the Ph.D. at Oxford University in 1965. He studied also in Belgium and Spain.

He taught English and Latin at Fordham University High School (1947–50) and English at Fordham University (1955–69). At Fordham he was executive vice president from 1965. In 1969 Healy went to the City University of New York as vice chancellor for academic affairs. In his seven years in that role its minority student enrollment rose from 5 percent to 30 percent. Healy tried unsuccessfully to found a liberal arts college in the New York slums. He was the forty-sixth president of Georgetown University (1976–89) and president of the New York Public Library from 1989 until his death. At both institutions, Healy strove to ensure that diverse points of view could be heard.

He was chairman of the American Council on Education (1983–84) and served on many public boards and commissions. He wrote *John Donne: Ignatius His Conclave* (1969) and coedited *John Donne: Selected Prose* (1967).

REFERENCES: CA (NR-46, 140); CB (1993); CHE, November 22, 1989, p. A3; LE (1974); NYT, January 1, 1993, p. 21, March 27, 1977, p. 32, and March 24, 1989, p. B1; WW (1990–91); *Library Journal* 118 (February 1, 1993): 15; NYT *Magazine*, September 23, 1990, p. 46; *Newsmakers* (Gale Research, 1990); *Time* 116 (May 28, 1990): 54–56.

HEFFERNAN, Helen. b. January 25, 1896, Lawrence, Massachusetts, to Michael John and Margaret Ann (Collins) Heffernan. Married: no. d. August 26, 1987, Sacramento, California.

Helen Heffernan spent almost forty years with the California State Department of Education (1926–65), where she developed educational programs. She was a strong proponent of progressive education. In addition to an interest in rural education she was a supporter of kindergarten education.

Heffernan graduated from high school in Goldfield, Nevada, in 1912 and from the Nevada Normal School in 1915. She received B.A. (1923) and M.A. (1925) degrees from the University of California at Berkeley. From 1915 to 1922 she taught in schools in Nevada, Utah, and Idaho. She was supervisor of rural schools in Kings County, California (1923–26). In 1926 she became chief of the Bureau of Elementary Education for California. Under her guidance rural demonstration schools were established as well as schools for migrant farmworkers' children. She worked to establish kindergartens, child care centers during World War II, and Head Start programs later.

Because of her belief in the importance of the role of supervisors, Heffernan began summer classes for them, first at the University of California at Berkeley, then for many years at the University of California at Los Angeles. She helped to develop the California School Supervisors Association and the California Rural School Supervisors Association and was president of the Rural Supervisors Section of the National Education Association.

In 1942 Heffernan served as a field representative of the Inter-American Education Project of the U.S. Office of Education. Following World War II she was elementary schools officer in Tokyo, Japan, on the staff of General Douglas MacArthur. She also worked for six months in Africa with an Agency for International Development program.

Heffernan founded the *California Journal of Elementary Education* in 1931 and edited it until 1963. With Vivian Edmiston Todd she wrote *The Kindergarten Teacher* (1960), *The Years before School: Guiding Preschool Children* (1964), and *Elementary Teacher's Guide to Working with Parents* (1969). She coauthored *Curriculum and the Elementary School Plant* (1958) with Charles Bursch. She was editor of *Guiding the Young Child* (1951) and with others edited the *Golden Road to Reading* series.

Heffernan became a target of conservatives in the 1960s. After the election of Max Rafferty (q.v.) as California commissioner of education her influence declined, and she retired in 1965.

REFERENCES: WEUS; WWAW (1972–73); Paul E. Blackwood, ''Helen Heffernan, 1896–1987,'' *Childhood Education* 65 (Winter 1988): 101–4; Ruth Wright Morpeth, ''Dynamic Leadership: Helen Heffernan and Progressive Education in California'' (Ph.D. diss., University of California, Riverside, 1989).

HENDERSON, Edwin Bancroft. b. November 24, 1883, Washington, D.C. Married to Mary Ellen Henderson. Children: two. d. February 3, 1977, Tuskegee, Alabama.

Edwin Bancroft Henderson introduced regular programs of physical education, including intramural and interscholastic sports, to public schools for African Americans in an era when resources available for those schools and their students had been very limited. Henderson founded the Negro Public School Athletic League in 1910. When he wrote *The Negro in Sports* (1939), major professional sports careers still were closed to African Americans, and the subject was little studied.

Henderson graduated with a diploma from the Washington Normal School (later, University of the District of Columbia) and earned A.B. and A.M. degrees at Howard University. He began teaching at M Street (later, Dunbar) High School in the District of Columbia in 1904. The next year he organized African-American sporting officials in the mid-Atlantic region, and in 1906 he participated in the launching of a school sports association. In 1925 he became director of physical training for District of Columbia high schools. From 1951 until his retirement in 1954, he was director of physical education and safety and athletics for all schools in the district.

Henderson was a leader of the National Association for the Advancement of Colored People (NAACP) in the Washington, D.C., area. For his educational work, in 1954 he received the National Honor Fellowship of the American Association for Health, Physical Education, and Recreation.

REFERENCES: CA (116); WP, February 5, 1977, p. B6; WWBA (1975); Frank P. Bolden, ''In Memoriam: Edwin Bancroft Henderson,'' *Journal of Physical Education and Recreation* 48 (May 1977): 6–7; Leon N. Coursey, ''The Life of Edwin Bancroft Henderson and His Professional Contributions to Physical Education'' (Ph.D. diss., Ohio State University, 1971).

HENNE, Frances Elizabeth. b. October 11, 1906, Springfield, Illinois, to J. Z. and Laura (Taylor) Henne. Married: no. d. December 21, 1985, Greenfield, Massachusetts.

Frances Henne had a leadership role in the development of school libraries and in preparing standards for them. She was a teacher and course designer of children's and young adult services in school and public libraries.

Henne received A.B. (1929) and M.A. (1934) degrees from the University of Illinois. From 1930 to 1934 she was at the Lincoln Public Library in Springfield, Illinois. She earned the B.S.L.S. degree from Columbia University in 1935 and worked at the New York Public Library while a student. Henne was a reference and circulation librarian at the New York State College for Teachers in Albany (later, State University of New York at Albany) from 1935 to 1938. She had a Carnegie Fellowship at the University of Chicago Graduate Library School (1938–39).

Louis Round Wilson (BDAE) invited her to become a librarian at the University High School at the University of Chicago, and she also served part-time at the Chicago Library School. Henne was the first woman on the faculty of the Graduate Library School. She was also associate dean and dean of students (1947–50) and acting dean (1951–52). She received the Ph.D. degree in 1949 from the University of Chicago. Henne helped to establish the Center for Children's Books and its *Bulletin*.

Henne went to Columbia University in 1954 as visiting associate professor, becoming a regular faculty member in 1955. She was a professor from 1961 until her 1975 retirement and then served as a lecturer for two years. Henne established annual Book Discussion Days. She was a lecturer on children's services throughout the United States and Canada.

Henne was on the committee that prepared standards for school libraries in 1945 and had a major role in preparation of *School Libraries for Today and Tomorrow, Functions and Standards*. She was cochair of the National Standards Revision Committee (1954–60), which wrote *Standards for School Library Programs*, regarded as a landmark for school library development in the United States. She also chaired the 1965–69 Standards Revision Committee.

Henne was a member of the Knapp School Library Development Project Advisory Board and the New York Regents Advisory Council on Libraries (1964–74). She was on the Board of Directors of the Association for Library Service to Children and Library Educators Development and was adviser for the Educational Media Selection Centers Project (1968–73). She was a consultant to the U.S. Office of Education and the New York State Education Department.

Henne wrote articles for professional journals, coauthored *A Planning Guide for the High School Library Program* (1951), and edited *Youth, Communication and Libraries* (with others, 1949). She received the American Library Association (ALA) Lippincott Award (1963), an honorary award from the American Association of School Librarians (AASL) (1968), ALA Centennial Citation (1976), and AASL/Baker and Taylor's President's Award (1979). *Frontiers of Library Service for Youth* (1979) was a festschrift in her honor.

REFERENCES: CA (118); FWC; NYT, December 25, 1985, p. 20; WWW (9); WWAW (1975–76); *The ALA Yearbook* (American Library Association, 1977); *School Library Journal* 32 (February 1986): 12–13; Wayne A. Wiegand, ed., *Supplement to the Dictionary of American Library Biography* (Libraries Unlimited, 1990).

HERRNSTEIN, Richard Julius. b. May 20, 1930, New York City, to Rezso and Flora Irene (Friedman) Herrnstein. Married May 28, 1951, to Barbara Brodo; November 11, 1961, to Susan Chalk Gouinlock. Children: three. d. September 13, 1994, Belmont, Massachusetts.

Richard Herrnstein's theory on the inheritability of intelligence and its consequence, "hereditary meritocracy," found its most controversial expression in *The Bell Curve: Intelligence and Class Structure in America* (with Charles Murray, 1994), which appeared soon after Herrnstein's death. Reactions to the book appeared in the opinion columns of newspapers and newsmagazines nationwide. Herrnstein's research on the subject of intelligence was controversial because of its implications for national social and educational policies, particularly as it suggested that compensatory educational programs could not succeed. Although Herrnstein did not discuss racial differences directly, his research was widely assumed to involve the assertion that African Americans were less intelligent than European Americans.

A child of Jewish Hungarian immigrants, Herrnstein graduated from the High School of Music and Art in Manhattan, New York. He earned the B.A. degree at the City College of New York in 1952 and the Ph.D. at Harvard University in 1955. He fulfilled military service as a research psychologist at the Walter Reed Army Medical Center in Washington, D.C. (1956–58) and lectured concurrently at the University of Maryland (1957–58). He taught at Harvard University from 1958 until his death.

Herrnstein was also author of *I.Q. in the Meritocracy* (1973) and *Crime and Human Nature* (with James Q. Wilson, 1985). From 1975 to 1981 he was editor of *Psychological Bulletin*. He was a Guggenheim fellow during 1977–78 and a Sloan Foundation Fellow during 1982–83.

REFERENCES: CA (107); CHE, October 26, 1994, p.12; NYT, September 16, 1994, p. B8; WW (1994); Constance Holden, ''R. J. Herrnstein: The Perils of Expounding Meritocracy,'' *Science* 181 (July 6, 1973): 36–39.

HERSKOVITS, Melville Jean. b. September 10, 1895, Bellefontaine, Ohio, to Herman and Henrietta (Hart) Herskovits. Married July 12, 1924, to Frances S. Shapiro. Children: one. d. February 25, 1963, Evanston, Illinois.

Melville Herskovits established the first American university program in African studies. It grew out of his anthropological studies of African-American families, which he extended steadily with investigations of African populations in the Caribbean, South America, and Africa.

Herskovits studied briefly at Hebrew Union College, the University of Cincinnati, and the University of Poitiers and served in the U.S. Army before earning the Ph.B. degree at the University of Chicago (1920). He studied under Franz Boas (BDAE) at Columbia University, where he received M.A. (1921) and Ph.D. (1923) degrees. With a three-year fellowship from the National Academy of Sciences, he remained at Columbia as a lecturer and conducted anthropometric research on African Americans.

In 1927 Herskovits joined the Anthropology Department of Northwestern University, where he would remain all of his career. During the next two decades he completed *The American Negro: A Study in Racial Crossing* (1928), *Anthropometry of the American Negro* (1930), *Acculturation* (1938), *The Economic Life of Primitive Peoples* (1940), and *The Myth of the Negro Past* (1941), as well as six anthropological studies on Caribbean, South American, and West African themes, most of them coauthored with Frances S. Herskovits, his wife. He undertook assignments with the U.S. Departments of Agriculture and State and with the Board of Economic Warfare during the war years of 1939–45.

From the late 1940s there was a strong African emphasis in Melville Herskovits' work. He directed the Program of African Studies at Northwestern University beginning in 1951. He was professor of African studies at Northwestern from 1960 until his death. In the second half of his career, his books included *Man and His Works* (1948), *Economic Anthropology* (1952), *Franz Boas* (1953), *Cultural Anthropology* (1955), and *The Human Factor in Changing Africa* (1962), as well as three posthumous volumes. He also edited the journal *American Anthropologist* (1949–52).

Herskovits was a Guggenheim fellow in 1937–38. He chaired the American

Council of Learned Societies Committee on Negro Studies (1939–50), was vice president of the American Academy of Arts and Sciences (1934), president of the American Folklore Society (1945), and president of the African Studies Association (1957–58), among many service roles. He was decorated by the governments of Haiti and the Netherlands.

REFERENCES: CB (1948); EAB; ECP; NYT, February 27, 1963, p. 16; PR; WWW (4); *American Anthropologist* 29 (April 1964): 278; Joseph H. Greenburg, ''Melville Jean Herskovits,'' *National Academy of Sciences Biographical Memoirs*, vol. 42 (National Academy of Sciences, 1971), pp. 77–93.

HESBURGH, Theodore Martin. b. May 25, 1917, Syracuse, New York, to Theodore Bernard and Anne Marie (Murphy) Hesburgh. Married: no.

Theodore Hesburgh was among the longest serving, best-known, most influential, and most popular university presidents in the twentieth century.

He began baccalaureate study at the University of Notre Dame (1934–37) before completing the Ph.B. degree at the Gregorian University in Vatican City (1939). He earned the S.T.D. degree at the Catholic University of America (1945). Hesburgh joined the Congregation of the Holy Cross in 1934 and was ordained a priest in the Roman Catholic Church in 1943, upon completion of three years of study at Holy Cross College in the District of Columbia.

He served as chaplain of the National Training School for Boys in Washington, D.C. (1943–44). Although he volunteered for foreign mission work, his order sent him to the University of Notre Dame, where he was chaplain to returned war veterans (1945–47) and taught religion (1945–48). He became department chair in 1948 and executive vice president of the university in 1949. He was president for thirty-five years, from 1952 until his retirement in 1987. Thereafter he held the title of president emeritus. During his presidency the university became known for its academic quality as well as its athletics, transferred governance from the Congregation of the Holy Cross to a lay board, and admitted women as students beginning in 1972.

Hesburgh sat on the U.S. Civil Rights Commission for fifteen years (1957–72), chairing it during the last three years. He served on many boards, including the National Science Foundation, Rockefeller Foundation, Carnegie Foundation for the Advancement of Teaching, Woodrow Wilson National Fellowship Foundation, Institute of International Education, United Negro College Fund, and American Council on Education. He chaired the Select Commission on Immigration and Refugee Policy (1978–81). He was awarded the Presidential Medal of Freedom in 1964 and received many other honors.

He was the author of *The Theology of Catholic Action* (1945), *God and the World of Man* (1950), *Patterns for Educational Growth* (1958), *Thoughts for Our Times* (1962) and four sequels, *The Humane Imperative: A Challenge for the Year 2000* (1974), *The Hesburgh Papers: Higher Values in Higher Education* (1979), and *God, Country, Notre Dame* (with Jerry Reedy, 1990), among other works.

REFERENCES: CA (13–16R); CB (1982); CHE, May 13, 1987, p. 3; LE (1974); NCAB (I: 256); NYT, October 10, 1967, p. 35, and May 23, 1977, p. 13; WW (1996); *Time* 129 (May 18, 1987): 168+, and 79 (February 9, 1962): 48+ (cover story); Charlotte A. Ames, comp., *Theodore M. Hesburgh: A Bio-Bibliography* (Greenwood Press, 1989).

HESS, Robert Lee. b. December 18, 1932, Asbury Park, New Jersey, to Henry and Ada (Davis) Hess. Married April 9, 1960, to Frances H. Aaron. Children: four. d. January 12, 1992, New York City.

Robert Hess led the revitalization of Brooklyn College of the City University of New York, instituting an acclaimed general education program and easing racial and ethnic conflict. The college under Hess' leadership became a model of effective higher education in a metropolitan setting.

Hess earned B.A. (1954), M.A. (1955), and Ph.D. (1960) degrees at Yale University. A scholar of African history, he taught at Carnegie Institute of Technology (1958–61, later, Carnegie–Mellon University), Mount Holyoke College (1961–62, 1963–64), Boston University (1962–63), and Northwestern University (1964–65), before joining the faculty of the University of Illinois at Chicago (1966–79), where he was also associate dean of liberal arts and sciences (1970–72) and associate vice chancellor for academic affairs (1972–79). He was president of Brooklyn College from 1979 until his death in 1992. By the late 1980s the general education program at Brooklyn College was considered the best nationally at a public institution.

Among Hess' scholarly books were *Italian Colonialism in Somalia* (1966), *Ethiopia: The Modernization of Autocracy* (1970), *Semper ex Africa: Bibliography of Primary Sources for 19th Century Tropical Africa* (coauthored, 1972), and the *Dictionary of African Biography: Ethiopia* (1977), which he edited.

He was a Fulbright scholar (1956–58) in Italy and a Guggenheim fellow (1968–69). He served as chair of the Board of Directors of the Museum of the Borough of Brooklyn (1986–92) and participated in a study on coherence in the baccalaureate degree by the Association of American Colleges, (later, and Universities), among many civic and professional contributions.

REFERENCES: CA (29–32R, 136); NYT, January 13, 1992, p. B11; WD (1994–96); WWW (10); *Who's Who in American Jewry* (Standard Who's Who, 1980).

HIGHET, Gilbert Arthur. b. June 22, 1906, Glasgow, Scotland, to Gilbert and Elizabeth Gertrude (Boyle) Highet. Married September 22, 1932, to Helen Clark MacInnes. Children: one. d. January 20, 1978, New York City.

In *The Art of Teaching* (1950), the classicist Gilbert Highet took a humanist swipe at the scientific conceits of educators. Highet argued that teaching involves emotions and values, two aspects of being human ''quite outside the grasp of science.'' At Columbia University and on his weekly radio program, *People, Places and Books* (1952–59), Highet practiced his preaching about the essential elements of a good teacher: strong memory, determined will, and large capacity for kindness.

Highet received the M.A. degree from the University of Glasgow in 1929 and the B.A. from Balliol College of Oxford University in 1932. He was a fellow of St. John's College, Oxford (1932–38), and editor of the *New Oxford Outlook*. He received the M.A. degree at Oxford (1936). Nicholas Murray Butler (BDAE) invited Highet to Columbia University in 1937. Except during the war years, when he served in the British army (1941–46), Highet was at Columbia until his 1972 retirement. From 1950 he was Anthon Professor of Latin Language and Literature, and he chaired the Greek and Latin Department from 1965 to 1972. He became a U.S. citizen in 1951.

Among Highet's books were *Beginning Latin* (1938), a school textbook; *The Classical Tradition* (1949); *Juvenal the Satirist* (1954); *The Anatomy of Satire* (1962), which won an award of merit from the American Philological Association; and *The Immortal Profession: The Joy of Teaching* (1976). He was a translator of books, editorial board member of *Horizon* magazine, and judge for the Book-of-the-Month Club.

REFERENCES: CB (1964, 1978); CA (NR-6, 73–76); DAB (supp. 10); NCAB (61: 191); NYT, June 30, 1972, and January 21, 1978, p. 24; WWW (7).

HILDRETH, Gertrude Howell. b. October 11, 1898, Terre Haute, Indiana, to Frederick Foster and Fannie (Smith) Hildreth. Married: no. d. March 6, 1984, Bethesda, Maryland.

Gertrude Hildreth coauthored the Metropolitan Achievement and Reading Readiness Tests (1933–68). She wrote extensively on early learning and the education of gifted children.

Hildreth received the A.B. degree from North Central College (1920) and the M.A. from the University of Illinois (1921). From 1921 to 1923 she was a psychologist in Oklahoma schools. In 1925 Hildreth received the Ph.D. from Columbia University. She served as staff psychologist at Columbia's Lincoln School and taught at Columbia from 1925 to 1945. At Brooklyn College of the City University of New York, she was professor of education until her 1965 retirement. She taught for four years at American University in Beirut, Lebanon, and one year (1969–70) at Voorhees College.

Hildreth was a fellow of the American Psychological Association and was active in founding the American Association of Applied Psychology. She was a Fulbright lecturer at the University of Istanbul, Turkey (1959–60). Among her books were *Psychological Service for School Problems* (1930), *Learning the Three R's* (1936), *Helping Children to Read* (with Josephine L. Wright, 1940), *The Child Mind in Evolution: A Study of Developmental Sequences in Drawing* (1941), *Child Growth through Education: Effective Teaching in the Modern School* (1948), *Readiness for School Beginners* (1950), *Teaching Spelling: A Guide to Basic Principles and Practices* (1955), *Teaching Reading* (1958), and *Introduction to the Gifted* (1966). With others she wrote the fourteen-volume *Easy Growth in Reading* (1940–45).

REFERENCES: CA (112); NYT, March 9, 1984, p. D15; PR; WWAW (1964); WP, March 10, 1984, p. B4.

HILL, Martha. b. December 1900, East Palestine, Ohio, to Grant and Grace (Todd) Hill. Married October 3, 1952, to Thurston J. Davies. Children: no. d. November 19, 1995, Brooklyn, New York.

Martha Hill was a pioneer of dance education in the United States. She was a founder of the Bennington School of the Dance, Connecticut College School of the Dance, and Juilliard School of Music Dance Department. She also established the graduate program in dance at New York University.

Hill was a graduate of the Kellogg School of Physical Education in Battle Creek, Michigan. She was director of dance there (1920–23), director of physical education at Kansas State Teachers College (later, Fort Hays State University, 1923–26), and dance instructor at the University of Oregon (1927–29) and Lincoln School of Teachers College, Columbia University (1929–30). Her dance instructors included Martha Graham and Margaret H'Doubler (q.v.), and she performed with the Graham troupe (1929–31). She received the B.S. degree from Columbia University in 1929.

Hill was brought to New York University (NYU) in 1930 by Jay B. Nash (BDAE); she directed the NYU dance program from 1931 to 1951. The Bennington School of the Dance was founded by Hill, Mary Shelly (q.v.), and Robert Leigh (BDAE), first president of Bennington College. Hill taught part-time at Bennington, while continuing her work at NYU. With Shelly she sought to make dance a central part of American theater. She received the M.A. degree from NYU in 1941.

Hill founded the Connecticut College School of the Dance in 1948 and served as codirector. With support from Ernest Melby (BDAE), dean of the NYU School of Education, she initiated a summer school of modern dance. Rosemary Park (q.v.), president of Connecticut College for Women, agreed to collaborate with NYU in establishing the American Dance Festival.

In 1951 Hill became founding director of the Dance Department at the Juilliard School of Music; she retired in 1985. She was a visiting instructor at a number of colleges and consultant to the U.S. Office of Education. She was on the editorial board of *Dance Observer*. She received the American Dance Guild Award (1974).

REFERENCES: NYT, November 21, 1995, p. B9; WW (1978–79); WWAW (1972–73); Thomas P. Brockway, *Bennington College in the Beginning* (Bennington College Press, 1981); Barbara Naomi Cohen-Stratyner, *Biographical Dictionary of Dance* (Schirmer Books, 1982); *Dance Magazine* 59 (April 1985): 120, and 70 (February 1996): 116–17; Sali Ann Kriegsman, *Modern Dance in America—the Bennington Years* (G. K. Hall, 1981); *Notable Names in the American Theatre* (James T. White, 1976); Walter Rigdon, ed., *The Biographical Encyclopaedia and Who's Who of the American Theatre* (J. H. Heineman, 1966).

HILL, Mozell Clarence. b. March 27, 1911, Anniston, Alabama, to Humphrey and Anna (Taylor) Hill. Married May 5, 1935, to Marnesba Davis. Children: four. d. March 26, 1969, New York City.

After attending public schools in Kansas City, Kansas, Mozell Hill earned A.B. (1933) and M.A. (1937) degrees at the University of Kansas. The University of Chicago awarded him the Ph.D. degree in 1946. He undertook postgraduate study at the London School of Economics during 1952–53.

Hill's subject was sociology. Initially, he studied African-American communities. Later, he focused on the sociology of education. He was an early participant in school desegregation studies, working with Harry Ashmore under sponsorship of the Ford Foundation's Fund for the Advancement of Education (1953–55) and with the Unitarian Service Committee (1955–56). During the decade of the 1960s he was a consultant on desegregation and delinquency in Connecticut, New York, and Missouri.

After college graduation he worked with the Indiana Governor's Commission on Unemployment and U.S. Resettlement Administration. At Langston University he was a member of the faculty (1937–46) and director of research (1940–42). In 1946 he went to Atlanta (later, Clark–Atlanta) University to teach. He served as chairman of the Department of Sociology and editor of the university's review, *Phylon* (1948–58). Hill was the first African-American professor at Teachers College of Columbia University (1958–62), where he taught sociology of education. He was professor of educational sociology at New York University from 1963 until his death six years later.

Hill was a U.S. Agency for International Development adviser at the University of Nigeria in Nsukka (1960–62). He was author of *Culture of a Contemporary Negro Community* (1943).

REFERENCES: DANB; NYT, March 28, 1969, p. 50; WWW (5).

HINTON, Carmelita Chase. b. April 1890, Omaha, Nebraska, to Clement and Lula Bell (Edwards) Chase. Married April 1916 to Sebastian Hinton. Children: three. d. January 16, 1983, Concord, Massachusetts.

Carmelita Hinton founded and directed the Putney School, an influential coeducational boarding school in Vermont. It was a progressive institution intended to be a utopian community where individuals concerned themselves with creativity rather than competition. Hinton believed school should be exciting.

Hinton attended public schools in Omaha. She graduated from Bryn Mawr College in 1912 and worked one year for her father. Then she worked in Chicago with Jane Addams at Hull House, where she became interested in the Gary Plan for schools. After marriage and the birth of three children, Hinton opened a nursery school in her home in Winnetka, Illinois. When her husband died in 1923, she taught at the North Shore Country Day School in Winnetka. She soon moved to Massachusetts, where she taught at the Shady Hill School in Cambridge (1925–35). When her children were of the age to attend public high school, she opened her own secondary school.

Hinton purchased a farm in 1934 and held a summer labor camp on the site in 1935. Putney School opened on September 9, 1935, with 54 students in grades eight through twelve and nine full-time teachers. By the early 1940s there were 150 students. The seventh and eighth grades were later dropped. Students participated in the work program, with jobs on the farm and in the kitchen, forest, garden, and other sites.

Because salaries were poor, a Putney Teachers Union was organized with Congress of Industrial Organizations (CIO) affiliation. The union went on strike. Millicent McIntosh (q.v.), parent of a student, mediated the controversy. Many teachers left, and in 1949 the school year began with twenty new teachers.

The school remained strong with a Board of Trustees organized, to which Hilton gave up her corporate stock in the institution. In 1951 the school purchased a nearby estate where the Putney Graduate School for teacher training was organized, offering a master's degree. After fourteen years Antioch College's teacher education division absorbed the graduate school.

During the McCarthy era the school came under attack because two of Hinton's children were working in China. Hinton retired in 1954. Later, she worked in Philadelphia for the Women's International League for Peace and Freedom.

REFERENCES: NYT, January 23, 1983, p. 28; Christopher Fairbairn Armstrong, ''Privilege and Productivity: The Cases of Two Private Schools and Their Graduates'' (Ph.D., diss., University of Pennsylvania, 1974); Susan McIntosh Lloyd, *The Putney School: A Progressive Experiment* (Yale University Press, 1987); Mary Margaret Stroh, *Eyes to See* (Delta Kappa Gamma Society, 1947); *Time* 64 (November 15, 1954): 52.

HIRSCH, Eric Donald, Jr. b. March 22, 1928, Memphis, Tennessee, to Eric Donald and Leah (Aschaffenburg) Hirsch. Married 1958 to Mary Pope. Children: three.

E. D. Hirsch was founder and president (from 1987) of the Cultural Literacy Foundation, which aimed to improve literacy and influence the school curriculum.

Hirsch received the B.A. degree (1950) from Cornell University. He served in the U.S. Navy from 1950 to 1952. He earned M.A. (1953) and Ph.D. (1957) degrees from Yale University, where he served on the faculty from 1956 to 1966. In 1966 he went to the University of Virginia, where in 1973 he was named William R. Kenan Professor of English. He was chair of the English Department (1968–71 and 1981–82) and director of composition from 1971. From 1989 to 1994 he was Linden Kent Professor of English.

Hirsch's concern with cultural literacy led to publication of *Cultural Literacy: What Every American Needs to Know* in 1987. With Joseph Kett and James Trefil, Hirsch compiled a list of information deemed necessary for cultural literacy, published in 1988 as *The Dictionary of Cultural Literacy*. Hirsch's foundation wanted to have a core of knowledge taught in schools. He considered reading meaningless without the basic information provided in his list and urged that schools supply information while they taught reading.

Hirsch's scholarship was in literary criticism. He was a Fulbright Fellow (1955), Guggenheim fellow (1964–65), senior fellow of the National Endowment for the Humanities (1971–72 and 1980–81), and fellow at the Center for Advanced Study in the Behavioral Sciences at Stanford University (1980–81), and at the Australian National University Humanities Research Centre (1982). Among his books were *Wordsworth and Schelling: A Typological Study of Romanticism* (1960), *Innocence and Experience: An Introduction to Blake* (1964), *Validity in Interpretation* (1967), *The Aims of Interpretation* (1976), *The Philosophy of Composition* (1977), *The Schools We Need and Why We Don't Have Them* (1996), and *What Your Kindergartner Needs to Know* (1996).

REFERENCES: CA (NR-27); WD (1994–96); WW (1996); *Dictionary of Literary Biography*, vol. 67 (Gale Research, 1988); *Newsweek* 109 (April 20, 1987): 72–73; *Who's Who in American Jewry* (Standard Who's Who, 1980).

HOFSTADTER, Richard. b. August 6, 1916, Buffalo, New York, to Emil A. and Katherine (Hill) Hofstadter. Married October 3, 1936, to Felice Swados; January 13, 1947, to Beatrice Kevitt. Children: two. d. October 24, 1970, New York, New York.

Richard Hofstadter was a noted historian of intellectual and political life in the United States who took special interest in the history of higher education.

Hofstadter earned the B.A. degree at the University of Buffalo (1937, later, State University of New York at Buffalo) and, after a one-semester interlude in law school, M.A. (1938) and Ph.D. (1942) degrees at Columbia University. He taught at the University of Maryland (1942–46). In 1946 he joined the faculty at Columbia, where he remained until his death. He was the DeWitt Clinton Professor of American History there from 1959. Hofstadter was Pitt Professor of American History and Institutions at Cambridge (England) University (1958–59) and Visiting Senior Fellow of the Humanities Council, Princeton University (1962–63).

He was coauthor of *The Development and Scope of Higher Education* (1952), *The Development of Academic Freedom in the United States* (1955), and *American Higher Education: A Documentary History* (1961). All three were commissioned studies: the first by the Commission on Financing Higher Education, which the Association of American Universities organized; the second by the American Academic Freedom Project conducted at Columbia University; and the third by the Committee on the Role of Education in American History.

Other works for which Hofstadter was better known treated education within broad contexts. They included *Social Darwinism in American Thought* (1944), *The Age of Reform: From Bryan to F.D.R.* (1955), for which he won the Pulitzer Prize in American history, and *Anti-Intellectualism in American Life* (1963), for which he won the Pulitzer Prize in general nonfiction, and six other books.

REFERENCES: ASL; CB (1956, 1970); CA (NR-4, 29–32R); DAB (supp. 8); IESS; WWW (5); Susan Stout Baker, *Radical Beginnings: Richard Hofstadter and the 1930s* (Greenwood Press, 1985); Lawrence A. Cremin (q.v.), *Richard Hofstadter (1916–1970):*

A Biographical Memoir (National Academy of Education, 1972); Daniel Joseph Singal, "Beyond Consensus: Richard Hofstadter and American Historiography," *American Historical Review* 89 (October 1984): 976–1004.

HOLLAND, Annie Welthy Daughtry. b. c. 1871, Isle of Wight County, Virginia, to John Daughtry and Margaret Hill. Married 1888 to Willis Bird Holland. Children: one. d. January 6, 1934, Louisburg, North Carolina.

Annie Holland was a teacher and organizer of African Americans in North Carolina. She founded the North Carolina Colored Parent-Teacher Association.

Sources differ on the names of Holland's parents. Holland attended schools of Isle of Wight and Southampton counties, Virginia. During her teenaged years she studied for two years at Hampton Institute (later, University). She was a teacher in county elementary schools. In New York City she took a course in dressmaking and worked at that occupation.

Returning to Virginia, she married Willis B. Holland, a school principal. In the 1890s she served as his assistant in a Franklin, Virginia, school and then taught in rural schools. Discovering the extreme poverty of her students, Holland organized cooperatives to purchase items they needed. She passed the examination for a teaching certificate after taking a teacher training course at Virginia Normal and Industrial Institute in Petersburg (later, Virginia State University). In 1905 she succeeded her husband as principal in Franklin and helped to organize industrial classes. Holland went to Gates Institute in Sunbury, North Carolina, in 1911 to be the county rural school supervisor; in 1912 she went to Corapeake.

In 1915 Holland became the state home demonstration agent, a Jeanes Fund supervisor. The Jeanes Fund and the North Carolina Negro Teachers' Association paid her salary. She oversaw forty-five county supervisors and demonstrated such household arts as gardening and canning. Through Holland's efforts Jeanes supervisors later oversaw health workers in schools and cooperatives. In 1921 Holland's title became state supervisor of Negro elementary schools. She organized parent–teacher groups and in 1927 helped to found the North Carolina Congress of Parents and Teachers. At its first meeting in Raleigh in 1928, Holland was elected president. In 1934 Holland collapsed while speaking to a countywide meeting and died minutes later.

REFERENCES: BWA; NBAW; N. C. Newbold, *Five North Carolina Negro Educators* (University of North Carolina Press, 1939).

HOLLAND, (George) Kenneth. b. May 10, 1907, Los Angeles, to Charles Alfred and Cora Effie (Spring) Holland. Married June 11, 1936, to Mary Frances Kimball. Children: four. d. December 9, 1977, Bronxville, New York.

In the period after World War II, Kenneth Holland led the development of educational exchanges, particularly for students, between the United States and other countries. He built his work in international education on an extensive foundation of government service that focused on youth programs and international relations.

He earned the A.B. degree in 1929 at Occidental College, where he was student body president, and the M.A. at Princeton University in 1931. As an American Field Service fellow he studied in Grenoble and Paris, France (1931–32).

He was secretary of the International Student Service (1932–33) and educational adviser in New England for the Civilian Conservation Corps (1933–35). At the American Council on Education, Holland was associate director of its Youth Commission starting in 1935. He administered education programs in the Office of Inter-American Affairs from 1941 to 1945.

Holland was president of the Inter-American Foundation (1945–46). He was assistant director of the Office of International Information and Cultural Affairs in the U.S. Department of State (1946–48) and first U.S. permanent representative to UNESCO in Paris, France (1948–50). He served concurrently as first executive secretary of the Board of Foreign Scholarships from 1947 and director of the State Department's Office of Educational Exchange during 1948–49. In 1950 he began his long service as third president of the Institute of International Education, the position from which he retired in 1973. He was president of La Napould Art Federation (1973–77).

Holland was a U.S. delegate to UNESCO conferences in London, Mexico City, Beirut, and Florence (1945–50). He wrote *Youth in European Labor Camps* (1939) and *Youth in the CCC* (with Frank Ernest Hill, 1942). He was decorated by the governments of Brazil, Colombia, France, and Germany.

REFERENCES: CB (1952, 1978); NYT, December, 10, 1977, p. 28; WW (1974–75); *Library Quarterly* 28 (October 1958): 358.

HOLMES, Dwight Oliver Wendell. b. November 5, 1877, Lewisburg, West Virginia, to John Alexander and Sarah (Bollin) Holmes. Married June 24, 1907, to Lucy C. Messer; 1957 to Alverta Morsell Jones. Children: one. d. September 7, 1963, Baltimore.

Dwight O. W. Holmes was a teacher and college administrator who gained notice as the first African American on the Maryland State Board of Education. Both of his parents were former slaves. Although his father was a Methodist minister, Holmes attended a Catholic school in Annapolis, Maryland, because public schools would not admit African Americans. The family spent one year in New York City, then moved to Staunton, Virginia. No high school was provided for African Americans, so Holmes attended the preparatory school at Howard University in Washington, D.C. In 1901 he received the A.B. degree from Howard University as valedictorian. He taught English at Sumner High School in St. Louis, Missouri, in 1902, then was vice principal and head of the Science Department at Douglass High School in Baltimore, where he remained to 1917. He was president of the Baltimore Education Association from 1915 to 1917.

Holmes earned master's degrees at Howard University in 1912 and Columbia University in 1915. At Miner Normal School (later, part of the University of the District of Columbia) Holmes taught education and psychology (1917–19). In 1919 he went to Howard University as registrar and professor of education. He served as dean of the College of Education (1920–34) and dean of the newly established Graduate School (1934–37). He was president of the Association of Negro Colleges for three years and chair of their rating committee. In 1934 he received the Ph.D. degree from Columbia University. His thesis was published as *Evolution of the Negro College*.

Holmes went to Morgan College in Baltimore in 1937 to be the institution's first African-American president, remaining until his retirement in 1948 at the age of seventy. The college had been founded by Methodists to train young African Americans for the ministry. During Holmes' tenure the state of Maryland purchased the institution (1939), and it became Morgan State College (later, University).

In 1953 Governor Theodore R. McKeldin appointed Holmes, then seventy-three years old, as the first African American on the Maryland State Board of Education. He was reappointed in 1958. The board supervised public schools and five state teachers colleges, including those historically black. While Holmes was a member, the board adopted a resolution to abolish segregation in public schools and teachers colleges.

REFERENCES: DANB; WWW (5); Frederick H. Diamond, "The Educator—D.O.W. Holmes," *The Crisis* 60 (January 1953): 9–14; Betty Jean Jackson, "Dwight Oliver Wendell Holmes: A Pioneer in Negro Education" (M.A. thesis, Morgan State College, 1972); *Who's Who in Colored America* (Christian E. Burkel and Associates, 1950).

HOLT, John Caldwell. b. April 14, 1923, New York City, to Henry and Elizabeth (Crocker) Holt. Married: no. d. September 14, 1985, Boston.

During the 1960s John Holt rose to prominence as a major critic of the negative effects he believed schools had on children's learning.

Holt graduated from Yale University in 1943 with the B.S. degree in industrial engineering, then was a submarine officer during three years of service in the U.S. Navy. He was on the staff of World Federalists for six years (1946–52) and during the last year was executive director of the New York chapter. For the next year, he traveled in Europe.

On returning to the United States, Holt worked at the private Colorado Rocky Mountain School in Carbondale as a high school teacher and coach (1953–57). Later, he taught and developed curricula in the elementary grades at the Shady Hill (1957–59) and Lesley Ellis (1959) schools in Cambridge, Massachusetts, where his principal subjects were mathematics and reading. He returned to teaching briefly (1965–67) at the Commonwealth School in Boston, this time teaching English in high school grades.

From the early 1960s until his death, Holt was engaged principally as a writer and lecturer on educational issues. He was also briefly a visiting lecturer in education at Harvard University (1968) and the University of California at Berkeley (1969). His books included *How Children Fail* (1964), *How Children Learn* (1967), *The Underachieving School* (1969), *Freedom and Beyond* (1972), *Escape from Childhood* (1974), *Instead of Education: Ways to Help People Do Things Better* (1976), *Never Too Late: My Musical Life Story* (1978), and *Teach Your Own: A Hopeful Path for Education* (1981).

REFERENCES: CA (NR-32, 117); CB (1981, 1985); NYT, March 25, 1968, p. 54, and September 15, 1985, p. 44; David DeLeon, ed., *Leaders from the 1960s* (Greenwood Press, 1994); Susannah Sheffer, ed., *A Life Worth Living: Selected Letters of John Holt* (Ohio State University Press, 1990).

HOPPOCK, Robert. b. December 24, 1901, Lambertville, New Jersey, to David Wilson and Margaret (Dalrymple) Hoppock. Married 1923 to Margaret Emily Thornton. Children: one. d. August 5, 1995, Vista, California.

Robert Hoppock was an early leader in vocational guidance and the study of occupations. Hoppock graduated from Lambertville (New Jersey) High School. He attended Lafayette College (1919–21) and received the B.S. degree (1923) from Wesleyan University with a major in economics. He worked at many jobs before deciding he wanted to teach. His own indecision about occupations led him to his interest in vocational guidance.

Hoppock taught English at Lambertville High School (1924–26). From 1927 to 1930 he was a vocational counselor in Rahway, New Jersey, and from 1930 to 1932 a field secretary for the National Vocational Guidance Association. He was assistant director (1933–39) of the Carnegie Corporation's National Occupational Conference, which studied and forecast employment trends during the 1930s. At Columbia University he received the M.A. degree in educational psychology (1932) and the Ph.D. in educational research (1935). Hoppock helped to organize and chaired the guidance department at New York University, where he was professor of education from 1939 to 1972. In order to acquaint students with the work world, he took them on field trips to offices and factories.

Hoppock organized the New Jersey Vocational Guidance Association. He was president of the National Vocational Guidance Association (1950) and Academy of Teachers of Occupations (1960) and a fellow of the American Psychological Association. He was a consultant to the U.S. Department of Labor, U.S. Office of Education, and state education departments.

Hoppock edited *Occupational Abstracts* and *Occupational Index*. He wrote *Job Satisfaction* (1935), *Occupational Orientation of College Students* (with others, 1939), and *Group Guidance: Principles, Techniques, and Evaluation* (1947). In 1957 *Occupational Information* was named one of the outstanding educational books by the National Education Association, and in 1966 Hoppock received the annual award of the New York Personnel and Guidance Association.

REFERENCES: CA (1–4R); LE (1974); NYT, August 17, 1995, p. B13; WD (1994–96).

HORN, Ernest. b. July 17, 1882, Mercer County, Missouri, to Asa and Lillie Mariah (Canady) Horn. Married June 4, 1914, to Madeline Daggett Darrough. Children: two. d. November 9, 1967, Iowa City, Iowa.

Ernest Horn had already taught school for five years in the rural Missouri community where he grew up and served for one year as principal of University Elementary School at the University of Missouri before receiving B.A. (1907) and M.A. (1908) degrees there. In 1914 he earned the Ph.D. at Columbia University.

Horn taught at the Colorado State Normal School (later, University of Northern Colorado) in Greeley (1909–12) and was principal of the Speyer School (1913–15), an experimental institution conducted by Columbia University. From 1915 until his retirement, he was professor of education at the University of Iowa, where he established the University Elementary School.

In 1934 Horn was among four dissenters on the sixteen-member Social Studies Commission of the American Historical Association. Although he would not sign the commission's report, which forecast "in the United States and other countries . . . a new age of collectivism," three years later the association published Horn's comprehensive follow-up study, *Methods of Instruction in the Social Studies*. It became the standard work on the subject.

From his dissertation, a statistical study of pupil participation in class, through later publications that focused on spelling and reading, Horn's scholarship emphasized practicality. His five-step method for learning the spelling of individual words was widely used for many years.

Horn was president of the Association for Supervision and Curriculum Development (1932–33) and American Educational Research Association (1946). He was a laureate member of Kappa Delta Pi.

REFERENCES: LE (1948); NYT, May 13, 1934, p. B1; WWW (7); *Akron* (Ohio) *Beacon Journal*, September 26, 1993, p. D7; Leo J. Alilunas, "Finds Ernest Horn 'Surprisingly Relevant,' " *Social Education* 70 (November 1970): 819–20; Stephen Richard Kaufmann, "Choosing the Middle Way: Ernest Horn's Contribution to the Commission on the Social Studies in the Schools" (Ph.D. diss., University of Iowa, 1983); Harold Ordway Rugg, *Foundations for American Education* (World Book, 1947).

HORTON, Myles. b. July 5, 1905, Savannah, Tennessee, to Perry and Elsie (Falls) Horton. Married 1935 to Zilphia Mae Johnson; Aimee Isgrig. Children: two. d. January 19, 1990, New Market, Tennessee.

The Highlander Folk School, which Myles Horton founded in Monteagle, Tennessee, in 1932 was based on the Danish folk school idea. It emphasized literacy training, leadership development, and labor education. The school held residential workshops with no grades or degrees. Through its programs poor residents of the Tennessee mountain area were helped in finding solutions to their social problems.

Horton graduated from Cumberland College in 1928. He studied at Union Theological Seminary (1929–30), the University of Chicago (1930–31), and in

Denmark (1931–32). In its early years Highlander Folk School helped with labor organizing and held workshops on school integration. The school itself was integrated and in the early 1950s held interracial workshops for community leaders. Septima Clark (q.v.) directed its educational programs. A Citizenship School Project on the South Carolina Sea Islands (1957–61) taught blacks to read and write so they could vote.

Opponents termed the institute a ''communist training school.'' In 1960 state courts closed the school because of its integration policies. The state of Tennessee revoked its charter in 1961 and confiscated its property. Highlander Research and Education Center was opened in Knoxville, Tennessee, in 1961, and in 1971 the facility was moved to a site in New Market, Tennessee. With Judith and Herbert Kohl, Horton wrote *The Long Haul: An Autobiography* (1990), which received the Robert F. Kennedy Award in 1991.

REFERENCES: CA (140); NYT, January 20, 1990, p. 30; Frank Adams, with Myles Horton, *Unearthing Seeds of Fire: The Idea of Highlander* (J. F. Blair, 1975); Brenda Bell, John Gaventa, and John Peters, eds., *We Make the Road by Walking: Conversations on Education and Social Change* (Temple University Press, 1990); John M. Glen, *Highlander: No Ordinary School, 1932–1962* (University Press of Kentucky, 1988); Aimee Isgrig Horton, *The Highlander Folk School: A History of Its Major Programs, 1932–1961* (Carlson, 1989).

HORWICH, Frances Rappaport. b. July 16, 1908, Ottawa, Ohio, to Samuel and Rosa (Gratz) Rappaport. Married July 11, 1931, to Harvey L. Horwich. Children: no.

Frances Horwich gained fame as Miss Frances of *Ding Dong School*, a popular children's television program in the 1950s. She was an experienced nursery, kindergarten, and elementary teacher when asked by Judith Waller of the National Broadcasting Corporation to develop and conduct the program. It received excellent comments from children, parents, and television critics. Begun on a Chicago station, it soon became a network show, airing five mornings a week. Horwich demonstrated lessons to children and asked them to participate at home. The last minutes each day were for parents, with activities summarized and preparation offered for the next day's lesson. The program aired from 1952 to 1956 on the network, in Chicago from 1957 to 1959, and in syndication from 1959 to 1965. It received many awards, including a Peabody Award.

Horwich received the Ph.B. degree from the University of Chicago (1929) and taught first grade in Evanston, Illinois (1929–32). She served as supervisor of Works Progress Administration nursery schools in Chicago from 1932 to 1935 and earned the A.M. degree from Columbia University in 1933. From 1935 to 1938 she was director of junior kindergartens in Winnetka, Illinois. She was dean of education at Pestalozzi-Froebel Teachers College in Chicago (1938–40). Horwich earned the Ph.D. degree from Northwestern University in 1942, while counselor (1940–43) of student teachers at Chicago Teachers College (later, State University). She spent two years each directing the Hessian Hills

School at Croton-on-Hudson, New York, and teaching at the University of North Carolina. Previous to the television program she was professor of education and department chairman at Roosevelt College (later, University) in Chicago (1946–52).

Horwich presented many workshops and speeches. She served as secretary/treasurer, director, and president of the National Association for the Education of Young Children. She wrote many "Ding Dong School Books," *Nursery First, Then Kindergarten* (1947), *Have Fun with Your Children* (1954), *The Magic of Bringing Up Your Child* (1959), and *Stories and Poems to Enjoy* (1962). Beginning in 1965 Horwich served as an educational consultant to publishers. She also advised Chicago Head Start (1968–70).

REFERENCES: CA (P–1); CB (1953); FWC; LE (1948); LW; NYT, January 4, 1953, p. B11, and January 18, 1953, p. B13; WW (1976–77); WWAW (1972–73); *Life* 34 (March 16, 1953): 123; Robert Lewis Shayon, "Miss Frances from Chicago," *Saturday Review* 36 (April 18, 1953): 32; *Time* 60 (October 27, 1952): 67.

HOWE, Harold, II. b. August 17, 1918, Hartford, Connecticut, to Arthur and Margaret Marshall (Armstrong) Howe. Married September 4, 1940, to Priscilla Foster Lamb. Children: three.

As director of the Learning Institute of North Carolina (1964–65), Harold Howe II ran programs that effectively integrated black and white students and teachers at a time when racial segregation was the norm. Howe succeeded Francis Keppel (q.v.) as U.S. commissioner of education (1965–68). He incurred the wrath of southern politicians, many of whom opposed his aggressive guidelines for school desegregation. In *Thinking about Our Kids: An Agenda for American Education* (1993), Howe criticized the narrowness of the National Education Goals of 1989 and urged recognition of the family as a central educational institution.

Howe was a grandson of Samuel Chapman Armstrong (BDAE), the Union general who founded Hampton Institute (later, University). He graduated from the Taft School in Watertown, Connecticut. After receiving the B.A. degree from Yale University (1940) he taught at Darrow School in Lebanon, New York (1940–41), and then spent the World War II years in the navy (1941–45). He taught at Phillips Academy in Andover, Massachusetts, and earned the M.A. degree (1947) from Columbia University.

Howe served as principal of high schools in Andover, Massachusetts (1950–53); Cincinnati, Ohio (1953–57); and Newton, Massachusetts (1957–60). In Newton he developed a house system, each house within the school having separate faculty and advisers. From 1960 to 1964 he was superintendent of schools in Scarsdale, New York. After leaving government service in 1968 Howe was a Ford Foundation adviser in India and from 1971 to 1981 Ford Foundation vice president in charge of the education and research division. From 1982 he was a senior lecturer at the Harvard Graduate School of Education.

Howe was author of *Picking Up the Options* (1968). He was chair of the

National Council on Educational Research (from 1980) and chair of the board of the Institute of Educational Leadership (1982). New York University gave him a gold medal for public service (1968).

REFERENCES: CB (1967); CHE, January 16, 1985, p. 26; NYT, December 19, 1965, p. 1+, and July 20, 1970, p. 10; RPE; WW (1984–85); Nancy Hoffman and Robert Schwartz, ''Remembrance of Things Past: An Interview with Francis Keppel (q.v.) and Harold Howe II,'' *Change* 22 (March/April 1990): 52–57.

HUGGINS, Nathan Irvin. b. January 14, 1927, Chicago, to Winston John and Marie (Warsaw) Huggins. Married July 18, 1971, to Brenda Carlita Smith. Children: no. d. December 5, 1989, Cambridge, Massachusetts.

Through his publications and administrative endeavors, Nathan Huggins helped to establish African-American studies as a scholarly field. He was the founding president during 1966–69 of the Museum of Afro-American History in Boston.

Huggins served in the U.S. Army during 1945–46. He earned the A.B. degree at the University of California, Berkeley, in 1954 and the M.A. there in 1955. He received A.M. (1959) and Ph.D. (1962) degrees at Harvard University. He taught at California State College (later, University), Long Beach (1962–64); Lake Forest College (1964–66); and the University of Massachusetts, Boston (1966–70). He was professor of history at Columbia University (1970–80). At Harvard from 1980 until his death, he was W.E.B. Du Bois Professor of History and African-American Studies and director of the W.E.B. Du Bois Institute. He was often a visiting professor at universities in the United States and abroad, including Heidelberg University in 1979 and Leiden University in 1988.

Huggins was author of *Protestants against Poverty: Boston's Charities, 1870–1900* (1971), *Harlem Renaissance* (1971), *A World in Shadow: The Free Black in Antebellum South Carolina* (1973), *Black Odyssey: The Afro-American Ordeal in Slavery* (1977), and *Slave and Citizen: The Life of Frederick Douglass* (1980) and the editor of several other books.

He held Guggenheim and Ford Fellowships (1971–72) and a Fulbright Senior Fellowship (1974–75). He was a fellow of the Center for Advanced Study in the Behavioral Sciences (1979–80) and a Rockefeller Foundation Humanities fellow (1983–84). For many years he was vice president of the Howard Thurman Educational Trust and a member of the Board of Advisors of Children's TV Workshop. He was a director of the American Council of Learned Societies (1985–89).

REFERENCES: CA (NR-25, 130); NYT, December 7, 1989, p. D22; WWW (10).

HUNGERFORD, Richard H. b. September 3, 1903, Concord, Michigan, to Harold H. and Eva (Tewksbury) Hungerford. Married: no. d. April 12, 1974, Jackson, Michigan.

Richard Hungerford gained recognition for his work with the mentally handicapped. He believed that with proper training many of them could assimilate into communities. He developed curricula for mentally deficient persons, emphasizing occupational and social competencies.

Hungerford received the A.B. degree from Albion College (1926) and the A.M. from the University of Michigan (1931). Beginning his career as a teacher in Detroit (1922–42), he became supervisor of the city's special education program (1939–42). He was director of the New York City Board of Education Bureau for Children with Retarded Mental Development (1942–53) and superintendent of a state school in Laconia, New Hampshire (1953–60). He served as executive director of the Gulf Bend Center for Children and Youth in Victoria, Texas (1963–66), and Mental Health and Mental Retardation Services of the Diocese of Galveston-Houston (1966–68). From 1968 to 1971 Hungerford was professor of special education at Boston University, and from 1971 he directed a Work Opportunity Center project in Springfield, Massachusetts.

With Chris J. DeProspo, Hungerford founded *Occupational Education* (1943). He was editor of the *American Journal of Mental Deficiency* (1948–59) and president of the American Association on Mental Deficiency (1950–51).

REFERENCES: NYT, April 14, 1974, p. 49; WW (1974–75); *American Journal of Mental Deficiency* 79 (September 1974): 111–12; *Journal of Special Education* 11 (Summer 1977).

HUNT, Charles Wesley. b. October 20, 1880, Charlestown, New Hampshire, to Wesley Abel and Rosie Jane (Bailey) Hunt. Married August 8, 1912, to Helen Elizabeth True; June 5, 1915, to Edna Margaret Klaer. Children: four. d. September 3, 1973, Oneonta, New York.

Charles W. Hunt brought together varied types of institutions of higher education into the American Association of Teachers Colleges (later, the American Association for College Teachers of Education, AACTE).

Hunt attended school in Saxtons River, Vermont. He received the B.A. degree from Brown University (1904) and M.A. (1910) and Ph.D. (1922) degrees from Columbia University. He taught in Saxtons River (1904–6), Providence (1906–8), and at the Horace Mann School of Columbia University (1908–9). He was a principal in Briarcliff Manor, New York (1910–13) and supervisor at the Children's Aid Society in New York City (1913–14). He returned to Columbia as secretary of Teachers College and vice-principal of the Horace Mann School (1918–21).

At the University of Pittsburgh (1921–24), Hunt directed extramural education and was acting dean of the School of Education (1923–24). He was dean of the Cleveland (Ohio) School of Education (1924–28) and professor and dean (1928–33) of the School of Education at Western Reserve (later, Case Western Reserve) University. Becoming principal of the Oneonta (New York) Normal School in 1933, Hunt remained until his 1951 retirement. When the school became a four-year college in 1938 Hunt's title changed to president. In 1948 the college became part of the State University of New York system, and it was renamed State University of New York College at Oneonta in 1961.

Hunt wrote *Costs of Secondary Schools in New York State* (1924) and *Everyday Reading* (with Henry C. Pearson, 1927), a three-volume workbook used in many school systems. In 1959 the AACTE established a lecture series named for Hunt. At Oneonta, the faculty established the Charles W. Hunt Scholarship for Teacher Preparation, and a student union was named for him.

REFERENCES: NCAB (58: 497); NYT, September 4, 1973, p. 34; WWW (6).

HUNT, Herold Christian. b. February 9, 1902, Northville, Michigan, to George E. and Katherine E. (Herold) Hunt. Married August 24, 1927, to Isabel Lucile Wright. Children: one. d. October 17, 1976, Lexington, Massachusetts.

Herold C. Hunt was an effective administrator of city school systems, which he headed in Kalamazoo, Michigan; New Rochelle, New York; Kansas City, Missouri; and Chicago. He was known as a reformer who eliminated patronage in the Chicago schools.

Hunt was educated in the public schools of Holland, Michigan. He received the A.B. degree from the University of Michigan in 1923 and taught social studies in the Hastings, Michigan, public schools from 1923 to 1927. After earning the M.A. degree from Teachers College of Columbia University in 1927, he became principal of St. Johns, Michigan, High School (1927–28 and 1929–31) and then superintendent (1931–34).

While superintendent in Kalamazoo (1934–37), Hunt was credited with mending a poor system. He served as superintendent in New Rochelle from 1937 to 1940, leading planning for a new curriculum that included vocational education. In 1940 Hunt received the Ed.D. degree from Teachers College and became superintendent of schools in Kansas City.

Both San Francisco and Chicago sought Hunt as superintendent in 1947. He became general superintendent in Chicago, in charge of business and financial affairs as well as education. Under his lead, teacher examinations were reformed, and teachers were hired from outside the city from approved teachers colleges, in addition to those trained at Chicago Teachers College (later, State University). Teachers participated in curriculum planning and textbook selection. Hunt established a Teachers Advisory Council.

In 1953 Hunt was named Charles W. Eliot Professor of Education in the Harvard Graduate School of Education. During 1956 he served as undersecretary of the U.S. Department of Health, Education, and Welfare. He retired from Harvard in 1970. Hunt was president of the American Association of School Administrators (1947–48), second vice president of the National Congress of Parents and Teachers (1948–51), chair of the American Council on Education (1948–49), and chair of the Board of Trustees of the Educational Testing Service (1949–50). He coauthored *The Practice of School Administration* (1958) and *The School Personnel Administrator* (1965).

REFERENCES: CB (1956, 1977); NYT, September 13, 1955, p. 16, and October 22, 1976, p. A25; WWW (7); *Newsweek* 37 (April 23, 1951): 92–93; William Max Staerkel, ''A Case Study in Public School Leadership: Herold C. Hunt'' (Ed.D. thesis, Stanford

University, 1953); *Time* 66 (September 12, 1955): 30; H. B. Wilson, "Toughest School Job in the Country," *Saturday Evening Post* 223 (October 7, 1950): 29.

HUNT, Joseph McVicker. b. March 19, 1906, Scottsbluff, Nebraska, to Robert Sanford and Carrie Pearl McVicker (Loughborough) Hunt. Married December 25, 1929, to Esther Dahms. Children: two. d. January 9, 1991, Urbana, Illinois.

J. McVicker Hunt conducted research on the early development of children. As a developmentalist he believed in the combined effects of environment and experience on intelligence. His book *Intelligence and Experience* (1961) was influential in early education. Project Head Start was in part prompted by Hunt's research.

Hunt was raised on a Nebraska farm. He received B.A. (1929) and M.A. (1930) degrees from the University of Nebraska and the Ph.D. degree from Cornell University (1933). He had a National Research Council Postdoctoral Fellowship at New York State Psychiatric Institute and Columbia University (1933–34) and at Worcester (Massachusetts) State Hospital and Clark University (1934–35). He then spent six months at the University of Nebraska and six months at Saint Elizabeth's Hospital in Washington, D.C.

From 1936 to 1946 Hunt was on the faculty at Brown University. He served as a consultant (1944–46) to the Community Service Society of New York, Institute of Welfare Research, and directed the agency (1946–51). With others he developed the Movement Scale to evaluate change in clients resulting from supportive intervention.

At the University of Illinois (1951–74) Hunt was professor of psychology and professor of elementary education (1967–74). He headed the clinical psychology training program, directed the doctoral program (1951–61), coordinated training in clinical and counseling psychology, and coordinated the Ford Grant Program in Behavioral Science (1951–55). He served as psychological consultant to the School of Aviation Medicine at Randolph Air Force Base (1951–54).

Hunt received numerous awards. He was a member of the Board of Trustees (1953–59) and president (1953–54 and 1958–59) of the American Psychological Foundation and received its Gold Medal. He received an award for excellence in research from the National Personnel and Guidance Association (1960), the Research Career Award from the National Institute of Mental Health (1962), and the Kurt Lewin Award from the Society for the Psychological Study of Social Issues (1981). The American Psychological Association gave Hunt the Distinguished Contribution Award from the Division of Clinical Psychology (1973) and the G. Stanley Hall (BDAE) Award from the Division of Developmental Psychology (1976).

Hunt contributed articles to journals of sociology, education, psychology, and psychiatry. He edited the *Journal of Abnormal and Social Psychology* (1950–56). Among his books were *The Challenge of Incompetence and Poverty* (1969), *Assessment in Infancy* (with Ina C. Uzgiris, 1975), and *Early Psychological*

Development and Experience (1980). A festschrift in his honor, *The Structuring of Experience* was edited by Ina C. Uzgiris and Fredric Weizmann (1977).

REFERENCES: CA (37–40R, 133); LE (1974); NYT, January 11, 1991, p. B6; WD (94–96N); WWW (10); *American Journal of Psychology* 105 (Fall 1992): 471–76; *American Psychologist* 35 (January 1980): 93–96, and 47 (August 1992): 1050–51; *Journal of Social Issues* 38 (1982): 159–61.

HUNTER, Madeline Cheek. b. c. 1916, Regina, Saskatchewan, Canada. Married to Robert Hunter. Children: two. d. January 27, 1994, Los Angeles.

After two successful decades as principal of the laboratory school at the University of California, Los Angeles (UCLA), Madeline Hunter became a leading proponent during the 1980s of direct instruction theory and practice. Her seven-step model of effective lesson design—anticipatory set, objective and purpose, input, modeling, check for understanding, guided practice, independent practice—became standard material in educational psychology textbooks and teacher education programs.

Raised in Santa Monica, California, Hunter received the B.S., B.A., M.Ed., and Ed. D. degrees from UCLA. She was a psychologist and principal in the Los Angeles public schools. From 1963 to 1982 she was principal of the Corinne A. Seeds Elementary School at UCLA. In 1982 she became professor of administration and teacher education and director of Project Linkage, also at UCLA.

During 1973–74, Hunter wrote a monthly column, ''Blueprints for State Meetings,'' in *Instructor*. In addition to many articles, she was author of *Teach More—Faster: A Programmed Book* (1967), *Teach for Transfer: A Programmed Book* (1971), *Rx: Improved Instruction* (1976), *Improving Your Child's Behavior* (with Paul V. Carlson, 1977), *Parent–Teacher Conferencing* (with Gerda Lawrence, 1978), *Mastery Teaching* (1982), *How to Change to a Nongraded School* (1992), and *Enhancing Teaching* (1994).

Hunter received a Certificate of Merit for Outstanding Service from Phi Delta Kappa (1969) and a presidential citation from the American Association for Health, Physical Education, and Recreation.

REFERENCES: ECE; NYT, February 3, 1994, p. B7; *Educational Leadership* 42 (February 1985): 61–66, 44 (February 1987): 46–71, 47 (February 1990): 41–43, and 51 (April 1994): 83; David L. Kirp, ''The Classroom According to Hunter,'' *Los Angeles Times Magazine*, August 12, 1990, pp. 16+; *Newsmakers* (Gale Research, 1991); John G. Ramsay, ''Madeline Hunter's Model,'' *Urban Education* 24 (January 1990): 476–87.

I

ILG, Frances Lillian. b. October 11, 1902, Oak Park, Illinois, to Joseph and Lennore (Peterson) Ilg. Married: no. Children: one adopted. d. July 26, 1981, Manitowish Waters, Wisconsin.

Frances L. Ilg founded the Gesell Institute of Child Development (later, Gesell Institute of Human Development) with Louise Bates Ames (q.v.) in 1950 and served as its director until 1970. It was organized to carry on the work begun at the Yale Clinic of Child Development directed by Arnold Gesell (BDAE) from 1911 to 1948. Ilg and Ames wrote a widely published newspaper column, "Child Behavior."

Ilg received the B.A. degree from Wellesley College (1925) and the M.D. degree from Cornell University (1929). She interned in New York City at St. Mary's Hospital for Children (1929–30) and Bellevue Hospital (1930–31), and at Boston's Northeastern Hospital for Women and Children (1931–32). In 1932 Ilg went to Yale University as a visiting pediatrician. She became a research assistant at the Clinic of Child Development (1933–36) and assistant professor of child development (1937–50). In 1936–37 Ilg was in Stockholm, Sweden, where she engaged in child health work and adopted a daughter.

Ilg wrote *The Gesell Institute Party Book* (1956) and was coauthor of many books on child development. With Arnold Gesell she wrote *Infant and Child Care in the Culture of Today* (1943) and *The Child from Five to Ten* (1946); with Arnold Gesell and Louise Bates Ames, *Youth: the Years from Ten to Sixteen* (1956); with Louise Bates Ames, *Child Behavior* (1955), *Parents Ask* (1962), *School Readiness* (1965), *Your Two-Year-Old: Terrible or Tender* (1976), *Your Three-Year-Old: Friend or Enemy* (1976), *Your Four-Year-Old: Wild and Wonderful* (1976), *Your Five-Year-Old: Sunny and Serene* (1979), and *Your Six-Year-Old: Loving and Defiant* (1979); and with Louise Bates Ames and Carol Chase Haber, *Your One-Year-Old* (1982).

REFERENCES: CA (104, 107); CB (1956, 1981); NYT, July 28, 1981, p. B8; WR; WWAW (1974); WWW (8).

IRWIN, Agnes. b. December 30, 1841, Washington, D.C., to William Wallace and Sophia Arabella Dallas (Bache) Irwin. Married: no. d. December 5, 1914, Philadelphia.

Agnes Irwin led model institutions for the education of women and girls at the end of the nineteenth and beginning of the twentieth century.

Educated at a private girls' school in Washington, D.C., and at home, she began teaching in the early 1860s at a school in New York City conducted by Mrs. Ogden Hoffman. In 1869 she took up the principalship of Penn Square Seminary, a private school for girls in Philadelphia, which she conducted as the Agnes Irwin School.

The excellence of the school and Irwin's effective leadership became well known, attracting the attention of President Charles W. Eliot (BDAE) of Harvard University as well as leaders of the Society for the Collegiate Education of Women, also known as the Harvard Annex. When the society was chartered as Radcliffe College, with Elizabeth Cary Agassiz (BDAE) as its president, Irwin was appointed dean (1894–1909). Because Agassiz never engaged herself fully in college administration, Irwin was the effective chief officer, representing Radcliffe on the Harvard Academic Board, broadening the Radcliffe curriculum, directing the construction of its first residence halls and other college facilities, and introducing graduate study leading to the Ph.D. degree.

To her disappointment, Irwin was passed over for the college presidency when Agassiz retired in 1903. While she served six more years as dean, her attention shifted to a concurrent role, president of the Women's Education Association of Boston (1901–7). After leaving Radcliffe, Irwin was founding president of the Head Mistresses' Association of Private Schools, located in Philadelphia (1911–14). She was coauthor of *Worthy Women of Our First Century* (1877).

REFERENCES: AWM; LW; NAW; NYT, December 6, 1914, p. 2; WR; WWW (1); Joanne Loewe Neel, *Miss Irwin's of Philadelphia: A History of the Agnes Irwin School* (Livingston, 1969); Agnes Repplier, *Agnes Irwin: A Biography* (Doubleday, Doran, 1934).

IVEY, John Eli, Jr. b. January 21, 1919, Raleigh, North Carolina, to John Eli and Vera (House) Ivey. Married July 25, 1942, to Melville Corbett. Children: three. d. May 24, 1992, Chapel Hill, North Carolina.

John E. Ivey, Jr., was a leader in the use of modern technology in education. He was the founding president of the Learning Resources Institute (1959–60) and of the Midwest Program on Airborne Television Instruction (1959–62).

Ivey received the B.S. degree from Alabama Polytechnic Institute (later, Auburn University) in 1940 and taught sociology at the University of North Carolina from 1941 to 1943. He earned the Ph.D. degree there in 1944 as a student of Howard Odum (BDAE). After two years with the Tennessee Valley Authority as an evaluator of education, he returned to the University of North Carolina as an associate professor. Appointed professor of city and regional planning in 1948, he also was a research professor at the Institute for Research in Social Sciences.

Ivey was director of the Board of Control for Southern Regional Education from its establishment in 1948 to 1957. The member states of the board cooperated in sharing facilities and programs. Ivey served as executive vice president of New York University from 1957 to 1959. The Learning Resources Institute promoted technology in classrooms, and the Midwest Program on Airborne Television served rural schools in six midwestern states. Ivey served as dean of the College of Education at Michigan State University from 1962 to 1971, then was research professor of higher education until his retirement in 1976.

As a consultant for school systems, Ivey participated in surveys in many cities and states, including North Carolina, Florida, Puerto Rico, and Atlanta, Georgia. His activity in professional associations included serving as secretary of the American Council on Education. He contributed articles to professional journals and wrote *Channeling Research into Education* (1944) and *Education for the Use of Regional Resources* (1945). He coauthored *Exploring the South* (1949), *Building Atlanta's Future* (1948), and *Community Resources* (1951). In 1951 Ivey received the Freedoms Foundation Medal. He was the recipient of an Eisenhower Exchange Fellowship in 1956 and studied educational systems abroad.

REFERENCES: CB (1960, 1992); LE (1974); NYT, May 30, 1992, p. 26; WW (1976–77); *Time* 69 (April 15, 1977): 88.

J

JACKSON, Philip Wesley. b. December 2, 1928, Vineland, New Jersey, to Raymond and Estelle (Sword) Jackson. Married May 1, 1948, to Josephine Dandrea. Children: three.

In his book *Life in Classrooms* (1969), Philip Jackson argued for the significance of crowds, praise, and power for children's learning. With these concepts he set in motion twenty-five years of research and debate on the ''hidden'' curriculum. Jackson was considered one of his generation's most astute scholars on the mutual work of teachers and students. The literary quality of his writings extended his influence. He had a major impact on the growth and stature of ethnographic studies in education.

Jackson served briefly in the U.S. Naval Reserve (1947–48) and graduated from Glassboro (New Jersey) State College (later, Rowan College) with the B.S. degree in 1951. He earned the M.Ed. a year later at Temple University and the Ph.D. at Teachers College, Columbia University, in 1954. After one year teaching educational psychology at Wayne State University, he went to the University of Chicago in 1955. He was principal of the laboratory nursery school (1966–70), director of laboratory schools (1970–75), chair of the Department of Education and Human Development (from 1973), and dean of the Graduate School of Education (from 1973). In 1973 he was named David Lee Shillinglaw Distinguished Service Professor.

His writings included *Creativity and Intelligence* (with Jacob W. Getzels, 1962), *The Teacher and the Machine* (1968) and *The Moral Life of Schools* (with Robert E. Boostrom and David T. Hansen, 1993). His essays, which were acclaimed, appeared in two collections, *The Practice of Teaching* (1986) and *Untaught Lessons* (1992). He was editor of the *Handbook of Research on Curriculum* (1992), a project of the American Educational Research Association.

He was a fellow of the Center for Advanced Study in the Behavioral Sciences (1962–63) and served as vice president of the National Academy of Education (1975–77).

REFERENCES: CA (21–24R); LE (1974); RPE; WW (1984–85).

JACOBS, Leland Blair. b. February 12, 1907, Tawas City, Michigan. Married 1930 to Beatrice Houghton. Children: one. d. April 4, 1992, Englewood, New Jersey.

Leland B. Jacobs was influential in finding ways of teaching literature to young children. He wrote and edited many children's books, including *Adventure Lands* and *Enchanted Isles* (both with Eleanor Johnson, q.v., 1954), *Just around the Corner* (1964), *Is Somewhere Always Far Away?* (1967), and *Poetry for Space Enthusiasts* (1971). At Teachers College, Columbia University, he taught in the field of curriculum, especially in reading and language arts.

Jacobs graduated from Michigan State Normal College (later, Eastern Michigan University). He received a master's degree from the University of Michigan and the Ph.D. from Ohio State University (1949). Jacobs began teaching in a one-room school in New Boston, Michigan. In Ypsilanti, Michigan, beginning in 1930, he taught most grades and served as an elementary school principal. Jacobs was an assistant professor of elementary education at Ohio State University from 1946 and consultant to the Ohio School of the Air.

He went to Columbia University in 1953. After his retirement in 1972 he continued to visit schools to teach writing to children. In addition to his children's books, Jacobs wrote *Using Literature with Young Children* (1965) and *Student Teaching in the Elementary School* (with James B. Burr and Lowry W. Harding, 1950) and edited *Children and the Language Arts* (with Virgil E. Herrick, 1955). He was elected to the Reading Hall of Fame in 1979.

REFERENCES: CA (73–76R; 137); NYT, April 7, 1992, p. B7; Doris Bergen, "Leland B. Jacobs: Fostering the Authority of Childhood," *Childhood Education* 69 (Fall 1992): 33–35; *Education* 80 (January 1960): 316; *Teaching K-8* 20 (April 1990): 39–40.

JANSON, Horst Woldemar. b. October 4, 1913, St. Petersburg, Russia, to Friedrich and Helene (Porsch) Janson. Married August 14, 1941, to Dora Jane Heineberg. Children: four. d. September 30, 1982, traveling between Milan, Italy, and Zurich, Switzerland.

H. W. Janson developed the program in art history at New York University into one of the most recognized in the United States. The *History of Art* (1962), written by Janson and his wife, Dora Jane Janson, was used extensively in art history courses and was translated into more than fourteen languages.

Janson was born in Russia of Latvian parents. The family moved to Finland and then to Germany, where Janson attended school in Hamburg. He was a student at the Universities of Hamburg and Munich. Coming to the United States, Janson received M.A. (1938) and Ph.D. (1942) degrees from Harvard University. He was a lecturer at the Worcester (Massachusetts) Art Museum (1936–38), an instructor at the University of Iowa (1938–41), and an associate professor of art at Washington University in Missouri (1941–49).

Janson was professor of fine arts at the Washington Square College of New York University from 1949 to 1979, serving as department chair (1949–74). He also was professor at New York University's Institute of Fine Arts. In 1974 he gave the Andrew W. Mellon Lectures at the National Gallery of Art in Washington, D.C.

Janson was a Guggenheim fellow in 1948 and 1955. He received the Charles

R. Morey Award from the College Art Association in 1952 and 1957 and the Art Dealers Association of America Award in 1981. He was president of the College Art Association of America (1970–72) and edited its publication, *Art Bulletin* (1962–65).

Among Janson's books were *Apes and Ape Lore in the Middle Ages and the Renaissance* (1952), *The Picture History of Painting, from Cave Painting to Modern Times* (with Dora Jane Janson, 1957), *A History of Art and Music* (with Dora Jane Janson and Joseph Kerman, 1968), *Basic History of Art* (with Samuel Cauman, 1971), *16 Studies* (1974), and *Art of the Nineteenth Century* (with Robert Rosenblum, 1984). He edited *Key Monuments of the History of Art* (with Dora Jane Janson, 1959), organized and edited *The Romantics to Rodin* (with Peter Fusco, 1980), and was a consulting editor for *Time-Life Library of Art*. Moshe Barasch and Lucy Freeman Sandler edited *Art, the Ape of Nature: Studies in Honor of H. W. Janson* (1981).

REFERENCES: CA (NR-4, 107); NYT, October 3, 1982, p. 5; WD (1982–84); WP, October 4, 1982, p. D4; WW (1976–77); Milton Esterov, ''Conversation with H. W. Janson,'' *Art News* 74 (September 1975): 59–63.

JARRELL, (Helen) Ira. b. July 27, 1896, Meriwether County, Georgia, to William Henry and Emma (Hutchison) Jarrell. Married: no. d. August 27, 1973, Little Rock, Arkansas.

During a career spent entirely in the Atlanta, Georgia, school system, Ira Jarrell rose from teacher to be superintendent for sixteen years. She was also president of the Atlanta teachers' union, which became one of the largest units in the country.

Jarrell graduated from Girls' High School in Atlanta in 1914 and received a diploma from the Atlanta Normal Training School in 1916. She began as a fifth and sixth grade teacher in 1916 and became a senior teacher in 1930. She earned the A.B. (1928) and M.A. (1931) degrees at Oglethorpe University. Jarrell was principal of Sylvan Hills School (1934–36) and W. F. Slaton School (1936–44).

In the Atlanta Public School Teachers' Association, Jarrell was recording secretary, vice president, and, from 1936, president. She advocated higher salaries for teachers and better working conditions. In 1936 she assisted in the mayoral election of William B. Hartsfield and in 1937 in the election of a school board supportive of teachers. She received the Ed.D. degree from Oglethorpe University in 1951.

Chosen the first woman superintendent of the Atlanta schools in 1944, Jarrell served in that role to her retirement in 1960. During her tenure enrollment increased and she oversaw a building program made possible by the passage of bond issues. For the first time male teachers were appointed as principals of elementary schools, and programs were established for handicapped and gifted students. Jarrell advocated the use of educational radio and television. Under her leadership the Atlanta Board of Education owned and operated its own television station. Ten coeducational high schools replaced separate schools for boys and girls, a change that brought criticism. Jarrell also faced criticism from African Americans, who questioned her commitment to equality.

After retirement from the Atlanta system, Jarrell directed the division of curriculum development services of the Georgia Department of Education. She served on the executive board of *The School Executive* and was a Sunday school teacher for fifty years.

REFERENCES: AWMA; NAW (Mod); WW (1964–65); WWAW (1966); *Atlanta Constitution*, August 21, 1973, p. 1+; Melvin W. Ecke, *From Ivy Street to Kennedy Center: Centennial History of the Atlanta Public School System* (n.p., 1972).

JOHNSON, Eleanor Murdock. b. December 10, 1892, Washington County, Maryland, to Richard and Emma (Shuff) Johnson. Married: no. d. October 8, 1987, Gaithersburg, Maryland.

Eleanor Johnson influenced many schoolchildren who read the *Weekly Reader*. It first appeared in 1928 and was published weekly after that. By the late 1960s it had a circulation of 13 million copies and was said to have been read by two-thirds of all schoolchildren in the United States.

Johnson was a graduate of the University of Chicago and held a master's degree from Columbia University. She taught in Oklahoma in Lawton, Chickasha, and Oklahoma City and was supervisor of elementary schools in Drumright and Oklahoma City. While assistant superintendent of schools for curriculum in York, Pennsylvania, she conceived the idea of a newspaper for elementary school children. Johnson believed they needed real-world knowledge, not just myths and folklore. William C. Blakey of the American Education Press in Columbus, Ohio, was interested and became the publisher. The first four-page issue appeared on September 21, 1928, and included articles on presidential candidates Herbert Hoover and Al Smith.

Johnson was assistant superintendent for curriculum in the Lakewood, Ohio, schools for four years. From the initial publication of *My Weekly Reader*, she trained others to edit it while she served as consultant. By 1935 she worked on the newspaper full-time as editor in chief. The Xerox Corporation purchased the *Weekly Reader* company in the 1940s; it became American Education Publications and was moved to Middletown, Connecticut. Johnson served concurrently as director of elementary school services at Wesleyan University. She retired as editor in 1961 but continued as a consultant to the newspaper until 1978. In the 1960s it was expanded to seven editions for each grade from preschool through six.

Johnson was author of *Child Story Readers*, *Treasury of Literature Readers*, *Word Mastery Spellers* (1953), and more than fifty elementary school workbooks. She served on the editorial board of *Education* and with Leland Jacobs (q.v.) edited *Adventure Lands* and *Enchanted Isles* (1954).

REFERENCES: CA (123); FWC; LE (1974); NYT, October 10, 1987, p. 40; WP, October 8, 1978, p. L1, and October 10, 1987, p. C8; *Education* 80 (December 1959): 251.

JONES, Franklin Ross. b. January 3, 1921, Charlotte, North Carolina, to William Morton and Olive Ruth (Moser) Jones. Married December 19, 1949, to Jane White. Children: three.

Franklin Ross Jones received the A.B. degree from Lenoir-Rhyne College in 1941. In North Carolina he taught in public schools (1944–47), was science teacher and principal of the junior high school in Henderson (1949–54), district school principal in Wake County (1954–56), and district superintendent in Roxboro (1956–58). He earned the A.M. degree from the University of North Carolina in 1951 and the D.Ed. degree from Duke University in 1960.

While professor of education and department chair at Randolph-Macon College (1956–64), Jones helped to establish the Virginia College Student Association. Among his innovations at the college were programmed instruction for student teachers, microteaching, and television teaching models.

Jones was dean of the School of Education at Old Dominion University from 1964 to 1969, when he was named Distinguished Professor of Human Development. In 1965 he founded the Child Study Center, which offered opportunities to observe classes for the visually impaired, mentally retarded, emotionally disturbed, and learning disabled. He also led the social foundations program (1973–77).

Jones was president of the North Central Teachers Association (1952), North Central Principals Association (1956), and South Atlantic Philosophy of Education Society (1966–68). The Virginia Research Association named Jones a distinguished researcher in education in 1972, 1973, and 1978. He was a member of the White House Conference on Children and Youth (1968–71) and chair of the Governor's Regional Implementation Commission on Children and Youth (1971–73).

Jones was the author of *Psychology of Human Development* (with Karl C. Garrison, 1969).

REFERENCES: CA (53–56R); LE (1974); WW (1996).

JONES, Virginia Mae Lacy. b. June 25, 1912, Cincinnati, Ohio, to Edward and Ellen Louise (Parker) Lacy. Married November 27, 1941, to Edward Allen Jones. Children: no. d. December 3, 1984, Atlanta, Georgia.

Virginia Lacy Jones gave forty years of service to library education, particularly helping to develop library education for African Americans.

Jones attended school in Clarksburg, West Virginia, and graduated from Sumner High School in St. Louis, Missouri. After receiving a bachelor of library science degree from Hampton Institute (later, University) in 1933, she was employed by Louisville (Kentucky) Municipal College, a component of the University of Louisville. During summers she taught school librarians at Prairie View (Texas) A&M College (1936–39). She attended Hampton again, receiving the B.S. degree in education in 1936, and returned to Louisville. With a fellowship from the General Education Board, Jones attended the University of Illinois, where she completed the M.L.S. degree in 1938.

When the Hampton Library School was closed in 1939, limiting opportunities for blacks to train in library science, Rufus Clement (BDAE) recruited Jones to help in the development of a new library school at Atlanta (later Clark–Atlanta) University. It was opened in 1941, with support from the Carnegie Corporation and Jones on the original faculty. Another General Education Board Fellowship in 1943 enabled Jones to attend the University of Chicago, where she received the Ph.D. degree in 1945. She was the second African American in the United States to earn a doctorate in library science.

Returning to Atlanta, she succeeded Eliza Atkins Gleason (q.v.) as dean of the university library school in 1945. Under Jones' leadership the curriculum was broadened, and in 1949 the degree earned was changed from bachelor to master of library science. The library sponsored conferences to aid in library development. With Carnegie Corporation support, a Field Service Program made professional consultations available to libraries for African Americans in the South. Jones left the deanship in 1981 and was named director of the new Robert W. Woodruff Library of the Atlanta University Center. It merged the libraries of six institutions constituting the center, formed in 1967. Jones retired in 1983.

Jones served on the editorial board of *Phylon* and was an editorial consultant to the *Library Journal.* She was on the President's Advisory Council on Library Research and Training Project (1967–70), was vice chair of the Georgia State Board for Certification of Librarians, and was a member of the Committee on Interstate Library Cooperation. She chaired the American Library Association's (ALA) Committee on Opportunities for Negro Students in the Library Profession. In the ALA Jones was a council member for four terms and on the executive board (1970–76). She served as secretary-treasurer (1948–54), board director (1960–64), and president (1967) of the Association of American Library Schools. The ALA presented her the Melvil Dewey (BDAE) Award in 1973 and the Joseph W. Lippincott Award in 1977 for distinguished librarianship. She was the first African American to receive either award. She wrote *Reminiscences in Librarianship and Library Education* (1979).

REFERENCES: BWA; HAWH; NBAW; WWW (8); *The ALA Yearbook of Library and Information Services* (American Library Association, 1985); *American Libraries* 16 (January 1985): 11; E. J. Josey, ed., *The Black Librarian in America* (Scarecrow, 1970); *Library Journal* 110 (February 15, 1985): 94; Robert Wedgeworth, ed., *ALA World Encyclopedia of Library and Information Services* (American Library Association, 1986); Wayne A. Wiegand, ed., *Supplement to the Dictionary of American Library Biography* (Libraries Unlimited, 1990).

K

KARPLUS, Robert. b. February 23, 1927, Vienna, Austria, to Hans and Isabella Lucie (Goldstern) Karplus. Married December 27, 1948, to Elizabeth Jane Frazier. Children: seven. d. March 20, 1990, Moraga, California.

Robert Karplus was a theoretical physicist and an expert in quantum electrodynamics. He became noted as an innovator in teaching physics and a proponent of making physics understandable for elementary school children through the Science Curriculum Improvement Study (SCIS).

As a Jewish youth in Vienna under Nazi occupation, Karplus fled with his family to the United States in 1938. At the age of sixteen he enrolled at Harvard University, where he received all of his academic degrees: the B.S. in 1945, M.A. in chemistry in 1946, and Ph.D. in 1948. From 1948 to 1950 he held a Frank M. Jewett Fellowship at the Institute for Advanced Study in Princeton, New Jersey. He was assistant professor of physics at Harvard from 1950 to 1954, when he was named associate professor at the University of California, Berkeley. He became a professor in 1958 and remained at Berkeley until his death.

During the 1960s, influenced by the studies of Jean Piaget in developmental psychology, Karplus began studying how young children learn science. Karplus taught experimental classes in physics in elementary schools. The SCIS developed from his Elementary School Science Project. In 1969 he was founder and associate director of the Intellectual Development Project at Lawrence Hall of Science at Berkeley. The SCIS developed instructional materials for children, using observation and model making. Findings from SCIS were used in developing new elementary science curricula.

Karplus was a Guggenheim fellow (1960–61 and 1973–74) and a Fulbright research scholar at the University of Vienna (1960–61). He served on the Science Education Advisory Committee of the National Science Foundation (1974–76) and was vice president (1975) and president (1977–78) of the American Association of Physics Teachers. He was a consultant to several industries and school districts.

Karplus wrote many articles and papers, several with his wife, Elizabeth F. Karplus. Among his books were *Advanced Quantum Mechanics of Atoms, Molecules and Solids* (1954), *One Physicist Looks at Science Education* (1963), *Introductory Physics for Liberal Arts Students* (1966), *A New Look at Elemen-*

tary School Science (1967), *Introductory Physics, A Model Approach* (1969), *Physics and Man* (1970), *Science Curriculum Improvement Study* (1970), and *Science Teaching and the Development of Reasoning* (1977). Karplus received the Distinguished Service Citation (1972) and Oerstad Medal (1980) from the American Association of Physics Teachers and the Distinguished Service Award (1978) from the National Science Teachers Association.

REFERENCES: LE (1971); NYT, March 24, 1990, p. 43; WW (1976–77); Robert Karplus, ''Beginning a Study in Elementary School Science,'' *American Journal of Physics* 30 (January 1962): 1–9, and 49 (September 1981): 810–14; *Physics Teacher* 10 (May 1952): 258, 15 (February 1977): 70+, and 19 (April 1981): 245; *Physics Today* 38 (March 1975): 71, and 45 (March 1992): 80; *Who's Who in American Jewry* (Standard Who's Who, 1980).

KATZ, Lilian Gonshaw. b. June 7, 1932, London, England, to Joseph and Eva (Freidine) Gonshaw. Married November 8, 1952, to Boris I. Katz. Children: three.

Lilian G. Katz was a scholar of early childhood education and teacher training. She wrote about the developmental stages of a teacher. Katz believed children learned best in informal environments and interactive situations. She was a proponent of the project approach in early childhood education, feeling it was more purposeful than play.

Katz came to the United States in 1947. She graduated from Wilson High School in Los Angeles in 1950 and attended Whittier College (1950–52). She taught nursery school in Redwood City, California (1962–64) and received the B.A. degree from San Francisco State College (later, University) in 1964. In 1968 she earned the Ph.D. degree from Stanford University.

From 1968 Katz taught at the University of Illinois at Urbana–Champaign, where from 1970 she was director of the Educational Resources Information Center (ERIC) on Early Childhood Education and research professor at the Institute for Research on Exceptional Children. She chaired the Department of Elementary and Early Childhood Education (1979–81) and cochaired a research unit on teacher education from 1979.

Katz received a Fulbright grant to India in 1983. She served as a member of the Illinois Governor's Advisory Council to the Department of Children and Family Services (1974), was chairperson of the National Task Force on Child Development (1980–81), and was cochair of the preprimary project of the International Evaluation Association (1980). She was on the editorial advisory board of the National Association for the Education of Young Children (1969–71) and editorial board of *Children in Contemporary Society* (1981).

In addition to articles in professional journals, Katz wrote *Talks with Teachers: Reflections on Early Childhood Education* (1977), *Ethical Behavior in Early Childhood Education* (with Evangeline H. Ward, 1978), *Talks with Parents: On Living with Preschoolers* (1983), *Engaging Children's Minds: The Project Approach* (with Sylvia C. Chard, 1989), and *The Case for Mixed-Age Grouping in Early Education* (with others, 1990). She edited *Current Topics in Early Childhood Education* and wrote monthly columns for *Parents Magazine* and *Instructor*.

REFERENCES: CA (111); ECE; LE (1974); WWAW (1985).

KELIHER, Alice Virginia. b. January 23, 1903, Washington, D.C., to James A. and Ida E. (Crow) Keliher. Married: no. d. July 11, 1995, Tucson, Arizona.

For her early work in establishing day care centers, Alice V. Keliher was known as "the grandmother of day care." During World War II, while directing child and youth services for the New York City Office of Civilian Defense, she guided the development of centers that cared for the children of women engaged in war work. Two decades later, she lent her expertise to the establishment of the Head Start program.

Keliher began teaching in Washington, D.C., in 1923 after completing the two-year teacher training program at the Wilson Normal School there. Her first supervisor had been her second grade teacher. While teaching, Keliher took courses at George Washington University. In 1927 she enrolled at Teachers College, Columbia University, where she studied under William H. Kilpatrick (BDAE), John Dewey (BDAE), and Goodwin Watson (q.v.) and earned B.S. (1928), M.A. (1929), and Ph.D. (1930) degrees.

In 1929 Keliher participated in a study tour of child care in Europe, making films of the programs she visited. The films impressed Arnold Gesell (BDAE), who invited Keliher to conduct research on child development with him at Yale University (1930–33). She left Yale to be elementary supervisor in Hartford, Connecticut, and concurrently part-time director of parent education in the Connecticut State Education Department, under the Federal Emergency Relief Administration.

In 1935 Keliher returned to New York City to chair the Commission on Human Relations of the Hanover Group, founded by Lawrence Frank. Between 1936 and 1940 Keliher continued that work and taught child development at New York University. She joined the university faculty on a full-time basis in 1940 and remained until her retirement in 1960. She also served for a time during the 1940s as part-time educational director of Walden School in New York City, established by Margaret Naumberg (BDAE). From 1960 to 1964 Keliher was Distinguished Service Professor at Jersey City State College, helping to develop it from a teachers college into a comprehensive institution. She was a Distinguished Professor at Wheelock College from 1964 to 1969.

She was a training officer for New England Head Start at Wheelock College and consultant to the national Head Start program. Keliher worked with Edward Zigler (q.v.) on the development of certification standards for child care workers. She was a member of the planning committee for the 1940 White House Conference on Children and Youth and served on many other national service committees. Keliher wrote *A Critical Study of Homogeneous Grouping* (1931), *Life and Growth* (1937), *Society and Family Life* (1937), and *Talks with Teachers*

(1958). With Laura Zirbes (BDAE) she wrote *The Book of Pets* (1928) and *Animal Tales* (1930).

REFERENCES: FWC; NYT, July 14, 1995, p. A23; WWAW (1970); *Childhood Education* 69 (1993): 300–303; *Young Children* 51 (November 1995): 57+.

KELLER, Franklin Jefferson. b. July 2, 1887, New York City, to Martin Christian and Katie (Stetzer) Keller. Married September 1, 1914, to Evelyn Miles. Children: two. d. April 19, 1976, Columbus, Ohio.

Franklin Jefferson Keller was an early advocate of vocational education in New York City. Keller received the B.S. degree from the College of the City of New York (later, City College, City University of New York, 1906), the M.A. from Columbia University (1910), and the Ph.D. from New York University (1916). He taught in New York City schools (1906–17) and was an assistant principal (1917–18). After two years (1918–20) as a reporter for the *New York Times*, he returned to the city school system as principal of Public School No. 7 (1920–25).

He was principal of the East Side Continuation School, later called the Metropolitan Vocational High School. In 1930 there were four vocational schools in the city; by Keller's retirement in 1957 there were thirty-one. During World War II he helped to create training facilities for trades used in national defense. After the war he was head of the vocational and technical section of the Education and Religious Affairs Branch of the American zone in Germany. Keller established a floating training school for maritime education in 1946 on the Liberty Ship *John W. Brown*. In 1948 he helped to establish the School of Performing Arts, later a division of LaGuardia High School of Music and Arts in New York City.

Keller directed the Vocational Survey Commission of the New York Board of Education (1930–31) and the National Occupational Conference (1933–36). He was a member of the governor's Commission on Education in Correctional Institutions (1936–42) and president of the National Vocational Guidance Association (1937–38). He wrote *Day Schools for Young Workers* (1924), *Vocational Guidance throughout the World* (with Morris S. Viteles, 1947), *Principles of Vocational Education* (1948), *The Double-Purpose High School* (1953), and *The Comprehensive High School* (1955).

REFERENCES: CA (65–68); NYT, April 21, 1976, p. 40; WWW (8).

KELLER, Fred Simmons. b. January 2, 1899, Rural Grove, New York, to Vrooman Barney and Minnie Vanderveer (Simmons) Keller. Married 1936 to Frances Scholl. Children: two. d. February 2, 1996, Chapel Hill, North Carolina.

With the publication of *Principles of Psychology: A Systematic Text in the Science of Behavior* (1950), Fred Keller and his Columbia University colleague William Schoenfeld initiated the teaching of psychology as a laboratory science in the United States. Keller also developed the Personalized System of Instruction (sometimes known as the Keller Plan), which for a time was influential among educators. Within psychology he was a behaviorist.

Keller left high school without graduating, to become a telegraph operator. He served in the U.S. Army (1918–19) and studied at Goddard Seminary (later, College) in Barre, Vermont (1919–20). He received the B.S. degree (1926) from Tufts College (later, University) and taught at Tufts (1926–28) while studying at Harvard University for M.A. (1928) and Ph.D. (1931) degrees. He was instructor of psychology at Colgate University (1931–38) and taught at Columbia University (1938–64), becoming professor in 1950. During World War II Keller worked in the Wartime Office of Scientific Research and Development. His methods for Morse Code training became widely used. From 1964 to 1967 he taught at Arizona State University, and between 1968 and 1973 he was adjunct and visiting professor at several universities.

His book *The Definition of Psychology* first appeared in the Century Psychology Series in 1937 and was republished in 1973. He also wrote *Learning: Reinforcement Theory* (1954), *PSI: The Keller Plan Handbook* (with J. G. Sherman, 1974), *Summer and Sabbaticals: A Collection of Papers* (1977), and *Pedagogue's Progress* (1982). He coedited *Behavior Modification* (1974).

Keller received a Fulbright-Hays Fellowship to Brazil in 1961 and helped to organize the psychology department at the University of Brasilia in 1964. He was a fellow of the Eastern Psychological Association (president 1956–57) and American Psychological Association, which gave him awards in 1974 for teaching and in 1976 for contributions to psychology. He received a Presidential Certificate of Merit from Harry Truman (1948) and the Distinguished Behavioral Scientist Medal from the Institute for Behavioral Research (1973).

REFERENCES: CA (NR-11); NYT, February 11, 1996, p. 56; WW (1978); *American Psychologist* 32 (January 1977): 68–71.

KELLER, Robert John. b. May 25, 1913, White Bear Lake, Minnesota, to John Joseph and Lillie (Olson) Keller. Married December 29, 1943, to Alice Maurine Fawcett. Children: two.

Robert J. Keller was a leading advocate in the 1950s of an enlarged role for junior colleges in Minnesota. In 1958 he coauthored a report on junior college development in the state.

Keller began his teaching career in Minnesota as a rural school teacher (1931–32), elementary teacher/principal in White Bear Beach School (1932–38), and high school teacher in North St. Paul (1938–40). He received the B.E. degree (1937) from Winona (Minnesota) State Teachers College (later, State University) and M.A. (1940) and Ph.D. (1947) degrees from the University of Minnesota. He was a serviceman in the U.S. Air Force (1942–45) and civilian research psychologist with the force (1946–47).

At the University of Minnesota he was a teaching research assistant (1940–42 and 1945–46), associate director (1947–50) and director (1950–54) of the Bureau of Institutional Research, and director of University High School (1956–

64). He was professor of education (1951–82) and dean of the College of Education (1964–70).

Among Keller's publications were *A University Looks at Its Program* (editor with Ruth E. Eckert, 1954), *Higher Education for Our State and Times* (1959), *Higher Education in Korea* (1974), *The Korean Higher Education Reform Project in Transition* (1975), and *Higher Education and National Development in Southeast Asia* (1977). He directed educational surveys for several states and was president of the American Association for Higher Education (1969–70).

REFERENCES: LE (1974); WW (1990–91).

KEMENY, John George. b. May 31, 1926, Budapest, Hungary, to Tibor and Lucy (Fried) Kemeny. Married November 5, 1950, to Jean Alexander. Children: two. d. December 26, 1992, Lebanon, New Hampshire.

John Kemeny was fourteen years old when he immigrated to the United States from Hungary. His family, being Jews, fled their homeland when its invasion by Nazi Germany became imminent. After learning English quickly as his fourth language, Kemeny graduated as valedictorian of his high school class and enrolled at Princeton University, where he earned the B.A. (1947) and Ph.D. (1949) degrees.

Kemeny's mathematical brilliance showed itself during his U.S. Army service when he worked on the theory of the atomic bomb and later at Princeton in his role as research assistant to Albert Einstein. Kemeny was a reformer of the calculus curriculum, an advocate of "new math" in schools, coinventor with Thomas E. Kurtz of the BASIC computer language, and an early proponent of computer time-sharing for educational purposes.

After four years of teaching mathematics and philosophy at Princeton, Kemeny went to Dartmouth College, where he stayed for the remainder of his career. He was professor of mathematics and philosophy (1953–70), coordinator of educational plans and development (1967–71), Albert Bradley Third Century Professor (1969–72), president (1970–81), and professor again (1981–90) until his retirement. During Kemeny's presidency, Dartmouth began admitting women as baccalaureate students, increased the enrollment of minority students, reestablished its historical commitment to the education of Native Americans, and adopted a trimester calendar in order to increase off-campus opportunities for students.

Kemeny chaired the Presidential Commission on the Accident at Three Mile Island (1979). He was a consultant to the Rand Corporation, fellow of the American Academy of Arts and Sciences, trustee of the Carnegie Foundation for the Advancement of Teaching, and New Hampshire state chairman of the United Negro College Fund, in addition to many other public service roles.

Kemeny was author of *A Philosopher Looks at Science* (1959) and *Random Essays on Mathematics, Education, and Computers* (1964) and coauthor of many other books, including *Introduction to Finite Mathematics* (1957), *Mathematical Models in the Social Sciences* (1962), and *Basic Programming* (1967).

References: CA (NR-46, 140); CB (1971, 1993); CHE, October 1, 1979, pp. 3–5; LE (1974); NYT, January 24, 1970, p. 1, and December 27, 1992, p. 40; WD (1994–96); WW (1986–87).

KEPPEL, Francis. b. April 16, 1916, New York City, to Frederick Paul and Helen Tracy (Brown) Keppel. Married July 19, 1941, to Edith Moulton Sawin. Children: two. d. February 19, 1990, Cambridge, Massachusetts.

During Francis Keppel's long tenure as dean of the Harvard Graduate School of Education, he bolstered its master of arts in teaching program and created its School and University Program for Research and Development. He earned a reputation as an innovator in teaching excellence and institutional collaboration. In 1962 President John Kennedy appointed him U.S. commissioner of education. Reappointed by President Lyndon Johnson, he became assistant secretary of health, education and welfare. Keppel led the fight for the passage of the Elementary and Secondary Education Act of 1965 and created the National Assessment of Educational Progress.

Keppel grew up in Montrose, New York. He received the A.B. degree from Harvard University (1938); studied sculpture for one year in Rome, Italy; and was assistant dean of freshmen at Harvard College (1939–41). He was secretary of the Joint Army and Navy Committee on Welfare and Recreation (1941–46) and served in the U.S. Army Information and Education Division (1944–46).

Keppel was assistant to the provost of Harvard (1946–48) until his appointment as dean of the Graduate School of Education (1948–62) by James B. Conant (BDAE). In 1957 he formed the School and University Program for Research and Development. He was in government service from 1962 to 1966.

Keppel was chair of the General Learning Corporation, vice chair of the New York City Board of Higher Education, director of the Aspen Institute (1974–90), member of the Twentieth Conference on Public Education in Switzerland (1957), and member of the American Academy of Arts and Sciences.

References: CB (1963, 1990); CHE, January 16, 1985, p. 26; NYT, February 21, 1990, p. A22; WWW (10); Nancy Hoffman and Robert Schwartz, "Remembrance of Things Past: An Interview with Francis Keppel and Harold Howe II [q.v.]," *Change* 22 (March/April 1990): 52–57; Franklin Parker (q.v.), "Francis Keppel of Harvard: Pied Piper of American Education," *School and Society* 91 (March 9, 1963): 126–30; *Saturday Review* 45 (December 15, 1967): 41.

KINGSBURY, Cyrus. b. November 22, 1786, Alstead, New Hampshire. Married: no. d. June 27, 1870, Boggy Depot, Indian Territory (Oklahoma).

For more than fifty years Cyrus Kingsbury served as a missionary to the Cherokee and Choctaw Indians. He established mission stations and schools, including one at Brainerd, near Chattanooga, Tennessee, for the American Board of Commissioners for Foreign Missions (ABCFM). Kingsbury used the Lancastrian system of education, which required few textbooks. He believed that instruction should be in the Indian languages.

Kingsbury graduated in 1812 from Brown University and in 1815 from Andover Theological Seminary, after which he was ordained. His first missionary efforts were in Tennessee. Later, he went to Cherokee lands in Virginia. After Indian resettlement Kingsbury worked with Choctaws in Indian Territory. The ABCFM's sponsorship of Kingsbury's mission to Indians ended in 1859, but he refused to retire and continued his work with support from a Presbyterian group.

REFERENCES: Arlene Hirschfelder and Paulette Molin, *The Encyclopedia of Native American Religions* (Facts on File, 1992); Rossiter Johnson, ed., *The Twentieth Century Biographical Dictionary of Notable Americans* (Biographical Society, 1904, reprinted by Gale Research 1968); Arminta Scott, ''Cyrus Kingsbury: Missionary to the Choctaws'' (Ph.D. diss., University of Oklahoma, 1975); Carl Waldman, *Who Was Who in Native American History* (Facts on File, 1990); James Grant Wilson and John Fiske, eds., *Appleton's Cyclopaedia of American Biography* (D. Appleton, 1888).

KINGSBURY, Susan Myra. b. October 18, 1870, San Pablo, California, to Willard Belmont and Helen Shuler (De Lamater) Kingsbury. Married: no. d. November 28, 1949, Bryn Mawr, Pennsylvania.

At Bryn Mawr College Susan Kingsbury headed the first graduate department in the United States that trained for careers in social services. Kingsbury helped to design a curriculum that included practical experience. She was an advocate of equal economic and political rights for women.

Kingsbury was raised in Stockton, California. In 1890 she graduated from the College (later, University) of the Pacific, where her mother was dean of women. After two years as a teacher in a country school, she taught history from 1892 to 1899 at Lowell High School in San Francisco, a boys' school. In 1899 she received a master's degree in history from Stanford University. She then attended Columbia University as a fellow of the Women's Education Association of Boston. She studied in England (1903–4), taught one year at Vassar College, and earned the Ph.D. degree from Columbia in 1905. At Simmons College in Boston Kingsbury taught economics from 1906 to 1915. In 1906 she also became director of the Massachusetts Commission on Industrial and Technical Education and director of research at the Women's Educational and Industrial Union of Boston.

M. Carey Thomas (BDAE), president of Bryn Mawr College, heard an address by Kingsbury in 1912 and invited her to join the Bryn Mawr faculty. In 1915 Kingsbury went to Bryn Mawr as director of the Carla Woerishoffer Graduate Department of Social Economy and Social Research (later, Graduate School of Social Work) and professor of social economy. She remained until her retirement in 1936.

Thomas and Kingsbury established the Bryn Mawr Summer School for Women Workers in 1921; Kingsbury directed the first session. The school provided 100 women working in industry the opportunity to study a variety of subjects. It remained on the Bryn Mawr campus until 1935, with Hilda Worthington Smith (q.v.) as director.

Kingsbury helped to found the American Association of Schools of Social Work in 1919 and was vice president of the American Economic Association (1919) and the American Sociological Society. In the American Association of University Women, she was chair of the Committee on Economic and Legislative Status of Women and president of the Philadelphia branch (1936–40). She traveled widely to observe living and working conditions of women. These travels included trips to China, India, and four times to the Soviet Union. She headed Pennsylvania's first minimum wage board.

Among her publications were *Factory, Family and Woman in the Soviet Union* (with Mildred Fairchild, 1935), *Employment and Unemployment in Pre-War and Soviet Russia* (with Mildred Fairchild, 1932), and *Newspapers and the News* (1937).

REFERENCES: BDSW; NAW; NYT, November 29, 1949, p. 30; WWW (2); Mary Jo Deegan, ed., *Women in Sociology* (Greenwood Press, 1991); *Social Service Review* 24 (March 1950): 107.

KLINE, Morris. b. May 1, 1908, Brooklyn, New York, to Bernard and Sarah (Spatt) Kline. Married September 4, 1939, to Helen Mann. Children: three. d. June 9, 1992, Brooklyn, New York.

Morris Kline was a critic of "new math," finding that it created new problems as serious as the ones it addressed. Kline believed mathematics should be taught not as an isolated subject, but in the context of its applications to other fields.

Kline graduated from Boys High School in Brooklyn, New York. He was an instructor at New York University (NYU), while earning B.Sc. (1930), M.Sc. (1932), and Ph.D. (1936) degrees there. From 1936 to 1938 he was a research assistant at the Institute for Advanced Study in Princeton, New Jersey. He returned to NYU in 1938 and taught mathematics there until 1975. He chaired the Mathematics Department at NYU's Washington Square College from 1959 to 1970. During World War II Kline was a physicist at the U.S. Army Signal Corps Engineering Laboratories in New Jersey.

Among his books were *Mathematics in Western Culture* (1953), *Mathematics and the Physical World* (1959), *Mathematics: A Cultural Approach* (1962), *Mathematics for Liberal Arts* (1967), *Why Johnny Can't Add: The Failure of the New Math* (1971), *Why the Professor Can't Teach* (1977), *Mathematics: The Loss of Certainty* (1980), and *Mathematics and the Search for Knowledge* (1985). He edited *Mathematics in the Modern World* (1968), *Mathematical Thought from Ancient to Modern Times* (1972), and *Mathematics: An Introduction to Its Spirit and Use* (1979). In 1958–59 he was a Guggenheim fellow and a Fulbright lecturer in Germany.

REFERENCES: CA (NR-2, 139); NYT, June 10, 1992, p. D23; WD (1994–96); WWW (10).

KNOWLES, Asa Smallidge. b. January 15, 1909, Northeast Harbor, Maine, to Jerome Henry and Lilla Belle (Smallidge) Knowles. Married March 24, 1930, to Edna Irene Worsnop. Children: two. d. August 11, 1990, Boston.

An educational entrepreneur, Asa S. Knowles had an exceptional gift for developing new types of institutions to meet new needs. He developed a variety of programs to bring the curriculum of Rhode Island College to the people it was meant to serve during World War II. In upstate New York on twelve weeks' notice, he established three community colleges to educate returning military personnel. Later in his career, he guided Northeastern University to leadership in cooperative education.

Knowles graduated from Thayer Academy in South Braintree, Massachusetts. After receiving the A.B. degree from Bowdoin College in 1930, he studied at the Harvard Business School (1930–31). In 1931 he became an instructor at Northeastern University. He earned the M.A. degree at Boston University in 1935. From 1936 to 1939 Knowles was head of the Department of Industrial Engineering at Northeastern. While on leave in 1938 he served in Washington, D.C., as a member of the secretariat of the International Management Congress. Returning to Northeastern, from 1939 to 1942 Knowles was dean of the College of Business Administration, director of the Bureau of Business Research, and professor of industrial administration. At Rhode Island College (1942–46) he founded a College of Business Administration and established wartime training and extension programs.

From 1946 to 1948 he was president of the Associated Colleges of Upper New York, comprising Mohawk, Champlain, and Sampson Colleges. At Cornell University he was vice president for university development (1948–51). In 1951 Knowles became the ninth president of the University of Toledo (Ohio), serving until 1958. He was president of the Greater Toledo Television Foundation (1955–58) and a member of the Ohio Commission on Education beyond the High School (1957–58).

Knowles returned to Northeastern University to serve as its third president from 1959 to 1975. Knowles organized University College to serve part-time students and employed people in evening programs. The New England College of Pharmacy was acquired, and in 1964 a College of Nursing was established. Knowles foresaw interest in law enforcement education and founded the College of Criminal Justice in 1967. Northeastern established satellite campuses in area high schools. After retiring as president Knowles served again as dean of the School of Business Administration.

Knowles was author of bulletins for the Bureau of Business Research at Northeastern and *Shawmut: 150 Years of Banking, 1836–1986* (1986). With Robert D. Thomson he wrote *Management of Manpower* (1943) and *Industrial Management* (1944). He coauthored the *Handbook of Cooperative Education* (1971). He was editor in chief of the *Handbook of College and University Administration* (1970) and *International Encyclopedia of Higher Education* (1977).

Knowles was president (1971–72) of the New England Association of Schools and Colleges, vice chair (1962–75) and chair (1975) of the National Commission for Cooperative Education, chair (1970–72) of the council of the Federal Regional Accreditation Commission on Higher Education, and chair (1968–69) of the Massachusetts Higher Education Facilities Commission. Knowles was a fellow of the American Academy of Arts and Sciences. He received many awards, including the Bowdoin Prize in 1978 for outstanding service to humanity and the Cooperative Education Association Herman Schneider (BDAE) Award in 1977.

REFERENCES: CA (29–32R, 132); LE (1974); NCAB (I: 300); NYT, August 15, 1990, p. D21; WWW (10); Rudolph M. Morris, *Where? On Huntington Avenue: Narratives of Northeastern* (Christopher Publishing House, 1977); Richard Thruelsen, ''The Man Who Astonished the Educators,'' *Saturday Evening Post* 219 (February 22, 1947): 24+.

KOHLBERG, Lawrence. b. October 25, 1927, Bronxville, New York, to Alfred and Charlotte (Albrecht) Kohlberg. Married June 12, 1955, to Lucille Stigberg. Children: two. d. c. January 17, 1987, Boston.

Lawrence Kohlberg was a noted researcher on moral education whose scholarship contributed to the growth of the field of developmental psychology. His theory of moral development postulated seven stages. He began moral development projects in schools and prisons.

After high school Kohlberg served in the U.S. Merchant Marine. At the University of Chicago he obtained credits by examination and earned the B.A. degree in one year (1948). He was a clinical trainee at the Boston Veterans Administration (1952–53). After receiving the Ph.D. degree from the University of Chicago in 1958 he taught psychology at Yale University (1959–61) and was a fellow at the Center for Advanced Study in the Behavioral Sciences (1961–62). Returning to the University of Chicago in 1962, Kohlberg was assistant and associate professor of psychology and human development. He founded and directed the Child Psychology Training Program.

Kohlberg went to Harvard University in 1968 as professor of education and social psychology. At Harvard he established the Center for Moral Development and Education.

Kohlberg's article ''Stage and Sequence: The Cognitive-Developmental Approach to Socialization'' in the *Handbook of Socialization Theory and Research* (David A. Goslin, ed., 1969) was regarded as a classic in developmental psychology. Among his writings were *The Meaning and Measurement of Moral Development* (1981), *The Philosophy of Moral Development* (1981), *The Psychology of Moral Development* (1984), *Programs of Early Education: The Constructivist View* (with Rheta DeVries, 1987), and *Child Psychology and Childhood Education: A Cognitive-Developmental View* (1987).

In 1973 Kohlberg contracted a parasitic disease in Central America, which impaired his health in later years. On January 17, 1987, he was reported missing from Cambridge (Massachusetts) Mount Auburn Hospital. His body was discovered in the Boston Harbor several months later, the death attributed to drowning. The October 1988 issue of the *Journal of Moral Education* was issued in his honor.

REFERENCES: CA (122, 125); ECE; NYT, January 31, 1987, p. 10, and April 8, 1987,

p. D30; WWW (9); *American Psychologist* 43 (May 1988): 399–400; *Human Development* 31 (May–June 1988): 191–93; *Journal of Counseling and Development* 72 (January/February 1994): 261–65; *Zygon* 22 (September 1987): 387; Sohan Modgil and Celia Modgil, eds., *Lawrence Kohlberg: Consensus and Controversy* (Falmer Press, 1986); Dawn Schrader, ed., *The Legacy of Lawrence Kohlberg* (Jossey-Bass, 1990); F. Clark Power, Ann Higgins, and Lawrence Kohlberg, *Lawrence Kohlberg's Approach to Moral Education* (Columbia University Press, 1989); Lisa Kuhmerker, *The Kohlberg Legacy for the Helping Professions* (R. E. P. Books, 1991).

KOONTZ, Elizabeth Duncan. b. June 3, 1919, Salisbury, North Carolina, to Samuel Edward and Lena Bell (Jordan) Duncan. Married November 26, 1947, to Harry Lee Koontz. Children: no. d. January 6, 1989, Salisbury, North Carolina.

Elizabeth Duncan Koontz was the first African American to serve as president of the National Education Association (NEA). She was an advocate of "teacher power." Previously, she had been president of the NEA Department of Classroom Teachers (1965–66), following terms as secretary and vice president. Her professional association activities had begun in 1952 on the local and state levels, including service as president of the North Carolina Teachers Association from 1959 to 1963.

Elizabeth (Libby) Duncan was raised in Salisbury, North Carolina, where she attended segregated schools. She graduated from Price High School as salutatorian in 1935. In 1938 she received the B.A. degree from Livingstone College. Her first position was teaching a special education class at the Harnett County Training School in Dunn, North Carolina (1938–40). Teachers lived in a boardinghouse owned by the school. When Duncan protested the lodging charges, she was dismissed.

At Atlanta (later, Clark–Atlanta) University she earned the M.A. degree in 1941. She studied special education at North Carolina State College in Durham (later, North Carolina Central University). During 1941–42 she taught in Landis and from 1942 to 1945 in Winston-Salem, North Carolina. Returning to Salisbury, she taught at Price Junior-Senior High School (1945–49) and at Monroe School (1949–65). When special classes were established in 1957 for slow learners, she became the special education teacher.

In 1964 Koontz was one of sixteen educators *Saturday Review* invited to visit the Soviet Union. While NEA president (1968–69), she started its Center for Human Relations. In 1969 President Richard Nixon named Koontz director of the Women's Bureau in the Department of Labor, where she advocated equal pay for women. In 1970 she was a delegate to the United Nations Commission on the Status of Women. On leaving the Bureau, Koontz returned to North Carolina, where she coordinated nutrition programs for the state Department of Human Resources. Her last position was as assistant state schools superintendent in North Carolina from 1975 to her 1982 retirement.

REFERENCES: BWA; CB (1969, 1989); LE (1974); NBAW; NYT, January 8, 1989, p.

26; WWAW (1977); WP, January 7, 1989, p. B6; WWW (9); Lynn Gilbert and Gaylen Moore, *Particular Passions: Talks with Women Who Have Shaped Our Times* (C. N. Potter; distributed by Crown, 1981), pp. 129–33; *Journal of Home Economics* 81 (Summer 1989): 58; Gayle J. Hardy, *American Women Civil Rights Activists* (McFarland, 1993).

KOTLER, Aaron. b. 1891 or 1892, Russian Poland (later, Belarus). Married 1913 to Chana Perl Meltzer. Children: two. d. November 29, 1962, New York City.

Sources differ on the places and dates of Rabbi Aaron Kotler's early life, before his immigration to the United States. Son of a rabbi, from youth he was known for his great knowledge of Torah. Married to a rabbi's daughter, while still in his twenties he led a yeshiva variously given as in Kletsk or Slutzk, in the vicinity of Minsk.

Kotler fled German armies and the annihilation of Jewish communities, going first to Vilna, Lithuania, in 1939, then in 1941 across Asia and the Pacific Ocean to the United States. He had first visited this country in 1936, when he encouraged the founding of an Orthodox institute for advanced rabbinical and Talmudic studies in Spring Valley, New York. On his return he founded a like institution, Beth Medrash Govoha, in Lakewood, New Jersey, in 1943. It grew to be the largest advanced yeshiva in the world. Kotler served as its director until his death. His successors were his son, Rabbi Schneur Kotler, and grandson, Rabbi Malkiel Kotler.

Aaron Kotler was chairman of the Rabbinical Council of Torah Umisorah, a national association of Jewish day schools, and led the Union of Orthodox Rabbis of the United States and Canada. He chaired the Council of Torah Sages of Agudath Israel and helped to found an independent Orthodox school system in Israel.

REFERENCES: NYT, November 30, 1962, p. 33; *American Jewish Year Book* 65 (Jewish Publication Society of America, 1964); *The Encyclopedia of Jewish Institutions: United States and Canada* (Mosadot, 1983), p. 210; Alex J. Goldman, *Giants of Truth* (Citadel Press, 1965); Sidney R. Lewitter, ''A School for Scholars: The Beth Medrash Govoha, The Rabbi Aaron Kotler Jewish Institute of Higher Learning in Lakewood, New Jersey'' (Ed.D diss., Rutgers University, 1981).

KRANZBERG, Melvin. b. November 22, 1917, St. Louis, Missouri, to Samuel and Rose (Fitter) Kranzberg. Married 1943 to Nancy Lee Fox; 1956 to Eva Mannering; 1962 to Adelaide H. Waltz; 1972 to Dolores Campen; 1985 to Louise Clark Catlett. Children: two. d. December 6, 1995, Atlanta, Georgia.

Melvin Kranzberg established the history of technology as a field of study. He received the B.A. degree (1935) from Amherst College and M.A. (1938) and Ph.D. (1942) degrees from Harvard University. He served with military intelligence in the U.S. Army (1943–46) and received a Bronze Star. He taught

European history at Harvard (1946), Stevens Institute of Technology (1946–47), and Amherst College (1947–52).

While at Case Institute of Technology (later, Case Western Reserve University) from 1952 to 1962, Kranzberg developed a history course for engineering students. He directed the graduate program in history of science and technology (1963–72). In 1972 he became Callaway Professor of the History of Technology at Georgia Institute of Technology. After his 1988 retirement, a professorship was named in his honor.

In 1958 Kranzberg cofounded the Society for the History of Technology, which he served as secretary. He founded the society's journal, *Technology and Culture*, and was its editor from 1958 to 1984. He also cofounded the International Committee for the History of Technology and was its vice president. Later, he was its first honorary president. He was chair of the History Advisory Committee of the National Aeronautics and Space Administration (NASA) and president of Sigma Xi (1979–80).

Among Kranzberg's publications were *By the Sweat of Thy Brow: Work in the Western World* (with Joseph Geis, 1975) and *Innovation at the Crossroads between Science and Technology* (1989). He coedited *Technology in Western Civilization* (1967), *Technology and Culture: An Anthology* (1972), *Technological Innovation* (1978), *Energy and the Way We Live* (1980), and *Bridge to the Future: A Centennial Celebration of the Brooklyn Bridge* (1984). He edited *Ethics in an Age of Pervasive Technology* (1980). His books were translated into Spanish, Italian, Japanese, and Arabic.

Awards received by Kranzberg included the Leonardo da Vinci Medal from the Society for the History of Technology (1967), NASA Apollo Achievement Award (1970), Roe Medal of the American Society of Mechanical Engineers (1980), Jabotinsky Centennial Medal from Israel (1980), Olmstead Award from the American Society of Engineers, and Bernal Award from the Society for the Social Studies of Science (1991). In 1989 Stephen H. Cutcliffe and Robert C. Post prepared *In Context: History and the History of Technology: Essays in Honor of Melvin Kranzberg*.

REFERENCES: CA (NR-11); NYT, December 9, 1995, p. 52; WD (1994–96); WW (1996); *Cleveland* (Ohio) *Plain Dealer*, December 14, 1995; *Science, Technology, and Human Values* 17 (Summer 1992): 386–89; John M. Staudenmaier, *Technology's Storytellers* (MIT Press, 1985).

KRUG, Edward August. b. September 26, 1911, Chicago, to Rudolph Hugo and Anna (Wendt) Krug. Married April 10, 1937, to Annie Ellen McDonald. Children: three. d. July 30, 1979, Madison, Wisconsin.

Edward A. Krug was the author of *The Shaping of the American High School, 1880–1920* (1964) and *The Shaping of the American High School, 1920–41* (1972), regarded as the definitive histories of American secondary education.

Krug attended schools in Chicago and received B.S. (1933) and M.S. (1934) degrees from Northwestern University. From 1935 to 1938 he taught social studies at Evanston (Illinois) Township High School. He earned the Ed.D. degree at Stanford University in 1941. While studying at Stanford, he served as an evaluator on the Motion Picture Project of the American Council on Education and on the staff of the Stanford Social Education Investigation (1941–43). Krug was assistant professor of education at the University of Montana (1943–45).

He was associate professor of education at the University of Wisconsin (1945–47) while also serving as Wisconsin state curriculum coordinator (1945–46). He spent one year at Stanford, then returned to Wisconsin in 1948, where he remained until his retirement in 1976. Beginning in 1966, he was the first Virgil Herrick Professor of Educational Policy Studies.

A prolific writer, Krug served on the editorial board of *History of Education Quarterly*. He wrote *Curriculum Planning* (1950), *The Secondary School Curriculum* (1960), and *Salient Dates in American Education* (1966) and edited *Charles W. Eliot* (BDAE) *and Popular Education* (1961). With F. L. Bacon he wrote *Our Life Today* (1939) and *Outwitting the Hazards* (1941); with Paul Hanna (BDAE), *Marketing the Things We Use* (1943); and with I. J. Quillen (BDAE), *Living in Our Communities* (1946) and *Living in Our America* (1951). He coauthored many other books, including *Schools and Our Democratic Society* (1952), *Administering Curriculum Planning* (1956), and *The College-Preparatory Function in Wisconsin High Schools* (1959).

REFERENCES: CA (NR-4); LE (1974); NCAB (62: 7); WWW (7); *History of Education Quarterly* 19 (Winter 1979): 523–24.

L

LABATUT, Jean. b. May 10, 1899, Martres-Tolosane, Haute-Garonne, France, to Dominique and Gabrielle (Clarac) Labatut. Married June 10, 1929, to Mercedes Terradell. Children: no. d. November 26, 1986, Princeton, New Jersey.

A leader in architectural education in the United States, Jean Labatut guided the Princeton University School of Architecture to become one of the foremost in the nation. Labatut established the first doctoral program in architecture in the country.

Labatut's early career was spent in France and Spain. He became professor of architecture at Princeton University in 1928 and was director of graduate studies in architecture there for a number of years. In 1941 he founded the Bureau of Urban Research. The architecture school's program came to include urban planning. The effects of environment on building materials were studied by the architecture laboratory, which Labatut established in 1949. He retired in 1967.

Labatut wrote articles for professional journals and *The University's Position with Regards to the Visual Arts* and was editor of *Highways in Our National Life* (with Wheaton J. Lane, 1950). He served as a consultant to the Board of Design for the New York's World Fair (1937–40), was the architect for the José Martí Monument Plaza and Park in Havana, Cuba, and was architect in residence at the American Academy in Rome several times. He received the Thomas Jefferson Memorial Foundation Medal in Architecture. In 1976 he was the first recipient of a joint award from the American Institute of Architects and the Association of Collegiate Schools of Architecture for lasting achievement in architectural education.

REFERENCES: CA (121); NYT, November 29, 1986, p. 36; WW (1978–79); *AIA Journal* 65 (June 1976): 18.

LARRICK, Nancy Gray. b. December 28, 1910, Winchester, Virginia, to Herbert S. and Nancy (Nulton) Larrick. Married February 15, 1958, to Alexander L. Crosby. Children: no.

Nancy Larrick was an expert in the field of children's literature and reading and wrote many books about or for children. She was a critic of racial biases in children's books.

Larrick received the A.B. degree from Goucher College in 1930 and taught in the Winchester, Virginia, schools from 1930 to 1942. She received the M.A. degree from Columbia University in 1937. From 1942 to 1945 she was education director of the War Bond Division of the U.S. Treasury Department. She was editor of *Young America Readers*, weekly newsmagazines (1946–51); and education director in the children's books department at Random House, Inc. (1951–59). She earned the Ed.D. degree at New York University in 1955.

From 1954 to 1979 Larrick was an adjunct professor of education at Lehigh University. She also taught at many other institutions. Larrick compiled several anthologies of poetry for children. Among her books for children were *See for Yourself: A First Book of Science Experiments* (1952), *Junior Science Book of Rain, Hail, Sleet and Snow* (1961), *Rivers, What They Do* (1961), and *Let's Do a Poem!* (1991). Her other books included *Printing and Promotion Handbook* (with Daniel Melcher, 1949), *A Parent's Guide to Children's Reading* (1958), *A Teacher's Guide to Children's Books* (1960), *A Parent's Guide to Children's Education* (1963), *Children's Reading Begins at Home* (1980), and *Encourage Your Children to Read* (1981). She edited *Better Readers for Our Times* (with William S. Gray, 1956), *Reading in Action* (1957), and *Reading: Isn't It Really the Teacher?* (with Charles J. Versacci, 1968).

Larrick was editor (1950–54) and editorial adviser (1970–76) of *The Reading Teacher* and editor of *English Journal* (1974–76). She was president of the International Reading Association (1956–57). She received the Edison Foundation Award (1959), the Carey-Thomas Award (1959), and a Certificate of Merit from the International Reading Association (1977). She became a member of the Reading Hall of Fame in 1977.

REFERENCES: CA (NR-1); LE (1974); RPE; WD (1994–96); *Dictionary of Literary Biography*, vol. 61 (Gale Research, 1987).

LAZARSFELD, Paul Felix. b. February 23, 1901, Vienna, Austria, to Robert and Sofie (Munk) Lazarsfeld. Married 1928 to Marie Jahoda; February 29, 1936, to Herta Herzog; November 21, 1949, to Patricia Kendall. Children: two. d. August 30, 1976, New York City.

Paul Lazarsfeld was an expert on mass communications media and an authority on American popular culture. He conducted extensive research on radio and its influence on the public and was recognized for his public opinion research. His panel studies were first used in the 1940 presidential campaign to interpret voters' decision making. He also helped to open the field of mathematical sociology.

Lazarsfeld studied psychology and mathematics at the University of Vienna, where he received the doctor of philosophy degree in applied mathematics in 1925. He taught mathematics at a junior college in Vienna. In 1929 he became an instructor at the Psychological Institute of the University of Vienna, where he founded and directed the Division of Applied Psychology. His first books were *Jugend und Beruf* (1931) and *Die Arbeitslosen in Marienthal* (with Marie Jahoda and Hans Zeisel, 1933). After the Rockefeller Foundation gave him a travel grant in 1933 to study psychology and observe research techniques, Lazarsfeld chose to remain in the United States. At the University of Newark (later, Rutgers University, Newark) he established and directed a research center. From 1937 to 1940 he was at Princeton University as director of the Rockefeller Foundation's Office of Radio Research. He collaborated with Frank Stanton of the Columbia Broadcasting System in analyzing radio listening habits and the sociological effects of programs. They developed the Lazarsfeld–Stanton program analyzer and wrote *Radio Research 1941.*

The Office of Radio Research was moved to Columbia University in 1940. While continuing as its director, Lazarsfeld was also associate professor of sociology (1940–62). At Columbia he began his research into voting patterns. In the mid-1940s the office expanded into the Bureau of Applied Social Research, with Lazarsfeld as director until 1950. He developed latent structure analysis, a mathematical technique applied to sociological findings. In 1963 he became Quetelet Professor of Social Science at Columbia, a chair created for him. He was a Distinguished Professor at the University of Pittsburgh from 1970 to 1976.

Lazarsfeld was the author of many books, including *Radio and the Printed Page* (1940), *The People's Choice* (1944), *Voting* (1954), *Mathematical Thinking in the Social Sciences* (1954), *The Language of Social Research* (with Morris Rosenberg, 1955), *Personal Influence* (with Elihu Katz, 1966), and *Qualitative Analysis* (1972). In 1979 Robert K. Merton, James S. Coleman (q.v.), and P. H. Rossi edited *Qualitative and Quantitative Social Research: Papers in Honor of Paul F. Lazarsfeld.* Lazarsfeld was the first recipient of the Julian L. Woodward Award from the American Association for Public Opinion Research in 1955.

REFERENCES: CA (NR-29, 69–72); CB (1964, 1976); DAB (supp. 10); EAB; IESS (18); NCAB (59: 331); NYT, September 1, 1976, p. 38; WWW (7); James S. Coleman, ''Paul F. Lazarsfeld: The Substance and Style of His Work,'' in Robert K. Merton and Matilda White Riley, eds., *Sociological Traditions from Generation to Generation* (Ablex, 1980); Paul F. Lazarsfeld, ''An Episode in the History of Social Research: A Memoir,'' in Donald Fleming and Bernard Bailyn, eds., *Perspectives in American History*, vol. 2 (Charles Warren Center for Studies in American History; Harvard University, 1968); Donald Paneth, *The Encyclopedia of American Journalism* (Facts on File, 1983); *Public Opinion Quarterly* 40 (Winter 1976–77): 556–57; David L. Sills, ''Paul F. Lazarsfeld,'' *National Academy of Sciences Biographical Memoirs*, vol. 56 (National Academy of Sciences, 1987), pp. 250–82; Nico Stehr, ''A Conversation with Paul F. Lazarsfeld,'' *The American Sociologist* 17 (August 1982): 150–55.

LEFKOWITZ, Abraham. b. October 17, 1884, Revish, Hungary. Married to Esther Lefkowitz. Children: four. d. November 7, 1956, New York City.

A champion of teachers' rights and academic freedom, Abraham Lefkowitz helped to found and lead the American Federation of Teachers (AFT), which he served as vice president (1920–34). He was known for his knowledge of financial and budgetary matters and his support for federal aid to education.

Lefkowitz received the A.B. degree (1904) from the City College of New York and A.M. (1907) and Ph.D. (1914) degrees from New York University.

He began teaching in the New York City school system in 1903. He taught at Public School 147 in Brooklyn (1911–15), at DeWitt Clinton High School, and at the High School of Commerce. In 1926 Lefkowitz was passed over for promotion to first assistant in history (head of a department), although he was first on the list of eligibility. The reason given was his radicalism, which raised questions concerning the freedom of teachers. After he was given the promotion one and one-half years later, he headed the Department of History and Civics at the High School of Commerce (1928–38). At his installation as principal of Samuel J. Tilden High School (1938–55) he was praised by city officials and many in the school system.

Lefkowitz was a leader of the New York City Teachers Union and was their legislative representative in Albany. From 1916 to 1926 he was coeditor of *The American Teacher*, the journal of the AFT. He and Henry Linville (BDAE) were active in supporting the civil rights of teachers. In 1935 Lefkowitz and Linville withdrew from the New York City Teachers Union because of its alleged communist leanings and helped to establish the Teachers Guild. Lefkowitz was legislative representative for the guild and editor of its bulletin. After the local Teachers Union was expelled from the AFT, Lefkowitz and Linville rejoined the AFT. Lefkowitz served as vice president and legislative representative of the Joint Committee of Teachers' Organizations in New York and in the 1940s as legislative representative of the Empire State Federation of Teachers Unions. He helped to organize and represented the Central Trades and Labor Council of New York.

Lefkowitz was active in reform movements. He was a director of Brookwood Labor College from its establishment in 1921 to 1935 and of Malumit Experimental School (1925–29). He was on the executive board of the National Urban League from its beginning in 1910.

REFERENCES: LE (1948); NYT, November 8, 1956, p. 39; Solon De Leon, ed., *American Labor Who's Who* (Hanford Press, 1925); Philip Taft, *United They Teach* (Nash, 1974).

LERNER, Gerda. b. April 30, 1920, Vienna, Austria, to Robert and Ilona (Neumann) Kronstein. Married October 6, 1941, to Carl Lerner. Children: two.

Gerda Lerner was a pioneer in women's history, creating courses and establishing doctoral programs. Her writings on the subject had a wide impact.

Born in Vienna, Austria, Lerner came to the United States in 1939 at the age of nineteen, the only member of her family to escape the annihilation of European Jews by national socialism. She became a U.S. citizen in 1943. As an adult student she received the B.A. degree from the New School for Social Research in 1963 and lectured there from 1963 to 1965. Her M.A. (1965) and Ph.D. (1966) degrees were earned at Columbia University. From 1966 to 1968 Lerner taught at Long Island University.

On the history faculty of Sarah Lawrence College from 1968 to 1980, Lerner directed programs in women's history. In 1980 she became Robinson–Edwards

Professor of History at the University of Wisconsin–Madison. Lerner served as president of the Organization of American Historians (1981–82), the first woman in that office in fifty years. She was a fellow of the National Endowment for the Humanities (1976) and Ford (1978–79), Lilly (1979), and Guggenheim (1980–81) Foundations.

Among her books were *The Grimke Sisters from South Carolina: Rebels against Slavery* (1967), *The Woman in American History* (1971), *Black Women in White America* (1972), *Women Are History: A Bibliography in the History of American Women* (1975), *The Majority Finds Its Past: Placing Women in History* (1979), *Women and History*: vol. 1, *The Creation of Patriarchy*, and vol. 2, *The Creation of Feminine Consciousness* (1986), and *United States History as Women's History* (1995). She wrote of her husband's illness and death in *A Death of One's Own* (1978).

REFERENCES: CA (NR-45); CHE, June 8, 1981, pp. 7–8; NYT, April 28, 1986, p. B4; WW (1990–91); WWAW (1989–90); Lina Mainiero, ed., *American Women Writers*, vol. 2 (Ungar, 1980).

LEWIS, Inez Johnson. b. 1875, Stone County Missouri, to John Mitchell and Florence Adah (Nelson) Johnson. Married December 26, 1910, to Harry Loring Lewis. Children: no. d. January 1964.

During sixteen years as the Colorado state superintendent of public instruction, Inez Johnson Lewis was known for improving school curricula, developing nursery school and day-care programs, and bringing library materials to remote locations via bookmobiles. Her statewide service followed fourteen years as a county superintendent. In that role she was an early proponent of consolidating small rural schools in order to improve their quality and the variety of their programs.

As a girl Inez Johnson moved with her family from Missouri to Kansas and later to Colorado Springs, Colorado, where she graduated from the city high school. From 1914 she studied at Colorado College, earning the B.A. degree there in 1928. She received the M.A. degree in school administration from Teachers College, Columbia University in 1930.

Information on Inez Johnson Lewis' early career is sketchy. She taught school in Colorado Springs before winning election in 1908 to the county superintendency, a post she held until 1912. After losing that office, she gained it again for the years 1915–28. She failed on her first try for election as state superintendent (1928) but was successful in 1930 and won reelection biennially until 1946. When she lost the 1946 election, at the age of seventy-one, she retired. During the 1940s there was increasing political controversy about Lewis' role and work, as the state legislature considered tenure and pensions for teachers. Two years after she retired, the position she had held was abolished, replaced by a state commissioner whom an elected board of education appointed.

Lewis was author of *Elementary Courses of Study for Colorado Schools* (1936) and *Colorado's Wealth: A Bulletin on Conservation of Natural Resources*

(1942). She was president of the National Council of Administrative Women in Education (1937–39), chair of the Division on Public Instruction of the General Federation of Women's Clubs (1939–41), president of the Colorado Education Association, and vice president of the National Council of Chief State School Officers.

REFERENCES: WW (1950–51); *Colorado and Its People* (1948), vol. 3, pp. 28–30; Colorado College, Tutt Library, Inez Johnson Lewis Collection; *Thirty-Third and Thirty-Fourth Biennial Reports of the State Superintendent of Public Instruction of the State of Colorado* (1942–44).

LIEBERMAN, Myron. b. April 30, 1919, St. Paul, Minnesota. Married to Mary Elizabeth Arthur. Children: four.

Beginning with publication of *The Future of Public Education* (1960), Myron Lieberman was a well-known advocate for rigorous standards and greater professionalism in American education. In *Public Education: An Autopsy* (1993) he argued that public schooling was in irreversible decline and proposed a three-sector education industry of public, nonprofit, and for-profit schools. Lieberman was both a university professor and a collective bargaining consultant and negotiator for teachers, school boards, and school board organizations.

He earned the B.S. in law degree from the University of Minnesota (1941), served in the U.S. Army during World War II (1942–46), and was with the U.S. War Department in Japan (1946–47). After receiving the B.S.Ed. degree from the University of Minnesota (1948), he was a high school teacher in St. Paul (1948–49).

Lieberman taught at the University of Illinois (1949–52) and University of Oklahoma (1953–56) and chaired the Department of Education at Yeshiva University (1956–59). He directed basic research for the Educational Research Council of Greater Cleveland (Ohio) for one year, taught at Rhode Island College (1963–69) and City College of New York (1969–75), and was Distinguished Professor of Education at the University of Southern California (1975–77). From 1976 Lieberman was president of Educational Employment Services, Inc.

Among his books were *Education as a Profession* (1956), *Educational Accountability* (1971), *Bargaining Before, During, and After* (1979), *Public-Sector Bargaining* (1980), *Beyond Public Education* (1986), *Privatization and Educational Choice* (1989), and *Public School Choice* (1990). He coauthored *Social Forces Influencing Public Education* (1961) and *Collective Negotiations for Teachers* (1966).

REFERENCES: CA (NR-8); LE (1974); WW (1996).

LLOYD, Alice Spencer Geddes. b. November 13, 1876, Athol, Massachusetts, to William Edwin and Ella Mary (Ainsworth) Geddes. Married February 16, 1914, to Arthur Lloyd. Children: no. d. September 4, 1962, Pippa Passes, Kentucky.

In 1916 Alice Lloyd moved from New England to the eastern Kentucky mountains, an impoverished area with almost no educational opportunities. There Lloyd founded a school and devoted her life to the establishment of schools to train mountain youth of Knott County. During her lifetime the county's literacy rate rose from 10 to 98 percent.

Born Alice Spencer Geddes, she was a graduate of Chauncey Hall in Boston and studied for a time at Radcliffe College. In Massachusetts towns she was publisher of the *Cambridge Press* and managing editor of the *Wakefield Citizen and Banner* (1905). In 1916 Lloyd went with her mother to Kentucky, seeking a warmer climate because of partial paralysis caused by spinal meningitis. A landowner at Caney Creek offered her fifty acres in exchange for teaching his children. She solicited Radcliffe College friends for funds to build a school. Caney Creek Community Center was founded in 1918, and a building soon was erected. It provided home management classes for women, vocational training for men, and education for children.

A high school was opened in 1919 with two students; it became the Knott County High School in 1924. The community she had started acquired the name Pippa Passes. Lloyd continued to garner funds to open other high schools in the area. Caney Junior College was established in 1923 to serve mountain youth. Students paid for their education with farm products and labor, no tuition being charged. A traditional curriculum was offered, and strict codes of conduct were followed. It became a fully accredited school. By 1956 the community center had forty-four buildings. Public funds paid for grade and high school teachers.

After Lloyd died in 1962, the college was renamed Alice Lloyd College. It became a four-year college in 1980.

REFERENCES: NAW (Mod); WWAW (1964); WR; "Alice Lloyd College," PCU; *Newsweek* 47 (September 2, 1956): 54; P. David Searles, *A College for Appalachia: Alice Lloyd on Caney Creek* (University Press of Kentucky, 1995); Robert W. Sloane, ed., *Alice Lloyd—Boston's Gift to Caney Creek* (Thoroughbred Press, 1982); *Time* 35 (April 8, 1940): 52–53.

LLOYD, Wesley Parkinson. b. June 16, 1904, Ogden, Utah, to Charles E. and Lucy (Parkinson) Lloyd. Married December 30, 1926, to Lillie Murdock. Children: two. d. March 7, 1977, La Jolla, California.

Wesley Lloyd was a leader in administrative services to college students and an international adviser on student counseling and educational administration.

After early schooling in St. Anthony, Idaho, Lloyd graduated from Latter Day Saints' High School in Salt Lake City. He earned B.S. (1927) and M.S. (1934) degrees at Brigham Young University. Lloyd taught social science and coached athletics at Rexburg (Idaho) High School (1927–30) and was principal of Latter Day Saints' seminaries in the Idaho towns of Grace (1930–33) and Oakley (1931–32). At the University of Chicago he completed the Ph.D. degree in education and religion in 1937.

From Chicago he returned to Brigham Young University, where he was dean of men (1937–44), dean of students (1944–60), chair of the Department of Philosophy of Education (1937–50), dean of the Graduate School (1960–69), and professor of education (1939–69). He was dean of the Graduate School of Arts and Sciences at United States International University from 1969 to 1972 and director of California Western College from 1972 to 1974. He chaired the Center for Leadership Education from 1974 until his death, applying the Lloyd Education Values Profile, which he had invented.

He served as president of the Utah Conference on Higher Education (1946–47), National Association of Student Personnel Administrators (1949–50), National Association of Deans and Advisors to Men (1950–51), and Western Association of Graduate Schools (1967–68). During the U.S. military occupation of Japan, Lloyd was twice director of the Japanese Institutes Personnel Services (1951–52 and 1954–55), which provided advice on the development of student services and organizations in higher education. He consulted also on educational issues in Burma, Colombia, Venezuela, and the Bahamas.

He was author of *Learning to Live* (1940), *Student Counseling in Japan: A Two-Nation Project in Higher Education* (1953), *Student Personnel Services in Japan* (1957), *Student Personnel Services in Universities of the World* (1957), and *The University in the Changing Community* (1961).

REFERENCES: CB (1952, 1977); LE (1974); NCAB (60: 247); NYT, March 10, 1977, p. 38; WWW (7); Ernest L. Wilkinson, *Brigham Young University: A School of Destiny* (Brigham Young University Press, 1976).

LOCKE, Bessie. b. August 7, 1865, West Cambridge (later, Arlington), Massachusetts, to William Henry and Jane MacFarland (Schouler) Locke. Married: no. d. April 9, 1952, New York City.

While not a kindergarten teacher herself, Bessie Locke founded the National Kindergarten Association, which helped to establish kindergartens throughout the United States. She served as its director and executive secretary for many years. More than 3,200 kindergartens were opened due to her efforts and those of the association.

Locke attended public school in Brooklyn, New York, and took business courses at Columbia University. She worked as a bookkeeper in her father's factory and served as pastor's assistant at All Souls Church. She helped to organize industrial classes for women. Later, she operated a millinery store in North Carolina.

Returning from North Carolina, Locke visited a friend's kindergarten class in a New York City slum area and was impressed with the impact the class had on the children's lives. From then on she devoted her life to the establishment of kindergartens.

Soliciting funds to found a kindergarten, Locke formed the East End Kindergarten Union of Brooklyn. She was founding secretary and, later, trustee of the Brooklyn Free Kindergarten Society and secretary of the New York Kindergarten Association. John D. Archbold of the Standard Oil Company donated

$250,000 to acquire land and build a structure to house the association. In 1909 Locke organized the National Association for the Promotion of Kindergarten Education (renamed the National Kindergarten Association in 1911).

Philander P. Claxton (BDAE), U.S. commissioner of education, asked the association to assist in forming a kindergarten division in the U.S. Bureau of Education in 1912; Locke served as chief from 1913 to 1919. Under her leadership the division improved kindergarten teacher training courses and published home education articles for parents that had a wide distribution for many years.

Locke was chairman of the kindergarten division of the National Congress of Parents and Teachers (1913–22) and a director of the National Council of Women (1921–46). She served on the governing board of the National College of Education in Evanston, Illinois (from 1920).

REFERENCES: BCAW; DAB (supp. 5); LW; NCAB (39: 14); NYT, April 11, 1952, p. 23; WWW (3); Durwood Howes, ed., *American Women 1935–1940* (Gale Research, 1981); Gloria Williams Ladd, "The National Kindergarten Association, 1909–1976: Its Place in Early Childhood Education" (Ed.D. diss., Columbia University Teachers College, 1982).

LORGE, Irving Daniel. b. April 19, 1905, New York City, to Solomon and Frieda (Katz) Lorge. Married August 13, 1939, to Sarah Wolfson. Children: two. d. January 23, 1961, New York City.

Irving Lorge was a psychologist interested in gifted children, psychological training, and psychology of aging. He developed readability and intelligence tests and questioned the constancy of intelligence quotients.

Lorge graduated from Townsend Harris High School, a secondary school for gifted students in New York City. He was a fellow of the School of Education at City College of New York (1925–27), where he received the B.S. degree in 1926. He spent his career at Columbia University, where he earned M.A. (1927) and Ph.D. (1930) degrees. Beginning as research assistant with the Institute of Educational Research of Teachers College, he became a professor of education in 1946.

Edward L. Thorndike (BDAE) interested Lorge in psychological research. Lorge succeeded Thorndike as executive officer of the Institute of Educational Research (1939–46). They developed the Lorge–Thorndike Intelligence Tests. In 1946 Lorge became executive officer of the Institute of Psychological Research at Columbia.

During World War II Lorge initiated changes in the teaching of illiterates in the service. He served as a consultant to several governmental agencies. His testing of the readability of regulations of the Office of Price Administration led to their revision.

Among his books were *Rural Trends in Depression Years* (with Edmund deS. Brunner, 1937), *The Semantic Count of English Words* (with Edward L. Thorndike, 1938), *The Teacher's Word Book of 30,000 Words* (with Edward L. Thorndike, 1944), *Retirement and the Industrial Worker* (with Jacob Tuckman, 1953),

The Lorge Formula for Estimating Difficulty of Reading Materials (1959); *Psychology of Adults* (with others, 1963), and *Terminology and Concepts in Mental Retardation* (with Joel R. Davitz and Lois J. Davitz, 1964).

REFERENCES: BDP; CB (1959, 1961); ECP; NYT, January 24, 1961, p. 29; WWW (4); *American Men of Science* (1956, vol. 3); *Encyclopaedia Judaica* (Macmillan, 1971).

LOVE, Ruth Burnett. b. April 22, 1932, Lawton, Oklahoma, to Alvin E. and Burnett C. Love. Married to James A. Holloway.

Ruth B. Love headed the Right-to-Read program of the U.S. Office of Education and served as superintendent of two urban school systems: Oakland, California, and Chicago.

Love received the B.A. degree in elementary education from San Jose State University in 1954 and the M.A. in guidance and counseling from San Francisco State University in 1959. She was a teacher in Oakland Unified School District (1954–59), served as a counselor/consultant for a Ford Foundation project (1960–62), and was an adult education teacher. In 1960 she was an exchange teacher in Cheshire, England. In the summer of 1962 she served as a project director for Operation Crossroads in Ghana. With the California State Department of Education, she was a consultant to the Bureau of Pupil Personnel Services (1963–65) and director of the Bureau of Compensatory Education (1965–71). Love received the Ph.D. degree in 1970 from United States International University.

In 1971 Love was chosen by Sidney Marland (q.v.), U.S. commissioner of education, to head the Right-to-Read program of the U.S. Office of Education. Because the program did not secure the funding she had been promised, Love resigned after six months, but she was persuaded to return and served to 1975. She favored a decentralized structure, with states developing literacy programs, her goal being to eliminate illiteracy by 1980. She encouraged states to require reading instruction in teacher education programs and advocated staff development.

The Oakland School District chose Love as superintendent in 1975, to succeed recently assassinated Marcus Foster (q.v.). When Love went to Chicago as superintendent in 1981, the board was split on the decision to hire her, amid a struggle for control of the school system. Love introduced the ''Adopt-a-School'' program, which attracted funds from individuals and corporations. She was criticized for her management style, in a system that was very large and intractable. Leaving the superintendency in 1984, Love was a commentator for a Chicago television station. She returned to California and conducted Ruth Love Enterprises, a consulting firm.

Love served on the President's Mental Health Commission and was on the Boards of Directors of the National Urban League (1977–82) and Reading Is Fundamental. She wrote *Strengthening Counseling Services for Disadvantaged Youth* (1966), *Hello World: A Career Exploration Program* (nine volumes, 1973), and *Johnny Can Read—So Can Jane* (1982). While Love was divorced and used her maiden name, some references to her are under the surname Holloway.

REFERENCES: AWM; LE (1974); NBAW; WW (1984–85); WWBA (1994–95); Nancy L. Arnez, "Selected Black Female Superintendents of Public School Systems," and Deanne M. Pindehughes, "Black Women and National Educational Policy," *Journal of Negro Education* 51 (Summer 1982): 301–17; Ruth Love Holloway, "Right to Read—a Chance to Change: Report from Washington," *Reading Teacher* 27 (October 1973): 33–36; *Wall Street Journal*, April 4, 1984, p. 1.

LUMIANSKY, Robert Mayer. b. December 27, 1913, Darlington, South Carolina, to Maurice Saul and Miriam (Witcover) Lumiansky. Married April 18, 1946, to Janet Schneider. Children: no. d. April 3, 1987, New York City.

Robert Lumiansky was a skilled translator into modern English of the works of Geoffrey Chaucer and Sir Thomas Malory and a champion of the place of the humanities in American scholarship and public life.

He graduated with the B.A. degree from the Citadel at the age of nineteen in 1933 and earned the M.A. at the University of South Carolina in 1935 and the Ph.D. at the University of North Carolina at Chapel Hill in 1942. He began his career teaching English at Walhalla (North Carolina) High School (1934–38).

Lumiansky had received a lieutenant's commission in the U.S. Army upon graduation from the Citadel. He entered active duty in 1942, rose to the rank of major, and was decorated with the Bronze Star of the United States and the Croix de Guerre of France.

He was a member of the faculty in English at Tulane University from 1946, serving as graduate dean (1954–63) and provost (1960–63). After two years as a professor of English at Duke University, he moved to the University of Pennsylvania as chair of the English Department (1965–73). He was a professor of English at New York University from 1975 to 1983.

Lumiansky's most notable achievements came in service to national humanities organizations. He chaired the board of the American Council of Learned Societies for fifteen years (1959–74), then served for almost a decade as its president (1974–82); he returned as president pro tempore during 1985–86. During the early 1960s, he organized a National Commission on the Humanities, which called for the creation of a new foundation, realized in 1965 through establishment of the National Endowments for the Arts and Humanities. He was a founding member of the national council overseeing the work of the National Endowment for the Humanities (1965–67). He served as a director of the National Humanities Center in Research Park, North Carolina, from 1976 until his death. Among many other service roles, Lumiansky was a member of the President's Task Force on the Arts and Humanities in 1981.

He was awarded a Guggenheim Fellowship in 1968–69. He served as president of the Medieval Academy of America (1981–82) and the United Chapters of Phi Beta Kappa (1976–79). He was a chevalier of the Legion of Honor of France and honored with the Phi Beta Kappa Award for Distinguished Service to the Humanities.

Lumiansky wrote *Chaucer's Canterbury Tales in Modern English* (1948), *Chaucer's Trolius and Criseyde in Modern English* (1952), and *Of Sondry Folk: The Dramatic Principle in the Canterbury Tales* (1955). He also prepared several critical and facsimile editions of medieval literary works.

REFERENCES: CA (122); NYT, April 5, 1987, p. 36; WWW (9); *R. M. Lumiansky: Scholar, Teacher, Spokesman for the Humanities*, American Council of Learned Societies Occasional Paper, no. 3 (1987); *Speculum* 63 (July 1988): 765–66.

LUSK, Georgia Lee Witt. b. May 12, 1893, near Carlsbad, New Mexico, to George and Mary Isabel (Gilreath) Witt. Married August 1915 to Dolph Lusk. Children: three. d. January 5, 1971, Albuquerque, New Mexico.

During three four-year terms as state superintendent of public instruction in New Mexico between 1931 and 1959, Georgia Lusk raised the quality of state schools, began a program to provide schoolchildren with free textbooks, and initiated a teachers' retirement program.

Lusk grew up on a ranch and completed high school in Carlsbad. She graduated from New Mexico State Teachers College (later, Western New Mexico University) in 1914. Her graduate work was done at Highlands (later, New Mexico Highlands) University and Colorado State Teachers College (later, University of Northern Colorado). She taught in Eddy County, New Mexico, until her marriage in 1915. She was widowed in 1919 with three sons, one born after her husband's death. Lusk then returned to teaching, in addition to running a ranch. In 1924 she was elected superintendent of schools for Lea County; she was reelected in 1926.

After losing the campaign for state superintendent of public instruction in 1928, she was elected in 1930 and held the position from 1931 to 1935 and again from 1943 to 1947. Under her leadership teachers' salaries were raised, an equalization fund was begun, and the school law was recodified. A state sales tax provided funds for schools. In 1941 and 1942 Lusk was rural school supervisor in Guadalupe County. She was a participant in the White House Conference on Rural Education in 1944, which produced the Charter for Rural Education.

In 1946 Lusk was elected at-large to the U.S. House of Representatives, but she was defeated for renomination in 1948. She served on the War Claims Commission (1949–53). She was state superintendent in New Mexico again from 1955 to 1959.

REFERENCES: AWM; CB (1947, 1971); HAWH; NYT, January 6, 1971, p. 40; WWW (5); *Biographical Directory of the American Congress 1774–1971* (U.S. Government Printing Office, 1971); Hope Chamberlin, *A Minority of Members: Women in the U.S. Congress* (Praeger, 1973); Roger D. Hardaway, ''New Mexico Elects a Congresswoman,'' *Red River Valley Historical Review* 4 (Fall 1979): 75–89; Eleanor Roosevelt and Lorena A. Hickok, *Ladies of Courage* (Putnam, 1954).

LYLE, Guy Redvers. b. October 31, 1907, Lloydminster, Saskatchewan, Canada, to John Percival and Mary (Lynch) Lyle. Married November 27, 1930, to Margaret White. Children: four.

Guy R. Lyle was a leader in the development of administrative policies and procedures that facilitated the educational effectiveness of the college library. He was recognized for the excellence of his staff development and his inspirational leadership of college librarianship as a profession. He was author of *Administration of the College Library*, first published in 1944, which defined librarianship as an extension of teaching.

After earning the A.B. degree at the University of Alberta in 1927, Lyle went to New York and worked at the New York Public Library (1927–29) while studying library science at Columbia University, where he earned B.S. (1929) and M.S. (1932) degrees. He was librarian of Antioch College (1929–35) and librarian and professor at the Women's College of the University of North Carolina (later, University of North Carolina at Greensboro, 1936–44). He taught librarianship at the University of Illinois during 1935–36 and 1942–43.

He was director of libraries at Louisiana State University (1944–54) and professor of library science and director of libraries at Emory University (1954–72). He held visiting appointments at several American universities, as well as at the Japan Library School at Keio University in Tokyo (1957) and at the University of Puerto Rico (1973).

Lyle wrote the "Crow's Nest" column in the *Wilson Library Bulletin* (1935–42). His publications included *Classified List of Periodicals for the College Library* (1934), *College Library Publicity* (1935), *Bibliography of Christopher Morley* (with H. Tatnall Brown, Jr., 1952), *The President, The Professor, and the College Library* (1963), *The Librarian Speaking* (1970), and a memoir titled *Beyond My Expectation: A Personal Chronicle* (1981). During the 1930s he also produced a movie, *Found in a Book*, on use of the library.

Lyle was frequently sought to survey college libraries. He chaired the College Library Advisory Board (1938–40), Association of College and Reference Libraries (1954), and Association of Southeastern Research Libraries (1964–65). He received the Lippincott Award from the American Library Association (1972). In 1974 Evan Ira Farber and Ruth Walling edited *The Academic Library: Essays in Honor of Guy R. Lyle.*

REFERENCES: CA (61–64); LE (1974); WW (1976–77); Wayne A. Wiegand, ed., *Leaders in American Academic Librarianship, 1925–1975* (Beta Phi Mu, 1983).

M

MAEDER, Hans Karl. b. December 29, 1909, Hamburg, Germany. Married May 29, 1947, to Ruth Gordon. Children: one. d. September 9, 1988, New York City.

Hans Maeder founded and directed the Stockbridge School, a progressive, interracial, and international preparatory institution dedicated to education for world understanding and based on ideals in the United Nations Charter. Maeder wanted to create a learning community that encompassed individual freedom and individual responsibility.

Maeder received the M.A. degree from the University of Hamburg. He was active in the underground resistance to national socialism and left Germany in 1933. For four years he was a teacher at the Udlose Boys Home, a school for problem boys in Denmark. In the late 1930s he traveled to Kenya, Singapore, and the Philippines, and he taught in Hawaii. After Pearl Harbor, he was interned as an enemy alien. Released in 1943, Maeder directed boys' work at a Brooklyn, New York, Young Men's Christian Association (YMCA). During 1944–45 he taught at Windsor Mountain School in Lenox, Massachusetts.

Beginning in September 1945, Maeder taught German and the history of language at the Walden School in New York City. When Alice Keliher (q.v.) left the Walden directorship, Maeder served two years as interim director (1947–49). Walden was an integrated day school; Maeder wanted to found a boarding school. He searched New England and in 1948 purchased the Dan R. Hanna estate at Interlaken, Massachusetts, near Stockbridge. The mansion needed extensive repairs, and students from Walden volunteered to work on it during the summer. This was the beginning of summer work camps at Stockbridge.

Hans and Ruth Maeder opened Stockbridge School in 1949, with six faculty and sixteen students, including three African Americans and three foreigners. In its first year the school had grades seven through eleven. Later, the school offered grades nine through twelve. The highest enrollment, reached in the late 1960s, was 150. Stockbridge was a structured school with students helping with all work. Teachers were meant to be advisers, friends, and disciplinarians and were addressed by first names.

In 1971 Maeder retired as director while continuing on the Board of Trustees. Enrollment declined to fifty-five, and the school's debts increased. After twenty-six years Stockbridge School was closed in 1975. Maeder was an educational consultant in New York City. In 1951 he served on a UNESCO commission to explore development of an international baccalaureate degree.

REFERENCES: LE (1974); NYT, September 11, 1988, p. 46; John Beaufort, "School Dedicated to Practicing Democracy," *Christian Science Monitor*, January 7, 1950; Gunter Nabel, *A Fight for Human Rights: Hans Maeder's Politics of Optimism for World Understanding through Education Documents of the Stockbridge School* (Dipa-Verlag, 1986).

MANN, Albert Russell. b. December 26, 1880, Hawkins, Pennsylvania, to William Imrie and Sarah Malinda (Lansing) Mann. Married August 23, 1906, to Mary Douglass Judd. Children: five. d. February 21, 1947, New York City.

Albert Mann was a leader in the development of higher education in agriculture and allied fields. For many years he was dean of agriculture and then provost of Cornell University. He applied his expertise about agricultural education also in government and philanthropic service.

Mann earned the bachelor of science in agriculture degree in 1904 at the New York State College of Agriculture, a statutory college of Cornell. He earned the A.M. degree at the University of Chicago in 1916.

After graduation from Cornell, Mann was assistant superintendent of the Boston Farm and Trades School (1904–5). He returned to Cornell (1905–8) as secretary to the dean of agriculture, Liberty Hyde Bailey (BDAE), who was then readying the *Cyclopedia of American Horticulture* for publication.

Mann was secretary to the New York state commissioner of agriculture for several months during 1908 but returned to the College of Agriculture at Cornell as secretary, registrar, and editor (1908–15). He became professor of rural social organization in 1915 and acting dean in 1916. In 1917 he was named dean, director of extension, and director of the agricultural experiment station. Under Mann's leadership, the agricultural extension service developed into a statewide activity sponsored by the university. He served concurrently as dean of the newly established College of Home Economics from 1925. He was Cornell's provost from 1931 to 1937.

In 1937 he resigned from the administration at Cornell to become vice president and director for southern education of the Rockefeller Foundation-sponsored General Education Board, a post he retained until his retirement in 1946. As at Cornell, he emphasized the utility of research in guiding development of the rural economy.

Mann's public service roles included secretary of the New York State Food Commission and federal food administrator in New York during the war years of 1917–18, director of agricultural education in Europe for the International Education Board while on leave from Cornell during 1924–26, chair of the committee on farm and village housing of the President's Conference on Home Building and Home Ownership (1930–31), and chair of the New York State Planning Board (1934–36). He was a manager on the education board of the Northern Baptist Convention. He was chair of the executive committee of the

Association of Land Grant Colleges and Universities (later, National Association of State Universities and Land Grant Colleges, 1935–37) and president of the American Country Life Association, among many other appointments.

Mann was inducted into the Order of the White Rose of Finland and the Order of the White Lion of Czechoslovakia; awarded an honorary degree from the University of Sofia, Bulgaria; and bestowed with the Agricultural Decoration, First Class, of Belgium. He wrote *Beginnings in Agriculture* (1911) and was a contributor on agriculture and agricultural education to reference books.

REFERENCES: NCAB (36: 47); NYT, February 22, 1947, p. 11; WWW (2); *General Education Board Review and Final Report, 1902–1964* (1964); *School and Society* 65 (March 1, 1947): 163.

MANN, Henri. *See* WHITEMAN, Henrietta V.

MARCUS, Jacob Rader. b. March 5, 1896, Connellsville, Pennsylvania, to Aaron and Jennie (Rader) Marcus. Married December 30, 1925, to Antoinette Brody. Children: one. d. November 14, 1995, Cincinnati, Ohio.

Over a long career devoted to research and writing, Jacob Marcus established and defined the field of American Jewish history.

Marcus was born of immigrant parents from Lithuania. The family moved to Wheeling, West Virginia, and sometime later Marcus went by himself to Cincinnati, where he began rabbinical study while a high school student, aged fifteen. He earned the A.B. degree at the University of Cincinnati in 1917. After service in the U.S. Army (1917–19), he completed rabbinical study at Hebrew Union College in 1920. At the University of Berlin, where he studied during 1922–25, he received the Ph.D. degree. He continued his studies in France and Palestine.

Marcus spent all of his professional life at Hebrew Union College–Jewish Institute of Religion in Cincinnati. He joined the faculty in 1920 in the fields of the Bible and rabbinics. He became professor of Jewish history in 1934 and Adolph S. Ochs Professor of American Jewish History in 1959. From 1965 he held the Milton and Hattie Kutz Distinguished Service Chair in American Jewish History. He founded the American Jewish Archives in 1947 and from 1956 until his death directed the American Jewish Periodical Center.

Among his many books were *Die handelspolitischen Beziehungen zwischen England und Deutschland in den Jahren 1576–1585* (1925), *The Rise and Destiny of the German Jew* (1934), *Communal Sick-Care in the German Ghetto* (1947), *Early American Jewry* (2 volumes, 1951–53), *Studies in American Jewish History* (1969), *The Colonial American Jew 1492–1776* (3 volumes, 1970), *The American Jewish Woman* (1981), and his monumental work, *United States Jewry* (4 volumes, 1989–93). He was also the editor of many documentary collections.

Marcus was president of the Central Conference of American Rabbis (1949–

50) and the American Jewish Historical Society (1956–59). He received many honors.

REFERENCES: CA (NR-28); CB (1960, 1996); CHE, November 18, 1992, p. A11; NYT, November 16, 1995, p. B16; WW (1996); Stanley F. Chyet, ''Jacob Rader Marcus: A Biographical Sketch,'' in American Jewish Archives, *Essays in American Jewish History* (Ktav, 1958), pp. 1–22; *Encyclopedia Judaica* (Macmillan, 1972); Randall M. Falk, *Bright Eminence: The Life and Thought of Jacob Rader Marcus* (Pangloss Press, 1994); *Perspectives* [American Historical Association newsletter], February 1996, pp. 38–39.

MARLAND, Sidney Percy, Jr. b. August 19, 1914, Danielson, Connecticut, to Sidney Percy and Ruth (Johnson) Marland. Married June 29, 1940, to Virginia Partridge. Children: three. d. May 26, 1992, Hampton, Connecticut.

Although labor unions opposed his appointment as U.S. commissioner of education, in that office (1970–72) and later as assistant secretary of health, education, and welfare (1972–73), Sidney Marland put his emphasis on vocational education. He criticized too much reliance on college-preparatory high school curricula that served the needs of only a minority among youth. Marland's government service capped a varied career as high school teacher, military officer, superintendent in suburban and urban communities, and educational consultant.

He graduated in 1936 from the University of Connecticut with the B.A. degree and returned to earn the M.A. degree in 1950. From New York University he received the Ph.D. degree in 1955.

He was a high school teacher of English in West Hartford, Connecticut (1938–41), before entering the U.S. Army, where he directed Pacific military intelligence research. He remained in military service until 1947, achieving the rank of colonel.

Marland's administrative career in education followed immediately. He was superintendent of schools in Darien, Connecticut (1948–56), and Winnetka, Illinois (1956–63). With Carleton W. Washburne (BDAE), who had preceded him as Winnetka superintendent, Marland wrote *Winnetka: The History and Significance of an Educational Experiment* (1963). Marland was superintendent of schools in Pittsburgh for five years (1963–68), earning a reputation as a strong opponent of teachers' organizations and labor unions generally. He resigned when a teachers' strike led to unionization. In Pittsburgh Marland also participated in the development of the Community College of Allegheny County. For two years before his appointment as commissioner of education, he was president of the Institute for Educational Development in New York City. Beginning in 1973 he was president of the College Entrance Examination Board.

At the request of then-commissioner of education Francis Keppel (q.v.), in 1963 Marland served as vice chair of the President's Conference on Education chaired by John Gardner (q.v.), which prepared the Elementary and Secondary Education Act of 1965. He served on the boards of the National Merit Scholarship Corporation (1963–68) and National Educational Television (1965–70), among many public service roles.

Marland's writings included *Religion in the Public Schools* (1963) and *Career Education: A Proposal for Reform* (1974). For his military service he was decorated with the Distinguished Service Cross, Legion of Merit, and Bronze Star.

REFERENCES: CA (53–56, 137); CB (1972, 1992); CHE, January 6, 1985, p. 26; LE (1974); NYT, September 24, 1970, p. 26, and May 27, 1992, p. D20; WWW (10).

MARSHALL, Clara. b. May 8, 1847, West Chester, Pennsylvania, to Pennock and Mary (Phillips) Marshall. Married: no. d. March 13, 1931, Bryn Mawr, Pennsylvania.

Clara Marshall advanced opportunities for women in medicine during her career at the Woman's Medical College of Pennsylvania. The college received an A rating from the American Medical Association, in a time when Abraham Flexner (BDAE) was highly critical of many medical schools.

After several years as a teacher, at the age of twenty-four Clara Marshall began medical study at the Woman's Medical College of Pennsylvania, where she was a member of Ann Preston's (q.v.) last class. After graduation in 1875, she pursued graduate study at the Philadelphia College of Pharmacy, being the first woman admitted to the college. She arranged the pharmaceutical display at the 1876 Centennial Exhibition in Philadelphia. From 1876 to 1905 she was professor of materia medica and therapeutics at the Woman's Medical College of Pennsylvania.

In 1888 Marshall became dean of the college, serving in that position until 1917. During her tenure scholastic standards were raised, the course was extended from three to four years, and a bacteriology laboratory was built.

Marshall determined that there should be a teaching hospital connected to the college to make clinical facilities available to women. A campaign for funds was begun, and a college hospital was erected story by story, completed in 1913. Marshall was the first woman on the staff of the Philadelphia Hospital, where she was a lecturer in obstetrics in 1882. Beginning in 1886 she was girls' attending physician at the Philadelphia House of Refuge.

In 1898 Marshall addressed the National Woman Suffrage Association meeting. She wrote articles for professional journals. Her book, *Woman's Medical College of Pennsylvania: An Historical Outline*, was published in 1897.

REFERENCES: DAB; LW; NAW; WWW (5); Gulielma Fell Alsop, *History of the Woman's Medical College, 1850–1950* (Lippincott, 1950); Martin Kaufman, Stuart Galishoff, and Todd L. Savitt, eds., *Dictionary of American Medical Biography* (Greenwood Press, 1983).

MARSHALL, Florence M. b. c. 1870, Shirley, Kansas, to William Henry and Ruhamah A. (Walker) Marshall. Married: no. d. January 27, 1947, Belfast, Maine.

Florence Marshall was instrumental in establishing vocational education for girls. Marshall objected to the lack of further education for girls not attending college. In response she founded the Boston Trade School and was principal of the Manhattan Trade School for twenty-five years.

Marshall's family moved from Kansas to Massachusetts when she was a child. She graduated from Boston University in 1899 and attended Barnard College for one year and Teachers College of Columbia University from 1901 to 1903. In 1903 she founded the Boston Trade School, serving as its director until 1908. Marshall served on the Douglas Committee in 1905, which studied the need for vocational education as part of the Massachusetts public school system. As a result the State Board of Education was reorganized to include vocational education. In 1908 the Boston Trade School was the first of its type to become part of a public school system.

Marshall became Massachusetts state director of vocational education for girls in 1908. She went to Europe to study vocational education and while there was invited to go to New York City to become principal of the Manhattan Trade School, a private school that later became part of the city system. The rented building used for the school being inadequate, Marshall persuaded municipal officials to erect a new building. Graduates of the school were readily employed.

In 1914 Marshall was appointed to a commission to study vocational education for the nation. The result was the 1917 Federal Vocational Education Act, which provided grants to states to assist in vocational education. During World War I Marshall organized and began the work of the Women's Bureau.

In 1906 she organized a girls' camp in Maine. Later, she bought a farm near Stamford, Connecticut, as a place of study and recreation for students of the Manhattan Trade School. She served on the National Education Committee of the Girl Scouts.

REFERENCES: BCAW; NYT, January 19, 1947, p. 25; *School and Society* 65 (March 19, 1947): 226.

MAYER, Clara Woollie. b. June 1, 1895, New York City, to Bernhard and Sophia (Buttenwieser) Mayer. Married: no. d. July 16, 1988, Los Angeles.

In the early years of the New School for Social Research, Clara Mayer played a major role. From 1919, when Alvin Johnson (BDAE) and others conceived of the idea for the school, Mayer helped to shape its direction. She was assistant director (1931–36) and associate director (1937–43) under Johnson, dean of the school of philosophy and liberal arts (1943–60), vice president (1950–62), and dean of the school (1960–62).

Daughter of a well-to-do New York realtor, Mayer received the A.B. degree from Barnard College in 1915, then did graduate study at Columbia University (1915–19). When the New School was founded, Mayer became a student. She was appointed to the board, became engaged in its administration, and assisted in development of the undergraduate program. During her years as assistant and associate director, Mayer became the appointing officer selecting professionals who taught part-time.

When Alvin Johnson retired in 1945, Bryn Hovde was his successor. Finding it difficult to work with Mayer, he resigned in 1949. When a later director, Henry David, requested Mayer's resignation as dean of the adult division, it caused loss of faculty support and financial support from the Mayer family.

Mayer was assistant editor of the *Encyclopedia of Social Sciences* (1928–29) and author of *The Manmade Wilderness* (1963).

REFERENCES: CA (P-2); NYT, September 22, 1943, p. 21, and July 19, 1988, p. B8; WW (1960); WWAW (1966); Esther Raushenbush, "Three Women: Creators of Change," in Helen S. Astin and Werner Z. Hirsch, eds., *The Higher Education of Women: Essays in Honor of Rosemary Park* (q.v.) (Praeger, 1978); Peter M. Rutkoff and William B. Scott, *New School: A History of the New School for Social Research* (Free Press, 1986).

MAYER, Jean. b. February 19, 1920, Paris, France, to André and Jeanne Eugénie (Veille) Mayer. Married March 16, 1942, to Elizabeth Van Huysen. Children: five. d. January 1, 1993, Sarasota, Florida.

Jean Mayer had two careers in American higher education, first as a leading scholar of the emerging field of nutrition, then as transformative president of Tufts University.

Mayer was a child of prominent French physiologists. As a lycée student in Paris he won prizes for excellence in the study of history. At the University of Paris he studied mathematics and philosophy at first, earning the B.Litt. degree in 1937. The next year he took the B.S. degree and in 1939 he completed the M.Sc. His service during World War II as a French army officer and intelligence agent won him the Croix de Guerre, Resistance Medal, and Chevalier of the Legion of Honor.

After the war Mayer moved to the United States. At Yale University he was a Rockefeller Foundation fellow (1946–48) and took the Ph.D. degree (1948). He served as a research associate at George Washington University (1948–49), then returned briefly to France, where in 1950 the University of Paris awarded him the D.Sc. degree.

Mayer served on the faculty at Harvard University from 1950 to 1976 and was president of Tufts University from 1976 until his retirement in 1992. At Harvard his scholarship brought physiology, population studies, and public policy to bear on the problem of hunger and its amelioration. At Tufts Mayer established programs in nutrition, veterinary medicine, and environmental management.

Mayer cofounded the National Council on Hunger and Malnutrition and organized the 1969 White House Conference on Food, Nutrition, and Health. In part through Mayer's influence, food stamps were introduced, and school lunch programs expanded. Mayer was associate editor of *Nutrition Review* and on the editorial boards of a number of journals, including *American Journal of Physiology*, *American Journal of Public Health*, and *Family Health*. Among his books were *Appetite and the Many Obesities* (1964), *Human Nutrition*, and *A Diet for Living* (1975). He edited *United States Nutrition Policies in the Sev-*

enties (1973) and *Health and Patterns of Life* (1974). He was adviser to three presidents.

REFERENCES: CA (129, 140); CB (1970, 1993); NYT, January 2, 1993, p. 9, April 1, 1992, p. B9, and June 8, 1986; WW (1992–93).

McALLISTER, Jane Ellen. b. October 24, 1899, Vicksburg, Mississippi, to Richard Nelson and Flora (McClellan) McAllister. Married: no. d. January 10, 1996, Vicksburg, Mississippi.

Jane Ellen McAllister trained African-American teachers in the South and encouraged innovation in teacher training programs. She was the first African American to receive a doctorate from Teachers College of Columbia University (1929).

McAllister attended a Catholic elementary school in Vicksburg, Mississippi, and graduated from Cherry Street High School in 1915. She received the A.B. degree from Talladega (Alabama) College in 1919 and taught at Southern University in Baton Rouge, Louisiana (1919–20 and 1921–22). The University of Michigan awarded her the M.A. degree in history and English in 1921. She served as principal of the Training School at Virginia State College (1922–24). As director of teacher training at Southern University (1924–28) she began the first extension class for African-American teachers. During 1926–27 she held a fellowship from the General Education Board. After receiving her doctorate from Columbia University, she was professor of education at Fisk University (1929–30).

McAllister was professor of education and department head at Miner Teachers College (later, part of the University of the District of Columbia) from 1930 to 1951. She was a consultant on rural teacher education for the General Education Board and the Rosenwald Fund. Under her guidance in 1937 the teacher training program at Louisiana Negro Normal and Industrial Institute (later, Grambling State University) was revised, and in 1941 a curriculum revision at the Mississippi Negro Training School (later, Jackson State University) resulted in a degree program in elementary education. McAllister was a consultant to Jeanes supervisors in Mississippi.

From 1950 to 1967 McAllister was professor of education at Jackson State College, where she initiated the Institute for Teachers of Disadvantaged Youth, College Readiness Program, and Continuing Education Enrichment Program. She secured funds for in-service training of teachers and helped to organize a Self Help Opportunity Project for unemployed high school dropouts.

McAllister wrote extensively for professional journals and was author of *The Training of Negro Teachers in Louisiana* (1929). She was a delegate to the 1960 White House Conference on Children and Youth. At Jackson State the Jane Ellen McAllister Lecture Series was established in her honor.

REFERENCES: NBAW; WWAW (1961); George A. Sewell and Margaret L. Dwight, *Mississippi Black History Makers* (University Press of Mississippi, 1984); Winona Williams-Burns, "Jane Ellen McAllister: Pioneer for Excellence in Teacher Education," *Journal of Negro Education* 51 (Summer 1982): 342–57.

McCARTHY, Charles. b. June 29, 1873, North Bridgewater (later, Brockton), Massachusetts, to John and Katherine (O'Shea) Desmond McCarthy. Married September 26, 1901, to Lucile Howard Schreiber. Children: one. d. March 26, 1921, Prescott, Arizona.

In 1901 Charles McCarthy became head of the Department of State Documents in Madison, Wisconsin, and in 1907 chief of the Wisconsin Legislative Reference Library. He taught political science at the University of Wisconsin from 1905. As librarian he researched and helped to draft bills for legislators. He also put forward his own ideas in several areas, including education. McCarthy helped to revitalize a program of short courses and farmers' institutes offered by the University of Wisconsin. He surveyed commercial correspondence courses to demonstrate that much money went out of state for them. In 1905 the Regents of the University of Wisconsin provided money for extension courses, and in 1907 the legislature appropriated money for an Extension Division.

When a committee was formed in 1909 to look into part-time schools for working youth and adult evening schools, McCarthy was its secretary. While traveling in Germany, McCarthy observed trade schools. Through his efforts, in 1911 Wisconsin passed the first law in the country to establish statewide continuation schools for persons who had left high school without a diploma. These schools became compulsory for youth between the ages of fourteen and sixteen. McCarthy lobbied also for passage of the Smith-Hughes Act, which provided federal aid for vocational education.

McCarthy graduated in 1892 from a nonpreparatory course at Brockton High School. He worked his way through college and received the Ph.B. degree with a major in history from Brown University in 1897. He coached the University of Georgia football team for two years, then went to Wisconsin. He received the Ph.D. degree from the University of Wisconsin in 1901. His dissertation won a prize from the American Historical Association.

In 1914, on the recommendation of John R. Commons (q.v.), McCarthy became director of the Federal Commission on Industrial Relations. During World War I he served under Herbert Hoover in the Food Administration, while the University of Wisconsin continued to provide his salary. McCarthy was interested in politics, particularly the progressive movement. He wrote *The Wisconsin Idea* (1912) and coauthored *An Elementary Civics* (1916).

REFERENCES: AR; BDSW; DAB; DALB; NCAB (19: 251); WWW (1); Marion Casey, *Charles McCarthy: Librarianship and Reform* (American Library Association, 1981); Edward A. Fitzpatrick, *McCarthy of Wisconsin* (Columbia University Press, 1944); *Dictionary of Wisconsin Biography* (State Historical Society of Wisconsin, 1960); Frank J. Woerdehoff, "Dr. Charles McCarthy's Role in Revitalizing the University Extension Division," *Wisconsin Magazine of History* 40 (Autumn 1956): 13–18; Frank J. Woerdehoff, "Dr. Charles McCarthy: Planner of the Wisconsin System of Vocational and Adult Education," *Wisconsin Magazine of History* 41 (Summer 1958): 270–74.

McCASLIN, Nellie. b. August 20, 1914, Cleveland, Ohio, to Paul Giles and Nellie (Wagner) McCaslin. Married: no.

A proponent of creative dramatics, Nellie McCaslin improved children's theater in the United States through her college-level teaching, educational workshops, and adaptation of children's stories for performance. Many of her plays were based on American legends.

McCaslin graduated from Western Reserve (later, Case Western Reserve) University with B.A. (1936) and M.A. (1937) degrees. At Tudor Hall, a girls' preparatory school in Indianapolis, McCaslin worked in theater with pupils from kindergarten through twelfth grade. In Hollywood she studied improvisation under Maria Ouspenskaya. She taught theater from 1944 to 1954 at the National College of Education in Evanston, Illinois, where she organized a children's theater company.

In 1957 McCaslin earned the Ph.D. degree from New York University and began teaching at Mills College of Education in New York City. There she organized a Saturday children's theater workshop. Her book *Creative Dramatics in the Classroom* was first published in 1968. After Mills College of Education closed in 1972, McCaslin taught educational theater at New York University.

In addition to writing plays, McCaslin wrote extensively on theater. Her publications included *Theatre for Children in the United States: A History* (1971), *Act Now! Plays and Ways to Make Them* (1975), *Historical Guide to Children's Theatre in America* (1977), *Shows on a Shoestring: An Easy Guide to Amateur Productions* (1979), and *Children and Drama* (1981). She was a consultant on establishing arts programs, conducted workshops on creative drama, sat on the advisory boards of several presses, and coordinated children's programs for WABC radio. McCaslin was a fellow of the American Theatre Association. She was president of the Children's Theatre Association (1973–75) and regional governor (1959–62) of the Children's Theatre Conference. She received the Jennie Heiden Award (1976) for excellence in children's theater.

REFERENCES: CA (33–36R); WD (1994–96); WWAW (1977–78); Alice M. Robinson, Vera Mowry Roberts, and Milly S. Barranger, eds., *Notable Women in the American Theatre* (Greenwood Press, 1989).

McINTOSH, Millicent Carey. b. November 30, 1898, Baltimore, to Anthony Morris and Margaret Cheston (Thomas) Carey. Married June 25, 1932, to Rustin McIntosh. Children: five.

Millicent Carey McIntosh was known for her leadership in the education of women at the Brearley School and at Barnard College. Her advocacy of women's education embraced both careers and useful citizenship.

She was raised in Baltimore, where both parents were Quaker ministers. She graduated from the Bryn Mawr School in Baltimore in 1916. In 1920 she received the A.B. degree from Bryn Mawr College, where her aunt, M. Carey Thomas (BDAE), was president. Further study was at Newnham College of

Cambridge University in England. She taught at Rosemary Hall in Greenwich, Connecticut (1922–23), and at the Summer School for Women Workers (1923). Johns Hopkins University awarded her the Ph.D. degree in English in 1926.

At Bryn Mawr College from 1926 to 1930, Millicent Carey was instructor in English, dean of freshmen, and then acting dean of the college. In 1930 she became headmistress of the Brearley School, a girl's preparatory school in New York City; she remained there until 1947. She was married in 1930 to Dr. Rustin McIntosh, a pediatrician, and bore five children (one set of twins) between 1933 and 1939. Among the courses she taught at Brearley were ethics, physiology, and general languages. She introduced aptitude and psychological tests, remedial courses as needed, music, art, dramatics, and sports.

Barnard College chose McIntosh to succeed Virginia Gildersleeve (BDAE) as dean in 1947, a position with similar duties to those of a college president. The title was changed to president in 1952. At Barnard she broadened the curriculum in many fields and strengthened ties with Columbia University, with more Barnard students attending classes at Columbia. She began the Barnard Forum in 1949. McIntosh believed strongly that women could combine motherhood and career and that a liberal arts education was a woman's best preparation for both.

McIntosh retired in 1962. She served on many boards and wrote *Women and Success: The Anatomy of Achievement* (1974).

REFERENCES: CB (1947); NYT, September 14, 1961, p. 1; WW (1960); WWAW; Anne L. Goodman, "Mrs. Mac of Barnard," *Harper's* 202 (May 1951): 92–100; *Newsweek* 38 (October 15, 1951): 48–50; William P. Rayner, *Wise Women* (St. Martin's Press, 1983).

McLAREN, Louise Leonard. b. August 10, 1885, Wellsboro, Pennsylvania, to Fred Churchill and Estella (Cook) Leonard. Married 1930 to Myron McLaren. Children: no. d. December 16, 1968, East Stroudsburg, Pennsylvania.

Louise Leonard McLaren founded the Summer School for Women Workers. It first met at Sweet Briar College in Virginia in 1927 and in succeeding years used rented facilities in different locations. McLaren was director from its inception to its closing in 1944. Women attended from several southern states. For many it was their first experience outside local mills and factories. Sessions were six weeks long. Economics and industrial history were taught, communication skills were stressed, and students wrote and produced several plays. There was no academic hierarchy. Women were encouraged to share their experiences. Much of organized labor lent support, and the school had a commitment to trade unions. Beginning in 1938 men were included in the program, and by 1940 more than one-half of the people attending were men.

McLaren was a graduate of Miss Beret's School for Girls in Harrisburg, Pennsylvania, and Vassar College (1907). She taught at Watertown (New York) High School and Lock Haven (Pennsylvania) Teachers College (later, Lock Haven University of Pennsylvania). Before founding the summer school she served as a Young Women's Christian Association industrial secretary; metropolitan industrial secretary in Baltimore and in Wilkes-Barre, Pennsylvania; and southern national industrial secretary. After the summer school closed, McLaren was employed by the American Labor Education Service.

REFERENCES: BDAL; NAW (Mod); Joyce Kornbluh and Mary Frederickson, eds., *Sisterhood and Solidarity* (Temple University Press, 1984).

MEGEL, Carl J. b. December 3, 1899, Hayden, Indiana, to Peter and Lena (Kirsch) Megel. Married April 1925 to Marion Stewart; October 1962 to Beverly Falk. Children: two. d. September 18, 1992, Rockville, Maryland.

Carl Megel served as the first full-time president of the American Federation of Teachers (AFT) during a period when its membership and influence developed rapidly. He was later the principal AFT representative in Washington, D.C.

After earning the B.A. degree at Franklin College in 1923, Megel taught mathematics and science and directed athletics in Toluca, Casey, and Palatine, Illinois, public schools. He was on the faculty of Lake View High School in Chicago from 1935 until his retirement in 1965, although from the early 1950s he was on leave because of his union duties.

Megel began his union activity out of concern for teachers' low salaries. In the Chicago Teacher's Union he was successively trustee (1943–46), treasurer (1946–48), and vice president (1949–51). In the national organization, he was president from 1952 to 1964 and Washington representative from 1964 to 1982. His cooperation with the American Federation of Labor–Congress of Industrial Organizations (AFL–CIO) brought financial and organizational support that contributed to the AFT's success during the 1950s. His successor as president was David Selden (q.v.), a New York union official, elected when urban teacher unionists found Megel's approach too moderate.

Megel participated in the White House Conference on Education in 1955 and represented the United States at conferences of UNESCO.

REFERENCES: BDAL; NYT, September 20, 1992, p. 54; WW (1966–67); *American School and University* 36 (November 1963): 42–46; William Edward Eaton, *The American Federation of Teachers, 1916–1961* (Southern Illinois University Press, 1975).

MEIER, Deborah Willen. b. 1931, New York City, to Joseph and Pearl (Larner) Willen. Married to Fred Meier. Children: three.

As an elementary and secondary school principal, Deborah Meier worked to reform school bureaucracies and to encourage disciplined inquisitiveness among students. Beginning in 1985, with teachers of Central Park East Secondary School in New York City, she organized teaching around cultivation of "habits of mind": evaluating evidence, appraising viewpoints, detecting patterns, entertaining counterfactual ideas, and assessing significance. In 1987, she became the first schoolteacher/principal to receive a MacArthur Foundation Fellowship.

Meier attended Ethical Culture Schools in New York City. She was a student at Antioch College for two years and then attended the University of Chicago graduate school, where she received a master's degree in American history. After working as a substitute teacher, she enrolled in education courses at Chicago Teachers College. She was a part-time kindergarten teacher in 1964. In Philadelphia, she attended the University of Pennsylvania and Temple University and taught in a Head Start program. As a kindergarten teacher in the Harlem neighborhood of New York City, she conducted a four-room school for children from the ages of four to seven in one section of a public school. She took additional courses at Bank Street College of Education and City College of the City University of New York.

In 1970 Lillian Weber (q.v.) asked Meier to work with teacher trainees. In 1972 an invitation followed to start an alternative primary school, Central Park East. After two years Meier became its director.

On the advice of Theodore Sizer (q.v.) to continue the school through grade twelve, in 1985 Central Park East Secondary School (CPESS) was opened. Teams of teachers created the curriculum in consultation with Meier. Meier was coprincipal of the school, which was a member of Sizer's Coalition of Essential Schools. In 1992 Meier and Sizer received $3 million from foundations to found ten new high schools in New York City. Meier directed the Central Park East schools until 1994, when she became a senior fellow of the Annenberg Institute for School Reform at Brown University.

Meier helped to found the North Dakota Study Group in 1970 with Vito Perrone and Lillian Weber. She was a founding member of the National Board for Professional Teaching Standards. She organized and was president of the Center for Collaborative Education. She was a contributing editor to *Dissent* and the *Nation* and wrote *The Power of Their Ideas* (1995).

REFERENCES: NYT, August 10, 1992, p. B3, and September 7, 1994, p. B11; WEUS; Naomi Barko, "Salute to Success," *New Choices* 31 (January 1991): 81–83; Mark F. Goldberg, "Portrait of Deborah Meier," *Educational Leadership* 48 (December 1990/January 1991): 26–28; Deborah Meier, "How Our Schools Could Be," *Phi Delta Kappan* (January 1995): 369–73; Marge Scherer, "On Schools Where Students Want to Be: A Conversation with Deborah Meier," *Educational Leadership* 52 (September 1994): 4–8; Hedrick Smith, *Rethinking America* (Random House, 1995), chapter 6.

MERRIAM, Harold Guy. b. September 6, 1883, Westminster, Massachusetts, to Joel Hervey and Anna Parkhurst (Mansfield) Merriam. Married August 3, 1915, to Doris Woodward Foote; March 9, 1974, to Frances Dummer Logan. Children: two. d. March 26, 1980, Missoula, Montana.

Founder of the Montana Institute of the Arts, longtime editor of regional literary journals, and director of the Federal Writers' Project in Montana, H. G. Merriam gave shape to arts education and creative writing in the Northwest.

After graduation from high school in Denver, Merriam attended the University of Wyoming, from which in 1905 he graduated with the A.B. degree. He was a Rhodes scholar at the University of Oxford during 1904–7, taking B.A. (1907) and M.A. (1912) degrees there. He was briefly a graduate student of drama at

Harvard University in 1910 and later studied for one year at Columbia University (1925–26), but not until 1939 did he receive the Ph.D. degree from Columbia. His thesis, published that year, was titled *Edward Moxon: Publisher of Poets*.

Merriam was a member of the faculty at Whitman (1908–10), Beloit (1911–13), and Reed (1913–19) Colleges before becoming professor of English at Montana State University (later, University of Montana). He remained there from 1919 until his 1954 retirement, except for one year (1939–40) at the University of Oregon. During World War I he served for one year with the Young Men's Christian Association (YMCA) in France and England, teaching English and facilitating American admissions to English universities.

As department chair in Montana, Merriam inaugurated formal study of creative writing before the subject was common. One year after his arrival he began editing *The Frontier*, later called *The Frontier and Midland* (1920–39).

Merriam was founding president of the Montana Institute of the Arts (1948–50). His publications included *Northwest Verse: An Anthology* (editor, 1931), *Montana Institute of Arts Quarterly* (editor, 1957–64), *Seed in the Soil* (1967), *The University of Montana: A History* (1970), *Frontier Woman: The Story of Mary Ronan* (1973), *The Golden Valley: Missoula to 1883* (1977), and *The Long Friendship* (1979). He received the Montana Arts Council Award and Governor's Citation in 1975.

REFERENCES: CA (NR-10); WWW (7); Esther Warford, "He Had a Wider Vision," *Montana Arts* 5 (July 1968); papers furnished by Brian Shovers, reference historian, Montana Historical Society Library.

MERRITT, Emma Frances Grayson. b. January 11, 1860, Dumfries, Virginia, to John and Sophia (Cook) Merritt. Married: no. d. June 8, 1933, Washington, D.C.

Emma Merritt was a teacher well before she received any higher education. She taught first grade in the public schools of the District of Columbia beginning in 1875, when she was fifteen years old. She continued to teach while completing the normal school program (1883–87) at Howard University. In 1887 she was appointed an elementary school principal. She continued intermittent study of the social sciences at Columbian (later, George Washington) University until the end of the century.

Merritt established the first kindergarten for African-American children in 1897. She became director of primary instruction in the District of Columbia in 1898 and a supervising principal in 1927, remaining in that role until her retirement in 1930.

At historically black universities and colleges throughout the country, Merritt was a prized lecturer on the education of young children. She was an organizer and director of the Teachers' Benefit and Annuity Association in the District of Columbia and president of the capital branch of the National Association for the Advancement of Colored People (NAACP), among many civic responsibilities.

REFERENCES: BWA; DANB; EBA; NBAW; Estelle W. Taylor, "Emma Frances Grayson Merritt: Pioneer in Negro Education," *Negro History Bulletin* 38 (August/September 1975): 434–35.

MEYER, Estelle Reel. *See* REEL, Estelle.

MIEL, Alice Marie. b. February 21, 1906, Six Lakes, Michigan, to Lucas M. and Ane Marie (Jensen) Miel. Married: no.

Alice Miel's primary concern was education for democracy. She stressed cooperation in schools, among teachers, between teachers and administrators, and with the community. She believed youth needed to learn to live democratically but also acknowledged limitations to freedom.

Miel was born on a farm in Michigan. Her interest in languages began at home when she learned Danish from her Danish-born mother and relatives. Miel completed a two-year course at Central State Normal School (later, Central Michigan University) and received A.B. (1928) and A.M. (1931) degrees from the University of Michigan. She taught high school Latin, Greek, and social studies in schools in Vicksburg, Farmington, and Rogers City, Michigan.

From 1930 to 1939 she was a teacher of Latin and social studies and teaching principal in Ann Arbor, Michigan, schools, where cooperation was stressed. *Democracy in School Administration*, which Miel wrote with G. R. Koopman and Paul J. Misner (1943), was based on those experiences. At Mount Pleasant, Michigan, Miel was an elementary coordinator (1939–42). She served on a state committee that studied the application of research findings to child development.

Miel received the Ed.D. degree from Teachers College, Columbia University, in 1944. In 1945 she joined the staff of Teachers College, at first at the Horace Mann–Lincoln Institute of School Experimentation. Miel and associates published *Cooperative Procedures in Learning* (1952). From 1960 to 1967 she was chair of the Department of Curriculum and Teaching. She retired in 1971 and in 1978 received the Teachers College Medal for Distinguished Service.

Miel's educational services included a curriculum survey in Puerto Rico, projects in Uganda and Tanzania, work as a social studies specialist helping educators to write textbooks in Afghanistan, and six months in postwar Japan assisting educators in developing leadership skills. Miel helped to found and served as first president of the World Council for Curriculum and Instruction (WCCI). She held leadership positions in the Association for Childhood Education International (president, 1953–54), Association for Supervision and Curriculum Development, World Education Fellowship, and National Education Association.

Among her writings were *Changing the Curriculum: A Social Process* (1946), *More than Social Studies* (with Peggy Brogan, 1957), *Supervision for Improved Instruction* (with Arthur J. Lewis, 1972), and *Education for World Cooperation* (with Louise Berman, 1983). Her edited works included *Toward Better Teaching* (with Kimball Wiles, BDAE, 1949), *Creativity in Teaching* (1961), and *Individualizing Reading Practices* (1958).

REFERENCES: CA (NR-20); FWC; LE (1974); RPE; WD (1994–96); Louise M. Berman, "Alice Miel: Leader in Democracy's Ways," *Childhood Education* 66 (Winter 1989): 98–102; Alice Miel, "Roaming through a Life-Space," *The Educational Forum* 56 (Summer 1992): 457–63; Elizabeth Anne Yeager, "Alice Miel's Contributions to the Curriculum Field" (Ph.D. diss., University of Texas at Austin, 1995).

MILLETT, John David. b. March 14, 1912, Indianapolis, Indiana, to Grover Allan and Helen Elizabeth (Welch) Millett. Married September 2, 1934, to Catherine Letsinger. Children: three. d. November 14, 1993, Cincinnati, Ohio.

John D. Millett was an expert in higher education finance and administration and a prolific author on both subjects. He received the A.B. degree from DePauw University (1933) and earned A.M. (1935) and Ph.D. (1938) degrees from Columbia University. Millett was employed in New York City by the Social Science Research Council (1939–41) and in Washington, D.C., by the National Resources Planning Board (1941–42). He served in the U.S. Army (1942–45 and 1947).

At Columbia again from 1945 to 1953, Millett taught public administration. While on leave he was executive director of the Commission on Financing Higher Education (1949–52). Two books resulted from the commission's work, both published in 1952: *Nature and Needs of Higher Education*, by the group, and *Financing Higher Education in the United States*, written by Millett. In 1952 Millett became director of Columbia University's Center of Administrative Studies.

While president of Miami University in Oxford, Ohio (1953–64), Millett chaired the Ohio Commission on Education beyond High School (1962–63) and was a leader in the development of two-year branch campuses. In 1964 he was named first chancellor of the Ohio Board of Regents. Higher education in Ohio expanded during his tenure. In 1972 Millett became senior vice president of the Academy for Educational Development in Washington, D.C. He returned to Miami University as professor of educational leadership and adjunct professor of political science (1980–84) and later was an independent consultant.

Millett was a trustee of the Educational Testing Service (1959–63 and 1966–70) and served twice as its chairman (1962–63 and 1969–70). He was a trustee of the College Entrance Examination Board (1961–64) and Institute of American Universities (1963–80) and a member of the National Board of Graduate Education and National Commission for UNESCO (1965–70). He was president of the American Society of Public Administrators (1960–61), secretary of the National Association of State Universities (1955–61), and chair of the National Academy of Public Administrators (1966–72).

Among Millett's publications were *Management in Public Service* (1954), *Organization for the Public Service* (1966), *Decision Making and Administra-*

tion in Higher Education (1968), *Mergers in Higher Education* (1976), *New Structures of Campus Power* (1978), and *Organization and the University* (1980).

REFERENCES: CA (104, 143); CB (1953, 1994); LE (1974); NYT, November 16, 1993, p. B4; *PS* 27 (March 1994): 119; WW (1988–89); Jean Elizabeth Dye, ''Administrative Leadership in the Academic Community: John David Millett, 1953–1964'' (Ph.D. diss., Miami University, 1986).

MILLS, Cyrus Taggart. b. May 4, 1819, Paris, New York, to William and Mary Mills. Married September 11, 1848, to Susan Lincoln Tolman (BDAE). Children: no. d. April 20, 1884, Oakland, California.

Cyrus Taggart Mills was raised by an aunt after being orphaned. He graduated from Williams College in 1844 and from Union Theological Seminary in 1847. He was ordained a Presbyterian minister in 1848. Beginning with his junior year in college, for four winters he taught in Plainfield, Massachusetts. He studied Tamil to prepare for missionary work in Ceylon.

Mills and his bride were sent by the American Board of Commissioners for Foreign Missions to Ceylon in 1849. He was in charge of Batticotta Seminary, an institution to prepare native teachers and clergy. Ill health forced the couple to return to the United States in 1854. They settled in Ware, Massachusetts, and Mills traveled and spoke on missions. In 1856 he resigned as a missionary. He served a church in Berkshire, New York (1856–58), then established a business in Ware. From 1860 until 1864 he was president of Oahu College near Honolulu, Hawaii, which he led to self-supporting status. After leaving Hawaii, Mills and his wife returned to Ware.

In 1865 they went to Benicia, California, where they purchased the Young Ladies' Seminary from Mary Atkins, renaming it Benicia Seminary for Young Ladies. They sold the seminary in October 1870 and built a new one near Oakland, California; it opened in 1871. Cyrus Mills was principal, and Susan Mills was associate principal. The institution was incorporated in 1877 as Mills Seminary-College. Cyrus Mills was an organizer and president of the Pomona Land and Water Company (1882–84), and he speculated in land while he conducted the seminary. The school continued under the direction of Susan Mills, who served as president of Mills College from 1890 to 1909.

REFERENCES: DAB; NCAB (25: 107); WWW (H); Elias Olan James, *The Story of Cyrus and Susan Mills* (Stanford University Press, 1953); Rossiter Johnson, ed., *The Twentieth Century Dictionary of Notable Americans* (Biographical Society, 1904, reprinted by Gale Research, 1968).

MITCHELL, Lucy Sprague. b. July 2, 1878, Chicago, to Otho S. A. and Lucia (Atwood) Sprague. Married May 8, 1912, to Wesley Clair Mitchell. Children: four. d. October 15, 1967, Palo Alto, California.

In 1916, when Lucy Sprague Mitchell established the Bureau of Educational Experiments in New York City, she secured her place as a pioneer of progressive education. The bureau became Bank Street College of Education in 1950. Mitchell oversaw its innovations in early childhood education, teacher education, urban schooling, and children's literature until her retirement in 1956. She stood with progressive educators who believed in the importance of creative self-expression and the play impulse of children and against the advocates of "life adjustment."

Lucy Sprague came from an affluent family and was tutored at home until the age of twelve. In Chicago, family friends she met included John Dewey (BDAE) and Alice Freeman Palmer (BDAE). Her family moved in 1893 to Los Angeles, where Mitchell attended the Marlborough School for two years. She moved to Cambridge, Massachusetts, to live with George (BDAE) and Alice Palmer and attend Radcliffe College, from which she graduated in 1900 with honors in philosophy.

In 1906 Benjamin Wheeler (BDAE) invited her to the University of California at Berkeley, where she became dean of women and assistant professor of English. Women's organizations there were strengthened through her leadership. In 1911 she visited New York City to work with Lillian Wald (BDAE), Julia Richman (BDAE), and others. She resigned as dean the next year, married, and moved to New York City. Later, she took courses from John Dewey at Columbia University and taught at the kindergarten of Caroline Pratt's (BDAE) Play School, which was relocated to space at the Mitchell residence.

Lucy and Wesley Mitchell founded the Bureau of Educational Experiments, helped with money provided by her cousin, Elizabeth Sprague Coolidge. Lucy Mitchell's first publication, *Here and Now Story Book* (1921), was a new form for children's books, focusing on the real experiences of children rather than on fairy tales. With others she established the Cooperative School for Teachers in 1931 as a teacher training institution. In 1938 she founded the Writers Workshop for authors of children's books, and in 1943 she began public school workshops. She was president of the Bank Street College of Education from 1950 to 1956.

Among other children's books, Mitchell wrote *The Here and Now Primer* (1924), *Manhattan: Now and Long Ago* (1934), and *Red, White and Blue Auto* (1944), and she edited *Believe and Make Believe* (with Irma Simonton Black, 1956). Her adult books included *Young Geographers* (1934), *Our Children and Our Schools* (1950), and *Know Your Children in School* (with others, 1954). She also wrote *Two Lives: The Story of Wesley Clair Mitchell and Myself* (1953).

REFERENCES: AWM; DAB (supp. 8); NAW; NCAB (53: 375); NYT, October 17, 1967, p. 44; WEUS; WR; Joyce Antler, *Lucy Sprague Mitchell: The Making of a Modern Woman* (Yale University Press, 1987); Emily Pond Matthews, "Lucy Sprague Mitchell: A Deweyan Educator" (Ed. D. diss., Rutgers University, the State University of New Jersey, 1979).

MONRO, John Usher. b. December 23, 1912, North Andover, Massachusetts, to Clayton and Frances (Sutton) Monro. Married June 21, 1936, to Dorothy Stevens Foster. Children: two.

In 1967 John Monro caught national attention when he resigned as dean of Harvard College to direct freshman studies at Miles College, a small, poor, historically black college in Birmingham, Alabama, which had lost its accreditation for a time. He had been teaching at Miles during the summer for several years, having been invited there by the college president, Lucius Pitts (q.v.).

Monro attended Phillips Academy in Andover, Massachusetts, working to pay his fees, and needed a scholarship to attend Harvard College, where he earned the A.B. degree in 1935.

His first career was journalism. From college graduation until Navy service during World War II, he was a reporter for the *Boston Transcript*. In 1946 he was about to return to newswriting when at the last moment he accepted an offer to advise returning veterans at Harvard. He later was director of financial aid (1950–58) and dean of the college (1958–67). Monro was a vigorous recruiter of African-American students to Harvard College.

Monro took with him to Miles College an interracial group of young teachers with whom he began a program for freshmen in the humanities and social sciences. It emphasized writing, which Monro taught regularly, and African-American authors. In 1977 Monro moved to Tougaloo College, where he was professor of writing until 1996. He also served as a consultant to the Urban Affairs Center at the University of Alabama at Birmingham.

REFERENCES: NYT, March 10, 1967, p. 1; Linda Greenhouse, ''The Reincarnation of John Monro,'' NYT, March 15, 1970, p. 56; *Intellect* 101 (November 1972): 129.

MORGAN, Lucy Calista. b. September 20, 1889, Murphy, North Carolina, to Alfred and Fannie Eugenia (Siler) Morgan. Married: no. d. July 3, 1981, Webster, North Carolina.

Penland School of Handicrafts, founded by Lucy Morgan in North Carolina, became internationally known as a handicrafts center. Morgan dated the school's founding to 1929, when outsiders first arrived to be students. They had learned of the center in an article in the *Handicrafter*. Morgan had begun a handicrafts program in 1924.

Morgan first went to Penland in 1920 to be teacher and principal at the Appalachian School. It had been founded in 1913 by her brother, Rufus Morgan, an Episcopalian minister. While there she became interested in hand-weaving. In 1923 she took a nine-week course in weaving at Berea (Kentucky) College and at the conclusion had three looms shipped to Penland. Twelve more were shipped soon, while later the men of the community made looms. Morgan wanted to revive the weaving craft, believing it could provide mountain women with income-producing work. She taught women in their homes.

Morgan acquired a car so she could get to resort areas to sell the goods. She also was able to sell weavings at the General Convention of the Episcopal Church, at the state fair in Raleigh, and in state parks.

In 1928 Olive Dame Campbell (q.v.) of the John C. Campbell School, Morgan, and other representatives from craft schools at Penland formed the Southern Highland Handicraft Guild.

When the outside students came, they first were housed at Appalachian School and in a farmhouse Morgan had purchased with contributions from industry. Morgan built other structures; by 1981 there were forty-four buildings on 440 acres. Other crafts such as pottery and metalwork were added to the curriculum.

Penland was incorporated as a nonprofit educational institution in 1938 with a Board of Trustees. The school had no requirements and no grades. In the 1940s students came under the GI Bill of Rights. Students visited from around the world, particularly Scandinavia.

Morgan's early years were spent in the North Carolina mountains. In 1915 she graduated from the two-year teacher training course at Central State Normal School (later, Central Michigan University). She taught in public schools in Michigan and Illinois and worked for the Chicago Children's Bureau (1918–19). After a year of teaching in Havre, Montana, Morgan went to Penland in 1920. She retired in 1962.

REFERENCES: CB (1959); NYT, July 5, 1981, p. 14; WR; WWAW (1958–59); Linda Darty, ''The Dream of Miss Lucy Morgan,'' *American Craft* 41 (October/November 1981): 2–3; Lucy Morgan and LeGette Blyth, *Gift from the Hills: Miss Lucy Morgan's Story of Her Unique Penland School* (University of North Carolina Press, 1971); *Who's Who in the South and Southeast* (1959).

MORGAN, Mary Kimball. b. December 8, 1861, Janesville, Wisconsin, to Freeman Aaron and Helen Maria (Chapin) Kimball. Married December 15, 1885, to William Edgar Morgan. Children: two. d. October 13, 1948, Elsah, Illinois.

Mary Kimball Morgan was a Christian Science educator responsible for establishing the Principia schools. She began with an elementary school, added a high school, then a junior college, and later founded Principia College in Elsah, Illinois. All were based on Christian Science principles. While owned and operated by Christian Scientists, the schools were not formally affiliated with the Church of Christ, Scientist.

Mary (Nellie May) Kimball's family moved from Wisconsin to St. Louis, Missouri, when she was six years old. She was educated in public schools and at home. In 1888 she joined the Christian Science Church. With her husband, William E. Morgan, she assisted in organizing a Christian Science church in St. Louis. She became a practitioner in 1896.

Morgan taught her two sons at home. Family friends asked her to include their children, and they were added to what became her kindergarten. A school opened in October 1898 with elementary grades added. The school, named Principia, was endorsed by Mary Baker Eddy, founder of Christian Science. In 1899 a dormitory was opened for boarding students. Within a few years the school owned an entire block of St. Louis. The first high school class graduated in

1906. The junior college began in 1910, one of the earliest established in the United States. Principia was incorporated in 1912.

In 1932 a four-year liberal arts college was founded, the first bachelor of arts degrees being awarded in 1934. Principia College moved to Elsah, Illinois, in 1935, while the elementary and high schools remained in St. Louis. Morgan served as president of the college until 1938; her son, Frederic Morgan, succeeded her. She retired as chairman of the Board of Trustees in 1942.

REFERENCES: LW; NAW; NYT, October 14, 1948, p. 29; ''Principia College,'' PC; WR; Edwin S. Leonard, Jr., *As the Sowing: The First Fifty Years of the Principia* (Principia, 1948).

MORLEY, Margaret Warner. b. February 17, 1858, Montrose, Iowa, to Isaac and Sarah Robinson (Warner) Morley. Married: no. d. December 12, 1923, Washington, D.C.

A prolific author of children's books, Margaret Morley wrote on nature and on how to teach youngsters about sex and birth. In a time when such subjects were generally taboo, her writings were known for their discretion.

Morley attended school in Brooklyn, New York, and the Oswego Normal School (later, State University of New York College at Oswego). In 1878 she graduated from New York City Normal (later, Hunter) College. She conducted further studies in biology at Armour Institute (later, part of Illinois Institute of Technology) and Woods Hole Marine Laboratory.

Morley taught at the Oswego Normal School; the State Normal School in Milwaukee, Wisconsin (later, University of Wisconsin–Milwaukee); and Leavenworth (Kansas) High School. She was a biology teacher in Chicago at the Armour Institute and the Free Kindergarten Training Class. Later, she lectured in Boston on nature topics.

Many of her books were used as texts in nature study, including *Seed Babies* (1896), *Flowers and Their Friends* (1897), *The Bee People* (1897), *The Insect Folk* (1903), *Little Mitchell: The Story of a Mountain Squirrel* (1904), *Grasshopper Land* (1907), and *Will O'the Wasps* (1913). Books for young people on sex and birth included *A Song of Life* (1891) and *Life and Love* (1895). *The Spark of Life: The Story of How Living Things Came into the World, as Told for Girls and Boys* (1913) was meant for parents. For part of each year Morley resided in Tyron, North Carolina, where she was able to observe nature.

REFERENCES: DAB; LW; NYT, December 15, 1923, p. 13; WWW (1); John W. Leonard, ed., *Woman's Who's Who of America* (American Commonwealth, 1914).

MORRISON, Philip. b. November 7, 1915, Somerville, New Jersey. Married 1965 to Phyllis Singer. Children: one.

Philip Morrison was a nuclear and theoretical astrophysicist who became interested in teaching young children the fundamentals of science. He reformed science curricula. Morrison also was an advocate of academic and intellectual freedom.

Morrison attended public schools of Pittsburgh. He received the B.S. degree (1936) from Carnegie Institute of Technology (later, Carnegie-Mellon University) and the Ph.D. degree in theoretical physics (1940) from the University of California, Berkeley, where he was a graduate student of J. Robert Oppenheimer (BDAE). He taught physics at San Francisco State College (later, University, 1941) and at the University of Illinois (1941–42).

Morrison worked on the Manhattan Project as a physicist in the Metallurgical Laboratory at the University of Chicago (1943–44) and as a group leader at the Los Alamos (New Mexico) Science Laboratory (1944–46). Later in life he refused to do weapons research. From 1946 to 1965 Morrison was professor of physics and nuclear studies at Cornell University. During those years he became active in the peace movement and advocated nuclear arms control. In 1965 he was invited to Massachusetts Institute of Technology (MIT) by Jerrold R. Zacharias (q.v.). He was Francis L. Friedman Lecturer and in 1973 became an Institute Professor.

An active member of the Physical Science Study Committee (PSSC), Morrison wrote much of the PSSC high school physics course and the secondary school textbook, *Physics*. He wanted pupils to have direct experience of science. In 1948 Morrison helped to found the Federation of American Scientists, which he later chaired (1973–76). From its beginning in 1960, Morrison was a member of the Commission on College Physics.

His April 30, 1960, *Saturday Evening Post* article, "Cause, Chance, and Creation," received an American Association for the Advancement of Science-Westinghouse Award for science writing. Morrison wrote book reviews for *Scientific American*, including an annual appraisal of science books for children, which he prepared with his wife. He wrote *Elementary Nuclear Theory* (with Hans Bethe, 1956), *Cosmic Rays* (with others, 1961), *My Father's Watch: Aspects of the Physical World* (with Donald F. Holcomb, 1969), *Winding Down* (1979), *Powers of Ten* (with others, 1982), *The Price of Our Defense* (with others, 1979), *The Ring of Truth* (a public television series, with Phyllis Morrison, 1987), and *Nothing Is Too Wonderful to Be True* (1995). With others, he edited *The Search for Extraterrestrial Intelligence* (1977) and *Search for the Universal Ancestors* (1985).

Awards received by Morrison included the Pregel Prize (1955) from the New York Academy of Science, Babson Prize (1957) from the Gravity Foundation, Oerstad Medal (1965) from the American Association of Physics Teachers, and Germant Award (1987) from the American Institute of Physics.

REFERENCES: CA (106); CB (1981); WW (1990–91); *American Journal of Physics* 33 (September 1965): 702; Anne Eisenberg, "Philip Morrison: A Profile," *Physics Today* 35 (August 1982): 36–41; Dana Roberts, "Talks with Great Teachers: Philip Morrison," *The Physics Teacher* 20 (January 1982): 21–27; David W. Swift, *SETI Pioneers: Sci-*

entists Talk about Their Search for Extraterrestrial Intelligence (University of Arizona Press, 1990).

MUSSEY, Ellen Spencer. b. May 13, 1850, Geneva, Ohio, to Platt Rogers (BDAE) and Persis (Duty) Spencer. Married June 14, 1871, to Reuben Delavan Mussey. Children: two. d. April 21, 1936, Washington, D.C.

At a time when most law schools barred women, Ellen Spencer Mussey founded the Washington (D.C.) College of Law as the first law school in the world primarily for women. In 1896 three women had begun reading law during evenings in Mussey's office. The lecturers included some male lawyers. Washington College of Law was incorporated in 1898 by Mussey and Emma Gillett. Mussey served as dean, the first woman law school dean in the world. While the school was begun for women, men attended, and by 1913, when Mussey resigned as dean, half of the 150 students were men. Mussey continued to be active in the school, and in 1933 she was still signing the diplomas. The school later became a part of American University.

Mussey's father, Platt Spencer, developed the Spencerian system of penmanship. He gave his daughter lessons from the time she was four years old. Because the family moved frequently, and she was sometimes ill, she had little formal schooling. After her mother's death when she was twelve, she ran the household and taught penmanship at a school. After her father's death two years later, she moved around, living with her siblings. In Rockford, Illinois, she attended Rockford Seminary (later, College) as a student/teacher.

Mussey moved to Washington, D.C., in 1869 to be principal of the ladies' department of the Spencerian Business College. After her marriage she studied law with her husband. When he was ill, she ran his office, and she handled claims cases successfully. After his death she continued the law office. Both National University and Columbian College (later, George Washington University) refused her admission because of her gender. She was able to take an oral examination for the bar and was admitted on March 23, 1893, using the name E. S. Mussey.

In 1896 Mussey was admitted to practice before the U.S. Supreme Court and in 1897 before the Court of Claims. Mussey crusaded to change gender-biased divorce laws, the bill doing so being signed by President Grover Cleveland in 1896. She worked for the establishment of kindergartens in the District of Columbia; appropriations for them came in 1898. When Mussey learned that American women lost their citizenship if they married foreigners, she drew up a citizenship bill enacted in 1922.

In 1906 Mussey was appointed to the District Board of Education. For some years she was counsel for Norway and Denmark in the District.

REFERENCES: AR; BCAW; DAB (supp. 2); LW; NAW; NCAB (A: 402 and 47: 578); WR; WWW (1); Grace Hathaway, *Fate Rides a Tortoise: A Biography of Ellen Spencer Mussey* (John C. Winston, 1937); Rossiter Johnson, ed., *The Twentieth Century Biographical Dictionary of Notable Americans* (Biographical Society, 1904, reprinted by Gale Research 1968).

N

NABRIT, James Madison, Jr. b. September 4, 1900, Atlanta, Georgia, to James Madison and Augusta Gertrude (West) Nabrit. Married December 30, 1924, to Norma Clarke Walton. Children: one.

James M. Nabrit, Jr., attended Morehouse College High School in Atlanta, Georgia, and Morehouse College, from which he received the B.A. degree in 1923. He earned the J.D. from Northwestern University in 1927. From 1925 to 1927 Nabrit taught at Leland College in Baker, Louisiana. He served as dean of the Agricultural, Mechanical and Normal College (later, University of Arkansas–Pine Bluff) for two years (1928–30). In private law practice in Houston, Texas, from 1930 to 1936, Nabrit handled numerous civil rights cases.

He went to Howard University in 1936 as a law professor. The first civil rights course in an American law school was organized by Nabrit. In addition to teaching, Nabrit was assistant to the president (1938–39), secretary of the university (1939–60), director of public relations (1940–50 and 1955–58), and dean of the law school (1958–60). With Thurgood Marshall, Nabrit argued the *Bolling v. Sharpe* case before the Supreme Court, which resulted in the prohibition of racial discrimination in District of Columbia schools in 1954.

In 1960 Nabrit was named president of Howard University to succeed Mordecai Johnson (BDAE). While on leave from the university, from 1965 to 1967 he served as deputy representative for the United States on the United Nations Security Council. In the late 1960s Howard University was a center of student protest. Nabrit announced in 1968 he would resign in 1969. James E. Cheek (q.v.) was his successor.

Nabrit served as an adviser to the Virgin Islands government on reorganization of the executive branch. He wrote articles for legal and educational journals.

REFERENCES: CB (1961); NCAB (J: 490); WW (1976–77); WWBA (1994–95); Walter Christmas, ed., *Negro Heritage Library*, vol. 1 (Educational Heritage, 1966), pp. 34–36; Juan Williams, ''District Schools: From Victory to Failure,'' WP, January 17, 1979, p. A19; Stanton L. Wormley and Lewis H. Fenderson, eds., *Many Shades of Black* (Morrow, 1969), pp. 61–71.

NABRIT, Samuel Milton. b. February 21, 1905, Macon, Georgia, to James Madison and Augusta Gertrude (West) Nabrit. Married August 8, 1927, to Constance T. Crocker. Children: no.

Samuel M. Nabrit was a scientist and college president who sought to improve educational standards for African Americans. He was the first African American to receive the Ph.D. degree from Brown University and the first Morehouse College graduate to receive one.

Nabrit's family moved from Macon to Augusta, Georgia, when he was seven years old. He attended Walker Baptist Institute, where his father taught. After receiving the B.S. degree from Morehouse College in 1925, Nabrit remained there to teach biology (1925–31). In 1928 he received the M.Sc. degree from Brown University and in 1932 the Ph.D. His summers were spent doing research at the Marine Biological Laboratory in Woods Hole, Massachusetts. In 1932 Nabrit became chair of the Atlanta (later, Clark–Atlanta) University Biology Department and in 1947 dean of the Graduate School of Arts and Sciences. Under his third grant from the General Education Board, he studied science education at Teachers College of Columbia University in 1944. In 1949–50 he studied at the University of Brussels, Belgium. He was the second president of Texas Southern University, serving from 1955 to 1966.

Nabrit was a founder of the National Institute of Science in 1943 and later its president (1945–46). He also served on the National Committee for Research in Science Teaching and the Committee on Training of College Teachers of the American Council on Education. Nabrit was a member of the Administrative Committee of the Southern Fellowships Fund (1954–61) and sat on the advisory committee to its parent body, the Council of Southern Universities (1963–64). Later, he became executive director of the Southern Fellowships Fund.

In 1964 Nabrit and Jerrold R. Zacharias (q.v.) developed a plan to upgrade historically black colleges. The Carnegie Corporation and Rockefeller Foundation funded the plan, which provided college teachers the opportunity to work with leading professors. Nabrit was named to the National Science Board in 1956. He was the first African American appointed to the Atomic Energy Commission when he succeeded Mary Bunting (q.v.) in 1966. He wrote *Inventory of Academic Leadership* (1969). Science buildings were named in his honor at Texas Southern University and Morehouse College.

REFERENCES: CB (1963); LE (1948); WW (1976–77); WWBA (1994/95); Stanton L. Wormley and Lewis H. Fenderson, eds., *Many Shades of Black* (1969), pp. 159–72; Vivian Ovelton Sammons, *Blacks in Science and Medicine* (Hemisphere, 1990).

NASH, Alice Ford Morrison. b. March 3, 1878, Northwood, New Hampshire, to Frank and Eva (Carr) Morrison. Married January 27, 1909, to Charles Emerson Nash. Children: no. d. March 3, 1966, Pittsgrove Township, New Jersey.

Alice Morrison began teaching at the Training School at Vineland, New Jersey, in 1900, immediately upon completing two years of teacher training at the New Hampton (New Hampshire) Literary and Biblical Institution. She remembered later that her preparation had been as a teacher of children with normal mental abilities, not retarded. She had expected to be at Vineland only long enough to earn money for college studies but stayed more than fifty years.

Along with her husband, who was first a teacher and then superintendent of the Training School, and Edgar A. Doll (q.v.), who directed the research program, Alice Morrison Nash endeavored to improve public perceptions of mental retardation. She worked particularly to make the case that retarded persons are like other people in significant ways. In the late 1940s and early 1950s, a new group of administrators, with graduate training and a research focus, replaced her generation in leading the school. Yet it was Nash whose gentle advocacy had helped to make the Training School a model for care and education of mentally retarded children.

Nash was a teacher at Vineland until 1909, when she became principal of the school department. From 1925 to 1952 she was director of education, and from 1952 until her death her title was educational consultant. She was a frequent contributor to the *Training School Bulletin* from its founding in 1904 until 1957, when its focus changed from being a record of the school to a research journal. She continued serving on the editorial board until her death in 1966.

REFERENCES: "Commemorative Issue Honoring Alice Morrison Nash for Fifty Years Service to the Training School and the Cause of Mental Deficiency," *Training School Bulletin* 46 (January 1950): 145–73; Alice Fleming, *Great American Teachers* (Lippincott, 1965); *Time* 55 (January 23, 1950): 46.

NAUMBURG, Margaret. b. May 24, 1890, New York City, to Max and Therese (Kahnweller) Naumburg. Married June 29, 1916, to Waldo Frank. Children: one. d. February 26, 1983, Needham, Massachusetts.

Margaret Naumburg combined ideas from progressive education, psychoanalytic theory, and an emphasis on artistic creation at the Walden School in New York City.

Naumburg was a student of John Dewey (BDAE) at Barnard College, where she earned the A.B. degree in 1911. She continued her studies at the London School of Economics with Sidney and Beatrice Webb; at the school of Maria Montessori, Casa dei Bambini; and with Marietta Johnson (BDAE). She founded the Children's (later, Walden) School in 1915, serving as its director until 1922.

In her first book, *The Child and the World* (1928), Naumburg emphasized individualism and creativity in a way that set her apart from the socially based progressivism of John Dewey. Naumburg favored allowing children to discover interests and develop skills for themselves, rather than through curricula that were formalized and depended on books. Dewey in turn criticized the path taken by his former student, in a series of articles he wrote in 1929. In 1930 at the invitation of *The New Republic* both of them contributed essays to the magazine, Dewey emphasizing what was taught and how, Naumburg warning that the group orientation Dewey favored resulted in herd behavior.

Naumburg joined the New York Psychiatric Institute in the 1930s and specialized in art therapy there. In her later years she also taught at the New School for Social Research. Books she wrote on art therapy included *Schizophrenic Art*

(1950), *Psychoneurotic Art* (1953), *Dynamically Oriented Art Therapy* (1966), and *An Introduction to Art Therapy* (1973).

REFERENCES: CA (109); NYT, March 6, 1983, p. 44; WWAW (1961–62); Robert H. Beck, "Progressive Education and American Progressivism: Margaret Naumburg," *Teachers College Record* 60 (January 1959): 198–208; Lawrence A. Cremin (q.v.), *The Transformation of the American School* (Vintage Books, 1961), pp. 211–14, 277; Clarence J. Karier, *Scientists of the Mind: Intellectual Founders of Modern Psychology* (University of Illinois Press, 1986).

NEF, John Ulric, Jr. b. July 13, 1899, Chicago, to John Ulric and Louise Bates (Comstock) Nef. Married November 19, 1921, to Elinor Henry Castle; April 21, 1964, to Evelyn Stefansson. Children: no. d. December 25, 1988, Washington, D.C.

John Ulric Nef, Jr., was an economic historian interested in educational reforms and relationships between disciplines. He was instrumental in organizing a new kind of graduate department at the University of Chicago, interdisciplinary and bridging the sciences and the arts.

Nef attended the University of Chicago High School. His father had been founder and chair of the Chemistry Department at the University of Chicago. When Nef was sixteen years old, his father died, and the philosopher George Herbert Mead became Nef's guardian. Nef received the S.B. degree from Harvard University in 1920. He studied in France and then at the Robert Brookings Graduate School, where he received the Ph.D. degree in 1927. He began his teaching career as an assistant professor at Swarthmore College (1927–28).

At the University of Chicago from 1929, Nef taught economics and economic history. In 1945 he worked with Robert Maynard Hutchins (BDAE), president of the university, to set up a graduate department that brought together many disciplines. Called the Committee on Social Thought, Nef provided its initial funding and served as its chair until 1964.

An outgrowth of the committee was the Center for Human Understanding, which Nef also chaired from 1958 to 1968. He edited two books based on the center's work: *Bridges of Human Understanding* (1964) and *Towards World Community* (1968). Later, Nef established the John and Evelyn Nef Foundation and served as its president. Nef was vice chair of the American Council of Learned Societies (1952). Among his publications were *The Rise of the British Coal Industry* (1932), *Industry and Government in France and England, 1540–1640* (1940), *The United States and Civilization* (1942), *The Universities Look for Unity* (1943), *War and Human Progress* (1950), *Cultural Foundations of Industrial Civilization* (1958), and *The Conquest of the Material World, Essays on the Coming of Industrialism* (1964). He also wrote *Search for Meaning: The Autobiography of a Nonconformist* (1973). The Society for the History of Technology awarded Nef the Leonardo da Vinci Medal in 1979.

REFERENCES: CA (NR-20, 127); NYT, December 27, 1988, p. A19; WWW (9); *Technology and Culture* 21 (July 1980): 437–45, and 31 (October 1990): 916–20.

NEYHART, Amos Earl. b. November 22, 1898, South Williamsport, Pennsylvania, to Simon Peter and Agnes Clara (Eck) Neyhart. Married June 20, 1923, to Mary Helen Leinbach. Children: three. d. July 5, 1990, State College, Pennsylvania.

School-based driver education in the United States began through the efforts of Amos Neyhart. In 1933 Neyhart offered a systematic course, combining classroom lectures and driving practice, to twenty students at State College (Pennsylvania) High School. He wrote "The Safe Operation of an Automobile" (1934), the first instructional text on the subject. In 1936 he offered a summer course to high school teachers from seventeen states to prepare them as instructors of driver education. The American Automobile Association (AAA) published his revised booklet, first in 1938 as a pamphlet and later as a central chapter of *Sportsmanlike Driving*.

Neyhart was a graduate of Pennsylvania State University, where he earned a bachelor's degree in industrial engineering and a master's degree in applied psychology. He was a member of the university's faculty beginning in 1929. For two years (1936–38) he took leave to work full-time as consultant on road training for the AAA. He continued as an adviser to AAA all of his life. He directed the Institute of Public Safety at Pennsylvania State University from 1938 until his retirement in 1964. He also developed curricula on motor fleet supervision, maintenance, and safety.

Neyhart traveled widely as a speaker, consultant, and instructor on driver education. He was a consultant to the National Commission on Safety Education of the National Education Association and served on presidential committees on traffic safety issues. He received the Pennsylvania Meritorious Medal (1956) and the Richard Kaywood Memorial Award of the American Driver and Traffic Safety Education Association (1987), as well as other honors.

REFERENCES: NYT, July 13, 1990, p. B8; James E. Aaron and Marland K. Strasser, *Driver and Traffic Safety Education* (Macmillan, 1966), pp. 27–29; American Automobile Association, "How to Drive," Sportsmanlike Driving Series, No. 5 (1938), unpaged introduction; American Automobile Association, *Sportsmanlike Driving* (1947), unpaged foreword; Margaret B. Duda, "Father of Driver Training," *NRTA Journal* (September–October 1980): 39–40; *Journal of Traffic Safety Education* 35 (Fall 1987): 22, and 37 (Winter 1989): 22; U.S. Congress, House Committee on Interstate and Foreign Commerce, "Driver Education Hearings," 85th Cong., 1st sess. (1957), pp. 59–60.

NOAH, Harold Julius. b. January 21, 1925, London, England, to Abraham and Sophia (Cohen) Noah. Married October 20, 1945, to Norma Mestel; October 14, 1966, to Helen Claire Chisnall. Children: four.

Harold J. Noah wrote extensively on the economics of education and on comparative education. Noah received the B.Sc. degree in 1946 from the London School of Economics and Political Science. He studied at Kings College of the University of London (1948–49 and 1952–54) and received a teacher's diploma. Noah taught economics at the Southwest London College of Commerce (1948–

49) and was assistant master and head of the Economics Department at the Henry Thornton School in London (1949–60). He was an exchange teacher in Newark, New Jersey (1958–59).

Noah came to the United States again in 1960 and taught economics for one year at Fairleigh Dickinson University. In 1962 he joined the faculty of Teachers College, Columbia University. He was professor of economics and education from 1969. He held the Arthur I. Gates Professorship of the Economics of Education (1980–83) and the Gardner Cowles Chair of Education (1983–87). He also directed the Institute of Philosophy and Politics of Education (1974–76) and was dean of Teachers College (1976–81).

From 1971 to 1982 Noah was a consultant to the Organization for Economic Cooperation and Development (OECD). He participated in International Education Association (IEA) studies. He wrote *Financing Soviet Schools* (1966) and *The National Case Study: An Empirical Comparative Study of Twenty-One Educational Systems* (with A. Harry Passow, q.v., and others, 1976). With Max A. Eckstein he wrote *Toward a Science of Comparative Education* (1969) and *Secondary School Examinations: International Perspectives on Policies and Practice* (1993), and they edited *Scientific Investigations in Comparative Education* (1969). He was editor of the *Comparative Education Review* (1966–71) and *Soviet Education* (1970–78). He was president of the Comparative and International Education Society (1973–74).

REFERENCES: CA (NR-30); LE (1974); WD (1994–96); WW (1984–85); Harold J. Noah, ''Reflections,'' *Comparative Education Review* 31 (February 1987): 137–49.

NOYES, Arthur Amos. b. September 13, 1866, Newburyport, Massachusetts, to Amos and Anna Page (Andrews) Noyes. Married: no. d. June 3, 1936, Pasadena, California.

Arthur Amos Noyes founded the Laboratory of Physical Chemistry at Massachusetts Institute of Technology (MIT). Many leading scientists received their training there. The chemistry textbooks he wrote had a revolutionary impact on the teaching of the subject. At the California Institute of Technology he helped to develop the school into a leader in physics and chemistry education and a center for research in technology and science.

Noyes attended high school in Newburyport, Massachusetts. He entered the sophomore class at MIT on a scholarship after studying first-year subjects on his own because of a lack of funds. He received a bachelor's degree in 1886 and the M.S. degree in 1887, then taught at MIT for a year. One of his students, George Ellery Hale, became a friend and close associate. In 1888 Noyes went to Europe, where he studied under Wilhelm Oswald at Leipzig. There his interest turned from organic to physical chemistry, and he was awarded a doctorate in 1890.

Returning to MIT, Noyes taught analytical, organic, and physical chemistry from 1899 to 1919. He founded the *Review of American Chemical Research* (later, *Chemical Abstracts*) in 1895 and served as its editor for a number of years. His proposal to establish a research laboratory in physical chemistry was accepted in 1903. He became director of the laboratory, providing some of the budget himself. Aid also came from the Carnegie Institution of Washington. Noyes served as acting president of MIT from 1907 to 1909. His book *The General Principles of Physical Science* (1902) was expanded (with M. S. Sherrill) into *A Course of Study in Physical Principles* (1922).

Noyes was associated part-time with the Throop (later, California) Institute of Technology beginning in 1913. From 1919, working with Robert Millikan (BDAE) and George E. Hale, he developed the school into an institute of national prominence. Noyes' role was to develop policies for the institute. Under his guidance, humanities were emphasized, the number of undergraduates was limited, and research was stressed at all levels. He was director of the Gates Laboratory.

Noyes served as president of the American Chemical Society (1904), chair of the National Research Council (1918), and president of the American Association for the Advancement of Science (1927). Among his many books were *A Course of Instruction in the Qualitative Chemical Analysis of Inorganic Substances* (1915), and *A System of Qualitative Analysis for the Rare Elements* (with William C. Bray, 1927). His awards included the Willard Gibbs Medal of the American Chemical Society (1915), Davy Medal of the Royal Society of London (1927), and Richards Medal of the American Chemical Society (1932). The California Institute of Technology was the beneficiary of his estate, to be used to support research in chemistry.

REFERENCES: DAB (supp. 2); NCAB (13: 284); NYT, June 4, 1936, p. 23; WAB; WWW (1); Charles Coulston Gillespie, ed., *Dictionary of Scientific Biography* (Charles Scribner's Sons, 1974); Linus Pauling, ''Arthur Amos Noyes,'' *National Academy of Sciences Biographical Memoirs* (National Academy of Sciences, 1958).

NYQUIST, Ewald Berger. b. November 1, 1914, Rockford, Illinois, to Carl Gustaf and Nellie Mathilda (Anderson) Nyquist. Married to Janet Nyquist. Children: three. d. July 24, 1987, Grafton, New York.

Ewald Nyquist held leadership roles in the New York State Department of Education for more than twenty years. As James E. Allen, Jr.'s (BDAE) successor as New York commissioner of education, Nyquist sought to make education more humanistic and advocated open education. Nyquist began the Regents Competency Test program. He supported busing for desegregation of schools and ordered school districts to pay for education of handicapped students. As an advocate of students' rights, Nyquist opposed dress codes. He began the evaluation of doctoral programs at universities within the state and called for abolition of free tuition at the City University of New York. In his inaugural address he proposed a nontraditional degree program, which resulted in the Regents External Degree Program.

Nyquist attended the schools of Rockford, Illinois. He received the B.S. degree from the University of Chicago in 1936. He pursued graduate work but did not complete a doctorate. In World War II he served as an ensign in the U.S. Naval Reserve. At Columbia University, he was assistant director (1945–48) and director (1948–51) of university admissions. In 1951 he began his tenure with the New York State Department of Education, serving as assistant commissioner of higher education (1951–55), associate commissioner of higher education and professional education (1955–57), deputy commissioner of education (1957–70), and commissioner (1970–77).

From 1977 to 1987 Nyquist was vice president for academic development at Pace University. He wrote *College Learning, Anytime, Anywhere* (1977) and edited *Open Education: A Source Book for Parents and Teachers* (with Gene R. Hawes, 1972).

REFERENCES: CA (113); LE (1974); NYT, September 16, 1970, p. 49, December 8, 1970, p. 1+, September 28, 1975, p. IV6, and July 25, 1987, p. 11; WWW (9).

O

OBERHOLTZER, Kenneth Edison. b. December 22, 1903, Carbon, Indiana, to Edison Ellsworth and Myrtle May (Barr) Oberholtzer. Married October 22, 1928, to Florence Craver. Children: no. d. December 17, 1993, Walnut Creek, California.

Kenneth E. Oberholtzer was credited with modernizing the Denver school system, which he served as superintendent for twenty years.

Oberholtzer attended schools in Indiana and Oklahoma. In 1924 he received the B.S. degree from the University of Illinois. He was a teacher and coach in Bellville, Texas, and became superintendent there in 1926. After receiving the M.S. degree in 1928 from Texas A&M University, he was superintendent of schools in Texas at El Campo (1928–34) and Lubbock (1934–37). Oberholtzer earned the Ph.D. degree from Teachers College of Columbia University in 1937, where Jesse Newlon (BDAE) was his adviser. He served as superintendent of schools in Long Beach, California, from 1937 to 1947. During World War II he was in the U.S. Army Education Branch of the Department of Defense.

In 1947 Oberholtzer became superintendent of schools in Denver, where he saw an opportunity to change the system. Oberholtzer was recognized as a leader and featured on a *Time* magazine cover (February 20, 1950). Gaining passage of three bond issues allowed salaries to be raised and new schools built. Oberholtzer initiated the weekly *Superintendent's Bulletin* for staff and the *School Review* for parents. He began public opinion surveys, a Program for Gifted Students, and School–Business visitations.

During the 1960s he faced opposition due to a divided school board and groups opposed to "general" education. He retired at the end of his contract in 1967 and for a few years was a consultant in Danville, California.

Oberholtzer was president of the American Association of School Administrations (1951–52), a member of the Commission of Educational Organizations, a director of the National Merit Scholars Program (1959), and vice president of the National Congress of the Parent Teacher Association. He wrote *American Agricultural Problems in the Social Studies* (1937) and was on the education advisory board of *Nation's Schools*.

REFERENCES: NYT, December 23, 1993, p. B6; WW (1960–61); *Nation's Schools* 47 (February 1951): 86; Patricia Ann Shikes, "Three Denver School Superintendents: A Historical Study of Educational Leadership" (Ph.D. diss., University of Denver, 1987).

O'CONNOR, Clarence Daniel. b. March 25, 1898, Pembina, North Dakota, to Archie M. and Amelia (Brennan) O'Connor. Married June 30, 1941, to Helen Pumphrey. Children: no. d. June 29, 1990, New York City.

Clarence D. O'Connor was a noted advocate of oral education for deaf children. He was superintendent of the Lexington School for the Deaf in New York City from 1935 to 1967. With Scott Reger he developed the Reger–O'Connor electronic hearing aid for group training.

O'Connor was principal of schools in Woodworth (1917–18) and McGregor (1918–19), North Dakota. In 1921 he graduated from the University of North Dakota. He served as high school principal in East Grand Forks (1921–23). After teaching voice at the University of North Dakota (1923–25), he studied voice in New York City. With a new interest in deaf education, he attended Clarke School for the Deaf in Lexington, Massachusetts (1930–31). O'Connor went to Lexington School for the Deaf in 1931 as assistant to the superintendent, was principal (1933–35), and became superintendent in 1935. He expanded the teacher preparation program. In 1934 he received the M.A. degree from Teachers College of Columbia University.

O'Connor served as president of the Alexander Graham Bell (BDAE) Association for the Deaf (1945–57). In 1967 the association honored him for distinguished service for the deaf. He wrote articles for journals about the deaf and served on many committees concerning deafness and education for the deaf.

REFERENCES: NYT, July 8, 1990, p. 18; WWW (10); *Volta Review* 69 (September 1967): 435, 69 (November 1967): 584, and 76 (March 1974): 167.

P

PALEY, Vivian Gussin. b. January 25, 1929, Chicago, to Harry A. and Yetta (Meisel) Gussin. Married June 20, 1947, to Irving Paley. Children: one.

While a kindergarten teacher at the University of Chicago's Laboratory School, Vivian Paley wrote books drawn from tape recordings of her classes. Using an approach that was deliberately "subjective and personal," she focused on what she called the "three f's"—fantasy, friends, and fairness—to reveal the thinking of children between the ages of three and five. Paley believed it was possible to fashion a common ground with children through their stories and play.

She earned the B.A. degree at the University of Chicago in 1947, another B.A. at Tulane University in 1950, and the M.A. at Hofstra University in 1962. She was a teacher in New Orleans (1952–56) and Great Neck, New York (1963–70), before going to the Chicago laboratory school in 1971.

Paley's books included *White Teacher* (1979); *Wally's Stories: Conversations in the Kindergarten* (1981); *Boys and Girls: Superheroes in the Doll Corner* (1984); *Mollie Is Three: Growing Up in School* (1986); *Bad Guys Don't Have Birthdays: Fantasy Play at Four* (1988); *The Boy Who Would Be a Helicopter* (1990); *Teaching Young Children* (1990); and *You Can't Say You Can't Play* (1992). In *Kwanzaa and Me: A Teacher's Story* (1995), Paley returned to questions of race, identity, and schooling that she had addressed in her first book.

She received the Erikson Institute Award for service to children (1987) and a MacArthur Foundation Fellowship (1989).

REFERENCES: CA (NR-30); WD (1994–96).

PAPERT, Seymour Aubrey. b. March 1, 1928, Pretoria, South Africa, to Jack and Betty Papert. Married April 10, 1963, to Androula Christofides; December 18, 1977, to Sherry Turkle. Children: one.

Seymour Papert created LOGO, a computer programming language suitable for children. He wished to change the culture of education and wanted to use computers to do that. Through LOGO Papert sought to promote self-directed learning.

Papert was raised in South Africa. He earned B.A. (1949) and Ph.D. (1952) degrees from Witwatersrand University and the Ph.D. degree from Cambridge University in England (1959). In 1959 Jean Piaget invited Papert to Switzerland to work with him on the nature of thinking. Papert remained there until 1964. After meeting Marvin Minsky in England, Papert went to the Massachusetts Institute of Technology (MIT), where he was professor of mathematics and education and Cecil and Ida Green Professor of Education (1974–80). He also was codirector of the Artificial Intelligence Laboratory (1967–73), director of the LOGO group (1970–81), and director of the Epistemology and Learning Research Group.

Papert and Minsky worked together to create a children's learning environment. The development of LOGO came with support from the National Science Foundation.

Papert was a Guggenheim fellow (1980) and a Marconi International fellow (1981). In 1982–83 he was science director of the Centre Mondial Informatique et Ressource Humaine in Paris. Among his publications were *Perceptrons: An Introduction to Computational Geometry* (with Marvin Minsky, 1969), *Counter-free Automata* (with Robert McNaughton, 1971), *Artificial Intelligence* (with Marvin Minsky, 1973), *Mindstorms: Children, Computers, and Powerful Ideas* (1980), and *The Children's Machine: Rethinking School in the Age of the Computer* (1993). With Idit Harel he edited *Constructionism* (1991).

REFERENCES: WW (1996); Mark F. Goldberg, ''Portrait of Seymour Papert,'' *Educational Leadership* 48 (April 1991): 68–70; David Hill, ''Professor Papert and His Learning Machine,'' *Teacher Magazine* 5 (January 1994): 16–19; Seymour Papert, ''New Views of LOGO,'' and Fran Reinhold, ''An Interview with Seymour Papert,'' *Electronic Learning* 5 (April 1986): 33–36+; *U.S. News and World Report* 109 (July 16, 1990): 56–57.

PARK, Rosemary. b. March 11, 1907, Andover, Massachusetts, to John Edgar and Grace Lina (Burtt) Park. Married July 31, 1965, to Milton Vasil Anastos. Children: no.

Rosemary Park was a distinguished women's college president and champion of scholarly excellence. At Radcliffe College she graduated with the A.B. degree in 1928 and the A.M. in 1929. She studied at the University of Bonn (Germany) the following year, returned to Germany for further study in 1932, and was awarded the Ph.D. degree magna cum laude at the University of Cologne (Germany) in 1934.

Park was instructor of German at Wheaton (Massachusetts) College (1930–32) and acting dean of freshmen (1934–35). In 1935 she began a long association with Connecticut College, first as a member of the faculty, soon also as dean of freshmen (1941–45), and finally as acting president (1946–47) and president (1947–62). With Mary Shelly (q.v.) she inaugurated the American Dance Festival and an associated summer school. Park also established a laboratory high school. From 1962 to 1967 she was president of Barnard College. She was vice chancellor for educational planning and programs (1967–70) and professor of education (1970–74) at the University of California at Los Angeles (UCLA). In retirement she founded the Plato Society of UCLA, a continuing study organization for senior citizens.

Elected a fellow of the American Academy of Arts and Sciences in 1956, Park was president of United Chapters of Phi Beta Kappa (1970–73) and served on the National Council on the Humanities as chair of its research committee. She was chair of the Association of American Colleges (later, and Universities, 1965–66) and a director of the American Council on Education, among many other service roles. She was author of *Das Bild Richard Wagners Tristan und Isolde in der deutschen Literatur* (1935) and coeditor of *Deutsche Erleben die Zeit, 1914–1945* (1949), a textbook. Park wrote a book review column for *Change* magazine. In 1978 Helen S. Astin and Werner Z. Hirsch edited *The Higher Education of Women: Essays in Honor of Rosemary Park.*

REFERENCES: CB (1964); LE (1974); NCAB (J: 378); NYT, September 18, 1961, p. 1, and March 20, 1967, p. 33; WW (1978–79); *Modern Maturity* (August–September 1991); Patricia Ann Sullivan, ''Rosemary Park: A Study of Educational Leadership during the Revolutionary Decades'' (Ph.D. diss., Boston College, 1982).

PARKER, Franklin. b. June 2, 1921, New York City. Married June 12, 1950, to Betty June Parker. Children: no.

Franklin Parker received the B.A. degree from Berea College in 1949 and the M.S. degree from the University of Illinois in 1950. He taught speech and was librarian at Ferrum College (1950–52) and librarian at Belmont College (1952–53). At George Peabody College for Teachers (later, part of Vanderbilt University), Parker was a circulation librarian (1955–56) and received the Ed.D. degree there (1956). He spent one year (1956–57) at the State Teachers College at New Paltz, New York (later, State University of New York College at New Paltz), then was associate professor of education at the University of Texas (1957–64). Parker was a professor of education at the University of Oklahoma (1964–68), Claude Worthington Benedum Professor of Education at West Virginia University (1966–86), and Distinguished Visiting Professor at Northern Arizona University (1986–89) and Western Carolina University (from 1989).

Parker was a Fulbright senior research scholar in Zambia (1961–62). He wrote extensively, particularly in the field of comparative education. Among his books were *African Development and Education in Southern Rhodesia* (1960) and *George Peabody: A Biography* (1971). He wrote a number of Phi Delta Kappa fastbacks, contributed to many volumes, and compiled many annotated bibliographies, some with his wife, Betty June Parker. Their joint publications included *Education in the People's Republic of China, Past and Present: An Annotated Bibliography* (1986) and *U.S. Higher Education: A Guide to Information Sources* (1980).

Parker was a fellow of the African Studies Association and Philosophy of Education Society. He was president (1963–64) of the History of Education Society and vice president (1963–64) and secretary (1965–68) of the Comparative and International Education Society.

REFERENCES: CA (NR-22); LE (1974); WD (1994–96); WW (1996).

PASSOW, Aaron Harry. b. December 9, 1920, Liberty, New York, to Morris and Ida (Wiener) Passow. Married July 2, 1944, to Shirley Siegel. Children: three. d. March 28, 1996, Englewood, New Jersey.

A. Harry Passow promoted quality education for all children while he specialized in education of the gifted. He was interested in the totality of experiences for students, pointing out that individuals are gifted always, not only during short periods of the day devoted to gifted education. He believed there are various kinds of giftedness, evident not only in a high intelligence quotient (IQ). Passow began the Talented Youth Project (TYP) while at the Horace Mann-Lincoln School of Experimentation of Teachers College, Columbia University. In 1958 he disputed as antidemocratic the proposal of Admiral Hyman G. Rickover that a small number of national high schools be established for youth with the greatest ability in science and mathematics.

Passow attended school in Liberty, New York, and studied at the New York State Teachers College in Albany (later, State University of New York at Albany) where he received B.A. (1942) and M.A. (1947) degrees. He was a teacher of mathematics and science at Stony Point (New York) High School (1942–43). From 1943 to 1946 he served in the U.S. Army Air Force. There followed two years in Eden, New York (1946–48), as a science teacher and counselor. He returned to the Albany Teachers College as mathematics teacher and supervisor of student teachers (1948–51). In 1951 Passow was awarded the Ph.D. degree by Teachers College of Columbia University. He spent one year as a curriculum associate with the Citizenship Education Project (CEP).

From 1952 to 1965 Passow was a research associate at the Horace Mann–Lincoln School, where the TYP was developed. He conducted research projects on education for the gifted and developed an interest in gifted disadvantaged students. He became a professor of education at Teachers College in 1952. From 1968 to 1977 he served as chair of the Department of Curriculum and Teaching and was head of the Committee on Urban Education (1965–77). In 1972 he became Jacob H. Schiff Professor of Education.

Passow was a Fulbright scholar in Sweden (1967–68) and visiting professor in Israel (1973 and 1981). He was director of an eighteen-month study of the Washington, D.C., school system, which resulted in publication of *Toward a Modern Urban School System* (1967). Passow was president of the World Council for Gifted and Talented Children. He wrote *Secondary Education for All: The English Approach* (1981), coauthored *Improving the Quality of Public School Programs* (with Harold J. McNally, 1960), and edited *Curricular Crossroads* (1962), *Developing Programs for the Disadvantaged* (1968), *Urban Education in the 1970s* (1971), *The Gifted and the Talented* (1979), and *Reforming the Schools in the 1980s* (1984).

REFERENCES: CA (NR-3); LE (1974); NYT, March 29, 1996, p. D19; RPE; WD (1994–96); WW (1996); Shari Stoddard and Trudy Wilson, ''Profiles and Prospectives,'' *Roeper Review* 13 (January 1991): 106.

PATRICK, Mary Mills. b. March 10, 1850, Canterbury, New Hampshire, to John and Harriet (White) Patrick. Married: no. d. February 25, 1940, Palo Alto, California.

For a half century Mary Mills Patrick worked to bring education to women in Turkey. As principal of the American College for Girls she opened higher education to women in the Middle East.

Patrick's family moved from New Hampshire to Lyons (later, Clinton), Iowa, in 1865. She graduated from the Lyons Collegiate Institute in 1869. In 1871 she went to Erzurum, Turkey, to teach at an American mission school where the students were primarily Armenian. During summer vacations she traveled widely and helped to open schools. Moving to Scutari, a suburb of Constantinople (Istanbul) in 1875, Patrick taught at the American High School for Girls, often called the Home School. It had been founded in 1871 by the Woman's Board of Missions of the American Board of Commissioners for Foreign Missions. Patrick lived in nearby Greek villages during vacations, adding proficiency in Greek to her Turkish.

In 1883 Patrick became coprincipal of the school. She studied in the United States during 1888–89 and on her return in 1889 became sole principal. The University of Iowa granted her the M.A. degree in 1890. The school received a charter in 1890 from the Commonwealth of Massachusetts as the American College for Girls, often referred to as Constantinople Woman's College. Patrick served as president from 1890 to 1924. She studied summers at various European universities and received the Ph.D. degree in 1897 from the University of Bern.

In 1905 a fire destroyed one of the two college buildings. The school purchased new property in 1908, and plans were made for a new campus. With a new charter in 1908 the school ended its affiliation with the mission board. Grace H. Dodge (BDAE) served as president of the trustees. Before 1908 the students were primarily Armenian, Greek, and Bulgarian Christians in western Turkey. After that date the government permitted Turkish students to enroll; a few had done so previously.

The move to new quarters on the European side of the Bosporus came in 1914. Patrick traveled to the United States to raise funds and meet with the trustees. When she retired in 1924, the school had 400 students of many nationalities. It affiliated later with Robert College for Men.

In 1914 Patrick received the Third Order of the Shefakat from Sultan Mehmed V of Turkey. She was the author of *Sextus Empiricus and Greek Scepticism* (1899), *Sappho and the Island of Lesbos* (1912), *The Greek Sceptics* (1929), *Under Five Sultans* (1929), and *Bosporous Adventure* (1934). She contributed the article on Anaxagoras to the *Encyclopedia of Religion and Ethics* (1910).

REFERENCES: AWM; CB (1940); DAB (supp. 2); LW; NAW; NYT, February 27, 1940, p. 21; Hester D. Jenkins, *An Educational Ambassador to the Near East* (Fleming H. Revell, 1925); Rossiter Johnson, ed., *The Twentieth Century Biographical Dictionary of Notable Americans* (Biographical Society, 1904, reprinted by Gale Research, 1968); John W. Leonard, ed., *Woman's Who's Who of America* (American Commonwealth, 1914); Ethel Nichols Thomas, ''Mary Mills Patrick and the American College for Girls at Istanbul in Turkey'' (Ed.D. diss., Rutgers, the State University of New Jersey–New Brunswick, 1979).

PATTERSON, Frederick Douglass. b. October 10, 1910, Washington, D.C., to William Ross and Mamie Lucille (Brooks) Patterson. Married June, 12, 1935, to Catherine Elizabeth Moton. Children: one. d. April 26, 1988, New Rochelle, New York.

As founder and president of the United Negro College Fund, Frederick D. Patterson was a leader in black higher education in the United States. The organization initiated cooperative fund-raising for historically black colleges and universities. In the 1970s he established the College Endowment Funding Plan.

Orphaned at the age of two, Patterson was raised by a sister in Texas. He attended Prairie View (Texas) College (later, Prairie View A & M University) from 1915 to 1919. At Iowa State University, he received the D.V.M. degree in 1923 and M.S. in 1927. In 1923 he became an instructor of veterinary science and chemistry at Virginia State College (later, University) in Petersburg, and in 1927 director of agriculture. He earned the Ph.D. degree from Cornell University in 1932.

Patterson went to Tuskegee (Alabama) Normal and Industrial Institute (later, University) in 1928 as head of the veterinary division. He was director of the School of Agriculture from 1933 to 1935, when he became third president of the institute. During his tenure as president (to 1953), the school gained national recognition.

Other institutions sought Patterson's advice on raising funds. In 1942 he proposed creating a consortium of black colleges to raise money for their needs. Founded in 1944 with twenty-seven colleges, the United Negro College Fund became a major source of money for private historically black colleges and universities in the United States. Its motto was, ''A mind is a terrible thing to waste.''

In 1953 Patterson left the Tuskegee presidency to become president of the Phelps-Stokes Fund, serving to 1970. The fund, founded in 1911, sought to improve conditions of African Americans and Africans and to improve the welfare of American Indians. Patterson later worked with the Robert R. Moton (BDAE) Memorial Institute.

In 1947 Patterson was a member of President Harry Truman's Commission on Higher Education, which supported federal aid to education and elimination of segregation. Patterson received the Presidential Medal of Freedom in 1987 and many other awards. He contributed a chapter to *What the Negro Wants*, edited by Rayford Logan (1944), and was an editor of *Robert Russa Moton of Hampton and Tuskegee* (with William H. Hughes, 1956).

REFERENCES: CB (1947, 1988); LE (1948); NYT, April 27, 1988, p. B8; WW (1954–

55); WWBA (1988); Martia Graham Goodson, ed., *Chronicles of Faith: The Autobiography of Frederick D. Patterson* (University of Alabama Press, 1991).

PEAKE, Mary Smith Kelsey. b. 1823, Norfolk, Virginia. Married 1851 to Thomas D. Peake. Children: one. d. February 22, 1862, Hampton, Virginia.

Mary S. Peake was one of the first teachers of slaves in the South. Her parents were a free black woman and an Englishman. At the age of six she began living with an aunt in Alexandria, Virginia, in order to attend school. Returning to Norfolk when her mother married, she worked as a seamstress. In 1847 the family moved to Hampton, Virginia, where the young woman founded the Daughters of Zion, a charitable organization. In 1851 she married Thomas Peake, a freeman.

Mary Peake began teaching slaves and freemen illegally. During the Civil War, when Hampton was burned in 1861, the Peakes moved across the James River. At Fortress Monroe, in September 1861, Peake resumed her teaching in Brown Cottage. When Lewis Lockwood of the American Missionary Society came to the area, he learned of Peake's school and brought it under the auspices of the society. By 1862 Peake was educating fifty children and twenty adults. Peake provided both academic and religious training, and founded a Sunday school for children. She died of tuberculosis at the age of thirty-nine.

Peake received the American Tract Society Medal of Praise. Peake Point, a housing project in Norfolk, was named for her.

REFERENCES: AAW; BWA; DANB; NBAW; Sing-Nan Fen, ''Mary S. Peake, 1823–62,'' *School and Society* 90 (April 6, 1963): 171–72; Lewis C. Lockwood, *Mary S. Peake, The Colored Teacher at Fortress Monroe* (American Tract Society, 1863; reprinted by Arno Press and New York Times, 1969).

PEI, Mario Andrew. b. February 16, 1901, Rome, Italy, to Francesco and Luisa (Ferri) Pei. Married June 25, 1924, to Pearl Glover. Children: no. d. March 2, 1978, Glen Ridge, New Jersey.

Concerned by the lack of communication in the world, Mario Pei believed that beginning in kindergarten, all children should be taught a common language in addition to their native one. It was to be selected by the nations of the world. Pei was a noted linguist who made the study of languages pleasurable and popular. His book *The Story of Language* (1949), influenced the study of linguistics. Pei was fluent in many languages, wrote extensively, and originated the branch of linguistics termed geolinguistics.

Pei's family moved to the United States when he was seven years old. In New York City he attended St. Francis Xavier High School on a scholarship and graduated in 1918. While attending evening classes at City College (later, of the City University of New York), he taught sixth grade at St. Francis Xavier Grammar School (1918–20). For one year he was a tutor in Havana, Cuba.

Pei reentered City College while he taught foreign languages at Fordham Preparatory School, Regis High School, and Franklin School. From 1923 to

1937 he taught at City College and its Townsend Harris High School. In 1925 he received the B.A. degree from City College and became a U.S. citizen. He received the Ph.D. degree from Columbia University in 1932. Pei taught Romance philology and comparative linguistics at Columbia from 1937 to 1970. He was a visiting lecturer at several universities, visiting professor of English and linguistics at Seton Hall University (1970–72), and North Atlantic Treaty Organization (NATO) lecturer in Portugal.

During World War II Pei was a consultant to the Office of War Information and Office of Strategic Services. He was a consultant and lecturer at the U.S. Army Language School in Monterey, California. He devised a thirty-seven-language course, War Linguistics, which led to the World's Chief Languages course.

Pei wrote and translated many books. Among them were *Languages for War and Peace* (1943, later titled *The World's Chief Languages*), *The Story of English* (1952), *All about Language* (1954), *Language for Everybody* (1957), *One Language for the World* (1958), *Talking Your Way around the World* (1961), *The Families of Words* (1962), *How to Learn Languages and What Languages to Learn* (1966), *The Many Hues of English* (1967), *Words in Sheep's Clothing* (1969), *Double-Speak in America* (1973), and *Weasel Words: The Art of Saying What You Don't Mean* (1978). He was associate editor of *Romanic Review*, *Modern Language Journal*, and *Symposium* and was on the editorial board of *Romance Philology*. He also wrote novels, including *Swords of Anjou* (1953).

Pei founded and was president (1964–66) of the American Society of Geolinguistics. Among awards he received were the Peace Treaty Contest Award from the Ziff-Davis Company (1945), George Washington Honor Medal from the Freedom Foundation (1957), the David Mckay Humanities Award from Brigham Young University (1970), and an award from the Italian Republic.

REFERENCES: CA (NR-5, 77–80); CB (1968, 1978); DAB (supp. 10); NCAB (60: 277); NYT, March 5, 1978, p. 36; WD (1976–78); WWW (7); Paul A. Gaeng, "In Memoriam: Mario A. Pei," *Italica* 55 (Summer 1978): 298–300; Theodore Huebener, "Mario A. Pei," in John Fisher and Paul A. Gaeng, eds., *Studies in Honor of Mario A. Pei* (University of North Carolina Press, 1972); Warren F. Kuehl, ed., *Biographical Dictionary of Internationalists* (Greenwood Press, 1983).

PERLMAN, Selig. b. December 9, 1888, Bialystok, Poland, to Mordecai and Paulina (Blankstein) Perlman. Married June 23, 1918, to Eva Shaber; August 22, 1930, to Fannie Shaber. Children: four. d. August 14, 1959, Philadelphia.

Selig Perlman was a pioneer in the study of labor economics and a leading student of the labor movement. He had a longtime association with John R. Commons (q.v.) and always referred to his theory of the labor movement as the Commons-Perlman theory. He guided the development of the University of Wisconsin School for Workers.

Perlman attended a Jewish day school in Bialystok, Poland, and then a local school of commerce on a scholarship. In 1906 he began the study of medicine at the University of Naples, Italy. Coming to the United States in 1908, he enrolled as a junior at the University of Wisconsin, where he studied economics under Commons and Richard Ely (BDAE). Perlman received the A.B. degree in 1910. He was a special investigator for the U.S. Commission on Industrial Relations (1913–15), where he worked under Charles McCarthy (q.v.).

Perlman received the Ph.D. degree from the University of Wisconsin in 1915 and was a research assistant to Commons. In 1919 he was appointed to the faculty, becoming professor in 1927. Later, he was named the John R. Commons Research Professor. He was principal author of Commons' *History of Labor in the United States* (1918). The acclaimed *A Theory of the Labor Movement* (1928) established him as a leading labor scholar. He also wrote *A History of Trade Unionism in the United States* (1922), *Labor Movements, 1896–1932* (with Philip Taft, 1935), and *Postwar Problems* (1945) and contributed to *Organized Labour in Four Continents* (H. A. Marquand, editor, 1939).

In 1947 he was a founder and a member of the Wisconsin Commission on Human Rights. After his retirement in June 1959, Perlman accepted an endowed chair at the Wharton School at the University of Pennsylvania, but he died in August of the same year.

REFERENCES: BDAL; DAB (supp. 6); IESS; NYT, August 15, 1959, p. 19; WWE; WWW (3); "A Memoir of Selig Perlman and His Life at the University of Wisconsin: Based on an Interview of Mark Perlman Conducted and Edited by Leon Fink," *Labor History* 32 (Fall 1991): 503–25; Leon Fink, " 'Intellectuals' versus 'Workers': Academic Requirements and the Creation of Labor History," *American Historical Review* 96 (April 1991): 395–421; Philip Taft, "Reflections on Selig Perlman as a Teacher and Writer," *Industrial and Labor Relations Review* 29 (January 1976): 249–57; Edwin E. Witte, "Selig Perlman," *Industrial and Labor Relations Review* 13 (April 1960): 335–37.

PETERSON, Martha Elizabeth. b. June 2, 1916, Jamestown, Kansas, to Anton R. and Gail (French) Peterson. Married: no.

Martha Peterson was a leader in higher education, a strong advocate for the liberal arts, and a champion of students. She advocated free expression for students, alongside reasonable limits put on student freedom.

Raised in Kansas, Peterson received B.A. (1937), M.A. (1943), and Ph.D. (1959) degrees from the University of Kansas. From 1937 to 1942 she was a teacher of Latin, German, and physical education at high schools in Kansas and from 1942 to 1946, an instructor in mathematics at the University of Kansas. Her administrative career began when she was named assistant dean of women at the University of Kansas in 1946. She was dean of women from 1952 to 1956.

At the University of Wisconsin–Madison Peterson served first as dean of women (1957–63), then as assistant to President Fred Harrington and university system dean for student affairs (1963–67). She formed student–faculty committees and advocated a stronger voice for students in campus affairs. In 1967 Peterson was named president of Barnard College, succeeding Rosemary Park (q.v.). During a time of student unrest, Peterson maintained communication and good relationships with students. Beloit College named her its president in 1975. She retired in 1981.

Peterson served as president of the National Association of Women Deans and Counselors (1965–67), chair of the executive committee of the American Council on Education, trustee of the College Entrance Examination Board, director of the American Arbitration Association, and member of the National Board on Graduate Education.

REFERENCES: CB (1969); LE (1974); NYT, May 19, 1967, p. 41, and June 25, 1975, p. 49; WW (1982–83); WWAW (1983–84).

PHINAZEE, (Alethia) Annette Lewis Hoage. b. July 25, 1920, Orangeburg, South Carolina, to William Charles and Alethia Minnie (Lightner) Lewis. Married April 29, 1944, to George Lafayette Hoage; July 14, 1962, to Joseph Phinazee. Children: one. d. September 17, 1983, Durham, North Carolina.

Annette L. Phinazee was instrumental in the training of many African-American librarians. She strove to improve library service in historically black colleges. As dean of the library school at North Carolina Central University, she worked to develop the curriculum and secured accreditation for the school.

Phinazee attended schools in Orangeburg, South Carolina. She was a student at South Carolina State College and received the B.A. degree from Fisk University in 1939 with a major in modern foreign languages. During 1939–40 she was a teacher/librarian at the Caswell County Training School in Yanceyville, North Carolina. In 1941 she was awarded the bachelor of science in library science degree from the University of Illinois. After one year as a cataloger in the Talladega (Alabama) College library, Phinazee was a journalism librarian at Lincoln University in Missouri (1942–44). She was employed by the Los Angeles County Library during 1944–45. Widowed in 1945, she returned to Orangeburg.

From 1946 to 1957 she was an assistant professor in the School of Library Service at Atlanta (later, Clark–Atlanta) University. In 1948 she earned the master of science in library science degree from the University of Illinois. While cataloger at Southern Illinois University (1957–62), in 1961 Phinazee was the first African-American woman to receive a doctorate in library science from Columbia University.

Phinazee returned to Atlanta University in 1962 and until 1967 headed special services at the Trevor Arnett Library, which included administering the Negro Collection. She also served as professor in the School of Library Service from 1963 to 1969. In 1965 Phinazee moderated and edited the proceedings of the Institute on Materials by and about Negroes, held in Atlanta. For one year she was associate director of the Cooperative College Library Center in Atlanta (1969–70).

In 1970 Phinazee became dean of the School of Library Science (later, Library and Information Sciences) at North Carolina Central University. She served there until her death in 1983. A program there in Early Childhood Library Specialists, established in 1970, was unique in the nation. In 1979 Phinazee headed the North Carolina delegation to the White House Conference on Library and Information Services. On the board of the Southeastern Black Press Institute, she arranged its transfer from the University of North Carolina to North Carolina Central University.

Phinazee was chair of the Classification Commission (1962–67) and first chair of the Standing Committee on Library Education of the American Library Association. In 1978 she was chair of the Council of Deans and Directors of the Association of American Library Schools (later, Association for Library and Information Science Education). She was the first African-American president of the North Carolina Library Association (1975–77) and served on the North Carolina Librarian Certification Commission.

Phinazee edited *The Black Librarian in the Southeast* (1980). She was a consultant to the Ford Foundation on improving library service in black colleges. She served on the Board of Christian Education of the United Presbyterian Church in the U.S.A. (1968–72).

REFERENCES: BWA; NBAW; WW (1984–85); WWBA (1981–82); *The ALA Yearbook of Library and Information Services* 9 (American Library Association, 1984): 27; *American Libraries* 14 (November 1983): 636; *School Library Journal* 30 (December 1983): 12; Benjamin F. Speller, Jr., ed., *Educating Black Librarians* (McFarland, 1991).

PINTNER, Rudolf. b. November 16, 1884, Lytham, Lancashire, England, to William and Irma Pintner. Married August 15, 1916, to Margaret M. Anderson. Children: two. d. November 7, 1942, Yonkers, New York.

A noted psychologist, Rudolf Pintner pioneered in the field of differential psychology and was a major contributor to the field of measurement. Interested in improving education for handicapped children, he developed intelligence tests for handicapped, deaf, and foreign-born individuals.

Pintner received the A.M. degree from Edinburgh University (1906) and the Ph.D. from the University of Leipzig (1913). He came to the United States in 1912 and was professor of psychology at the University of Toledo (1912–13). At Ohio State University (1913–21), he rose from instructor to professor. From 1921 to 1942, at Teachers College of Columbia University, he was professor of education and associate director of the Advanced School of Education.

Pintner studied individual differences. He conducted many surveys, including one on personalities of hard-of-hearing children. In 1917 he published *A Scale of Performance Tests* with Donald G. Paterson (BDAE). It served as a model for others, including the Army Beta tests. Pintner developed both verbal and nonverbal tests, among them the Pintner-Cunningham Primary Mental Test, Pintner–Durost Elementary Test, and Pintner Adjustment Inventory for the Deaf. He was an early developer of group tests and taught a training course in group and individual testing.

Pintner wrote extensively for educational journals, especially the *Journal of*

Applied Psychology, *Journal of Educational Psychology*, *Journal of Genetic Psychology*, and *American Annals of the Deaf*. He translated psychology works from German. Among his books were *The Mental Survey* (1918), *Intelligence Testing: Methods and Results* (1923), *Mental Tests and Measurements* (1925), *A Survey of American Schools for the Deaf, 1924–1925* (with others, 1928), *Educational Psychology* (1929), and *The Psychology of the Physically Handicapped* (with others, 1941). He was on the editorial board of *Psychology Bulletin*.

REFERENCES: BDP; ECP; NYT, November 8, 1942, p. 51; PR; WWW (2); *American Journal of Psychology* 56 (April 1943): 303–5; Seth Arsenian, ed., *Rudolf Pintner: In Memoriam* (Gallaudet College Press, 1951); *Journal of Counseling Psychology* 7 (January–February 1943): 50–52; *Teachers College Record* 44 (December 1942): 204–11.

PITKIN, Royce Stanley. b. June 7, 1901, Marshfield, Vermont, to Ozias Cornwall and Olive Jane (Severance) Pitkin. Married 1924 to Helen Kathleen McKelvey. Children: three. d. May 3, 1986, Burlington, Vermont.

Royce S. "Tim" Pitkin was founding president of Goddard College in Plainfield, Vermont. From that position he was a leading voice for progressive collegiate education.

Pitkin was the seventh child of a farmer and rural engineer who made a meager living. As a boy he attended local public schools until the age of fifteen. Following two years at Goddard Seminary, a private high school in nearby Barre, Vermont, he studied briefly at Cornell University. He continued his studies in agriculture at the University of Vermont, from which he graduated in 1923.

After several summers of study, Pitkin earned the M.A. degree at Teachers College of Columbia University in 1928. He taught science in Plymouth, New Hampshire (1923–24); was high school principal in Hyde Park, Vermont (1924–26), and Groveton, New Hampshire (1926–27); and was superintending principal in Wallingford, Vermont (1927–31). Enrolling full-time at Teachers College, he earned the Ph.D. degree in educational administration in 1933. He was high school headmaster and elementary school principal in New London, New Hampshire, from 1932 to 1935.

In 1935 he was asked to return to Goddard, which had become a junior college for women. Under Pitkin's leadership the institution was moved to Plainfield, Vermont, in 1938; admitted men again; and in 1944 became a four-year baccalaureate college. Calling it a "school for living," and an "experimental college," Pitkin emphasized community connections, instituted a work-study program, and offered short courses for adults based loosely on the Danish folk school model. From 1963 there was also an Adult Degree Program. During Pitkin's long presidency (1938–69), Goddard College was financially poor and academically progressive, a combination that made its accreditation, achieved in 1959, always uncertain.

Pitkin was a founder of the Union for Experimenting Colleges and Universities and president of the Vermont and Quebec Unitarian-Universalist Convention. He was author of a children's book, *Maple Sugar Time*, as well as articles on education.

REFERENCES: NYT, May 6, 1986, p. B8; Ann Giles Benson and Frank Adams, *To Know for Real: Royce S. Pitkin and Goddard College* (Adamant Press, 1987); Vermont Historical Society, Royce Stanley "Tim" Pitkin Papers (Document 351); *Who's Who in the East* (1968–69).

PITTS, Lucius Holsey. b. 1915, in James, Georgia. Married to Dafferneeze Pitts. Children: four. d. February 26, 1974, Augusta, Georgia.

Lucius Pitts distinguished himself by his heroic efforts to improve two historically black institutions, Miles College in Birmingham, Alabama, and Paine College in Augusta, Georgia.

Pitts was born a child of poor tenant farmers in rural Georgia and was the first person in his family to attend high school. He earned the B.A. degree at Paine College in 1941. His baccalaureate study had been interrupted by an injury that cost him the sight in one eye. He was principal of Milan (Georgia) Public School (1936–39). After serving as assistant to the dean of the chapel at Fisk University and earning the M.A. degree there (1945), Pitts returned to Augusta, where he taught at Paine College until 1948 and engaged in youth work. He was principal of Holsey–Cobb Institute in Cordele, Georgia, for the next seven years.

Moving to Atlanta, Pitts was executive secretary of the Georgia Teachers and Education Association (1955–61), whose members were African-American teachers in the state. In those years he was also vice president of the Georgia chapter of the National Association for the Advancement of Colored People (NAACP) and president of the Georgia Council on Human Relations.

Pitts went to Miles College as president in 1961, three years after it had lost its accreditation. The college applied three times for reinstatement, succeeding in 1969. Pitts oversaw construction of nine new buildings, dramatic expansion of library holdings, and increased enrollment. He also recruited John U. Monro (q.v.) from Harvard University to be director of freshman studies.

In 1971 Pitts moved to his alma mater, Paine College, as its first African-American president. He died there two and a half years later.

REFERENCES: LE (1971); NYT, December 24, 1970, p. 41, February 27, 1974, p. 42, and March 2, 1974, p. 30; WWBA (1975–76); John Egerton, *A Mind to Stay Here*, (Macmillan, 1970), pp. 107–27.

PLAYER, Willa Beatrice. b. August 9, 1909, Jackson, Mississippi, to Clarence E. and Beatrice (Day) Player. Married: no.

In October 1955, Willa Player became the nation's first black woman to lead a four-year women's college when she accepted the presidency of Bennett College in Greensboro, North Carolina. She believed strongly in liberal arts education and was known as a staunch advocate for women.

Player attended school in Akron, Ohio. She received the B.A. degree from Ohio Wesleyan University (1929) and M.A. from Oberlin (Ohio) College (1930). She studied further at the Universities of Chicago and Wisconsin and the University of Grenoble, France, from which she received the Certificat d'Etudes (1935). She had General Education Board Fellowships (1945 and 1947) and a Frank Ross Chambers Fellowship at Columbia University, earning the Ed.D. degree there (1948).

Player began her career as a Latin and French instructor at Bennett College in 1929 and served the college as director of admissions, coordinator of instruction, and vice president. When president, she supported Bennett students in their protests of racial segregation at Greensboro's lunch counters during the civil rights movement. In 1966 she left the presidency to be director of the Division of Institutional Development in the Bureau of Postsecondary Education, U.S. Office of Education, in Washington, D.C. The division had been established by the Higher Education Act of 1965. Player divided the program into Advanced and Basic Institutional Development programs. After her retirement in 1977 she served as a consultant in higher education.

Player was president of the National Association of Schools and Colleges of the Methodist Church (1962–63) and a member of the Commission on Funding Black Colleges (1976–84). The U.S. Department of Health, Education and Welfare gave her the Superior Service Award (1970) and Distinguished Service Award (1972). She was inducted into the Ohio Women's Hall of Fame (1984). Bennett College endowed a chair in her honor (1988).

REFERENCES: BWA; EBA; LE (1974); NBAW; WW (1976–77); WWAW (1972–73); WWBA (1994/95).

POUSSAINT, Alvin Francis. b. May 15, 1934, New York City, to Christopher Thomas V. and Harriet (Johnston) Poussaint. Married November 4, 1973, to Ann Ashmore; 1993 to Tina Young. Children: one.

Alvin F. Poussaint developed the theory of ''aggression-rage'' in African Americans. He was a vigorous opponent of arguments that there were inherent racial differences, based on psychiatry, neuromedicine, or intelligence research that disadvantaged African Americans in education and social relations.

Poussaint graduated from Peter Stuyvesant High School in New York City. He received the B.S. degree from Columbia University in 1956 and the M.D. degree from Cornell University in 1960. At the University of California at Los Angeles (UCLA) he interned with the Center for the Health Sciences (1960–61) and was a psychiatric resident at the Neuropsychiatric Institute (1961–64) and chief resident (1964–65). He received the M.S. degree in 1964 in psychopharmacology. In 1965 he served with the Student Nonviolent Coordinating Committee (SNCC) as medical field director in the South.

Poussaint taught at the medical school of Tufts University from 1966 to 1969. At Harvard Medical School he was clinical professor of psychiatry, associate dean (1969–75), and dean (1975–78) of student affairs.

In 1969 Poussaint was a charter member of the Black Academy of Arts and Letters and served as its treasurer. He was national treasurer of the Medical Committee for Human Rights, on the board of Operation PUSH (1971–85), and a consultant to the U.S. Department of Health, Education, and Welfare (1969–73). In 1987 he helped to found the Camille Cosby Center, part of Judge Baker Children's Center in Boston. He served as a script consultant for *The Cosby Show* and wrote the introduction and afterword to Bill Cosby's book *Fatherhood*.

Poussaint was a contributor to many books and wrote *Why Blacks Kill Blacks* (1972). With James P. Comer (q.v.) he authored *Black Child Care* (1975) and *Raising Black Children* (1992). He received many awards, including the Michael Schwerner Award in 1968 for contributions to civil rights.

REFERENCES: CA (53–56); CB (1973); EBA; WW (1996); WWBA (1994/95); George Metcalf, *Up from Within: Today's New Black Leaders* (McGraw-Hill, 1971); Emily Rovetch, ed., *Like It Is: Arthur E. Thomas Interviews Leaders on Black America* (E. P. Dutton, 1981).

PRESCOTT, Daniel Alfred. b. March 18, 1898, Manassas, Virginia, to Daniel Howard and Eva Mary (Foote) Prescott. Married June 25, 1920, to Eleanor Richardson; November 26, 1934, to Ruth Sharrett; January 3, 1950, to Annalise Boehmer Wagner. Children: no. d. May 7, 1970, Munich, Germany.

In the development of child study programs, Daniel Prescott played an instrumental role, particularly at the Institute for Child Study, which he founded at the University of Maryland in 1947. The institute became a national center for in-service training of teachers.

Prescott grew up in Manassas, Virginia. During World War I he served with the American Field Service in France. He attended Tufts College (later, University), where he received the B.S. degree in 1920. He taught science for one year at La Grange College in Georgia. His Ed.M. (1922) and Ed. D. (1923) degrees were earned at the Harvard Graduate School of Education, where he taught from 1923 to 1927. During his last year at Harvard Prescott went to Europe as a research fellow. He remained during 1927–28 at the Rousseau Institute in Geneva, Switzerland, where he worked with Jean Piaget. In 1927 he participated in the International Congress on Peace through Education in Prague, Czechoslovakia.

Returning to the United States, Prescott was professor of education at Rutgers University from 1928 to 1931. He spent the next year with the General Education Board of New York City as a research investigator, returned to Rutgers in 1932, and remained until 1939. As chair of an American Council on Education committee (1934–38) Prescott edited *Emotion and the Educative Process* (1938). He served the Commission on Teacher Education as chairman of its Division on Child Development and Teacher Education (1938–44).

At the University of Chicago as professor of education from 1939 to 1944, Prescott directed the Collaboration Center in Human Development, aided by the

General Education Board. *Helping Teachers Understand Children* (1945) was published by the center and used for in-service training of teachers.

Prescott went to the University of Maryland in 1947 to establish the Institute for Child Study, which he directed until 1960. *The Child in the Educative Process* (1957) was regarded as a classic text for teachers. He was professor of education at the university until 1968.

Prescott served as a consultant to many child-study programs in the United States and abroad. The State Department employed him as a specialist. With his wife, Annalise Boehmer Prescott, he conducted a child-study program in Omaha, Nebraska (1964–69), and helped to design an experimental school. His other books included *Education and International Relations* (1930), *Factors That Influence Learning* (1958), *The Elementary School Child* (1961), *High School Youth* (1962), *The Impact of Child Study on Education* (1962), and *The Emergent Middle School* (with others, 1968).

REFERENCES: NCAB (56: 259); WWW (5); *Education* 80 (April 1960): 507; *Psychological Reports* 59 (December 1986): 1321–22.

PRESTON, Ann. b. December 1, 1813, Westgrove, Pennsylvania, to Amos and Margaret (Smith) Preston. Married: no. d. April 18, 1872, Philadelphia.

Ann Preston was a pioneer in providing medical education for women and a noted advocate for women's participation in hospital clinics. Her 1867 reply to opponents of women in medicine became well known and helped to alleviate prejudice against female physicians.

Preston was raised in a Quaker family and because of her mother's poor health helped to raise her six brothers. The family was active in abolitionist and temperance movements. In 1849 she wrote *Cousin Ann's Stories for Children*, a book of juvenile poems. Concerned about women's physiology and health but refused entrance by other medical colleges, she entered the first class of the Female (later, Woman's) Medical College of Philadelphia in 1850. She graduated in 1851 at the age of thirty-eight. Her thesis was titled "General Diagnosis."

In 1853, when she taught physiology and hygiene at the college, she was the first woman to have a chair at a medical school. Because clinical training was not available for women, Preston led the organization of a Board of Lady Managers to found a hospital for women. In 1861 they obtained a charter and rented a house for the hospital. The college closed but reopened in 1862, with classes held on the first floor of the hospital.

In 1866 Preston became the first woman to serve as a medical school dean; she continued teaching physiology. She became a member of the Board of Incorporators of the hospital in 1867. A demonstration against women in medicine by male medical students in 1867 resulted in her noted reply in Philadelphia newspapers. She arranged for women students to obtain clinical training at other facilities in 1868 and 1869. Preston suffered from rheumatism and died in 1872.

By then 138 women had received medical degrees from the Woman's Medical Hospital.

REFERENCES: DAB; HAWH; LW; NAW; NCAB (10: 467); NYT, April 19, 1872, p. 1; WR; WW (H); Gulielma Fell Alsop, *History of the Woman's Medical College, 1850–1950* (Lippincott, 1950); Pauline Poole Foster, "Ann Preston, M.D. (1813–1872): A Biography" (Ph.D. diss., University of Pennsylvania, 1984); Rossiter Johnson, ed., *The Twentieth Century Biographical Dictionary of Notable Americans* (Biographical Society, 1904; reprinted by Gale Research, 1968); Martin Kaufman, Stuart Galishoff, and Todd L. Savitt, eds., *Dictionary of American Medical Biography* (Greenwood Press, 1983); Frances E. Willard (BDAE) and Mary A. Livermore, eds., *A Woman of the Century* (C. W. Moulton, 1893; reprinted by Gale Research, 1967).

PUSEY, Nathan Marsh. b. April 4, 1907, Council Bluffs, Iowa, to John Marsh and Rosa (Drake) Pusey. Married June 10, 1936, to Anne Woodward. Children: three.

Nathan Pusey was known particularly for his commitment to general education and the importance of the humanities in baccalaureate study. An early reputation for brilliance as a classroom teacher and scholar led him quickly into the role of college and university president, although he would recall later that he had really wanted a career in publishing.

Pusey attended public high school in Council Bluffs, Iowa, then enrolled at Harvard College as a scholarship student, earning the A.B. degree in 1928, with a major in English and comparative literature. Three years later he returned to Harvard, taking the A.M. degree in ancient history in 1932. He was awarded the Ph.D. in 1937, writing his dissertation in classical Greek, a language he had taken up only six years earlier.

Between his periods of study, Pusey traveled and studied in Europe (1928–29) and taught at the Riverdale (New York) Country School (1929–31). He went to Lawrence College (later, University) in 1935, staying for three years as sophomore tutor in a new experimental general education program. He taught history and literature at Scripps College (1938–40) and founded a general liberal arts program at Wesleyan University (1940–44) before being called back to Lawrence as president (1944–53). There he led the development of a "freshman studies" program that endured for many decades with few changes.

From 1953 to 1971, Pusey was president of Harvard University. A traditionalist in matters of learning and faith, he paid particular attention to strengthening Harvard's undergraduate program. He also served as president of the Andrew W. Mellon Foundation (1971–75) and the United Board for Christian Higher Education in Asia (1979–83).

Pusey was author of *The Age of the Scholar: Observations on Education in a Troubled Decade* (1963), *American Higher Education 1945–1970: A Personal Report* (1978), and *Lawrence Lowell* (BDAE) *and His Revolution* (1980). He was a member of the American Academy of Arts and Sciences.

REFERENCES: CA (109); CB (1953); LE (1974); NCAB (I: 292); WW (1978–79).

R

RAFFERTY, Maxwell Lewis, Jr. b. May 7, 1917, New Orleans, Louisiana, to Maxwell Lewis and De Etta (Cox) Rafferty. Married June 4, 1944, to Frances Luella Longman. Children: three. d. June 13, 1982, Troy, Alabama.

During eight years as California state superintendent of public instruction, Max Rafferty became nationally known for his very conservative positions on educational and social issues and his dramatic manner of stating them. He opposed school busing, fair housing legislation, strikes by teachers, sex education, the theory of evolution, and the influence of John Dewey on schooling, while he supported censorship of school library collections, education in patriotism, and homework. He cited moral grounds when he revoked the credentials of some 1,000 teachers.

Rafferty received B.A. (1938) and M.A. (1949) degrees at the University of California at Los Angeles and the Ed.D. (1955) degree at the University of Southern California. Before his election to the state superintendency, he served as a teacher in Trona (1940–48); principal in Big Bear Lake (1948–51); and superintendent in Saticoy (1951–55), Needles (1955–61), and La Canada (1961–62) school districts, all in California.

At La Canada Rafferty delivered a speech on "The Passing of the Patriot," reprinted in *Reader's Digest*, which made him a state and national figure. Rafferty won elections as state superintendent in 1962 and 1966. His accomplishments in office were largely exhortatory, since the state board of education and local school administrators often had more direct authority than he did. In 1968 Rafferty won the Republican nomination to be U.S. Senator from California, but he lost the general election narrowly. In 1970 he lost to Wilson Riles in his bid for a third term as superintendent. The next year Rafferty became dean of education at Troy State University in Alabama, where he remained until his death by accidental drowning in 1982.

Rafferty wrote *About Our Schools* (1955), *Practices and Trends in School Administration* (1960), *Home Discipline* (1961), *Suffer, Little Children* (1962), *What They Are Doing to Your Children* (1964), *Max Rafferty on Education* (1968), *Classroom Countdown* (1971), and *Handbook of Educational Administration* (1971). He received the Shankland Memorial Award of the American Association of School Administrators in 1955 and George Washington Gold Medal Awards of the Freedom Foundation in 1962, 1963, and 1965.

REFERENCES: CA (NR-1, 107); CB (1969, 1982); LE (1974); NYT, June 14, 1982, p. D11; NYT *Magazine*, September 1, 1968, pp. 6–7; WWW (8).

RANDOLPH, Virginia Estelle. b. June 8, 1874, Richmond, Virginia, to Edward Nelson and Sarah Elizabeth (Carter) Randolph. Married: no. d. March 16, 1958, Richmond, Virginia.

In 1908 Virginia E. Randolph became the first Jeanes supervisor in the United States in Henrico County, Virginia. Randolph stressed the overall development of children. The methods she developed served as a model for others. She assisted small rural schools for blacks in the South with money she received from the Jeanes foundation. Anna T. Jeanes had established the foundation in 1907 with a $1 million endowment. It became known as the Negro Rural School Fund.

Randolph graduated from Richmond Normal School (later, Armstrong High School). She taught in Goochland County, Virginia, and in the 1890s began teaching at the Mountain Road School in Henrico County. Finding the school in poor shape, she improved the grounds and had trees planted. While teaching regular subjects, she added classes in manual arts, taught cleanliness, and had students prepare hot lunches. She visited students' homes, organized a Patrons Improvement League, and generally helped to improve the community.

Jackson Davis (q.v.), superintendent of schools in Henrico County, visited Randolph's school and was impressed by her methods. He requested that she serve as supervisor of the Negro schools in the county. On October 26, 1908, she accepted. With funds from the Jeanes Foundation, she began industrial arts programs in the schools. The first Arbor Day program in Virginia was conducted by Randolph. In 1912 she explained her methods in a speech to southern superintendents meeting at Hampton. Within a few years there were many Jeanes agents. Eventually, they functioned like general supervisors for county Negro schools. Jeanes methods were spread to Liberia, British Commonwealth countries, and elsewhere. In 1936 the National Association of Jeanes Supervisors was organized.

In 1926 Randolph was the first African American to receive the William E. Harmon Award in education. She was named honorary president of the Association of American Jeanes Teachers for Liberia, which was organized in 1927. The Virginia Randolph Fund was established in 1936, with money raised by Jeanes teachers of the South. In 1938 it became part of the Southern Education Foundation, Inc. Randolph retired in 1948. A new school erected on the site of the Mountain Road School was named the Virginia Randolph County Training School. In 1970 the old school became a museum named in her honor, and in 1976 it was made a National Historic Landmark.

REFERENCES: BWA; NBAW; NYT, March 18, 1958, p. 29; WR; Walter Russell Bowie, *Women of Light* (Harper & Row, 1963); *The Jeanes Story: A Chapter in the History of American Education, 1908–1968* (Jackson State University Press, 1979); Frank Lincoln Mather, ed., *Who's Who of the Colored Race* (1915, reprinted by Gale Research, 1976).

RAUP, Robert Bruce. b. March 21, 1888, Clark County, Ohio, to Gustavus Philip and Fanny (Mitchell) Raup. Married August 23, 1924, to Clara Eliot. Children: four. d. April 13, 1976, Palo Alto, California.

As a critic of American public schools in the 1930s, R. Bruce Raup's views received a wide audience. At Teachers College, Columbia University, he helped to formulate the foundations courses curriculum.

Raup attended public schools in Lagonda and Springfield, Ohio. He earned the A.B. degree from Wittenberg College (later, University) in 1909. After receiving the B.D. degree from McCormick Theological Seminary (1914), he served as a minister of the American Presbyterian Church in Havana, Cuba (1914–15). From 1916 to 1918 Raup was instructor of ethics and college pastor at Bellevue (Nebraska) College. During World War I he was a military chaplain. He taught psychology and education at Blackburn College (1919–21) and then did graduate study at Teachers College, where he was a student of John Dewey (BDAE). Raup earned the Ph.D. degree from Teachers College in 1926 and remained there until his retirement in 1953 as professor emeritus of the philosophy of education. Among the courses he taught was Character and Moral Judgment in Education.

Raup was active in the Progressive Education Association. He was president (1941) of the Philosophy of Education Society and on the committee on education of the Federal Council of Churches in America. A prolific author, among his books were *Complacency: The Foundation of Human Behavior* (1925), *Toward a New Education* (1930), and *Education and Organized Interests in America* (1936). He wrote *Discipline of Practical Judgment* (1943) and *The Improvement of Practical Intelligence* (1950) with George E. Axtelle (BDAE), Kenneth D. Benne (BDAE), and B. Othanel Smith (BDAE). He contributed to *The Educational Frontier* (1950), edited by William H. Kilpatrick (BDAE). For his contribution to educational theory he received the Nicholas Murray Butler (BDAE) Medal in Silver from Columbia University.

REFERENCES: CA (65–68); NCAB (59: 426); NYT, April 15, 1976, p. 36; WWW (7).

RAY, Henry William. b. June 16, 1909, Caldwell, Ohio, to David L. and Anna K. (Spies) Ray. Married August 1945 to Esther Smith. Children: one.

Henry Ray believed in the interrelatedness of environment and learning. He emphasized the importance of a proper learning environment and criticized schools as containment centers for memorization of facts and figures. Ray wanted to develop children's perceptual abilities and help them learn to learn. He worked particularly in the fields of gifted and handicapped education.

Ray spent one year in study at the Canfield (Ohio) Normal School and was certified to teach. He earned another certificate after two years at Kent State Normal School (later, University). He was an elementary school teacher in Lake Milton, Ohio (1929–31), and teacher (1931–36) and principal (1936–45) in Sebring, Ohio. After earning the B.S. degree in elementary education from Kent State University in 1945, Ray was an elementary principal in Oak Ridge, Tennessee (1945–46), and coordinator of instruction in Alliance, Ohio (1946–57). He received M.A. (1951) and Ph.D. (1955) degrees from Teachers College, Columbia University.

From 1955 to 1963 Ray was assistant superintendent of Bucks County Schools in Doylestown, Pennsylvania. While on leave he was an instructional materials specialist with a U.S. Agency for International Development team in Afghanistan (1958–59). In 1963 he became director of teaching and learning resources in Warminster, Pennsylvania. At an age when most people would be retired, he continued there as coordinator of special projects (1979–94). He also lectured at Lehigh University, beginning in 1965.

At the Centennial School District in Warminster Ray created the Special Experience Room, an audiovisual facility used according to the needs of children. Having seen little change in classroom design over many years, Ray used the Special Experience Room to encourage children to make their own discoveries about their environment.

Ray conducted workshops and demonstrations on educating handicapped children. He was a consultant to the Bureau of Education of Handicapped in the U.S. Office of Education. The Pennsylvania State Department of Education awarded him a citation for his outstanding work in establishing a facility to aid children in making personal investigations. He wrote articles in *Audiovisual Instruction*, *Focus on Exceptional Children*, and *American Annals of the Deaf*, among other journals.

REFERENCES: LE (1974); Rebecca F. Dailey, ''Media in the Round: Learning in the Special Experience Room,'' *Teaching Exceptional Children* 4 (Fall 1971): 4–9; ''Learning in the Round: a Multi-Media Experiment,'' *Smithsonian* 1 (April 1970): 54–57.

READ, Sister Joel. b. December 30, 1925, Chicago. Married: no.

As president of Alverno College for more than a quarter century, Sister Joel Read led the development of an outcomes-based curriculum that attracted national attention and was often praised but seldom emulated. Begun in 1973, the curriculum required students at the women's college to demonstrate mastery of eight ability areas. Because of its outcomes orientation, students received no course grades.

Sister Joel Read was a member of the Order of St. Francis. She earned the B.S. degree in education at Alverno in 1948 and the M.A. in history at Fordham University in 1951. After teaching history and chairing the department at Alverno, she became president of the college in 1968.

Her national professional service included president of the American Association for Higher Education (1976–77), chair of the Commission on the Status of Education for Women of the Association of American Colleges (later, and Universities, 1971–77), and member of the National Council on the Humanities (1977–83) and of the Board of Directors of the Educational Testing Service (1987–93). She was the first recipient of the Anne Roe Award presented by the Harvard Graduate School of Education (1980).

REFERENCES: CHE, February 1, 1989, pp. A10–13; LE (1974); WW (1996); WWAW (1995–96); Joy K. Rice, "Reflections on the Mission and Future of the Catholic Women's College: Sister Joel Read Interviewed," *Initiatives* 53 (Fall 1991): 41–51.

REDDING, (Jay) Saunders. b. October 13, 1906, Wilmington, Delaware, to Lewis Alfred and Mary Ann (Holmes) Redding. Married July 19, 1929, to Esther Elizabeth James. Children: two. d. March 2, 1988, Ithaca, New York.

Until the appointment of Saunders Redding to the faculty of Brown University as visiting professor during 1949–50, no African American had taught on the faculty of an Ivy League university. Redding spent most of his career at historically black institutions, but in the five years before he retired he held an endowed professorship at Cornell University.

Redding was exceptional for the range of his writings in the broad area of black studies and for his mobility between historically black colleges and predominantly white institutions. In a novel, *Stranger and Alone* (1950), he addressed in frank terms the shortcomings of historically black colleges. Previously, Redding had written *No Day of Triumph* (1942), partly autobiography and partly a critical commentary on African-American culture and values. He also wrote literary criticism in *To Make a Poet Black* (1939), history in *They Came in Chains* (1950) as well as later books, and biography in *The Lonesome Road: The Story of the Negro's Part in America* (1958).

Redding studied briefly at Lincoln (Pennsylvania) University (1923–24), then at Brown University (Ph.B., 1928; M.A., 1932). At Columbia University he pursued graduate study during 1933–34. He taught at Morehouse College (1928–31), Louisville Municipal College (1934–36), Southern University (1936–38), and Hampton Institute (later, University, 1943–66). He was the first director of the Division for Research and Publication of the National Endowment for the Humanities (NEH, 1966–70) before going to Cornell University (1970–75). From 1970 until his death he also held the title of conservator of NEH. He lectured on behalf of the U.S. Department of State in Asia, Africa, and South America.

Redding served on the Board of Fellows of Brown University (1969–81) and was a director of the American Council of Learned Societies (1976–88), among other professional services. He received fellowships from the Rockefeller (1939–40), Guggenheim (1944–45, 1959–60), and Ford (1964–65) Foundations; citations from the National Urban League and New York Public Library; and the Mayflower Award for distinguished writing (1944). He was honorary conservator of the Library of Congress (1973–77).

REFERENCES: CA (NR-26, 124); CB (1969, 1988); NYT, March 5, 1988, p. 33; WP, August 14, 1968, p. B1; WW (1984–85); *Dictionary of Literary Biography*, vol. 63 (Gale Research, 1988).

REEL, Estelle. b. November 26, 1862, Pittsfield, Illinois, to M.A.L. and Jane (Scandland) Reel. Married 1910 to Cort Frederick Meyer.

Estelle Reel was a pioneering woman administrator in education, first in the state of Wyoming, then in Washington, D.C. Raised and educated in Illinois, Missouri, and Massachusetts, as a young woman she moved to Wyoming and taught school for five years (1886–91) in Cheyenne.

She was superintendent of schools for Laramie County (1891–95) until her election as state superintendent of public instruction. She was the first woman in the country elected to a statewide office.

In 1898 President William McKinley appointed Reel U.S. superintendent of Indian schools. She left that role in 1910, when she married and moved with her husband to Toppenish, Washington.

REFERENCES: Marie H. Erwin, *Wyoming Historical Blue Book* (1946); John W. Leonard, ed., *Woman's Who's Who of America* (American Commonwealth, 1914).

REES, Mina Spiegel. b. August 2, 1902, Cleveland, Ohio, to Moses and Alice Louise (Stackhouse) Rees. Married June 24, 1955, to Leopold Brahdy. Children: no.

Mina Rees achieved many firsts as a woman in mathematics with a notable talent for research administration. Her area of specialty was abstract algebra.

As a small child, Rees moved to New York City. She was valedictorian at Hunter High School and graduated from Hunter College (A.B., 1923), where she was president of her class and editor of the yearbook. From her sophomore year she also taught mathematics in the college. She received the A.M. degree from Columbia University (1925) and the Ph.D. from the University of Chicago (1931).

For much of her career Rees was affiliated with Hunter College, as a teacher in its high school (1923–26) and then member of the collegiate faculty (1926–50). Beginning in 1943 she was on leave from Hunter College for government service. She served on the staff of the Office of Scientific Research and Development (1943–46) and directed the mathematics division in the newly established Office of Naval Research (1946–52) before serving one year (1952–53) as its deputy science director. Rees returned to Hunter College in 1953 as dean of faculty, a post she held until 1961. She concluded her career as chief officer of the graduate entity of the City University of New York, under successive titles of dean (1961–68), provost (1968–69), and president (1969–72) when it became the Graduate School and University Center.

Rees was a leader in the development of the concept of the mathematical sciences, reflecting the growing importance of applications of mathematics, many of them using computers. She chaired the Advisory Commission for Mathematics of the National Bureau of Standards (1954–57), served on the National Science Board (1964–70), chaired the Council of Graduate Schools (1970), and was president (1971) and chair (1972) of the American Association for the Advancement of Science, among many other services to government and academe. She was awarded the President's Certificate of Merit (1948), the first Award for Distinguished Service of the Mathematical Association of America

(1962), and the Public Welfare Medal of the National Academy of Sciences (1983).

REFERENCES: AWM; AWS; CB (1957); LE (1974); WW (1994); Phyllis Fox, ''Mina Rees,'' in Louise S. Grinstein and Paul J. Campbell, eds., *Women of Mathematics* (McFarland, 1987), pp. 175–81; *Science* 167 (February 20, 1970): 1149–51.

REESE, Gustave. b. November 29, 1899, New York City. Married 1974 to Carol Truax. Children: no. d. September 7, 1977, Berkeley, California.

Gustave Reese led the development of musicology as a subject in the humanities. He was cofounder of the American Musicological Society.

Reese attended Horace Mann School in New York City. He received the LL.B. degree in 1921 from New York University and was admitted to the bar. He worked as an apprentice to the director of publications at G. Schirmer, Inc., music publishers. He began teaching at New York University in 1927 and received the Mus. Bac. degree there in 1930. Continuing to work at Schirmer's, he was director of publications from 1940 to 1945 and then director of publications at Carl Fischer music publishers from 1945 to 1955. He taught at New York University except for the years 1937–45 and retired in 1973.

Reese taught at the Juilliard School of Music and was visiting professor at other institutions. He was associate editor (1933–44) and editor (1944–45) of *Musical Quarterly*. With others he founded the American Musicological Association (later, Society); he served as its first secretary (1934–46) and was vice president (1946–50) and president (1950–52). He was a council member of the International Musicological Society (1967–72), vice president of the Plainsong and Mediaeval Music Society, and president of the Renaissance Society of America (1971–73).

Reese wrote for professional journals, contributed to music encyclopedias, and in 1949 participated in revising *Baker's Biographical Dictionary of Musicians*. His best-known books, *Music in the Middle Ages* (1940) and *Music in the Renaissance* (1954), were regarded as classics. He also wrote *Fourscore Classics of Music Literature* (1957). He edited *The Commonwealth of Music: In Honor of Carl Sachs* (with R. Brandel, 1965), and *Essays in Musicology* (with Robert J. Snow, 1969). *Aspects of Medieval and Renaissance Music: A Birthday Offering to Gustave Reese* (1966), edited by Jan LaRue and others, honored Reese's sixty-fifth birthday.

REFERENCES: BBD; CA (73–76); NGD; NYT, September 13, 1977, p. 34, and October 2, 1977, p. 19; *American Musicological Society Journal* 30 (Fall 1977): 359; *Musical Quarterly* 63 (October 1977): 579; *Renaissance Quarterly* 31 (Spring 1978): 48–49.

REEVES, Floyd Wesley. b. November 16, 1890, Castalia, South Dakota, to Charles Edward and Ella T. (Ogilvee) Reeves. Married September 11, 1915, to Hazel Beatrice Flint. Children: three. d. August 20, 1979, East Lansing, Michigan.

Floyd W. Reeves was a specialist in curriculum development and an expert on administration of school districts and colleges. He was influential in adult education, especially in the development of the GI Bill of Rights.

Reeves taught in rural schools of South Dakota before completing high school. He received the B.S. degree from Huron (South Dakota) College in 1915. In South Dakota he was a principal in Huron (1915–17) and superintendent in Gregory (1917–20) and Winner (1920–22). In 1918 he established the first vocational education program in the state.

Reeves received the M.A. degree from the University of Chicago (1921). After two years at Transylvania College (later, University, 1923–25) as director of the School of Education, he completed the Ph.D. degree at the University of Chicago (1925).

At the University of Kentucky (1925–29) Reeves was professor of education, director of the Bureau of School Service (1927–29), and head of the Department of Educational Administration. In 1929 he returned to the University of Chicago, first as professor of education and later as professor of administration (1938–53). He directed the university's self-survey, which became a model for other self-surveys. He also directed the Rural Education Project, which led to revisions of school curricula. The curriculum of junior colleges was influenced by his work with the Institute for Administrative Officers of Higher Education.

Reeves took leave from Chicago to serve as first director of personnel of the Tennessee Valley Authority (1933–36). He was chair of the President's Advisory Committee on Education (1936–39), which called for federal aid to education, and he participated in the White House Conference on Children in a Democracy (1939–41). As director of the American Youth Commission of the American Council on Education (1939–42), in 1939 Reeves called for lowering the voting age to eighteen. He was director of labor supply in the federal Office of Production and Management (1940–41).

Reeves was chair of the Conference on Postwar Readjustment of Civilian and Military Personnel (1942–43), charged with devising a plan for reentry into civilian life. Many of its proposals were included in the GI Bill of Rights. Before and after its passage he spoke throughout the nation on its purposes.

In 1948 Reeves headed a UNESCO consultative mission to the Philippines, and in 1956 and 1957 he headed teams on rural development in Pakistan. After his retirement from Chicago, Reeves went to Michigan State University in 1953 as professor of educational administration and consultant to the president. He was Distinguished Professor of Education from 1957 until his retirement in 1962. He served on the Board of Trustees of the National Institute of Public Affairs.

Reeves wrote *The Liberal Arts College* (with others, 1932), *Adult Education* (with Thomas Fansler and Cyril O. Houle, 1938), and *College Organization and Administration* (with John Dale Russell, 1929). He edited *Education for Rural America* (1945). With others, he edited and coauthored many volumes of University of Chicago surveys.

REFERENCES: CA (89–92); NYT, August 31, 1979, p. B5; WWW (7); Robert H. Beck,

''Educational Leadership, 1906–1956,'' *Phi Delta Kappan* 37 (January 1956): 164; Barbara Ann Nicholas, ''Floyd W. Reeves on Curriculum'' (Ph.D. diss., Michigan State University, 1971); Richard O. Niehoff, *Floyd W. Reeves* (University Press of America, 1991); Carl T. Pacacha, ''Floyd Wesley Reeves and the GI Bill of Rights: A Bicentennial Reflection,'' *Adult Leadership* (September 1976): 9–11.

REGAN, Agnes Gertrude. b. March 26, 1869, San Francisco, to James and Mary Ann (Morrison) Regan. Married: no. d. September 30, 1943, Washington, D.C.

The influence of Agnes Regan on social work education came through her many years with the National Catholic School of Social Service (NCSSS) in Washington, D.C. The school had opened in 1921 under sponsorship of the National Council of Catholic Women. Regan became a faculty member in 1922 and for many years was assistant director (1925–41). As acting director (1935–37) she led its reorganization.

Regan grew up in San Francisco, where she graduated from Saint Rose Academy and in 1887 from the San Francisco Normal School (later, State University). She taught elementary grades (1887–1900) and was a principal (1900–1914) and a school board member (1914–19). She also served on the San Francisco Playground Commission (1912–19). With Governor Hiram Johnson, Regan lobbied for successful passage of the first teacher pension law in California.

In 1920 she was a delegate to the organizational meeting of the National Council of Catholic Women, who were responsible for training laywomen in social work. She was chosen second vice president of the Board of Directors and soon after was named executive secretary, a post she held until 1941. The school, founded in 1921, opened with sixteen students. Until 1925 it was named the National Catholic Service School for Women. Regan lived at the school, which was a residential facility offering one- and two-year courses. In 1923 Catholic University of America awarded M.A. degrees to college graduates of the NCSSS who had completed the two-year course. In 1925 the school was incorporated, and a Board of Trustees was formed.

Regan lobbied for laws prohibiting child labor and for changes in restrictive immigration laws. She received a papal decoration in 1933. In 1939 and 1940 Regan was a member of the White House Conference on Children in a Democracy. A residence hall at Catholic University of America was named in her memory. The NCSSS merged with Catholic University of America in 1947.

References: AR; BDSW; DAB (supp. 3); NAW; WR; Aaron I. Abell, *American Catholicism and Social Action* (Hanover House, 1960); Loretto R. Lawler, *Full Circle: The Story of the National Catholic School of Social Service, 1918–1947* (Catholic University of America Press, 1951); *New Catholic Encyclopedia* (McGraw-Hill, 1967).

RENNE, Roland Roger. b. December 12, 1905, Bridgeton, New Jersey, to Fred Christian and Caroline A. (Young) Renne. Married August 9, 1932, to Mary Kneeland Wisner. Children: four.

During Roland R. Renne's twenty-year tenure leading Montana State College (later, University) the institution grew into a university. As an agricultural economist he emphasized the increasing importance of technology and international perspective as transformative influences on the agricultural curriculum.

Renne grew up on a dairy farm and graduated from high school in Shiloh, New Jersey, in 1923. He received the B.S. degree from Rutgers University (1927) and M.Sc. (1928) and Ph.D. (1930) degrees from the University of Wisconsin. He went to Montana State College in 1930 as assistant professor of economics and agricultural economics, rising to professor in 1936. He headed the Departments of Economics (1938–39) and Economics and Agricultural Economics (1939–43) and was acting president (1943–44). He became president of Montana State in 1944 and held the post until 1964. Renne farmed eighty acres while president.

Renne served on the Bozeman School Board (1936–43), Montana State Planning Board (1937–42 and 1954–62), Pacific Northwest Planning Council (1937–41), and state price office of the Montana Office of Price Administration (1942–43). He participated in missions to the Philippines, Peru, Ethiopia, and India. On leave from the university, he was U.S. assistant secretary of agriculture for international affairs (1963–64). Renne was a candidate for governor of Montana in 1964 but lost. He served on the National Forest Advisory Board (1948–54), U.S. Advisory Council on Indian Affairs (1949–52), President's Water Resources Policies Commission (1950–51), and National Manpower Council (1950–62) and was director of water resources research for the U.S. Department of the Interior (1964–69).

He was professor of agricultural economics and associate dean of agriculture at the University of Illinois, Urbana, from 1969 to 1974. Returning to Montana State University in 1974, he was director of foreign trade study. He was a vice president of the American Farm Economic Association (1941) and president of the Western Agricultural Economic Association (1939). He wrote experiment station bulletins, *The Tariff on Dairy Products* (1933), *The Montana Citizen* (with J. Wesley Hoffmann, 1937), *Land Economics* (1947), and *The Government and Administration of Montana* (1958).

REFERENCES: CA (1–4R); CB (1963); WW (1978–79); Paul Friggens, ''Hay-Pitching 'Prexy': Head of Montana State College Is Progressive and Practical,'' *Christian Science Monitor Magazine*, August 14, 1948, p. 6; Robert Rydell, Jeffrey Safford, and Pierce Mullen, *In the People's Interest: A Centennial History of Montana State University* (Montana State University Foundation, 1992).

RICHARDS, Robert Hallowell. b. August 26, 1844, Gardiner, Maine, to Francis and Anne Hallowell (Gardiner) Richards. Married June 4, 1875, to Ellen Henrietta Swallow; June 8, 1912, to Lillian Jameson. Children: no. d. March 27, 1945, Natick, Massachusetts.

Robert Richards spent his entire career at the Massachusetts Institute of Technology (MIT), where he introduced laboratory methods of experimentation and research into the teaching of mining engineering and metallurgy. He was credited with revolutionizing instruction in those fields. Richards advocated teaching students how to think so they could then do problem solving themselves.

Born in Maine, Richards was educated at a school in England, at a private school in Boston, by tutors, and for two years at Phillips Academy in Exeter, New Hampshire. When MIT opened in 1865, he was the seventh student to register, graduating in 1868 with the bachelor of science degree. Beginning in 1868, when he had an appointment as assistant in chemistry, he taught at MIT until his retirement in 1914 at the age of seventy. From 1873 to 1914 he was professor of mining engineering. He headed the Department of Mining Engineering for forty-one years.

Inventions to his credit included machines for ore dressing, a jet aspirator for laboratories, ore separators, and a prism for stadia surveying. He worked to improve metallurgical processes and became an authority on the ore dressing of copper.

Richards was married to Ellen Henrietta Swallow Richards (BDAE) from 1875 until her death in 1911. She was one of his students and the first woman admitted to MIT. Richards was president of the American Institute of Mining Engineers in 1886. He conducted summer classes in various locations, visiting mining sites. In addition to more than 100 scientific articles, Richards wrote the four-volume *Ore Dressing*, in its time the only study in English on the subject. *A Textbook of Ore Dressing* was first published in 1909. He served on many boards and received numerous awards. The Mining and Metallurgical Society of America gave him a gold medal in 1915. His autobiography, *His Mark*, was published in 1936. At his death in 1945 Richards was the oldest living graduate of MIT and the last member of its first class.

REFERENCES: DAB (supp. 3); NCAB (12: 347); NYT, March 28, 1945, p. 23; WWW(2).

RISLING, David, Jr. b. April 4, 1921, Weitchpec, California.

A pioneer educator in Native American studies, David Risling, Jr., was instrumental in developing organizations that furthered the cause of Indian education.

Risling was raised on the Hoopa Reservation in California and graduated from the Hoopa Valley High School. He served as an officer in the U.S. Navy (1943–45). In 1947 he received the B.S. degree from California Polytechnic University, San Luis Obispo, credited as the first Native American in California to receive a degree. The M.A. degree was awarded to him by the same university in 1953. He taught science and was director of agricultural studies at Caruthers High School (1947–51). From 1951 to 1970 Risling was at Modesto Junior College, where he taught science and agriculture and was a counselor. He taught in the Department of Native American Studies at the University of California, Davis, from 1970 to 1991 and was coordinator of the Tecumseh Center.

Risling founded the California Indian Education Association in 1967 and served as president (1968–70). He also founded California Indian Legal Services and served as chair. He was an organizer of the National Indian Education Association in 1969 and was on its board (1970–77). With others he established Degoniwida-Quetzalcoatl (D-Q) University in Davis, where he served as chair of the Board of Directors and taught courses on Native American law and culture. Risling coauthored *The Establishment of D-Q University* (with Jack D. Forbes, q.v., and Kenneth R. Martin, 1972). He was a founder of the Native American Rights Fund and the American Indian Higher Education Consortium. Risling served on the National Advisory Commission on Indian Education (1973–81). In 1990 he was named American Indian Educator of the Year by the California Legislature.

REFERENCES: Juan L. Gonzales, Jr., *The Lives of Ethnic Americans* (Kendall/Hunt, 1994); Barry T. Klein, *Reference Encyclopedia of the American Indian* (Todd, 1995); Sharon Malinowski, ed., *Notable Native Americans* (Gale Research, 1995).

RIVERA, Tomás. b. December 22, 1935, Crystal City, Texas, to Florencio M. and Josefa (Hernández) Rivera. Married November 27, 1958, to Conceptión Garza. Children: three. d. May 16, 1984, Fontana, California.

Tomás Rivera was the first Chicano-American to head a major research university. He also helped to develop Mexican-American literature.

As a child Rivera traveled in the Midwest with his family, who were migrant workers. He graduated from Crystal City High School in 1954 and received the A.A. degree from Southwest Texas Junior College in 1954 and the B.A. degree from Southwest Texas State University in 1956. He began his teaching career as an English instructor in a San Antonio high school (1957–58) and taught Spanish at Crystal City (1958–60) and League City (1960–65), Texas. He earned the M.Ed. degree at Southwest Texas State University in 1964. Rivera chaired the Department of Foreign Languages at Southwest Texas Junior College in 1965–66.

At the University of Oklahoma he was a teaching assistant and instructor and received M.A. and Ph.D. degrees in 1969. From 1969 to 1971 he taught Spanish at Sam Houston State University and spent summers in a university program in Puebla, Mexico. Rivera then went to the University of Texas at San Antonio, where he helped to organize the curriculum of the university. He served there as director of the Division of Foreign Languages, Literature and Linguistics (1971–73), associate dean of the College of Multidisciplinary Studies (1973–76), and vice president for administration (1976–78). He was also professor of Spanish literature. At the University of Texas at El Paso, he was executive vice president (1978–79).

In 1979 Rivera became chancellor of the University of California, Riverside, where he served until his death in 1984. He was also a corporate officer of the Times Mirror Company.

Rivera was on the executive committee of the Western College Association, on the Boards of Trustees of the Carnegie Foundation for the Advancement of

Teaching and Educational Testing Service, and on the Boards of Directors of the American Association for Higher Education and American Council on Education. He was a founding member and vice president of the National Council of Chicanos in Higher Education. He served on the Commission on a National Agenda for the 1980s.

Rivera was a respected author of prose and poetry. The Quinto Sol National Chicano Prize was awarded to him for *And the Earth Did Not Part* (1971). He wrote *Always and Other Poets* (1973) and *A Public Trust* (with others, 1979). His works appeared in many anthologies, and he served on editorial boards of *MICTLA* and *El Magazin*. Julian Oliveres edited *The Harvest: Short Stories by Tomás Rivera* (1989) and *The Searchers: Collected Poetry by Tomás Rivera* (1990). The Tomás Rivera Institute in Claremont, California, named in his honor, was established in 1985.

REFERENCES: CA (NR-32); CHE, February 15, 1984, p. 1+; WWW (8); Juan D. Bruce-Novoa, *Chicano Authors* (University of Texas Press, 1980); Vernon E. Lattin, Rolando Hinojosa, and Gary D. Keller, eds., *Tomás Rivera, 1935–1984: The Man and His Work* (Bilingual Review/Press, 1988); *Los Angeles Times*, May 17, 1984, p. I3; Julio A. Martinez, *Chicano Scholars and Writers* (Scarecrow Press, 1979); Matt S. Meier, *Mexican–American Biographies* (Greenwood Press, 1988).

ROBERTS, Lydia Jane. b. June 30, 1879, Hope Township, Michigan, to Warren and Mary Jane (McKibbin) Roberts. Married: no. d. May 28, 1965, Rio Piedras, Puerto Rico.

Lydia Roberts studied nutrition, especially of children. Her career was spent in research on the subject and in efforts to improve the nutrition of children and families in the United States and Puerto Rico. She developed workshops for teacher education and public health nutrition.

Roberts graduated in 1899 from the one-year course of Mount Pleasant Normal School (later, Central Michigan University). She taught in Michigan in rural schools and in Mount Pleasant and Cadillac. She moved to Montana, where she taught in Miles City and Great Falls. After a short time in Virginia, Roberts went to Dillon, Montana. She served as a critic teacher for the State Normal College (later, Western Montana College) and taught third grade in a Dillon school.

In 1915 Roberts enrolled at the University of Chicago, where she earned the Ph.B. degree in 1917. She had become interested in nutrition in Montana and studied it at Chicago, where Katharine Blunt (BDAE) was a member of the Department of Home Economics. Roberts' master's thesis was published in the *Journal of Home Economics* in 1919, the year she received the M.S. degree.

Beginning as an instructor in 1918, Roberts rose through academic ranks at the University of Chicago, becoming a professor in 1930. She was awarded the Ph.D. degree in 1928. In 1930 she succeeded Blunt as department head. She remained at Chicago until mandatory retirement in 1944. Her book *Nutrition Work with Children* (1927) was considered a classic in the field. In addition to her administrative duties Roberts continued research in nutrition and conducted surveys on nutrition of children. She prepared government bulletins, and with members of the Children's Bureau staff she wrote *The Road to Good Nutrition* (1942).

Roberts served on committees of the White House Conference on Child Health and Protection in 1929. She was a member of the Council on Foods and Nutrition of the American Medical Association (1934–48) and the Food and Nutrition Board of the National Research Council. In 1943 in Puerto Rico, she conducted a survey of nutrition and a workshop on nutrition education. She accepted an invitation to teach at the University of Puerto Rico in Rio Piedras, going there in 1944; from 1946 to 1952 she chaired the Home Economics Department, revising the curriculum and strengthening the instructional program. Nutrition workers from Central and South America were trained in her workshops. Among her books were *Patterns of Living in Puerto Rican Families* (with Rosa L. Stefani, 1949) and *The Doña Elena Project: Better Living Program in an Isolated Rural Community* (1963). Roberts received numerous awards, including the Marjorie Hulsizer Copher Award from the American Dietetic Association (1952) and the Marshall Field Award for nutrition services to children (1957).

REFERENCES: AWS; NAW; WW (1940); *American Dietetic Association Journal* 47 (August 1965): 127–28, and 49 (October 1966): 299–301; Franklin C. Bing, "Lydia Jane Roberts: A Biographical Sketch," *Journal of Nutrition* 93 (September 1967): 1–13.

ROGLER, Lloyd Henry. b. July 21, 1930, Santurce, Puerto Rico, to Charles C. and Carmen (Canino) Rogler. Married to Susan Shapiro. Children: two.

Lloyd H. Rogler was a sociologist who gained a national reputation as a leader in Latino scholarship. His research emphasized mental health.

Rogler graduated from Iowa City (Iowa) High School. He received B.S. (1951), M.A. (1952), and Ph.D. (1957) degrees from the University of Iowa. In 1952 he was drafted into the army, serving until 1954 in a military research group investigating the impact of the Korean War on public opinion.

From 1957 to 1960 Rogler taught at the University of Puerto Rico. Under August B. Hollingshead, he directed a project on mental illness and its effect on families. At Yale University (1960–68) Rogler directed the Latin American Studies Program and published papers on his Puerto Rican studies. With Hollingshead he wrote *Trapped: Families and Schizophrenia* (1965). He taught at Case Western Reserve University from 1968 to 1974. In 1974 Rogler became Albert Schweitzer Professor in the Humanities at Fordham University, where he founded and directed the Hispanic Research Center (1977–90).

Rogler's publications included *Migrant in the City: The Life of a Puerto Rican Action Group* (1972), *The Puerto Rican Child in New York City* (with others, 1980), *Unitas—Hispanic and Black Children in a Healing Community* (with Anne Farber, 1981), *Conceptual Framework for Mental Health Research on Hispanic Populations* (with Rosemary Santana Cooney, 1983), *Puerto Rican*

Families in New York City (with Cooney, 1984), and *Hispanics and Mental Health: A Framework for Research* (with others, 1989).

Among awards Rogler received were the Hubert Humphrey Chair of International Renowned Scholars (1972), Academic Excellence Award from the National Coalition of Hispanic Mental Health and Human Services Organization (1980), Hostos and Marti Award from the New York Society of Clinical Psychologists (1981), and first Lifetime Honorary Membership from the Association of Hispanic Mental Health Professionals (1985).

REFERENCES: CA (17–20R); WD (1994–96); WW (1988–89); Juan L. Gonzalez, Jr., *The Lives of Ethnic Americans* (Kendall/Hunt, 1994); Amy L. Unterburger, ed., *Who's Who among Hispanic Americans* (Gale Research, 1994–95).

RUDOLPH, Frederick. b. June 19, 1920, Baltimore, to Charles Frederick and Jennie Hill (Swope) Rudolph. Married June 18, 1949, to Dorothy Dannenbaum. Children: two.

Frederick Rudolph wrote the standard works on the development of higher education in the United States and on courses of study in colleges and universities. His histories covered the entire period from the early seventeenth to the mid-twentieth century.

Rudolph was a graduate of Williams College (B.A., 1942), where he also taught for all of his career. After four years' service in the U.S. Army, rising to the rank of captain, and one year as history instructor at Williams (1946–47), he earned M.A. (1949) and Ph.D. (1953) degrees from Yale University. He returned to the Williams faculty in 1951 and was Mark Hopkins Professor of History from 1964 to 1982.

Rudolph's books included *Mark Hopkins and the Log* (1956), *The American College and University: A History* (1962), *Curriculum: A History of the American Undergraduate Course of Study since 1636* (1977), *Essays on Education in the Early Republic* (editor, 1965), and *Perspectives: A Williams Anthology* (1983). He held grants from the Guggenheim Foundation (1958–59 and 1968–69) and Fund for the Advancement of Education (1960–61). He served on the Commission on Baccalaureate Degrees of the Association of American Colleges (later, and Universities) during 1981–85. He was executive editor (1980–84) and consulting editor (1985–92) of *Change* magazine. The Association of American Colleges awarded him its Frederic Ness Book Award in 1980.

REFERENCES: CA (9–12R); WW (1996).

RYAN, Sister John Gabriel. b. Mary Ann Ryan, August 30, 1874, Manville, Rhode Island, to Thomas and Mary (Dwyer) Ryan. Married: no. d. December 25, 1951, Seattle.

During a period of rapid change in educational expectations for nurses, Sister John Gabriel Ryan initiated improvements in the professional training of nursing sisters in Roman Catholic congregations. Through short courses and textbooks, she influenced the development of nursing education nationally.

Her mother having died giving her birth, Mary Ann Ryan, the future Sister John Gabriel, was raised by her father, a blind shopkeeper. She completed the normal training course at St. James School in her hometown of Manville, Rhode Island, then remained there as a teacher.

At the age of nineteen, she defied her father's wish that she continue to care for him and marry a suitor of his choosing. Instead, she went to Canada, where she joined the Order of St. Anne as a novice, though illness soon compelled her to return home. On regaining her health, in 1899 she went again to Canada and joined the Sisters of Providence. In Great Falls, Montana, she worked from 1901 at Columbus Hospital, where she studied pharmacy and passed the state board examination in the subject (1904). She graduated from Columbus Hospital School of Nursing (1908). She taught at St. Vincent Hospital School of Nursing in Portland, Oregon (1913–15). Later studies in summer sessions at several universities and colleges led to the A.B. degree from the University of Washington (1927) and the M.A. from Seattle College (later, University, 1937).

In 1917 Sister John Gabriel was appointed general supervisor of training schools in the west, operated by the Sisters of Providence. She was later named directress of schools of nursing (1924) and hospital consultant (1933) in the western provinces of the order. She taught short courses on hospital administration nationally during the 1930s, using 200 instructional booklets she had written. In cooperation with state officials and national associations, Sister John Gabriel standardized the nursing curricula of Sisters of Providence hospitals. Ill health compelled her retirement in 1938.

Sister John Gabriel was author of *Principles of Teaching in Schools of Nursing* (1928), *Practical Methods of Study* (1931), *Teacher's Work Organization Book* (1931), *Professional Problems—A Textbook for Nurses* (1932), and *Through the Patient's Eyes* (1935). She served on the board of the *American Journal of Nursing* (1931–35). She was an honorary fellow of the American College of Hospital Administrators (1935) and honorary president of the Washington State Hospital Association (1938).

REFERENCES: Margaret Felton, *Sister John Gabriel*, National League of Nursing Education (1952); "Sister John Gabriel—Leader in a Time of Change," *Sisters of Providence Caritas* 14 (January 1976): 1+; Sister John Gabriel, personal papers collection, Sisters of Providence Archives, Seattle.

S

SAMORA, Julian. b. March 1, 1920, Pagosa Springs, Colorado. Married to Betty Samora. Children: five. d. February 2, 1996, Albuquerque, New Mexico.

In 1964 the Rosenberg Foundation commissioned Julian Samora to organize a conference of Spanish-speaking scholars. The result was *La Raza: Forgotten Americans* (1966), a collection of essays on the history, religion, culture, politics, and demography of Mexican Americans. It established Samora as an intellectual leader of Chicano studies in higher education. He also helped to establish medical sociology as a discipline.

Samora received the B.A. degree in 1942 from Adams State College in Colorado. He taught for one year in Herfano County and then at Adams State (1944–45). He received the M.A. degree from Colorado State University (1947) and was a teaching assistant at the University of Wisconsin (1948–49). He earned the Ph.D. degree (1953) in sociology and anthropology from Washington University. Samora taught at the University of Colorado Medical School (1955–57) and at Michigan State University (1957–59). From 1959 to 1985 he was a professor at Notre Dame University, where he directed the Mexico Border Studies Project, sponsored by the Ford Foundation. The program attracted many Mexican-American graduate students.

Samora held a National Endowment for the Humanities Fellowship (1979) and was a National Association for Chicano Studies scholar (1983). He was a fellow of the Whitney Foundation (1951–52) and American Sociological Association (1978) and sat on the U.S. Commission on Civil Rights and on the President's Commission on Rural Poverty. He edited *International Migration Review* and *Nuestro* and coauthored *Mexican-Americans in a Midwest Metropolis* (1967), *Mexican-Americans in the Southwest* (1969), *Los Mojados: The Wetback Story* (1971), *A History of the Mexican-American People* (1977), and *Gunpowder Justice* (1979).

Politically committed to social justice and equal opportunity for Mexican Americans, Samora was a founder of the National Council of La Raza. In 1989 Michigan State University established the Julian Samora Research Institute. Samora received the Order of the Aztec Eagle in 1993 from the Mexican government.

REFERENCES: CA (37R); NYT, February 6, 1996, p. D23; WW (1990–91); Matt S.

Meier, *Mexican-American Biographies* (Greenwood Press, 1988); Roberto Rodriquez, "Chicano Studies Pioneer Praised," *Black Issues in Higher Education* 12 (October 5, 1995): 34–37; Amy L. Unterburger, ed., *Who's Who among Hispanic Americans* (Gale Research, 1994–95).

SARASON, Seymour Bernard. b. January 12, 1919, Brooklyn, New York, to Max and Anna (Silverlight) Sarason. Married May 22, 1943, to Esther Kroop. Children: one.

Seymour Sarason was a noted psychologist, a founder of community psychology, and a critic of American psychology. Among his interests was anxiety in the learning of schoolchildren. He directed a research program of test anxiety in children and adults.

Sarason's family moved to Newark, New Jersey, when he was six years old. He skipped some grades and went to summer school for additional credits. While in high school he contracted polio. At the age of sixteen he entered the University of Newark (later, Rutgers University, Newark), where he received the B.A. degree in 1939. He earned M.A. (1940) and Ph.D. (1942) degrees from Clark University.

Sarason's first professional position was at Southbury (Connecticut) Training School, where he was chief psychologist (1942–46). In 1946 he went to Yale University; there he became professor of psychology in 1954. He was director of graduate programs in clinical psychology (1949–62), director of the psychoeducational clinic (1963–70), and IBM Professor of Urban Education (1975–77). At Yale he helped to create the clinical training program. He retired in 1989. He also served as adjunct professor at Southern Connecticut State College (1958–61) and visiting lecturer at Boston University (1961–65).

Sarason was a prolific writer. Two of his books, *The Culture of the School and the Problem of Change* (1971) and *Schooling in America: Scapegoat and Salvation* (1983), had particularly strong impacts. Among his other books were *Psychological Problems in Mental Deficiency* (1949), *The Clinical Interaction* (1954), *Anxiety in Elementary School Children* (with others, 1960), *The Preparation of Teachers* (with Kenneth S. Davidson and Burton Blatt, 1962), *The Creation of Settings and the Future Societies* (1972), *The Psychological Sense of Community* (1974), *Educational Handicap, Public Policy and Society History* (with John Doris, 1979), *Psychology Misdirected* (1981), and *Psychology and Mental Retardation* (1983). Sarason received awards from the American Psychological Association in 1969 for contributions to psychology, in 1974 for contributions to community psychology, and in 1984 for contributions to psychology in the public interest. The American Association on Mental Deficiency honored him in 1973 and 1974. Sarason's *The Making of an American Psychologist* was published in 1988.

REFERENCES: CA (120); WW (1984–85); *American Journal of Community Psychology* 18 (June 1990): 341–82; *American Psychologist* 40 (March 1985): 332–36.

SCHOFIELD, Martha. b. February 1, 1839, near Newton, Pennsylvania, to Oliver and Mary (Jackson) Schofield. Married: no. d. January 13, 1916, Aiken, South Carolina.

Martha Schofield taught African Americans for fifty years in South Carolina. She believed that racial equality would come through education and economic independence. She established the Schofield Normal and Industrial School in Aiken. It became one of the outstanding schools for African Americans in the country. Vocational skills were stressed as a way to obtain employment.

Schofield was raised in Newton and Darby, Pennsylvania. She taught for a short time at the Bell School on Long Island; at a seminary in Harrison, New York; and at a school for African Americans in Philadelphia. In 1864 she attended a teachers' institute. In 1865 she received an appointment to teach on the Sea Islands off the South Carolina coast. Her first year was on Wadmelaw Island, where former slaves, both adults and children, learned to read and write. She taught on other islands and in Charleston. In 1867 on Saint Helena she worked with Laura Towne (q.v.). In 1868 Schofield went to Aiken to teach in a Freedmen's School, but the Freedmen's Bureau ended its educational work two years later.

Schofield bought land in Aiken, one-half of the deed held by others, to be used for school purposes forever. A schoolhouse was erected with help from the Freedman's Bureau, with the goal of training African-American teachers. Pupils ranging in age from five to thirty-five studied in three departments: primary, intermediate, and grammar. The grammar department, grades eight to ten, was certified as a normal school, with practice teaching done in the lower grades. The first two graduates completed the normal program in 1885.

In the 1880s vocational subjects were introduced into the curriculum and more buildings were erected. A print shop was begun; then a blacksmithy and courses in cobbling, carpentry, wheelwrighting, and harness-making were added. Girls learned housekeeping arts.

In 1881 a Colored Teacher's Institute for Aiken County was held at the school; it became an annual event. Schofield Normal and Industrial School was incorporated in 1886. In 1892 Schofield resigned, but she returned the next year and remained until 1912.

REFERENCES: NAW; WR; Katherine Smedley, *Martha Schofield and the Re-education of the South, 1839–1916* (E. Mellen Press, 1987); Katherine Smedley, ''Martha Schofield and the Rights of Women,'' *South Carolina Historical Magazine* 85 (July 1984): 195–210.

SCHOMBURG, Arthur Alphonso. b. January 24, 1874, San Juan, Puerto Rico, to Carlos Federico and Mary (Joseph) Schomburg. Married June 30, 1895, to Elizabeth Hatcher; March 17, 1902, to Elizabeth Morrow Taylor; c. 1914 to Elizabeth Green. Children: eight. d. June 10, 1938, Brooklyn, New York.

Arthur Schomburg was a noted bibliophile, amassing a collection of materials on persons of African descent throughout the world. He was an authority in the field of black history, and the Schomburg collection came to be used extensively by scholars and researchers. Schomburg wanted an accurate history portrayed and sought to refute legends about blacks.

Schomburg attended public schools in Puerto Rico and graduated from the Institute de Instruccion. He attended Saint Thomas College in the Virgin Islands. In 1891 he went to New York City, where until 1896 he was secretary of the Los Dos Antillas Cuban Revolutionary Party. For five years (1901–6) he worked as a clerk/manager in a law firm and taught Spanish. From 1906 to 1929 Schomburg was a clerk at Bankers Trust Company, becoming supervisor of the mailing department.

From his early years, Schomburg collected information on blacks. He contributed items from his collection to exhibitions. He lectured on black history for the Universal Negro Improvement Association. With John E. Bruce, in 1911 he founded the Negro Society for Historical Research. In 1916 Schomburg's *Bibliographical Checklist of Negro Poets* was published.

The Division of Negro History, Literature and Prints was begun at New York's 135th Street Public Library in 1925. In 1926 the Carnegie Corporation provided $10,000 to purchase Schomburg's collection for the library. Schomburg traveled to Europe in 1926 to search for more historical materials and on his return donated them to the Schomburg collection. After retirement from Bankers Trust in 1929, Schomburg was curator of the Negro collection at Fisk University (1930–32), working under Louis Shores (BDAE). In 1932 he accepted an invitation to become curator of his own collection in New York, which had been named the Schomburg Collection of Negro History and Literature. He served in that role until his death in 1938.

Schomburg was president of the American Negro Academy (1921–26). He was active in Masonry and was editor of *Transaction* and coeditor of the *Odd Fellows Journal*, Masonic publications. He wrote many articles. "The Negro Digs Up His Past" was included in *Anthology of American Negro Literature*, edited by Sylvestre C. Watkins (1944). In 1927 Schomburg received the William E. Harmon Award for outstanding work in the field of education. The Schomburg collection continued to expand and in 1973 was named the Schomburg Collection for Research in Black Culture.

REFERENCES: DALB; DANB; NYT, June 11, 1938, p. 15; Ralph L. Crowder, "Street Scholars: Self-Trained Black Historians," *The Black Collegian* (January/February 1979): 14, 16; Jean Blackwell Hutson, "The Schomburg Collection," in John Henrik Clarke, ed., *Harlem: A Community in Transition* (Citadel Press, 1964); Donald Franklin Joyce, "Arthur Alonzo Schomburg: A Pioneering Black Bibliophile," *Journal of Library History* 10 (April 1975): 169–76; Yusef A. Salaam, "The Schomburg Library Then and Now," *Freedomways* 23 (First Quarter 1983): 29–36; Elinor Des Verney Sinnette, *Arthur Alfonso Schomburg, Black Bibliophile and Collector: A Biography* (New York Public Library and Wayne State University Press, 1989).

SCHULTZ, Theodore William. b. April 30, 1902, Arlington, South Dakota, to Henry Edward and Anna Elizabeth (Weiss) Schultz. Married 1930 to Esther Florence Werth. Children: three.

Theodore W. Schultz was called the father of the economics of education. He worked to make agricultural economics a part of general economics. He shaped the Department of Economics and Sociology at Iowa State College (later, University) and as chairman of the Department of Economics at the University of Chicago made it a center for agricultural economics. Schultz's research interests included the analysis of human capital and economic growth. He received the Nobel Prize in economics in 1979.

Schultz was raised on a South Dakota farm. He received the B.S. degree from South Dakota State College (later, University) in 1926 and M.S. (1928) and Ph.D. (1930) degrees from the University of Wisconsin. At Iowa State College Schultz was professor of agricultural economics and chairman of the Department of Economics and Sociology (1934–43). When administrators at the university removed a colleague's article on oleomargarine—a controversial topic in a dairy region—from a bulletin board, Schultz resigned in protest.

At the University of Chicago from 1943, Schultz was professor of economics, chairman of the department (1946–61), and Charles L. Hutchinson Distinguished Professor of Economics (1952–72). He was a research fellow at the Center for Advanced Study in the Behavioral Sciences (1956–57).

Schultz conducted studies throughout the world and was an adviser to U.S. government organizations. He served as editor of the *Journal of Farm Economics* (1939–42). Textbooks he wrote that were used extensively were *Economic Organization of Agriculture* (1953) and *Economic Value of Education* (1963). Among his other publications were *Prospects for Agricultural Recovery* (1934), *Redirecting Farm Policy* (1943), *Food for the World* (1944), *Investment in Human Capital: The Role of Education and of Research* (1971), *Investing in People: The Economics of Population Quality* (1981), and *The Economics of Being Poor* (1993). He edited *Investment in Education* (1972).

Schultz received many honors, including the Francis A. Walker (BDAE) Medal from the American Economic Association (1972) and the Leonard Elmhirst Medal from the International Agricultural Economics Association (1976). He was president of the American Economic Association (1960), a director of the National Bureau of Economic Research (1949–67), and a founding member of the National Academy of Education (1965).

REFERENCES: CA (85–88); IESS; LE (1974); NYT, October 17, 1979, p. 1+; WD (1994–96); WW (1996); WWE; *Journal of Farm Economics* 39 (December 1957): xv; Tyler Wasson, ed., *Nobel Prize Winners* (H. W. Wilson, 1987).

SCHUMAN, William Howard. b. August 4, 1910, New York City, to Samuel and Ray (Heilbrunn) Schuman. Married March 27, 1936, to Frances Prince. Children: two. d. February 15, 1992, New York City.

Though he was foremost a composer, William Schuman was also an innovator in music education. His presidency of the Juilliard School of Music brought the first significant revisions to its curriculum in half a century, with a new attention to American music and culture. As founding president of the Lincoln Center for the Performing Arts, Schuman underscored the educational function and public responsibilities of an artistic organization.

He studied in the School of Commerce at New York University but withdrew one day after hearing a New York Philharmonic concert in Carnegie Hall. He studied harmony and counterpoint privately, then enrolled in 1933 at Teachers College, Columbia University, where he earned B.S. (1935) and M.A. (1937) degrees.

In the first decade of his career, Schuman directed the chorus and taught at Sarah Lawrence College. He briefly held a concurrent appointment as director of publications at G. Schirmer, Inc. (1944–45). He was president of the Juilliard School from 1945 to 1962. Under Schuman's leadership, Juilliard added academic courses to its performance training, offered a five-year bachelor of science degree, and instituted programs in opera and dance, the latter directed by Martha Hill (q.v.). The "Literature and Materials of Music" curriculum that Schuman inaugurated at Juilliard became a model for other conservatories. He was president of Lincoln Center from 1962 until he retired in 1969.

Schuman was a member of the advisory committee on cultural information to the U.S. Information Agency (USIA) and was vice chair of the U.S. delegation to the UNESCO International Conference of Creative Artists held in Venice, Italy, in 1952. He was a prolific composer, awarded the Pulitzer Prize in 1943 and 1985 and Guggenheim Fellowship in 1939 and 1941.

REFERENCES: BBD; CB (1962, 1992); EAB; NGD; NYT, February 16, 1992, p. 48; WAB; WWW (10); Christopher Rouse, *William Schuman Documentary* (G. Schirmer, 1980); Flora Rheta Schreiber and Vincent Persichetti, *William Schuman* (G. Schirmer, 1954).

SCHWAB, Joseph Jackson. b. February 2, 1909, Columbus, Mississippi, to Samuel Buchsbaum and Hortense (Jackson) Schwab. Married September 13, 1932, to Rosamond Martin McGill. Children: one. d. April 13, 1988, Lancaster, Pennsylvania.

Joseph Schwab modeled an inclusive approach to educational questions across an unusually broad spectrum of subjects. He was the principal motivator and organizer of the Biological Sciences Curriculum Study, one of several post-Sputnik reviews of science and mathematics learning in American schools. He was also a noted philosopher of education who drew upon the traditions of both Robert Maynard Hutchins (BDAE), with a focus on great books and ideas, and John Dewey (BDAE), with an emphasis on the social context of learning.

Schwab entered the University of Chicago when he was fifteen years old and received all of his degrees there. After earning the Ph.B. degree (1930) with majors in English literature and physics, he turned his attention to biology. He took the S.M. degree in 1936 and the Ph.D. in 1938 for studies in mathematical genetics. During 1936–37 he studied educational testing and measurement under Irving Lorge (q.v.) at Teachers College, Columbia University. From 1938 to 1974 Schwab taught at the University of Chicago, where he held appointments in both biology and education. At Chicago he worked in collaboration with Ralph Tyler (BDAE).

The Biological Sciences Curriculum Study at Schwab's initiative offered three alternative concepts of the discipline for high school study, with molecular, organic, and ecological emphases. As an exponent of free play with ideas in academic discourse, Schwab regretted the anti-intellectual tendency he perceived in student protest movements of the late 1960s, an issue he engaged in his book *College Curriculum and Student Protest* (1969). During the 1950s and 1960s he advised the Jewish Theological Seminary on an inquiry-based approach to biblical study. Schwab's seminal essays on curricula and classroom teaching appeared in the collection *Science, Curriculum, and Liberal Education* (1978). He was coauthor of *The Teaching of Science* (1962).

After retiring from the University of Chicago, Schwab was a visiting fellow of the Center for the Study of Democratic Institutions (1973–88). He was Inglis Lecturer at Harvard University (1960) and held fellowships from the Center for Advanced Study in the Behavioral Sciences (1958–59) and the Guggenheim Foundation (1971–72).

REFERENCES: CA (NR-5); LE (1974); NYT, April 18, 1988, p. B8; WWW (9); *Science Education* 72 (July 1988): n.p.; Lee S. Shulman, ''Joseph Jackson Schwab,'' in Edward Shils, ed., *Remembering the University of Chicago* (University of Chicago Press, 1931), 452–68.

SEARS, Jesse Brundage. b. September 25, 1876, Kidder Missouri, to William Wallace and Angeline Augusta (Johnson) Sears. Married June 22, 1904, to Stella Louise Richardson. Children: three, including Robert Richardson Sears (q.v.). d. December 7, 1973.

Jesse Sears was a leader in the school survey movement. Through surveys he sought to evaluate schools scientifically and improve them.

Seats was raised on a Missouri farm. He taught in a nearby rural school before graduating from the Kidder, Missouri, high school. Then he taught in Daviess County rural schools (1897–1900) and at an elementary school in Kidder (1902–3) and was a supervising principal of Kingston, Missouri, schools (1903–5), and principal of Hamilton High School (1905–6).

Sears was a student and assistant of Elwood Cubberly (BDAE) at Stanford University, where he received the A.B. degree in 1909. He spent one year as instructor in the history of education at the University of Wisconsin (1909–10) and one year studying with Paul Monroe (BDAE) at Teachers College of Columbia University (1910–11). He returned to Stanford, where he became a professor in 1921 and retired in 1942.

Sears received the Ph.D. degree from Columbia University in 1920. His study, *Philanthropy in the History of Higher Education*, published in 1922 by the U.S.

Bureau of Education, was the first major study of the subject. In 1925 Sears published a guide, *The School Survey*. Many of his school surveys were published. He also wrote *Classroom Organization and Control* (1918), *The Place of Research in Educational Reconstruction* (1936), *City School Administrative Controls* (1938), *Public School Administration* (1947), *The Nature of the Administrative Process* (1950), and *Cubberly of Stanford and His Contribution to American Education* (with Adin D. Henderson, 1957). He edited *School Administration in the Twentieth Century* (1934).

In 1937 Sears was a consultant to the Educational Policies Commission and a staff member of the American Council on Education.

REFERENCES: LE (1948); NCAB (E: 79); WWW (5).

SEARS, Robert Richardson. b. August 31, 1908, Palo Alto, California, to Jesse Brundage (q.v.) and Stella Louise (Richardson) Sears. Married June 25, 1932, to Pauline Kirkpatrick Snedden. Children: two. d. May 22, 1989, Menlo Park, California.

Robert R. Sears conducted studies in the psychological development of children, child-rearing practices, aggression in children, and mother-child relationships. He continued the intelligence quotient (IQ) studies of Lewis Terman (BDAE).

Sears was raised in Palo Alto, California, where his father was on the faculty of Stanford University. He received the A.B. degree from Stanford (1929) and the Ph.D. degree from Yale University (1932), where he studied with Clark L. Hull (BDAE). He was instructor in psychology at the University of Illinois (1932–36) and concurrently clinical psychologist at the Institute for Juvenile Research in Chicago. Sears returned to Yale as assistant and associate professor of psychology (1936–42) and a staff member of the Institute for Human Relations.

At the University of Iowa (1942–49), Sears was professor of child psychology, successor to George D. Stoddard (BDAE) as director of the Child Welfare Research Station, and editor of the *Iowa Studies in Child Welfare*. He studied the discipline of children at home in preschool programs. Sears was professor of education and child psychology at the Harvard Graduate School of Education (1949–53), where he organized and directed the Laboratory of Human Development.

Sears returned to Stanford in 1953 as professor of psychology. He headed the Psychology Department (1953–61) and was dean of the School of Humanities and Sciences (1961–70) and David Starr Jordan Professor of Psychology (1970–75). He helped to establish and was a trustee of the Center for Advanced Study in the Behavioral Sciences. He organized the Stanford Boys' Town Center for Youth Development (later, Center for the Study of Children, Youth, and Families).

His writings included *Frustration and Aggression* (with others, 1939), *Objective Studies of Psychoanalytic Concepts* (1943), *Patterns of Child Rearing* (with E. Maccoby and Harry Levin, 1957), and *Identification and Child Rearing* (with Lucy Rau and Richard Alpert, 1965). He edited *Seven Ages of Man* (with S. Feldman, 1973).

Sears was chair of the Committee on Child Development (1947–50) of the National Research Council and vice chair of the Board of Directors of the Social Science Research Council (1950–53). He was president of the American Psychological Association (1951), Western Psychological Association (1964), and Society for Research in Child Development (1973–75). He received the Distinguished Scientific Contribution Award from the American Psychological Association in 1975. In 1980 the American Psychological Foundation gave its Gold Medal for lifetime contributions to psychology to Robert and Pauline Sears.

REFERENCES: CA (17–20R, 128); CB (1951, 1989); ECE; IESS; LE (1974); NYT, May 26, 1989, p. A18; WWW (10); *American Psychologist* 31 (January 1976): 60–64, 36 (January 1981): 88–91, and 45 (May 1990): 663–64; *Gifted Child Quarterly* 34 (Spring 1990): 83; Joan E. Grusec, ''Social Learning Theory and Developmental Psychology: The Legacies of Robert Sears and Albert Bandura (q.v.),'' *Developmental Psychology* 28 (1972): 776–85; Gardner Lindzey, ed., *A History of Psychology in Autobiography*, vol. 7 (W. H. Freeman, 1980); Henry W. Maier, *Three Theories of Child Raising: The Contributions of Erik H. Erikson* (q.v.), *Jean Piaget, and Robert R. Sears and Their Applications* (Harper and Row, 1969).

SELDEN, David Seeley. b. June 5, 1914, Dearborn, Michigan, to Arthur Willis and Florence Loretta (Seeley) Selden. Married 1932 to Isabel L. Igel; 1946 to Dolores Velez; March 22, 1956, to Bernice Cohen. Children: three.

David Selden followed a short career as a school teacher with a long career as an organizer of teachers' unions.

He earned the B.A. degree in education at Michigan State Normal College (later, Eastern Michigan University) in 1936 and the M.A. at Wayne State University in 1940. He taught social studies in Dearborn, Michigan (1936–43), where he was a charter member and local chapter president of the American Federation of Teachers (AFT, 1940–43). After wartime naval service, he was a writer and founder of a short-lived experimental college in Jacksonville, Florida.

Selden taught school briefly in upstate New York (1947–48) before going to work for the American Federation of Labor and its affiliate, the AFT. During the 1950s he teamed with Charles Cogen and Albert Shanker (q.v.) in leading the United Federation of Teachers (UFT), New York City branch of the AFT. In 1961 the UFT won an election to be bargaining agent for New York teachers. Selden sought unsuccessfully to have a role in the national union while Carl J. Megel (q.v.) was its president. In 1964, Charles Cogen became AFT president, and Selden became his special assistant. In 1968 and 1970 Selden won close elections as AFT president; in 1972 he lost a bid for a third two-year term and retired from the union.

During Selden's four-year presidency he initiated, but could not conclude, discussions with Elizabeth Koontz (q.v.), president of the National Education

Association (NEA), about a merger of AFT and NEA. His militancy as a unionist and his strong positions on national political issues made him a controversial figure. He was author of *The Teacher Rebellion* (1985), a memoir.

REFERENCES: BDAL; LE (1974); *American School and University* 36 (November 1963): 44; Maurice R. Berube, *Teacher Politics: The Influence of Unions* (Greenwood Press, 1988); Robert J. Braun, *Teachers and Power: The Story of the American Federation of Teachers* (Simon and Schuster, 1972); William Edward Eaton, *The American Federation of Teachers, 1916–1961* (Southern Illinois University Press, 1975); Marjorie Murphy, *Blackboard Unions: The AFT and the NEA, 1900–1980* (Cornell University Press, 1990).

SHANE, Harold Gray. b. August 11, 1914, Milwaukee, Wisconsin, to Bert L. and Grace (Gray) Shane. Married September 1, 1938, to Ruth Marion Williams; July 6, 1974, to Catherine McKenzie. Children: four. d. July 12, 1993, Bloomington, Indiana.

Harold Gray Shane did pioneering work in educational futurism. He believed educators helped to create the future and believed there was a need to redesign the school curriculum. He advocated teaching transferable vocational skills and skills in critical thinking.

Shane attended schools in Detroit, Chicago, Los Angeles, and Milwaukee. In 1935 he received the B.E. degree from Milwaukee State Teachers College (later, University of Wisconsin–Milwaukee). He taught several grade levels in the schools of Cincinnati, Ohio (1935–37). While a principal in Toledo, Ohio, from 1937 to 1941, he received the M.A. degree from Ohio State University (1939). Shane was supervisor of elementary education for the state of Ohio (1942–43). In 1943 he earned the Ph.D. degree from Ohio State University. During U.S. Navy service (1943–46) he wrote fourteen navy textbooks and manuals.

Shane succeeded Carleton Washburne (BDAE) as superintendent of schools in Winnetka, Illinois (1946–49), then was professor of education at Northwestern University (1949–59). In 1959 he went to Indiana University as dean of the School of Education. The school experimented with changes in the teacher education program through a Ford Foundation grant. Leaving the deanship in 1965, Shane continued as professor of education until 1983.

Shane was a visiting professor at several universities and a consultant to many local school systems and the U.S. Office of Education. He served on the Board of Directors of the Center for Applied Research in Education. In addition to writing several hundred articles for professional and popular journals, he wrote, coauthored, edited, and contributed to numerous books. Among the books were *Creative School Administration in Elementary and Junior High Schools* (with Wilbur A. Yauch, 1954), *Improving Language Arts Instruction through Research* (with June Grant Mulry, 1963), *Linguistics and the Classroom Teacher* (1967), *The Educational Significance of the Future* (1973), *Curriculum Change* (editor, 1977), *Educating for a New Millennium: Views of 132 International Scholars* (with M. Bernadine Tabler, 1981), *Teaching and Learning in a Mi-*

croelectronic Age (1987), and *Curriculum for a New Millennium* (with Wilma S. Longstreet, 1993). He served on the editorial boards of *Childhood Education* (1947–49) and *Phi Delta Kappan* (1961–80).

Shane received two Educational Press Association awards and two Enoch Pratt Memorial Library Outstanding Educator Book of the Year awards. He was president of the Association for Supervision and Curriculum Development (1973–74) and a director of the National Society for the Study of Education (1968–78).

REFERENCES: CA (NR-21, 141); ECE; LE (1974); NYT, July 16, 1993, p. D20; RPE; WW (1990–91); Ron Brandt, ''On Education and the Future: A Conversation with Harold Shane,'' *Educational Leadership* 41 (September 1983): 11–13; Sandra M. Long, ''Reflections on the Past and Visions of the Future: An Interview with Harold G. Shane,'' *Phi Delta Kappan* 67 (March 1986): 527–31.

SHANKER, Albert. b. September 14, 1928, New York City, to Morris and Mamie (Burko) Shanker. Married March 18, 1961, to Edith Gerber. Children: four. d. February 22, 1997, New York City.

Albert Shanker began his career as a beleaguered sixth grade teacher on Manhattan's Upper West Side in 1952. He led the United Federation of Teachers (UFT) in its successful campaign to win the right to collective bargaining in 1960. As national president of the American Federation of Teachers (AFT), Shanker used his weekly, syndicated column, ''Where We Stand,'' to define and defend the teaching profession to the American public. He was known for the courage to speak his mind even in the face of contrary professional opinion. He opposed school vouchers and privatization of education but was also a strong advocate for discipline and standards in schools.

Shanker graduated from Stuyvesant High School in New York City. He received the B.A. degree from the University of Illinois in 1949 and the M.A. from Columbia University for studies in philosophy and mathematics and completed course work for the doctorate. While teaching in New York City (1952–59) he joined the New York Teachers Guild (later, UFT). He was an organizer for the AFT (1959–60). He worked with David Selden (q.v.) and assisted Charles Cogen in the UFT, succeeding Cogen as president (1964–85). Shanker built the local AFT unit into the largest teachers' union anywhere. In the 1968 controversy over decentralization of the New York City schools, Shanker was concerned that excessive local control would threaten teachers' rights and job security. He edited the UFT publication, *United Teacher.*

Shanker became president of the AFT in 1974. He was outspoken on educational issues and in 1985 advocated national examinations for beginning teachers. He was interested in the professionalization of teachers and served on the National Board for Professional Teaching Standards. Shanker also was a vice president of the American Federation of Labor–Congress of Industrial Organizations (AFL–CIO). He was a charter member of the Congress of Racial Equality (CORE) and a member of the educational task force of the Committee for Economic Development. He served on many national boards and committees and wrote extensively for periodicals and newspapers.

REFERENCES: BDAL; CB (1969); CHE, November 21, 1990, p. A3; LE (1974); NYT, February 24, 1997, pp. A9, A12; RPE; WW (1996); *Education Week* 15 (February 21, 1996): 31–37; *Educational Leadership* 50 (March 1993): 46–49; George R. Kaplan, ''Shining Lights in High Places: Education's Top Four Leaders and Their Heirs,'' *Phi Delta Kappan* 67 (September 1985): 7+; Dickson A. Mungazi, *Where He Stands: Albert Shanker of the American Federation of Teachers* (Praeger, 1995); A. H. Raskin, ''Shanker's Great Leap,'' NYT *Magazine* (September 9, 1993): 64+; Diane Ravitch, ''In Memoriam: Albert Shanker, 1928–1997,'' *New Leader* 80 (February 24, 1997): 3–4.

SHAPLEY, John. b. August 7, 1890, Jasper County, Missouri, to Willis Harlow and Sarah (Stowell) Shapley. Married September 19, 1918, to Fern Helen Rusk. Children: two. d. September 8, 1978, Washington, D.C.

John Shapley was instrumental in developing art history as a discipline in colleges and universities.

Shapley received the A.B. degree from the University of Missouri in 1912 and the M.A. degree from Princeton University in 1913. He assisted John Pickard in founding the College Art Association in 1912. He was a fellow of the American Academy in Rome (1913–14) and a Proctor fellow (1914–15). In 1914 he earned the Ph.D. degree from the University of Vienna. Shapley was assistant professor of art at Brown University from 1915 to 1924. During World War I he taught mathematics to military personnel.

From 1924 to 1929 he was professor of art at New York University. The Carnegie Corporation financed, and Shapley directed, a project that supplied art history materials to high schools and colleges in the United States and Great Britain. Shapley wrote the captions for the colored art reproductions of the Carnegie Sets. These materials provided a start for the widespread study of art history. In 1929 Shapley went to the University of Chicago and in 1939 to Johns Hopkins University. He moved to Washington, D.C., and taught art and archaeology in area universities, first at Catholic University of America (1952–60). He spent three years at the University of Baghdad in Iraq (1960–63). After returning to Washington, he taught at Howard University (1963–70), George Washington University (1972–75), and Federal College (1976–77, later, University of the District of Columbia.)

Shapley contributed to the *Encyclopedia Britannica*, the *Dictionary of Religion and Ethics*, and the sixteen-volume *A Survey of Persian Art*. With his wife he coauthored *Comparisons in Art* (1957). He was president of the College Art Association (1923–38) and edited the *Art Bulletin* (1921–39), helping with its financing in the 1930s. For his contributions to the understanding of Persian culture, he was decorated by the shah of Iran in 1960. He received the Carnegie Corporation Medal. Shapley served as president of the Byzantine Institute and associate director of the Iranian Institute.

REFERENCES: CA (81–84); WP, September 13, 1978, p. C8; WWW (8); *Who's Who in American Art* (R. R. Bowker, 1978).

SHARP, Zerna A. b. August 12, 1889, Hillisburg, Indiana, to Charles and Lottie (Smith) Sharp. Married: no. d. June 17, 1981, Frankfort, Indiana.

Zerna Sharp conceived the idea for Dick and Jane reading textbooks, which teachers in many elementary schools used from the 1930s to 1972. The method used with Dick and Jane books was known as ''look-say'' and involved repetition of words. Only one new word was introduced on each page, and only five in each story. While Sharp did not write the books, she worked with others who did. Among them were William S. Gray (BDAE), and Eleanor B. Campbell, an illustrator, whose pictures showed the actions used in the stories.

Sharp graduated from high school in Hillisburg. She studied at Marion Normal College (later, Indiana Wesleyan University) and was a teacher in Indiana in Hillisburg, Kirklin, and La Porte. She also attended Columbia University. The idea for the textbooks was developed when Sharp served as a reading consultant and textbook editor for the Scott Foresman Company.

In her later years critics of her concept objected that the parents were stereotyped and that many students could not relate to a family with two children, a dog named Spot, and a cat named Puff.

REFERENCES: CA (104); NYT, June 19, 1981, p. B6; WP, June 20, 1981, p. C4; *AB Bookman's Weekly* 68 (July 27, 1981): 419; *Time* 117 (June 29, 1981): 67.

SHAW, Pauline Agassiz. b. February 6, 1841, Neuchâtel, Switzerland, to Jean Louis Rodolphe (BDAE) and Cécile (Braun) Agassiz. Married November 30, 1860, to Quincy Adams Shaw. Children: five. D. February 10, 1917, Boston.

An educational and social pioneer, Pauline Agassiz Shaw began movements to establish kindergartens and day nurseries. She advocated manual training and vocational guidance.

She began her schooling in Switzerland. Her mother died when she was seven years old, and her father, a professor of natural science, came to the United States. After his remarriage, his children joined him in 1850. Shaw attended a school conducted by her stepmother, Elizabeth Cabot Cary Agassiz (BDAE).

After her own marriage Pauline Agassiz Shaw established a school in Boston for her children and their friends at 6 Marlboro Street, where she introduced progressive methods. In 1877 she opened two kindergartens, in Jamaica Plain and Brookline, which began the kindergarten movement in the East. Also in that year she established the first day nursery.

By 1883 Shaw supported thirty-one free kindergartens in the Boston area. Many were located in public schools with her financing. Mothers' meetings and parents' clubs were included in them. Boston had earlier discontinued the public kindergartens established by Elizabeth Peabody (BDAE) and others. In 1888 fourteen of Shaw's kindergartens were accepted into the Boston public school system.

Many of the day nurseries evolved into settlement houses. Shaw's Civic Service House opened in 1901 to train immigrants in citizenship. It provided a link between schools and the community. Shaw also established the Cottage Place

Neighborhood House (1876), Children's House (later, Roxbury Neighborhood House, 1878), Ruggles Street Neighborhood House, (1879), and Moore Street Neighborhood House (later, Cambridge Neighborhood House, 1879).

In 1888 Shaw financed the Sloyd Training School of Boston, for teaching sloyd (manual training) and training sloyd teachers. It developed into a school of craftsmanship and design. Shaw endowed a course in vocational guidance at Harvard University's Department of Education. In 1901 Shaw founded the Boston Equal Suffrage Association for Good Government; she served as its president for ten years.

REFERENCES: BCAW; DAB; NAW; NCAB (27: 485); NYT, February 11, 1917, p. 23; WR; *Pioneers of the Kindergarten in America* (Century, 1924); Robert A. Woods and Albert J. Kennedy, eds., *Handbook of Settlements* (Arno Press, 1970).

SHEATS, Paul Henry. b. December 5, 1907, Tiffin, Ohio, to Edward Hamlin and Katherine Ann (Koch) Sheats. Married 1929 to Dorothea Burns; November 21, 1942, to Helen Johnson Taylor; June 16, 1967, to June Maseeger Dow. Children: three. d. August 12, 1984.

Paul Sheats sought to bridge the gap between vocational and liberal education. Believing that a one-fifth participation rate in adult education was too low, he urged that continuing education for adults be made part of the standard workweek. His writing emphasized the importance of education for responsible citizenship, which he argued was achievable through forums for youth and further education for adults.

Sheats earned the A.B. degree at Heidelberg College (1929), the A.M. at Columbia University (1930), and the Ph.D. at Yale University (1936). He served as instructor of government at the New York State College for Teachers (later, State University of New York at Albany, 1930–34), directed the Federal Forum Project in Chattanooga, Tennessee (1936–37), and taught on the faculty of education at the University of Wisconsin (1937–40).

From 1940 his career focused on adult education. He was successively editor of the *Adult Education Bulletin* (1940–42), administrative assistant for the Federal Forum demonstration project in the U.S. Office of Education (1942–43), director of New Tools for Learning (1943–44) and Town Hall Inc. (1944–46) in New York City, and associate director of University Extension at the University of California at Berkeley (1946–49). At Berkeley from 1949 until his retirement in 1975 he was professor of education.

Among many public service roles, Sheats was a consultant on adult education to the Ford Foundation in 1951, was vice chair of the U.S. National Commission to UNESCO (1954–56), and member of the President's Panel on Vocational Education (1961–62). He served on the Board of Directors of National Testing Laboratories (1961–64) and was resident fellow of the Oxford (England) University Extra-Mural Delegacy (1967) and senior consultant to the Southern Regional Education Board (1970–73). He was president of the Department of Adult Education, National Education Association (1942–44); American Adult Education Association (1953–54); and National University Extension Association (1962–63). He sat on the executive committee of the National Association of State Universities and Land Grant Colleges (1963–66).

Sheats wrote *Citizenship Education through the Social Studies* (with R. W. Frederick, 1936), *Forums for Young People* (with J. W. Studebaker, BDAE, and C. S. Williams, 1937), *Education and the Quest for a Middle Way* (1938), *Forums on the Air* (1939), *Adult Education* (with others, 1953), *The Case against the Adult Dropout* (1965), *Developing Community Service and Continuing Education Programs in California Higher Education Institutions* (with others, 1972), and *Developing Community Services in the Seventies* (1975). He served on the editorial board of *Lifelong Learning, The Adult Years* (1977–80). He received the Delbert Clark (1970) and Julius M. Nolte (1975) Awards.

REFERENCES: WWW (9); Who's Who in the World (1984–85).

SHEDD, Mark Redans. b. June 1, 1926, Quincy, Massachusetts, to Guy Vaughn and Sarah Kathryn (Redans) Shedd. Married October 18, 1968, to Shirley Greene. Children: six. d. November 17, 1986, Portland, Maine.

Mark R. Shedd was an innovative, progressive, and controversial administrator, especially during his tenure as superintendent of the Englewood, New Jersey, and Philadelphia school systems. At one time he suggested that the federal government nationalize operation and funding of the nation's largest school systems.

Shedd received the A.B. degree from the University of Maine in 1950 and the M.Ed. from Harvard University in 1954. From 1950 to 1960 he served as a school administrator in Maine at Bangor, Caribou, and Auburn. After receiving the Ed.D. degree from Harvard in 1960, he was a rural district superintendent with the Connecticut Department of Education.

Shedd became superintendent of the Englewood schools in 1962. While he worked to lessen racial imbalance, Shedd's progress was considered too slow by black parents, who initiated boycotts and sit-ins in 1963 and 1966.

In 1967 Shedd became superintendent of the Philadelphia schools. During his five-year tenure the school budget doubled, teachers salaries increased significantly, and a building program was begun. Students gained a bill of rights and places on curriculum committees. During the 1971 mayoral election Frank Rizzo, then police commissioner, stated that, if elected, he would fire Shedd for being too innovative and too easy on troublemaking students. Shedd resigned but remained as a special assistant until his contract was fulfilled.

From 1972 to 1974 Shedd served as visiting professor at the Harvard Graduate School of Education. He was commissioner of education in Connecticut from 1974 to 1983. He advocated a work-study program for high school students and developed a statewide school desegregation plan. In 1983 he went to the University of Southern Maine as professor of public policy and management.

In 1968 President Lyndon Johnson named Shedd to head a fourteen-member advisory committee to secure good teachers for schools serving disadvantaged students. While in Philadelphia, he received the A. Philip Randolph Award of the Negro Trade Union Leadership Council (1968), the Man of the Year Award of the Educational Equality League (1971), and the Distinguished Service Award of the Philadelphia Urban Coalition (1972).

REFERENCES: NYT, November 19, 1986, p. D27; WW (1986–87); Wallace Roberts, "Can Urban Schools Be Reformed?" *Saturday Review* 52 (May 17, 1969): 70+.

SHELLY, Mary Josephine. b. February 17, 1902, Grand Rapids, Michigan, to James Robert and Mary Isabelle (Hayes) Shelly. Married: no. d. August 6, 1976, New York City.

Mary Josephine Shelly was a leader in the physical education and dance education of women in two quite different settings: Bennington College and the military.

Shelly taught in the public schools of Grand Rapids (1922–23) and Battle Creek (1923–24), Michigan. She was an instructor at the University of Oregon (1924–28) and received the B.A. degree there in 1926. She earned the M.A. degree at Teachers College of Columbia University (1929), continuing there as an instructor (1929–32), then was administrative assistant and instructor in physical education at New College of Columbia University (1932–35). At the University of Chicago, Shelley taught physical education, chaired the Women's Physical Education Department, and was assistant to the dean of students (1935–38).

Shelly was cofounder with Martha Hill (q.v.) of the School of the Dance at Bennington (Vermont) College. She was administrative director of the school (1934–38) and educational assistant to the president (1928–42) and also served as administrative director of the Bennington School of the Arts.

In 1942 Shelly took a leave of absence from Bennington to take charge of physical training in the Women's Naval Reserve. She was commissioned in the WAVES as assistant for the women's reserve to the director of training of the navy. She directed educational programs and assisted with demobilization after the war. She returned to Bennington in 1946 as educational assistant to the president. In the Korean conflict she commanded the WAF (Women in the Air Force). Returning to Bennington once again, she was director of student personnel (1953–54).

Shelly was director of public relations for the Girl Scouts of America from 1954 to 1956. She was decorated with a commendation medal from the navy and the Legion of Merit from the air force. She and Martha Hill both served on the editorial board of *Dance Observer*.

REFERENCES: CB (1951, 1976); NYT, August 7, 1976, p. 22; WWAW (1968–69); WWW (7); Sali Ann Kriegsman, *Modern Dance in America—The Bennington Years* (G. K. Hall, 1981).

SILBER, John Robert. b. August 15, 1926, San Antonio, Texas, to Paul G. and Jewell (Joslin) Silber. Married July 12, 1947, to Kathryn Underwood. Children: seven.

John Silber worked at only two universities in his career, first the University of Texas at Austin, where he joined the faculty in 1955 and served as dean of arts and sciences (1967–70), then Boston University, where he was president (1971–96). At both institutions his outspoken views on education, politics, and American life and values made him a very controversial public figure. At Texas he was widely believed to be a liberal and at Boston equally judged a conservative, though his positions were usually less notable for easy classification than for the strength with which he held and expressed them. He propounded a vigorous, confrontational Socratic teaching method, insisted that only excellent faculty were welcome under his leadership, and criticized the lifestyles and moral character of college students.

At the University of Texas he conflicted with the chancellor and chair of the Board of Regents and was dismissed after three years as dean. At Boston University he survived repeated efforts by faculty and deans to have him dismissed, particularly during the late 1970s, when he successfully resisted creation of a faculty union and broke a strike by faculty, librarians, and other employees. During his presidency the stature and resources of Boston University increased dramatically.

Silber earned the B.A. degree with highest honors at Trinity University (Texas) in 1947 when he was twenty years old. He spent one year studying divinity at Yale University and one year studying law at the University of Texas at Austin before entering the graduate program in philosophy at Yale. There he was awarded the M.A. degree in 1952 and the Ph.D. in 1956.

Silber gained renewed national attention when he arranged in 1989 to have the School of Education of his university manage the public schools of Chelsea, Massachusetts, and when he was Democratic nominee for governor of the state in 1990.

His writings included *The Ethical Significance of Kant's Religion* (1960) and *Straight Shooting: What's Wrong with America and How to Fix It* (1989). He was chair of the Texas Society to Abolish Capital Punishment (1960–69) and served on the boards of the National Humanities Faculty (1968–73), WGBH Educational Foundation (from 1971), National Association of Independent Colleges and Universities (1976–81), and National Captioning Institute (from 1985), among others. He served on the National Bipartisan Commission on Central America (1983–84) and the Presidential Advisory Board on Radio Broadcasting to Cuba (1985–92). Among many honors and awards, he received a Fulbright scholar grant to the Federal Republic of Germany (1959–60), a Guggenheim Fellowship (1963–64), the Harbison Award for distinguished teaching (1966), the Distinguished Public Service Award of the Anti-Defamation League of B'nai B'rith (1989), and the Horatio Alger Award (1992).

REFERENCES: CB (1984); LE (1974); NYT, March 30, 1996, p. 10; WD (1994–96); WW (1996); Helen Epstein, "Crusader on the Charles," NYT *Magazine*, April 23, 1989, pp. 26–29+; *Newsmakers* (Gale Research, 1990); *Time* 135 (June 18, 1990): 19.

SIZEMORE, Barbara Ann Laffoon. b. December 17, 1927, Chicago, to Sylvester Walter and Delila Mae (Alexander) Laffoon. Married June 28, 1947, to Furman E. Sizemore; September 29, 1979, to Jake Milliones, Jr. Children: two.

The first African-American woman to lead a major urban school system, Barbara Sizemore was a persuasive advocate for the "effective schools" movement. As an administrator she emphasized the need for focus and accountability in schools in low-income neighborhoods. Her two-year term as superintendent in the District of Columbia (1973–75) was punctuated by disputes with the school board rooted in part in her commitment to decentralization and community involvement but also in citywide politics.

Sizemore attended public schools in Terre Haute, Indiana, and graduated with the B.A. degree from Northwestern University in 1947. She earned the M.A. degree at Northwestern in 1954 and the Ph.D. in educational administration at the University of Chicago in 1979.

Sizemore taught English and reading in public elementary and junior high schools of Chicago (1950–63) and was a principal of elementary (1963–65) and high schools (1965–67). She also served as an adjunct faculty member at Northeastern Illinois University (1965–71). In 1969, after two years of graduate study at the University of Chicago, she became district superintendent of the Woodlawn Experimental Schools, under a grant in cooperation with community activists and the Midwest Administration Center of the University of Chicago, directed by Roald Campbell (q.v.). She was proposal development coordinator for the Chicago public schools (1971–73).

In 1973 Sizemore was briefly associate secretary of the American Association of School Administrators before accepting appointment as superintendent of schools in Washington, D.C. Following her dismissal in October 1975, she was an independent consultant and campaigned unsuccessfully for a seat on the city council in Washington, then joined the faculty of the University of Pittsburgh (1977–92). She was dean of the School of Education at DePaul University from 1992.

Sizemore's doctoral thesis was published as *The Ruptured Diamond: The Politics of Decentralization of the District of Columbia Public Schools* (1981). She received the Human Rights Award of the United Nations Association (1985).

REFERENCES: BWA; NBAW; WWAW (1993–94); WWBA (1993–94); *Education Week*, March 13, 1996; Nancy L. Arnez, "Selected Black Female Superintendents of Public Schools Systems," *Journal of Negro Education* 51 (Summer 1982): 311–14; *Phi Delta Kappan* 57 (February 1976): 425.

SIZER, Theodore Ryland. b. June 23, 1932, New Haven, Connecticut, to Theodore and Carolina Wheelwright (Foster) Sizer. Married July 2, 1955, to Nancy Ellen Faust. Children: four.

Theodore Sizer's broad experience as a teacher, administrator, researcher, and theorist of effective schooling made him an influential school reformer. The nine educational principles Sizer articulated in *Horace's Compromise: The Dilemma of the American High School* (1984) became the organizing framework for his Coalition of Essential Schools, which included 940 schools in thirty-seven states and two foreign countries. His initiative attracted a $500 million gift from Walter H. Annenberg and made Brown University a national center for collaborative reform and professional renewal in schooling.

Sizer received the A.B. degree from Yale University in 1953 and served in the U.S. Army from 1953 to 1955. He taught in West Roxbury, Massachusetts, and Melbourne, Australia. He earned M.A.T. (1957) and Ph.D. (1961) degrees from Harvard University. Sizer was an assistant professor and director of the M.A.T. program at Harvard (1961–64). As dean of the Harvard Graduate School of Education from 1964 to 1972, he guided expansion of research and led the faculty to national prominence. From 1972 to 1981 Sizer was headmaster at Phillips Academy in Andover, Massachusetts.

In 1981 Sizer became chair of the Study of High Schools group, which led to publication of *Horace's Compromise*. He went to Brown University in 1984 as professor and chair of the Education Department. He founded the Coalition of Essential Schools with seven public and private schools. Sizer felt fewer subjects should be taught in high schools, but in greater depth. He hoped teachers would have fewer students throughout the day and wanted a personalized education. In 1988 the coalition received support from the Education Commission of the States. After the Annenberg gift it was renamed the Annenberg National Institute for School Reform.

Sizer was author of *Secondary Schools at the Turn of the Century* (1964), *Places for Learning, Places for Joy* (1973), *Horace's School: Redesigning the American High School* (1992), and *Horace's Hope* (1996). He edited *The Age of the Academies* (1964) and *Religion and Public Education* (1967). He was a Guggenheim fellow in 1971 and in 1991 was one of three educators to receive the Harold W. McGraw Prize in Education.

REFERENCES: CA (NR-13); CHE, November 7, 1990, p. A3; LE (1974); WD (1994–96); WW (1996); *Educational Leadership* 51 (September 1993): 53–56; *Time* 123 (February 20, 1984): 81; *U.S. News and World Report* 108 (February 26, 1990): 50–55.

SLOWE, Lucy Diggs. b. July 4, 1885, Berryville, Virginia, to Henry and Fannie (Potter) Slowe. Married: no. d. October 21, 1937, Washington, D.C.

Lucy Diggs Slowe influenced women's education as the first dean of women at Howard University. Her innovations in the position and her beliefs about the role of deans had an influence beyond the Howard campus.

Slowe was orphaned at the age of six and was raised by an aunt. They lived in Alexandria, Virginia, and in Baltimore, where Slowe graduated from the Colored (later, Douglass) High School in 1904. She attended Howard University on a scholarship, graduating in 1908, and then taught English at Douglass High School in Baltimore from 1908 to 1915. After earning the M.A. degree in English from Columbia University in 1915, she taught at Armstrong High School in the District of Columbia (1915–19). In 1919 Slowe was asked to organize the district's first junior high school for blacks. She served as principal of the new Shaw Junior High School (1919–22). While at Shaw she began the first integrated in-service training extension course for junior high school teachers.

Slowe became Howard University's first dean of women in 1922, serving until her death in 1937. She was also associate professor of English. She believed women needed to be prepared for the job market and wanted careers available to women outside the traditional ones. She wanted to foster initiative in women and desired that the content of courses be related to the community. A Women's Vocational Seminar was organized, and she formed the Women Students' Cultural Series in 1929. She urged more dormitories for women. After Mordecai Johnson (BDAE) became Howard's president in 1926, Slowe had serious disagreements with him. Johnson removed her from the Council of Deans.

While a student Slowe was cofounder of Alpha Kappa Alpha, a black sorority. She was first president of the National Association of Colored Women (1923–29), while also a member of its counterpart, the American Association of University Women. With Mary McLeod Bethune (BDAE), in 1935 she founded the National Council of Negro Women, which she served as its first secretary. She was chair of the Association of Advisors to Women in Colored Schools.

In her younger years Slowe was a national tennis champion. Howard University named a dormitory for her, and a stained glass window in the university chapel was dedicated to her. Slowe Elementary School in the District of Columbia was also named for her.

REFERENCES: AAW; BWA; DANB; NAW; NBAW; WEUS; WR; Patricia Bell-Scott, ''The Business of Being Dean of Women,'' *Initiatives* 54 (Summer 1991): 35–41; Geraldine J. Clifford, ed. *Lone Voyagers: Academic Women in Coeducational Universities, 1890–1937* (Feminist Press at the City University of New York, 1989); Geneva C. Turner, ''School Names,'' *The Negro History Bulletin* 18 (January 1955): 90–91.

SMITH, Hilda Worthington. b. June 19, 1888, New York City, to John Jewell and Mary Helen (Hall) Smith. Married: no. d. March 3, 1984, Washington, D.C.

Hilda ''Jane'' Worthington Smith was a pioneer in labor education, which she believed should be separate from regular adult education programs. She helped to plan and for thirteen years was director of the Bryn Mawr Summer School for Women Workers. The idea of the school was conceived by M. Carey Thomas (BDAE), president of Bryn Mawr College. Opened in 1921, the school was a pioneer in the labor education movement and became a model for similar labor schools. Students from diverse backgrounds came from throughout the United States for eight-week sessions. Women studied nonvocational subjects and were trained in skills of participation through self-government.

Smith was raised in New York City where she graduated from the Veltin School. She received B.M. (1910) and M.A. (1911) degrees from Bryn Mawr

College and a diploma from the New York School of Philanthropy (later, Columbia University Graduate School of Social Work). In 1916 she was invited back to Bryn Mawr to develop a community center devised by Susan Kingsbury (q.v.), which proved to be very successful. It provided after-school activities for children, classes in English, a kindergarten, and hot lunches for schoolchildren. In 1919 Smith became dean at Bryn Mawr; she left that post in 1922, when the summer school offices were established in New York City.

As other labor schools were organized, Smith helped to establish the Affiliated Schools for Workers and served as chairman. For four years (1929–33) she operated the Vineyard Shore School at the Smith family's summer home on the Hudson River at West Park, New York. Women industrial workers attended eight-month sessions. The school had to close because of financial problems during the depression. The facility later housed the Hudson Shore Labor School.

Virginia Gildersleeve (BDAE), president of Barnard College, asked Smith's assistance in planning the Barnard Summer School. Smith served as an adviser. Columbia University established workers' morning classes, which Smith had proposed.

In 1933 Harry Hopkins hired Smith for the Worker's Education Section, Emergency Education Division, of the Federal Emergency Relief Administration (FERA). She helped with development of a new national policy to use unemployed teachers to instruct unemployed workers. She also directed Camps and Schools for Unemployed Women, established in 1934. Known as "She-she-she" camps, these did not garner the support that Civilian Conservation Corps (CCC) camps won, and the program ended in 1937.

During World War II Smith served with Community Services in War Housing projects in public housing developments. In 1965 Smith was hired as a consultant in the Office of Economic Opportunity in the Training and Technical Assistance Division. She retired in 1972 at the age of eighty-four. Smith wrote *Women Workers at the Bryn Mawr Summer School* (1929), *Education and the Worker-Student* (with Jean Carter Ogden, 1934), and *Opening Vistas in Workers' Education: An Autobiography* (1978).

REFERENCES: CA (112); NYT, March 14, 1984, p. B10; WEUS; WP, March 6, 1984, p. B7; Joyce L. Kornbluh, *A New Deal for Workers' Education: The Workers' Service Program, 1933–1942* (University of Illinois Press, 1987); Joyce L. Kornbluh and Mary Frederickson, eds., *Sisterhood and Solidarity: Workers' Education for Women, 1914–1984* (Temple University Press, 1984); Susan Ware, *Beyond Suffrage: Women in the New Deal* (Harvard University Press, 1981).

SOLOMON, Barbara Miller. b. February 12, 1919, Boston, to Benjamin Allen and Bessie (Pinsky) Miller Skirball. Married May 13, 1940, to Peter Herman Solomon. Children: three. d. August 20, 1992, Cambridge, Massachusetts.

Barbara Solomon was a leader in women's studies, teaching the first course on the history of American women at Harvard University, where she was the first woman assistant dean. She received the A.B. degree from Radcliffe College in 1940 and Ph.D. from Harvard in 1953. She taught history at Wheelock College in Massachusetts (1957–59) before going to Radcliffe in 1960, where she was associate dean (1963–70). She lectured on history and literature at Harvard (1965–74) and was a research fellow (1968–69), assistant dean (1970–74), and senior lecturer (1974–85).

Solomon was on the advisory committee for the Schlesinger Library on the History of Women in America from 1965, chaired it during 1975–76, and was scholar in residence from 1985. She held a Guggenheim Fellowship (1976–77) and was a Radcliffe Mellon scholar (1979–80). Her books included *Pioneers in Service: The History of the Associated Jewish Philanthropies of Boston* (1956); *Ancestors and Immigrants: A Changing New England Tradition* (1965), used as a college textbook; and *In the Company of Educated Women* (1985), which won the Frederic W. Ness Award of the Association of American Colleges (later, and Universities). She edited *Travels in New England and New York by Timothy Dwight* (BDAE, four volumes, 1969) and the twelve-volume *Educated Women* (1987).

REFERENCES: NYT, August 23, 1992, p. 46; WWAW (1972); WWW (10).

SOWELL, Thomas. b. June 30, 1930, Gastonia, North Carolina. Married to Alma Jean Parr. Children: two.

In an era when most African Americans who achieved prominence through academic careers were liberal, Thomas Sowell took strongly conservative positions on issues concerning economics, education, and race in the United States. Sowell was a severe critic of the ineffectiveness of American education. He disputed prevalent assumptions about the inferiority of educational opportunity for African Americans and the need for affirmative action programs as too simplistic and contrary to empirical evidence.

Sowell dropped out of Stuyvesant High School in New York City. He completed his schooling while serving in the U.S. Marine Corps. He earned the A.B. degree at Harvard University (1958), the A.M. at Columbia University (1959), and the Ph.D. in economics at the University of Chicago (1968). He was an economist with the U.S. Department of Labor (1961–62), taught economics at Douglass College of Rutgers University (1962–63) and Howard University (1963–64), and was an economic analyst with the American Telephone and Telegraph Company (AT&T, 1964–65). He served on the faculties of Cornell University (1965–69), Brandeis University (1969–70) and the University of California at Los Angeles (1970–74). He was concurrently a project director for the Urban Institute (1972–74). During 1976–77 Sowell was a fellow of the Center for Advanced Study of the Behavioral Sciences. From 1980, he was a senior fellow at the Hoover Institution.

In addition to many books on economic topics, he was author of *Black Education: Myths and Tragedies* (1972), *Education: Assumptions versus History* (1986), *Choosing a College* (1989), *Inside American Education: The Decline, the Deception, the Dogmas* (1993), and *Race and Culture* (1994).

REFERENCES: CA (NR-26); CB (1981); EBA; WD (1994–96); WW (1996); WWE; WWBA (1994/95); Barbara Carlisle Bigelow, ed., *Contemporary Black Biography*, vol. 2 (Gale Research, 1992); Peter Brimelow, "A Man Alone," *Forbes* 140 (August 24, 1987): 40+; *Newsweek* 97 (March 9, 1981): 29+; Alan Wolfe, "School Daze," *New Republic* 208 (February 8, 1993): 25+.

SPEARE, Frank Palmer. b. 1869, Boston, to Charles and Jeanette (Palmer) Speare. Married December 24, 1897, to May Cushing Whiting; July 6, 1914, to Katharine May Vinton. Children: one. d. May 28, 1954, Boston.

The founder of Northeastern University, Frank Speare held various employment in the first half-dozen years after his college graduation: as a teacher in school programs of the Boston Young Men's Christian Association (YMCA), evening school administrator in nearby Medford, Massachusetts, and high school principal. The Evening Institute of the Boston YMCA, which he directed beginning in 1896, evolved gradually into an institution of higher education. Speare was president until he retired in 1940.

Speare graduated from Bridgewater (Massachusetts) State Teachers College (later, State College) in 1889 and undertook further studies at Harvard University.

His educational experiment evolved rapidly. A YMCA Department of Law, which would develop into the Northeastern University School of Law, opened in 1898. Within a decade, Speare added courses of study in commerce and engineering and a pioneering work-study program. The institution was renamed Northeastern College in 1916 and University in 1923.

Speare received the master of humanics degree from the International YMCA Training School (later, Springfield College) in 1911. He was president of the Massachusetts Schoolmaster's Club during 1933–34. He served concurrently as chairman of the board and president of Chandler Secretarial School in Boston, retiring from it in 1947.

REFERENCES: NYT, May 30, 1954, p. 45; WWW (5); Everett C. Marston, *Origin and Development of Northeastern University, 1898–1960* (Northeastern University, 1961).

SPINDLER, George Dearborn. b. February 28, 1920, Stevens Point, Wisconsin, to Frank Nicholas and Winifred (Hatch) Spindler. Married May 29, 1942, to Louise Schaubel. Children: one.

George D. Spindler was a cultural anthropologist interested particularly in education and schooling as cultural institutions. He wrote extensively on these topics.

Spindler received the B.S. degree from Central State Teachers College (later, University of Wisconsin–Stevens Point) in 1940, the M.A. from the University of Wisconsin in 1947, and the Ph.D. from the University of California at Los Angeles in 1952. He served with U.S. Army Intelligence (1942–45). At Stanford University he was a member of the faculty in anthropology (1952–78). He was visiting professor at several other universities.

Spindler served as editor of *American Anthropologist* (1962–67). He was president of the Southwest Anthropology Association (1963–64) and the Council for Anthropology and Education (1982). With Holt, Reinhart, and Winston publishers, he was a series editor from 1960 and consulting editor from 1965. He wrote *Dreamers without Power: The Menomini Indians* (with Louise Spindler, 1971) and *Burgbach: Urbanization and Identity in a German Village* (with student collaborators, 1973). Among books he edited were *Education and Anthropology* (1955), *Education and Culture: Anthropological Approaches* (1963), *Education and Cultural Process: Toward an Anthropology of Education* (1974), *Doing the Ethnography of Schooling* (1982), and *Cultural Therapy and Culturally Divergent Schools* (1994). With Louise Spindler he edited *Interpretive Ethnography of Education: At Home and Abroad* (1987), *Cultures around the World* (1977), *Native North American Cultures* (1977), and *Urban Anthropology in the United States* (1978).

REFERENCES: CA (21–24R); LE (1974); WD (1994–96); WW (1994).

SPOCK, Benjamin McLane. b. May 2, 1903, New Haven, Connecticut, to Benjamin Ives and Mildred Louise (Stoughton) Spock. Married June 25, 1927, to Jane Davenport Cheney; October 24, 1976, to Mary Morgan Councille. Children: two.

Although his principal work was in pediatric medicine, through his writing Benjamin Spock was one of the nation's most influential parent educators. During 1939–41, while participating in Caroline Zachry's (q.v.) Seminar for the Study of Personality Development, he contributed a series of articles on school health to *Progressive Education*. His famous book, *The Common Sense Book of Baby and Child Care*, first appeared in 1946 and became the all-time bestseller among books originally published in the United States. The book spawned an extended national debate about whether parents and schools were raising American children in an overly permissive manner.

Spock attended Hamden (Connecticut) Hall Country Day School and Phillips Academy in Andover, Massachusetts. He graduated with the B.A. degree (1925) from Yale University, continued there as a student of medicine for two years, and received the M.D. degree from Columbia University (1929). His medical residencies were in pediatrics and psychiatry. He remained in New York City from 1933 to 1947 as a pediatrician in private practice and a member of the faculty of the Cornell University School of Medicine.

While serving as a psychiatrist in the U.S. Naval Reserve (1944–46) he wrote the book that would make him famous. He taught psychiatry at the Mayo Foundation for Medical Education and Research (later, Mayo Medical School, 1947–51) and child development in the medical schools at the University of Pittsburgh (1951–55) and Western Reserve (later, Case Western Reserve) University (1955–67).

Spock was a columnist for *Ladies Home Journal* (1954–63) and *Redbook* magazines. He cochaired the National Committee for a Sane Nuclear Policy, achieved notoriety during the 1960s for his public opposition to the war in Vietnam, and was the People's Party candidate for president of the United States in 1972.

Among his other books were *Dr. Spock Talks with Mothers* (1961), *Caring for Your Disabled Child* (with Marion Lerrigo, 1965), *A Teenager's Guide to Life and Love* (1970), *Raising Children in a Difficult Time* (1974), *Spock on Spock* (with Mary Morgan, 1985), and *A Better World for Our Children* (1994).

REFERENCES: ASL; CA (NR-35); CB (1969); NYT, March 5, 1992, p. C1+; WD (1994–96); WW (1996); Lynn Z. Bloom, *Doctor Spock: Biography of a Conservative Radical* (Bobbs-Merrill, 1972); David DeLeon, ed., *Leaders from the 1960s* (Greenwood Press, 1994); Mary Ellen Hubbard, ''Benjamin Spock, M.D.: The Man and His Work in Historical Perspective'' (Ph.D. diss., Claremont Graduate School, 1981).

SPODEK, Bernard. b. September 17, 1931, Brooklyn, New York, to David and Esther (Lebenbaum) Spodek. Married June 21, 1957, to Prudence Debb. Children: two.

An expert in early childhood education, Bernard Spodek brought increased visibility to the field. He advocated a more intellectual purpose for schooling in early childhood, in addition to its social and personal objectives. In Spodek's view kindergarten should provide a basis for further learning. He was interested in teacher preparation and open education and wrote prolifically on early childhood education.

Spodek received the B.A. degree from Brooklyn College (1952) and M.A. (1955) and Ph.D. (1962) degrees from Teachers College of Columbia University. He was an early childhood teacher at the Beth Hayeled School in New York City (1952–56), a public school elementary teacher in New York City (1956–57), and a teacher in the laboratory school of Brooklyn College (1957–60). Spodek was an assistant professor of elementary education at the University of Wisconsin–Milwaukee from 1960 to 1965.

In 1965 Spodek became associate professor of early childhood education at the University of Illinois, Urbana–Champaign. He was a professor in the Department of Curriculum and Instruction from 1968, director of graduate programs (1986–87), department chair (1987–89), director of honors in the College of Education (1984–86), and a faculty member in the Bureau of Educational Research (1981–85). He was codirector of the Program for Teacher Trainers in Open Education.

Spodek chaired the early childhood and child development special interest group (1983–84) of the American Educational Research Association. In the National Association for the Education of Young Children he served as secretary (1965–68) and president (1976–78). He served on the 1972 yearbook committee of the National Society for the Study of Education. He headed the Task Force on Preschool Education of the American Society for Curriculum and Development.

Spodek was consulting editor for *Young Children* (1985–87) and *Early Child-*

hood Research Quarterly (1987–90). He coauthored *New Directions in the Kindergarten* (1965), *Teaching in the Early Years* (1972), *Mainstreaming Young Children* (1984), *Foundations of Early Childhood Education* (1987), *Right from the Start* (1994), and *Dealing with Individual Differences in the Early Childhood Classroom* (1994). Spodek edited *Educationally Appropriate Kindergarten Practices* (1991) and *Handbook of Research on the Education of Young Children* (1993). He coedited *Early Childhood Education: Issues and Insights* (1977), *Understanding the Multicultural Experience in Early Childhood Education* (1983), *Professionalism and the Early Childhood Practitioner* (1988), *Issues in Early Childhood Curriculum* (1991), and *Early Childhood Special Education* (1994).

REFERENCES: CA (NR-49); ECE; LE (1974); WW (1996).

SPOFFORD, Grace Harriet. b. September 21, 1887, Haverhill, Massachusetts, to Harry Hall and Sarah G. (Hastings) Spofford. Married: no. d. June 5, 1974, New York City.

Grace Spofford directed the Music School of the Henry Street Settlement in New York City from 1935 to 1954. Lillian Wald (BDAE) had founded the settlement in 1893. The neighborhood service first added music to its offerings in 1927. During Spofford's tenure the enrollment increased, with individual lessons offered at minimal cost to students ranging in age from five to sixty-five. Spofford, who lived at the settlement, stressed learning over competition. She was also head of the music division of the National Federation of Settlements (1938–42).

Spofford graduated from Haverhill (Massachusetts) High School. She spent one year at Mount Holyoke College, then went to Smith College, receiving the B.A. degree in 1909. From 1910 to 1912 she taught piano at Heidelberg College in Tiffin, Ohio. At the Peabody Conservatory of Music she received degrees in piano and organ. She taught piano at Peabody and was its executive secretary (1917–24). From 1924 to 1931 she was the first dean of the Curtis Institute of Music. From 1934 to 1938 she was associate director of the New York College of Music. She managed the Curtis String Quartet and was executive secretary of Olga Samaroff's (BDAE) Layman's Music Courses in the 1930s.

Spofford represented the United States at the 1953 meeting of UNESCO in Brussels, at which the International Society for Music Education was founded. She was twice a delegate to the International Music Council. Active in music organizations, Spofford was chair of music of the International Council of Women (1954–63) and of the National Council of Women of the United States (1954–64). She wrote *A Guide for Beginners in Piano Playing* (with Elizabeth Coulson, 1916). In 1968 she was honored by the National Association of Music Clubs.

REFERENCES: NAW (Mod); NGD; NYT, June 7, 1974, p. 38; WWAW (1974–75); WWW (6); *Christian Science Monitor*, April 26, 1952; *Newsweek* 39 (June 2, 1952): 78.

STALNAKER, John Marshall. b. August 17, 1903, Duluth, Minnesota, to William E. and Sara (Tatham) Stalnaker. Married July 29, 1933, to Ruth Elizabeth Culp; August 21, 1969, to Edna Remmers. Children: three. d. August 19, 1990, Sarasota, Florida.

In 1955, when the Ford Foundation and Carnegie Corporation of New York made grants to establish the National Merit Scholarship Corporation, John Stalnaker was its founding president. He brought to the new enterprise a diverse set of experiences as an administrator, tester, and teacher in higher education. The program that Stalnaker led for the next fourteen years met the dual needs of providing financial support for college education and motivating the most able high school graduates to consider attending college. It provided a professionally designed and administered examination as the basis for making scholarship decisions.

After teaching at a one-room schoolhouse in Alberta, Canada, Stalnaker attended the University of Chicago, where he earned the B.S. degree with honors in 1925. He taught mathematics and science at the Harvard School for Boys in Chicago (1925–26), then went to Purdue University as instructor and special assistant to the president (1926–30), while he pursued further studies at the University of Chicago that led to the A.M. degree in psychology in 1928. He worked at the University of Minnesota for one year (1930–31) on a research team on athletics, then returned to the University of Chicago as a member of the Board of Examiners (1931–36).

Known as an expert on testing, Stalnaker joined the College Entrance Examination Board (CEEB) in 1936, remaining on its staff for nine years. During his last three years with CEEB he developed and administered tests for the U.S. armed forces. He was dean of students and professor of psychology at Stanford University from 1945 to 1949 and coordinator of psychological services and professor of psychology at the Illinois Institute of Technology from 1949 to 1951. Concurrently, he served as director of studies for the Association of American Medical Colleges (1949–55). Stalnaker was a consultant to the Ford Foundation's Fund for Advancement of Education (1952–55) immediately before taking up his leadership role at the new National Merit Scholarship program. Stalnaker's many public service roles included membership on the advisory committee for foreign service examinations (1941–51) and Science Advisory Board for the U.S. Air Force, chairman of the Board of Foreign Scholarships overseeing Fulbright programs (1962–65), and membership on the Illinois Board of Higher Education (1969–75) and Institute for Lifetime Learning (1962–87).

He received a Presidential Certificate of Merit in 1948 and CEEB's Distinguished Service Medal in 1976.

REFERENCES: CB (1958, 1990); LE (1948); NYT, August 22, 1990, p. D21; WWW (10); *American Men of Science*, vol. 3 (1956); *American Psychologist* 46 (December 1991): 1344.

STANLEY, Julian Cecil, Jr. b. July 9, 1918, Macon, Georgia, to Julian Cecil and Ethel (Cheney) Stanley. Married August 18, 1946, to Rose Roberta Sanders; January 1, 1980, to Barbara Sprague Kerr. Children: one.

Julian C. Stanley, Jr., was an expert on the development of mathematically gifted students. He founded (1971) and directed the Study of Mathematically and Scientifically Precocious Youth (SMPY) and conducted talent searches for gifted youth. He was interested in identifying them by the age of thirteen and providing special and accelerated help for them.

Stanley graduated from high school at the age of fifteen. He attended West Georgia Junior College (later, West Georgia College) and received the B.S.Ed. degree from South Georgia Teachers College (later, Georgia Southern University) in 1937. He taught science and mathematics in high schools in Atlanta, Georgia (1937–42), and served in the U.S. Army Air Force (1942–45). His Ed.M. (1946) and Ed.D. (1950) degrees were earned at Harvard University. He was a psychology instructor at Newton (Massachusetts) Junior College (1946–48) and instructor in the Graduate School of Education at Harvard (1948–49).

Stanley taught educational psychology at George Peabody College for Teachers (later, part of Vanderbilt University) from 1949 to 1953. At the University of Wisconsin–Madison (1953–67), he taught in the faculty of education (1953–62). At Wisconsin he organized the Department of Educational Psychology (1962) and served as director of the Laboratory of Experimental Design (1961–67).

In 1967 Stanley went to Johns Hopkins University, where he was professor of education and psychology. In 1979 he established the Office of Talent Identification and Development (later, Center for the Advancement of Academically Talented Youth). He assisted in the establishment of similar talent search groups elsewhere. Stanley's center put mathematically gifted children into fast-paced classes and academic summer programs.

Stanley was a Fulbright research scholar at the University of Louvain (1958–59) and lectured in Australia and New Zealand (1974). He was a fellow of the Center for Advanced Study in the Behavioral Sciences (1965–67). He served as president of the Tennessee Psychological Association (1951), National Council on Measurement in Education (1963–64), American Educational Research Association (1966–67), and the Divisions of Educational Psychology (1965–66) and Evaluation and Measurement (1972–73) of the American Psychological Association.

Stanley wrote *Statistical Methods in Education and Psychology* (with Gene V. Glass, 1970). He edited many of the proceedings of the Hyman Blumberg Symposia on Research in Early Childhood Education and coedited several other volumes, including *Improving Experimental Design and Statistical Analysis* (1967), *Perspectives in Educational and Psychological Measurement* (1972), and *Educational Programs and Intellectual Prodigies* (1978).

He received the American Psychological Association's Edward L. Thorndike (BDAE) Award for Distinguished Psychological Contributions to Education

(1978), American Educational Research Association Award for Distinguished Contributions to Research in Education (1980), and the J. McKeen Cattell (BDAE) Award from the American Psychological Society (1994).

REFERENCES: CA (NR-8); RPE; WD (1994–96); WW (1996); *The Gifted Child Today* 15 (July/August 1992): 42–45, and (September/October 1992): 12–14; *People Weekly* 17 (April 19, 1982): 47+.

STERN, Catherine Brieger. b. January 6, 1894, Breslau, Germany, to Oskar and Hedwig (Lyon) Brieger. Married April 19, 1919, to Rudolf Alfred Stern. Children: two. d. January 8, 1973, New York City.

Catherine Brieger Stern was an innovator in teacher education and mathematics education. She devised teaching materials—blocks in mathematics and picture cards for sounds in reading—and was an opponent of rote learning and drill.

Käthe Brieger was raised in Breslau, Germany, where she attended the Mädchen Gymnasium (high school for girls) and Breslau University. She taught at the school and worked in a hospital during World War I. In 1918 she received the Ph.D. degree from Breslau University in physics and mathematics. She studied the Montessori method of teaching during the early 1920s. In 1924 she opened a Montessori kindergarten in her home and began developing her materials for use in teaching reading and mathematics.

In 1938 Stern and her family came to the United States, where she took the name Catherine. Specializing in the teaching of reading and mathematics, she taught at the Windward School in White Plains, New York, and at the Woods Schools in Langhorne, Pennsylvania. From 1940 to 1943 she was a research assistant to Max Wertheimer at the New School for Social Research and studied Gestalt psychology. Wertheimer named her mathematical teaching devices "structural arithmetic." Stern founded the Castle School in New York City in 1944 and served as its director until 1951. It was an experimental school for preschool children.

The structural arithmetic devices were known as the Stern apparatus in Europe. Stern's approach to teaching was used widely in England and Sweden. She was a consultant on mathematics to the Carnegie Corporation and the School Mathematics Study Group. Stern wrote *Children Discover Arithmetic* (1949), *The Early Years of Childhood: Education through Insight* (with Toni S. Gould, 1955), *Children Discover Reading* (with Gould, 1965), *Structural Reading Series* (with others, 1963), and *Structural Reading Program* (with others, 1973). Many of her articles appeared in *Mathematics Teacher*.

REFERENCES: CA (37–40R); NAW (Mod); NCAB (57: 661); NYT, January 9, 1973, p. 42; Martin Mayer, *The Schools* (Harper, 1961), Chapter 12, "On the Teaching of Mathematics."

STOLZ, Lois Hayden Meek. b. October 19, 1891, Washington, D.C., to Alexander Kennedy and Fannie Virginia (Price) Meek. Married March 7, 1938, to Herbert Rowell Stolz. Children: no. d. October 24, 1984, Palo Alto, California.

Lois Meek Stolz was a leader in early childhood education and a researcher in child development. She graduated from Washington (D.C.) Normal School in 1912 and taught in the Washington schools for four years. She received the A.B. degree (1921) from George Washington University and M.A. (1922) and Ph.D. (1925) degrees from Columbia University, where she received assistance from Patty Smith Hill (BDAE). Her dissertation, *A Study of Learning and Retention in Young Children*, was published by Columbia in 1925.

She was educational secretary for the American Association of University Women (AAUW) from 1924 to 1929, setting up an adult educational program in child development. In 1929 she visited Russia to observe infant day care centers. Meek assisted Helen Thompson Woolley (BDAE) at the Institute of Child Development of Teachers College, Columbia University, in 1929 and became director in 1930. After the institute closed, Meek was director of the Department of Child Development and Guidance.

After her 1938 marriage to Herbert Stolz, she moved to California. She was a research associate of the Institute for Child Welfare that her husband directed at the University of California, Berkeley. During World War II, at the request of the governor, she also coordinated emergency day care services in the state. In 1943 she organized and directed the Kaiser Child Service Centers in Portland, Oregon. The centers operated twenty-four hours a day, took children from the age of eighteen months, contained infirmaries, and provided emergency care. Stolz began teaching at Stanford University in 1945; there she developed a graduate program in child development and guidance. She retired in 1957.

Her book *Your Child's Development and Guidance Told in Pictures* (1940) won an award from *Parents Magazine*. She participated in a project of the Progressive Education Association (PEA) to design a secondary school curriculum based on principles of adolescent development. Her study of the effects of war service on veterans and children resulted in *Father Relations of War-Born Children* (with others, 1954).

Her books included *How Children Build Habits* (1925), *Your Child's Development and Guidance* (1940), *Interpersonal Relations of Boys and Girls* (1943), *Somatic Development of Adolescent Boys* (with Herbert Stolz, 1951), *The Causes of Behavior* (1962), *The Employed Mother in America* (1963), *Influences on Parent Behavior* (1967), and *The Course of Human Development* (1971). She was the first woman to edit a yearbook of the National Society for the Study of Education, the twenty-eighth, *Preschool and Parental Education* (1929).

Stolz was first president of the National Association for Nursery Education (1929–31), which became the National Association for the Education of Young Children. She was a member of President Herbert Hoover's National Committee for the Advancement of Education (1926–28), member and chairperson (1926–29) of the National Committee of Nursery Schools, president of the Mental Hygiene Society of California (1946–47), and member of the council (1955–61) of the Society for Research in Child Development. She was on the Board of Directors (1927–37) and vice president (1937) of PEA. Stolz received the G.

Stanley Hall (BDAE) Award from the American Psychological Association (1967).

REFERENCES: CA (P-2); PR; WEUS; WWAW (1964); WWW (9); Gwendolyn Stevens and Sheldon Gardner, *Women of Psychology*, vol. 2 (Schenkman, 1982); *Young Children* 40 (January 1985): 24.

STONE, Arthur L. b. August 17, 1865, Spencer, Massachusetts, to Emerson and Charlotte C. (Boyden) Stone. Married December 23, 1889, to Adelia S. Norwood. Children: six. d. March 19, 1945, Missoula, Montana.

From 1914 to 1942, Arthur L. Stone served as founding dean of the University of Montana School of Journalism. In that role he used his practical experience as a journalist as a basis for his leadership, instead of advanced study in the field of journalism.

Stone graduated from Spencer (Massachusetts) High School. He earned the A.B. degree with a major in chemistry at Worcester Polytechnic Institute in 1884, taught there in 1885, then attended Yale University briefly as a graduate student. From 1886 to 1888 he was a field chemist in Laramie, Wyoming, for the Union Pacific Railway.

Moving to Montana, Stone taught science in Helena (1889) and was superintendent of schools in Anaconda (1889–91). He began his journalism career in 1891 as a reporter with the *Anaconda Standard* and rose to be managing editor. In 1907 he moved to Missoula, where he was editor and manager of the *Missoulian* until he became dean.

In 1917 the Montana journalism school joined with nine other schools of journalism to found the American Association of Schools and Departments of Journalism. Stone served as secretary (1925–27) and president (1928) of the association. He was the author of *Following Old Trails* (1913).

REFERENCES: *Daily Missoulian*, March 20, 1945, p. 1; Montana State University catalogs; Albert Alton Sutton, *Education for Journalism in the United States from Its Beginning* (Northwestern University, 1945, reprinted by AMS Press, 1968).

STONE, Mason Sereno. b. December 14, 1859, Waterbury Center, Vermont, to Orson Newell and Candace (Mason) Stone. Married April 6, 1904, to Alma Gertrude Wright. Children: no. d. July 13, 1940, Montpelier, Vermont.

Mason Stone graduated with the A.B. degree from the University of Vermont in 1883 and received the A.M. there in 1909. Between 1883 and 1889, he was principal of Williston Academy, Bristol High School, and People's Academy in Morrisville, all in Vermont. In the several years following, Stone rose quickly in school administration. He served for two years as supervisor of schools in Orleans County, Vermont (1889–91). Declining an offer to direct the education division of the U.S. Bureau of Indian Affairs, he moved to Massachusetts and was briefly superintendent of Easthampton school district (1891–92).

Stone returned to Vermont upon his election by the legislature as state superintendent of education, holding that post from 1892 to 1900 and again from

1905 to 1916. The interruption in his long period of state service came when he superintended public schools of Manila, the Philippines, which had become a U.S. possession at the conclusion of the Spanish-American War.

As Vermont state superintendent, Stone promoted dramatic changes in schooling. Working with the legislature, he achieved consolidation of tiny school districts, raised taxes in support of schools, achieved standardization in the high school curriculum with free textbooks, lengthened the school year, and improved the condition of rural schoolhouses. He was less effective in the second period he held office. An opponent of centralization, he tried to defeat a 1915 law that established a state board of education, which in turn selected the state superintendent. He continued only briefly as superintendent after its passage.

Stone was later assistant to the state fuel administrator and lieutenant governor (1919–21). He was author of *History of Education: State of Vermont* (1934).

REFERENCES: WWW (4); Michele A. Cross, "Mason S. Stone and Progressivism in Vermont Public Education, 1882–1916," *Vermont History* 62 (Winter 1994): 26–40.

STOREY, Thomas Andrew. b. January 29, 1875, Burden, Kansas, to Riley Clark and Rose Margaret (Schafer) Storey. Married June 26, 1899, to Parnie Olive Hamilton. Children: three. d. October 28, 1943, Atlanta, Georgia.

Thomas A. Storey was a pioneer in teaching hygiene and a leader in physical education. Storey received A.B. (1896), A.M. (1900), and Ph.D. (1902) degrees from Stanford University and was assistant professor of hygiene there. In 1905 he earned the M.D. degree from Harvard University. He was a resident in medical service at Boston Children's Hospital in 1906.

At the College of the City of New York (later, City College of the City University of New York) Storey organized the Department of Hygiene. He was associate professor of physical instruction and training (1906–10), professor of physical instruction and hygiene (1910–13), and professor of hygiene (1913–26). In 1914 Storey and others urged the New York Department of Instruction to have physical education within schools as a state function. Two years later Storey was named state physical education director; New York was the first state to have the position. During World War I Storey was executive secretary of the Government Interdepartmental Hygiene Board. He was state inspector of physical training with the Military Training Commission in Albany (1917–21) and executive secretary of the U.S. Interdepartmental Social Hygiene Board in Washington, D.C. (1918–21).

Storey returned to Stanford University, where he was professor and director of hygiene and physical education (1926–29) and general director of the School of Hygiene and Physical Education (1929–40). From 1940, when he retired from Stanford, he was special consultant for the American Social Hygiene Association.

Storey's books included *A General Outline and Syllabus on Hygiene* (1919), *General Hygiene* (1924), *Constructive Hygiene* (1926), *The Status of Hygiene Programs in Institutions of Higher Education in the United States* (1927), *De-*

fensive Hygiene (1928), *Individual Hygiene* (1928), *Group Hygiene* (1929), and *Principles of Hygiene* (1930). He received an award from the American Physical Education Association in recognition of distinguished service in the cause of physical education and the Luther Halsey Gulick (BDAE) Medal (1926).

REFERENCES: NYT, October 29, 1943, p. 19; WWW (2); Alida G. Currey, "The Life and Educational Services of Thomas Andrew Storey" (Ph.D. diss., Stanford University, 1951); Mabel Lee (BDAE), *A History of Physical Education and Sports in the U.S.A.* (John Wiley and Sons, 1983); Arthur Weston, *The Making of American Physical Education* (Appleton-Century-Crofts, 1962).

STUART, Moses. b. March 26, 1780, Wilton, Connecticut, to Isaac and Olive (Morehouse) Stuart. Married January 1, 1805, to Abigail Clark. Children: nine. d. January 4, 1852, Andover, Massachusetts.

Moses Stuart was a gifted teacher known as the father of biblical science and Hebrew literature in the United States. During his years (1810–48) as professor of sacred literature at Andover (Massachusetts) Theological Seminary he taught some 1,500 future ministers. He was the first theologian in the nation to teach Hebrew and wrote the standard Hebrew grammar textbook.

Stuart attended an academy in Norwalk, Connecticut. He entered the sophomore class at Yale College (later, University) in 1797 and graduated in 1799. For one year he taught in North Fairfield (later, Eaton), Connecticut. He served briefly as principal of a high school in Danbury; studied law in Newtown, Connecticut (1801–2); and was admitted to the bar in 1802. Appointed tutor in Greek and Latin at Yale (1802–4), Stuart came under the influence of Yale's president, Timothy Dwight (BDAE), and studied theology.

Stuart was licensed to preach in 1803 and served as a supply pastor (1804–6). After his 1806 ordination he was pastor of the First Congregational Church in New Haven. In 1810 he became professor of sacred literature at Andover Seminary. He studied Hebrew, German, and Semitic languages. For his Hebrew grammar, written in 1812, he set the type himself. A revised grammar appeared in 1821. He was a prolific writer, credited with forty books and brochures, including many commentaries and translations. Stuart also spoke out on public issues, particularly temperance. After his 1848 retirement from Andover he continued writing.

REFERENCES: DAB; DARB; NCAB (6: 244); WWW (H); John H. Giltner, *Moses Stuart: The Father of Biblical Science in America* (Scholars Press, 1988); Mark Edward Lender, *Dictionary of American Temperance Biography* (Greenwood Press, 1984); James Grant Wilson and John Fiske, eds., *Appleton's Cyclopaedia of American Biography* (D. Appleton, 1888).

T

TAFT, (Julia) Jessie. b. June 24, 1882, Dubuque, Iowa, to Charles Chester and Amanda May (Farwell) Taft. Married: no. Children: two adopted. d. June 7, 1960, Philadelphia.

Influenced by the work of George Herbert Mead, W. I. Thomas, Jane Addams, and Otto Rank, Jessie Taft became the nation's leading theoretician and teacher of the functional approach to social casework. *Dynamics of Therapy in a Controlled Relationship* (1953) led to her appointment as director of the School of Social Work at the University of Pennsylvania. She cofounded the *Journal of Social Work Process* (1937) and gave the school's curriculum its distinctive Rankian shape and emphasis.

Taft graduated from West Des Moines (Iowa) High School. After receiving the A.B. degree from Drake University (1904) and the Ph.B. from the University of Chicago (1905), she taught in West Des Moines for four years. She received the Ph.D. degree from the University of Chicago in 1913, and in 1915 her dissertation was published. She was assistant superintendent of the New York State Reformatory for Women (1913–15) in Bedford Hills and director of the Social Services Department of the New York State Charities Aid (1915–18). She developed educational programs for mental hygiene. In 1918 she moved to Philadelphia as director of the Department of Child Study of the Seybert Institution and then in 1920 to the Bureau of Children of the Pennsylvania Department of Welfare.

Taft was director of the Pennsylvania School of Social Work (later, University of Pennsylvania School of Social Work) from 1934 to 1950. She taught social casework and developed the school's curriculum. She translated two of Rank's books and wrote his biography in 1958. Among her other books were *A Functional Approach to Family Case Work* (editor, 1944), *Counseling and Protective Service as Family Case Work* (1946), and *Family Casework and Counseling* (1948).

References: BDSW; ESW; NAW (Mod); PR; WWW (7); Mary Jo Deegan, ed., *Women in Sociology* (Greenwood Press, 1991); Virginia P. Robinson, *Jessie Taft, Therapist and Social Work Educator* (University of Pennsylvania Press, 1962); *Social Service Review* 34 (September 1960): 345–46.

TAYLOR, Alrutheus Ambush. b. November 22, 1893, Washington, D.C., to Lewis and Lucy (Johnson) Taylor. Married September 9, 1919, to Harriet Ethel

Wilson; September 9, 1943, to Catherine Buchanan. Children: no. d. June 4, 1954, Nashville, Tennessee.

During A. A. Taylor's long tenure as dean of the College of Liberal Arts at Fisk University (1930–51), it became the first historically black institution to achieve full accreditation from the Southern Association of Secondary Schools and Colleges. Taylor was known also for his scholarship on the history of the Reconstruction era.

After public schooling in the nation's capital, Taylor earned the A.B. degree at the University of Michigan in 1916, with a major in mathematics. He studied at Harvard University during 1922–23 and received the A.M. then. He returned for a further year during 1925–26, and received the Ph.D. in 1935.

Taylor taught English at the Tuskegee Institute (later, University, 1914–15) and worked for the Urban League on the resettlement of black migrants to the North (1917–19), then taught mathematics at West Virginia Collegiate Institute (later, State College, 1919–22). After his first year of study at Harvard, he became a research associate with Carter G. Woodson (BDAE) in Washington, D.C., at the Association for the Study of Negro Life and History (1923–25). In 1926 he became chair and professor of history at Fisk University. Four years later he was named dean of arts and sciences.

He was author of *The Negro in South Carolina during Reconstruction* (1924), *The Negro in the Reconstruction of Virginia* (1926), and *The Negro in Tennessee, 1865–1880* (1941). He served from 1937 to 1950 on the executive council of the Association for the Study of Negro Life and Culture.

REFERENCES: DANB; WWW (3); John Hope Franklin (q.v.), "Alrutheus Ambush Taylor," *Journal of Negro History* 39 (July 1954): 240–42; August Meier and Eliot Rudwick, *Black History and the Historical Profession, 1915–1980* (University of Illinois Press, 1986), pp. 75–77.

THAYER, Vivian Trow. b. October 13, 1886, Tamora, Nebraska, to Oscar Benjamin and Rose Standish (Munson) Thayer. Married April 18, 1914, to Florence Amelia Adams. Children: three. d. July 19, 1979, Winter Haven, Florida.

V. T. Thayer served for two decades as educational director of the Ethical Culture Schools and was a leader in both the Ethical Culture Society and the Progressive Education Association (PEA).

Thayer studied at the University of Wisconsin from 1909 to 1912. He received degrees of A.B. (1916), A.M. (1917), and Ph.D. (1922) there. After his initial period of study he was superintendent of schools in Ashland, Wisconsin (1912–16 and 1918–19).

Upon completing the doctorate, Thayer became principal of the Ethical Cultural High School in New York City (1922–24). He soon left to join the faculty of Ohio State University (1924–28) but returned and remained with the Ethical Culture Schools as educational director from 1928 to 1948. In retirement he taught at the Universities of Hawaii (1948–49) and Virginia (1951–56) and at Fisk University (1956–57).

Thayer served as managing editor of the *American Review* (1923–27) and was an editor of the *Journal of Educational Research* (1929–31). He was author of *The Passing of the Recitation* (1928), *Supervision in the Secondary School* (with H. B. Alberty, BDAE, 1931), *The Educational Frontier* (1933), *Reorganizing Secondary Education* (with others, 1939), *American Education under Fire* (1944), *Religion in Public Education* (1947), *The Attack upon the American Secular School* (1951), *Public Education and Its Critics* (1954), *The Role of the School in American Society* (1960), and *Formative Ideas in American Education* (1965). He chaired the Committee on Secondary School Curriculum of the PEA (1933–40). He was named Pioneer Humanist of the Year by the American Humanist Association (1964) and received the Distinguished Lifetime Service to Education Award from the John Dewey (BDAE) Society (1969).

REFERENCES: CA (P-2, 89–92); LE (1971); NCAB (61: 42); NYT, July 22, 1979, p. 34; WWW (7); John T. Zepper, "V. T. Thayer: Progressive Educator," *Educational Forum* 34 (May 1970): 495–504.

THORNDIKE, Robert Ladd. b. September 22, 1910, Montrose, New York, to Edward Lee (BDAE) and Elizabeth (Moulton) Thorndike. Married June 10, 1933, to Dorothy Vernon Mann. Children: three. d. September 21, 1990, Olympia, Washington.

Robert L. Thorndike was an outstanding teacher of psychology and noted in the field of measuring scholastic achievement. He helped to develop intelligence tests of reading comprehension and also worked in mathematics achievement. He was coauthor of the Lorge-Thorndike Intelligence Tests with Irving Lorge (q.v.) and Elizabeth P. Hagen. Later called Cognitive Ability Tests, they measured scholastic ability in children.

Thorndike received the B.A. degree from Wesleyan University in 1931 and M.A. (1932) and Ph.D. (1935) degrees from Columbia University. He taught psychology at George Washington University from 1934 to 1936. Then he went to Columbia, where he remained until his 1976 retirement. He spent the war years (1942–46) in the U.S. Army Air Force. *Personnel Selection: Test and Measurement Techniques* (1949) resulted from his work on air crew selection and was regarded as a classic in the field. At Columbia he was chairperson of the Division of Psychology (1957–64), coordinated the Measurement and Evaluation program, and became Richard March Hoe Professor at Teachers College. He participated in the 1966 revision of the Stanford-Benet intelligence test.

Thorndike wrote articles for psychology and education journals. Among his books were *The Human Factor in Accidents* (1951), *The Concepts of Over- and Under-Achievement* (1963), *Reading Comprehension Education in Fifteen Countries* (1973), and *Applied Psychometrics* (1982). With Elizabeth Hagen he wrote *Measurement and Evaluation in Psychology and Education* (1955), *Ten Thousand Careers* (1959), and *Characteristics of Men Who Remained in and Left Teaching* (1961). Many of his works were translated into other languages.

He was a leader in the International Educational Achievement Association and represented the United States at its meetings from 1969 to 1976. Thorndike was active in the American Psychological Association (president of three divisions and director 1958–61), American Educational Research Association (president 1974–75), and Psychometric Society (treasurer 1940–53 and president 1953). He received the Nicholas Murray Butler (BDAE) Medal from Columbia University and an award from the Educational Testing Service.

REFERENCES: CA (NR-1, 132); LE (1974); NYT, September 25, 1990, p. B12; WP, September 26, 1990, p. D4; WWW (10); *American Psychologist* 47 (October 1992): 1237; *Educational Researcher* 20 (April 1991): 22–23.

THURSTON, Lee Mohrmann. b. August 7, 1895, Central Lake, Michigan, to George Lee and Lenore Mary (Mohrmann) Thurston. Married December 26, 1921, to Jessie Holmes Gothro. Children: two. d. September 4, 1953, Washington, D.C.

Lee M. Thurston was a prominent administrator of Michigan public schools. He advocated decentralizing control of schools to put local communities in charge.

Thurston received the A.B. degree from the University of Michigan in 1918 and served in the U.S. Marine Corps (1918–19). In Michigan he taught in the public schools of Boyne City, Manistee (1920–22), and Owosso (1922–26). His A.M. (1929) and Ph.D. (1935) degrees were earned at the University of Michigan. From 1926 to 1931 Thurston was superintendent of the Perry, Michigan, schools and from 1931 to 1935 assistant superintendent in Ann Arbor. He served as Michigan state deputy superintendent of public instruction (1935–38 and 1944–48) and professor of education at the University of Pittsburgh (1938–44).

Thurston was state superintendent of Michigan schools from 1948 to 1953 and concurrently a lecturer at the University of Michigan. He was to have become dean of education at Michigan State University in 1953, when President Dwight D. Eisenhower named him U.S. commissioner of education to succeed Earl J. McGrath (BDAE). Thurston died, however, after two months in office.

Thurston served as president of the National Council of Chief State School Officers (1950–51) and chairman of the Educational Policies Commission. He was on the editorial board of *Nation's Schools* and wrote *State School Administration* (with William H. Roe). *General School Laws* (1952) was compiled under his direction.

REFERENCES: CHE, January 16, 1985, p. 26; NYT, September 5, 1953, p. 16; WWW (3); *Higher Education* 10 (September 1953): 1–2; *Nation's Schools* 52 (October 1953): 120–21; *Newsweek* 41 (June 29, 1953): 62.

TORRANCE, (Ellis) Paul. b. October 8, 1915, Milledgeville, Georgia, to Ellis Watson and Jimmie Pearl (Ennis) Torrance. Married November 25, 1959, to Jessie Pansy Nigh. Children: no.

Paul Torrance was known for his research and writing on creativity. He devised tests to measure creativity and conducted a twenty-two-year longitudinal study, published as the *Torrance Tests of Creative Thinking*.

Torrance was raised on a farm. He had problems with spatial relations, considered himself learning disabled, and never drove an automobile. He attended Georgia Military College for two years, taught at the Vocational High School in Milledgeville (1936–37), then returned to Georgia Military College as a teacher of eighth and ninth grade history, Latin, and English.

Torrance studied at Georgia State College for Women (later, Georgia College) in Milledgeville and at Mercer University, where he received the A.B. degree in 1940. At the University of Minnesota, he studied counseling psychology and earned the M.A. degree in 1944. He was principal of Georgia Military College (1941–44) before serving in the U.S. Army (1945–46).

Torrance was a counselor at Kansas State College (later, University) from 1946 to 1948 and directed counseling and taught psychology there from 1949 to 1951. He received the Ph.D. degree from the University of Michigan in 1951. In the U.S. Air Force, Torrance was director of the Survival Research Field Unit at Stead Air Force Base in Nevada (1951–57), where he developed training programs.

Torrance returned to the University of Minnesota in 1958 as professor of educational psychology. In 1966 he went to the University of Georgia, where he was head of the Department of Educational Psychology (1966–78) and Alumni Distinguished Professor of Educational Psychology (1973–84). The Torrance Center for Creative Studies at the university was named for him.

Among Torrance's many publications were *Guiding Creative Talent* (1962), *Education and the Creative Potential* (1963), *Gifted Children in the Classroom* (1965), *Dimensions of Early Learning: Creativity* (1969), *Encouraging Creativity in the Classroom* (1970), *Creative Learning and Teaching* (1974), *Discovery and Nurturance of Giftedness in the Culturally Different* (1977), and *Why Fly: Philosophy of Creativity* (1995). The *Torrance Tests of Creative Thinking* were translated into more than forty languages.

Torrance served on the editorial boards of *Gifted Child Quarterly*, *Highlights for Children*, and *Journal of Creative Behavior*. He received citations for contributions to the education of gifted children from the Council for Exceptional Children and the Association for Gifted Children.

REFERENCES: CA (NR-40); ECE; LE (1974); WW (1996); Garnet W. Millar, *E. Paul Torrance, "The Creativity Man"* (Ablex, 1995); Jack H. Presbury and Morgan W. Henderson, "E. Paul Torrance," *G/C/T* 32 (March/April 1984): 2–8.

TOWLE, Charlotte Helen. b. November 17, 1896, Butte, Montana, to Herman Augustus and Emily (Kelsey) Towle. Married: no. d. October 1, 1966, North Conway, New Hampshire.

Charlotte Towle led development of social work education during the middle decades of the twentieth century. She earned the B.A. degree in education from Goucher College (1919). While a student her participation in fieldwork at the

Baltimore Prisoners' Aid Society and the American Red Cross led her to a career in social work. She was a caseworker for the Red Cross (1919–21) in Baltimore and Denver, the U.S. Veterans Bureau in San Francisco (1921–24), and U.S. Neuropsychiatric Hospital in Tacoma, Washington (1924–26). Towle studied at the New York School of Social Work (later, Columbia University Graduate School of Social Work), under a Commonwealth Fund Fellowship, earning certification in psychiatric social work in 1927.

She was director of the Home Finding Department of the Children's Aid Society in Philadelphia and taught part-time at the Pennsylvania School of Social Work (1927–28). Later she worked with students from the New York and Smith Colleges of social work as a clinical fieldwork supervisor at the Institute for Child Guidance in New York City (1928–32).

Towle taught psychiatry and social work at the University of Chicago School of Social Service Administration from 1932 until her retirement in 1962. At Chicago she developed a social casework curriculum, the Chicago Pattern, that drew from many disciplinary sources for teaching diagnosis and treatment. It served as a national model.

Her second book, *Common Human Needs in Public Assistance* (1945), defined public assistance as a citizen's right, an idea that the American Medical Association attacked as socialistic. As a result of the ensuing controversy, the Government Printing Office, which had issued the book, destroyed the remaining copies. The American Association of Social Workers reissued it in 1952; several translations appeared, and it remained in print forty years later. Her other books were *Social Case Records from Psychiatric Clinics* (1941) and *The Learner in Education for the Professions* (1954). She served on the editorial board of *Social Service Review* (1944–62).

Towle was a Fulbright scholar at the London School of Economics (1955–56). She received the Florina Lasker Award for distinguished service to social welfare (1956) and the Distinguished Service Award of the National Conference of Social Work (1962). In retirement Towle was affiliated with the Scholarship and Guidance Association.

REFERENCES: BDSW; NAW (Mod); NYT, October 2, 1966, p. 86; WWW (4); *Encyclopedia of Social Work* (National Association of Social Workers, 1977); Helen Harris Perlman, *Helping: Charlotte Towle on Social Work and Social Casework* (1969); Wendy Beth Posner, "Charlotte Towle: A Biography" (Ph.D. diss., University of Chicago, 1986); *SSA Newsletter* 13 (Autumn/Winter 1966/67), entire issue.

TOWNE, Laura Matilda. b. May 3, 1825, Pittsburgh, to John and Sarah (Robinson) Towne. Married: no. d. February 22, 1901, Saint Helena Island, South Carolina.

Laura M. Towne went to Saint Helena Island in South Carolina in 1862 to teach freed slaves. She founded the Penn School, which continued in existence until 1948, when it became part of the state system. Towne believed in adhering to a traditional curriculum.

Towne was educated first in Boston. When her family moved to Philadelphia, she attended medical classes there. In 1862 she volunteered to go to the Sea Islands to teach, soon joined by a friend, Ellen Murray. Their classes in Brick Church began with 80 students; by 1864 there were 194. Towne also served as physician to residents of the island.

Her curriculum encompassed academic subjects, health habits, and, later, sewing classes. In 1870 she added a normal department. Financing came at first from the Freedmen's Bureau and later from the Benezet Society of Pennsylvania. Following Towne's death, Rossa B. Cooley (q.v.) and Grace B. House took over Penn School and changed its curriculum to emphasize agriculture and trades.

REFERENCES: LW; NAW; WR; Rupert Sargent Holland, ed., *Letters and Diary of Laura M. Towne* (Riverside Press, 1912; reprinted by Negro Universities Press, 1969); Guion Griffis Johnson, *A Social History of the Sea Islands* (University of North Carolina Press, 1930; reprinted by Negro Universities Press, 1969); Lina Mainiero, ed., *American Women Writers*, vol. 4 (Ungar, 1982); Gerald Robbins, "Laura Towne: White Pioneer in Negro Education, 1862–1901," *Journal of Education* 143 (April 1961): 40–54.

TUMIN, Melvin Marvin. b. February 10, 1919, Newark, New Jersey, to Robert M. and Rose (Yawitz) Tumin. Married June 18, 1948, to Sylvia Yarost. Children: two. d. March 3, 1994, Princeton, New Jersey.

As a sociologist and anthropologist, Melvin Tumin studied the interactions of social class, educational attainment, and tolerance of cultural diversity. After attending the University of Newark (later, Rutgers University, Newark) from the age of fifteen, Tumin studied at the University of Wisconsin, where he was awarded B.A. (1939) and M.A. (1940) degrees. In 1944 he received the Ph.D. degree from Northwestern University.

He taught for three years at Wayne State University before going to Princeton University, where he was on the faculty in sociology and anthropology from 1947 until his retirement in 1989. In Detroit he was research director of the Mayor's Commission on Race Relations (1945–47). He was also a visiting professor at Teachers College, Columbia University, during 1963–68 and a visiting research sociologist at the Educational Testing Service from 1969.

His many written works included *Social Life, Structure and Function* (with J. W. Bennett, 1948), *Caste in a Peasant Society* (1952), *Segregation and Desegregation* (1957), *Desegregation: Resistance and Readiness* (1958), *An Inventory and Appraisal of Research on American Anti-Semitism* (1961), *Social Class and Social Change in Puerto Rico* (with A. S. Feldman, 1961), *Education, Social Class, and Intergroup Attitudes in England, France, and Germany* (1964), *Quality and Equality in American Education* (edited with Marvin Bressler, 1967), *Social Stratification* (1967), *Evaluation of the Effectiveness of Educational Systems* (with Marvin Bressler, 1969), *Comparative Perspective on Race Relations* (editor, 1969), *Patterns of Society* (1973), and *Male and Female in Today's World* (1980).

Tumin was president of the Society for the Study of Social Problems (1966–

67) and Eastern Sociological Society (1967–68), a visitor at the Institute for Advanced Study (1973–74), Guggenheim fellow (1969–70), and National Endowment for the Humanities faculty fellow (1973–74).

REFERENCES: CA (45–48, 144); NYT, March 5, 1994, p. 12; WD (1994–96); WW (1988–89); *Who's Who in American Jewry* (Standard Who's Who, 1980).

TURNER, Clair Elsmere. b. April 28, 1890, Harmony, Maine, to Fred Orrison and Mary Frances (Chalmers) Turner. Married December 24, 1924, to Naomi Elsie Cocke. Children: two. d. November 27, 1974, Arlington, Massachusetts.

C. E. Turner was a pioneer of international reputation in the field of health education. From 1914 to 1944 he taught at Massachusetts Institute of Technology (MIT). He taught the first college course in public health at the Harvard-MIT School of Public Health (1914–22) and established the master of public health degree with a specialization in health education.

Turner graduated from Bates College in 1912 with the A.B. degree and received the M.A. from Harvard University in 1913. He was a teacher in Maine at an ungraded school in Harmony, a grammar school in St. Albans and a high school in Wellington and instructor in biology in Lewiston (1913–14). Turner directed the Malden (Massachusetts) Study in Health Education and Growth (1921–31). He developed a series of grade school textbooks published as the Malden Health Series. He also taught at Tufts University Dental School and Medical School (1917–29) and lectured at many universities throughout the world.

Turner was first president (1951–56) of the International Union for Health Education and Society of Public Health Educators (1950–51). The Eastman Kodak Company sought Turner's help in developing films to teach public health in schools. During World War II Turner was chief of health education in the U.S. Office of Inter-American Affairs.

In 1973 Turner received the first Parisot Medal of the International Union for Public Health. His books included *Hygiene, Dental and General* (1920); *Personal and Community Health* (1925); with Georgie B. Collins, *Health* (1924), *Cleanliness and Health* (1926), and *Community Health* (1928); *Principles of Health Education* (1932); *Personal Hygiene* (1937); *School Health and Health Education* (1970); and an autobiography, *I Remember*. Many of his books were translated into other languages.

REFERENCES: CA (P-1); NYT, November 28, 1974, p. 36; WWW (6); Paul August Knipping, ''Clair E. Turner and the Growth of Health Education'' (Ph.D. diss., University of Wisconsin–Madison, 1970); Elaine Shaw Sorensen, ''Clair E. Turner: Pioneer in Health Education, 1890–1974,'' *Health Education* 18 (February/March 1987): 37–39.

TURNER, Thomas Wyatt. b. March 16, 1877, Hughesville, Maryland, to Eli and Linnie (Gross) Turner. Married December 28, 1907, to Laura Elaine Miller; 1936 to Louise Wright. Children: no. d. April 21, 1978, Washington, D.C.

Thomas Wyatt Turner assisted many historically black colleges in the establishment of science programs. He developed the natural science program at Hampton Institute (later, University), where he taught from 1924 to 1945.

Turner was the son of former slaves. His early education was in Maryland in Charles County and at Charlotte Hall. He attended Howard University Preparatory School and received A.B. (1901) and M.A. (1905) degrees from Howard. He taught science at Tuskegee Institute (later, University, 1901–2) and at Baltimore High School for Negroes (1902–14), except for one year (1910–11) when he taught in Saint Louis. From 1914 to 1924 he taught biology at Howard University, where he served as acting dean of the College of Education (1914–20). In 1921 he received the Ph.D. degree from Cornell University, where he had studied summers.

At Hampton Institute, Turner's research led to published papers. He traveled to other black colleges to observe their teaching of science. In retirement he served as a consultant to colleges and organized the Science Department at Texas Southern University. In 1978 the science building at Hampton Institute was named Turner Hall.

Turner was active in civil rights and Catholic organizations. He was a founding member of the National Association for the Advancement of Colored People (NAACP) in 1909 and served it in leadership positions in Baltimore and Virginia. He was founding president of Federated Colored Catholics (1925–34) and organized the Virginia Conference of College Science Teachers.

REFERENCES: NCAB (61: 10); NYT, April 25, 1978, p. 40; Frank Lincoln Mather, ed., *Who's Who of the Colored Race* (1915; Gale Research, 1976); Mary Anthony Scally, *Negro Catholic Writers, 1900–1943* (Walter Romig, 1945), pp. 115–18.

TYACK, David B. b. November 17, 1930, Beverly, Massachusetts. Married 1951. Children: two.

David B. Tyack was a noted social and cultural historian of American education and a prolific writer on the subject. He received B.A. (1952), M.A.T. (1953), and Ph.D. (1958) degrees from Harvard University and was an instructor of history and education there (1958–59). At Reed College (1959–66) he taught the history of education and American intellectual history and was director of the Master of Arts in Teaching Program. He was associate professor of the history of education at the University of Illinois (1967–69). In 1969 he went to Stanford University as associate professor, and in 1980 he became professor of education and history.

Tyack wrote articles on the history of education and the education of teachers. Among his many books were *George Ticknor and the Boston Brahmins* (1967), *Nobody Knows* (1969), *The One Best System* (1974), *Educational Reform* (with Michael Kirst and Elisabeth Hansot, 1979), *Managers of Virtue* (with Hansot, 1982), *Public Schools in Hard Times* (with Robert Lowe and Elisabeth Hansot, 1984), *Law and the Shaping of Public Education, 1785–1954* (with Thomas James and Aaron Benavot, 1987), *Learning Together* (with Hansot, 1990), and

Tinkering toward Utopia (with Larry Cuban, q.v., 1995). He edited *Turning Points in American Educational History* (1967) and *Work, Youth, and Schooling* (with Harvey Kantor, 1982) and contributed chapters to several volumes.

REFERENCES: LE (1974); WW (1996).

V

VARS, Gordon Forrest. b. February 10, 1923, Erie, Pennsylvania, to Ethan Wiard and Mildred Fredrica (Place) Vars. Married August 22, 1949, to Annis Tallentire; December 21, 1975, to Alice McVetty. Children: two.

Gordon Vars led in the development of curricular theory for junior high schools and middle schools, particularly with the concept of the core curriculum.

Vars was raised in Bellefonte, Pennsylvania. After service in the U.S. Army, he completed studies for the A.B. degree at Antioch College in 1948. He earned the M.A. in science education at Ohio State University in 1949 and the Ed.D. at George Peabody College for Teachers (later, part of Vanderbilt University) in 1958. Vars taught public school in Bel Air, Maryland (1949–52), and at the Peabody Demonstration School (1952–56). He taught at the State University of New York College at Plattsburg (1956–60), Cornell University (1960–66), and Kent State University (1966–93). He was coordinator of the Middle School Division, Kent State University School (1966–76). Vars served as executive secretary, treasurer, and editor of the National Association for Core Curriculum (from 1959) and was first president of the National Middle School Association (1973–74).

He was coauthor with William Van Til (BDAE) and John H. Lounsbury of *Modern Education for the Junior High School Years* (1961) and with John H. Lounsbury, *A Curriculum for the Middle School Years* (1978). Vars also edited *Common Learnings: Core and Interdisciplinary Team Approaches* (1969) and wrote *Interdisciplinary Teaching in the Middle Grades: Why and How* (1987). He was named Ohio Middle School Educator of the Year in 1980 and in 1986 received the Lounsbury Award for Excellence in Middle School Education from the National Middle School Association.

REFERENCES: CA (21–24R); LE (1974); WW (1996); Daniel Dyer, ''Gordon F. Vars: The Heart and Soul of Core Curriculum,'' *Middle School Journal* 24 (January 1993): 30–38; ''Mr. Middle School,'' *Record-Courier* (Ravenna-Kent, Ohio), December 7, 1993, p. C5.

VINCENT, George Edgar. b. March 21, 1864, Rockford, Illinois, to John Heyl (BDAE) and Elizabeth (Dusenbury) Vincent. Married January 8, 1890, to Louise Mary Palmer. Children: three. d. February 1, 1941, New York City.

George Vincent was a vigorous exponent of community education and a builder of educational and philanthropic institutions. His opportunities came to him through other persons, including his father, a cofounder of the Chautauqua Institution; William Rainey Harper (BDAE), founding president of the University of Chicago; and John D. Rockefeller, Sr., creator of the Rockefeller Foundation. Nonetheless, Vincent was an accomplished public servant in his own right.

After attending public schools and the Pingry School in Elizabeth, New Jersey, Vincent enrolled at Yale College (later, University), earning the A.B. degree in 1885. He undertook further study in sociology at the University of Chicago, from 1892 when it opened until 1896, when he received the Ph.D. degree.

For most of his life Vincent held leadership roles at the Chautauqua Institution, alongside other responsibilities. He was literary editor of the Chautauqua Press (1886), vice principal (1888–98) and principal (1898–1907) of instruction, president (1907–15), and honorary president (1915–37). He also was briefly a newspaper journalist in New York City (1885–86).

Vincent stayed at the University of Chicago after completing the doctorate, teaching sociology, psychology, and social psychology. He was dean of the junior college (1900–1907), then dean of arts, literature, and sciences (1907–11). In 1911 he became president of the University of Minnesota. In a six-year period Vincent raised the profile of graduate and professional education, increased the public presence of the institution, and professionalized its administration. He was president of the Rockefeller Foundation from 1917 until his retirement in 1929, emphasizing health and medicine in its grants and restoring its reputation.

Vincent wrote *An Introduction to the Study of Society* (with Albion W. Small, BDAE, 1895) and *Social Mind and Education* (1896). He served on the editorial board of the *American Journal of Sociology* from its founding in 1895 to 1914. He served also on the General Education Board (1914–29) and was a U.S. representative at the 1923 Pan-American Conference in Chile. The National Institute of Social Science presented him its Gold Medal (1935).

REFERENCES: CB (1941); DAB (supp. 3); NCAB (15: 236); NYT, February 2, 1941, p. 45; WWW (1); *American Journal of Sociology* 46 (March 1941): 734–35.

W

WALCUTT, Charles Child. b. December 22, 1908, Montclair, New Jersey, to Henry Leeds and Clara (Child) Walcutt. Married January 5, 1934, to Sue Grundy Bonner; 1962 to Jeanne H. Bocca. Children: two. d. April 11, 1989, Great Neck, New York.

A strong advocate of teaching reading by basic methods, Charles C. Walcutt opposed the ''look-say'' approach to reading used in the 1940s. Walcutt received the A.B. degree from the University of Arizona (1930) and M.A. (1932) and Ph.D. (1937) degrees from the University of Michigan, where he remained one year as an instructor. Walcutt taught at the University of Oklahoma (1938–44), Michigan State Normal College (later, Eastern Michigan University, 1944–47), and Washington and Jefferson College (1947–51). In 1951 he began teaching English at Queens College of the City University of New York (CUNY), and from 1964 to 1984 he was also at the CUNY Graduate School and University Center.

Among Walcutt's publications were *Reading: Chaos and Cure* (with Sibyl Terman, 1958), *Tomorrow's Illiterates: The State of Reading Instruction Today* (1961), *An Anatomy of Prose* (1962), *Your Child's Reading* (with J. C. Daniels and Hunter Diack, 1964), *Teaching Reading: A Phonic/Linguistic Approach to Developmental Reading* (with Glen McCracken and Joan Lamport, 1974), and *The Dilemma of Private Economy and Public Waste* (1979). With Glen McCracken he wrote the Lippincott Basic Reading Series. He edited many volumes, including *The Mind in the Making* (with L. F. Dean, 1939), the three-volume *Explicator Cyclopedia* (with J. Edwin Whitesell, 1966–68), and *Seven Novelists in the American Naturalist Tradition* (1974).

Walcutt held Fulbright awards to the American Institute of the University of Oslo (1957–58) and the University of Lyon (1965–66) and received a research award from the Council for Basic Education (1960–61). He was a member of the advisory committee of the American Reading Reform Foundation and the advisory council of the National Council of Teachers of English.

REFERENCES: CA (128, NR-3); NYT, April 12, 1989, p. B5; WD (1990–92); *Who's Who in the East* (1962–63).

WARRINER, John E. b. 1907, Michigan. Married: yes. Children: two. d. July 29, 1987, Saint Croix, Virgin Islands.

John Warriner wrote a series of textbooks for English grammar and composition that were used widely in American classrooms.

Little information is available concerning Warriner's life. He received a bachelor's degree from the University of Michigan and master's degree from Harvard University. He taught at New Jersey Teachers College (later, Montclair State University) and at Garden City (New York) High School.

His textbook series, *Warriner's English Grammar and Composition*, was used in grades six through twelve. His approach focused on traditional exercises; it included sentence diagramming and the identification of parts of speech. After his retirement in 1962 Warriner continued to revise the books, the last being issued shortly before his death in 1987. Warriner also wrote *Handbook of English* (two volumes, 1953), *Advanced Composition: A Book of Models for Writing* (1961), *Short Stories: Characters in Conflict* (1981), and *English Workshop* (1986).

REFERENCES: CA (123); NYT, August 8, 1987, p. 32; *Curriculum Review* 26 (September/October 1986): 41–42.

WATSON, Goodwin Barbour. b. July 9, 1899, Whitewater, Wisconsin, to Walter S. and Ellen D. (Goodwin) Watson. Married June 14, 1923, to Gladys M. Hipple; 1946 to Barbara Bellow; to Doris Watson. Children: six. d. December 30, 1976, Longboat Key, Florida.

Dynamic, opinionated, and controversial, Goodwin Watson's scholarship in educational psychology led him to doubt the results of standardized tests before criticizing them became popular. He was a founding member, with Paul Lazarsfeld (q.v.), of the Society for the Psychological Study of Social Issues (SPSSI), first editor of the *Journal of Applied Behavioral Science* (1965–70), and founder of the Union Graduate School of the Union for Experimenting Colleges and Universities (1970). His social and political activism, combined with travel to Mexico and the Soviet Union during the 1930s, brought attacks on his patriotism from members of Congress and the American Legion, though he was vindicated judicially.

While still in his teen years, Watson was a principal and assistant principal in Albion and Madison, Wisconsin (1916–18), and received a license to preach. He graduated with the A.B. degree from the University of Wisconsin in 1920. Over the next several years he directed religious education programs in Denver and New York City (1920–22), was ordained a minister in the Methodist Church, studied at Union Theological Seminary (1921–24), and earned M.A. (1923) and Ph.D. (1925) degrees in educational psychology at Teachers College of Columbia University. He undertook postdoctoral study at the Universities of Vienna and Berlin during 1931–32.

Watson remained on the faculty at Teachers College from 1925 to 1962. He also codirected the Institute for Group Psychotherapy. On leave during 1941–44, he was chief analyst in the foreign intelligence section of the Federal Communication Commission, a position that Congress eliminated when unable to dismiss him. After retirement from Teachers College, he was Distinguished Service Professor at Newark (New Jersey) State College. Watson was on the faculty of Union Graduate School from its founding in 1970 until his death. He was author of *Action for Unity* and *Youth after Conflict* (both 1947) and *Social Psychology: Issues and Insights* (1966), as well as research reports and journal articles.

REFERENCES: CA (69–72); NYT, January 5, 1977, p. B18; PR; WWW(7); *Journal of Social Issues* 42 (1986): 49–67; *Journal of Applied Behavioral Science* 13 (January–February–March 1977): back cover.

WATTENBARGER, James Lorenzo. b. May 2, 1922, Cleveland, Tennessee, to James Claude and Lura G. (Hambright) Wattenbarger. Married June 11, 1947, to Marion Swanson. Children: three.

In the rapid development of community colleges during the decades after World War II, James Wattenbarger was a leading advocate for statewide systems and an expert on their financing. He was principal planner and administrator of Florida's community colleges. Wattenbarger emphasized the responsibility of community colleges to serve the people of their communities in all stages of life.

Wattenbarger graduated with the A.A. degree from Palm Beach Junior College in 1941 and received the B.A. degree in education from the University of Florida in 1943. After service in the U.S. Army Air Force (1943–45) he resumed studies at the University of Florida, where he earned M.A. (1947) and Ed.D. (1950) degrees. His doctoral thesis was published as *A State Plan for Public Junior Colleges, with Special Reference to Florida* (1953). While a graduate student, Wattenbarger taught in Palm Beach (1946–47) and was an assistant principal in Gainesville (1948–49).

After service on the faculty in education at the University of Florida (1950–55), Wattenbarger directed the Division of Community and Junior Colleges in the Florida Department of Education (1955–67). He returned to the University of Florida as professor of education and director of the Institute for Higher Education, remaining from 1968 until his retirement in 1992. Until 1988 he also chaired the Department of Educational Administration.

He coauthored *The Community College in the South* (1962), *The Community Junior College* (1970), *More Money for More Opportunity* (1974), *Improving State-wide Planning* (1974), *Financing Community Colleges* (1988), and *America's Community Colleges: The First Century* (1994).

REFERENCES: CA (106); LE (1974); *Who's Who in the South and Southeast* (1993–94); Ron Stanley, "James L. Wattenbarger," *Community College Journal* 64 (June/July 1994): 5.

WEBER, Lillian. b. February 7, 1917, New York City, to Samuel and Celia (Levine) Dropkin. Married 1935 to Frederick Palmer Weber. Children: two. d. February 22, 1994, Bronx, New York.

Lillian Weber was a leading advocate of open education and publicly funded preschool education. She studied at Hunter College and received the B.S. degree from the University of Virginia (1938). She earned the M.A. from Bank Street College of Education (1959). From the 1940s she was associated with the Spuyton-Duyvil Pre-School, which she eventually directed.

In 1965 she went to England where she studied infant and nursery schools for a year and a half. From that experience she wrote *The English Infant School and Informal Education*, published in 1971.

Weber was on the faculty of City College of the City University of New York from 1967 to 1987 as professor of elementary education. She directed the City College Workshop Center for Open Education (from 1972). The work of the Advisory Services to the Open Corridor Project in New York City schools, directed by Weber, was described in *Use and Setting: Development in a Teacher's Center*, coauthored with Beth Alberty and James Neujahr (1982). With Deborah Meier (q.v.) and Vito Perrone, Weber was a founder of the North Dakota Study Group.

In 1973 Weber became the first woman to deliver the John Dewey Society Annual Lecture. City College honored her in 1987 as City Woman of the Year.

REFERENCES: ECE; NYT, February 24, 1994, p. D20; *Young Children* 50 (November 1994): 57.

WECHSLER, David. b. January 12, 1896, Lespedi, Romania, to Moses and Leah (Pascal) Wechsler. Married July 21, 1939, to Ruth Ann Halpern. Children: two. d. May 2, 1981, New York City.

David Wechsler was a critic of conventional intelligence quotient (IQ) tests. He developed other intelligence tests, which were widely used in mental measurement. He believed intelligence tests separated emotions and mental traits. The intelligence scales he developed included verbal and performance dimensions. They were intended to provide content suitable for adults and were designed to be administered individually.

Born in Romania, Wechsler came to the United States at the age of six. In 1916 he graduated from City College (later, of the City University of New York) with the A.B. degree. He earned the M.A. degree in experimental psychopathology from Columbia University in 1917 under Robert S. Woodworth (BDAE). During service with the Army Signal Corps in World War I, Wechsler was assigned to test draftees. He studied in London and Paris as an army student and, after his discharge in 1919, at the University of Paris (1920–22). From 1922 to 1924 he was a psychologist at the Bureau of Child Guidance. In 1925 he earned the Ph.D. degree at Columbia University. He served with the Psychological Corporation of New York (1925–27). Wechsler was a research associate at the Institute of Child Welfare Research, Teachers College of Columbia University, from 1928 to 1932.

Wechsler became chief psychologist at Bellevue Hospital in New York City in 1932 and remained there until 1967. He was a clinical psychologist at New York University School of Medicine from 1942 to 1970 and professor from

1970. Tests he developed that became known internationally included the Bellevue-Wechsler I (1939), Army Wechsler (1942), Wechsler Intelligence Scale for Children (1949), Wechsler Adult Intelligence Scale (1955), and Wechsler Preschool and Primary Scale of Intelligence (1967), designed for children from four to six and one-half years of age.

Wechsler helped to found the Department of Psychology at Hebrew University in Jerusalem, Israel. His books included *The Range of Human Capacities* (1935); *The Measurement of Adult Intelligence* (1939), which became *The Measurement and Appraisal of Adult Intelligence* (1958); and *Selected Papers of David Wechsler* (1974). In 1973 he received a Distinguished Professional Contribution Award from the American Psychological Association.

REFERENCES: BDP; CA (103); IESS, vol. 18; NYT, May 4, 1981, p. B10; PR; WW (1976); *American Psychologist* 29 (January 1974): 44–47, and 36 (December 1981): 1542–43; *Encyclopedia Judaica* (Macmillan, 1972); Raymond E. Francher, *The Intelligence Men* (W. W. Norton, 1985); *Journal of Special Education* 21 (Fall 1987): 6–7.

WEIKART, David Powell. b. August 26, 1931, Youngstown, Ohio, to Hubert James and Catherine (Powell) Weikart. Married August 24, 1957, to Phyllis Saxton. Children: four.

A disciple of Jean Piaget, David P. Weikart studied early childhood education in an ever-widening circle. He began in the 1960s with research on preschool intervention programs. His Perry Preschool Project in Ypsilanti, Michigan, was offered to three- and four-year-old African-American children from poor families. The program suggested that ''verbal bombardment'' enhanced their prospects for success in later schooling. In follow-up studies Weikart tracked their progress into adulthood.

Weikart broadened his work to cognitively oriented preschools for children of all backgrounds, and eventually extended it to cross-cultural study of early childhood programs in Europe, Africa, and Asia. The work of the High Scope Educational Research Foundation, which he founded and directed, encompassed curriculum development, teacher training, program evaluation, and cost-benefit analysis. Its findings were a major basis for the development and revision of programs such as Head Start.

Weikart earned the A.B. degree at Oberlin College (1953) and M.A. (1957) and Ph.D. (1966) degrees at the University of Michigan. He served as a first lieutenant in the U.S. Marine Corps (1953–55).

He was director of special services in the Ypsilanti (Michigan) Public Schools (1957–70) and also director of research and development, before founding the High Scope Educational Research Foundation (1970), of which he was president. He was director of its affiliate, the High Scope Institute, in London, England, from 1991.

Weikart's books included *Preschool Intervention: Preliminary Report of the Perry Preschool Project* (editor, 1967), *The Cognitively Oriented Curriculum;*

A Framework for Preschool Teachers (with others, 1971), *Young Children in Action: A Manual for Preschool Educators* (with Mary Hohmann and Bernard Banet, 1979), *Young Children Grow Up: The Effects of the Perry Preschool Program on Youths through Age 15* (with L. J. Schweinhart, 1980), *High/Scope Early Childhood Policy Papers* (from 1985), *Quality in Early Childhood Programs: Four Perspectives* (with others, 1985), *How Nations Serve Young Children: Profiles of Child Care and Education in 14 Countries* (editor with Patricia P. Olmsted, 1989), and *Quality Preschool Programs: A Long Term Social Investment* (1989).

He received the Lela Rowland Award of the National Mental Health Association in 1987.

REFERENCES: ECE; LE (1974); WW (1996).

WEXLER, Jacqueline Grennan. b. August 2, 1926, Sterling, Illinois, to Edward W. and Florence (Dawson) Grennan. Married June 1969, to Paul J. Wexler. Children: no.

Jacqueline Wexler was born Jean Marie Grennan. She was educated in Catholic schools in Sterling, Illinois, and at Webster College (later, University), where she earned the B.A. degree in 1948. One year later, she adopted the name Jacqueline upon taking religious vows as a Sister of Loretto. After further study summers, she was awarded the M.A. degree by the University of Notre Dame in 1957.

First as Sister Jacqueline, then as Miss Grennan, and later as Mrs. Wexler, Jacqueline Grennan Wexler was a college president who pressed her institutions and their communities to embrace fundamental change in admissions, curriculum, and governance.

At Catholic high schools for girls in El Paso, Texas, and St. Louis, Missouri, she taught English and mathematics from 1951 to 1959. At Webster College, she rose from assistant to the president (1959) to vice president for development (1960–62), executive vice president (1962–65), and president (1965–69). Under her leadership, the college recruited a lay faculty and was the first Roman Catholic institution in the United States to sever all legal connections with the church. Webster developed an innovative teacher training program; established the Webster Institute of Mathematics, Science, and the Arts; abolished most graduation requirements; and extended its programs into the urban community.

After half a year as vice president and director of international university studies at the Academy for Educational Development (1969), Wexler was named president of Hunter College of the City University of New York (1969–79). She was a strong proponent of New York's open college admissions program as a means to serve the metropolis. She was also known for her skillful negotiation of conflicts between students, faculty, and community members during the 1970s.

Wexler was an adviser to the chief of naval operations (1978–81) and a member of the Foreign Service Board of Examiners of the U.S. Department of

State (1981–83). She was president of a private firm, Academic Consulting Associates, and president of the National Conference of Christians and Jews, both from 1982 to 1990.

She received many public appointments and honors, including membership on the President's Advisory Panel on Research and Development in Education (1961–65), the Elizabeth Cutter Morrow Award of the Young Women's Christian Association (1968), and the Abram Sachar (BDAE) Silver Medallion of the National Women's Committee of Brandeis University (1988). She was author of the book *Where I Am Going* (1968).

REFERENCES: CB (1970); LE (1974); NYT, January 12, 1967, p. 43, November 14, 1978, p. C8, January 9, 1979, p. C8, and July 30, 1982, p. B1; WW (1996); WWAW (1995–96); Patricia Jansen Doyle, "The Real World of Jacqueline Grennan," *Saturday Review* 50 (July 15, 1967): 58+; *Life* 57 (October 23, 1964): 53+; *Time* 89 (January 20, 1967): 66.

WHARTON, Clifton Reginald, Jr. b. September 13, 1926, Boston, to Clifton Reginald and Harriet (Banks) Wharton. Married 1950 to Dolores Duncan. Children: two.

As a chief executive in higher education, Clifton R. Wharton, Jr., distinguished himself by adept leadership on difficult financial issues and by promoting flexibility in complex bureaucratic organizations.

After early education overseas and high school studies at the Boston Latin School, Wharton enrolled at Harvard University, where he earned the B.A. degree in 1947. He received the M.A. in international relations from Johns Hopkins University the following year. He trained in international economics at the University of Chicago, where he was awarded the Ph.D. in 1958.

From 1948 to 1953, Wharton was on the staff of the American International Association of Economic and Social Development, an endeavor led by Nelson Rockefeller with programs in Latin America. In 1957 he joined the Agricultural Development Council (ADC) under John D. Rockefeller, Jr. He directed its Southeast Asian programs and was concurrently visiting professor of economics at the University of Malaya (1958–64). Upon returning to the United States, he was the ADC's director of American university research (1964–67) and vice president (1967–69). He also taught at Stanford University during 1964–65.

Wharton became president of Michigan State University (1970–78) after a difficult search in which state and campus politics predominated. Although much public attention was paid to his being the first African American to head a large, predominantly white university, on the job he was known for his adeptness at building institutional cohesion. As chancellor of the State University of New York (1978–87) and later as chairman and chief executive officer of the Teachers Insurance and Annuity Association and College Retirement Equities Fund (TIAA-CREF, 1987–93) again his achievements were in institutional reform: introducing flexibility in decision making and improving institutional finances.

Wharton served as deputy secretary of state in the first year of the William Clinton presidency.

Wharton's publications included *Subsistence Agriculture and Economic Development* (editor, 1969), *Continuity and Change: Academic Greatness under Stress* (1971), and *Patterns for Lifelong Learning* (with Theodore M. Hesburgh, q.v., and others, 1973).

He chaired the board of the Rockefeller Foundation (1982–87) and was a trustee of the Asia Society (1967–77), Carnegie Foundation (1970–79), Aspen Institute (1980–93), and Council on Foreign Relations (1983–93), among others. He received the Joseph C. Wilson Award for achievement and promise in international affairs in 1977 and the President's Award on World Hunger in 1983.

REFERENCES: CA (41–44R); CB (1987); CHE, January 6, 1993, p. A15+; LE (1974); NYT, October 18, 1969, p. 1, and October 27, 1977, p. 1+; WW (1996); WWBA (1995/96); Edgar A. Toppin, *A Biographical History of Blacks in America Since 1528* (David McKay, 1971).

WHITE, Edna Noble. b. June 3, 1879, Fairmount, Illinois, to Alexander L. and Angeline E. (Noble) White. Married: no. d. May 4, 1954, Highland Park, Michigan.

Edna Noble White was named director of the newly founded Merrill-Palmer Institute in 1919. Funded with $3 million from Lizzie Merrill Palmer, the institute was opened in Detroit in 1920. Its purposes were to train young women in home economics and to be a child development training school and center for family education. A laboratory nursery school was added in 1922, providing a place for child study and research. The staff used an interdisciplinary approach in the study of child development. White retired as director in 1947.

White graduated from Fairmount (Illinois) High School and in 1906 received the A.B. degree from the University of Illinois. She taught at Danville (Illinois) High School and at the Lewis Institute (later, part of Illinois Institute of Technology) in Chicago. At Ohio State University, where she went in 1908, she became professor, head of the Home Economics Department, and supervisor of the extension service. During World War I White served as director of Ohio food conservation for the Council of National Defense. In 1929 she was a participant and speaker at the Fifth World Conference of the New Education Fellowship in Denmark.

After her retirement from the Merrill-Palmer Institute White helped to organize the study of child development in Greek universities and developed a gerontology program in Detroit. White was president of the American Home Economics Association (1918–20) and chair of the National Council on Parent Education (1925–37). She advised the Rockefeller institutes on child development research. During the 1930s she served the Works Progress Administration as chair of the National Advisory Committees on Nursery Schools and Parent Education.

REFERENCES: AWM; NAW (Mod); WW (1934–35); Harry A. Overstreet and Bonaro

W. Overstreet, *Leaders for Adult Education* (American Association for Adult Education, 1941); Dorothy Tyler, ''Edna Noble White, 1880–1954,'' *Merrill-Palmer Quarterly* 1 (Fall 1954): 3.

WHITEMAN, Henrietta V. [Henri Mann]. b. 1934, Clinton, Oklahoma, to Henry and Leonora Mann.

As a leading advocate for the development of Native American studies programs in universities, Henrietta Whiteman emphasized the value of such programs as a means to self-awareness and self-determination for Native American peoples. She underscored the importance of supportive orientation programs for native students in predominantly European-American institutions, while she called for community involvement as a necessary component of Native American studies.

Whiteman grew up among her people, the Cheyenne, in a farming community in rural Oklahoma. She earned the B.A. degree at Southwestern State College (later, Southwestern Oklahoma State University), the M.A. at Oklahoma State University, and the Ph.D. at the University of New Mexico (1982).

She taught and coordinated Native American studies at the University of California, Berkeley (1970–72), before becoming director of Native American studies at the University of Montana, where she received promotion to professor of Native American studies in 1991. On leaves of absence, she taught at Harvard University and served in the Indian Education Office of the U.S. Bureau of Indian Affairs (1986–87).

Whiteman was named Cheyenne Indian of the Year in 1982; Outstanding Woman in the greater Missoula, Montana, area in 1987; and American Indian Heritage Foundation Woman of the Year in 1988.

REFERENCES: Gretchen M. Bataille, ed., *Native American Women: A Biographical Dictionary* (Garland, 1993); Henrietta V. Whiteman, ''Native American Studies, the University, and the Indian Student,'' in Thomas Thompson, ed., *The Schooling of Native America* (American Association of Colleges for Teacher Education, 1978), pp. 104–16.

WILLIAMS, William Taylor Burwell. b. July 3, 1869, Stonebridge, Virginia, to Edmund and Louisa (Johnson) Williams. Married June 29, 1904, to Emily A. Harper; October 27, 1937, to Kate Ruff Green. Children: no. d. March 26, 1941, Tuskegee, Alabama.

William T. B. Williams was a proponent of industrial education and influential in black education in the South.

Williams began teaching in a county school at the age of seventeen, attended Hampton Institute (later, University, 1886–88), and taught elementary school (1889). He graduated from Phillips Academy in Andover, Massachusetts, in 1893 and received the B.A. degree from Harvard University in 1897.

After serving as principal of an Indianapolis public school (1897–1902), he became a field agent for the Southern Education Board and Hampton Institute (1903–6). As agent for the John F. Slater Fund, beginning in 1906, he helped to establish a county training school for Negro youth. He also was agent for the Anna T. Jeanes (or Rural School) Fund, directing work of Jeanes teachers. In 1918 he was assistant supervisor of vocational training in Negro schools for the Committee on Education and Special Training of the War Department.

In 1919 Robert R. Moton (BDAE) asked Williams to be a consultant on teacher training at Tuskegee Institute (later, University). Williams was Tuskegee's first dean of the College Department (1927–36) and then vice president (1936–41). He served on educational commissions to the Virgin Islands (1928) and Haiti (1930).

Williams was an editorial staff member of *Southern Workman* and associate editor of *Cyclopedia of the Colored Race*. He helped to organize and was president of the National Association of Teachers in Colored Schools and received the Spingarn Medal in 1934.

REFERENCES: DANB; EBA; NYT, March 27, 1941, p. 23; WWW (1); *Journal of Negro History* 26 (July 1941): 411–12.

WILLIAMSON, John Finley. b. June 23, 1887, Canton, Ohio, to William and Mary (Finley) Williamson. Married June 20, 1912, to Rhea Beatrice Parlette. Children: three. d. May 28, 1964, Toledo, Ohio.

John Finley Williamson was a noted choral director who established Westminster Choir College to train ministers of music for Protestant churches. The Westminster Plan, which he developed, had a major influence on the teaching of choral music.

Williamson graduated from the conservatory of Otterbein College in 1911. He studied voice and organ in New York City and Leipzig, Germany. In 1920, while minister of music at Westminster Presbyterian Church in Dayton, Ohio, he formed a choir that became well known. Other churches sought training in the methods used by Williamson. In 1926 he responded by founding Westminster Choir School at the church. At the start there were ten faculty members, with Williamson as president and his wife as dean. The school was independent and interdenominational. Williamson moved it to Ithaca, New York, in 1929, as the Ithaca Conservatory; he served as dean.

In 1932 Williamson received an invitation from the presidents of Princeton University and Princeton Seminary and the governor of New Jersey to move the school to Princeton, New Jersey. In the new location, students were able to participate in musical events in New York City and Philadelphia. In 1938 the school was named Westminster Choir College. It offered baccalaureate and master's degrees. Williamson was president until 1958. In 1991 the college became a part of Rider University.

Williamson edited the *Westminster Series of Choral Music*. After retirement he conducted workshops, including one in Japan. He died while at a clinic for church choirs.

REFERENCES: BBD; NGD; NYT, May 29, 1964, p. 29; ''Westminster Choir College,''

PC; WWW (4); Lee Hastings Bristol, Jr., *Westminster Choir College* (Newcomen Society in North America, 1965); Paul Hutchinson, "Ten Years of Westminster," *Christian Century* 53 (June 17, 1936): 870–72; *International Cyclopedia of Music and Musicians* (Dodd, Mead, 1975); David A. Wehr, "John Finley Williamson (1887–1964): His Life and Contribution to Choral Music" (Ph.D. diss., University of Miami, 1971).

WILLIS, Benjamin Coppage. b. December 23, 1901, Baltimore, to Clarence Milton and Elizabeth Estelle (Coppage) Willis. Married January 24, 1925, to Rachel Davis Webster. Children: one. d. August 27, 1988, Plantation, Florida.

Benjamin C. Willis was superintendent of the Chicago public schools from 1953 to 1966. He was lauded in his early years for rebuilding the system, but later he was criticized for refusing to move African-American children into white schools.

Willis studied at St. John's College in Maryland and received the B.A. degree from George Washington University in 1922. In Maryland he was a teacher/principal in Henderson (1922–23) and principal in Federalsburg (1923–27), Denton (1927–31), and Catonsville (1932–34). He received the M.A. degree from the University of Maryland in 1926. Willis was superintendent of schools in Caroline (1934–40) and Washington (1940–47) counties, Maryland, and in New York state at Yonkers (1947–50) and Buffalo (1950–53). At Columbia University he earned the Ed.D. degree in 1950.

In 1953 Willis succeeded Herold Hunt (q.v.) as superintendent of Chicago schools. In his first seven years many new schools were erected, summer school was restarted, and a junior college was expanded. Willis became the highest paid educator in the United States. With a neighborhood system, Chicago schools were segregated. Willis considered schools places of learning, not social change, and would not compromise with demands to reduce racial imbalances. In 1963 there were protests against Willis, with classes boycotted and his home picketed. He agreed to retire in 1965.

Willis later was professor of educational administration at Purdue University Calumet campus (1966–70) and superintendent of schools in Broward County, Florida (1969–72). He wrote *Social Problems in Public School Administration* (1966). From 1955 to 1960 he was president of the Great Cities School Improvement Study. He was president of the American Association of School Administrators (1961–62), executive director of the Massachusetts Educational Survey (1963–65), chairman of the President's Panel of Consultants on Vocational Education, chairman of the Educational Policies Commission of the National Education Association (NEA) (1962–67), a member of the President's Science Advisory Committee (1962–66), and consultant to the Peace Corps.

REFERENCES: LE (1974); NYT, August 31, 1988, p. D21; WWW (9); Larry Cuban (q.v.), *Urban School Chiefs under Fire* (University of Chicago Press, 1976); *Education* 81 (December 1960): 352; *Newsweek* 56 (December 12, 1960): 97–98, 65 (June 7, 1965): 52, and 67 (May 23, 1966): 98; *Saturday Review* 43 (September 17, 1960): 75+.

WILSON, Logan. b. March 6, 1907, Huntsville, Texas, to Samuel Calhoun and Sammie (Logan) Wilson. Married December 27, 1932, to Myra Marshall. Children: two. d. November 7, 1990, Austin, Texas.

Logan Wilson was a sociologist known particularly for his book *The Academic Man* and a leader of higher education in the South.

He received the A.B. degree from Sam Houston State Teachers College (later, State University) in 1926 and the A.M. degree from the University of Texas in 1927. He was a reporter for the *Houston Press* and taught at East Texas State Teachers College (later, State University) at Commerce. He received M.A. (1938) and Ph.D. (1939) degrees from Harvard University. Wilson taught sociology at the University of Maryland (1939–41) and headed Departments of Sociology at Tulane University (1941–43) and the University of Kentucky (1943–44). He served as dean of Newcomb College, Tulane University (1944–51) and as vice president and provost of the University of North Carolina (1951–53).

In 1953 Wilson returned to Texas as president of the University of Texas at Austin. The next year he became president of the University of Texas system. Under his leadership all academic programs were opened to African-American students in 1956, and entrance examinations were required for all potential students, with admission based on merit. He was president of the American Council on Education from 1961 to 1971.

Wilson wrote *The Academic Man: A Study in the Sociology of a Profession* (1942), *Sociological Analysis: An Introductory Text and Case Book* (with William L. Kolb, 1949), *Shaping American Higher Education* (1971), and *American Academics: Then and Now* (1979). He was editor of *Emerging Patterns in American Higher Education* (1965) and *Universal Higher Education: Costs, Benefits, Options* (with Olive Mills, 1972). He served as president of the Council of Southern Universities (1953–54).

REFERENCES: CA (45–48); CB (1956, 1991); LE (1974); NCAB (I: 56); NYT, November 9, 1990, p. B7; WWW (10).

WITMER, Lightner. b. June 28, 1867, Philadelphia, to David Lightner and Katherine (Huchel) Witmer. Married June 11, 1904, to Emma Repplier. Children: no. d. July 19, 1956, Philadelphia.

The work of Lightner Witmer, founder of clinical psychology, bore on education in fundamental ways. He established the Witmer School and introduced the concept of diagnostic teaching, both of them important in special education. Particularly through the work of his students, he helped to shape school psychology. Yet he was an unpopular outsider in his own discipline and was soon surpassed in the subfield that he had inaugurated.

Upon graduation from the Episcopal School in Philadelphia, Witmer enrolled at the University of Pennsylvania, where he earned the A.B. degree in 1888. During the next two years he continued to study there, first in law, then in political science, while teaching at Rugby Academy in Philadelphia. He left the preparatory school job in 1890 to train under James McKeen Cattell (BDAE) in psychology, then enrolled in 1891 at the University of Leipzig, which awarded him the degree of *Magister* in 1892 and a doctorate in philosophy in 1893.

Witmer returned to the University of Pennsylvania in 1892 and taught there for the next forty-five years. He founded its psychological clinic in 1896. He also held appointments at Bryn Mawr College (1896–98) and Lehigh University (1903–5), establishing psychology laboratories at both of them.

From 1907 he conducted a school outside Philadelphia for the education of resident retarded children; it came to be called the Witmer School. From that year he was also editor of *The Psychological Clinic* until he discontinued it in 1935. He served briefly with the American Red Cross in Italy during 1917–18.

Witmer was the author of many articles, most of them published in his own journal. He also wrote *Analytical Psychology* (1902) and *The Special Class for Backward Children* (1911) and edited *Experimental Studies in Psychology*.

REFERENCES: BDP; ECP; NYT, July 21, 1956, p. 15; PR; WWW (3); *American Journal of Psychology* 69 (December 1956): 680–82; Paul McReynolds, "Lightner Witmer: Little-Known Founder of Clinical Psychology," *American Psychologist* 42 (September 1987): 849–58.

WOOD, Stella Louise. b. September 2, 1865, Chicago, to Abraham Wilder and Abie Fales (Walker) Wood. Married: no. d. February 11, 1949, River Forest, Illinois.

Stella Wood went to Minneapolis in the 1890s to head a kindergarten. It became Miss Wood's Kindergarten and Primary Training School. It had a two-year curriculum, and its graduates found employment in many school systems. Minority students were welcomed, which was unusual for a private school at that time. In 1922 Wood declined an offer for the school to become a department of elementary education at the University of Minnesota. However, from 1944 the university granted graduates of Miss Wood's sixty credit hours toward a bachelor's degree in its College of Education. Other institutions had done this previously. In 1945 the school was incorporated as a nonprofit institution. Macalester College in St. Paul, Minnesota, made an offer in 1948 for the school to affiliate, which was accepted.

Wood grew up in Chicago, Evanston, and Oak Park, Illinois. Interested in kindergartens, in 1882 she attended the Cook County Normal School, where one of her instructors was Francis Parker (BDAE). Wood was an assistant at a Chicago kindergarten and after her graduation spent six years as director of the Hobby Street Kindergarten, which enrolled many immigrant children. After one year at the University of Michigan she was a supervisor of kindergartens and training of kindergarten teachers in Muskegon, Michigan (1891–95). In Dubuque, Iowa, for one year she headed a kindergarten demonstration school.

The Minneapolis Kindergarten Association, founded in the early 1890s, supported a charity kindergarten and maintained a kindergarten training school.

Wood went to Minneapolis to head the training school, housed in the Universalist Church of the Redeemer. By 1913 it was located at Wells Memorial Settlement House. David L. Kiehle (BDAE) of the University of Minnesota heard Wood speak and asked her to teach a summer school class in kindergarten theory. In 1897 the Minneapolis schools opened their first public school kindergarten at the Sheridan School, with financial help from the Kindergarten Association. Other kindergartens followed under Wood's supervision.

Wood was active in the International Kindergarten Union, in 1903 became its secretary-treasurer, and later was recording secretary and vice president. In 1917 she was elected president. She was a vice president of the kindergarten section of the National Education Association and represented it at the World Federation of Education Associations in Switzerland in 1929.

REFERENCES: WWW (3); Marguerite N. Bell, *With Banners: A Biography of Stella L. Wood* (Macalester College Press, 1954); *Minneapolis Morning Tribune*, February 12, 1949, p. 1.

WOODRING, Paul Dean. b. July 16, 1907, Delta, Ohio, to Peter David and Ethel (Gormley) Woodring. Married September 19, 1938, to Jeanette McGraw. Children: no. d. November 12, 1994, Bellingham, Washington.

Paul Woodring wrote extensively about American education for the general reading public. His column ''Woodring on Education'' appeared in thirty-six newspapers between 1958 and 1962. From 1960 to 1966 he served as the education editor of *Saturday Review*. He wrote particularly about the teaching profession's problems of knowledge, status, and work conditions. He urged that entrance standards be raised for the profession to attract outstanding candidates and improve the quality of teaching.

Woodring attended Bowling Green (Ohio) State Normal School (later, State University) for two years and taught in a country elementary school. He received the B.S.Ed. degree from Bowling Green (1930) and M.A. (1934) and Ph.D. (1938) degrees from Ohio State University. He was a high school teacher and a criminal courts psychologist in Detroit (1937–39). Except for service in the U.S. Army (1942–46), he spent his career at Western Washington University. He was Distinguished Service Professor from 1962 to 1986 and served as interim president during 1964–65.

Among his books were *Let's Talk Sense about Our Schools* (1953), *A Fourth of the Nation* (1957), *New Directions for Teacher Education* (1958), *Education in a Free Society* (with others, 1958), *The Higher Learning in America: A Reassessment* (1968), *Investment in Innovation* (1970), *Who Should Go to College* (1972), and *The Persistent Problems of Education* (1983). He edited *American Education Today* (with John Scanlon, 1963), and *Education in America* (four volumes, with James Cass, 1971),

Woodring was an educational adviser for the Ford Foundation's Fund for the Advancement of Education (1956–62). He was a fellow of the American Psychological Association and president of the State Psychology Association of

Washington. He received the Bell Award from the National Education Association (1962 and 1963), Educational Press Association Award (1963, 1964, and 1966), and Education Writers Association Award (1964). The Woodring College of Education at Western Washington University was named in his honor.

REFERENCES: CA (17–20R); LE (1974); NYT, November 18, 1994, p. B10; WD (1994–96); WW (1980–81).

WOODY, (Walter) Thomas. b. November 3, 1891, Thorntown, Indiana, to Mahlon and Matilda (Shafer) Woody. Married June 12, 1920, to Wilhelmine A. Lawton. Children: two. d. September 11, 1960, Upper Darby, Pennsylvania.

Thomas Woody wrote with exceptional versatility on education, historically and in comparative perspective. His work was known for its thorough grounding in original sources read in many languages.

Woody earned the A.B. degree at Indiana University in 1913 and A.M. (1916) and Ph.D. (1918) degrees in the history of education at Teachers College, Columbia University, where he was a student of Paul Monroe (BDAE). As a Quaker, Woody did not enlist for military service but instead conducted relief work among prisoners of war in Russia and France during 1917–19 for the International Committee of the Young Men's Christian Association.

Woody was a high school teacher of German from 1913 to 1915. From 1919 until his death he taught the history of education at the University of Pennsylvania.

His books included *Early Quaker Education in Pennsylvania* (1920); *Fürstenschulen in Germany after the Reformation* (1920); *Quaker Education in the Colony and State of New Jersey* (1923); *A History of Women's Education in the United States* (two volumes, 1929), which remained the authoritative work for many years; *The Educational Views of Benjamin Franklin* (edited, 1931); *New Minds: New Men? The Emergence of the Soviet Citizen* (1932), which followed a stay of twenty months in the Soviet Union, first on a study tour with John Dewey (BDAE) and other American educators, then with a Guggenheim Fellowship (1929–30); *Life and Education in Early Societies* (1949), largely about physical education; and *Liberal Education for Free Men* (1951). The American Academy of Physical Education honored Woody with its Publications Award in 1952.

REFERENCES: NYT, September 13, 1960, p. 37; WWW (4); William W. Brickman (BDAE), "Thomas Woody—Educational Historian and International Educator," *Educational Forum* 28 (March 1964): 267–75; R. Baird Schuman, "Thomas Woody, 1891–1960," *School and Society* 89 (March 11, 1961): 109–10.

WRIGHT, Benjamin Fletcher. b. February 8, 1900, Austin, Texas, to Benjamin Fletcher and Mary (Blandford) Wright. Married June 9, 1926, to Alexa Foote Rhea. Children: two. d. November 28, 1976, Austin, Texas.

Benjamin F. Wright attended schools in Austin, Texas, and served in the U.S. Army infantry during World War I. He received A.B. and A.M. degrees from the University of Texas in 1921 and was an instructor (1922–24) and adjunct professor of government (1925–26) there. He earned the Ph.D. degree from Harvard University in 1925. Beginning as an instructor at Harvard in 1926, he became professor of government in 1945 and served as department chair (1942–46).

At Harvard, Wright helped to establish a graduate program to study American civilization. He was one of twelve persons appointed by President James B. Conant (BDAE) to the Committee on the Objectives of a General Education in a Free Society. They prepared the report *General Education in a Free Society* (1945). Wright chaired a committee to put the recommendations into operation. In 1949 a new undergraduate program was established at Harvard that required all students to include humanities, social sciences, and natural sciences in their courses of study.

Wright became the fifth president of Smith College in 1949 and served for a decade. In 1959–60 he was a fellow of the Center for Advanced Study in the Behavioral Sciences. He was professor of government at the University of Texas from 1960 until he retired in 1975.

Among his publications were *American Interpretations of Natural Law* (1931), *The Contract Clause of the Constitution* (1938), *The Growth of American Constitutional Law* (1942), *Consensus and Continuity, 1776–1787* (1958), and *Five Public Philosophies of Walter Lippmann* (1973).

REFERENCES: CA (77–80, 69–72); CB (1956, 1977); NCAB (I: 224); NYT, November 30, 1976, p. 42; WWW (7).

WRIGHT, Elizabeth Evelyn. b. April 3, 1872, Talbotton, Georgia, to John Wesley and Virginia (Rolfe) Wright. Married June 2, 1906, to Martin Menafee. Children: no. d. December 14, 1906, Battle Creek, Michigan.

Elizabeth Wright admired Booker T. Washington (BDAE) and established a school in Denmark, South Carolina, based on his principle of combining practical training with academic subjects.

Wright was the daughter of a former slave and a Cherokee. She used the name Lizzie. At the age of five she went to live with her grandmother. Her early education was sporadic. Hearing about Tuskegee Institute (later, University), she applied and was admitted in 1888 to the preparatory class. At first she attended night school in order to work during the day, but later she was able to attend day classes, with her expenses paid by Judge George W. Kelley of Massachusetts. During 1892–93 she taught school in McNeill's, South Carolina, until arsonists destroyed the school in April 1893. She returned to Tuskegee, graduating in 1894. Her diploma entitled her to teach in public schools.

Wright returned to McNeill's, where she intended to build a school on land Judge Kelley had purchased. The materials were burned before the school could be erected. Because of frail health Wright spent some time at the Battle Creek (Michigan) Sanitarium.

On April 14, 1897, Wright opened a school with fourteen pupils in Denmark,

South Carolina, above a store. With a loan from state senator Stanwix Mayfield, she was able to purchase twenty acres of land with three buildings, and she moved the school in October 1897. Soon there were 236 day students and fourteen boarders, with Wright as principal. Pupils worked on the premises. In 1899 a deed was granted for Denmark Industrial School for Colored Youth. Bylaws were adopted in 1901.

In honor of Ralph Voorhees of Clinton, New Jersey, who made a gift of $4,500, the school was named Voorhees Industrial School. It was incorporated in 1904.

In June 1906 Wright married Martin Menafee, a Tuskegee graduate who had come to the Denmark school in 1900 as treasurer and, later, business manager. Wright returned to Battle Creek for surgery in November 1906, but her health declined, and she died at the age of thirty-four. In 1929 the Voorhees School added a junior college, and in 1964 it became a four-year institution, Voorhees College.

REFERENCES: BWA; NBAW; WR; Albert Emil Jabs, ''The Mission of Voorhees College: Its Roots and Its Future'' (Ed.D. diss., University of South Carolina, 1983); J. Kenneth Morris, *Elizabeth Evelyn Wright, 1872–1906, Founder of Voorhees College* (University Press, 1983).

WRIGHT, Sophie Bell. b. June 5, 1866, New Orleans, Louisiana, to William Haliday and Mary (Bell) Wright. Married: no. d. June 10, 1912, New Orleans.

Sophie Bell Wright was instrumental in providing night classes in New Orleans for employed men and boys who were poor and did not have the opportunity to secure an education.

Wright was crippled in a childhood accident. She attended schools in New Orleans, graduating from high school in 1880. Shortly afterward she opened the Day School for Girls in her parents' home. It was chartered in 1883 as the Home Institute and was expanded into a boarding school in 1885. By 1900 there were about 200 pupils. Wright attended Peabody Normal Seminary in New Orleans, teaching mathematics in exchange for instruction in foreign languages.

Young men wanted an education, and Wright began instructing them evenings, free of charge. She began with 20 students and volunteer teachers. The evening school eventually grew to 1,500 pupils. She continued to run the Home Institute. Because of lack of space, Wright first rented a larger house, then purchased one to house the Home Institute and the Free Night School.

In 1903 Wright received an award for outstanding service to the community, and money was raised to pay off her mortgage. The city of New Orleans opened its own night schools in 1909. Wright was active in community and charity organizations, including the Louisiana branch of the King's Daughters (president 1906). She established the Upper Bethel Mission Sabbath-School. In 1911 a New Orleans high school was named for Wright.

REFERENCES: NAW; NCAB (10: 51); WR; Margaret Evelyn Gardner, ''Sophie Bell Wright: A Biography'' (M.A. thesis, Louisiana State University, 1959); Mary Margaret Stroh, *Eyes to See* (Delta Kappa Gamma Society, 1947).

Y

YOAKAM, Gerald Alan. b. November 18, 1887, Eagle Grove, Iowa, to Eugene George and Olive Louisa (Mason) Yoakam. Married August 2, 1911, to Helen Marie Swain. Children: two. d. May 17, 1963, Clinton, Maryland.

The Yoakam readability formula, developed by Gerald A. Yoakam, evaluated the difficulty of children's books. Yoakam wrote extensively in the field of reading.

Yoakam received the A.B. degree from the University of Iowa in 1910. From 1910 to 1918 he served in Iowa as a principal, superintendent, and county superintendent of schools. After receiving the A.M. degree from the University of Iowa in 1919, he remained one year as principal of University Elementary School. He directed teacher training at the State Teachers College in Kearney, Nebraska (later, University of Nebraska at Kearney), from 1920 to 1923 and earned the Ph.D. from the University of Iowa in 1922.

In 1923 Yoakam went to the University of Pittsburgh, where he remained until 1955 as professor of education and director of elementary education. He conducted reading conferences, served as a consultant to public schools in western Pennsylvania, and was on a commission surveying the schools of Washington, D.C. Yoakam was president of the International Council for the Improvement of Reading (1950–53) and National Council on Research in English.

He contributed to the twenty-fourth and thirty-sixth yearbooks of the National Society for the Study of Education. Among his many books were *Reading and Study* (1928), *The Improvement of the Assignment* (1932), *An Introduction to Teaching and Learning* (with Robert G. Simpson, 1934), *The Laidlaw Basic Readers* (1940), *The Teacher and His Work* (with George Gould, 1947), and *Basal Reading Instruction* (1955). Yoakam compiled and edited *Current Problems of Reading Instruction* (1951) and *Providing for the Individual Reading Needs of Children* (1953). He was associate editor of the *Journal of Educational Research.*

In his honor the local council of the International Reading Association in Allegheny County, Pennsylvania, was named the Gerald A. Yoakam Reading Council.

REFERENCES: WWW (8); *Education* 79 (December 1958): 256–57.

YOUNG, Nathan Benjamin. b. September 15, 1862, Newbern, Alabama, to Frank and Susan (Smith) Young. Married December 30, 1891, to Emma May Garrette; November 15, 1905, to Margaret Amelia Bulkley. Children: seven. d. July 19, 1933, Tampa, Florida.

Nathan B. Young served as president of two historically black colleges. His advocacy of a liberal arts emphasis in the colleges, along with vocational training, made him a controversial figure.

Young was born in slavery. He received the A.B. degree from Talladega College (1884), then headed a high school in Jackson, Mississippi. He earned A.B. (1888) and A.M. (1891) degrees from Oberlin College. He was principal of Thomas School, a black elementary school in Birmingham, Alabama. From 1872 to 1897 he was head of the academic department at Tuskegee Institute (later, University). Young left because he disagreed with Booker T. Washington (BDAE) about the emphasis on vocational education for blacks. At Georgia State Industrial College for Negroes (later, Savannah State College) Young was director of teacher training (1897–1901) under Richard R. Wright (BDAE).

In 1901 Young became president of Florida State Normal and Industrial School (later, Florida Agricultural and Mechanical University), a land-grant institution. Under his leadership the academic programs were enhanced. He established farmers' institutes and a summer training school for teachers, began a nursing program in 1904 with assistance from the Slater Fund, and started an extension division. It was the first black college to have a Carnegie library. Young phased out the elementary unit and built a model training school. The State Board of Education wanted more emphasis on vocational subjects, but Young refused. He was ordered to stop advertising the institution as a college. Following a conflict over finances, Young was dismissed in 1923.

Young was president of Lincoln University in Missouri from 1923 to 1927 and from 1929 to 1931. He required graduate degrees for faculty, and he improved facilities. After he was dismissed at Lincoln University, he served as field representative for the National Association of Colored Teachers.

REFERENCES: EBA; Antonio F. Holland, "Education over Politics: Nathan B. Young at Florida A&M College, 1901–1923," *Agricultural History* 65 (Spring 1991): 131–48; Leedell W. Neyland and John W. Riley, *The History of Florida Agricultural and Mechanical University* (University of Florida Press, 1963).

Z

ZACHARIAS, Jerrold Reinach. b. January 23, 1905, Jacksonville, Florida, to Isidore A. and Irma (Kaufman) Zacharias. Married June 23, 1927, to Leona Hurwitz. Children: two. d. July 16, 1986, Belmont, Massachusetts.

During the late 1950s, Jerrold R. Zacharias led the Physical Science Study Committee (PSSC) in development of a new high school physics curriculum that for two decades was the prevailing approach to the subject. PSSC worked from the assumptions that students could learn from each other, and they should be directly engaged in the experimentation and discovery that are at the center of science. It favored principles over techniques and introduced atomic and nuclear physics into high school study. It provided an integrated set of teaching materials, including textbooks, workbooks, experiments, films, and tests.

After study at Columbia University, where he earned A.B. (1926), A.M. (1927), and Ph.D. (1933) degrees, Zacharias began his career at Hunter College (1931–40). At the Massachusetts Institute of Technology (MIT) he worked on the staff of the Radiation Laboratory (1940–45), developing radar. He directed the engineering division at the Los Alamos Laboratory during construction of the first atomic bombs, then returned to MIT, where he was professor of physics (1946–66), director of the Laboratory for Nuclear Science (1946–56), and Institute Professor (1966–70).

Zacharias was an outstanding experimental scientist as well as educator. In addition to his wartime work, he built the first effective atomic clock. He was a member of the President's Science Advisory Committee (1952–64). In 1960 he received the Oersted Medal of the American Association of Teachers of Physics. He was a fellow of the American Academy of Arts and Sciences.

REFERENCES: CB (1964, 1986); NYT, July 18, 1986, p. D17; WWW (9); Gloria Dapper and Barbara Carter, "Jerrold R. Zacharias: Apostle of the New Physics," *Saturday Review* 44 (October 21, 1961): 52+; Jack S. Goldstein, *A Different Sort of Time: The Life of Jerrold R. Zacharias* (MIT Press, 1992).

ZACHRY, Caroline Beaumont. b. April 20, 1894, New York City, to James Greer and Elise Clarkson (Thompson) Zachry. Married: no. Children: two adopted. d. February 22, 1945, New York City.

Caroline B. Zachry conducted major studies in progressive education and child guidance. She was active in the Progressive Education Association (PEA), especially in its psychologically oriented group. Zachry believed that the primary role of school was the social development of children.

Zachry was a graduate of the Spence School for Girls in New York City and received the B.S. degree (1924) from Teachers College of Columbia University. For two years she taught at the Lincoln School of Teachers College. Under William Heard Kilpatrick (BDAE), she received A.M. (1925) and Ph.D. (1929) degrees, also at Teachers College. In 1926 Zachry went to New Jersey State Teachers College (later, Montclair State University) to teach English. After becoming interested in psychology, she headed the Psychology Department. From 1930 to 1934 Zachry also directed the Mental Hygiene Institute. She studied for a year under Carl Jung in Vienna.

From 1934 to 1939 she directed a study of adolescence for the Commission on Secondary School Curriculum of the PEA. The result was *Emotion and Conduct in Adolescence* (1940), which was influential in the training of secondary school teachers. She was director of the Seminar for the Study of Personality Development, founded by the PEA. Its staff included Benjamin Spock (q.v.). After her death the seminar was renamed the Caroline B. Zachry Institute of Human Development. Zachry served as a mental health consultant to the Ethical Culture Schools of New York City (1935–42). In 1942 she became director of the Bureau of Child Guidance of the New York City Board of Education.

Her publications included *Personality Adjustments of School Children* (1929) and *Reorganizing Secondary Education* (with V. T. Thayer, q.v., and Ruth Kotinsky, 1939), and she contributed to *Democracy and the Curriculum* (1939).

REFERENCES: NAW; NYT, February 24, 1945, p. 11; PR; *American Men of Science* (1944); Gwendolyn Stevens and Sheldon Gardner, *Women of Psychology*, vol. 2 (Schenkman, 1982).

ZIGLER, Edward Frank. b. March 1, 1930, Kansas City, Missouri, to Louis and Gertrude (Gleitman) Zigler. Married August 28, 1955, to Bernice Gorelick. Children: one.

From 1970 to 1972 Edward F. Zigler served as first director of the Office of Child Development (later, Administration for Children, Youth and Families) and chief of the U.S. Children's Bureau. He was a counselor to agencies on the problems of children. He served on the National Planning and Steering Committee of Project Head Start (1965–70), on the Fifteenth Anniversary Head Start Committee (1980), and on the planning committee of Project Follow Through. In collaboration with Alice Keliher (q.v.), Zigler developed a certification program for child care workers, the Child Development Associate.

Zigler graduated from the University of Missouri at Kansas City in 1954. He received the Ph.D. degree at the University of Texas at Austin in 1958, after a psychological internship at Worcester (Massachusetts) State Hospital (1957–58). After teaching for one year (1958–59) at the University of Missouri at Columbia, Zigler went to Yale University. He became professor of psychology in 1967 and Sterling Professor in 1976. He headed the Psychology Section of the Child Study Center and helped to establish the Bush Center in Child Development and Social Policy, which he directed from 1977.

Zigler served as a consultant to secretaries of the U.S. Department of Health, Education and Welfare. His awards came from the American Psychological Association, American Academy of Pediatrics, American Association on Mental Deficiency, American Academy on Mental Retardation, National Association for Retarded Citizens, and Association for the Advancement of Psychology. Zigler contributed to many psychology texts and encyclopedias. He coauthored *Socialization and Personality Development* (1973), *Principles of General Psychology* (1980), *Understanding Mental Retardation* (1986), *Children, Development and Social Issues* (1987), and *Head Start: The Inside Story of America's Most Successful Educational Experiment* (1992). He edited *Project Head Start: A Legacy of the War on Poverty* (1979).

REFERENCES: CA (NR-33); ECE; WW (1996); *American Journal of Community Psychology* 18 (April 1990): 179–216; *American Psychologist* 38 (January 1983): 40–49, and 42 (April 1987): 315–19; *Mental Retardation* 15 (August 1977): n.p.; *Journal of Orthopsychiatry* 63 (July 1993): 330–32; Edward F. Zigler and Mary E. Lang, ''Head Start: Looking toward the Future,'' *Young Children* 38 (September 1983): 3–6.

Appendix A

PLACE OF BIRTH

UNITED STATES

Alabama

Hill, Mozell Clarence	Anniston
Young, Nathan Benjamin	Newbern

Alaska

Demmert, William G., Jr.	Klawock

Arkansas

Green, Richard Reginald	Mennifee

California

Andrus, Ethel Percy	San Francisco
Beatty, Willard Walcott	Berkeley
Cain, Leo Francis	Chico
Coons, Arthur Gardiner	Anaheim
Cooper, William John	Sacramento
Forbes, Jack D.	Long Beach
Fry, Edward Bernard	Los Angeles
Gardner, David Pierpont	Berkeley
Gardner, John William	Los Angeles
Grambs, Jean Dresden	Pigeon Point
Gross, Calvin Edward	Los Angeles
Holland, (George) Kenneth	Los Angeles
Kingsbury, Susan Myra	San Pablo
Regan, Agnes Gertrude	San Francisco

Risling, David, Jr.	Weitchpec
Sears, Robert Richardson	Palo Alto

Colorado

Casey, Ralph Droz	Aspen
Samora, Julian	Pagosa Springs

Connecticut

Burritt, Elihu	New Britain
Carroll, John Bissell	Hartford
Howe, Harold, II	Hartford
Marland, Sidney Percy, Jr.	Danielson
Sizer, Theodore Ryland	New Haven
Spock, Benjamin McLane	New Haven
Stuart, Moses	Wilton

Delaware

Redding, (Jay) Saunders	Wilmington

District of Columbia

Borchardt, Selma Munter
Brown, Sterling Allen
Gaver, Mary Virginia
Henderson, Edwin Bancroft
Irwin, Agnes
Keliher, Alice Virginia
Patterson, Frederick Douglass
Stolz, Lois Hayden Meek
Taylor, Alrutheus Ambush

Florida

Zacharias, Jerrold Reinach	Jacksonville

Georgia

Barker, Mary Cornelia	Atlanta
Benson, Charles Scott	Atlanta
Butler, Selena Sloan	Thomasville
Foreman, Stephen	Rome
Jarrell, (Helen) Ira	Merriwether County
Nabrit, James Madison, Jr.	Atlanta
Nabrit, Samuel Milton	Macon
Pitts, Lucius Holsey	James
Stanley, Julian Cecil, Jr.	Macon
Torrance, (Ellis) Paul	Milledgeville
Wright, Elizabeth Evelyn	Talbotton

Idaho

Bell, Terrel Howard	Lava Hot Springs

Illinois

Blackmer, Alan Rogers	Oak Park
Cobb, Jewell Plummer	Chicago
Cooper, (Jere) Frank Bower	Mount Morris Township
Crim, Alonzo Aristotle	Chicago
Eisner, Elliot Wayne	Chicago
Ellis, John Tracy	Seneca
Engelmann, Siegfried	Chicago
Gallagher, Buell Gordon	Rankin
Gentle, Thomas Higdon	Farmington
Gross, Richard Edmund	Chicago
Henne, Frances Elizabeth	Springfield
Huggins, Nathan Irvin	Chicago
Ilg, Frances Lillian	Oak Park
Krug, Edward August	Chicago
Mitchell, Lucy Sprague	Chicago
Nef, John Ulric, Jr.	Chicago
Nyquist, Ewald Berger	Rockford
Paley, Vivian Gussin	Chicago
Read, Sister Joel	Chicago

Reel, Estelle	Pittsfield
Sizemore, Barbara Ann Laffoon	Chicago
Vincent, George Edgar	Rockford
Wexler, Jacqueline Grennan	Sterling
White, Edna Noble	Fairmount
Wood, Stella Louise	Chicago

Indiana

Ackerman, Carl William	Richmond
Baird, Albert Craig	Vevay
Bloom, Allan David	Indianapolis
Brademas, (Stephen) John	Mishawaka
Coleman, James Samuel	Bedford
Comer, James Pierpont	East Chicago
Hildreth, Gertrude Howell	Terre Haute
Megel, Carl J.	Hayden
Millett, John David	Indianapolis
Oberholtzer, Kenneth Edison	Carbon
Sharp, Zerna A.	Hillisburg
Woody, (Walter) Thomas	Thorntown

Iowa

Bowman, John Gabbert	Davenport
Engle, Paul Hamilton	Cedar Rapids
Goodykoontz, Bess	Waukon
Haugen, Einar Ingvald	Sioux City
Morley, Margaret Warner	Montrose
Pusey, Nathan Marsh	Council Bluffs
Taft, (Julia) Jessie	Dubuque
Yoakam, Gerald Alan	Eagle Grove

Kansas

Douglass, Aubrey Augustus	Eureka
H'Doubler, Margaret Newell	Beloit
Marshall, Florence M.	Shirley

Peterson, Martha Elizabeth	Jamestown
Storey, Thomas Andrew	Burden

Louisiana

Clark, Felton Grandison	Baton Rouge
Rafferty, Maxwell Lewis, Jr.	New Orleans
Wright, Sophie Bell	New Orleans

Maine

Ames, Louise Bates	Portland
Bigelow, Karl Worth	Bangor
Campbell, Olive Dame	Medford
Copeland, Melvin Thomas	Brewer
Knowles, Asa Smallidge	Northeast Harbor
Richards, Robert Hallowell	Gardiner
Turner, Clair Elsmere	Harmony

Maryland

Johnson, Eleanor Murdock	Washington County
McIntosh, Milicent Carey	Baltimore
Rudolph, Frederick	Baltimore
Turner, Thomas Wyatt	Hughesville
Willis, Benjamin Coppage	Baltimore

Massachusetts

Bascom, Florence	Williamstown
Brewster, Kingman, Jr.	Longmeadow
Coles, Robert (Martin)	Boston
Coyle, Grace Longwell	North Adams
Dearborn, Walter Fenno	Marblehead
Donham, Wallace Brett	Rockland
Eliot, Abigail Adams	Boston
Haynes, Rowland	Worcester
Heffernan, Helen	Lawrence
Lloyd, Alice Spencer Geddes	Athol
Locke, Bessie	Cambridge (later, Arlington)

McCarthy, Charles	North Bridgewater (later, Brockton)
Merriam, Harold Guy	Westminster
Monro, John Usher	North Andover
Noyes, Arthur Amos	Newburyport
Park, Rosemary	Andover
Shedd, Mark Redans	Quincy
Solomon, Barbara Miller	Boston
Speare, Frank Palmer	Boston
Spofford, Grace Harriet	Haverhill
Stone, Arthur L.	Spencer
Tyack, David B.	Beverly
Wharton, Clifton Reginald, Jr.	Boston

Michigan

Begle, Edward Griffith	Saginaw
Carlson, William Samuel	Ironwood
Elkind, David	Detroit
Hungerford, Richard H.	Concord
Hunt, Herold Christian	Northville
Jacobs, Leland Blair	Tawas City
Miel, Alice Marie	Six Lakes
Roberts, Lydia Jane	Hope Township
Selden, David Seeley	Dearborn
Shelly, Mary Josephine	Grand Rapids
Thurston, Lee Mohrmann	Central Lake
Warriner, John E.	

Minnesota

Gans, Roma	St. Cloud
Giddings, Thaddeus Philander Woodbury	Anoka
Goldsmith, Grace Arabell	St. Paul
Hagerty, William Walsh	Holyoke
Keller, Robert John	White Bear Lake
Lieberman, Myron	St. Paul
Stalnaker, John Marshall	Duluth

Mississippi

McAllister, Jane Ellen	Vicksburg
Player, Willa Beatrice	Jackson

Missouri

Bruner, Herbert Bascom	Montserrat
Goslin, Willard Edward	Harrisburg
Horn, Ernest	Mercer County
Kranzberg, Melvin	St. Louis
Sears, Jesse Brundage	Kidder
Shapley, John	Jasper County
Zigler, Edward Frank	Kansas City

Montana

Towle, Charlotte Helen	Butte

Nebraska

Brownell, Samuel Miller	Peru
Hansen, Carl Francis	Wolbach
Hinton, Carmelita Chase	Omaha
Hunt, Joseph McVicker	Scotttsbluff
Thayer, Vivian Trow	Tamora

New Hampshire

Hunt, Charles Wesley	Charlestown
Kingsbury, Cyrus	Alstead
Patrick, Mary Mills	Canterbury

New Jersey

Anrig, Gregory Richard	Englewood
Cobb, Henry Van Zandt	East Orange
Cuban, Larry	Passaic
DuBois, Rachel Davis	near Woodstown
Gage, Nathaniel Lees	Union City
Hamilton, (Amy) Gordon	Tenafly

Hess, Robert Lee	Asbury Park
Hoppock, Robert	Lambertville
Jackson, Philip Wesley	Vineland
Morrison, Philip	Somerville
Renne, Roland Roger	Bridgeton
Tumin, Melvin Marvin	Newark
Walcutt, Charles Child	Montclair

New Mexico

Dozier, Edward Pasqual	Santa Clara Pueblo
Lusk, Georgia Lee Witt	near Carlsbad

New York

Adler, Mortimer Jerome	New York
Austin, Mary Carrington	Sherrill
Ausubel, David Paul	Brooklyn
Baker, Frank Elmer	Clymer
Berry, George Packer	Troy
Bestor, Arthur Eugene, Jr.	Chautauqua
Bishop, Nathan	Vernon
Boyce, Frank Gordon	Binghamton
Bronk, Detlev Wulf	New York
Bruner, Jerome Seymour	New York
Bunting, Mary Alice Ingraham	Brooklyn
Clapp, Hannah Kezia	near Albany
Cooley, Anna Maria	New York
Cooley, Rossa Belle	Greenport
Cremin, Lawrence Arthur	New York
D'Amico, Victor Edmond	New York
Diller, Angela	Brooklyn
Dorson, Richard Mercer	New York
Feldman, Marvin Jerome	Rochester
Fenichel, Carl	New York
Fisher, Welthy Blakesley Honsinger	Rome
Glazer, Nathan	New York
Greene, Maxine Meyer	New York
Hayes, Samuel Perkins, Sr.	Baldwinsville

Healy, Timothy Stafford	New York
Herrnstein, Richard Julius	New York
Hesburgh, Theodore Martin	Syracuse
Hofstadter, Richard	Buffalo
Holt, John Caldwell	New York
Keller, Franklin Jefferson	New York
Keller, Fred Simmons	Rural Grove
Keppel, Francis	New York
Kline, Morris	New York
Kohlberg, Lawrence	Bronxville
Lorge, Irving Daniel	New York
Mayer, Clara Woollie	New York
Meier, Deborah Willen	New York
Mills, Cyrus Taggart	Paris
Naumburg, Margaret	New York
Parker, Franklin	New York
Passow, Aaron Harry	Liberty
Poussaint, Alvin Francis	New York
Reese, Gustave	New York
Sarason, Seymour Bernard	Brooklyn
Schuman, William Howard	New York
Shanker, Albert	New York
Smith, Hilda Worthington	New York
Spodek, Bernard	Brooklyn
Thorndike, Robert Ladd	Montrose
Weber, Lillian	New York
Zachry, Caroline Beaumont	New York

North Carolina

Cheek, James Edward	Roanoke Rapids
Cooper, Anna Julia Haywood	Raleigh
Gleason, Eliza Valeria Atkins	Winston-Salem
Ivey, John Eli, Jr.	Raleigh
Jones, Franklin Ross	Charlotte
Koontz, Elizabeth Duncan	Salisbury
Morgan, Lucy Calista	Murphy
Sowell, Thomas	Gastonia

North Dakota

O'Connor, Clarence Daniel	Pembina

Ohio

Aikin, Wilford Morton	New Concord
Bowen, William Gordon	Cincinnati
Boyer, Ernest LeRoy	Dayton
Commons, John Rogers	Hollansburg
Cooke, Flora Juliette	Bainbridge
Doll, Edgar Arnold	Cleveland
Fry, Emma Viola Sheridan	Painesville
Glueck, Nelson	Cincinnati
Herskovits, Melville Jean	Bellefontaine
Hill, Martha	East Palestine
Horwich, Frances Rappaport	Ottawa
Jones, Virginia Mae Lacy	Cincinnati
McCaslin, Nellie	Cleveland
Mussey, Ellen Spencer	Geneva
Raup, Robert Bruce	Clark County
Ray, Henry William	Caldwell
Rees, Mina Spiegel	Cleveland
Sheats, Paul Henry	Tiffin
Weikart, David Powell	Youngstown
Williamson, John Finley	Canton
Woodring, Paul Dean	Delta

Oklahoma

Ballard, Louis Wayne	Devil's Promenade
Franklin, John Hope	Rentiesville
Love, Ruth Burnett	Lawton
Whiteman, Henrietta V. (Henri Mann)	Clinton

Pennsylvania

Alexander, (Richard) Thomas	Smicksburg
Becker, Gary Stanley	Pottsville
Bell, Derrick Albert, Jr.	Pittsburgh

Bloom, Benjamin Samuel	Lansford
Bok, Derek Curtis	Bryn Mawr
Congdon, Charles Harris	Nelson
Douglass, Sarah Mapes	Philadelphia
Drexel, Mary Katharine	Philadelphia
Fantini, Mario D.	Philadelphia
Gans, Bird Stein	Allegheny City
Goodenough, Florence Laura	Honesdale
Mann, Albert Russell	Hawkins
Marcus, Jacob Rader	Connellsville
Marshall, Clara	West Chester
McLaren, Louise Leonard	Wellsboro
Neyhart, Amos Earl	South Williamsport
Preston, Ann	Westgrove
Schofield, Martha	near Newton
Towne, Laura Matilda	Pittsburgh
Vars, Gordon Forrest	Erie
Witmer, Lightner	Philadelphia

Rhode Island

Doyle, Sarah Elizabeth	Providence
Ryan, Sister John Gabriel	Manville

South Carolina

Clark, Septima Poinsette	Charleston
Lumiansky, Robert Mayer	Darlington
Phinazee, (Alethia) Annette Lewis Hoage	Orangeburg

South Dakota

Anderson, Charles Arnold	Platte
Artichoker, John Hobart	Pine Ridge
Fairbank, John King	Huron
Flanagan, Hallie Mae Ferguson	Redfield
Reeves, Floyd Wesley	Castalia
Schultz, Theodore William	Arlington

Tennessee

Alexander, William Marvin	McKenzie
Hirsch, Eric Donald, Jr.	Memphis
Horton, Myles	Savannah
Wattenbarger, James Lorenzo	Cleveland

Texas

Brazelton, Thomas Berry, II	Waco
Caldwell, Bettye McDonald	Smithville
Cavazos, Lauro Fred	King Ranch
Rivera, Tomás	Crystal City
Silber, John Robert	San Antonio
Wilson, Logan	Huntsville
Wright, Benjamin Fletcher	Austin

Utah

Campbell, Roald Fay	Ogden
Eggertsen, Claude Andrew	Thistle
Lloyd, Wesley Parkinson	Ogden

Vermont

Pitkin, Royce Stanley	Marshfield
Stone, Mason Sereno	Waterbury Center

Virginia

Barnett, Marguerite Ross	Charlottesville
Booker, Matilda Moseley	Halifax County
Branch, Mary Elizabeth	Farmville
Burroughs, Nannie Helen	Orange Springs
Culbertson, Jack Arthur	Nickelsville
Davis, Jackson	Cumberland County
Drake, (John Gibbs) St. Clair	Suffolk
Foster, Luther Hilton, Jr.	Lawrenceville
Foster, Marcus Albert	Athens
Fred, Edwin Broun	Middleburg

Holland, Annie Welthy Daughtry	Isle of Wight County
Larrick, Nancy Gray	Winchester
Merritt, Emma Frances Grayson	Dumfries
Peake, Mary Smith Kelsey	Norfolk
Prescott, Daniel Alfred	Manassas
Randolph, Virginia Estelle	Richmond
Slowe, Lucy Diggs	Berryville
Williams, William Taylor Burwell	Stonebridge

Washington

Bond, Guy Loraine	Cooperville
Bowen, Howard Rothmann	Spokane
Buchanan, Scott Milross	Sprague

West Virginia

Boatwright, Frederic William	White Sulphur Springs
Farnsworth, Dana Lyda	Troy
Holmes, Dwight Oliver Wendell	Lewisburg

Wisconsin

Anderson, Robert Henry	Milwaukee
Buros, Oscar Krisen	Lake Nebagamon
Childs, John Lawrence	Eau Claire
Dumke, Glenn S.	Green Bay
Frazier, Maude	Sauk County
Morgan, Mary Kimball	Janesville
Shane, Harold Gray	Milwaukee
Spindler, George Dearborn	Stevens Point
Watson, Goodwin Barbour	Whitewater

Wyoming

Anderson, John Edward	Laramie

FOREIGN COUNTRIES

Australia

Conway, Jill Kathryn Ker	Hilston, New South Wales

Austria

Karplus, Robert	Vienna
Lazarsfeld, Paul Felix	Vienna
Lerner, Gerda	Vienna

Belarus

Kotler, Aaron	

Canada

Bandura, Albert	Mundare, Alberta
Goodlad, John Inkster	North Vancouver, British Columbia
Hayden, Philip Cady	Brantford, Ontario
Hunter, Madeline Cheek	Saskatchewan
Lyle, Guy Redvers	Lloydminster, Sasktchewan

China

Fahs, Sophia Blanche Lyon	Hangchow

Egypt

Gattegno, Caleb	Alexandria

England

Katz, Lilian Gonshaw	London
Noah, Harold Julius	London
Pintner, Rudolf	Lytham, Lancashire

France

Barzun, Jacques Martin	Creteil
Labatut, Jean	Martres-Tolosones, Haute-Garonne
Mayer, Jean	Paris

Germany

Albers, Josef	Bothrop, Westphalia
Erikson, Erik Homburger	Frankfurt on the Main
Gray, Hanna Holborn	Heidelberg
Maeder, Hans Karl	Hamburg
Stern, Catherine Brieger	Breslau

Hungary

Kemeny, John George	Budapest
Lefkowitz, Abraham	Revish

Iran

Galamian, Ivan Alexander	Tabriz

Israel

Ginott, Haim G.	Tel Aviv

Italy

Pei, Mario Andrew	Rome

Mexico

Carhart, Raymond Theodore	Mexico City

Norway

Foght, Harold Waldstein	Fredrikshald

Panama Canal Zone

Clark, Kenneth Bancroft	
Guinier, Ewart G.	Panama City

Poland

Baron, Salo Wittnayer	Tarnow, Austrian Galicia
Belkin, Samuel	Swislicz
Bereday, George Zygmunt Fijalowski	Warsaw
Chall, Jeanne Sternlicht	Shendisov
Perlman, Selig	Bialystok

Puerto Rico

Rogler, Lloyd Henry	Santurce
Schomburg, Arthur Alphonso	San Juan

Romania

Wechsler, David	Lespedi

Russia

Gingold, Josef	Brest-Litovsk
Janson, Horst Woldemar	St. Petersburg

Scotland

Highet, Gilbert Arthur	Glasgow

South Africa

Papert, Seymour Aubrey	Pretoria

Switzerland

Shaw, Pauline Agassiz	Neuchatel

Wales

Edwards, Richard	Cardiganshire

West Indies

Crogman, William Henry, Sr.	Phillipsburg, St. Martin

Appendix B

STATES OF MAJOR SERVICE

ALABAMA

Foster, Luther Hilton, Jr.
Gallagher, Buell Gordon
Monro, John Usher
Nabrit, Samuel Miller
Patterson, Frederick Douglass
Pitts, Lucius Holsey
Rafferty, Maxwell Lewis, Jr.
Williams, William Taylor Burwell
Young, Nathan Benjamin

ALASKA

Demmert, William G., Jr.

ARIZONA

Dozier, Edward Pasqual

ARKANSAS

Caldwell, Bettye McDonald

CALIFORNIA

Andrus, Ethel Percy
Bandura, Albert
Begle, Edward Griffith
Benson, Charles Scott
Bowen, Howard Rothmann
Boyer, Ernest LeRoy
Cain, Leo Francis
Cobb, Jewell Plummer
Coons, Arthur Gardiner
Cooper, William John
Cuban, Larry
Douglass, Aubrey Augustus
Drake, (John Gibbs) St. Clair
Dumke, Glenn S.
Eisner, Elliot Wayne
Erikson, Erik Homburger
Forbes, Jack D.
Foster, Marcus Albert
Gage, Nathaniel Lees
Gardner, David Pierpont
Glazer, Nathan
Goodlad, John Inkster
Goslin, Willard Edward
Gross, Richard Edmund
Heffernan, Helen
Hunter, Madeline Cheek
Karplus, Robert
Love, Ruth Burnett
Mills, Cyrus Taggart
Noyes, Arthur Amos
Park, Rosemary
Rafferty, Maxwell Lewis, Jr.
Regan, Agnes Gertrude
Risling, David, Jr.
Rivera, Tomás

Sears, Jesse Brundage
Sears, Robert Richardson
Sheats, Paul Henry
Sowell, Thomas
Spindler, George Dearborn
Stolz, Lois Hayden Meek
Storey, Thomas Andrew
Tyack, David B.

COLORADO

Lewis, Inez Johnson
Oberholtzer, Kenneth Edison

CONNECTICUT

Albers, Josef
Ames, Louise Bates
Begle, Edward Griffith
Brewster, Kingman, Jr.
Brownell, Samuel Miller
Burritt, Elihu
Cobb, Jewell Plummer
Comer, James Pierpont
Hill, Martha
Ilg, Frances Lillian
Johnson, Eleanor Murdock
Keliher, Alice Virginia
Park, Rosemary
Rogler, Lloyd Henry
Sarason, Seymour Bernard
Shedd, Mark Redans
Stuart, Moses
Zigler, Edward Frank

DELAWARE

Carlson, William Samuel

DISTRICT OF COLUMBIA

Ballard, Louis Wayne
Beatty, Willard Walcott
Bell, Terrel Howard
Borchardt, Selma Munter
Boyer, Ernest LeRoy
Brademas, (Stephen) John
Brown, Sterling Allen
Brownell, Samuel Miller
Burroughs, Nannie Helen
Cavazos, Lauro Fred
Cheek, James Edward
Cooper, Anna Julia Haywood
Cuban, Larry
Demmert, William G., Jr.
Ellis, John Tracy
Foght, Harold Waldstein
Gardner, John William
Goodykoontz, Bess
Hansen, Carl Francis
Healy, Timothy Stafford
Henderson, Edwin Bancroft
Howe, Harold, II
Keppel, Francis
Marland, Sidney Percy
McAllister, Jane Ellen
Merritt, Emma Frances Grayson
Mussey, Ellen Spencer
Nabrit, James Madison
Player, Willa Beatrice
Reel (Meyer), Estelle
Regan, Agnes Gertrude
Shapley, John
Slowe, Lucy Diggs
Smith, Hilda Worthington
Turner, Thomas Wyatt

FLORIDA

Alexander, William Marvin
Wattenbarger, James Lorenzo
Young, Nathan Benjamin

GEORGIA

Barker, Mary Cornelia
Butler, Selena Sloan
Crim, Alonzo Aristotle
Crogman, William Henry
Gleason, Eliza Valeria Atkins
Hill, Mozell Clarence
Jarrell, (Helen) Ira
Jones, Virginia Mae Lacy
Kranzberg, Melvin
Lyle, Guy Redvers
Phinazee, (Alethia) Annette Lewis Hoage
Pitts, Lucius Holsey
Torrance, (Ellis) Paul

HAWAII

Austin, Mary Carrington

IDAHO

Campbell, Roald Fay

ILLINOIS

Adler, Mortimer Jerome
Anderson, Charles Arnold
Anderson, Robert Henry
Ausubel, David Paul
Beatty, Willard Walcott
Becker, Gary Stanley
Bestor, Arthur Eugene, Jr.
Bloom, Allan David
Bloom, Benjamin Samuel
Campbell, Roald Fay
Carhart, Raymond Theodore
Coleman, James Samuel
Congdon, Charles Harris
Cooke, Flora Juliette
Drake, (John Gibbs) St. Clair
Edwards, Richard
Engelmann, Siegfried
Franklin, John Hope
Gleason, Eliza Veleria Atkins
Gray, Hanna Holborn
Hayden, Philip
Henne, Frances Elizabeth
Herskovits, Melville Jean
Hess, Robert Lee
Hill, Mozell Clarence
Horwich, Frances Rappaport
Hunt, Herold Christian
Hunt, Joseph McVicker
Jackson, Philip Wesley
Katz, Lilian Gonshaw
Marland, Sidney Percy, Jr.
McCaslin, Nellie
Megel, Carl J.
Morgan, Mary Kimball
Nef, John Ulric, Jr.
Paley, Vivian Gussin
Reeves, Floyd Wesley
Roberts, Lydia Jane
Schultz, Theodore William
Schwab, Joseph Jackson
Shane, Harold Gray
Sizemore, Barbara Ann Laffoon
Spodek, Bernard
Towle, Charlotte Helen

Vincent, George Edgar
Willis, Benjamin Coppage

INDIANA

Dorson, Richard Mercer
Gingold, Josef
Hesburgh, Theodore Martin
Samora, Julian
Shane, Harold Gray

IOWA

Baird, Albert Craig
Bowen, Howard Rothmann
Bowman, John Gabbert
Engle, Paul Hamilton
Hayden, Philip Cady
Horn, Ernest
Schultz, Theodore William
Sears, Robert Richardson

KANSAS

Foght, Harold Waldstein

KENTUCKY

Anderson, Charles Arnold
Clapp, Elsie Ripley
Lloyd, Alice Spencer Geddes

LOUISIANA

Clark, Felton Grandison
Goldsmith, Grace Arabell
Lumiansky, Robert Mayer
Lyle, Guy Redvers
Wright, Sophie Bell

MAINE

Shedd, Mark Redans

MARYLAND

Bronk, Detlev Wulf
Buchanan, Scott Milross
Coleman, James Samuel
Grambs, Jean Dresden
Holmes, Dwight Oliver Wendell
Prescott, Daniel Alfred
Stanley, Julian Cecil, Jr.

MASSACHUSETTS

Anrig, Gregory Richard
Bell, Derrick Albert, Jr.
Berry, George Packer
Blackmer, Alan Rogers
Bok, Derek Curtis
Brazelton, Thomas Berry, II
Bruner, Jerome Seymour
Buchanan, Scott Milross
Bunting, Mary Alice Ingraham
Carroll, John Bissell
Chall, Jeanne Sternlicht
Coles, Robert (Martin)
Conway, Jill Kathryn Ker
Copeland, Melvin Thomas
Dearborn, Walter Fenno
Donham, Wallace Brett
Eliot, Abigail Adams
Elkind, David
Erikson, Erik Homburger
Fairbank, John King
Fantini, Mario D.
Farnsworth, Dana Lyda
Flanagan, Hallie Mae Ferguson

Glazer, Nathan
Guinier, Ewart G.
Haugen, Einar Ingvald
Hayes, Samuel Perkins
Herrnstein, Richard Julius
Holt, John Caldwell
Howe, Harold, II
Huggins, Nathan Irwin
Hunt, Herold Christian
Irwin, Agnes
Keppel, Francis
Knowles, Asa Smallidge
Kohlberg, Lawrence
Maeder, Hans Karl
Marshall, Florence M.
Mayer, Jean
Monro, John Usher
Morrison, Philip
Noyes, Arthur Amos
Papert, Seymour Aubrey
Poussaint, Alvin Francis
Pusey, Nathan Marsh
Richards, Robert Hallowell
Rudolph, Frederick
Shaw, Pauline Agassiz
Silber, John Robert
Solomon, Barbara Miller
Speare, Frank Palmer
Stuart, Moses
Turner, Clair Elsmere
Wright, Benjamin Fletcher
Zacharias, Jerrold Reinach

MICHIGAN

Brownell, Samuel Miller
Eggertsen, Claude Andrew
Hungerford, Richard H.
Ivey, John Eli, Jr.
Miel, Alice Marie
Selden, David Seeley
Thurston, Lee Mohrmann
Weikart, David Powell
Wharton, Clifton Reginald, Jr.
White, Edna Noble

MINNESOTA

Anderson, John Edward
Bond, Guy Loraine
Casey, Ralph Droz
Congdon, Charles Harris
Giddings, Thaddeus Philander Woodbury
Goodenough, Florence
Goslin, Willard Edward
Green, Richard Reginald
Keller, Robert John
Torrance, (Ellis) Paul
Vincent, George Edgar
Wood, Stella Louise

MISSISSIPPI

McAllister, Jane Ellen
Monro, John Usher

MISSOURI

Aiken, Wilford Morton
Barnett, Marguerite Ross
Gross, Calvin Edward
Morgan, Mary Kimball
Wexler, Jacqueline Grennan
Young, Nathan Benjamin

MONTANA

Merriam, Harold Guy
Renne, Roland Roger
Stone, Arthur L.
Whiteman, Henrietta V. (Henri Mann)

NEBRASKA

Hansen, Carl Francis
Haynes, Rowland

NEVADA

Clapp, Hannah Kezia
Frazier, Maude

NEW HAMPSHIRE

Kemeny, John George

NEW JERSEY

Anrig, Gregory Richard
Bowen, William Gordon
Boyer, Ernest LeRoy
Buros, Oscar Krisen
Doll, Edgar Arnold
DuBois, Rachel Davis
Fry, Edward Bernard
Gaver, Mary Virginia
Kotler, Aaron
Labatut, Jean
Nash, Alice Ford Morrison
Shedd, Mark Redans
Stalnaker, John Marshall
Tumin, Melvin Marvin
Williamson, John Finley

NEW MEXICO

Ballard, Louis Wayne
Lusk, Georgia Lee Witt

NEW YORK

Ackerman, Carl William
Alexander, (Richard) Thomas
Ausubel, David Paul
Baron, Salo Wittmayer
Barzun, Jacques Martin
Beatty, Willard Walcott
Belkin, Samuel
Bereday, George Zygmunt Fijalowski
Bigelow, Karl Worth
Brademas, (Stephen) John
Bronk, Detlev Wulf
Bruner, Herbert Bascom
Caldwell, Bettye McDonald
Childs, John Lawrence
Clark, Kenneth Bancroft
Cobb, Jewell Plummer
Cooley, Anna Maria
Cremin, Lawrence Arthur
D'Amico, Victor Edmond
Davis, Jackson
Diller, Angela
Elkind, David
Fahs, Sophia Blanche Lyon
Fantani, Mario D.
Feldman, Marvin Jerome
Fenichel, Carl
Flanagan, Hallie Mae Ferguson
Fry, Emma Viola Sheridan
Galamian, Ivan Alexander
Gallagher, Buell Gordon
Gans, Bird Stein

Gans, Roma
Gardner, John William
Gattegno, Caleb
Ginott, Haim G.
Greene, Maxine Meyer
Guinier, Ewart G.
Hamilton, (Amy) Gordon
Healy, Timothy Stafford
Henne, Frances Elizabeth
Hess, Robert Lee
Highet, Gilbert Arthur
Hildreth, Gertrude Howell
Hill, Martha
Hill, Mozell Clarence
Hofstadter, Richard
Holland, (George) Kenneth
Hoppock, Robert
Howe, Harold, II
Hunt, Charles Wesley
Jacobs, Leland Blair
Janson, Horst Woldemar
Johnson, Eleanor Murdock
Keliher, Alice Virginia
Keller, Franklin Jefferson
Keller, Fred Simmons
Kline, Morris
Lazarsfeld, Paul Felix
Lefkowitz, Abraham
Lerner, Gerda
Locke, Bessie
Lorge, Irving Daniel
Lumiansky, Robert Mayer
Mann, Albert Russell
Marshall, Florence M.
Mayer, Clara Woollie
McCaslin, Nellie
McIntosh, Millicent Carey
Meier, Deborah Willen
Miel, Alice Marie
Mitchell, Lucy Sprague
Naumburg, Margaret
Noah, Harold Julius
Nyquist, Ewald Berger
O'Connor, Clarence Daniel
Park, Rosemary
Passow, Aaron Henry
Pei, Mario Andrew
Peterson, Martha Elizabeth
Pintner, Rudolf
Raup, Robert Bruce
Rees, Mina Spiegel
Reese, Gustave
Rogler, Lloyd Henry
Schomburg, Arthur Alphonso
Schuman, William Howard
Shanker, Albert
Sharp, Zerna A.
Spofford, Grace Harriet
Stern, Catherine Brieger
Stolz, Lois Hayden Meek
Storey, Thomas Andrew
Thayer, Vivian Trow
Thorndike, Robert Ladd
Vincent, George Edgar
Walcutt, Charles Child
Warriner, John E.
Watson, Goodwin Barbour
Weber, Lillian
Wechsler, David
Wexler, Jacqueline Grennan
Wharton, Clifton Reginald, Jr.
Zachry, Caroline Beaumont

NORTH CAROLINA

Albers, Josef
Campbell, Olive Dame
Carroll, John Bissell
Cheek, James Edward
Franklin, John Hope
Holland, Annie Welthy Daughtry
Ivey, John Eli, Jr.
Koontz, Elizabeth Duncan
McLaren, Louise Leonard
Morgan, Lucy Calista
Phinazee, (Alethia) Annette Lewis Hoage
Player, Willa Beatrice

OHIO

Carlson, William Samuel
Coyle, Grace Longwell
Cuban, Larry
Culbertson, Jack Arthur
Gingold, Josef
Glueck, Nelson
Kranzberg, Melvin
Marcus, Jacob Rader
Millett, John David
Spock, Benjamin McLane
Vars, Gordon Forrest
White, Edna Noble

OKLAHOMA

Bruner, Herbert Bascom
Foreman, Stephen
Kingsbury, Cyrus

OREGON

Engelmann, Siegfried
Gentle, Thomas Higdon

PENNSYVANIA

Bascom, Florence
Bowman, John Gabbert
Douglass, Sarah Mapes
Drexel, Mary Katharine
Foster, Marcus Albert
Gross, Calvin Edward
Hagerty, William Walsh
Kingsbury, Susan Myra
Larrick, Nancy Gray
Marland, Sidney Percy
Marshall, Clara
Neyhart, Amos Earl
Preston, Ann
Ray, Henry William
Shedd, Mark Redans
Sizemore, Barbara Ann
Smith, Hilda Worthington
Taft, (Julia) Jessie
Witmer, Lightner
Woody, (Walter) Thomas
Yoakam, Gerald Alan

RHODE ISLAND

Bishop, Nathan
Doyle, Sarah Elizabeth
Sizer, Theodore Ryland

SOUTH CAROLINA

Clark, Septima Poinsette
Cooley, Rossa Belle
Schofield, Martha
Towne, Laura Matilda
Wright, Elizabeth Evelyn

SOUTH DAKOTA

Artichoker, John Hobart
Cobb, Henry Van Zandt
Foght, Harold Waldstein
Reeves, Floyd Wesley

TENNESSEE

Clark, Septima Poinsette
Goslin, Willard Edward
Horton, Myles
Taylor, Alrutheus Ambush

TEXAS

Anderson, Robert Henry
Barnett, Marguerite Ross
Branch, Mary Elizabeth
Cavazos, Lauro Fred
Gross, Calvin Edward
Nabrit, Samuel Milton
Rivera, Tomás
Silber, John Robert
Wilson, Logan
Wright, Benjamin Fletcher

UTAH

Bell, Terrel Howard
Campbell, Roald Fay
Gardner, David Pierpont
Lloyd, Wesley Parkinson

VERMONT

Boyce, Frank Gordon
Hill, Martha
Hinton, Carmelita Chase
Pitkin, Royce Stanley
Shelly, Mary Josephine
Stone, Mason Sereno

VIRGINIA

Boatwright, Frederic William
Booker, Matilda Moseley
Davis, Jackson
Hirsch, Eric Donald, Jr.
Jones, Franklin Ross
Peake, Mary Smith Kelsey
Randolph, Virginia Estelle
Redding, (Jay) Saunders
Turner, Thomas Wyatt

WASHINGTON

Bestor, Arthur Eugene, Jr.
Cooper, (Jere) Frank Bower
Goodlad, John Inkster
Ryan, Sister John Gabriel
Woodring, Paul Dean

WEST VIRGINIA

Clapp, Elsie Ripley
Parker, Franklin

WISCONSIN

Baker, Frank Elmer
Commons, John Rogers
Fred, Edwin Broun
Haugen, Einar Ingvald
H'Doubler, Margaret Newell
Krug, Edward August
Lerner, Gerda
McCarthy, Charles
Perlman, Selig
Peterson, Martha Elizabeth

Pusey, Nathan Marsh
Read, Sister Joel
Stanley, Julian Cecil, Jr.

WYOMING

Reel (Meyer), Estelle

OVERSEAS

Fisher, Welthy Blakesley Honsinger
Patrick, Mary Mills

Appendix C

FIELD OF WORK

ADMINISTRATION OF EDUCATION, FEDERAL GOVERNMENT

Bell, Terrel Howard
Boyer, Ernest LeRoy
Brownell, Samuel Miller
Cavazos, Lauro Fred
Cooper, William John
Demmert, William G., Jr.
Gardner, John William
Goodykoontz, Bess
Howe, Harold, II
Keppel, Francis
Marland, Sidney Percy, Jr.

ADMINISTRATION OF EDUCATION, STATES

Anrig, Gregory Richard
Artichoker, John Hobart
Bell, Terrel Howard
Demmert, William G., Jr.
Heffernan, Helen
Holmes, Dwight Oliver Wendell
Lewis, Inez Johnson
Lusk, Georgia Lee Witt
Millett, John David
Nyquist, Ewald Berger
Rafferty, Maxwell Lewis, Jr.
Reel, Estelle
Shedd, Mark Redans
Stone, Mason Sereno
Thurston, Lee Mohrmann

ADMINISTRATION OF HIGHER EDUCATION

Baker, Frank Elmer
Barnett, Marguerite Ross
Belkin, Samuel
Boatwright, Frederic William
Bok, Derek Curtis
Bowen, Howard Rothmann
Bowen, William Gordon
Bowman, John Gabbert
Boyer, Ernest LeRoy
Brademas, (Stephen) John
Branch, Mary Elizabeth
Brewster, Kingman, Jr.
Bronk, Detlev Wulf
Bunting, Mary Alice Ingraham
Cain, Leo Francis
Carlson, William Samuel
Cavazos, Lauro Fred
Cheek, James Edward
Clark, Felton Grandison
Cobb, Jewell Plummer
Conway, Jill Kathryn Ker
Coons, Arthur Gardiner
Dumke, Glenn S.

Foght, Harold Waldstein
Foster, Luther Hilton, Jr.
Fred, Edwin Broun
Gallagher, Buell Gordon
Gardner, David Pierpont
Glueck, Nelson
Gray, Hanna Holborn
Hagerty, William Walsh
Haynes, Rowland
Healy, Timothy Stafford
Hesburgh, Theodore Martin
Hess, Robert Lee
Holmes, Dwight Oliver Wendell
Kemeny, John George
Knowles, Asa Smallidge
Lloyd, Alice Spencer Geddes
Mayer, Clara Woollie
Mayer, Jean
McIntosh, Millicent Carey
Millett, John David
Mills, Cyrus Taggart
Nabrit, James Madison, Jr.
Nabrit, Samuel Milton
Park, Rosemary
Patterson, Frederick Douglass
Peterson, Martha Elizabeth
Pitkin, Royce Stanley
Pitts, Lucius Holsey
Player, Willa Beatrice
Pusey, Nathan Marsh
Read, Sister Joel
Rees, Mina Spiegel
Renne, Roland Roger
Rivera, Tomás
Silber, John Robert
Speare, Frank Palmer
Vincent, George Edgar
Wexler, Jacqueline Grennan
Wharton, Clifton Reginald, Jr.
Wilson, Logan
Wright, Benjamin Fletcher
Young, Nathan Benjamin

ADMINISTRATION OF PUBLIC AND PRIVATE SCHOOLS

Bishop, Nathan
Brownell, Samuel Miller
Bruner, Herbert Bascom
Clapp, Elsie Ripley
Clapp, Hannah Kezia
Cooper, (Jere) Frank Bower
Cooper, William John
Crim, Alonzo Aristotle
Foster, Marcus Albert
Frazier, Maude
Goslin, Willard Edward
Green, Richard Reginald
Gross, Calvin Edward
Hansen, Carl Francis
Hinton, Carmelita Chase
Hunt, Herold Christian
Jarrell, (Helen) Ira
Love, Ruth Burnett
Maeder, Hans Karl
Marland, Sidney Percy, Jr.
Oberholtzer, Kenneth Edison
Sears, Jesse Brundage
Shedd, Mark Redans
Sizemore, Barbara Ann Laffoon
Willis, Benjamin Coppage

ADULT EDUCATION

Campbell, Olive Dame
Horton, Myles

McCarthy, Charles
Mitchell, Lucy Calista
Reeves, Floyd Wesley
Sheats, Paul Henry
Smith, Hilda Worthington
Vincent, George Edgar
Wright, Sophie Bell

ART AND ARCHITECTURE

Albers, Josef
D'Amico, Victor Edmond
Eisner, Elliot Wayne
Janson, Horst Woldemar
Labatut, Jean
Shapley, John

BUSINESS

Copeland, Melvin Thomas
Donham, Wallace Brett

COMMUNITY AND JUNIOR COLLEGES

Keller, Robert John
Wattenbarger, James Lorenzo

COMPARATIVE AND INTERNATIONAL EDUCATION

Alexander, (Richard) Thomas
Anderson, Charles Arnold
Bereday, George Zygmunt Fijalowski
Bigelow, Karl Worth
Boyce, Frank Gordon
Eggertsen, Claude Andrew
Holland, (George) Kenneth
Noah, Harold Julius
Parker, Franklin

COUNSELING AND GUIDANCE

Bloom, Benjamin
Hoppock, Robert
Lloyd, Wesley Parkinson
Zachry, Caroline Beaumont

CRITICS OF EDUCATION

Bestor, Arthur Eugene, Jr.
Bloom, Allan David
Boyer, Ernest LeRoy
Hirsch, Eric Donald, Jr.
Holt, John Caldwell
Lieberman, Myron
Sizer, Theodore Ryland
Sowell, Thomas

CURRICULUM

Alexander, William Marvin
Beatty, Willard Walcott
Bruner, Herbert Bascom
Bruner, Jerome Seymour
Eisner, Elliott Wayne
Grambs, Jean Dresden
Gross, Richard Edmund
Horn, Ernest
Miel, Alice Marie
Neyhart, Amos Earl
Reeves, Floyd Wesley
Thayer, Vivian Trow
Vars, Gordon Forrest

DANCE

H'Doubler, Margaret Newell
Hill, Martha
Shelly, Mary Josephine

EARLY CHILDHOOD EDUCATION

Ames, Louise Bates
Anderson, John Edward
Caldwell, Bettye McDonald
Eliot, Abigail Adams
Elkind, David
Engelmann, Siegfried
Hunt, Joseph McVicker
Ilg, Frances Lillian
Katz, Lilian Gonshaw
Keliher, Alice Virginia
Locke, Bessie
Mitchell, Lucy Sprague
Paley, Vivian Gussin
Prescott, Daniel Alfred
Shaw, Pauline Agassiz
Spodek, Bernard
Stolz, Lois Hayden Meek
Weber, Lillian
Weikart, David Powell
White, Edna Noble
Wood, Stella Louise

ECONOMICS

Becker, Gary Stanley
Benson, Charles Scott
Bowen, Howard Rothmann
Bowen, William Gordon
Commons, John Roger
Schultz, Theodore William

ELEMENTARY AND SECONDARY EDUCATION

Aiken, Wilford Morton
Blackmer, Alan Rogers
Campbell, Roald Fay
Clapp, Elsie Ripley
Clapp, Hannah Kezia
Cooke, Flora Juliette
Cooper, Anna Julia Haywood
Cooper, (Jere) Frank Bower
Cuban, Larry
Culbertson, Jack Arthur
Fantini, Mario D.
Goodykoontz, Bess
Maeder, Hans Karl
Meier, Deborah Willen
Merritt, Emma Frances Grayson
Naumberg, Margaret
Sears, Jesse Brundage
Sizer, Theodore Ryland

ENGINEERING

Hagerty, William Walsh
Richards, Robert Hallowell

HEALTH AND PHYSICAL EDUCATION

Farnsworth, Dana Lyda
Haynes, Rowland
Henderson, Edwin Bancroft
Morley, Margaret Warner
Shelly, Mary Josephine
Storey, Thomas Andrew
Turner, Clair Elsmere

HISTORY

Cremin, Lawrence Arthur
Ellis, John Tracy
Franklin, John Hope
Hofstadter, Richard

Krug, Edward August
Lerner, Gerda
Rudolph, Frederick
Tyack, David B.
Woody, (Walter) Thomas

HUMANITIES

Barzun, Jacques Martin
Crogman, William Henry
Highet, Gilbert Arthur
Lumiansky, Robert Mayer

JOURNALISM

Ackerman, Carl William
Casey, Ralph Droz
Stone, Arthur L.

LANGUAGE

Baird, Albert Craig
Brown, Sterling Allen
Carroll, John Bissell
Engle, Paul Hamilton
Haugen, Einar Ingvald
Hirsch, Eric Donald, Jr.
Jacobs, Leland Blair
Larrick, Nancy Gray
Merriam, Harold Guy
Pei, Mario Andrew
Warriner, John E.

LAW

Bell, Derrick Albert, Jr.
Nabrit, James Madison, Jr.
Mussey, Ellen Spencer

LIBRARY SCIENCE

Gaver, Mary Virginia
Gleason, Eliza Valeria Atkins
Henne, Frances Elizabeth
Jones, Virginia Mae Lacy
Lyle, Guy Redvers
Phinazee, (Alethia) Annette Lewis Hoage
Schomburg, Arthur Alphonso

MATHEMATICS

Begle, Edward Griffith
Gattego, Caleb
Kemeny, John George
Kline, Morris
Rees, Mina Spiegel

MEASUREMENT AND EVALUATION

Anrig, Gregory Richard
Buros, Oscar Krisen
Dearborn, Walter Fenno
Goodenough, Florence Laura
Lorge, Irving Daniel
Pintner, Rudolf
Stalnaker, John Marshall
Thorndike, Robert Ladd
Torrance (Ellis) Paul
Wechsler, David

MEDICINE AND NURSING

Berry, George Packer
Brazelton, Thomas Berry, II
Comer, James Pierpont
Marshall, Clara
Poussaint, Alvin Francis
Preston, Ann

Ryan, Sister John Gabriel
Spock, Benjamin McLane

MINORITY EDUCATION

Artichoker, John Hobart
Ballard, Louis Wayne
Beatty, Willard Walcott
Booker, Matilda Moseley
Branch, Mary Elizabeth
Burroughs, Nannie Helen
Butler, Selena Sloan
Clark, Septima Poinsette
Comer, James Pierpont
Cooley, Rossa Belle
Cooper, Anna Julia Haywood
Davis, Jackson
Douglass, Sarah Mapes
Drexel, Mary Katharine
Foreman, Stephen
Henderson, Edwin Bancroft
Holland, Annie Welthy Daughtry
Kingsbury, Cyrus
McAllister, Jane Ellen
Monro, John Usher
Peake, Mary Smith Kelsey
Randolph, Virginia Estelle
Risling, David, Jr.
Samora, Julian
Schofield, Martha
Slowe, Lucy Diggs
Taylor, Alrutheus Ambush
Towne, Laura Matilda
Turner, Thomas Wyatt
Williams, William Taylor Burwell
Wright, Elizabeth Evelyn
Young, Nathan Benjamin

MUSIC

Ballard, Louis Wayne
Congdon, Charles Harris
Diller, Angela
Galamian, Ivan Alexander
Giddings, Thaddeus Philander Woodbury
Gingold, Josef
Hayden, Philip Cady
Reese, Gustave
Schuman, William Howard
Spofford, Grace Harriet
Williamson, John Finley

NUTRITION AND HOME ECONOMICS

Cooley, Anna Maria
Goldsmith, Grace Arabell
Mann, Albert Russell
Mayer, Jean
Roberts, Lydia Jane
White, Edna Noble

PARENTAL EDUCATION

Brazelton, Thomas Berry, II
Gans, Bird Stein
Ginott, Haim G.
Spock, Benjamin McLane

PHILOSOPHY

Adler, Mortimer Jerome
Buchanan, Scott Milross
Childs, John Lawrence
Gattegno, Caleb
Gentle, Thomas Higdon
Greene, Maxine Meyer
Raup, Robert Bruce

POLITICS OF EDUCATION

Brademas, (Stephen) John
Frazier, Maude
Gardner, John William

PSYCHOLOGY

Anderson, John Edward
Ausubel, David Paul
Bandura, Albert
Bruner, Jerome Seymour
Carroll, John Bissell
Clark, Kenneth Bancroft
Coles, Robert (Martin)
Erikson, Erik Homburger
Gage, Nathaniel Lees
Goodenough Florence Laura
Herrnstein, Richard Julius
Hildreth, Gertrude Howell
Hunt, Joseph McVicker
Hunter, Madeline Cheek
Keller, Fred Simmons
Kohlberg, Lawrence
Lorge, Irving Daniel
Sarason, Seymour Bernard
Sears, Robert Richardson
Stanley, Julian Cecil, Jr.
Torrance, (Ellis) Paul
Watson, Goodwin Barbour
Witmer, Lightner
Zachry, Caroline Beaumont

READING

Austin, Mary Carrington
Bond, Guy Loraine
Chall, Jeanne Sternlicht
Fisher, Welthy Blakesley Honsinger
Fry, Edward Bernard
Gans, Roma
Hildreth, Gertrude Howell
Johnson, Eleanor Murdock
Sharp, Zerna A.
Walcutt, Charles Child
Yoakam, Gerald Alan

RELIGIOUS EDUCATION

Baron, Salo Wittmayer
Belkin, Samuel
Fahs, Sophia Blanche Lyon
Glueck, Nelson
Kotler, Aaron
Marcus, Jacob Rader
Morgan, Mary Kimball
Stuart, Moses

SCIENCE

Bascom, Florence
Bronk, Detlev Wulf
Cobb, Jewell Plummer
Fred, Edwin Broun
Karplus, Robert
Morrison, Philip
Nabrit, Samuel Milton
Noyes, Arthur Amos
Schwab, Joseph Jackson
Turner, Thomas Wyatt
Zacharias, Jerrold Reinach

SOCIAL SCIENCES

Coleman, James Samuel
Commons, John Rogers
Dorson, Richard Mercer
Dozier, Edward Pasqual

Drake, (John Gibbs) St. Clair
DuBois, Rachel Davis
Fairbank, John King
Forbes, Jack D.
Glazer, Nathan
Guinier, Ewart G.
Herskovits, Melville Jean
Hill, Mozell Clarence
Huggins, Nathan Irvin
Lazarsfeld, Paul Felix
Nef, John Ulric, Jr.
Perlman, Selig
Redding, (Jay) Saunders
Rogler, Lloyd Henry
Samora, Julian
Spindler, George Dearborn
Tumin, Melvin Marvin
Whiteman, Henrietta (Henri Mann)

SOCIAL WORK

Coyle, Grace Longwell
Hamilton, (Amy) Gordon
Kingsbury, Susan Myra
Regan, Agnes Gertrude
Taft, (Julia) Jessie
Towle, Charlotte Helen

SPECIAL EDUCATION

Cain, Leo Francis
Carhart, Raymond Theodore
Cobb, Henry Van Zandt
Doll, Edgar Arnold
Fenichel, Carl
Hayes, Samuel Perkins, Sr.
Hungerford, Richard H.
Nash, Alice Ford Morrison
O'Connor, Clarence Daniel
Passow, Aaron Henry
Pintner, Rudolf
Sarason, Seymour Bernard
Stanley, Julian Cecil, Jr.
Zigler, Edward Frank

TEACHER EDUCATION

Alexander, (Richard) Thomas
Anderson, Robert Henry
Baker, Frank Elmer
Bigelow, Karl Worth
Bloom, Benjamin Samuel
Douglass, Aubrey Augustus
Edwards, Richard
Foght, Harold Waldstein
Gage, Nathaniel Lees
Gentle, Thomas Higdon
Goodlad, John Inkster
Hunt, Charles Wesley
Hunter, Madeline Cheek
Jackson, Philip Wesley
Jones, Franklin Ross
Keppel, Francis
McAllister, Jane Ellen
Mitchell, Lucy Sprague
Shane, Harold Gray
Stern, Catherine Brieger
Woodring, Paul Dean

TECHNOLOGY

Horwich, Frances Rappaport
Ivey, John Eli, Jr.
Kranzberg, Melvin
Papert, Seymour Aubrey
Ray, Henry William

THEATER AND DRAMATIC ARTS

Flanagan, Hallie Mae Ferguson

Fry, Emma Viola Sheridan

McCaslin, Nellie

UNIONS AND TEACHER ORGANIZATIONS

Andrus, Ethel Percy

Barker, Mary Cornelia

Borchardt, Selma Munter

Koontz, Elizabeth Duncan

Lefkowitz, Abraham

Lieberman, Myron

Lumiansky, Robert Mayer

Megel, Carl J.

Selden, David Seeley

Shanker, Albert

VOCATIONAL EDUCATION

Burroughs, Nannie Helen

Feldman, Marvin Jerome

Hoppock, Robert

Keller, Franklin Jefferson

Marshall, Florence M.

McLaren, Louise Leonard

Morgan, Lucy Calista

Smith, Hilda Worthington

WOMEN'S EDUCATION

Bascom, Florence

Bunting, Mary Alice Ingraham

Conway, Jill Kathryn Ker

Doyle, Sarah Elizabeth

Irwin, Agnes

Lerner, Gerda

McLaren, Louise Leonard

Park, Rosemary

Patrick, Mary Mills

Slowe, Lucy Diggs

Solomon, Barbara Miller

Wexler, Jacqueline Grennan

Appendix D

CHRONOLOGY OF BIRTH YEARS

1780

Stuart, Moses

1786

Kingsbury, Cyrus

1806

Douglass, Sarah Mapes

1807

Foreman, Stephen

1808

Bishop, Nathan

1810

Burritt, Elihu

1813

Preston, Ann

1819

Mills, Cyrus Taggart

1822

Edwards, Richard

1823

Peake, Mary Smith Kelsey

1824

Clapp, Hannah Kezia

1825

Towne, Laura Matilda

1830

Doyle, Sarah Elizabeth

1839

Schofield, Martha

1841

Crogman, William Henry, Sr.
Irwin, Agnes
Shaw, Pauline Agassiz

1844

Richards, Robert Hallowell

1847

Marshall, Clara

1850

Mussey, Ellen Spencer
Patrick, Mary Mills

1854

Hayden, Philip Cady

1855

Cooper, (Jere) Frank Bower

1856

Congdon, Charles Harris

1858

Drexel, Mary Katharine
Morley, Margaret Warner

1859

Cooper, Anna Julia Haywood
Stone, Mason Sereno

1860

Merritt, Emma Frances Grayson

1861

Morgan, Mary Kimball

1862

Bascom, Florence
Commons, John Rogers
Reel, Estelle
Young, Nathan Benjamin

1864

Cooke, Flora Juliette
Fry, Emma Viola Sheridan
Vincent, George Edgar

1865

Locke, Bessie
Stone, Arthur L.
Wood, Stella Louise

1866

Noyes, Arthur Amos
Wright, Sophie Bell

1867

Witmer, Lightner

1868

Boatwright, Frederic William
Gans, Bird Stein

1869

Foght, Harold Waldstein
Giddings, Thaddeus Philander Woodbury
Regan, Agnes Gertrude
Speare, Frank Palmer
Williams, William Taylor Burwell

1870

Gentle, Thomas Higdon
Kingsbury, Susan Myra
Marshall, Florence M.

1871

Holland, Annie Welthy Daughtry

1872

Butler, Selena Sloan
Wright, Elizabeth Evelyn

1873

Cooley, Rossa Belle
McCarthy, Charles

1874

Cooley, Anna Maria
Hayes, Samuel Perkins, Sr.
Randolph, Virginia Estelle
Ryan, Sister John Gabriel
Schomburg, Arthur Alphonso

1875

Storey, Thomas Andrew

1876

Fahs, Sophia Blanche Lyon
Lloyd, Alice Spencer Geddes
Sears, Jesse Brundage

1877

Baker, Frank Elmer
Bowman, John Gabbert
Diller, Angela
Donham,Wallace Brett
Holmes, Dwight Oliver Wendell
Turner, Thomas Wyatt

1878

Dearborn, Walter Fenno
Haynes, Rowland
Mitchell, Lucy Sprague
Nash, Alice Ford Morrison

1879

Barker, Mary Cornelia
Burroughs, Nannie Helen
Fisher, Welthy Blakesley Honsinger
Roberts, Lydia Jane
White, Edna Noble

1880

Hunt, Charles Wesley
Mann, Albert Russell

1881

Branch, Mary Elizabeth
Frazier, Maude

1882

Aikin, Wilford Morton
Campbell, Olive Dame
Cooper, William John
Davis, Jackson
Horn, Ernest
Taft, (Julia) Jessie

1883

Baird, Albert Craig
Henderson, Edwin Bancroft
Merriam, Harold Guy

1884

Andrus, Ethel Percy
Copeland, Melvin Thomas
Lefkowitz, Abraham
Pintner, Rudolf

1885

McLaren, Louise Leonard
Slowe, Lucy Diggs

1886

Goodenough, Florence Laura
Thayer, Vivian Trow

1887

Alexander, (Richard) Thomas
Booker, Matilda Moseley
Douglass, Aubrey Augustus
Fred, Edwin Broun
Keller, Franklin Jefferson
Spofford, Grace Harriet
Williamson, John Finley
Yoakam, Gerald Alan

1888

Albers, Josef
Perlman, Selig
Raup, Robert Bruce
Smith, Hilda Worthington

1889

Childs, John Lawrence
Doll, Edgar Arnold
Flanagan, Hallie Mae Ferguson
H'Doubler, Margaret Newell
Morgan, Lucy Calista
Sharp, Zerna A.

1890

Ackerman, Carl William
Casey, Ralph Droz
Hinton, Carmelita Chase
Naumburg, Margaret
Reeves, Floyd Wesley
Shapley, John
Turner, Clair Elsmere

1891

Beatty, Willard Walcott
Kotler, Aaron
Stolz, Lois Mayden Meek
Woody, (Walter) Thomas

1892

Bruner, Herbert Bascom
Coyle, Grace Longwell
DuBois, Rachel Davis
Eliot, Abigail Adams
Hamilton, (Amy) Gordon
Johnson, Eleanor Murdock

1893

Anderson, John Edward
Lusk, Georgia Lee Witt
Taylor, Alrutheus Ambush

1894

Gans, Roma
Goodykoontz, Bess
Stern, Catherine Brieger
Zachry, Caroline Beaumont

1895

Baron, Salo Wittmayer
Borchardt, Selma Munter
Buchanan, Scott Milross
Herskovits, Melville Jean
Mayer, Clara Woollie
Thurston, Lee Mohrmann

1896

Heffernan, Helen
Jarrell, (Helen) Ira
Marcus, Jacob Rader
Towle, Charlotte Helen
Wechsler, David

1897

Bronk, Detlev Wulf

1898

Berry, George Packer
Bigelow, Karl Worth
Clark, Septima Poinsette
Hildreth, Gertrude Howell
McIntosh, Millicent Carey
Neyhart, Amos Earl
O'Connor, Clarence Daniel
Prescott, Daniel Alfred

1899

Goslin, Willard Edward
Keller, Fred Simmons
Labatut, Jean
McAllister, Jane Ellen
Megel, Carl J.
Nef, John Ulric, Jr.
Reese, Gustave
Watson, Goodwin Barbour

1900

Brownell, Samuel Miller
Coons, Arthur Gardiner
Glueck, Nelson
Hill, Martha
Nabrit, James Madison, Jr.
Wright, Benjamin Fletcher

1901

Brown, Sterling Allen
Hoppock, Robert
Lazarsfeld, Paul Felix
Pei, Mario Andrew
Pitkin, Royce Stanley
Willis, Benjamin Coppage

1902

Adler, Mortimer Jerome
Blackmer, Alan Rogers
Erikson, Erik Homburger
Hunt, Herold Christian
Ilg, Frances Lillian
Rees, Mina Spiegel
Schultz, Theodore William
Shelly, Mary Josephine

1903

Clark, Felton Grandison
Galamian, Ivan Alexander
Hungerford, Richard H.
Keliher, Alice Virginia
Oberholtzer, Kenneth Edison

Spock, Benjamin McLane
Stalnaker, John Marshall

1904

Bond, Guy Loraine
D'Amico, Victor Edmond
Gallagher, Buell Gordon
Goldsmith, Grace Arabell
Lloyd, Wesley Parkinson

1905

Buros, Oscar Krisen
Campbell, Roald Fay
Carlson, William Samuel
Ellis, John Tracy
Farnsworth, Dana Lyda
Fenichel, Carl
Horton, Myles
Lorge, Irving Daniel
Nabrit, Samuel Milton
Renne, Roland Roger
Zacharias, Jerrold Reinach

1906

Gaver, Mary Virginia
Hansen, Carl Francis
Haugen, Einar Ingvald
Henne, Frances Elizabeth
Highet, Gilbert Arthur
Hunt, Joseph McVicker
Miel, Alice Marie
Redding, (Jay) Saunders

1907

Anderson, Charles Arnold
Barzun, Jacques Martin
Fairbank, John King
Holland, (George) Kenneth
Jacobs, Leland Blair
Lyle, Guy Redvers
Park, Rosemary
Pusey, Nathan Marsh
Sheats, Paul Henry
Warriner, John E.
Wilson, Logan
Woodring, Paul

1908

Ames, Louise Bates
Bestor, Arthur Eugene, Jr.
Bowen, Howard Rothmann
Engle, Paul Hamilton
Horwich, Frances Rappaport
Kline, Morris
Sears, Robert Richardson
Walcutt, Charles Child

1909

Cain, Leo Francis
Cobb, Henry Van Zandt
Eggertsen, Claude Andrew
Gingold, Josef
Gleason, Eliza Valeria Atkins
Knowles, Asa Smallidge
Maeder, Hans Karl
Player, Willa Beatrice
Ray, Henry William
Schwab, Joseph Jackson

1910

Bunting, Mary Alice Ingraham
Guinier, Ewart G.

Larrick, Nancy Gray
Patterson, Frederick Douglass
Schuman, William Howard
Thorndike, Robert Ladd

1911

Belkin, Samuel
Gattegno, Caleb
Hill, Mozell Clarence
Krug, Edward August

1912

Alexander, William Marvin
Carhart, Raymond Theodore
Gardner, John William
Jones, Virginia Mae Lacy
Millett, John David
Monro, John Usher

1913

Bloom, Benjamin Samuel
Foster, Luther Hilton, Jr.
Janson, Horst Woldemar
Keller, Robert John
Lumiansky, Robert Mayer

1914

Begle, Edward Griffith
Clark, Kenneth Bancroft
Marland, Sidney Percy, Jr.
McCaslin, Nellie
Nyquist, Ewald Berger
Selden, David Seeley
Shane, Harold Gray

1915

Austin, Mary Carrington
Bruner, Jerome Seymour
Franklin, John Hope
Morrison, Philip
Pitts, Lucius Holsey
Torrancc, (Ellis) Paul

1916

Carroll, John Bissell
Dorson, Richard Mercer
Dozier, Edward Pasqual
Hagerty, William Walsh
Hofstadter, Richard
Hunter, Madeline Cheek
Keppel, Francis
Peterson, Martha Elizabeth

1917

Boyce, Frank Gordon
Dumke, Glenn S.
Gage, Nathaniel Lees
Greene, Maxine Meyer
Hesburgh, Theodore Martin
Kranzberg, Melvin
Rafferty, Maxwell Lewis, Jr.
Weber, Lillian

1918

Anderson, Robert Henry
Ausubel, David Paul
Brazelton, Thomas Berry, II
Culbertson, Jack Arthur
Howe, Harold, II
Stanley, Julian Cecil, Jr.

1919

Brewster, Kingman, Jr.
Grambs, Jean Dresden
Gross, Calvin Edward
Ivey, John Eli, Jr.
Koontz, Elizabeth Duncan
Lieberman, Myron
Sarason, Seymour Bernard
Tumin, Melvin Marvin
Solomon, Barbara Miller

1920

Bereday, George Zygmunt Fijalowski
Goodlad, John Inkster
Gross, Richard Edmund
Lerner, Gerda
Mayer, Jean
Passow, Aaron Harry
Phinazee, (Alethia) Annette Lewis Hoage
Rudolph, Frederick
Samora, Julian
Spindler, George Dearborn

1921

Bell, Terrel Howard
Chall, Jeanne Sternlicht
Jones, Franklin Ross
Parker, Franklin
Risling, David, Jr.

1922

Benson, Charles Scott
Ginott, Haim G.
Wattenbarger, James Lorenzo

1923

Foster, Marcus Albert
Glazer, Nathan
Healy, Timothy Stafford
Holt, John Caldwell
Vars, Gordon Forrest

1924

Caldwell, Bettye McDonald
Cobb, Jewell Plummer

1925

Bandura, Albert
Cremin, Lawrence Arthur
Fry, Edward Bernard
Noah, Harold Julius
Read, Sister Joel

1926

Coleman, James Samuel
Kemeny, John George
Shedd, Mark Redans
Silber, John Robert
Wexler, Jacqueline Grennan
Wharton, Clifton Reginald, Jr.

1927

Brademas, (Stephen) John
Cavazos, Lauro Fred
Fantini, Mario D.
Feldman, Marvin Jerome
Huggins, Nathan Irvin
Karplus, Robert
Kohlberg, Lawrence
Sizemore, Barbara Ann Laffoon

1928

Boyer, Ernest LeRoy
Crim, Alonzo Aristotle
Hirsch, Eric Donald, Jr.
Jackson, Philip Wesley
Papert, Seymour Aubrey
Shanker, Albert

1929

Coles, Robert (Martin)
Paley, Vivian Gussin

1930

Artichoker, John Hobart
Becker, Gary Stanley
Bell, Derrick Albert, Jr.
Bloom, Allan David
Bok, Derek Curtis
Gray, Hanna Holborn
Herrnstein, Richard Julius
Rogler, Lloyd Henry
Sowell, Thomas
Tyack, David B.
Zigler, Edward Frank

1931

Anrig, Gregory Richard
Ballard, Louis Wayne
Elkind, David
Engelmann, Siegfried
Meier, Deborah Willen
Spodek, Bernard
Weikart, David Powell

1932

Cheek, James Edward
Hess, Robert Lee
Katz, Lilian Gonshaw
Love, Ruth Burnett
Sizer, Theodore Ryland

1933

Bowen, William Gordon
Eisner, Elliot Wayne
Gardner, David Pierpont

1934

Comer, James Pierpont
Conway, Jill Kathryn Ker
Cuban, Larry
Demmert, William G., Jr.
Forbes, Jack D.
Poussaint, Alvin Francis
Whiteman, Henrietta V. (Henri Mann)

1935

Rivera, Tomás

1936

Green, Richard Reginald

1942

Barnett, Marguerite Ross

Appendix E

IMPORTANT DATES IN AMERICAN EDUCATION

1635	Boston Latin Grammar School established.
1636	Harvard College founded.
1642	Massachusetts law required education of children.
1647	Massachusetts law required employment of schoolmasters.
1690	(approximate date) *New England Primer* published.
1693	College of William and Mary established.
1701	Yale College founded.
1702	First schools established by Society for the Propagation of the Gospel in Foreign Parts.
1729	Isaac Greenwood wrote first American arithmetic book.
1751	Benjamin Franklin established first American academy.
1765	John Morgan established first school of medicine.
1776	Phi Beta Kappa, academic honor society, founded at College of William and Mary.
1779	Phillips Academy established at Andover, Massachusetts.
1783	Noah Webster's *American Spelling Book* published.
1784	Tapping Reeve opened Litchfield (Connecticut) Law School.
1789	North Carolina legislature chartered a state university.
1802	First federal land grant made to Ohio.
1805	Free School Society of New York founded.
1806	Lancastrian monitorial school established in New York City.
1809	Elizabeth Ann Bayley Seton founded the Sisters of Charity of St. Joseph, Roman Catholic teaching and nursing community.
1811	Albert Picket published the first educational periodical.
1812	New York established state office of superintendent of common schools.
1816	Infant school opened in Boston.
1817	Thomas Hopkins Gallaudet founded the first American school for the deaf in Hartford, Connecticut.

1819	*Dartmouth College v. Woodward* decision affirmed the independence of colleges established privately.
1819	University of Virginia founded, with Thomas Jefferson as rector.
1821	Free public high school opened in Boston.
1821	Emma Willard founded Troy Female Seminary, offering first collegiate education for women.
1823	Samuel Read Hall established a normal school near Concord, Vermont.
1826	First lyceum for adult education formed in Massachusetts.
1827	Massachusetts law required establishment of high schools.
1829	Samuel Read Hall's *Lectures on Schoolkeeping* published.
1832	School for the blind established by Samuel Gridley Howe in Boston; later, the Perkins Institute.
1837	Horace Mann became secretary of newly established Massachusetts Board of Education and began reforms of public schools.
1837	Calvin E. Stowe's *Report on Elementary Instruction in Europe* published.
1838	Henry Barnard organized the first teacher institute in Connecticut.
1839	First state normal school established in Lexington, Massachusetts.
1845	State teachers' associations organized in Massachusetts, New York, and Rhode Island.
1847	David P. Page's much-used *Theory and Practice of Teaching* published.
1848	Class for mentally retarded established in Boston.
1850	Female (later Woman's) Medical College of Philadelphia opened.
1851	Massachusetts School for the Idiotic and Feeble-Minded established.
1852	Compulsory school laws passed in Massachusetts.
1856	Margaretha Schurz established a German kindergarten in Milwaukee, Wisconsin.
1857	National Teachers' Association (later, National Education Association) founded.
1860	Elizabeth Peabody established the first English kindergarten in Boston.
1861	Edward A. Sheldon opened the Oswego (New York) Normal School.
1862	Morrill Act passed establishing land grant colleges.
1866	First American school of architecture opened.
1867	Howard University established in Washington, D.C.

1867	National Department of Education (later, U.S. Office of Education) established.
1872	Kalamazoo (Michigan) case established taxation for education beyond elementary school.
1873	Susan Blow opened the first public school kindergarten in St. Louis, Missouri.
1874	John H. Vincent established the Chautauqua (New York) Institution.
1876	*American Journal of Mathematics* appeared, the first scholarly journal in the United States.
1878	Johns Hopkins University awarded Ph.D. degrees.
1881	Booker T. Washington appointed head of the Tuskegee (Alabama) Normal and Industrial Institute (later, University).
1890	J. McKeen Cattell wrote *Mental Tests and Measurements.*
1892	National Herbartian Society (later, National Society for the Study of Education) founded.
1897	National Congress of Parents and Teachers founded.
1905	Institute of Musical Art (later, Juilliard Institute) established.
1906	Carnegie Foundation for the Advancement of Teaching established.
1909	First junior high school established in Berkeley, California.
1909	First remedial speech classes held in New York City.
1910	First junior college opened in Fresno, California.
1911	School surveys initiated in Montclair, New Jersey.
1913	Bureau of educational research established in New York City.
1914	Smith–Lever Act supported agricultural education.
1916	John Dewey wrote *Democracy and Education.*
1916	American Federation of Teachers organized.
1917	Smith–Hughes Act supported vocational education.
1918	American Council on Education founded.
1918	Commission on the Reorganization of Secondary Education published *Cardinal Principles of Secondary Education.*
1926	American Association for Adult Education founded.
1933	University in Exile established at New School for Social Research, in response to the purge of Jews from German universities.
1933	First driver education course offered.
1933	Institute for Advanced Study founded at Princeton, New Jersey.
1937	St. John's College, Annapolis, Maryland, initiated 100 Great Books program.
1940	Progressive Education Association completed Eight-Year Study of high schools.

1944	G.I. Bill enacted.
1944	United Negro College Fund founded.
1945	Harvard University's Committee on the Objectives of a General Education in a Free Society issued its report.
1948	Twenty-eight institutions reorganized as State University of New York.
1953	Department of Health, Education, and Welfare established.
1953	Station KUHT in Houston, Texas, inaugurated educational television.
1953	Advanced Placement examination program established.
1954	*Brown v. Board of Education of Topeka* decision ruled against racially segregated schools.
1954	B. F. Skinner wrote "The Science of Learning and the Art of Teaching" in the *Harvard Educational Review*.
1958	National Defense Education Act passed.
1958	School Mathematics Study Group organized.
1960	Master Plan for Higher Education in California issued.
1961	Collective bargaining election in New York City won by United Federation of Teachers.
1962	U.S. Supreme Court ruled against prayer in public schools.
1964	Free Speech movement began at the University of California, Berkeley.
1965	Elementary and Secondary Education Act passed.
1966	The Coleman Report on educational opportunity published.
1967	John Kemeny and Thomas E. Kurtz developed BASIC computer language.
1969	*Sesame Street* premiered on Public Broadcasting System.
1970	National student strike followed deaths by shooting of students at Kent State and Jackson State Universities.
1972	U.S. Supreme Court ruled Wisconsin compulsory schooling law violated Amish right to free exercise of religion.
1974	U.S. District Court ruled Boston public schools were deliberately segregated and ordered busing of students to achieve racial balance.
1976	Exclusion of women from Rhodes Scholarships remedied by act of British Parliament.
1977	Department of Education established.
1978	Hanna Holborn Gray became president of the University of Chicago.
1983	National Commission on Excellence in Education issued "A Nation at Risk: The Imperative for Educational Reform."

1984	Macintosh desktop computer marketed to college students.
1991	President George Bush issued ''America 2000,'' national education goals and implementation plan.
1994	New Jersey Supreme Court ruled state method of financing public schools unconstitutional.
1995	University of California Board of Regents eliminated affirmative action in admissions.

INDEX

The page numbers set in **boldface** indicate the location of a main entry.

About the Authors

FREDERIK OHLES is Vice President for Academic Affairs, Dean of the College, and Professor of History at Illinois College. Ohles has taught at the University of Melbourne and held administrative appointments at the Council for International Exchange of Scholars and St. Olaf College.

SHIRLEY M. OHLES is an independent researcher in education. She was coauthor with John F. Ohles of *Private Colleges and Universities* (Greenwood, 1982) and *Public Colleges and Universities* (Greenwood, 1986), and research associate in the preparation of the *Biographical Dictionary of American Educators* (Greenwood, 1978).

JOHN G. RAMSAY is Professor of Educational Studies and Coordinator of the Learning and Teaching Center at Carleton College. He has published in numerous journals.

ISBN 0-313-29133-0
90000>
EAN
9 780313 291333
HARDCOVER BAR CODE